FINANCIAL FUTURES, OPTIONS, AND SWAPS

FINANCIAL FUTURES, OPTIONS, AND SWAPS

Alan L. Tucker, Ph.D.
Temple University

WEST PUBLISHING COMPANY

St. Paul   New York   Los Angeles   San Francisco

Figure and Exhibit Credits

Chapter Five
Figure 5.1 From *Futures* Magazine, February 1987.
Exhibit 5.7 Reprinted by permission of Wall Street Journal ©Dow Jones and Company, Inc. (1988) All Rights Reserved Worldwide.
Exhibit 5.9 Reprinted by permission of Wall Street Journal ©Dow Jones and Company, Inc. (1988) All Rights Reserved Worldwide.
Chapter Six
Figure 6.2 L. Harris, "The October 1987 S & P 500 Stock-Futures Basis," *Journal of Finance* 44 (March 1989): 83. Reprinted with permission.
Figure 6.3 Wood "Do Yield Curves Normally Slope Up? The Term Structure of Interest Rates, 1862–1982" *Economic Perspectives*, Federal Reserve Bank of Chicago (July/August 1983), p. 18. Reprinted with permission.
Chapter Seven
Unnumbered Exhibit R. Kolb, G. Gay, and W. Hunter, "Liquidity and Capital Requirements for Futures Market Hedges." *Review of Research in Futures Markets*, 1985, Vol. 4, No. 1, pp. 1–25. Reprinted with permission.
Exhibit 7.1 B. Cornell and M. Reinganum. "Forward and Futures Prices: Evidence from the Foreign Exchange Markets," *Journal of Finance*, 36, (December 1981), p. 1041. Reprinted with permission.
Chapter Eight
Exhibit 8.2 Reprinted by permission of Wall Street Journal ©Dow Jones and Company, Inc. (1989) All Rights Reserved Worldwide.

continued following Index

Copyeditor   Margaret Jarpey
Artist   Katherine Townes Books
Text Designer   Lois Stanfield
Compositor   Carlisle Communications, Ltd.

Copyright © 1991 by WEST PUBLISHING COMPANY
50 West Kellogg Boulevard
P.O. Box 64526
St. Paul, MN 55164–1003

Library of Congress Cataloging-in-Publication Data

Tucker, Alan L.
   Financial futures, options, and swaps / Alan L.   Tucker.
      p.   cm.
   Includes index.
   ISBN 0-314-75279-X (hard)
      1. Financial futures.   2. Stock options.   3. Swaps (Finance)
4. Portfolio management.   I. Title.
HG6024.3.T83   1990
332.64'5 — dc20   90-12497
                                                                              CIP

To Wendy

CONTENTS

PREFACE

This book is intended to introduce the undergraduate or MBA student to financial futures, options, and swaps. These instruments represent derivative securities, meaning that they are derived from, or "written on," some other asset. Theory and application are equally stressed. The book assumes no knowledge of investments or portfolio theory, its only prerequisite is an introductory finance course. Elementary probability and statistical measures are reviewed, as is the limited calculus required.

The objective of this book is to clearly explain why these securities exist, where and how they are traded, how to employ them in managing risk, and how to accurately price them.

The book differentiates itself in a number of ways. First, an entire section is devoted to the relation between derivative securities and modern portfolio theory. This should enable the student to quickly understand the role of these securities in managing risk. Second, an analysis of swaps is presented, since interest rate and currency swaps are rapidly gaining prestige as important derivative securities. Third, a chapter is devoted to the concept of portfolio insurance, especially dynamic hedging, which is often practiced by institutional portfolio managers today. Finally, separate chapters are devoted to currency futures and options in recognition of the continuing internationalization of firms and security funds, and the globalization of the world's financial markets.

In Part 1, concerning the relation between derivative securities and modern portfolio theory, elementary probability and statistical concepts and measures are introduced, followed by a presentation of the theory of diversification and the important insurance opportunities offered by derivative securities. Part 2 concerns financial futures, while Part 3 covers options. Here the markets and instruments are detailed, followed by valuation theory and hedging applications. Separate chapters are devoted to popular instruments. Part 4 completes the book with an analysis of swaps.

Special features throughout illustrate real-world applications, research, innovations, successes, and failures. Key concepts and phrases with their definitions are highlighted in the page margins. Finally, a glossary of terms is provided. Selected references and self-test problems and solutions are offered at the end of most chapters, and appendices concerning simple linear regression and differentiation are provided.

Computer software that accompanies this book is also available from the publisher—specifically, two Lotus 1–2–3 templates. The first computes European option values using the seminal Black-Scholes model as extended for continuous dividends by Merton. It also computes corresponding American option values using the quadratic approximation of Barone-Adesi and Whaley. The second computes an implied standard deviation from the Black-Scholes model adjusted for continuous dividends. This software can be readily integrated into the course offering, providing students with the technology to rapidly compute the prices of popular and sophisticated option contracts.

In developing this book I received great help from a number of generous individuals. First, I would like to thank Jeff Madura for encouraging me to write this book. Second, I wish to thank my editor, Dick Fenton, who capably oversaw the book's development. I also want to thank my typing team of Mike and Sue Tucker, who are also my brother and sister-in-law. I also thank Jayne Lindesmith for her work on the book's production, and Paritosh Mehta for his help in designing the accompanying software. Finally, this book has benefited from the helpful suggestions of numerous reviewers. I am indebted to these scholars for their insights.

Mahmoud M. Haddad
Wayne State University

Richard J. Teweles
California State University—
Long Beach

Hung-Gay Fung
University of Baltimore

Patricia B. Smith
University of New Hampshire

Jacky C. So
Southern Illinois University at
Edwardsville

Nicolas Gressis
Wright State University

Paul J. Bolster
Northeastern University

Robert L. Losey
American University

Anthony F. Herbst
University of Texas at El Paso

Steven Freund
Pennsylvania State University

I hope that you enjoy this book and encourage you to write to me expressing your comments and suggestions.

A.L.T.

FINANCIAL FUTURES, OPTIONS, AND SWAPS

1

INTRODUCTION

Welcome to the exciting and fast-paced world of financial futures, options, and swaps. Collectively, these instruments are known as *derivative securities* because they are derived from, or "written on," some underlying asset. For instance, a stock option would no longer be traded if the underlying company, whose stock the option is written on, went bankrupt.

Because these instruments are derived from their underlying assets, their prices are intimately related to the prices of those assets. One of the central concerns of this book is the determination of the price of the derivative security given the current price, called the *spot price*, of its underlying asset. Another central concern involves the use of derivative securities to manage price uncertainty. The primary reason for the existence and growth of derivative securities is that they provide an efficient means of managing the risk associated with holding a position in the underlying spot asset. The concept of risk as it relates to price uncertainty, and the use of derivative securities to control it, is discussed more thoroughly in Chapters 2 through 4.

This book deals primarily with futures contracts traded on currencies, debt instruments, and stock indices, and with options traded on stocks, stock indices, currencies, and futures contracts. These are the best known and most traded derivative securities. However, an understanding of futures contracts necessitates the discussion of forward contracts as well, so this subject is touched on. Finally, currency and interest rate swaps are analyzed. Swaps are rapidly gaining prestige as important types of derivative securities.

This chapter presents a brief introduction to financial futures, options, and swaps. A discussion of each instrument's origin, growth, and use, is followed by a description of how derivative securities "fit" into our financial system. Important concepts relating spot assets and derivative securities are highlighted. Finally, career opportunities are outlined.

Spot Assets	Derivative Securities
Capital Market Assets	Forward Contracts
Common Stock	Commodities
Preferred Stock	Currencies
Bonds	Futures Contracts
Mortgages	Agricultural Commodities
Money Market Assets	Metallurgical Commodities
Federal Funds	Financial Assets
Commercial Paper	Interest Rates
Certificates of Deposit	Stock Indices
Treasury Bills	Currencies
Banker's Acceptances	Miscellaneous
Currency Market Assets	Option Contracts
Spot Exchange	Financial Assets
Nonfinancial Assets	Stocks
Spot Commodities	Stock Indices
Real Estate	Currencies
Collectables	Futures Contracts
	Miscellaneous
	Swap Contracts
	Currency
	Interest Rates
	Miscellaneous

MARKET CLASSIFICATION

To gain a broad perspective on derivative securities, it is useful to classify markets by one of two means: (1) by asset type—spot assets or derivative securities; and (2) by market microstructure—organized markets or over-the-counter (OTC) and cash markets.

Exhibit 1.1 presents a market classification by asset type. There are spot assets such as common stock, U.S. Treasury bills, and foreign exchange that are traded on financial markets. There are also spot assets such as real estate and collectibles that are traded on nonfinancial markets. The distinguishing feature of all spot assets is that their trading calls for *immediate delivery*. In other words, the purchase of these assets represents a transfer of ownership at the current price. For instance, the purchase of common stock represents a transfer of corporate ownership at the current share price.

Alternatively, there are derivative securities, including many different types of futures and option contracts. The distinguishing feature of these securities is that their trading calls for the *deferred delivery* of an underlying spot asset. For instance, the purchase of a currency futures

Organized Exchanges	OTC and Cash Markets
Stock Exchanges	OTC Stock Markets
Options Exchanges	OTC Bond Markets
Futures Exchanges	OTC Option Markets
	Commodity Cash Markets
	Spot
	Forward
	Currency Cash Markets
	Spot
	Forward
	OTC Swap Markets

Exhibit 1.2:

Markets Classified by Micro-structure

contract entails the obligation to trade some amount of designated foreign currency in the future. Thus, derivative securities represent contracts to trade spot assets at a deferred time.

From Exhibit 1.1, notice that a derivative security must evolve from a spot asset. But which spot assets tend to give rise to sustained derivative securities trading? The answer to this question is not fully known, but recent investigations suggest that at least two factors are important.[1] First is the variability of the price of the spot asset. Since the primary use of derivative securities is to manage price uncertainty, more spot price uncertainty should attract greater trading volume in the derivative instrument. In this book we provide numerous illustrations of risk management through derivative securities trading. Second, the size of the market for the spot asset is an important determinant. For example, gold futures contracts are successfully traded on a number of different futures markets throughout the United States and free world. The ability of several markets to offer futures trading on gold stems from its vast spot market.

Exhibit 1.2 presents a market classification by market microstructure. Markets can be *organized*, meaning that trading occurs at a physical location (a trading floor), and contracts exhibit standardized features. From Exhibit 1.2, notice that stocks and many types of options and futures contracts are traded on organized exchanges. These exchanges operate under an auction system where buyers and sellers compete intensely when setting contract prices.

On the other hand, markets can be less formally structured, meaning that trading may occur through an electronic network of market participants, and contracts are tailored to the specific needs of the client. From Exhibit 1.2, notice that some stocks, bonds, options, and swaps are traded on over-the-counter (OTC) markets, while commodity and

---

[1]See D. Black (1986) and D. Carlton (1984), for example.

currency contracts are traded on cash markets. Both OTC and cash markets are characterized by *negotiated trading,* meaning that contract prices are established through direct negotiations between clients and dealers. Dealers make a market by offering to buy and sell assets, and they earn profits by establishing spreads between selling and buying prices.

FUTURES CONTRACTS

A *forward contract* represents an agreement between two parties to trade a specified asset in the future for a price agreed upon today. Forward contracting in various assets has existed for centuries, and *futures contracts* currently represent an institutionalized form of forward contracting. With a futures contract, however, the contract terms are standardized, the contract trades on an organized exchange, and traders must realize any losses each and every trading day. These characteristics are not exhibited by forward contracts. Subsequent chapters (Chapters 6 and 8 especially) elaborate on these different characteristics.

The origins of modern futures trading can be traced back to the 1840s. At this time, the city of Chicago had emerged as the distribution center of our farming economy. However, Chicago's storage facilities were insufficient to warehouse the vast amounts of grain and other foodstuffs that were being shipped after harvesting. As a result, farmers were subjected to delivery delays that made the prices received for their commodities uncertain, since these prices varied over time. In other words, delays in distribution resulted in price uncertainty.

To alleviate this risk, the Chicago Board of Trade (CBOT) was formed in 1848 by a group of private businessmen. The CBOT offered trading in grain futures and other futures contracts with established quantities, maturities, and other features so that a farmer could agree to deliver his harvest at a future date for a price determined today. This way, the farmer that could not deliver his commodities to Chicago at harvest time because of distribution delays did not have to take a chance that the price would change by the time he did deliver it. This process helped to smooth the distribution of commodities by alleviating the burden on Chicago's storage facilities at harvest time.

As the years passed, the CBOT began to offer more and more futures contracts traded on different underlying commodities. And in 1874 the Chicago Mercantile Exchange (CME) was established as the second oldest futures exchange. The service that these exchanges offered was efficient risk reallocation. Farmers could transfer their price uncertainty by contracting to sell their commodities in the future at specified prices. The parties willing to purchase the commodities at these specified prices were typically food retailers. The exchanges facilitated contracting between farmers and food retailers. However, *speculators* soon discovered that they could use futures contracts as a means of trying to profit on commodity price movements, achieving the same "action" as on the underlying asset for a fraction of the capital. Further, by using futures, speculators did not have to take delivery and store the actual commodity. Speculators thus became active participants in futures trading.

Futures traders represented a source of credit risk to one another. This was especially true when speculators entered the market. For instance, a speculator might default on a contract to purchase grain from a farmer. To alleviate this risk, the CBOT created a *clearinghouse* in 1925. The role of the clearinghouse was to ensure that all traders made good on their obligations. It acted as a type of middleman in each trade, requiring all traders to post security deposits known as *margins*, and it proved successful in building market confidence and trading volume.

With the institution of the clearinghouse, futures exchanges became almost fully developed. The next major change was the introduction of a whole new class of futures contracts known as *financial futures*, beginning in the 1970s. Now futures contracts were traded on assets such as foreign exchange, U.S. Treasury securities, and stock market indices. Thus, futures contracts were introduced to help investors manage the price uncertainty of their financial asset portfolios. Speculators could also use a financial futures contract to wager on movements of the prices of financial assets.

Financial futures trading has proven very successful. Today the majority of all futures trading involves financial futures. Figure 1.1 shows that financial futures trading grew from 13 percent of total trading volume to 60 percent over the period of 1980 through 1986. In this book the application and pricing of financial futures contracts are stressed to reflect the popularity of these particular futures contracts.

From the previous discussion, it is obvious that futures contracts can be used to help manage price uncertainty or to speculate on subsequent price movements. A third use of futures contracts is price discovery. Given that futures contracts call for the trading of an underlying asset at a future date, the price at which the asset is agreed to be traded, called the *futures price*, likely reflects expectations about the asset's future value, that is, the price expected to prevail at the delivery date. Because of this, futures prices may be used as estimates of subsequent spot prices, and futures contracts can be used for price discovery.

OPTION CONTRACTS

An *option* is a contract between two parties that gives the buyer the right to trade an underlying asset at a fixed price in the future. For instance, you may buy an option that allows you to purchase Ford stock, at $80 per share, thirty days from now. Notice that you have the right, but not the obligation, to purchase the stock. For this right you would pay a price to the option seller. In this book we analyze how option prices are determined.

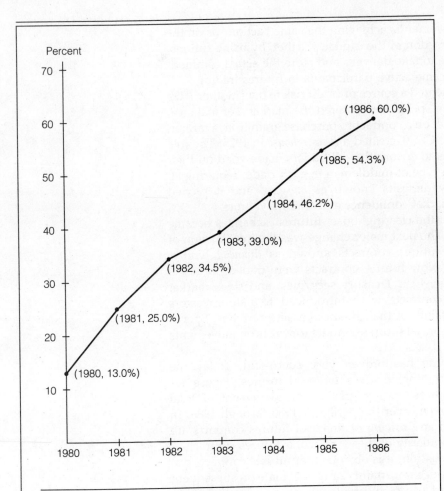

Year	Financial Futures Volume (Millions)	All Futures Volume (Millions)
1980	12	92
1981	25	100
1982	38	110
1983	50	128
1984	67	145
1985	88	162
1986	114	190

The origins of organized options trading on stocks and other assets can be traced back to the early 1900s. At that time a group of independent businessmen, known as the Put and Call Brokers and Dealers Association, created an over-the-counter (OTC) options market. Members of the association would link up traders who wanted to buy options on common stock with those who wanted to sell. If a seller could not be found for a buyer, or vice versa, the association member would act as a dealer—taking a position in one side of the contract until the member could off-load it.

Although the OTC stock options market operated continuously throughout the next several decades, it ultimately proved to have too many shortcomings. One was low liquidity resulting from the nonstandardized nature of the option contracts. Another was large transaction costs due to the high credit risk of option sellers and the association members.

In 1973 the CBOT developed and organized an exchange devoted strictly to stock options trading. This new exchange became known as the Chicago Board Options Exchange (CBOE), which is still the world's largest organized options exchange. The CBOE offered greater liquidity because of the standardized contracts it traded. Also, the CBOE established an options clearinghouse similar to that established by the CBOT in the 1920s to ensure the rights of market traders. Greater liquidity and lower credit risk together served to lower transaction costs, and the CBOE was soon dominating the OTC options market. Also, four other organized U.S. exchanges soon began to provide options trading: the American Stock Exchange (AMEX), the Philadelphia Stock Exchange (PHLX), the Pacific Stock Exchange (PSE), and the New York Stock Exchange (NYSE). While these four exchanges trade securities other than options, the CBOE continues to be the only organized exchange devoted strictly to options trading.

Figure 1.2 shows that option volume at these five exchanges grew rapidly during the period of 1980 through 1985, and the CBOE continues to lead the other four major exchanges. The primary reason for this is the popularity of the CBOE's option contract on the Standard and Poor's 100 Stock Index (SP100). This contract, which began trading on March 11, 1983, and is typically referred to as OEX, its ticker symbol, represents the first stock index option ever traded. Presently, contract volume in the OEX is over 20 million annually. We will analyze stock index options later in Chapter 18.

Besides stock and stock index options, options traded on financial futures contracts also exhibit strong volume. Nearly all organized futures exchanges now provide futures options trading. Also, options trading on foreign currency has shown tremendous volume growth. In this book we focus our analysis of options on those written on stocks, stock indices, currencies, and futures contracts.

Option contracts can be used to help manage price uncertainty. For instance, stock index options are popular because they can be used by *institutional investors* to reduce risk. Many institutional investors hold

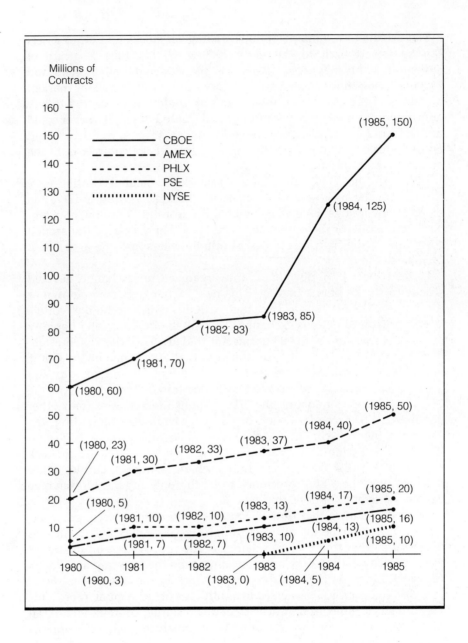

large stock portfolios that mimic broad market indices like the SP100 or SP500. By trading stock index options, they can help protect their equity portfolios from adverse market swings. As another example, U.S.–based exporters can use currency options to protect against exchange rate risk when international trade agreements are contingent. In this book we illustrate many applications of options to hedge against price uncertainty.

Like futures contracts, options can also be used to speculate on movements of the price of the underlying spot asset. For example, a speculator that anticipates a downturn in the stock market may want to trade index options in order to profit from this forecast. This book provides examples of both simple and advanced speculative strategies involving option contracts.

SWAPS

Swaps represent an important new development in derivative security markets. In its most general form, a *swap* involves a negotiated agreement between two parties to exchange cash flows at specified future dates according to a prescribed manner. In this book we focus our analysis on currency and interest rate swaps. A *currency swap* allows two firms to exchange foreign currencies at recurrent intervals, and is usually used in conjunction with debt issues. An *interest rate swap* occurs when a firm that has issued one form of debt agrees to swap interest payments with another firm that has issued a different form of debt denominated in the same currency. These swaps provide for the transfer of exchange rate and interest rate risk between the two firms involved. Furthermore, swaps can be used to create unique investment opportunities.

Currency swaps first appeared in 1981 when IBM and the World Bank entered into an agreement to swap debt obligations denominated in different currencies. In 1982 interest rate swaps evolved as a special case of a currency swap. Since that time, the markets for currency and interest rate swaps have grown substantially. For instance, the International Swap Dealers Association estimated that over $700 billion of swaps contracts were executed in 1987 alone.

PRICING LINKAGES

Spot assets and their derivative securities exhibit prices that are inextricably linked. Although several chapters of this book are devoted to pricing issues, it is beneficial to provide an overview of these issues now.

Linkages between Spot Assets and Their Derivative Instruments

Because derivative securities are written on underlying spot assets, there should exist well-defined pricing relations between derivative securities and their spot assets. For example, suppose that you own an option that gives you the right to buy IBM stock at $120 per share. You may exercise this right immediately or at any time until the option contract expires. Now suppose that IBM stock is currently selling for $125 per share. It follows that your option contract should have a value of at least $5 per share of IBM stock. After all, you could exercise the option, paying $120 per share, and in turn sell your IBM shares at the current market price of $125 per share.

As another example, consider a futures contract that is about to expire. At expiration, a futures contract entails the immediate delivery of the underlying asset. Hence, the price of an expiring futures contract must equal the asset's spot price. Futures and spot prices will converge as the maturity of the futures contract unwinds.

The mechanism that keeps prices of derivative securities and their underlying spot assets inextricably linked is known as *arbitrage*. An arbitrage restriction is a boundary that governs the pricing relation between a spot asset and its derivative instrument. Should this boundary be violated, a profit opportunity may arise. In other words, it may be possible to trade the spot and derivative securities in such a way that an abnormal profit is generated. If so, the market is revealed to be inefficient. An *arbitrager* is one who attempts to exploit any such inefficiencies.

To illustrate the concept of arbitrage, suppose that you observe a current market price of $4 (per share) for the previously mentioned IBM stock option. This price is a violation of a rational pricing boundary—the option should sell for at least $5. To profit, you could undertake the following arbitrage trading strategy: (1) purchase the option for $4; (2) immediately exercise your option, purchasing IBM stock for $120 per share; and (3) immediately sell your IBM stock for the current market price of $125 per share. Your proceeds from the transaction are therefore $1 per share, ignoring transaction costs. This $1 represents riskless profit, presuming that all transactions could take place at the market prices prevailing when the violation was detected. Of course, you would continue to execute your arbitrage trading strategy until market prices of IBM stock and the stock option were in line. Arbitrage is the mechanism that keeps prices in line.

This book will repeatedly demonstrate how the prices of derivative securities are determined by arbitrage restrictions present in efficiently operating markets. Thus, given the price of the underlying spot asset, we demonstrate how the price of the derivative security can be determined through the imposition of boundaries set by arbitrage trading strategies. Some of these strategies will be rather simple, like the one just described, while others are more elegant. The idea is for you not to merely memorize these strategies, but instead learn how to systematically undertake arbitrage transactions and even create new derivative security instruments.[2]

Finally, it is important to recognize that the concept of arbitrage is intimately related to the economic law known as the *Law of One Price:*

---

[2]Such a process is sometimes called "financial engineering."

two identical assets cannot sell for different prices. Many of our arbitrage strategies will entail holding a combination of the spot asset and its derivative security such that the resulting portfolio exhibits no risk. Therefore, by the Law of One Price the portfolio should earn the same return in equilibrium as does a risk-free security. Using this fact, we will be able to "back out" the price of the derivative security.

Linkages between Different Types of Derivative Securities

Spot assets and derivative securities exhibit well-defined pricing relations. But the prices of different types of derivative instruments are linked as well. In this book it will be demonstrated that synthetic forward contracts can be created by holding certain combinations of option contracts. Also, it will be shown that the cash flows associated with swaps can be replicated by combinations of forward contracts. Finally, it will be shown that futures and forward prices are equivalent under certain restrictions. Therefore, it should be noted that options, futures, forwards, and swaps are all related to one another through established mechanisms. Indeed, arbitrage restrictions should ensure the existence of these relations if markets operate efficiently.

Market Imperfections and Arbitrage

Market imperfections, or *frictions*, refer to transaction costs, taxes, imperfect security divisibility, trading delays, and other trading restrictions such as those on short selling.[3] These are real-world costs and barriers to individuals seeking to trade assets, including derivative securities. A consequence of such market imperfections is that arbitrage trading strategies are not implemented without commensurate costs or, at times, may not be readily implemented at all. For example, the $1-per-share proceeds from the above arbitrage strategy involving IBM stock options may be partially or completely eliminated by the transaction costs of trading. Also, executing the trades described may entail delays that make the proceeds uncertain.

Because of this, arbitrage restrictions do not hold exactly—that is, they do not hold the way they would if markets were perfect. Consequently, the pricing relations between spot assets and derivative securities, as well as those among different derivative securities, are somewhat inexact. This should be expected, however, given the realities of security trading. You should not be surprised by small pricing violations. The

---

[3]The concept of short selling and its restrictions are discussed in Chapter 3.

A Career Profile: Meet Paul Adair

Mr. Paul Adair, age 27, currently holds the job title of director of foreign currency products at the Philadelphia Stock Exchange, the world's leading trader of listed currency option contracts. Mr. Adair holds a B.S. in accounting (marketing minor) from LaSalle University (1983). His undergraduate G.P.A. was 3.26. He is married, has no children, and is currently pursuing an M.B.A. on a part-time basis.

Mr. Adair has been with the Philadelphia Stock Exchange for over five years. After graduating from college, he applied at the exchange for a position in the market surveillance department, entry level. He spent three years in surveillance and then moved to the exchange's marketing department.

As director of foreign currency products, Mr. Adair has the duty of marketing foreign currency options and futures. This entails educating potential market users, supporting current users, helping to enhance products for further growth, being involved in new-product development, and editing an exchange-published newsletter. In a typical workday, Mr. Adair interacts with market members and participants in product-related mat-

ters. He also spends a considerable amount of his day developing new business relations in an effort to enhance trading volume.

Mr. Adair's position also entails some travel, about twice per month to cities including New York and Washington. Because of the relatively small size of the Philadelphia Stock Exchange and the international flavor of the products Mr. Adair is involved in, combined with the great success of currency options trading at the exchange, he is highly visible, interacting with senior-level management at user firms. Mr. Adair contends that the intimacy of the PHLX places him in situations in which most other exchanges would utilize an employee with ten or more years of experience.

In the future, Mr. Adair expects to be working with a member firm marketing currency options or other foreign exchange–related products, or at the PHLX in a position of further responsibility—whether it be in marketing or another area of the exchange. Currently, Mr. Adair's salary range is $35,000 to $40,000 (1989).

---

markets are still considered efficient if the violations observed are insufficient to overcome the frictions associated with arbitrage.[4]

EMPLOYMENT OPPORTUNITIES IN DERIVATIVE SECURITIES

Individual investors, institutional investors, financial intermediaries, and corporations all trade derivative securities. For instance, equity

---

[4]Market imperfections result in the "apparent" breakdown of the Law of One Price in other markets as well. For instance, one can observe that big-ticket items, such as autos, are very similarly priced across different retailers. However, small-ticket items—razors, for example—exhibit greater price variation across retailers. Thus, it appears that the Law of One Price holds better for big-ticket items. This is because buyers are willing to search more, that is, to expend "search costs," for big-ticket items. Search costs represent a friction. One would find that the Law of One Price operates very well for small-ticket items, however, after controlling for search costs. For a fun way to learn more about the Law of One Price, search costs, and other related issues, read *The Fatal Equilibrium*, a murder mystery by Marshall Jevons, *Ballantine Books*, New York, 1985.

portfolio managers often trade stock index options to help manage their portfolios. Fixed-income fund managers often trade interest rate futures to hedge against adverse interest rate shifts. Banks and thrifts are major players in the interest rate swap market. Multinational corporations trade currency futures and options. For example, Chrysler Corporation presently uses currency options to hedge about half of its exchange exposure. Domestic corporations are also active in derivative instrument markets. For example, Archer Daniels Midland Co., a huge grain and soybean producer, is a major player in futures markets.

Employment in any of the above entities often commands at least a familiarity with derivative securities and their markets. But derivative instrument markets themselves offer many career opportunities, just a few of which are briefly described below. The opportunities described are oriented toward "new" labor, such as recent college or MBA graduates.

Brokerage Firms

Brokerage firms process securities transactions for their clients in return for a commission fee. They also offer related services, such as account management. These firms employ different personnel who specialize in derivative instruments, including

- *Account executives.* Account executives are salespeople and thus are crucial to the brokerage firm. Some account executives specialize in derivative securities.
- *Marketing personnel.* Customer turnover in derivative securities trading is high, so brokerage firms must aggressively pursue new clients. To do so, these firms employ marketing personnel who make seminar presentations and otherwise campaign for new derivative security clients.
- *Control personnel.* These employees are responsible for conducting customer credit analysis, setting position limits, and reviewing margin accounts for clients who trade derivative securities.
- *Research analysts.* Most large brokerage firms maintain research departments that provide recommendations to clients as a service or for a fee. Research analysts are often employed and trained to specialize in derivative instrument markets.

Government

Government bodies such as the Commodity Futures Trading Commission and the Securities and Exchange Commission (SEC) exist to regulate derivative securities trading. These bodies are invariably understaffed and suffer large turnover rates as their employees, after gaining valuable experience, opt for more lucrative careers in the private sector—for instance, as compliance personnel with brokerage firms. As a result, government regulators are often seeking employees, especially those who have legal expertise or can perform economic research and analysis on new contract proposals and the like.

Organized Exchanges

The exchanges that provide trading on listed futures and options have various labor needs, including

- *Marketing personnel.* Exchanges are incorporated entities that thrive on trading volume. And different exchanges frequently compete with one another to trade similar products. For instance, in January 1990 exchanges will compete against one another, for the first time, in trading stock options. To promote their instruments and enhance trading volume, exchanges employ marketing personnel to make seminar presentations, conduct research, publish brochures, design new products, and otherwise campaign for more clientele.

- *Surveillance personnel.* Besides government regulatory bodies, trading purity is preserved by surveillance conducted by the exchange itself. Every organized futures and options exchange has a surveillance department that employs personnel who oversee trading activity. These personnel exist to detect and help prevent abusive trading practices.

Entrepreneurial Careers

Derivative instrument markets are attractive grounds for sowing the entrepreneurial spirit. One who possesses a sound comprehension of derivative securities and an unwaning work ethic may be qualified for trading on the floor of an organized futures or options exchange. This is an exciting but stressful job that requires savvy and, typically, a good deal of experience. Also, floor trading requires substantial initial capital. For example, it currently costs about $21,000 per month to lease a seat on the CBOE. In subsequent chapters we study exchange members and the trading activity that occurs on the floor.

Another entrepreneurial career in the derivative securities arena is a *commodity pool operator.* Commodity pools operate somewhat like a mutual fund except that they exist for the purpose of trading options and futures. Most pools are limited partnerships in which small investors combine their capital and then employ an operator to manage the pool. An experienced derivative securities trader may be a candidate to manage a commodity pool.

SUMMARY

Financial futures, options and swaps are derivative securities that represent contracts to trade spot assets at a deferred time. Financial futures are standardized contracts traded on organized exchanges. Most options trading occurs on organized exchanges as well. Some options, forward contracts, and swaps are traded on over-the-counter (OTC) and cash markets.

Futures, options, and swaps represent efficient mechanisms for risk reallocation. Derivative instruments can also be used to speculate on subsequent spot price changes or for price discovery.

The prices of spot assets and their derivative securities are linked by arbitrage restrictions present in efficient markets. Arbitrage restrictions also help assure well-defined pricing relations among different types of derivative securities.

This chapter, in presenting a broad overview of derivative securities, serves as an introduction to the rest of this book. Part 1 examines the relation between derivative securities and modern portfolio theory. Here the role of derivative instruments in reducing the disutility associated with price uncertainty is explored. Parts 2, 3, and 4 are devoted to financial futures, options, and swaps, respectively. The markets and various instruments are defined. Pricing issues are investigated, and applications of derivative securities contracting are presented.

Selected References

Baer, J., and O. Saxon. *Commodity Exchanges and Futures Trading.* New York: Harper Brothers, 1949.

Beidleman, C. *Financial Swaps.* Homewood, Ill.: Dow Jones-Irwin, 1985.

Black, D. *Success and Failure of Futures Contracts: Theory and Empirical Evidence.* Salomon Brothers Monograph Series in Finance and Economics, Monograph 1986-1.

Carlton, D. "Futures Markets: Their Purpose, Their History, Their Growth, Their Successes and Failures." *Journal of Futures Markets* (Fall 1984), 237–271.

Finnerty, J. "Financial Engineering in Corporate Finance: An Overview." *Financial Management* 17 (Winter 1988): 14–33.

Galai, J. "Characterization of Options." *Journal of Banking and Finance* 1 (December 1977): 373–385.

Gastineau, G. *The Stock Options Manual.* New York: McGraw-Hill, 1979.

Hieronymous, T. *The Economics of Futures Trading.* New York: Commodity Research Bureau, 1977.

Horn, F. *Trading in Commodity Futures.* New York: New York Institute of Finance, 1984.

Irwin, H. *Evolution of Futures Trading.* Madison, Wisc.: Mimir Publishers, 1954.

Malkiel, B., and R. Quandt. *Strategies and Rational Decisions in the Securities Options Market.* Cambridge, Mass.: M.I.T. Press, 1969.

McMillan, L. *Options as a Strategic Investment.* New York: New York Institute of Finance, 1980.

Phillips, S., and C. Smith. "Trading Costs For Listed Options: The Implications for Market Efficiency." *Journal of Financial Economics* 8 (1980): 179–201.

Riess, M. "Employment Opportunities in the Commodity Business." Working Paper No. 4, Center for the Study of Futures Markets, Columbia University, 1981.

Stoll, H., and R. Whaley. "New Option Instruments: Arbitrage Linkages and Valuation." *Advances in Futures and Options Research* 1 (1986): 25–62.

Taylor, C. *History of the Board of Trade of the City of Chicago.* Chicago: Robert Law Company, 1917.

Questions and Problems

1. Define arbitrage and the Law of One Price. How do these concepts influence the pricing of derivative securities?

2. Define an option; a futures contract; a swap.

3. What do we mean by a *financial* futures contract? Provide examples of such contracts.

4. What are the three uses of futures contracts? What are the uses of options and swaps?

5. Suppose that you observed a small violation of an arbitrage restriction involving a derivative security. Why doesn't this imply an inefficient market?

6. Distinguish between derivative securities and spot assets.

7. Discuss the developments that led to the creation of the CBOT. Discuss those that led to the establishment of the CBOE.

8. What spot asset characteristics appear to promote volume in derivative securities trading?

9. Describe some differences between organized markets and OTC and cash markets.

10. Provide a numerical example of an arbitrage opportunity entailing a stock option. Show how you would trade in order to profit from this opportunity.

11. Why should the futures price at contract expiration be equal to the prevailing spot price of the underlying asset?

Appendix 1.A

INFORMATION SOURCES FOR DERIVATIVE SECURITIES

There exist many sources of information on derivative securities. One is the exchange where the security trades. Every organized exchange has a marketing department designed to promote the trading of its listed securities, and these departments publish brochures and other information forms that provide details about the contracts traded. This information typically includes contract specifications, contract innovations, volume, pricing, trading strategies, and the like, in addition to numerous interesting facts and details. It is usually free of charge.

Many of the facts concerning trading volume and contract specifications contained in this book were obtained from these information sources. Addresses and phone numbers of U.S.–based futures and options exchanges are provided at the end of this appendix so that you may write or call them to be placed on their mailing lists.

Although swaps are not currently traded on organized exchanges, information about these securities can be obtained from the International Swap Dealers Association. The address is International Swap Dealers Association, 1 Rockefeller Plaza, Suite 1505, New York, NY 10020.

Numerous periodicals provide price and other information regarding derivative securities. Some are listed below. Consult your library to obtain subscription information:

- *The Wall Street Journal.* This well-known newspaper provides daily price information on virtually all listed futures and option contracts. It also offers a daily column titled "Futures Markets."
- *Barron's.* This is a weekly newspaper that provides a column devoted to option markets titled "The Striking Price." It also provides columns devoted to futures markets—"Commodities Corner" and "The Current Yield."
- *Value Line Options.* Published forty-eight times each year, this periodical gives specific option trading recommendations.
- *Consensus.* This is a weekly newspaper devoted solely to the futures industry.
- *Futures.* This is a monthly magazine devoted to futures and options trading. It also provides information on suppliers of on-line computer services and software.

Various practitioner and academic journals also provide valuable information. Some focus exclusively on derivative securities, including *The Journal Of Futures Markets, Advances In Futures And Options Research, The Review Of Futures Markets,* and the *International Options Journal.* Many of the articles referenced in this book are found in these and other journals. Consult your library for subscription information.

U.S. Futures Exchanges

Chicago Board of Trade
141 W. Jackson Blvd.
Chicago, IL 60604
(312)435-3500

Chicago Mercantile Exchange
30 S. Wacker Drive
Chicago, IL 60606
(312)930-1000

Chicago Rice and Cotton Exchange
444 W. Jackson Blvd.
Chicago, IL 60604
(312)341-3078

Coffee, Sugar, and Cocoa Exchange
4 World Trade Center
New York, NY 10048
(212)938-2800

Commodity Exchange, Inc.
4 World Trade Center
New York, NY 10048
(212)938-2900

Kansas City Board of Trade
4800 Main Street
Suite 303
Kansas City, MO 64112
(816)753-7500

MidAmerica Commodity Exchange
444 W. Jackson Blvd.
Chicago, IL 60604
(312)341-3000

Minneapolis Grain Exchange
400 S. Fourth Street
Minneapolis, MN 55414
(612)338-6212

New York Cotton Exchange
4 World Trade Center
New York, NY 10048
(212)938-2650

New York Futures Exchange
4 World Trade Center
New York, NY 10048
(212)656-4949

New York Mercantile Exchange
4 World Trade Center
New York, NY 10048
(212)938-2222

Philadelphia Stock Exchange
1900 Market Street
Philadelphia, PA 19103
(215)496-5000

NOTE: Consult *The Wall Street Journal* to determine the types of futures
and futures options traded on each exchange.

U.S. Option Exchanges

American Stock Exchange
86 Trinity Place
New York, NY 10006
(212)306-1000

AMEX Commodities Corp.
86 Trinity Place
New York, NY 10006
(212)306-1000

Chicago Board Options Exchange
LaSalle at Van Buren
Chicago, IL 60604
(312)786-5600

New York Stock Exchange
11 Wall Street
New York, NY 10005
(212)263-8533

Pacific Stock Exchange
301 Pine Street
San Francisco, CA 94104
(415)393-4000

Philadelphia Stock Exchange
1900 Market Street
Philadelphia, PA 19103
(215)496-5000

NOTE: Consult *The Wall Street Journal* to determine the types of options
traded on each exchange. The AMEX Commodities Corp. is affiliated with
the American Stock Exchange.

Part One

DERIVATIVE SECURITIES AND MODERN PORTFOLIO THEORY

This part of the book is devoted to the relation between derivative securities and modern portfolio theory. It answers the question of why derivative securities exist and are rapidly gaining popularity among financial managers, portfolio managers, and investors of all types. Specifically, you will learn to think of financial futures, options, and swaps as types of insurance contracts, offering tremendous opportunities to reduce risk as measured by the variability of returns.

To begin, Chapter 2 offers some elementary probability and statistical concepts and measures required to understand modern portfolio theory. In Chapter 3 you will be exposed to this theory and to the very important concept that risk reduction through portfolio formation is greater when the portfolio's assets are less correlated. Unfortunately for risk-averse investors, most assets such as stocks and bonds exhibit a high degree of correlation.

Chapter 4 describes derivative securities and explains how they are designed to artificially introduce negative correlation not naturally found in stock, bond, and other asset markets. In this way, they better allow investors to limit the disutility associated with risk. Thus, derivative securities perform a valuable function; they improve social welfare by helping investors to insure their wealth. The markets in which these securities trade simply represent insurance markets that facilitate the transfer of unwanted risks.

Another issue dealt with in this part is how derivative securities help to complete the market, meaning that they provide investment opportunities that are otherwise unattainable. By helping to reduce risk and expand the investment opportunity set, derivative securities enhance investor utility.

2

STATISTICAL CONCEPTS AND MEASURES

In this book we are interested in how financial futures, options, and swaps can be employed to reduce the riskiness of financial assets and portfolios of financial assets. In securities markets, risk is typically measured by the dispersion of returns. In this chapter we introduce some important elementary risk concepts and measures.

SIMPLE PROBABILITY DISTRIBUTION

The *simple probability distribution* portrays the probabilities of obtaining various rates of return over some time period. Figure 2.1 presents a simple probability distribution for a security j. To ease exposition, presume that j is a common stock and that the time period is one year. Here $r_{j,i}$, on the horizontal axis, relates to the ith possible return that stock j may generate over the year. And $h_{j,i}$, on the vertical axis, represents the probability of earning any ith return. The distribution is drawn to appear continuous; the many possible discrete return outcomes exhibited by a stock are well approximated by a continuous distribution. Also, the entire region encompassed by the distribution (the shaded region in Figure 2.1) exhibits an area of 1.00, or 100 percent, representing the sum of the probabilities of all possible rates of return.

Expected Value and Variance of a Population

The distribution portrayed in Figure 2.1 is symmetrical and can be fully described by its mean and its variance. That is, if one knew the distribution's *mean*, its central location, and its *variance*, a measure of the dispersion of returns, then one would also know the entire shape of the symmetrical distribution itself. Here the mean represents the distribu-

Figure 2.1

Simple Probability
Distribution for Rates of
Return for Security j

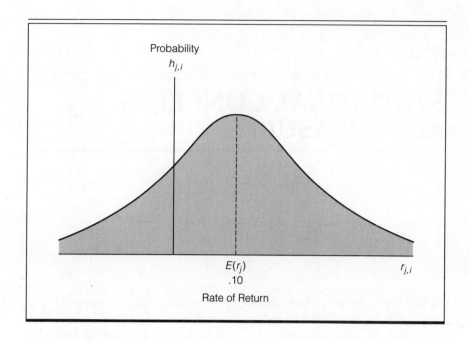

tion's expected value, or stock j's expected rate of return, $E(r_j)$. The formula to compute $E(r_j)$ is

(2.1)
$$E(r_j) = \sum_{i=1}^{n} h_{j,i} \cdot r_{j,i},$$

where n is all possible return outcomes. From Figure 2.1, $E(r_j) = .10$ for this stock.

The variance, represented by $\sigma^2_{r_j}$, tells us the potential for a particular return to deviate from the expected return. We measure $\sigma^2_{r_j}$ by the following formula:

(2.2)
$$\sigma^2_{r_j} = \sum_{i=1}^{n} h_{j,i}[r_{j,i} - E(r_j)]^2.$$

Mean and Variance of a Sample

Since, in reality, we cannot observe a financial security's return distribution, we must estimate it through sampling. This necessitates the assumption that the underlying probability distribution of returns is constant.

Figure 2.2 portrays a time series of annual returns for a stock j. There are six returns: 13%, 21%, 4%, −8%, 15%, and 12%. One can estimate

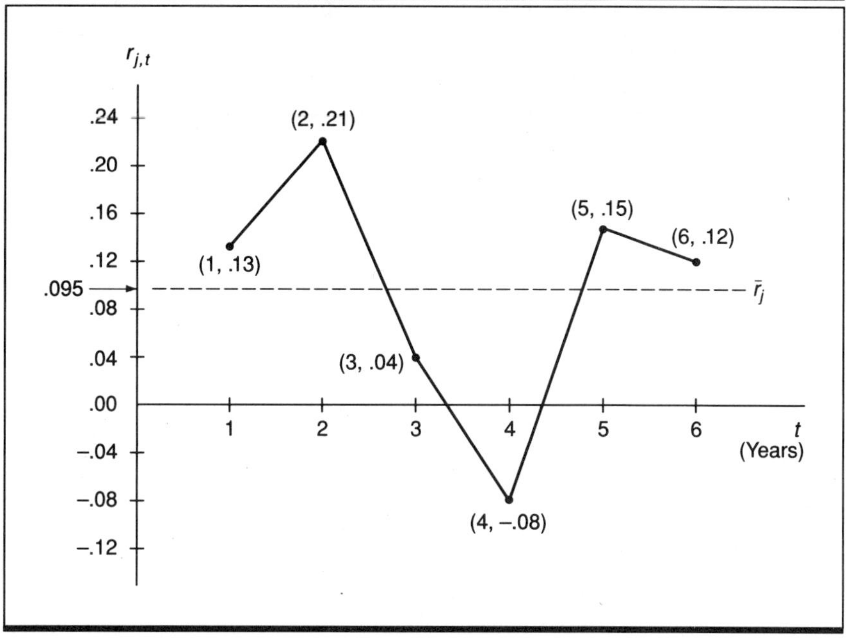

Figure 2.2
Time Series of Annual Rates of Return for Security j

the expected value of the underlying distribution by taking the *sample mean* of these returns:

(2.3)
$$\bar{r}_j = \sum_{t=1}^{N} r_{j,t}/N.$$

Here $\bar{r}_j$ is the sample mean return, 9.50%, and N is the number of sample years, 6.

Notice that the sample estimate, .095, differs from the actual, or true, expected rate of return assumed for this stock (.10 from Figure 2.1). Although the sample mean is an unbiased estimate of the expected value, it is not error-free. A more exact estimate may be obtained by increasing N, the size of our sample. However, as we increase N, we increase the risk that the underlying probability distribution of returns will change over the longer sample period. In general, one should obtain as large a sample as possible, presuming one is confident that changes in the shape of the underlying distribution are nominal.

To estimate return variance, we compute the *sample variance* as follows:

(2.4)
$$\sigma_{r_j}^2 = \sum_{t=1}^{N} (r_{j,t} - \bar{r}_j)^2/N - 1.$$

Here we divide by $N - 1$, since a sample estimate (the sample mean $\bar{r}_j$) is used in the computation. Dividing by $N - 1$ yields an unbiased variance estimate when utilizing small samples, as we do here. The resulting sample variance is .01035:

$$(.13 - .095)^2 = .001225$$
$$(.21 - .095)^2 = .013225$$
$$(.04 - .095)^2 = .003025$$
$$(-.08 - .095)^2 = .030625$$
$$(.15 - .095)^2 = .003025$$
$$(.12 - .095)^2 = \underline{.000625}$$
$$\text{Total} = .051750$$
$$(.051750)/6 - 1 = .01035 = \sigma^2_{r_j}$$

JOINT PROBABILITY DISTRIBUTION

The above measures provide information about the return distribution of a security, but not about the way different securities are interrelated. The probabilities of obtaining various pairs of returns on two securities at the same time are given by the *joint probability distribution*. Again, we are unable to observe the joint probability distribution for securities, so we instead compute the following sample estimates: the sample covariance, the sample correlation coefficient, and the sample coefficient of determination. These are important estimates of the interrelations between individual securities. They are also important in determining the variance of a portfolio of securities.

Sample Covariance

The **sample covariance** tells us how the returns of two different securities move together through time.

The *sample covariance* tells us how the returns of two different securities move together through time. Returns may move directly (positive covariance), inversely (negative covariance), or independently (zero covariance). The formula for sample covariance is

(2.5) $$COV(r_A, r_B) = \sum_{t=1}^{N} [(r_{A,t} - \bar{r}_A)(r_{B,t} - \bar{r}_B)]/N - 1.$$

Suppose we observe the following quarterly rates of return for two stocks, *A* and *B*:

	Quarter				
	1	2	3	4	Mean
Stock *A*	.09	.01	.04	.06	.050
Stock *B*	.06	.00	.05	.07	.045

From Equation 2.5, the sample covariance is .00087:

$$(.09 - .05)(.06 - .045) = .00060$$
$$(.01 - .05)(.00 - .045) = .00180$$
$$(.04 - .05)(.05 - .045) = -.00005$$
$$(.06 - .05)(.07 - .045) = \underline{.00025}$$
$$\text{Total} = .00260$$
$$.00260/(4 - 1) = .00087 = COV(r_A, r_B).$$

This suggests that assets A and B are directly related in the sense that if A earns a return above its mean, then there is a propensity for stock B to also earn a return above its mean (and vice versa). Typically, assets are indeed directly related—that is, they exhibit positive covariance—since securities tend to be similarly affected by macroeconomic factors and policies, including changes in interest rates, domestic and foreign trade deficits, and the like.

Sample Correlation Coefficient

Sample covariance is an unbounded measure; that is, it can range from $-\infty$ to $+\infty$. To bound (or "standardize") sample covariance, we can divide by the product $\sigma_{r_A}\sigma_{r_B}$:

(2.6) $$\rho_{A,B} = COV(r_A, r_B)/\sigma_{r_A}\sigma_{r_B}.$$

By dividing by the product of the sample standard deviations (the square root of sample variance), we obtain $\rho_{A,B}$, which is the *sample correlation coefficient*. It falls within the range -1 to $+1$, and thus represents a bounded measure of how the returns on two different assets move together through time.

> The **sample correlation coefficient** represents a bounded measure of how the returns on two different assets move together through time.

When $\rho_{A,B} = +1$, then we say that assets A and B are *perfectly positively correlated*. Here each sample pairing of returns lines up on a straight line with a positive slope. Figure 2.3 portrays the rare case of perfect positive correlation. Conversely, when $\rho_{A,B} = -1$, then stocks A and B are *perfectly negatively correlated*. As shown in Figure 2.4, here each sample pairing lines up on a straight line with a negative slope. If $\rho_{A,B} = 0$, then assets A and B are said to be *independent;* when the return on A is above its mean, there is no propensity for the return on B to be above or below its mean. Figure 2.5 portrays such independence. Notice that $\rho_{A,B} = 0$ only when $COV(r_A, r_B) = 0$, since $\sigma_{r_A}\sigma_{r_B}$ is by definition nonnegative and almost certainly positive.

Typically, securities exhibit positive, but not perfect positive, correlation. That is, $\rho_{A,B}$ usually lies somewhere between 0 and $+1$. In our case, $\rho_{A,B} = 0.83135$ (try to compute σ_{r_A} and σ_{r_B} yourself):

$$\rho_{A,B} = COV(r_A, r_B)/\sigma_{r_A}\sigma_{r_B} = .00087/(.03366)(.03109) = .83135.$$

Figure 2.6 portrays the more common *imperfect positive correlation*.

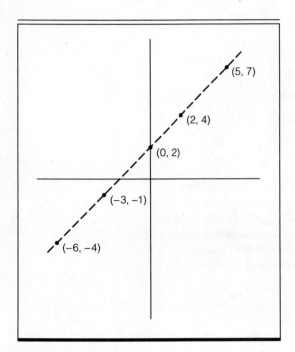

Figure 2.3
Perfect Positive Correlation

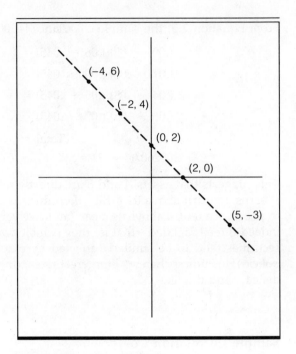

Figure 2.4
Perfect Negative Correlation

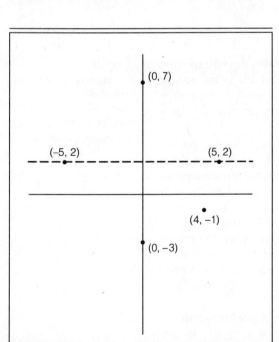

Figure 2.5
Zero Correlation

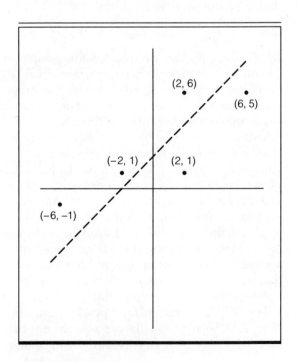

Figure 2.6
Imperfect Positive Correlation

Stock Correlations

In this chapter we contend that most stocks exhibit positive covariance such that the pairwise correlation coefficients lie somewhere between 0 and +1. Evidence supporting this contention is presented in the following pairwise correlation coefficients (a correlation matrix) for five well-known U.S. stocks. These sample correlations are based on a historical sample of 115 monthly returns ending December 1986. The five corporations are American Express (1), AT&T (2), Chevron (3), Coca-Cola (4), and Dow Chemical (5).

Company Number	Correlation Coefficients				
	1	2	3	4	5
1	1.000	0.286	0.136	0.443	0.496
2		1.000	0.188	0.336	0.311
3			1.000	0.018	0.374
4				1.000	0.348
5					1.000

Coefficient of Determination

The *sample coefficient of determination*, designated R^2, is obtained by squaring the sample correlation coefficient. Here $R^2 = (.83135)^2 = .69114$. This coefficient is an important measure of the strength of the association between the two securities. Specifically, R^2 tells us how much of the variability of returns of one asset can be associated with the variability of returns of the other asset. Thus, approximately 69 percent of the return variability of stock A is associated with the return variability of stock B.

> The **sample coefficient of determination** tells us how much of the variability of returns of one asset can be associated with the variability of returns of the other asset.

Variance as a Special Case of Covariance

Suppose that we were interested in the covariance of an asset with itself, or $COV(r_A, r_A)$. Clearly we know that $R^2 = 1.00$; 100 percent of the variability of the returns of A must be associated with the variability of returns of A. If $R^2 = 1$, then $\rho_{A,A} = +1$ ($\rho_{A,A}$ cannot be -1 here). But if $\rho_{A,A} = +1$, then $COV(r_A, r_A)$ must equal $\sigma_{r_A}^2$:

$$\rho_{A,A} = COV(r_A, r_A)/\sigma_{r_A}\sigma_{r_A} = COV(r_A, r_A)/\sigma_{r_A}^2 = 1$$

if and only if

$$COV(r_A, r_A) = \sigma_{r_A}^2.$$

Hence we can conclude that variance is a special case of covariance. Specifically, *variance* is the covariance of one asset with itself. This insight will prove useful when we analyze portfolio variance.

> **Variance** is the covariance of one asset with itself.

SECURITIES AND THE MARKET PORTFOLIO

In the previous part we analyzed the association between individual securities. Now we want to consider the relation between an individual stock and the *market portfolio*. Recall from your previous finance class(es) that the market portfolio is a theoretical portfolio containing all risky assets, where each asset is held in proportion to the total market value of that asset relative to the total market value of all other risky assets. Since this abstract portfolio is not observable, in practice we employ some observable proxy index, like the SP500, to represent the market portfolio.

A Stock's Characteristic Line

Suppose we observe the following pairs of monthly returns for a stock, j, and the market portfolio, m:

			Quarter		
	1	2	3	4	5
Stock j	.03	.04	.07	$-.03$	.09
Market portfolio m	.05	$-.01$	.09	$-.03$	.05

The **characteristic line** shows the return the stock is expected to produce given a particular market rate of return.

Figure 2.7 provides a diagram of these five sample pairings, along with a *line of best fit*, referred to as the stock's *characteristic line*. This line minimizes the sum of the squared vertical distances from each individual observation to the line.[1] Economically speaking, the characteristic line shows the return the stock is expected to produce given a particular market rate of return. For instance, from Figure 2.7 we see that if the market portfolio earns a 2 percent rate of return, then stock j is expected to earn a 3.3 percent rate of return.

A line can be fully described by its intercept and slope. Denoting A_j and β_j as the intercept and slope coefficients, respectively, of stock j's characteristic line, we can estimate these coefficients as follows:

(2.7)
$$\beta_j = COV(r_j, r_m)/\sigma_{r_m}^2$$

(2.8)
$$A_j = \bar{r}_j - \beta_j \bar{r}_m.$$

In our case, $\bar{r}_j = .04$, $\bar{r}_m = .03$, $COV(r_j, r_m) = .0017$, and $\sigma_{r_m}^2 = .0024$. (Try computing these yourself.) Thus the estimated slope and intercept coefficients are:

---

[1]See Appendix 1 of this book for a discussion of simple linear regression analysis and the least-squares criterion.

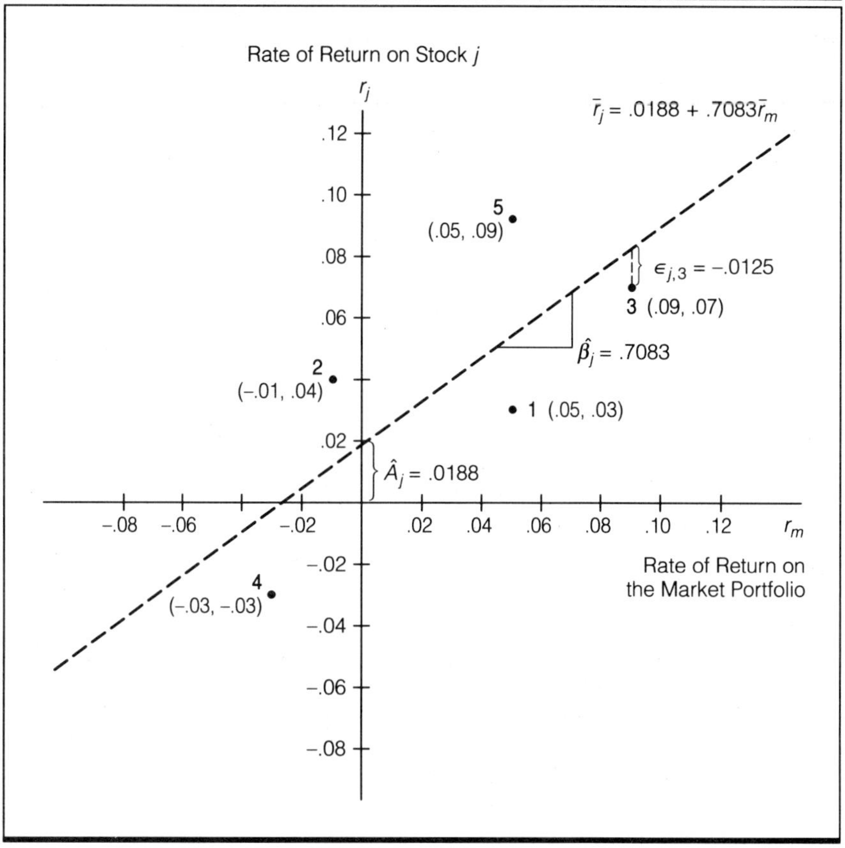

Figure 2.7
Stock j's Characteristic Line

Rate of Return on Stock j

$\bar{r}_j = .0188 + .7083\bar{r}_m$

5 (.05, .09)

$\epsilon_{j,3} = -.0125$

3 (.09, .07)

$\hat{\beta}_j = .7083$

2 (-.01, .04)

1 (.05, .03)

$\hat{A}_j = .0188$

Rate of Return on
the Market Portfolio

4 (-.03, -.03)

$$\hat{\beta}_j = .0017/.0024 = .7083$$
$$\hat{A}_j = .04 - (.7083).03 = .0188.$$

Given these estimates, we can write the equation for stock j's characteristic line:

$$\bar{r}_j = .0188 + .7083\,\bar{r}_m.$$

Beta

The estimated slope of the characteristic line, β_j, is referred to as the security's *beta*. It measures the degree to which a security responds to the changes in the return on the market portfolio. In our case, if the rate of return on the market portfolio increased by 2 percent next month, then we would expect stock j's rate of return to have increased by 1.417 percent (.02 × .7083). Notice that beta is positive because $COV(r_j, r_m)$ is positive (see Equation 2.6). Again, this is typical; most stocks tend to move together and thus with the market portfolio.

Beta measures the degree to which a security responds to changes in the return on the market portfolio.

Residuals and Residual Variance

A *residual*, denoted $\epsilon_{j,t}$, is the vertical distance between a returns pair $(r_{j,t}, r_{m,t})$ and the characteristic line. Mathematically, a residual is given by the following formula:

(2.9)
$$\epsilon_{j,t} = r_{j,t} - (\hat{A}_j + \hat{\beta}_j \, r_{m,t}).$$

For example, here stock j's residual for Month 3 is $-.0125$:

$$\epsilon_{j,3} = .07 - (.0188 + .7083(.09)) = -.0125.$$

Consequently, the stock's realized return, 7 percent, was 1.25 percent less than its expected return (given a market return of 9 percent for this sample month).

We may compute the variance of these residuals, which is simply called *residual variance*—a measure of a security's propensity to generate returns that deviate from expected returns, as given by its characteristic line. To compute stock j's residual variance, denoted $\sigma^2_{\epsilon_j}$, we use the following formula:

(2.10)
$$\sigma^2_{\epsilon_j} = \left(\sum_{t=1}^{N} \epsilon^2_{j,t} \right)/N - 2.$$

Here we divide by $N - 2$ to generate an unbiased estimate, since each residual is based on two sample estimates, $\hat{A}_j$ and $\hat{\beta}_j$. For our stock j, the residual variance is .0012:

Month	Residual	Squared Residual
1	$-.0242$	.000586
2	.0283	.000801
3	$-.0125$	.000156
4	$-.0275$	.000756
5	.0358	.001281
	Total =	.003580

$$.003580/(5 - 2) = .0012 = \sigma^2_{\epsilon_j}.$$

Some Diagnostics For Residual Variance Suppose that a security's covariance with the market portfolio is such that $\rho_{j,m} = +1$. That is, the security is perfectly positively correlated with the market portfolio. What is the security's residual variance? The obvious answer is zero, since each sample pair of returns would line up exactly on the characteristic line, and thus each $\epsilon_{j,t}$ would be zero. Adding such a security to the portfolio would have no effect on the portfolio's risk; the security is redundant, mirroring the risk-return pattern of the portfolio itself.

Now suppose that a stock's covariance with the market is zero, so $\rho_{j,m} = 0$. What is this stock's residual variance? To answer this question, recall Figure 2.5. Since the line of best fit—here stock j's characteristic line—has a zero slope, $\hat{\beta}_j = 0$, the equation for the characteristic line is simply $\bar{r}_j = \hat{A}_j$. That is, the expected return on stock j is a constant and is independent of r_m. Therefore, each residual $\epsilon_{j,t}$ is given by $r_{j,t} - \hat{A}_j$. Since $\hat{A}_j$ is a constant and therefore exhibits no variance, residual variance must approximately equal return variance: $\sigma^2_{\epsilon_j} \approx \sigma^2_{r_j}$.

To see this more formally, rewrite Equation 2.9 so that $\epsilon_{j,t} = r_{j,t} - \hat{A}_j = r_{j,t} - \bar{r}_j$:

$$\sigma^2_{\epsilon_j} = [\sum_{t=1}^{N} (r_{j,t} - \bar{r}_j)^2]/N - 2.$$

Now notice that this expression for residual variance is nearly identical to Equation 2.4, which gives stock j's sample return variance. Indeed, residual and return variance are nearly identical for large samples (i.e., large N), again given $\rho_{j,m} = 0$.

A security's *residual variance* represents the portion of a security's total return variance that is diversifiable. Simply put, it is the portion of a security's return variance that does not move systematically with the market specifically, nor, therefore, with other securities generally. So if $\rho_{j,m} = +1$, as in the first case above, then the stock exhibits no diversifiable risk ($\sigma^2_{\epsilon_j} = 0$). This is why the stock is redundant, and will not help to further reduce the risk of the well diversified market portfolio. For the second case above, where $\rho_{j,m} = 0$, so $\sigma^2_{\epsilon_j} \approx \sigma^2_{r_j}$, the stock's total risk is diversifiable. If this zero-beta stock were added to the portfolio, its return variance would be diversified away, and thus this stock would be risk-free. Hence, we can conclude that a *zero-beta asset* is a riskless asset that in equilibrium should earn the riskless rate of interest.

A security's **residual variance** represents that portion of a security's total return variance which is diversifiable.

A **zero-beta asset** is a riskless asset that in equilibrium should earn the riskless rate of interest.

SUMMARY

This chapter introduced some elementary probability and statistical measures and concepts. We reviewed the simple probability distribution and the associated concepts of population expected return and variance, and sample mean and variance. We also reviewed the joint probability distribution and the associated concepts of sample covariance, correlation, and the coefficient of determination. Finally, we examined the relation between an individual security and the market portfolio, in which context the characteristic line, beta, and residual variance of a security were reviewed.

The measures and concepts discussed in this chapter represent the foundation upon which the benefits of futures, options, and swaps can be understood. Thus, you must possess a working knowledge of these concepts and measures if you wish to seriously pursue the study of derivative securities.

Selected References

Daniel, W., and J. Terrell. *Business Statistics: Concepts and Methodology*. 2d ed. Boston: Houghton Mifflin, 1979.

Haugen, R. *Modern Investment Theory*. 1st ed. Englewood Cliffs: Prentice-Hall, 1986.

Levy, H., and M. Ben-Horim. *Statistics: Decisions and Applications in Business and Economics*. 1st ed. New York: Random House, 1984.

Reilly, F. *Investment Analysis and Portfolio Management*, 2d ed. Hinsdale: Dryden, 1985.

Wonnacott, T., and R. Wonnacott. *Introductory Statistics for Business and Economics*. 1st ed. New York: Wiley, 1984.

Questions and Problems

1. Under what conditions are a security's residual variance and return variance approximately equal?

2. Why do financial securities like stocks or bonds tend to exhibit positive covariance?

3. If $\rho_{A,B}$ = .81, then what is the coefficient of determination? What does this coefficient tell us?

4. Suppose you found the following pairings of returns for two stocks, A and B. What are $COV(r_A, r_B)$ and $\rho_{A,B}$?

		Month			
	1	2	3	4	5
Stock A	.02	.03	.04	.00	$-.03$
Stock B	.01	.03	.03	.01	$-.01$

Questions 5 through 10 refer to the following monthly return pairings for stock j and the market portfolio m:

		Month			
	1	2	3	4	5
Stock j	.03	$-.02$	.00	.01	.01
Market Portfolio	.03	.04	.02	.02	$-.01$

5. What are $\sigma_{r_j}^2$ and $\sigma_{r_m}^2$?

6. What is $COV(r_j, r_m)$?

7. What is stock j's characteristic line?

8. What is the correlation coefficient, $\rho_{j,m}$?

9. What is the coefficient of determination, R^2?

10. What is stock j's residual variance?

Self-Test Problems

Refer to the following quarterly returns for stock j and the market portfolio (m) for self-test (ST) problems 1 through 8:

	Quarter			
	1	2	3	4
Stock j	.05	.07	.02	.00
Market Portfolio	.04	.06	.03	−.01

ST-1. What are r_j and r_m?

ST-2. What are $\sigma_{r_j}^2$ and $\sigma_{r_m}^2$?

ST-3. What is $COV(r_j, r_m)$?

ST-4. What is $\hat{\beta}_j$?

ST-5. What is stock j's characteristic line?

ST-6. What is $\rho_{j,m}$?

ST-7. What is the coefficient of determination, R^2?

ST-8. What is $\sigma_{\epsilon_j}^2$?

Solutions to Self-Test Problems

ST-1. $\bar{r}_j = (.05 + .07 + .02 + .00)/4 = .035.$

$\bar{r}_m = (.04 + .06 + .03 - .01)/4 = .030.$

ST-2. $\sigma_{r_j}^2 = [(.0 - .035)^{22} + (.07 - .035)^2 +$

$(.02 - .035)^2 + (.00 - .035)^2]/3 = .001.$

$\sigma_{r_m}^2 = [(.04 - .03)^2 + (.06 - .03)^2 +$

$(.03 - .03)^2 + (-.01 - .03)^2]/3 = .0009.$

ST-3. $COV(r_j, r_m) = [(.05 - .035)(.04 - .03) + (.07 - .035)$

$(.06 - .03) + (.02 - .035)(.03 - .03) +$

$(.00 - .035)(-.01 - .03)]/3 = .0009.$

ST-4. $\hat{\beta}_j = .0009/.0009 = 1.00.$

ST-5. $\hat{A}_j = .035 - (1.00).03 = .005.$

$\bar{r}_j = .005 + 1.00\bar{r}_m.$

ST-6. $\rho_{j,m} = .0009/\sqrt{.001}\sqrt{.009} = .9487.$

ST-7. $R^2 = (.9487)^2 = .90.$

ST-8. $\epsilon_{j,1} = .05 - (.005 + 1.00(.04)) = .005.$

$\epsilon_{j,2} = .07 - (.005 + 1.00(.06)) = .005.$

$\epsilon_{j,3} = .02 - (.005 + 1.00(.03)) = -.015.$

$\epsilon_{j,4} = .00 - (.005 + 1.00(-.01)) = .005.$

$\sigma^2_{\epsilon_j} = [(.005)^2 + (.005)^2 + (-.015)^2 +$

$(.005)^2]/2 = .00015.$

3

PORTFOLIO DIVERSIFICATION

Modern portfolio theory asserts that assets should not be held in isolation. Rather, they should be held as parts of portfolios. Indeed, pension funds, mutual funds, insurance companies, banks, thrifts, and other institutions are required by law to hold diversified portfolios. Individual investors also are wise to hold diversified portfolios. The risk and return of an individual asset is therefore viewed in the context of how its inclusion in a portfolio affects the *portfolio's* risk and return.

Accepting the standard deviation of portfolio returns as a reasonable measure of portfolio risk, we demonstrate in this chapter how to compute the risk and expected return of a portfolio based on the characteristics of its component assets. In short, we investigate the theory of portfolio diversification. Our most important conclusion is that risk reduction through diversification is enhanced if individual assets exhibit low correlation with each other.

STANDARD DEVIATION AS A MEASURE OF RISK

If a portfolio's returns are normally distributed, only two measures are needed to describe its return distribution: its standard deviation and expected rate of return (mean).[1]

---

[1]Alternatively, we may be solely concerned with mean and standard deviation if investors are assumed to exhibit quadratic utility functions. Utility theory is described in Chapter 4. If investors have a quadratic utility function, then they are concerned only with mean and standard deviation, and do not "price" other statistics such as skewness or kurtosis. The assumption that investors have quadratic utility functions is typically not invoked, however, because of its restrictive and artificial nature.

It is well known that the normal distribution is robust to additivity. In other words, if two or more normal distributions are combined, the resulting distribution is also normal. So if individual asset returns are assumed to be normally distributed, then a mixture of those assets—a portfolio—also is assumed to have normally distributed returns.

The assumption of normally distributed asset returns is important to us because it underlies modern portfolio theory. By invoking this assumption, we can focus exclusively on the computation of mean and standard deviation, making the analysis of portfolio diversification easier and tractable, while retaining consistency with the notion that rational investors are risk averse.

THE EXPECTED RETURN OF A PORTFOLIO

The **expected rate of return to a portfolio** is a simple weighted average of the expected rates of return to the assets included in the portfolio.

The *expected rate of return to a portfolio* is a simple weighted average of the expected rates of return to the assets included in the portfolio:

(3.1)
$$E(r_p) = \sum_{j=1}^{M} w_j E(r_j),$$

where

$E(r_p)$ = the portfolio's expected rate of return,

$E(r_j)$ = asset j's expected rate of return,

w_j = the weight, defined as the fraction of money invested in asset j, and

M = the total number of assets in the portfolio.

For example, if we invest one-half of our wealth in an asset A, which has an expected return of 6 percent, and one-half of our wealth in asset B, with a 10 percent expected return, then our portfolio's expected return is 8 percent:

$$E(r_p) = .50(.06) + .50(.10) = .08.$$

A proof of Equation 3.1 is presented in Appendix 3.A.

The Budget Constraint

Each weight, w_j, represents the fraction of money invested in asset j. In other words, each w_j is determined by dividing the dollar amount invested in asset j by the total investment in the portfolio. It follows that the sum of all weights must be 1, representing 100 percent of the equity investment in the portfolio:

(3.2)
$$\sum_{j=1}^{M} w_j = 1.$$

Equation 3.2 is our *budget constraint*. It simply states that the sum of wealth invested in each asset must equal our total wealth invested.

Short Selling

A portfolio weight, w_j, can be either positive or negative. A positive weight implies that the asset is being purchased (a *long* position), while a negative weight means that you are taking a short position in the asset, or *short selling*, meaning you are borrowing the asset with the obligation to replace it at some time in the future.

Short selling occurs when you borrow an asset with the obligation to replace it at some time in the future.

You may choose to undertake a short position if you anticipate a price depreciation. This way you can "sell high and buy low." For example, suppose that you borrow 100 shares of IBM stock (a round lot). You borrow these shares from someone who owns IBM stock; a broker typically facilitates the transaction. You then sell the 100 shares in the open market for its current price, say, $120 per share. If IBM's price depreciates after a period of time, to say, $110 per share, then you can repurchase the shares in the open market and reverse your short position (return your borrowed shares). Your proceeds from the short sale are $1,000 [($120 − $110) × (100)]. If IBM paid a dividend during the period, you would have to pay cash in the amount of the total dividends to the original stock owner.

The proceeds from the short sale, here $12,000, usually have to be left with the broker. Further, you may have to deposit a fraction of the proceeds in your own money with the broker. This margin offers the broker protection from your credit risk should IBM's price appreciate during the period.

However, large financial institutions that are very creditworthy are not typically constrained as to use of proceeds. Thus, they may use the proceeds from the short sale to invest in other assets. Also, no margin deposit is required.

To illustrate short selling, suppose that you have equity of $10,000 and sell short $5,000 of stock A, a stock you expect to depreciate. In turn, you invest the entire $15,000 in another stock, B, which you expect to appreciate in value. Thus, it is assumed that you can fully use the proceeds from the short sale. The resulting weight in stock B is 150 percent, or $w_B = 1.5$. The weight in A is −50 percent, or $w_A = -.5$, indicating a short position. The weights sum to 1, satisfying the budget constraint. If B has a 10 percent expected return over the period, and stock A has a −8 percent expected return, then your "portfolio's" expected return is 19 percent:

$$E(r_p) = (1.5)(.10) + (-.5)(-.08) = .19.$$

Why not short sell more of stock A? Unlike strictly long positions, where the portfolio's expected return must lie somewhere between the returns on the two stocks, a portfolio's expected return is unlimited (in theory) when short selling occurs. You could continuously increase the portfolio's expected return by shorting more and more of stock A. However, such a strategy has two caveats. First, in reality short selling is indeed limited, often to 50 percent or less of an investor's equity position. Second, increasing the expected return of a portfolio usually implies that the portfolio's risk is also increasing. We discuss portfolio risk next.

THE RISK OF A PORTFOLIO

The **variance of returns of a portfolio** of assets is a weighted average of the covariance pairings of all assets included in the portfolio.

The *variance of returns of a portfolio* of assets is a weighted average of the covariance pairings of all assets included in the portfolio:

$$\sigma^2_{r_p} = \sum_{i,j=1}^{M^2} w_i w_j COV(r_i, r_j), \quad \textbf{(3.3)}$$

where $\sigma^2_{r_p}$ = the variance of portfolio returns. A proof of Equation 3.3 is presented in Appendix 3.A.

In order to compute $\sigma^2_{r_p}$, you need to obtain the *covariance matrix,* which gives you the covariance pairings of all assets in the portfolio. The covariance matrix for a two-stock portfolio is as follows:

Stock	w_A A	w_B B
w_A A	$COV(r_A, r_A)$	$COV(r_A, r_B)$
w_B B	$COV(r_B, r_A)$	$COV(r_B, r_B)$

Recall from Chapter 2 that variance is the covariance of an asset with itself. Thus, the diagonal terms in the above matrix are variance terms: $COV(r_A, r_A) = \sigma^2_{r_A}$ and $COV(r_B, r_B) = \sigma^2_{r_B}$. Because of this, the above matrix is often called the *variance-covariance matrix:*

Stock	w_A A	w_B B
w_A A	$\sigma^2_{r_A}$	$COV(r_A, r_B)$
w_B B	$COV(r_B, r_A)$	$\sigma^2_{r_B}$

Once the above matrix is determined, the computation of portfolio return variance is straightforward. From Equation 3.3, you first multiply each covariance term by the weight at the top of the column and then multiply again by the weight at the left side of the row. When such a product is obtained for each element of the matrix, you add the products. The resulting sum is $\sigma^2_{r_p}$. For our two-stock portfolio we have the following:

$$\sigma_{r_p}^2 = w_A^2\sigma_{r_A}^2 + w_Aw_BCOV(r_A,r_B) + w_Bw_ACOV(r_B,r_A) + w_B^2\sigma_{r_B}^2.$$

Recognizing that $COV(r_A,r_B) \equiv COV(r_B,r_A)$ gives us

$$\sigma_{r_p}^2 = w_A^2\sigma_{r_A}^2 + w_B^2\sigma_{r_B}^2 + 2w_Aw_BCOV(r_A,r_B).$$

Finally, from Equation 2.5 we know that $COV(r_A,r_B) = \rho_{A,B}\sigma_{r_A}\sigma_{r_B}$. Substituting gives us

$$\sigma_{r_p}^2 = w_A^2\sigma_{r_A}^2 + w_B^2\sigma_{r_B}^2 + 2w_Aw_B\rho_{A,B}\sigma_{r_A}\sigma_{r_B}.$$

Notice that a two-stock portfolio has four covariance terms. In general, there are M^2 covariance terms. Thus, the computation of portfolio return variance gets very messy as the number of portfolio assets grows. For example, for the SP500 Stock Index there are $(500)^2$, or 250,000 covariance terms. To illustrate the computation of $\sigma_{r_p}^2$, suppose that we have a simple two-stock portfolio where we have determined the following covariance matrix:

Stock	w_A A	w_B B
w_A A	.05	.03
w_B B	.03	.07

If this portfolio is equally weighted, meaning that $w_A = w_B = .50$, then the resulting portfolio variance is .045:

$$\sigma_{r_p}^2 = (.50)^2(.05) + (.50)^2(.07) + 2(.50)(.50)(.03) = .045.$$

Notice that the resulting portfolio's return variance, .045, is less than both the variance of A, .05, and the variance of B, .07. Thus, in this example, diversifying across both assets resulted in lower variance than holding either asset A or B (not diversifying).

Obviously, the portfolio's standard deviation is simply σ_{r_p}; here it is $\sqrt{.045}$, or .212. Also, it is possible to determine $\rho_{A,B}$ from the information provided, as follows:

$$.045 = (.50)^2(.05) + (.50)^2(.07) +$$
$$2(.50)(.50)\rho_{A,B}(.05)^{1/2}(.07)^{1/2},$$

or $\rho_{A,B} = .507$. Thus, stocks A and B exhibit positive correlation. Recall from Chapter 2 that this is typical.

PORTFOLIO RISK AND CORRELATION

Suppose that in the above illustration we allow the correlation coefficient, $\rho_{A,B}$, to vary. Obviously, we will obtain different measures of

Exhibit 3.1:
Portfolio Standard Deviations

$\rho_{A,B}$	σ_{r_p}
1.000	.244
.750	.228
.507	.212
.000	.173
−.500	.122
1.000	.020

The σ_{r_p} values are obtained from Equation 3.3 and the following parameters: $w_A = .50$; $w_B = .50$; $\sigma_{r_A}^2 = .05$; $\sigma_{r_B}^2 = .07$.

σ_{r_p}. In fact, we will obtain smaller values of σ_{r_p} as the correlation coefficient is reduced. Therefore, if we define risk by the standard deviation of portfolio returns, then portfolio risk is reduced as $\rho_{A,B}$ is reduced. This concept is exemplified in Exhibit 3.1, where values of σ_{r_p} are reported for given correlation coefficients. The standard deviation of portfolio returns decreases unidirectionally as $\rho_{A,B}$ is reduced.

To demonstrate this notion more formally, suppose that we differentiate $\sigma_{r_p}^2$ with respect to $\rho_{A,B}$.[2] We have:

$$\partial \sigma_{r_p}^2 / \partial \rho_{A,B} = 2w_A w_B \sigma_{r_A} \sigma_{r_B} > 0 \text{ if } w_A, w_B > 0.$$

This exercise demonstrates that there is a direct relationship between portfolio risk and asset correlation when the portfolio weights are positive. In other words, as $\rho_{A,B}$ goes up (down), σ_{r_p} increases (decreases). We can generally conclude, therefore, that risk reduction through diversification is enhanced if individual assets exhibit lower correlation with each other.

Perfect Positive Correlation

Risk reduction through diversification is enhanced if individual assets exhibit lower correlation with each other.

The above notion is affirmed by examining the special cases of perfect positive correlation ($\rho_{A,B} = +1$) and perfect negative correlation ($\rho_{A,B} = -1$). For $\rho_{A,B} = +1$, and recognizing that $w_B = 1 - w_A$, we have

$$\sigma_{r_p}^2 = w_A^2 \sigma_{r_A}^2 + (1 - w_A)^2 \sigma_{r_B}^2 + 2w_A(1 - w_A)\sigma_{r_A}\sigma_{r_B}.$$

---

[2]This represents the first time that the calculus process known as *differentiation* is used in this text. Understanding this process is very useful, although not imperative, in fully grasping some of the material presented. For this reason, it is reviewed in Appendix 2 in the back of this text.

Taking the square root of both sides of this expression gives us the following:[3]

$$\sigma_{r_p} = w_A\sigma_{r_A} + (1 - w_A)\sigma_{r_B}.$$

This expression states that the standard deviation of portfolio returns is a simple weighted average of the standard deviations of returns of the portfolio's component assets, when these assets are perfectly positively correlated. This can be confirmed by examining Exhibit 3.1 where $\rho_{A,B} = 1.000$. The corresponding value of σ_{r_p} is .244, which is the simple weighted average of σ_{r_A} and σ_{r_B}:

$$.244 = .50(.05)^{1/2} + .50(.07)^{1/2}.$$

When $\rho_{A,B} = +1$, portfolio diversification is not successful in reducing risk (at least when only long positions are taken). For example, from Exhibit 3.1, placing 100 percent of our wealth in stock A would have resulted in the lowest variance, .05. Since A had the lower variance, an undiversified portfolio consisting strictly of stock A exhibits less risk than any long combination of A and B.

Figure 3.1 graphically depicts this concept. Here we have two stocks, C and C', which are redundant with respect to their return profiles. Thus, these two stocks must exhibit perfect positive correlation. Figure 3.1 shows that a portfolio consisting of long positions in these two stocks is unsuccessful in reducing risk. The risk of the resulting two-stock portfolio is identical to that of stock C or C'.

Perfect Negative Correlation

For $\rho_{A,B} = -1$, we have

$$\sigma_{r_p}^2 = w_A^2\sigma_{r_A}^2 + (1 - w^A)^2\sigma_{r_B}^2 - 2w_A(1 - w_A)\sigma_{r_A}\sigma_{r_B}.$$

Taking the square root of both sides of this expression gives us[4]

$$\sigma_{r_p} = |w_A\sigma_{r_A} - (1 - w_A)\sigma_{r_B}|.$$

Now recognize that this expression for portfolio standard deviation yields lower values of σ_{r_p} than the expression corresponding to the case of perfect positive correlation:

$$\sigma_{r_p} = |w_A\sigma_{r_A} - (1 - w_A)\sigma_{r_B}| < \sigma_{r_p} = w_A\sigma_{r_A} - (1 - w_A)\sigma_{r_B}.$$
$$\rho_{A,B} = -1 \qquad\qquad \rho_{A,B} = +1$$

---

[3]Recognize that the expression is a perfect square of the form $(L + M)^2 = L^2 + M^2 + 2LM$. Here $L = w_A\sigma_{r_A}$ and $M = (1 - w_A)\sigma_{r_B}$. Thus, the resulting square root is just $L + M$, or $w_A\sigma_{r_A} + (1 - w_A)\sigma_{r_B}$.

[4]Recognize that the expression is a perfect square of the form $(L - M)^2$. Also, we use an absolute sign since σ_{r_p} must be nonnegative.

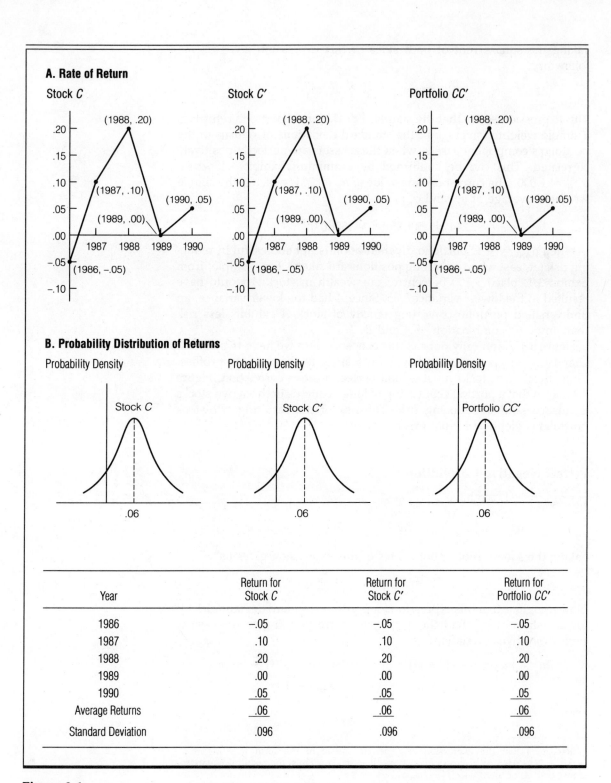

A. Rate of Return

Stock C

Stock C'

Portfolio CC'

B. Probability Distribution of Returns

Probability Density

Probability Density

Probability Density

Stock C

Stock C'

Portfolio CC'

.06

.06

.06

Year	Return for Stock C	Return for Stock C'	Return for Portfolio CC'
1986	−.05	−.05	−.05
1987	.10	.10	.10
1988	.20	.20	.20
1989	.00	.00	.00
1990	.05	.05	.05
Average Returns	.06	.06	.06
Standard Deviation	.096	.096	.096

Figure 3.1:
Rate of Return Distributions for Two Perfectly Positively Correlated Stocks ($\rho_{C,C'} = +1$) and an Equally Weighted Portfolio CC'

Thus, we again see that portfolio risk is lower when component assets are less correlated (presuming long positions are undertaken). This can be confirmed by examining Exhibit 3.1 where $\rho_{A,B} = -1.000$. The corresponding value of σ_{r_p} is .020, which is substantially lower than .244, the value of σ_{r_p} when $\rho_{A,B} - 1.000$:

$$\sigma_{r_p} = \left| (.50)(.05)^{1/2} - (.50)(.07)^{1/2} \right| = .020 < .244.$$

When $\rho_{A,B} = -1$, portfolio diversification is a powerful tool in reducing risk. Indeed, it is possible to eliminate all return dispersion by assigning the appropriate weights to each component asset. Setting $\sigma_{r_p} = 0$ and solving algebraically for w_A when $\rho_{A,B} = -1$ gives us

$$w_A = \sigma_{r_B}/(\sigma_{r_A} + \sigma_{r_B}).$$

This expression yields the weight in A that minimizes σ_{r_p}. Of course, w_B is just $(1 - w_A)$ by our budget constraint. In our illustration, $w_A = .542$, and $w_B = .458$ minimizes σ_{r_p}:

$$w_A = (.07)^{1/2}/[(.05)^{1/2} + (.07)^{1/2}] = .542; \; w_B = .458.$$

We can confirm this as follows:

$$\sigma_{r_p} = \left| (.542)(.05)^{1/2} - (.458)(.07)^{1/2} \right| = 0.$$

Notice that we placed a greater portion of our wealth (.542) in the lower variance stock, A.

The ability to completely eliminate portfolio risk through long positions when assets are perfectly negatively correlated is depicted graphically in Figure 3.2. Here we have two stocks, D and D', that are mirror opposites with respect to their return profiles. Thus, these two stocks must be perfectly negatively correlated. Figure 3.2 shows that a portfolio consisting of long positions in these two stocks exhibits no return dispersion.

Positive Correlation

As was discussed in Chapter 2, most assets exhibit some degree of positive correlation. This is because asset values are commonly influenced by the same macroeconomic factors, including monetary and fiscal policy as well as international trade policy. Consequently, combining assets into portfolios (via long positions) reduces risk but does not completely eliminate it. Figure 3.3 illustrates this point. Here an equally weighted portfolio of two stocks, A and B, is formed. Stocks A and B exhibit a correlation coefficient of .67. The portfolio's average return is .075, which is the same as the average return for each stock. However, the portfolio's standard deviation is .103, which is less than the standard deviation of either stock. The portfolio's risk is therefore less than the average of the risks of the component stocks. Thus, diversification has reduced, though not eliminated, risk.

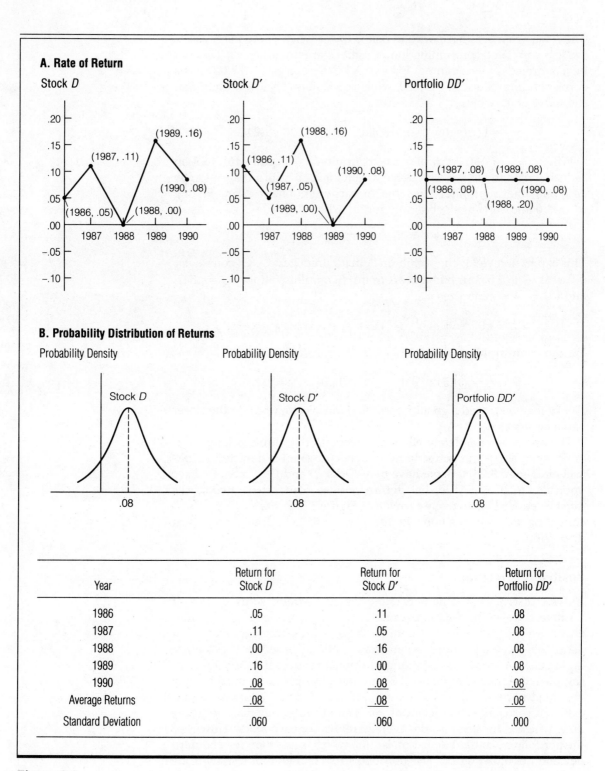

A. Rate of Return

Stock *D*

(1987, .11)
(1989, .16)
(1990, .08)
(1986, .05)
(1988, .00)

Stock *D'*

(1988, .16)
(1986, .11)
(1990, .08)
(1987, .05)
(1989, .00)

Portfolio *DD'*

(1987, .08)   (1989, .08)
(1986, .08)   (1990, .08)
(1988, .20)

B. Probability Distribution of Returns

Probability Density — Stock *D* — .08

Probability Density — Stock *D'* — .08

Probability Density — Portfolio *DD'* — .08

Year	Return for Stock *D*	Return for Stock *D'*	Return for Portfolio *DD'*
1986	.05	.11	.08
1987	.11	.05	.08
1988	.00	.16	.08
1989	.16	.00	.08
1990	.08	.08	.08
Average Returns	.08	.08	.08
Standard Deviation	.060	.060	.000

Figure 3.2

Rate of Return Distributions for Two Perfectly Negatively Correlated Stocks ($\rho_{D,D'} = -1$) and an Equally Weighted Portfolio, *DD'*

A. Rate of Return

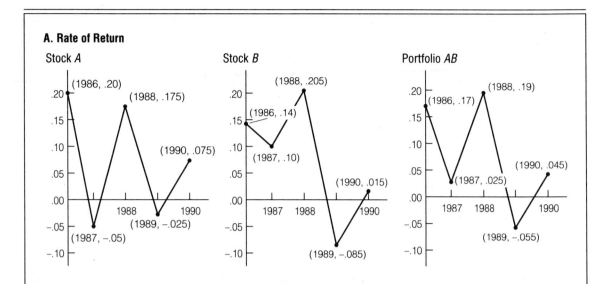

B. Probability Distribution of Returns

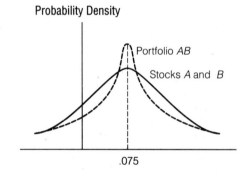

Year	Return for Stock A	Return for Stock B	Return for Portfolio AB
1986	.200	.140	.170
1987	−.050	.100	.025
1988	.175	.205	.190
1989	−.025	−.085	−.055
1990	.075	.015	.045
Average Returns	.075	.075	.075
Standard Deviation	.113	.113	.103

Figure 3.3

Rate of Return Distributions for Two Positively Correlated Stocks ($\rho_{A,B} = .665$) and an Equally Weighted Portfolio, AB

A RE-EXAMINATION OF SHORT SELLING

The concept of short selling was defined earlier in this chapter. At that time, we stated that while short selling may increase expected return, it can also increase a portfolio's risk. Now that the relation between portfolio risk and asset correlation has been explained we can expand on the practice of short selling.

Recall our illustration in which a weight of 1.5 was assigned to one stock, B, with an expected return of .10, and a weight of $-.5$ was assigned to another stock, A, with an expected return of $-.08$. The resulting portfolio's expected return was .19. Thus, short selling stock A increased our portfolio's expected rate of return. However, notice also that stocks A and B were likely negatively correlated, since B was expected to appreciate while A was expected to depreciate. By shorting stock A, we effectively made our positions in A and B *positively* correlated. In other words, we took two stocks that were negatively correlated and, by assuming a short position in one of them, created a positively correlated two-stock portfolio. The result, of course, is that while we increased our expected return through short selling, we also increased our portfolio risk, since positive correlation results in greater portfolio return variance.

To demonstrate this more precisely, again differentiate $\sigma_{r_p}^2$ with respect to $\rho_{A,B}$:

$$\partial\sigma_{r_p}^2/\partial\rho_{A,B} = 2w_A w_B \sigma_{r_A}\sigma_{r_B} < 0 \text{ if } w_A < 0 \text{ or } w_B < 0.$$

This expression states that portfolio risk *increases* as correlation is lowered if short selling occurs.

Short selling can reduce risk substantially if assets are positively correlated.

Does short selling always increase portfolio risk? The answer is no. In fact, short selling can reduce risk substantially if assets are positively correlated. Intuitively, we can take two assets that exhibit positive correlation and, by shorting one of them, create a negatively correlated two-asset portfolio. Indeed, we can completely eliminate portfolio return dispersion through short selling even if component assets are perfectly positively correlated.

Recall the expression for σ_{r_p} when $\rho_{A,B} = +1$:

$$\sigma_{r_p} = w_A\sigma_{r_A} + w_B\sigma_{r_B} = w_A\sigma_{r_A} + (1 - w_A)\sigma_{r_B}.$$

If we set $\sigma_{r_p} = 0$ and solve algebraically for w_A, we have

$$w_A = -\sigma_{r_B}/(\sigma_{r_A} - \sigma_{r_B}).$$

This expression yields the weight for asset A that will minimize portfolio risk when $\rho_{A,B} = +1$. Of course, $w_B = (1 - w_A)$. Notice, however, that w_A must be either negative, implying it should be sold short, or greater than 1, implying that asset B should be sold short. Thus, short selling is needed in order to minimize σ_{r_p} when $\rho_{A,B} = +1$.

As an example, suppose that two perfectly positively correlated assets have the following standard deviations of returns: $\sigma_{r_A} = .10$ and

σ_{r_B} = .15. The weights that minimize portfolio risk are $w_A = 3$ and $w_B = -2$:

$$w_A = (-.15)/(.10 - .15) = 3; w_B = (1 - w_A) = -2.$$

Thus, we short sell B, the higher variance asset, investing the proceeds along with our initial equity in asset A. We can confirm that this unique set of weights produces a zero portfolio standard deviation:

$$\sigma_{r_p} = (3.0)(.10) + (-2.0)(.15) = 0.$$

We see that through short selling an investor can artificially create negative correlation and thus reduce risk, if so desired. The investor takes assets that are naturally positively correlated, such as common stocks, and, by shorting one or more of these assets, introduces negative correlation. Of course, expected return will also typically decline as a result. Hence, short selling can be used to either increase expected return, with correspondingly higher risk, or reduce risk, with correspondingly lower return. In sum, we can say that short selling expands the investor's opportunity set.

Short selling expands the investor's opportunity set.

Short Selling and the Risk-Free Asset

As an illustration of how short selling can expand an investor's opportunity set, consider a two-asset portfolio in which one of the assets is risk-free. Recall from Chapter 2 that a risk-free asset is a zero-beta asset; it has no systematic risk, and its unsystematic risk can be diversified and eliminated. In equilibrium, the risk-free asset should earn the riskless rate of interest.

Consider Figure 3.4. A risky stock is plotted at Point A. It has an expected return of .10 and a standard deviation of .06. A risk-free asset is also plotted at Point B. It has a return of .05. This asset may be a bond guaranteed by the federal government, so the probability of earning a 5 percent return is 100 percent. This implies that the standard deviation of returns on the bond is zero.

Now recall the expression for the variance of a two-asset portfolio:

$$\sigma_{r_p}^2 = w_A^2 \sigma_{r_A}^2 + w_B^2 \sigma_{r_B}^2 + 2w_A w_B \rho_{A,B} \sigma_{r_A} \sigma_{r_B}.$$

Since $\sigma_{r_B} = 0$, we have

$$\sigma_{r_p}^2 = w_A^2 \sigma_{r_A}^2,$$

or

$$\sigma_{r_p} = w_A \sigma_{r_A}.$$

Given this expression, we can produce a schedule of portfolio expected returns and standard deviations for various values of w_A:

Figure 3.4:

The Effect of Short Selling on the Investment Opportunity Set

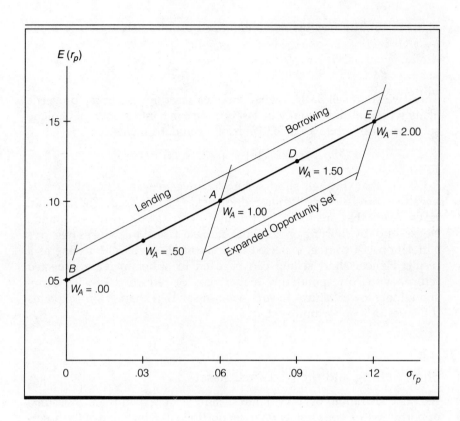

W_A	$E(r_p)$	σ_{r_p}
.00	.050	.000
.50	.075	.030
1.00	.100	.060
1.50	.125	.090
2.00	.150	.120

These points are plotted in Figure 3.4. The resulting plot is a straight line. If an investor takes a position between Points B and A, then he is investing money in both the risky stock and the risk-free bond; that is, he is taking a long position in both assets. He is lending money to the federal government—the bond issuer. If the investor assumes a position on the line to the northeast of Point A, then he is taking a short position in the risk-free asset. In other words, the investor borrows capital at the riskless rate of interest by selling guaranteed bonds. He then uses the borrowed capital to invest in stock A, increasing both risk and expected return.

The important point to this exercise is that an investor, through short selling, can achieve portfolio combinations to the northeast of Point A.

If short selling were prohibited completely, the investor could not achieve portfolios such as Points D or E in Figure 3.4. Hence, short selling expands the investor's opportunity set; it allows the investor to achieve points in expected return-standard deviation space that would otherwise be unattainable.

EFFICIENT PORTFOLIO FORMATION: A BRIEF DISCUSSION

Efficient portfolio formation refers to the creation of a frontier of investment portfolios that each produce the highest expected return for a given level of risk. Put another way, suppose that two investors, who are willing to tolerate the same degree of risk, are faced with the same investment opportunities. One investor may form a portfolio that meets her risk constraint by merely choosing random securities and equally weighting these securities. The more sophisticated investor can form a more efficient, dominating portfolio from this same opportunity set, however, by systematically choosing securities and weights. The resulting portfolio will exhibit a greater expected return for the same risk level. Indeed, an entire efficient frontier of portfolios can be determined to dominate any other portfolio combinations.

The science of portfolio management is largely concerned with the generation of this efficient frontier. Advances in theory, data resources, and technology have facilitated the practical aspects of portfolio management toward this end. Moreover, hundreds of services now exist that specialize in software routines that optimize portfolio composition.

The concepts presented in this chapter, and in Chapter 2, underlie not only efficient portfolio formation but also the development and application of derivative securities. This should be expected, since instruments such as financial futures and options can be employed to help manage portfolios and price uncertainty. Beginning in Chapter 4, the intimate relation between derivatives securities and the preceding concepts will become more and more apparent.

SUMMARY

Because assets are held as parts of portfolios, they should be analyzed with respect to how their inclusion affects the portfolio's risk and expected return. Assuming that risk can be reasonably measured by the standard deviation of portfolio returns, portfolio risk and expected return are computed based on the characteristics of the component assets.

The expected rate of return to a portfolio is a simple weighted average of the expected rates of return to the component assets. However, portfolio standard deviation is more complex than a simple weighted

A History of Modern Portfolio Theory

In 1952 H. Markowitz demonstrated how to create a frontier of efficient portfolios, each having the highest possible expected rate of return for a given level of risk—as measured by the standard deviation of portfolio returns. Markowitz's technique was so computationally demanding, however, given the available technology, that practical application of his optimal portfolio allocation model was precluded.

In 1963, however, W. Sharpe developed a simplified version of his mentor's model, less demanding with respect to computational effort. It was based on an approximating formula for portfolio return variance known as the single-index model. This model, combined with technologic advances, allowed modern portfolio theory to be readily applied in the real world. Today, Markowitz's model is widely used to allocate wealth across different types of assets, while Sharpe's model is widely used to allocate wealth within asset groups, especially common stock.

Also in the early 1960s, financial theorists began to investigate how Markowitz's model influenced the valuation of securities. The investigation focused on the impact of efficient portfolio formation within a frictionless marketplace. The result of the investigation became what is now known as the capital asset pricing model (CAPM), developed independently by W. Sharpe (1964), J. Lintner (1965), and J. Mossin (1966). This model demonstrates that an asset's equilibrium return is a linear function of its systematic risk. Specifically, an asset's return is equal to the riskless rate of interest plus a risk premium that depends on the asset's covariance with a broadly diversified market portfolio. The CAPM is still widely used today, despite a heated debate concerning its validity [R. Roll (1977)].

In the mid 1960s E. Fama provided an elegant definition of security market efficiency: If information is rapidly and effi-ciently digested by market analysts, it is impossible to generate abnormal returns through any form of security analysis. Also, since informational events occur randomly, security prices should move randomly such that technical analysis is fruitless. Fama's insights led to several new financial innovations, including stock index mutual funds ("no-brainers"). And since Fama's argument, hundreds of well-done empirical investigations have focused on market efficiency and the ability to detect abnormal profit opportunities. The evidence is, overall, very mixed.

In 1973 M. Black and F. Scholes developed an important and powerful model to value option contracts. The model is grounded in an elegant arbitrage argument that has served as a framework for more complex option pricing models developed over the last decade. The Black-Scholes model is widely used by option traders and, arguably, is the most employed financial model in the world.

In 1972 the Chicago Mercantile Exchange began to trade currency futures contracts. This was the first time a financial futures contract was ever traded. In 1975 the first interest rate futures appeared. And in 1982 the first stock index futures ("pinstripe pork bellies") appeared, encouraged by the work of S. Figlewski and S. Kon (1982).

Both the volume and variety of options and futures exploded in the 1980s. Also, currency and interest rate swaps were introduced in the early 1980s. Today these instruments provide investors with a powerful means to help manage security portfolios. From Markowitz to today, the management of security portfolios has been a dynamic and applied science motivated to helping well-intentioned investors make their money work harder so that people's lives are enriched.

average of the return standard deviations of the component assets, the reason being that most assets are less than perfectly positively correlated.

The formula used to compute portfolio return variance demonstrates that portfolio risk generally decreases as lower-correlated assets are combined to form the portfolio. This is an extremely important concept.

Through short selling an investor can expand his or her investment opportunity set. Short selling can help to reduce or eliminate portfolio risk by artificially introducing negative correlation.

The concepts presented in this chapter represent an epistemological vehicle for the understanding and use of derivative securities.

Selected References

Black, F., and M. Scholes. "The Pricing of Options and Corporate Liabilities." *Journal of Political Economy* (May–June 1973).

Evans, J., and S. Archer. "Diversification and the Reduction of Dispersion: An Empirical Analysis." *Journal of Finance* (December 1968).

Fama, E. "The Behavior of Stock Prices." *Journal of Business* (January 1965).

Fama, E. "Efficient Capital Markets: A Review of Theory and Empirical Work." *Journal of Business* (May 1970).

Figlewski, S., and S. Kon. "Portfolio Management with Stock Index Futures." *Financial Analysts Journal* (January 1982).

Lintner, J. "The Valuation of Risk Assets and the Selection of Risky Investments in Stock Portfolios and Capital Budgets." *Review of Economics and Statistics* (February 1965).

Markowitz, H. "Portfolio Selection." *Journal of Finance* (December 1952).

Mossin, J. "Equilibrium in a Capital Market." *Econometrica* (October 1966).

Roll, R. "A Critique of the Asset Pricing Theory's Tests: Part I: On the Past and Potential Testability of the Theory." *Journal of Financial Economics* (March 1977).

Sharpe, W. "A Simplified Model of Portfolio Analysis." *Management Science* (January 1963).

Sharpe, W. "Capital Asset Prices: A Theory of Market Equilibrium under Conditions of Risk." *Journal of Finance* (September 1964).

Sharpe, W. "Portfolio Analysis." *Journal of Financial and Quantitative Analysis* (June 1967).

Solnik, B., and B. Noetzlin. "Optimal International Asset Allocation." *Journal of Portfolio Management* (Fall 1982–83).

Wagner, W., and S. Lau. "The Effect of Diversification on Risk." *Financial Analysts Journal* (November–December 1971).

Questions and Problems

1. What is short selling? When can short selling increase portfolio risk? When can it reduce portfolio risk?

2. What would be the formula for portfolio variance for a three-asset portfolio?

3. Assume that two stocks are perfectly positively correlated. Is it possible to form a portfolio of these stocks that exhibits zero return dispersion? Explain your answer.

4. Consider two stocks with the following characteristics:

	Stock A	Stock B
Expected Return	.08	.12
Standard Deviation	.22	.25

Compute the expected return and variance of an equally weighted portfolio of these two stocks under the following correlation coefficients between A and B: 1.00, .50, .00, −.50, −1.00.

5. Two stocks, A and B, exhibit the following standard deviations of returns: $\sigma_{r_A} = .30$ and $\sigma_{r_B} = .25$. If these stocks are perfectly negatively correlated, what portfolio weights should be chosen to minimize portfolio risk?

6. In Problem 5, if stocks A and B were perfectly positively correlated, what portfolio weights should be chosen to minimize portfolio risk?

7. Why do most assets tend to exhibit positive, but less than perfect positive, correlation?

8. What are some of the consequences of using standard deviation as a measure of risk?

9. Why is the covariance matrix often referred to as the variance-covariance matrix? What do we know about the corresponding off-diagonal elements of this matrix?

10. Suppose that a risky stock, A, has an expected return of 12 percent and a standard deviation of .08. Also, suppose that a risk-free asset has a 5 percent return. A portfolio is constructed of these two securities. Provide a schedule of portfolio expected returns and standard deviations under the following values of w_A: .00, .50, 1.00, 1.50, 2.00.

11. Suppose that the following variables obtain:

Stock	E(r)	σ_r	Correlation Coefficients
1	.09	.12	1 with 2: .39
2	.14	.18	1 with 3: .46
3	.07	.12	2 with 3: .11

Assuming that an equally weighted portfolio of these three stocks is formed, what are the portfolio's expected return and return variance?

Self-Test Problems

Self-test problems 1 through 3 refer to the following information:

Stock	E(r)	σ_r	Correlation Coefficients
1	.06	.20	1 with 2: $-.10$
2	.08	.10	1 with 3: $+.60$
3	.15	.15	2 with 3: $+.05$

A portfolio is formed as follows: sell short $1,000 of Stock 1; buy $1,500 of Stock 2; buy $1,500 of Stock 3. The investor uses $1,000 on his own equity. The remaining $1,000 is borrowed at a risk-free interest rate of .04.

ST-1. Compute the weights for each component of the portfolio, assuming that there are no restrictions on the use of the short-sale proceeds.

ST-2. Compute the portfolio's expected rate of return.

ST-3. Compute the portfolio's standard deviation of returns.

Solutions to Self-Test Problems

ST-1. Owner's equity is $1,000. Therefore the weights are

$$
\begin{array}{rcll}
w_1 &=& -\$1,000/\$1,000 &= -1.00 \\
w_2 &=& \$1,500/\$1,000 &= 1.50 \\
w_3 &=& \$1,500/\$1,000 &= 1.50 \\
w_4 &=& -\$1,000/\$1,000 &= \underline{-1.00} \text{ (borrowings)} \\
&&& 1.00
\end{array}
$$

ST-2. $E(r_p) = -1.00(.06) + 1.50(.08) + 1.50(.15) - 1.00(.04) = .245.$

ST-3. Borrowing at the (constant) risk-free rate has no effect on the covariances between securities. Therefore,

$$
\begin{aligned}
\sigma_{r_p}^2 =\ & (-1.00)^2(.20)^2 + (1.50)^2(.10)^2 + (1.50)^2(.15)^2 \\
& + 2(-1.00)(1.50)(-.10)(.20)(.10) \\
& + 2(-1.00)(1.50)(.60)(.20)(.15) \\
& + 2(1.50)(1.50)(.05)(.10)(.15) \\
=\ & .0685.
\end{aligned}
$$

$$
\sigma_{r_p} = (.0685)^{1/2} = .262.
$$

Appendix 3.A

PORTFOLIO EXPECTED RATE OF RETURN

The rate of return to a portfolio in any ith state of nature is given by

(3.A–1) $\qquad r_{p,i} = w_A r_{A,i} + w_B r_{B,i} + \ - \ - \ - \ + \ w_M r_{M,i}.$

The statistical definition for the expected rate of return to a portfolio is given by

(3.A–2) $\qquad\qquad E(r_p) = \sum_{i=1}^{n} h_i r_{p,i}.$

Substituting Equation 3.A-1 into Equation 3.A-2 yields

(3.A–3) $\qquad E(r_p) = \sum_{i=1}^{n} h_i(w_A r_{A,i} + w_B r_{B,i} + \ - \ - \ - \ + w_M r_{M,i})$

$$= w_A \sum_{i=1}^{n} h_i r_{A,i} + w_B \sum_{i=1}^{n} h_i r_{B,i} + \text{---} + w_M \sum_{i=1}^{n} h_i r_{M,i}$$

$$= w_A E(r_A) + w_B E(r_B) + \text{---} + w_M E(r_M)$$

$$= \sum_{j=1}^{M} w_j E(r_j).$$

PORTFOLIO RETURN VARIANCE

The statistical definition of the variance of a portfolio is given by

(3.A–4)
$$\sigma_{r_p}^2 = \sum_{i=1}^{n} h_i [r_{p,i} - E(r_p)]^2.$$

Substituting Equations 3.A-1 and 3.A-3 into Equation 3.A-4 yields

(3.A–5)
$$\sigma_{r_p}^2 = \sum_{i=1}^{n} h_i \{ w_A r_{A,i} + w_B r_{B,i}) - [w_A E(r_A) + w_B E(r_B)] \}^2$$

for a two-asset portfolio. Factoring and rearranging algebraically yields

(3.A–6)
$$\sigma_{r_p}^2 = w_A^2 \sum_{i=1}^{n} h_i [r_{A,i} - E(r_A)]^2 + w_B^2 \sum_{i=1}^{n} h_i [r_{B,i} -$$

$$E(r_B)]^2 + 2 w_A w_B \sum_{i=1}^{n} h_i [r_{A,I} - E(r_A)][r_{B,i} - E(r_B)]$$

$$= w_A^2 \sigma_{r_A}^2 + w_B^2 + 2 w_A w_B COV(r_A, r_B).$$

Generalizing to a portfolio of M stocks, we obtain

(3.A–7)
$$\sigma_{r_p}^2 = \sum_{i,j=1}^{M^2} w_i w_j COV(r_i, r_j).$$

Appendix 3.B

THE SINGLE-INDEX MODEL

Equation 3.3, developed by H. Markowitz (1952), is a perfectly accurate estimate of portfolio return variance for the sample period. However, this equation has two shortcomings in practice. First, the number of covariance terms required by the model increases rapidly (at the rate of M^2) as the number of portfolio assets (M) increases. For instance, 250,000 covariance terms are required to compute the variance of the SP500. Second, to estimate the covariance matrix required, the number of sample observations in the time series of asset returns must be greater than M. This can present data problems when M is large.

To overcome these practical limitations, W. Sharpe (1963) developed an approximating formula to compute portfolio return variance. This formula, known as the *single-index model*, is easier to implement than the Markowitz model. The number of input parameters required by the single-index model increases only linearly with M. Thus, the single-index model represents a trade-off; it requires fewer terms and is more simple to implement, but it is only an approximation of portfolio return variance.

In developing his model, Sharpe invoked the following three assumptions:

- $COV(\epsilon_i, \epsilon_j) = 0$; the residuals, or abnormal returns, to different securities are independent.

- $E(\epsilon_{j,t}) = 0$; the expected residual, or abnormal return, at any time t is zero.

- $COV(\epsilon_j, r_m) = 0$; the residuals, or abnormal returns, are uncorrelated to the returns on a well-diversified market portfolio.

The resulting model for portfolio return variance is

(3.B–1)
$$\sigma_{r_p}^2 \approx \left(\sum_{j=1}^{M} w_j \beta_j \right)^2 \sigma_{r_m}^2 + \sum_{j=1}^{M} w_j^2 \sigma_{\epsilon_j}^2.$$

Equation 3.B-1, the single-index model, states that portfolio return variance is approximately equal to the portfolio's systematic risk, as captured by the first right-side term, plus the portfolio's unsystematic risk (residual variance), as captured by the second right-side term. It is this second right-side term that is reduced as the portfolio is diversified, assuming that the portfolio's component assets are less than perfectly positively correlated with each other.

4

THE FUNDAMENTAL ROLE OF DERIVATIVE SECURITIES

In the previous chapter we demonstrated that risk is progressively reduced as assets exhibit lower correlation, and substantial risk reduction is possible if assets exhibit negative correlation. However, most spot assets such as stocks and bonds exhibit positive correlation with each other. To reduce risk through combining spot assets, it is necessary to somehow introduce negative correlation not naturally found in their markets. Short selling, one possible way of introducing negative correlation, is hampered by restrictions. A more viable possibility is to trade derivative securities, which artificially introduce negative correlation not naturally found in spot asset markets. This, in turn, can enhance investor utility. So can the fact that the trading of derivative securities may expand the investor's opportunity set.

Before turning to these issues, however, it is useful to consider utility theory and to further examine why investors may seek to reduce risk.

UTILITY THEORY

Rational economic agents make decisions in such a way as to maximize their *utility*, which can be thought of as the satisfaction derived from the consumption of goods and services. If the decision outcomes are uncertain, then utility is a random variable, so rational agents act as to maximize their *expected utility*.

Utility theory concerns the study and modeling of rational economic behavior. Here we introduce the subject as it applies to consumption. After that, the theory is extended to incorporate utility derived from wealth. Risk represents a source of *disutility* (negative utility) for risk-averse investors.

Utility from Consumption

A **utility function** defines a relation between an individual's utility level and the amounts of goods and services consumed.

A *utility function* defines a relation between an individual's utility level and the amounts of goods and services consumed. For instance, if there are n different goods and services available to an agent for consumption, the agent's utility function may be written as

(4.1) $$U = f(Q_1, Q_2, \ldots, Q_n),$$

where U denotes utility (the number of "utiles" of satisfaction), and Q_i represents the quantity of good i consumed by the agent. Equation 4.1 represents a general utility function in that it is applicable to any agent. This general function differs across individual agents since agents exhibit heterogeneous tastes and preferences.

Nevertheless, all rational consumers tend to exhibit utility functions having three common properties:

- *Insatiability.* This means that no matter how much of a specific good a consumer already has, more of that good will increase total utility. Although one can think of goods that may eventually cause disutility by themselves (e.g. consuming too much alcohol), presumably an agent can trade such a good for other scarce goods (e.g. aspirin).
- *Diminishing marginal utility.* This means that while additional units of a specific good provide ever-increasing total utility, the marginal, or incremental, utility gained from each added unit will be progressively smaller. For example, the utility gained from watching the second game of a baseball doubleheader is positive but typically not as great as the utility gained from watching the first game.
- *Diminishing marginal substitutability.* This means that as successive units of a particular good are removed from a consumer, the consumer requires progressively larger quantities of another good in order to maintain the initial utility level. Presumably, the consumer chose the original mix of goods and services so as to maximize his or her unique utility function. Thus, by removing some quantity of a particular good, we disturb this utility maximizing mix. Simply replacing the displaced good with the same quantity of another good will not restore the optimal mix. The consumer will require relatively more of the new good.

To illustrate these three properties of rational utility, we invoke the simplifying assumption that the world consists of just two consumable goods. Under this assumption, our general utility function becomes

(4.2) $$U = f(Q_1, Q_2).$$

The properties above could be illustrated in a multi-good setting, but such an approach only serves to unnecessarily complicate the analysis. Thus, we shall stick to a two-good setting.

Only a limited number of specific forms of Equation 4.2 satisfy all three properties. One of these forms is the multiplicative form:

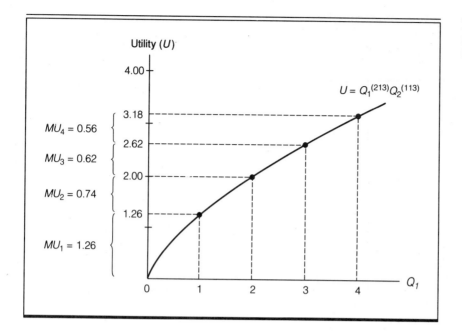

Figure 4.1:
Properties of Insatiability and Diminishing Marginal Utility

(4.3) $$U = Q_1^{(2/3)}Q_2^{(1/3)}.$$

Using Equation 4.3 we can illustrate the properties of insatiability, diminishing marginal utility, and diminishing marginal substitutability.

Figure 4.1 illustrates insatiability. It shows that utility rises as the quantity of Good 1 is increased while the quantity of Good 2 is held constant. A similar utility increase would obtain if Q_2 were increased while Q_1 were held constant. More quantity of a good (or service) results in greater utility.

Figure 4.1 also illustrates the principle of diminishing marginal utility. As each unit of consumption of Good 1 is realized, total utility increases at a decreasing rate. For example, the marginal utility gained from consuming a second unit of Good 1 (0.74 utiles) is greater than that from consuming a third unit (0.62 utiles), and so on. As Figure 4.1 shows, the utility function is concave to the origin. Thus, we can say that utility is concave in consumption.

Figure 4.2 employs an *indifference curve* to illustrate the principle of diminishing marginal substitutability in consumption. An indifference curve is a set of all combinations of goods and services that produce the same total utility for an individual consumer. Here it shows all combinations of Goods 1 and 2 that yield a utility level of 3. Since this utility level is the same along the curve, we can say that the agent is indifferent to any of these combinations, that is, has no preference among them. For instance, the following two combinations both provide three utiles:

An **indifference curve** is a set of all combinations of goods and services that produce the same total utility for an individual consumer.

Figure 4.2

Property of Diminishing
Marginal Substitutability of
Consumption

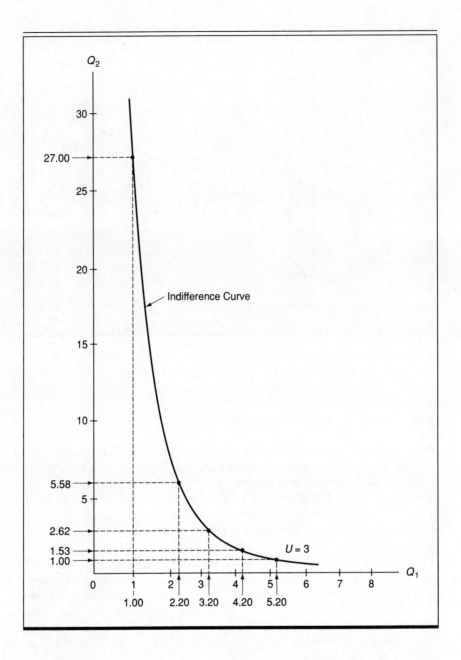

$(Q_1 = 1, Q_2 = 27)$ and $(Q_1 = 5.20, Q_2 = 1)$. Notice that the indifference curve is convex to the origin, which follows from the concavity of
the utility function in Figure 4.1. Such convexity implies diminishing
marginal substitutability. Thus, if we begin with a combination of
$(Q_1 = 5.20, Q_2 = 1)$, we can surrender one unit of Good 1 and still
maintain a utility level of 3 by obtaining 0.53 units of Good 2. If we give
up a second unit of Good 1, then we must obtain another 1.11 units of
Good 2 to remain indifferent. In general, we must obtain more and more

units of Good 2 as we surrender each additional unit of Good 1 in order to maintain the same utility level.

Utility from Wealth

We now extend the analysis of the utility derived from consumption to the utility derived from wealth. This is a natural extension in the sense that wealth makes consumption possible. Wealth therefore provides utility. Nonconsumable investment assets such as stocks and bonds also represent a source of utility, since the income they provide embellishes wealth. However, the risk associated with such assets—that is, the risk of wealth loss due to price declines—represents a source of disutility for the agent. This fact is what ultimately distinguishes the utility derived from consumption and the utility derived from wealth. We typically think of consumable goods as exhibiting no risk; they are certain and provide no potential disutility. On the other hand, the investments from which we draw wealth for consumption usually exhibit uncertain returns and therefore potential disutility.

The utility function with respect to wealth is commonly concave in wealth, just as utility is typically concave in consumption. This implies that more wealth yields more utility, and that each additional dollar of wealth results in progressively smaller utility gains (i.e. diminishing marginal utility of wealth). Figure 4.3 portrays a concave utility-of-wealth function that is based on the following functional form:

(4.4)
$$U = W^{(1/2)}.$$

Now suppose that an investor with this utility function (Equation 4.4) currently has $50 in wealth. This investor therefore has a utility level (with certainty) of 7.07. Suppose he or she is offered a lottery in which there is a 50 percent chance of winning $100 and a 50 percent chance of receiving nothing. The cost of the lottery ticket is $50. Should the investor play the lottery?

The answer to this question lies in the *expected utility* derived from the lottery. Since the lottery's outcome is uncertain, utility becomes a random variable; this is why we speak of "expected" utility. If expected utility is greater (or at least no less) than the current utility derived from $50 (7.07 utiles), then the investor will opt for the lottery. On the other hand, if expected utility is less than 7.07, the investor, who seeks to maximize expected utility, will forego the lottery.

If the investor wins, he will reap $100 in wealth and have a utility level of 10.00. If the investor loses, zero wealth and zero utility result. Since the probability of winning is 50 percent, the expected utility of the lottery is therefore $10.00(.50) + 0.00(.50) = 5.00$.[1] The investor should

---

[1]See J. Von Neumann and O. Morgenstern (1947) for the conditions under which expected utility represents a linear combination of the utilities of outcomes.

Figure 4.3:
A Risk-Averse Investor's Utility-of-Wealth Function

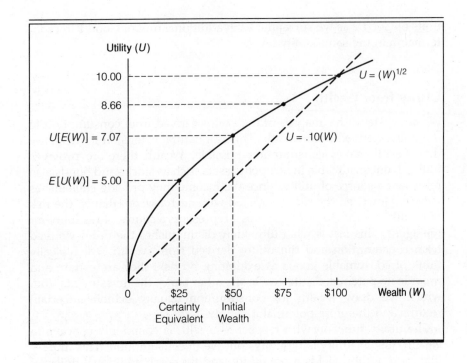

forego playing the lottery since the expected utility from the lottery, 5.00, is less than the utility associated with the lottery's cost, 7.07. This result obtains despite the fact that the lottery's expected dollar return is equivalent to the lottery's dollar cost ($50); that is, the lottery is a "fair game."[2]

An interesting question is, how much would the above investor be willing to pay to play the lottery? The answer is $25.00, since this is the level of wealth with associated utility of 5.00. Of course, different investors exhibit different utility-of-wealth functions and thus would pay different dollar amounts to engage in the lottery. In general, this dollar amount is called the *certainty equivalent*. It represents the point of indifference between utility associated with a *certain* level of wealth and utility associated with an *expected* level of wealth. Figure 4.3 labels the certainty equivalent for the above investor.

The **certainty equivalent** represents the point of indifference between utility associated with a certain level of wealth and utility associated with an expected level of wealth.

Establishing a Definition of Risk Aversion

Exhibit 4.1 shows different lotteries for the above investor, with the expected utility of each. Each lottery costs the same, $50, and each

---

[2]Most games of chance are not "fair games" since their expected dollar return is less than their dollar cost.

Lottery	Probability Win	Lose	Payoff Win	Lose	Utility Win	Lose	Expected Utility	Certainty Equivalent
1	.5	.5	$ 60	$40	7.75	6.32	7.04	$49.56
2	.5	.5	75	25	8.66	5.00	6.83	46.65
3	.5	.5	90	10	9.49	3.16	6.33	40.07
4	.5	.5	100	0	10.00	0.00	5.00	25.00

exhibits the same expected dollar return, $50. Despite this, the lotteries exhibit different expected-utility levels. Moving down Exhibit 4.1, note how the dollar outcomes associated with each lottery become more volatile. The win-lose payoff spread is $20 for Lottery 1, but $100 for Lottery 4. Also, the expected utilities decline, implying that expected utility and return dispersion are inversely related for this investor. In other words, risk is associated with disutility if the investor exhibits a concave utility-of-wealth function. We can conclude that an investor who exhibits a concave utility function is *risk averse*.

As the dispersion of wealth grows, the level of utility associated with any given level of expected wealth falls. This is confirmed by the pattern of certainty equivalents presented in Exhibit 4.1. The risk-averse investor is willing to pay less to play lotteries exhibiting more outcome dispersion.

A risk-averse individual exhibits a concave utility-of-wealth function. Another way of comprehending this is to examine investors who exhibit non-concave utility functions. For instance, consider an investor that has a linear utility function of the following form:

(4.5) $$U = .10W.$$

In this case, utility increases with wealth, but the investor does not exhibit diminishing marginal utility of wealth. Equation 4.5 is depicted by the broken line in Figure 4.3. Notice that for this investor, $U(\$100) = 10.00$, and $U(\$0) = 0.00$. These are the same utility levels, associated with $100 and $0, respectively, as exhibited by the risk-averse investor with utility function Equation 4.4. However, whereas the risk-averse investor is unwilling to engage in the lottery, the investor exhibiting the linear utility function is indifferent; for this investor, the expected utility from the lottery and the utility of $50 in initial wealth are the same, 5.00 utiles. In fact, this investor would be indifferent to *any* of the lotteries described in Exhibit 4.1. These lotteries, and their new expected utilities given a linear utility function, are presented in Exhibit 4.2. For each, the expected utility of wealth is 5.00, and the certainty equivalent is $50. Despite the fact that the four lotteries have widely dispersed win-lose dollar spreads, the investor with linear utility is

An investor who exhibits a concave utility function is **risk averse**.

Exhibit 4.2:

Lotteries and Their Expected Utilities for a Risk-Neutral Investor

Lottery	Probability		Payoff		Utility		Expected Utility	Certainty Equivalent
	Win	Lose	Win	Lose	Win	Lose		
1	.5	.5	$ 60	$40	6.0	4.0	5.0	$50
2	.5	.5	75	25	7.5	2.5	5.0	50
3	.5	.5	90	10	9.0	1.0	5.0	50
4	.5	.5	100	0	10.0	0.0	5.0	50

indifferent between them. Hence we can conclude that investors with linear utility functions are not risk averse, but instead are risk neutral. Using a similar analysis, it can be demonstrated that investors with convex utility-of-wealth functions are risk lovers. They prefer risk, so their certainty equivalents actually rise with outcome dispersion. Obviously, investors exhibiting linear or convex utility functions are not rational; they exhibit no disutility from risk.

More formally, we can state that

- If $U[E(W)] > E[U(W)]$, we have risk-aversion;
- If $U[E(W)] = E[U(W)]$, we have risk-neutrality; and
- If $U[E(W)] < E[U(W)]$, we have risk-loving,

wherein $U[E(W)]$ is the utility of expected wealth, and $E[U(W)]$ is the expected utility of wealth. For our risk-averse investor in Figure 4.3, $U[E(W)] = 7.07$, while $E[U(W)] = 5.00$:

$$U[E(W)] = U[.50(\$100) + .50(\$0)] = U[\$50] = 7.07 >$$

$$E[U(W)] = .50U(\$100) + .50U(\$0) = .50(10) + .50(0) = 5.00.$$

The Risk-Averse Investor's Indifference Map

Under utility gained from consumption we assumed, for simplicity, that the *consumer* lived in a two-good world. This was a convenient but unrealistic assumption. However, if returns are normally distributed, then the *investor* truly lives in a two-good world—the world of return and risk (as measured by the standard deviation of returns). Return provides positive utility while risk results in disutility. In general, a risk-averse investor's utility function may be written as follows:

(4.6) $$U = f[E(r), \sigma],$$

where utility is monotonically increasing in expected return and monotonically decreasing in standard deviation.

A consumer exhibits an indifference curve representing various combinations of two goods yielding the same utility level. Analogously, an investor possesses combinations of return and risk that afford the

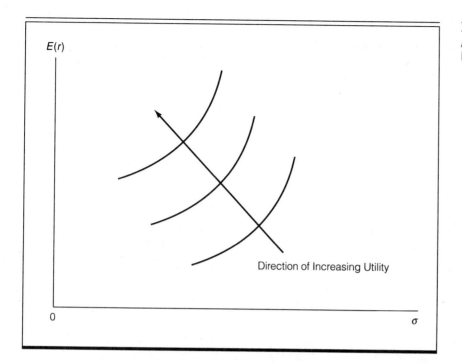

Figure 4.4:
A Risk-Averse Investor's
Indifference Map

E(r)

Direction of Increasing Utility

0   σ

same level of utility. Figure 4.4 provides a set of indifference curves (known as an *indifference map*) for a representative risk-averse investor. The utility of the rational investor increases as we move from one indifference curve to another in a northwesterly direction; increasing expected return and decreasing standard deviation of return provide more and more utility.

Of course, different investors exhibit different utility functions with respect to return and risk. Some investors are relatively more risk averse than others. Figure 4.5 portrays indifference maps for various investors. For a highly conservative investor (A), a large increase in expected return is required to offset the disutility associated with a small increase in standard deviation. For a relatively less risk-averse investor (C), a comparatively smaller increase in expected return is required to offset the same increase in standard deviation. The more aggressive investor possesses flatter indifference curves, corresponding to his flatter (more linear-like) utility function.

THE ROLE OF DERIVATIVE SECURITIES IN OPTIMIZING UTILITY

Armed with the concepts that (1) rational investors are utility maximizers who exhibit disutility from risk, and (2) risk is reduced with

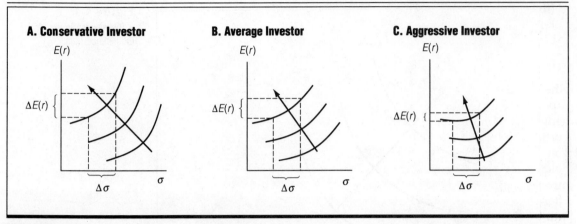

Figure 4.5:
Indifference Maps for Various Degrees of Risk Aversion

Through introducing negative correlation, derivative instruments provide added risk-reduction opportunities and, thereby, opportunities to enhance investor utility.

portfolios of less correlated assets, we are prepared to examine the role that derivative securities play in the investment marketplace. In general, we believe that derivative securities can be employed to reduce risk—and enhance investor utility—because they introduce negative correlation not found in spot asset markets.

To help demonstrate this important concept, let us consider one specific derivative security—the stock index futures contract, which represents an agreement to buy or sell an entire stock portfolio in the future for a specified price. For instance, the Chicago Mercantile Exchange presently trades futures contracts on the Standard and Poor's 500 (SP500) Stock Index. By employing this contract, you can arrange to buy or sell the SP500 in the future for a specified price and thus alter the risk associated with holding an equity portfolio.

Presume that you currently hold or manage a stock portfolio that mirrors the SP500, in other words, is perfectly positively correlated with it.[3] Let the current value of your stock portfolio be V_0, and let I_0 be the current level of the SP500. For instance, V_0 may be $5 million and $I_0 =$ 200.00. Thus, you currently hold 25,000 units of the SP500 Stock Index. Define N_S as the number of index units held. Hence, $N_S = 25,000$. Also, define N_f as the number of index units traded in the futures market. Finally, define h as N_f/N_S. We can refer to h as a *hedge ratio*. By varying

---

[3]For instance, you may be the manager of an index fund, which is a stock portfolio designed to mimic a broad market index such as the SP500. On Wall Street, index funds are often called "no-brainers," reflecting the simplicity in constructing and managing such a fund.

h (through varying N_f), you can obtain an entire set of portfolio risk-return combinations.

Let the expected return on a *hedged portfolio,* denoted $E(r_h)$, be given by

(4.7) $$E(r_h) = E(r_S) + hE(r_f),$$

where $E(r_S)$ is the expected return on your stock portfolio, and $E(r_f)$ is the expected return on an SP500 futures contract. You may think of this hedged portfolio as a type of two-asset portfolio; one asset is your stock portfolio, while the second is your position in SP500 futures contracts. You can use these futures contracts to alter the risk associated with holding your stock portfolio. The trick is to assume a position in the futures contracts such that you maximize your expected utility. This often entails assuming a futures position such that the returns on the futures contracts and on your stock portfolio are negatively correlated.

Using the equation for portfolio variance given in Chapter 3, the variance of return for the hedged portfolio is

(4.8) $$\sigma_{r_h}^2 = \sigma_{r_S}^2 + h^2\sigma_{r_f}^2 + 2hCOV(r_S,r_f).$$

Using Equations 4.7 and 4.8, Figure 4.6 shows the hedged portfolio risk-return possibilities for different levels of h under the following assumed parameter values: $E(r_S) = .18$, $E(r_f) = .10$, $\sigma_{r_S}^2 = .05$, $\sigma_{r_f}^2 = .05$, and $COV(r_S,r_f) = .05$. At the point where $h = 0$, $E(r_h) \equiv E(r_S)$, and $\sigma_{r_h}^2 \equiv \sigma_{r_S}^2$. In other words, the expected return and variance of the hedged portfolio are identical to the expected return and variance of your stock portfolio. This occurs since, at this point, you assume no position in the futures contracts; you hold an *unhedged portfolio.* By varying h, however, you can achieve other risk-return combinations. For instance, by setting h to be less than zero, you can reduce risk. At $h = -0.5$, for example, $\sigma_{r_h}^2 = .0125$, while at $h = -1$, $\sigma_{r_h}^2 = 0$. To achieve a hedge ratio less than zero, you must set N_f to be less than zero. This is done by agreeing to sell the SP500 in the future. We say that you undertake a *short position* in the futures contract. For example, at $h = -0.50$, $N_f = -12,500$; here you agree to sell 12,500 units of the index in the future at a specified price.

Since you currently hold a stock portfolio that mimics the behavior of the SP500, taking a short position in SP500 futures contracts introduces negative correlation. If the SP500 Stock Index level should fall, you would lose money on your stock position. However, you would experience an offsetting gain on your short futures position; as the SP500 falls, the value of your futures contracts grows, since you have contracted to sell the SP500 at a specified (i.e. fixed) price. This introduction of negative correlation reduces risk. Ultimately, this is how any derivative security can be employed to reduce risk. By taking an offsetting position in the derivative instrument, an investor introduces negative correlation and thus reduces return variance.

Derivative securities also can be used to increase expected return, but at the cost of increasing return variance as well. In Figure 4.6, setting a

Figure 4.6:
Portfolio Risk-Return
Possibilities for Different
Values of h, the Hedge Ratio

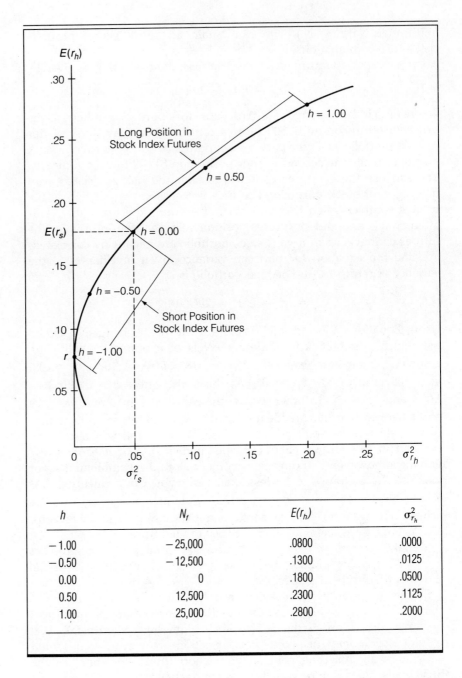

h	N_f	$E(r_h)$	$\sigma^2_{r_h}$
−1.00	−25,000	.0800	.0000
−0.50	−12,500	.1300	.0125
0.00	0	.1800	.0500
0.50	12,500	.2300	.1125
1.00	25,000	.2800	.2000

hedge ratio greater than zero results in increased expected return and risk. Here you assume a *long position* in the futures contract, agreeing to buy the SP500 in the future. Now your positions in stock and futures contracts are positively correlated. An increase (decrease) in the SP500

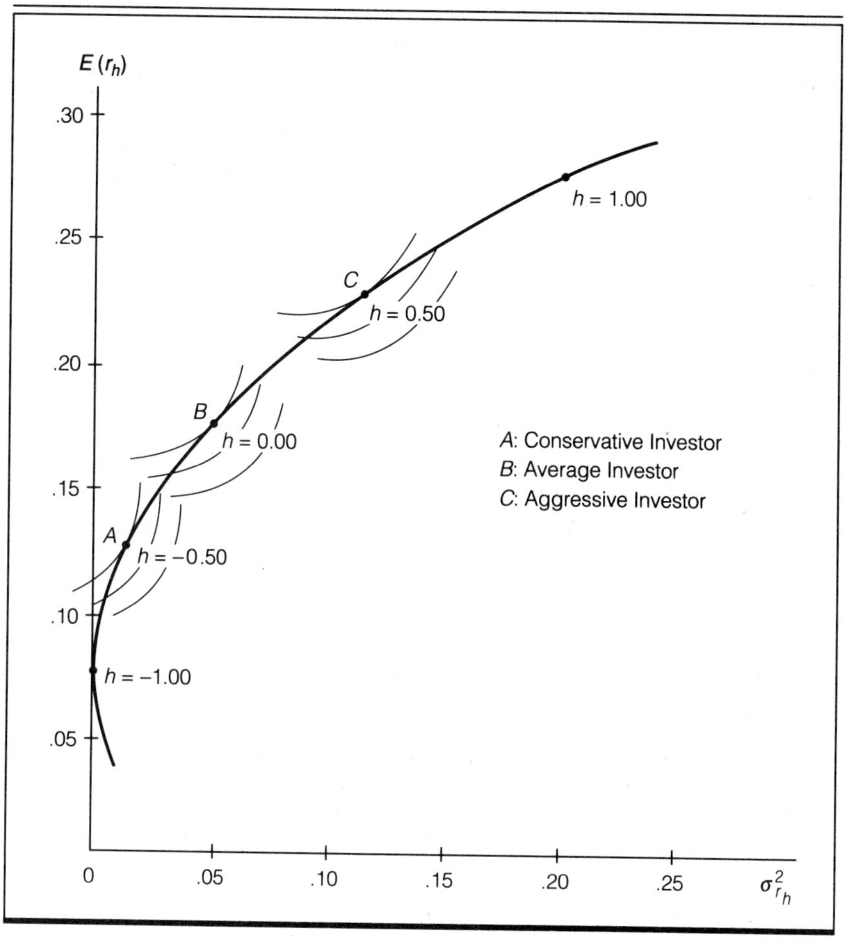

A: Conservative Investor
B: Average Investor
C: Aggressive Investor

increases (decreases) the returns on both your stocks and futures contracts. Such positive correlation inflates return dispersion.

An investor will ultimately choose a hedge ratio that maximizes his or her particular expected utility. This will depend on the investor's degree of risk aversion. Figure 4.7 superimposes the indifference maps of Figure 4.5 onto the portfolio risk-return combinations of Figure 4.6. An investor will maximize expected utility at the point where an indifference curve is just tangential to the frontier of risk-return possibilities. At this tangential point the investor holds a hedged portfolio that lies on the most northwesterly indifference curve attainable. From Figure 4.7, we see that a relatively conservative investor will set h to be less than zero, thereby reducing risk. On the other hand, a comparatively aggressive investor may exhibit a positive hedge ratio; the aggressive investor is willing to tolerate more risk in order to achieve a higher expected return. Although such an investor is still risk averse, we may

An investor will maximize expected utility at the point where an indifference curve is just tangential to the frontier of risk-return possibilities.

conclude that his or her resulting risk-return position is somewhat speculative. For an average investor, the hedge ratio will lie somewhere in between, perhaps at zero. Thus, each investor can achieve different risk-return combinations through trading SP500 Stock Index futures contracts, even though each holds exactly the same portfolio of stocks.

The notion that stock index futures contracts can be used to achieve different risk-return combinations is analogous to the notion that short selling expands an investor's opportunity set. Recall from Chapter 3 that through short selling an investor can attain points in risk-return space that he or she may not otherwise be able to attain if short selling was restricted. Similarly, the trading of stock index futures contracts and, more generally, any derivative instrument can expand the investment opportunity set. For instance, from Figure 4.7 we see that a conservative investor can achieve a risk-return combination given by Point A through assuming a short position in SP500 futures contracts. Such a risk-return combination might not have been attainable if futures contracts did not exist. Thus, the trading of derivative instruments serves to expand the investment opportunity set, allowing market participants to attain points in mean-variance space that maximize their particular utility function.

This argument has been expressed more formally by using the theory of *complete markets*. If markets are complete, then investors can contract to establish any risk-return combination desired.[4] The more complete the markets are, the more that investors, and thus society, benefit from the ability to optimize utility. From this perspective, we see that the trading of derivative securities can contribute to social welfare by making markets more complete.

A Word on The Minimum-Variance Hedge Ratio

A hedge ratio is used to determine the number of derivative securities to trade. In this book we will examine a variety of different hedge ratios, one of which is known as the *minimum-variance hedge ratio*. As its name implies, this hedge ratio is designed to minimize return variance. From Figure 4.6, the return variance of the hedged portfolio is minimized when $h = -1$. Thus, we can state that in this example the minimum-variance hedge ratio is $h = -1$.

To demonstrate this more formally, differentiate Equation 4.8 with respect to h:

$$\partial \sigma_{r_h}^2 / \partial h = 2h\sigma_{r_f}^2 + 2COV[E(r_S), E(r_f)].$$

---

[4]See S. Myers (1968) and G. Debreu (1959). More formally, we say that a market is complete when the number of unique linearly independent securities is equal to the total number of alternative future states of nature.

Setting the derivative equal to zero and solving for h yield:[5]

$$h = -COV[E(r_S), E(r_f)]/\sigma^2_{r_f}$$
$$= (-.05)/(.05) = -1.$$

The fact that variance is minimized when $h = -1$ in this example is very intuitive. Because the stock portfolio and the SP500 are perfectly positively correlated, and the SP500 and its futures contract are perfectly positively correlated,[6] the stock portfolio and the SP500 futures contract must be perfectly positively correlated. Therefore, by establishing a hedge ratio of -1 (contracting to sell a unit of the SP500 in the future for each of the 25,000 units currently held), you effectively make the stock portfolio and futures positions perfectly *negatively* correlated, locking out all return dispersion. Your certain return here is 8 percent. Since this is the return generated for a zero-risk portfolio, it must in equilibrium represent the risk-free rate of return. This is labeled as r in Figure 4.6.

Just as stock index futures contracts can be employed to eliminate risk and insure a risk-free rate of return, other derivative securities can be used to do the same. Later in this book we will use this result to help determine the prices of derivative securities.

OTHER DERIVATIVE SECURITIES AND THEIR ROLE

Earlier we showed that stock index futures contracts can

- Introduce negative correlation and reduce the risk associated with holding an equity portfolio.
- Expand the investment opportunity set, giving investors otherwise unattainable points in risk-return space.
- Help to provide market completion.
- Enhance investor utility and social welfare.

All of these points are interrelated. But more importantly, all of these points represent consequences derived from *any* derivative security examined in this book. Financial futures, options, and swaps all can be employed to reduce risk, expand the market, and improve investor utility, whether the "investor" be a stock portfolio manager, a bond

---

[5]We set the derivative equal to zero to determine an optimum. The second derivative is positive, $\partial^2\sigma^2_{r_h}/\partial h^2 > 0$, confirming a minimum.

[6]That the SP500 and its futures contract are perfectly positively correlated results from the following equation for the expected return on a long futures position: $E(r_f) = [E(I_T) - {}_Tf_0]/I_0$ where $E(I_T)$ is the expected level of the SP500 at the maturity of the futures contract (in T years), ${}_Tf_0$ is the price at which the SP500 will be traded in T years under the futures contract, and I_0 is the current index level. For instance, if $E(I_T) = 224$, ${}_Tf_0 = 204$, and $I_0 = 200$, then $E(r_f) = .10$. Since ${}_Tf_0$ and I_0 are currently known (i.e. they are constants), $E(r_f)$ and $E(I_T)$ must be perfectly positively correlated.

trader, a commercial bank, a multinational firm, or any other market participant.

For instance, consider the owner of a stock who purchases a *put option*, giving him or her the right to sell the stock in the future for a specified price. If the stock's value should decline, the value of the put option obviously increases. Thus, the positions in the stock and the put option are negatively correlated. Depending on the owner's degree of risk aversion, he or she may or may not use the put option to alter the risk associated with holding the stock. Just as with stock index futures, the put option can be employed to different degrees in order to achieve targeted risk-return combinations. The same can be said for each derivative instrument examined in this book.

COMPARING DERIVATIVE SECURITIES AND SHORT SELLING

In Chapter 3 it was demonstrated that short selling a spot asset could expand the investment opportunity set. Consequently, short selling provides for more nearly complete markets and can enhance investor utility. To this extent, short selling in the spot market and the trading of derivative securities can provide the same benefits. However, derivative securities and short selling are not perfect substitutes. Derivative securities do not represent a financial "excess."

This is because security markets impose restrictions on short selling in spot asset markets (described in Chapter 3) that are not applied to the trading of derivative securities. As a consequence, investors can undertake short positions and introduce negative correlation more readily in derivative instrument markets. Also, it is often less expensive to short sell in derivative security markets than in the underlying security markets.

Moreover, the trading of derivative securities provides investment opportunities that even unrestricted short selling may not be able to provide. For example, in Chapter 15 we will demonstrate that investors are able to form all kinds of investment strategies with options. The fact that straight short selling does not have this capacity indicates that derivative securities indeed make the market more complete. Thus, even if transaction costs were zero and restrictions on short selling were lifted, derivative securities would still add utility to investors and society as a whole.

SUMMARY

The trading of derivative securities yields the following related benefits: (1) the introduction of negative correlation and the associated ability to reduce risk; (2) the completion of markets and the associated ability to attain risk-return combinations that may be otherwise unattainable; and (3) the enhancement of investor utility and, thereby, social welfare.

We have come to the conclusion of Part 1 of this book, dealing with the relation between modern portfolio theory and derivative securities. It was designed to explore the fundamental role that derivative securities play in our financial system. At this point you should understand how derivative securities can be used to enhance investor utility. Often it is said that derivative securities represent insurance contracts, and the markets in which they trade are merely types of insurance markets. This is a reasonable statement. Derivative securities introduce negative correlation not found naturally in the markets for spot assets. As a result, investors can employ them to reduce the risk associated with holding a preexisting spot asset position. The investor insures against financial loss. For comparatively conservative investors, the consequence is greater expected utility.

Now that we have established the economic rationale for the existence of derivative securities, we can proceed to analyze such securities in greater detail. We begin with financial futures contracts in Part 2.

Selected References

Carlton, D. "Futures Markets: Their Purpose, Their History, Their Growth, Their Successes And Failures." *Journal of Futures Markets* 4 (Fall 1984): 237–271.

Debreu, G. *Theory of Value*. New Haven: Yale University Press, 1959.

Figlewski, S. and Kon, S. "Portfolio Management with Stock Index Futures." *Financial Analysts Journal* 38 (January 1982): 52–60.

Friedman, M. *Price Theory*. Chicago: Aldine, 1976.

Henderson, J., and Quandt, R. *Microeconomic Theory*. New York: McGraw-Hill, 1980.

MacMillan, L. *Options as a Strategic Investment*. New York: New York Institute Of Finance, 1980.

Myers, S. "A Time-State-Preference Model of Security Valuation." *Journal of Financial and Quantitative Analysis* 3 (March 1968): 1–33.

Van Horne, J. "Of Financial Innovations and Excesses." *Journal of Finance* 40 (July 1985): 621–631.

Von Neumann, J. and Morgenstern, O. *Theory of Games and Economic Behavior*. Princeton: Princeton University Press, 1947.

Questions and Problems

1. Discuss how the trading of derivative securities can reduce risk and enhance investor utility.

2. What is the shape of a risk-averse investor's utility-of-wealth function? What does this shape imply about the marginal utility of wealth?

3. For a consumer, a more northeasterly indifference curve is associated with greater utility. For an investor, a more northwesterly indifference curve is associated with greater utility. Resolve this contradiction.

4. Using the lotteries described in Exhibits 4.1 and 4.2, what are the associated certainty equivalents if an investor exhibits the following utility of wealth function:

$$U = (W)^{1.5}.$$

What is unusual about this utility function?

5. Explain the notions of insatiability, diminishing marginal utility, and diminishing marginal substitutability in consumption.

6. Explain why short selling and the trading of derivative securities are not perfect substitutes for each other.

7. Determine the expected utilities and certainty equivalents for the following lotteries if the utility of wealth function is given by $U = \sqrt{W}$. Assume that each lottery's cost is $25.

Lottery	Probability		Payoff	
	Win	Lose	Win	Lose
A	.5	.5	$ 30	$ 20
B	.5	.5	40	10
C	.5	.5	50	0

8. Suppose that $V_0 = \$1,000,000$, $I_0 = 100.00$, $h = -1$, and $_1f_0 = 102.00$. Also, suppose that your stock portfolio pays a constant dividend rate of 4 percent, or $40,000 in dividends for the year. What is the overall return to your hedged portfolio if $I_1 = 112.00$?

9. Now suppose that the stock market declines by 10 percent over the year so that $I_1 = 90.00$. What is the overall return to your hedged portfolio? How does this return relate to that in Problem 8?

10. Distinguish between utility and expected utility. Under what conditions do investors act so as to maximize their *expected* utility?

Self-Test Problems

ST-1. Suppose that $V_0 = \$5,000,000$, $I_0 = 200.00$, $h = -1$, and $_1f_0 = 204.00$. Also, suppose that your stock portfolio pays a constant dividend rate of 6 percent, or $300,000 in dividends for the year. What is the overall return to your hedged portfolio if $I_1 = 224.00$?

ST-2. Now suppose that the SP500 declines 10 percent over the year so that $I_1 = 180.00$. What is the overall return to your hedged portfolio?

ST-3. What are the expected utilities and certainty equivalents for the following lotteries if an investor's utility-of-wealth function is $U = ln(W)$:

Lottery	Cost	Probability		Payoff	
		Win	Lose	Win	Lose
1	$100	.5	.5	$120	$80
2	100	.5	.5	150	50
3	100	.5	.5	190	10

Solutions to Self-Test Problems

ST-1. Return to stock portfolio:

$300,000 in dividends, or	.06
+ $600,000 in capital gains, or	.12[a]
Total	.18

Return to futures position:

$500,000 in losses, or	−.10[b]

Total return to hedged portfolio:

$400,000, or	.08

[a][(224 − 200)/(200)] × $5,000,000 = $600,000.
[b](224 − 204) (−25,000) = −$500,000.

ST-2. Return to stock portfolio:

$300,000 in dividends, or	.06
$500,000 in capital losses, or	−.10[a]
Total	−.04

Return to futures position:

$600,000 in gains, or	.12[b]

Total return to hedged portfolio:

$400,000, or	.08[c]

[a][(180 − 200)/(200)] × $5,000,000 = −$500,000.
[b](180 − 204) (−25,000) = $600,000.
[c]Note the return to the hedged portfolio is the same, 8 percent, in both problems.

ST-3.

Lottery	Cost	Probability		Payoff		Utility		Expected Utility	Certainty Equivalent
		Win	Lose	Win	Lose	Win	Lose		
1	$100	.5	.5	$120	$80	4.8[a]	4.4	4.6[b]	$99.48[c]
2	100	.5	.5	150	50	5.0	3.9	4.5	90.02
3	100	.5	.5	190	10	5.3	2.3	3.8	44.70

[a]E.g. $U = \ln(\$120) = 4.8$.
[b]E.g. $E[U(W)] = .5(4.8) + .5(4.4) = 4.6$.
[c]E.g. $4.6 = \ln(W)$, $W = e^{4.6} = \$99.48$.

FINANCIAL FUTURES

After a sound examination of this part of the book, you should understand what financial futures are, how and where they are traded, how the futures price is determined, and how to employ these contracts to help manage risk. Chapter 5 begins with a description of futures markets and instruments. Chapter 6 is devoted to futures pricing, while Chapter 7 concerns the three uses of futures contracts: price discovery, speculation, and hedging. Chapters 8 through 10 provide detailed analyses of currency futures, stock index futures, and interest rate futures, respectively.

5

MARKETS AND INSTRUMENTS

This chapter on financial futures markets and instruments begins with a definition of financial futures, followed by a discussion of the markets on which they are traded. The different types of futures contracts are then presented. Together, this material provides an institutional framework for analyzing financial futures.

FINANCIAL FUTURES

A *futures contract* represents a contractual agreement to purchase or sell a specified asset in the future for a specified price that is determined today. The underlying asset could be a foreign currency, a stock index, a U.S. Treasury bill, or any number of other assets. The specified price is known as the *futures price*. Each contract also specifies a *delivery month*, which may be nearby or more deferred in time.

The buyer of a futures contract agrees to purchase the underlying asset and is said to have a *long position* in the contract. On the other hand, the writer or seller agrees to sell the asset and is said to have a *short position* in the contract. For example, a contract to sell 25,000 British pounds at $1.30/£1 in 90 days represents a short position.

Financial futures are futures contracts where the underlying asset is a financial asset, such as a stock index or Treasury security. Do not confuse these futures with agricultural or metallurgical futures. An agricultural futures contract is written on, say, wheat, and a metallurgical futures is written on, say, silver or gold. This book deals primarily with financial futures rather than agricultural or metallurgical futures.

Futures contracts represent a type of derivative security in that they are a derivative of the underlying asset, and the futures price depends critically on the current price of the asset. Again, we call this current

A **futures contract** represents a contractual agreement to purchase or sell a specified asset in the future for a specified price that is determined today.

The **spot price** refers to the underlying asset's current price.

price the underlying asset's *spot price*. Futures contracts also provide tremendous leverage; comparatively small percentage changes in the underlying asset's value can create large percentage changes in a futures position.

FUTURES MARKETS

Forward contracts represent obligations to trade assets in the future for specified prices. Each forward contract is unique, tailored to the specific needs of its customer. Forward contracting in currencies and other assets has existed for centuries. Futures contracts currently represent a standardized form of forward contracting; they are traded on an organized exchange, which is a physical place or trading floor where listed contracts are traded face to face. The oldest and largest organized futures exchange is the Chicago Board of Trade (CBOT), established in 1848. This not-for-profit association of members (those holding seats in the exchange) has been used as a model for the development of other organized futures exchanges, some of which are shown in Exhibit 5.1 along with their underlying assets traded.

Futures Players

If markets were frictionless, making transaction costs zero, then all profits (losses) earned by long futures traders would be offset by the losses (profits) experienced by short future traders. In this case futures trading would represent what is called a *zero-sum game*. However, transaction costs indeed exist, so futures trading represents a less than zero-sum game. Despite this, futures trading can be beneficial if it results in utility gains through the transfer of risk between market players. These players are futures hedgers and speculators.

Hedgers A futures trader who utilizes the contract to reduce risk is said to be a *hedger*. Examples of futures hedging are provided in subsequent chapters. In the classical hedge, the holder (or potential holder) of the underlying asset takes a position in the futures contract to reduce the price uncertainty associated with the spot position. For instance, a U.S.–based multinational corporation that expects to repatriate some amount of foreign currency in the future may employ a short futures position to lock into an exchange rate at which the currency can be exchanged for dollars.

A **hedger** utilizes a futures contract to reduce the risk associated with holding a preexisting position in the spot-asset market.

Speculators A futures trader who employs the contract primarily to profit is a *speculator*. In order to generate speculative profits in futures trading, the speculator must successfully forecast the direction of futures prices and, of course, undertake a contract position that can

A **speculator** utilizes a futures contract primarily to profit on a forecast of subsequent spot-price changes.

Futures Exchange (Year Founded)	Underlying Assets
Chicago Board of Trade (1848)	Silver, Gold, Corn, Oats, Soybeans, Soybean Meal, Soybean Oil, Wheat, U.S. Treasury Bonds and Notes, BNMA, GNMA CDR, Municipal Bond Index, Institutional Index, Major Market Index.
Chicago Mercantile Exchange (1919)	Currencies, U.S. Treasury Bills, Gold, CDs, Eurodollar Time Deposits, SP100, SP500 SP O-T-C, Nikkei 225, Feeder Cattle, Live Cattle, Live Hogs, Pork Bellies, Lumber.
London International Financial Futures Exchange (1982)	Time Stock Index, Japanese Government Bonds, U.S. Treasury Bonds, Currencies, 3-Month Eurodollar Interest Rate, 3-Month Sterling Interest Rate, 20-year U.K. Gilt Interest Rate, Short Gilt.
Mid-American Commodity Exchange (1880)	Currencies, U.S. Treasury Bonds and Bills, Gold, Silver, Platinum, Wheat, Oats, Corn, Soybeans, Soybean Meal, Live Cattle, Live Hogs.
New York Commodity Exchange (1933)	Gold, Silver, Copper, Aluminum.
Singapore International Exchange (1984)	Currencies, Eurodollars, Gold, Nikkei Stock Average, U.S. Treasury Bonds.
Sydney Futures Exchange (1960)	3-Month Eurodollar Interest Rates, U.S. Treasury Bonds, Australian Dollar, Gold, Wool, Live Cattle, All Ordinaries Share Price Index, 90-Day Bank-Accepted Bills of Exchange.
Toronto Futures Exchange (1984)	Canadian Bonds and Treasury Bills, Toronto Stock Exchange 300 Index, Oil and Gas Index, U.S. Dollar, Toronto 35 Index.

Exhibit 5.1:
Major Futures Exchanges and Their Instruments

Note: The Mid-American Commodity Exchange (Chicago) recently merged with the Chicago Board of Trade.

extract the profits from this forecast. Examples of speculative strategies involving futures contracts are provided in subsequent chapters.

For a *pure speculator*, the futures position is not offset by a spot position or an offsetting futures contract. On the other hand, *spreaders* utilize offsetting futures positions in order to speculate at lower risk levels. A futures spread involves a long position in one contract and a short position in another. Examples of spreads are provided in subsequent chapters.

Arbitrage plays an important role in determining futures prices. A futures player who engages in arbitrage activities should be considered a type of speculator. The *arbitrager* undertakes trading to exploit profit opportunities that are rarely risk-free.

Clearinghouses

Every organized futures exchange has a *clearinghouse* that guarantees contract performance to all market participants. It does so by breaking down each futures trade into two distinct contracts: one between the buyer and the clearinghouse acting as the seller, and one between the seller and the clearinghouse acting as the buyer. Hence each trader has obligations to the clearinghouse, and need depend on no one else's integrity except that of the clearinghouse. Clearinghouses do not default on contracts; to do so would deteriorate market confidence. Since the clearinghouse matches its long and short positions exactly, it is perfectly hedged; that is, its net futures position is zero.

The clearinghouse is organized as an independent corporation. Its stockholders are its *member clearing firms,* which facilitate the mechanics of futures trading, discussed below. All futures traders must maintain an account with a member clearing firm, either directly or through a brokerage firm.

Margin Requirements

Each futures trader represents a source of credit risk to the clearinghouse. For instance, the long futures trader may have insufficient capital to purchase the underlying asset at the specified futures price. Because of this, each trader is required to post *margin*, usually with a member clearing firm. A margin, which is often a cash deposit, insures the clearinghouse against credit risk.

Besides cash, the margin deposit may be met, at least in part, with liquid securities or a bank letter of credit. For example, U.S. Treasury bills may be posted. The initial margin varies somewhat across markets and contracts, but is often set equal to the contract's *maximum daily price limit.* Such maximum limits are instituted to help assure market safety and are related to a procedure known as *daily resettlement* (discussed below). Exhibit 5.2 displays daily limits and other information for selected financial futures. Margins also vary by the type of trading strategy involved. Hedging trades and spreads typically require lower margins than pure speculative trades. Upon completion of the futures contract, the margin is returned. If securities were posted, then the interest earned is paid to the trader.

Daily Resettlement

The initial margin is always a small fraction of the underlying asset's value. For instance, at the CBOT an initial margin of about $2,000 is

Commodity	Delivery Months	Contract Size	Minimum Price Fluctuation	Daily Limit
Chicago Board of Trade				
U.S. Treasury Bonds	Mar/Jun	$100,000	1/32 pt.	2 pts.
	Sept/Dec	8% coupon	= $31.25	= $2,000
U.S. Treasury Notes	Mar/Jun	$100,000	1/32 pt.	2 pts.
	Sept/Dec	8% coupon	= $31.25	= $2,000
Chicago Mercantile Exchange International Monetary Market Division				
British Pound	Jan/Mar	BP25,000	$.00005/BP1	None
	Apr/Jun		= $12.50	
	Jul/Sept			
	Oct/Dec			
Swiss Franc	-"-	SF125,000	$.0001/SF1	None
			= $12.50	
Chicago Mercantile Exchange Index and Option Market Division				
SP100	Next four months and Mar/Jun Sept/Dec	500 × SP100	5 pts. = $25	None

adequate security for a contract on $100,000 face-value U.S. Treasury notes. An initial margin can be small because of a procedure known as *daily resettlement*, or *marking-to-the-market*, a futures market requirement that traders realize losses daily.

To illustrate this procedure, assume that you have a long position in a Swiss franc futures contract traded on the International Monetary Market division of the Chicago Mercantile Exchange (CME). Assume that the futures price is $0.70/SF1, and that the contract entails SF125,000. Also assume that the initial margin is $2,000. If the contract (i.e., futures price) closes today at $0.694, down $0.006/SF1, then you suffer a one-day loss of $750 ($0.006 × 125,000). As the long trader, you lose because you contracted at a futures price of $0.70 and the current futures price is now $0.694. At the end of the trading day, the $750 is deducted from your margin deposited with the broker or member clearing firm. Then there is a *margin call*; you must replenish the margin to resume trading the next day. This is daily resettlement; you have realized your loss at the end of the trading day and, presuming you replenished your margin (i.e., met your margin call), the contract is now said to be marked-to-the-market. Here the $750 is credited to the seller's margin account.

Daily resettlement, or marking-to-the-market, is a futures market requirement that traders realize losses daily.

Exhibit 5.3:

A Self-Contained Illustration of Daily Resettlement

Assume that on Monday, March 1, you enter a futures contract to buy one CBOT March Treasury bond futures contract at the futures price of $98,156.25 (98 $\frac{5}{32}$). The initial margin is $2,500, and the maintenance margin is $2,000. For simplicity, you do not withdraw excess monies from your margin balance. All margin requirements are met with cash. You hold your long position through Friday, March 5. Then you sell the contract (a reversing trade) at the opening price on Monday, March 8. Below is a schedule of assumed prices and the associated margin requirements. Your gross profit on the entire transaction is ($1,062.50).

Trading Date	Settlement Price	Marked-to-the-Market	Other Entries	Account Balance
3/1	$98,250.00 (98 $\frac{8}{32}$)	+ $ 93.75	+ $ 2,500.00[a]	$2,593.75
3/2	96,687.50 (96 $\frac{22}{32}$)	− 1,562.50	+ 968.75[b]	2,000.00
3/3	97,000.00 (97 $\frac{0}{32}$)	+ 312.50		2,312.50
3/4	97,593.75 (97 $\frac{19}{32}$)	+ 593.75		2,906.25
3/5	96,937.50 (96 $\frac{30}{32}$)	− 656.25		2,250.00
3/8	97,093.75 (97 $\frac{3}{32}$)[c]	+ 156.25	− 2,406.25[d]	0.00
			+ $ 1,062.50[e]	

[a] $2,500 initial margin deposit.
[b] $968.75 deposit to meet $2,000 maintenance margin. This deposit is the variation margin.
[c] $97,093.75 opening futures price on March 8.
[d] Entire account balance withdrawn after reversing trade.
[e] Deposits less withdrawals. A positive amount indicates a loss. Also note that
$1,062.50 = $98,156.25 − $97,093.75

You may not have had to replenish the entire $750. In general a trader must deposit monies to restore a *maintenance margin*, which is often about 75 percent of the initial margin. For instance, here you would deposit just $250 [$2,000(1.00 − .75) − $750]. This $250 cash deposit is known as the *variation margin*. A broker or clearing firm normally has permission from the trader to withdraw the required deposit from the trader's established account; this facilitates the daily resettlement process, especially if a margin call should occur during the trading session. Such a call may be experienced if the futures price changes dramatically and no maximum daily price limit is applied to the contract.

Exhibit 5.3 provides another, self-contained illustration of the daily resettlement procedure. You should study it carefully in order to grasp this important process.

Daily Resettlement, Margins, and Leverage   The preceding discussion of the daily resettlement process prepares us to discuss its relation with margins and leverage. First, it should be obvious why the initial margin is so small. It need only cover one-day price changes, since contracts are marked-to-the-market each trading day. And one-day price changes are typically quite small, representing only a fraction of the futures price. Second, you should now understand why initial margins are often set equal to the contract's daily price limit. This limit bounds the daily price change, thus limiting the trader's potential one-day loss. Finally, it is now easy to understand why futures represent leveraged instruments. In the above illustration, a futures price change of less than 1 percent ($0.006/$0.700) resulted in a margin loss of over 37 percent ($750/$2,000).

Daily Price Limits and Position Limits

As noted above, exchanges impose daily price limits on some contracts to help ensure market safety. If the price of a futures contract hits a limit during a trading session, we have a *limit move*. Limit moves can be *limit up* or *limit down*. The exchange usually does not permit trading at prices above the limit up or below the limit down. However, the exchange's officials may elect to alter these limits if trading has ceased for a long period.

To also ensure contract performance and market safety, exchanges often impose *position limits* as to the number of contracts a trader can hold. Different exchanges impose different position limits on various futures contracts.

Delivery Terms

How a futures contract is delivered varies among contracts. With respect to the delivery date, some contracts may be delivered on any business day of the delivery month while others permit delivery after the last trading day, which also varies across contracts. With respect to the manner of delivery, most contracts call for the physical exchange of the underlying asset while others, such as stock index futures contracts, call for a *cash settlement*. Also, many futures contracts permit more than one deliverable asset. For instance, a short wheat trader may be allowed to deliver different qualities of wheat. When this occurs, the contract specifies a price adjustment reflecting the quality of the delivered asset.

Fortunately for us, however, most underlying assets are never delivered, because the vast majority of all futures traders engage in *reversing trades*. A reversing trade effectively makes a trader's net futures position equal to zero, thus absolving the trader from further trading requirements. For example, if you were long a SP500 futures contract with a March delivery month, you could enter a reversing trade by shorting one SP500 March futures contract. Since your net position is now zero, the clearinghouse absolves you from any further trading obligations. In futures markets, over 99 percent of all futures positions are closed out via a reversing trade.

Finally, while the vast majority of all futures are closed out (offset) via reversing trades, it is important to note that the method of actual

A **reversing trade** effectively makes a trader's net futures position equal to zero, thus absolving the trader from further trading requirements.

delivery still influences the futures price. This point will be made clearer later in this chapter, and in Chapter 6.

Executing Trades

Futures trades are executed in a similar manner across markets. To illustrate a trade, presume that you (the client or principal) wanted to assume a long position in a June British pound futures contract. This contract trades on the International Monetary Market division of the Chicago Mercantile Exchange. You are willing to assume the position "at market," meaning that you are seeking the best currently available price.

The process begins with a phone call to your agent (account executive or broker), who must trade through an exchange member. Exchange members are individuals who trade on the floor of the exchange. They hold seats in the exchange. A member may be a *commission broker* (more formally called a *futures commission merchant*), or a *local*. A commission broker's seat is usually financed by a trading firm, such as Shearson Lehman. Thus, calling an account executive or broker of a trading firm (with which you have an established account) effectively gives you access to a commission broker. Over the past decade, seat prices at the CME have ranged mainly between $200,000 and $300,000.

Your agent next places the order through to the commission broker, who in turn executes the trade and earns a commission. Commission brokers are therefore exchange members who execute trades for public clients for a fee.

The actual trading is conducted in a designated floor area, called a *pit*, for the particular futures contract involved. Trades are executed through the use of sophisticated hand signals. The commission broker confirms the trade with your agent, who then notifies you of your completed transaction and the futures price. You must then deposit your initial margin with a member firm of the clearinghouse. Typically, your broker or account executive handles this process, withdrawing funds from your established account.

The commission broker may have transacted in the pit with another commission broker who represented another public client. Alternatively, he may have transacted with a local. Locals are exchange members who trade for their own accounts. They earn a living by buying at one price, known as a *bid price*, and selling at a higher price, known as an *ask price*. Locals are sometimes called scalpers, day traders, or position traders, depending on their trading behavior. *Scalpers* trade actively, holding their positions for no more than a few minutes. Thus they attempt to profit from volume trading. *Day traders* hold their positions for a longer period, but less than a full trading session. They attempt to profit on price movement but do not wish to assume the risk of holding longer positions. *Position traders* assume longer-term positions. The roles that these different traders play are examined more closely in Chapter 7.

Traders on the floors of futures exchanges are allowed to trade both for themselves as locals as well as for public clients as commission brokers. This is known as *dual trading*.

Types of Orders

Besides placing a market order, a public futures trader can place any of the following order types:

- *Limit order.* Stipulates a specific price at which you will contract. It can be good only for a trading session (a *day order*), or until cancelled (an *open order*).
- *Fill-or-kill order.* Instructs the commission broker to fill an order immediately at a specified price. The order is canceled if it cannot be transacted quickly.
- *All-or-none order.* Allows the commission broker to fill part of an order at one specified price and the remainder at another price.
- *On-the-open* or *on-the-close order.* Represent orders to trade within a few minutes of opening or closing, respectively.
- *Stop order.* Triggers a reversing trade when prices hit a prescribed limit. Stop orders are used to protect against losses on existing positions.

Transaction Costs

Transaction costs in futures markets are very small, especially for exchange members. Presently it costs locals about 24¢ per round-trip trade. Of course, public traders incur other costs. The following transaction costs are realized from futures trading:

- *Floor trading and clearing fees.* These are the small fees charged by the exchange and its associated clearinghouse. If a trade is executed through a commission broker, these fees are built into the broker's commission. Locals pay the fees directly.
- *Commissions.* A commission broker charges a commission fee to transact a public order. It is paid at the order's inception and covers both the opening and reversing trades.
- *Bid-ask spreads.* Locals simultaneously quote bid and ask prices. The bid-ask spread represents a transaction cost when effecting a trade with a local. The spread represents the cost of obtaining trading immediacy, since locals offer the public trading liquidity. A bid-ask spread is typically equal to the value of the contract's minimum price fluctuation, called a *tick*.

- *Delivery costs.* A trader who holds a position until delivery is exposed to delivery costs. However, as noted above, the overwhelming majority of futures contracts never entail actual delivery of the underlying asset.

Taxes

Determining the tax consequences of futures trading can be complex, especially when spreads are involved. A few generally applicable tax guides follow:

- *Marking-to-the-market.* At the end of the calendar year every futures contract is marked-to-the-market so that any unrealized gains or losses are treated, for tax purposes, as though they were actually realized during the tax year.
- *Gains.* The realized and unrealized gains from futures trading are taxed at the ordinary personal income tax rate.
- *Losses.* The realized and unrealized losses are made deductible by offsetting them against any other investment gains. Losses exceeding gains by up to $3,000 can be deducted against ordinary income.
- *Commissions.* In general, brokerage commissions are tax-deductible.

Market Growth and Globalization

Futures trading has exhibited tremendous growth since the 1970s. Figure 5.1 portrays the growth in all U.S. futures trading for the period 1972 through 1986. During this period annual trading volume grew ten-fold, to nearly 200 million contracts. Also, eight new futures exchanges have developed in the free world since 1982. Exhibit 5.4 identifies these eight exchanges, all of which are outside the United States.

The advent of these foreign markets has given rise to cooperative linkages that facilitate international futures trading. Exhibit 5.5 presents current linkages between several organized exchanges. Here contracts can be opened on one exchange and closed out on the other. For example, Japanese yen futures may be traded on the Chicago Mercantile Exchange (CME) and the position closed on the Singapore International Monetary Exchange.

Also, some futures contracts are traded on several different (but not linked) markets. In addition to possibly providing opportunities for future cooperative links, such trading currently provides for more continuous market access. Exhibit 5.6 reports the different markets on which U.S. Treasury bond, Eurodollar, Deutsche mark, and gold futures are traded. Three of these contracts exhibit around-the-clock trading, with gold futures having nearly 24-hour trading. Also, the Philadelphia Exchange and CBOT have recently begun evening trading of currency

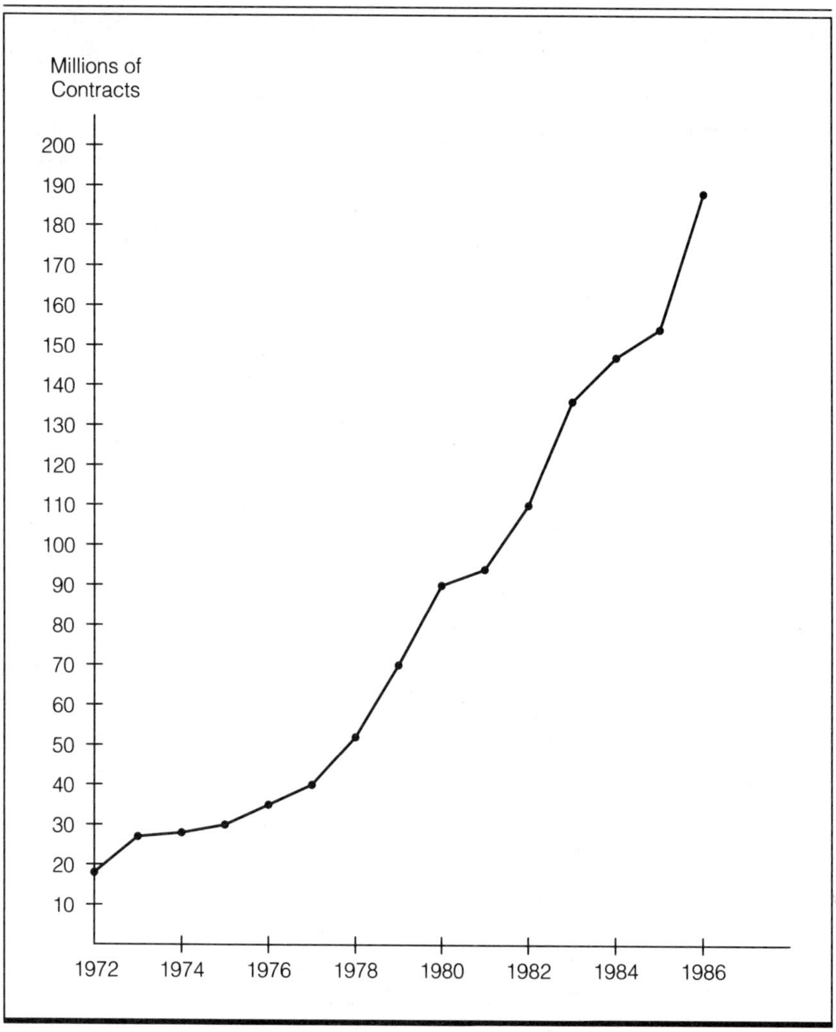

Figure 5.1:
Annual Volume for All U.S. Futures Trading

Millions of Contracts

and Treasury bond futures, respectively, in order to regain market share lost to overseas exchanges. Finally, the CME will soon institute an after-hours electronic futures trading system. This system, called *Globex*, is designed to recapture business from Japanese and other Far East futures traders.

Market Regulation

Organized futures markets are regulated to ensure contract performance and to prevent insider trading and price manipulation, such as *frontrun-*

Exchange	Year Founded
London International Financial Futures Exchange	1982
Bermuda International Futures Exchange	1984
Singapore International Monetary Exchange	1984
Toronto Futures Exchange	1984
Baltic International Freight Futures Exchange	1985
Kuala Lumpur Commodity Exchange	1985
New Zealand Futures Exchange	1985
Tokyo Financial Futures Exchange	1985

Exhibit 5.5:
Linked Futures Markets

Futures Contract	Linked Markets
Gold	New York Commodity Exchange and the Sydney Futures Exchange
U.S. Treasury Bonds 3-Month Eurodollars	London International Financial Futures Exchange and the Sydney Futures Exchange
Eurodollars British Pound Japanese Yen	Chicago Mercantile Exchange and the Singapore International Monetary Exchange

Frontrunning occurs when dual traders in some way give priority to their own trading at the expense of outside clients.

ning, which occurs when dual traders in some way give priority to their own trading at the expense of outside clients. For instance, if a dual trader knows that a client will soon enter a large order, then the trader can profit by assuming a prescribed position prior to executing the client's order.

Futures exchanges are regulated by a number of bodies, especially the Commodity Futures Trading Commission (CFTC) and National Futures Association (NFA). The CFTC was created by Congress in 1974. The NFA was established in 1982 as a private, self-regulatory agency funded by transaction fees assessed on futures trading. Together these two bodies are empowered to approve new contracts, set maximum daily price limits, ensure the competency of brokers, and the like. Each futures exchange also regulates trading by means of trading rules, and market surveillance. The goal is to assure orderly trading and prevent price manipulation.

Regulation and the 1987 Equities Market Crash The U.S. stock market, as measured by the SP500, declined in value by 21.6 percent

Futures Contract	Markets Traded
U.S. Treasury Bonds[a]	Chicago Board of Trade
	Sydney Futures Exchange
	London International Financial Futures Exchange
	Singapore International Monetary Exchange
Eurodollars[a]	International Monetary Market (CME)
	London International Financial Futures Exchange
	Singapore International Monetary Exchange
Deutsche Marks[a]	International Monetary Market (CME)
	MidAmerica Commodity Exchange (Chicago)
	Philadelphia Board of Trade
	London International Financial Futures Exchange
	Brazilian Futures Exchange
	Sao Paulo Commodities Exchange
	Bolsa Mercantile and Futures Exchange
Gold	Chicago Board of Trade
	New York Commodity Exchange
	Winnipeg Commodity Exchange
	Brazilian Futures Exchange
	Sao Paulo Commodities Exchange
	Bolsa Mercantile and Futures Exchange
	Singapore International Monetary Exchange

Exhibit 5.6:

Markets Trading Futures Contracts on U.S. Treasury Bonds, Eurodollars, Marks and Gold

[a]Around-the-clock trading is possible.

during the single month of October 1987. Most of this decline was concentrated on "Black Monday," October 19, 1987, when the DJIA fell by 508 points. A presidential commission known as the *Brady Commission* was assigned to investigate the causes of the crash. This commission concluded that stock index futures trading may have exacerbated the crash. Specifically, the initial market decline resulted in a wave of stock index futures selling. Recall from Chapter 4 that equity portfolio managers may sell (write) index futures to help insure their portfolio values. The Brady Commission reported that over $4 billion worth of stock index futures contracts were written by portfolio insurers on October 19 alone.

This wave of index futures selling drove futures prices down, and reportedly drove a wedge between spot index values and index futures prices. The result was a tremendous volume of index arbitrage as arbitragers attempted to profit by selling large blocks of stocks and purchasing index futures contracts. The Brady Commission reported that $1.7 billion in stock was sold by arbitragers on October 19 alone. However, the conclusion that such stock selling exacerbated the crash has been disputed by the CFTC and many others.

The commission's final report on the crash recommended that several regulatory measures be instituted in order to preclude a similar exacerbation, namely, the redesigning of derivative security instruments, coordinating trading halts, the institution of daily price change limits, and more effective monitoring of trading activities The commission was especially concerned with excessive frontrunning around the crash period. At the current time, however, it appears that most of these recommendations will not be instituted.

"Futuresgate" 1989   In January of 1989 the FBI disclosed a massive ongoing investigation of abusive futures trading practices at both the CBOT and CME. The investigation, with FBI agents posing as independent floor brokers and traders under assumed names, centered on the Japanese yen and Swiss franc futures pits at the CME, and the U.S. Treasury bond and soybean futures pits at the CBOT. One abusive practice discovered was an illegal trading scheme known as *bucket trading* in which two traders conspire to exploit profits on public market orders by delaying the order's execution. Here is how a bucket trade may be executed:

Bucket trading is an illegal scheme in which two traders conspire to exploit profits on public market orders by delaying the order's execution.

- First, a commission broker receives a client's market order. Suppose that the order is to buy 25 U.S. Treasury bond futures contracts at the best available price.

- Second, the commission broker signals a confederate, called a "bagman," to buy the contracts. Presume the bagman buys the 25 contracts at $90,000 per contract, or $2.25 million. The commission broker continues to hold the client's market order.

- Third, suppose the price rises shortly to, say, $90,062.50. The commission broker now executes the client's order; the client thinks that $90,062.50 was the best available price. The bagman sells the 25 contracts at $90,062.50 for a profit of $1,562.50. This profit should have been the client's. Instead, the profit is "bucketed" into the bagman's account, and he and the broker later split the monies. If the bond futures price had fallen, the customer would have bought the contracts from the bagman at the $90,000 price. The loss is bucketed into the customer's account, and the two illegal traders do not exhibit any losses.

Reportedly, the FBI's sting was instituted at the request of Archer Daniels Midland Co., a huge grain and soybean producer and active futures market participant. Although the investigation is still unfolding,

The CBOE 250 Futures Contract

On November 11, 1988, the Chicago Board of Trade (CBOT) and the Chicago Board Options Exchange (CBOE) jointly began trading a new stock index futures contract. Although it is a CBOT contract, it will be traded on the floor of the CBOE and regulated by both the Commodity Futures Trading Commission (CFTC) and the Securities and Exchange Commission (SEC). The CFTC normally regulates U.S. futures markets, while the SEC normally regulates U.S. options markets.

The stock index upon which the new futures contract is written is known as the CBOE 250. It is an arithmetic index of the 250 largest capitalized stocks traded on the New York Stock Exchange. As such, the new index is highly correlated with the SP100 and the SP500. Since options on the SP100 and SP500 are traded on the CBOE, side-by-side trading of these options and the new CBOE 250 futures contracts may contribute to the operational efficiency of the market. Investors should be able to use both the index options and futures contracts together in certain trading strategies.

But the truly unique aspect of the new CBOE 250 futures contract is that it allows for *cross margining*—that is, the ability to use realized profits on a position held in one market to satisfy margin requirements on a position held in another market by the same investor. For example, a trader could use realized profits from index put options (should the market fall) to satisfy margin calls on a long index futures position. During the October 1987 equities market crash, investors who were long on index futures, but who held index put options, could not employ their option profits immediately to cover their margin calls in the futures market. Now, with cross margining, investors can meet such margin calls. Cross margining was a recommendation offered by the Brady Commission assigned to analyze the October 1987 crash. Thus, the new CBOE 250 futures contract is the direct result of a Brady Commission recommendation. Investors can expect more cross margining as exchanges operate jointly to offer new securities that ease operational frictions.

---

it appears that the toll will be heavy. The government has issued scores of subpoenas to traders and others, and is apparently not offering full immunity for cooperation into the investigation.

The investigation raises some serious concerns about the integrity of the exchanges' *open-outcry* system. Some of the potential changes that could ensue as a result include

- *Banning dual trading.* Such a ban would help to reduce abusive practices like frontrunning and bucket trading. (Notice that the bagman in a bucket trade must be a dual trader.)

- *Increasing surveillance.* Greater scrutiny of trading would help to minimize abuses.

- *Precise trade recording.* Futures traders often argue that their markets move too rapidly to record trades precisely at execution, as is done in equity and other security markets. However, improved electronic technology should make it easier to institute tougher reporting requirements.

- *Abolishing the open-outcry system.* Technology advances can now facilitate fully computerized trading. An example is the CME's proposed Globex system, discussed earlier.

FUTURES INSTRUMENTS

Futures contracts are written on a variety of underlying assets. In order to differentiate financial futures, and to facilitate the determination of futures prices, we may categorize contracts as either *physical futures* or *financial futures*. Physical futures may be either agricultural or metallurgical, while financial futures refer to currency, interest rate, and index futures.

Physical Futures

Futures contracts were first traded on physical assets. Today agricultural contracts exist on textiles, poultry, oil and meal, grains, and other foodstuffs. In the metallurgical area there are contracts on genuine and precious metals and petroleum. Exhibit 5.7 reports *settlement futures prices* for many of these physical futures, for trading on November 16, 1988. A settlement price, which is used to quantify the resettlement cash flows each day, is determined by a *settlement committee*. Often the settlement futures price is determined by averaging the prices of the session's last few trades.

The first settlement price listed in Exhibit 5.7 is $2.6425 per bushel, occurring for December corn futures traded on the CBOT. There were 82,880 contracts outstanding (as of the beginning of the trading session) for December CBOT corn, as indicated by the *open interest* reported. Other price entries are similarly interpreted. Also, notice that several delivery months are available for each contract. For agricultural futures, these months tend to coincide with the underlying commodity's harvest pattern. For all physical futures the number of delivery months also depends on contract volume, with more months available for the more active contracts.

The two most important differences between agricultural and metallurgical futures contracts concern *storability* and *seasonality*. Metallurgical commodities, like gold and petroleum, are nearly indefinitely storable, whereas agricultural commodities have finite storable lines. For example, eggs have very short storable lives; and although other agricultural commodities store well for long periods (e.g. corn), their values depreciate during storage because of lost moisture content and other causes. Most agricultural commodities also exhibit seasonal production patterns, while metallurgical commodities do not.

Finally, it is important to note that physical futures contracts often are available for different qualities of the underlying commodity. For example, several different grain futures are traded that differ by protein content, texture, and taste. Grain texture and taste are important for human consumption, whereas only protein content is important for animal feeding.

Financial Futures

The CME successfully began futures trading on foreign exchange in 1972. Interest rate futures trading began in 1975 when the CME first

COMMODITY FUTURES PRICES

–GRAINS AND OILSEEDS–

CORN (CBT) 5,000 bu.; cents per bu.

	Open	High	Low	Settle	Change	Lifetime High	Lifetime Low	Open Interest
Dec	265	266½	263¾	264¼	– 1¾	370	184	82,880
Mr89	273	274¼	271¾	272½	– ¾	370	193½	94,689
May	277½	279	276¾	277½	– ½	369	207½	28,476
July	279	280½	278¼	279¼	....	360	233	18,495
Sept	268¼	268¾	266¼	267½	– ¾	317¾	245	4,397
Dec	261	261¾	258½	260	– ¾	295	234	13,656
Mr90	266	266	263½	264	– 2	270	258½	203

Est vol 55,000; vol Tues 47,428; open int 242,796, –4,654.

OATS (CBT) 5,000 bu.; cents per bu.

	Open	High	Low	Settle	Change	Lifetime High	Lifetime Low	Open Interest
Dec	209¾	211¾	205	205¼	– 4¾	389½	162	3,074
Mr89	219½	221	215	215	– 5	367¾	161	3,762
May	223½	224	218½	218½	– 4½	340	187	990
July	215½	216½	212¼	212¼	– 3¼	277	211½	1,382
Sept	214	214	210½	210½	– 4	231	209½	181

Est vol 1,500; vol Tues 1,312; open int 9,389, –314.

SOYBEANS (CBT) 5,000 bu.; cents per bu.

	Open	High	Low	Settle	Change	Lifetime High	Lifetime Low	Open Interest
Nov	745	750	740	744¼	+ ¾	1045	499½	1,740
Ja89	757	764¾	755	758	....	1034	553	47,021
Mar	770	777	767½	770¼	– ¾	1023	579	28,287
May	774	781	773	775½	+ ½	1003	647	10,929
July	774	782	773	776¼	+ 1	986	685	11,417
Aug	771	774	769	770	+ 4	951	725	1,291
Sept	740	742	737½	738	+ 1	835	701	2,109
Nov	716½	722¾	716	716¼	– 1	793	663	8,629
Ja90	728	728	723	723	– 1	748	722	303

Est vol 60,000; vol Tues 56,107; open int 111,726, +14.

SOYBEAN MEAL (CBT) 100 tons; $ per ton.

	Open	High	Low	Settle	Change	Lifetime High	Lifetime Low	Open Interest
Dec	245.50	249.20	245.20	246.50	....	318.70	159.00	19,779
Ja89	246.00	249.50	246.00	247.40	+ .40	313.00	177.00	25,118
Mar	245.20	248.50	245.00	246.20	+ .50	308.00	193.50	17,963
May	242.50	245.00	242.00	243.50	+ .80	304.00	200.50	7,229
July	239.50	241.50	239.00	240.20	+ .50	300.00	221.00	3,686
Aug	236.00	237.00	236.00	236.50	– .50	298.00	217.50	927
Sept	230.00	231.00	230.00	231.00	....	290.00	214.00	1,034
Oct	222.00	222.00	221.00	221.50	– .50	237.00	208.00	879
Dec	218.00	218.00	217.50	218.00	....	270.00	203.00	916

Est vol 30,000; vol Tues 28,506; open int 77,531, –1,634.

SOYBEAN OIL (CBT) 60,000 lbs.; cents per lb.

	Open	High	Low	Settle	Change	Lifetime High	Lifetime Low	Open Interest
Dec	22.18	22.30	21.90	21.91	– .28	34.25	18.30	28,173
Ja89	22.46	22.57	22.20	22.20	– .27	33.95	20.75	17,146
Mar	22.98	23.08	22.71	22.71	– .24	33.60	21.25	20,164
May	23.45	23.55	23.27	23.27	– .19	33.00	22.95	7,374
July	23.85	24.00	23.65	23.65	– .17	32.50	23.00	4,631
Aug	24.00	24.20	23.80	23.80	– .20	32.05	23.80	1,209
Sept	24.20	24.20	24.10	24.10	– .10	28.70	24.10	954
Oct	24.20	24.35	24.20	24.25	– .10	26.95	24.05	1,579
Dec	24.25	24.45	24.05	24.05	– .22	28.05	22.80	1,901

Est vol 20,000; vol Tues 16,611; open int 83,131, –70.

WHEAT (CBT) 5,000 bu.; cents per bu.

	Open	High	Low	Settle	Change	Lifetime High	Lifetime Low	Open Interest
Dec	412½	414	409½	410¾	– 3	438	289	28,151
Mr89	420¼	421½	417½	419¼	– 2	442	323	24,426
May	406	406	403	403½	– 2¾	420	330	5,043
July	382	384	381	383½	– ½	395	327	13,452
Sept	386½	389	386½	387	– ½	390	350½	537
Dec	393	399	393	399	+ 2	399	378	107

Est vol 20,000; vol Tues 15,392; open int 71,716, –431.

WHEAT (KC) 5,000 bu.; cents per bu.

	Open	High	Low	Settle	Change	Lifetime High	Lifetime Low	Open Interest
Dec	409	409¾	406	409	– 1¼	428½	301½	14,936
Mr89	414	417	412¼	416½	+ ¾	434	322¾	16,907
May	403	403	400	402	– 1	416	324	1,566
July	385	388	384	387	....	391	331	2,455
Sept	389	390	389	390	– 1	390	353	304

Est vol 6,442; vol Tues 5,641; open int 36,174, +229.

WHEAT (MPLS) 5,000 bu.; cents per bu.

	Open	High	Low	Settle	Change	Lifetime High	Lifetime Low	Open Interest
Dec	402	402½	387	397¾	– 5	473½	308¾	4,984
Mr89	415	416	412	412¼	– 4	472	347	3,428
May	416	418½	415	416	– 2	428	399	352
Sept	400	400	399½	399½	– 1½	405	397½	155

Est vol 1,720; vol Tues 1,185; open int 9,018, –263.

BARLEY (WPG) 20 metric tons; Can. $ per ton

	Open	High	Low	Settle	Change	Lifetime High	Lifetime Low	Open Interest
Nov	....	....	....	123.30	– 1.10	133.10	78.50	30
Dec	125.20	125.50	124.10	124.20	– 1.30	135.70	78.90	13,591
Mr89	132.50	132.60	131.40	131.50	– 1.20	142.00	105.00	7,064
May	135.30	135.80	134.80	134.80	– 1.10	148.50	125.50	2,928
July	138.00	138.00	137.60	137.60	– .40	147.00	135.00	1,492
Oct	131.00	131.00	130.80	130.80	– .20	140.00	129.70	263

Est vol 2,085; vol Tues 1,858; open int 25,368, –400.

FLAXSEED (WPG) 20 metric tons; Can. $ per ton

	Open	High	Low	Settle	Change	Lifetime High	Lifetime Low	Open Interest
Dec	387.00	391.00	381.00	382.00	– 8.00	482.00	242.10	4,319
Mr89	397.00	400.70	390.00	390.90	– 8.60	485.00	266.00	3,749
May	402.00	405.30	395.00	396.50	– 7.90	490.00	395.00	1,550
July	402.50	405.50	395.50	396.00	– 8.50	492.00	395.50	251
Oct	....	....	....	358.00	– 8.60	394.50	354.00	354
Dec	360.00	362.00	355.10	355.10	– 5.90	434.00	353.00	433

Est vol 790; vol Tues 845; open int 10,656, +14.

RAPESEED (WPG) 20 metric tons; Can. $ per ton

	Open	High	Low	Settle	Change	Lifetime High	Lifetime Low	Open Interest
Nov	329.00	331.70	326.50	326.50	– 6.70	482.00	261.00	156
Ja89	334.50	338.50	330.50	330.80	– 5.30	486.70	291.80	13,749
Mar	341.00	344.80	337.00	337.00	– 5.50	489.50	300.70	8,672
June	352.00	354.30	346.00	346.20	– 6.30	490.00	346.00	2,684
Sept	....	....	....	355.00	– 6.50	390.50	358.00	1,156
Nov	364.00	365.50	358.00	358.00	– 5.00	482.00	261.80	3,260

Est vol 2,340; vol Tues 3,591; open int 29,677, +41.

WHEAT (WPG) 20 metric tons; Can. $ per ton

	Open	High	Low	Settle	Change	Lifetime High	Lifetime Low	Open Interest
Nov	161.00	161.00	158.00	158.00	– 3.00	169.00	94.40	703
Dec	159.00	159.00	154.50	154.50	– 5.00	167.00	94.00	3,584
Mr89	161.50	161.50	159.10	159.10	– 2.90	170.50	103.50	8,004
May	161.00	161.00	159.00	159.00	– 2.20	168.50	135.50	3,324
July	157.50	157.70	157.00	157.50	– .60	166.50	144.30	639
Oct	....	....	....	151.50	– .50	152.00	151.00	100

Est vol 2,715; vol Tues 991; open int 16,354, –109.

RYE (WPG) 20 metric tons; Can. $ per ton

	Open	High	Low	Settle	Change	Lifetime High	Lifetime Low	Open Interest
Dec	157.50	158.10	157.50	158.00	+ .50	194.50	140.00	902
Mr89	160.00	160.50	160.00	160.50	+ .50	178.00	149.90	1,553
May	....	....	....	162.50	+ .50	171.50	156.00	312

Est vol 255; vol Tues 66; open int 2,767, –108.

–LIVESTOCK & MEAT–

CATTLE–FEEDER (CME) 44,000 lbs.; cents per lb.

	Open	High	Low	Settle	Change	Lifetime High	Lifetime Low	Open Interest
Nov	82.00	82.05	81.85	81.95	– .10	84.05	70.25	2,136
Ja89	83.55	83.75	83.45	83.55	– .20	85.05	74.00	5,913
Mar	82.75	82.95	82.52	82.92	+ .02	83.85	74.00	4,268
Apr	81.80	82.00	81.75	81.90	– .05	82.90	74.40	1,217
May	80.70	80.70	80.47	80.57	– .22	81.80	60.00	1,086
Aug	79.40	79.40	79.40	79.40	– .05	80.25	78.50	337

Est vol 1,521; vol Tues 2,528; open int 14,977, +197.

Wednesday, November 16, 1988.

Open Interest Reflects Previous Trading Day.

CATTLE–LIVE (CME) 40,000 lbs.; cents per lb.

	Open	High	Low	Settle	Change	Lifetime High	Lifetime Low	Open Interest
Dec	73.25	73.47	73.05	73.25	– .10	75.50	60.25	27,446
Fb89	73.85	74.22	73.70	74.07	+ .15	75.60	65.10	29,926
Apr	74.95	75.30	74.85	75.27	+ .20	76.47	67.20	16,663
June	73.40	73.65	73.35	73.57	....	75.20	68.75	5,053
Aug	71.25	71.35	71.00	71.30	– .02	73.20	69.70	4,259
Oct	70.40	70.45	70.27	70.30	– .07	74.00	69.50	1,116

Est vol 15,962; vol Tues 20,353; open int 84,471, +396.

HOGS (CME) 30,000 lbs.; cents per lb.

	Open	High	Low	Settle	Change	Lifetime High	Lifetime Low	Open Interest
Dec	41.00	41.40	40.87	41.35	+ .30	48.50	38.30	13,641
Fb89	45.15	45.50	45.05	45.37	+ .07	52.00	41.80	10,797
Apr	44.00	44.35	43.85	44.32	+ .25	51.65	40.60	6,259
June	48.35	48.40	48.10	48.32	+ .02	56.25	42.50	1,621
July	48.50	48.70	48.35	48.55	– .05	56.00	47.07	1,460
Aug	47.50	47.97	47.50	47.95	+ .25	51.00	45.97	249
Oct	....	....	....	44.65	....	47.00	43.50	211

Est vol 5,393; vol Tues 6,422; open int 34,246, –340.

PORK BELLIES (CME) 40,000 lbs.; cents per lb.

	Open	High	Low	Settle	Change	Lifetime High	Lifetime Low	Open Interest
Feb	44.45	44.67	44.15	44.45	– .42	67.00	43.75	10,693
Mar	45.00	45.15	44.65	45.05	– .42	66.35	44.25	3,526
May	46.65	46.80	46.40	46.67	– .70	65.50	45.87	2,451
July	47.85	48.20	47.75	47.90	– .47	64.50	47.30	2,509
Aug	47.25	47.45	46.82	46.82	– .70	58.25	46.50	541

Est vol 3,477; vol Tues 3,181; open int 19,720, +30.

–FOOD & FIBER–

COCOA (CSCE)–10 metric tons; $ per ton.

	Open	High	Low	Settle	Change	Lifetime High	Lifetime Low	Open Interest
Dec	1,365	1,406	1,364	1,392	+ 45	2,197	1,103	1,763
Mr89	1,410	1,450	1,410	1,445	+ 59	2,088	1,125	17,457
May	1,413	1,439	1,413	1,434	+ 44	2,088	1,152	5,747
July	1,418	1,442	1,418	1,438	+ 39	1,985	1,172	3,554
Sept	1,426	1,450	1,426	1,452	+ 42	1,850	1,206	1,816
Dec	1,441	1,456	1,441	1,458	+ 40	1,735	1,240	4,702
Mr90	1,480	1,480	1,480	1,483	+ 35	1,500	1,305	2,496

Est vol 7,046; vol Tues8,445; open int 37,535, –776.

COFFEE (CSCE)–37,500 lbs.; cents per lb.

	Open	High	Low	Settle	Change	Lifetime High	Lifetime Low	Open Interest
Dec	126.20	127.60	125.70	127.27	+ .33	150.25	101.00	5,563
Mr89	126.90	128.30	126.43	127.98	+ .60	150.50	112.44	10,382
May	126.25	127.45	125.75	126.97	+ .47	150.75	112.13	2,284
July	125.50	126.40	125.40	126.28	+ .48	145.00	114.00	1,303
Sept	125.75	125.75	125.75	125.63	+ .88	143.50	114.00	522
Dec	125.00	125.00	125.00	125.00	+ .70	129.25	118.00	106

Est vol 5,140; vol Tues3,484; open int 20,160, –112.

SUGAR–WORLD (CSCE)–112,000 lbs.; cents per lb.

	Open	High	Low	Settle	Change	Lifetime High	Lifetime Low	Open Interest
Jan	....	....	....	9.86	– .12	15.00	7.75	107
Mar	10.25	10.28	10.15	10.16	– .05	14.39	7.66	75,508
May	9.94	10.00	9.89	9.90	– .05	13.64	7.87	25,015
July	9.76	9.82	9.76	9.76	– .05	13.40	8.10	6,628
Oct	9.63	9.70	9.61	9.61	– .06	13.30	8.45	10,000
Mr90	9.32	9.32	9.32	9.32	– .04	9.70	8.75	279

Est vol 10,672; vol Tues10,952; open int 117,539, +1,551.

SUGAR–DOMESTIC (CSCE)–112,000 lbs.; cents per lb.

	Open	High	Low	Settle	Change	Lifetime High	Lifetime Low	Open Interest
Jan	21.65	21.75	21.65	21.73	+ .08	22.44	21.58	1,593
Mar	21.85	21.88	21.85	21.88	+ .04	22.50	21.75	1,829
May	....	....	....	21.98	+ .01	22.60	21.80	1,296
July	22.03	22.05	22.03	22.05	+ .04	22.60	21.80	751
Sept	22.00	22.00	22.00	22.01	+ .02	22.60	21.95	1,131
Nov	21.74	21.85	21.74	21.80	....	22.50	21.62	379

Est vol 597; vol Tues414; open int 6,979, –175.

COTTON (CTN)–50,000 lbs.; cents per lb.

	Open	High	Low	Settle	Change	Lifetime High	Lifetime Low	Open Interest
Dec	55.30	55.40	54.85	54.95	– .67	70.20	48.65	11,185
Mr89	56.25	56.40	56.10	56.17	– .44	68.90	48.90	13,963
May	56.40	56.90	56.35	56.80	+ .03	68.70	49.03	4,032
July	56.50	57.10	56.50	57.00	+ .29	65.73	49.26	3,125
Oct	56.75	56.75	56.75	56.75	+ .20	65.50	50.35	912
Dec	56.50	57.05	56.46	56.85	+ .24	65.50	50.75	3,337

Est vol 9,500; vol Tues 4,666; open int 36,587, +69.

ORANGE JUICE (CTN)–15,000 lbs.; cents per lb.

	Open	High	Low	Settle	Change	Lifetime High	Lifetime Low	Open Interest
Nov	181.00	181.75	180.00	179.60	– 2.70	192.00	132.00	523
Ja89	169.10	169.80	168.10	168.50	– 1.75	179.05	132.00	4,329
Mar	168.50	168.80	167.20	168.20	– 1.20	175.50	152.90	2,881
May	168.75	168.75	168.00	168.45	– .75	173.50	149.00	764
July	168.50	168.50	168.00	168.15	– .85	171.80	162.25	457
Sept	166.50	166.50	166.50	166.20	– .15	170.10	161.00	224

Est vol 2,500; vol Tues 2,165; open int 9,211, –329.

–METALS & PETROLEUM–

COPPER-STANDARD (CMX)–25,000 lbs.; cents per lb.

	Open	High	Low	Settle	Change	Lifetime High	Lifetime Low	Open Interest
Nov	135.00	135.00	135.00	135.00	– 1.90	153.80	135.00	164
Dec	130.12	131.50	125.75	128.00	– 1.90	148.20	64.70	17,272
Mr89	111.00	111.50	107.70	110.50	+ .50	122.90	66.50	12,949
May	105.50	106.20	103.40	105.80	+ .60	115.00	73.15	1,940
July	103.50	104.30	102.00	103.80	+ .80	112.80	76.00	1,530
Sept	101.50	101.50	101.00	102.50	+ 1.00	107.50	76.00	518
Dec	100.50	100.50	100.30	101.50	+ 1.50	106.50	77.45	991

Est vol 12,000; vol Tues 12,784; open int 35,423, –1,550.

GOLD (CMX)–100 troy oz.; $ per troy oz.

	Open	High	Low	Settle	Change	Lifetime High	Lifetime Low	Open Interest
Nov	424.00	424.00	424.00	424.50	+ .10	425.70	411.00	5
Dec	426.00	428.90	424.50	425.60	....	546.00	395.50	54,607
Fb89	431.50	434.00	429.50	430.50	+ .20	549.50	401.00	22,587
Apr	436.00	439.00	435.00	435.90	+ .30	550.00	407.00	10,226
June	440.60	444.40	440.60	441.30	+ .40	570.00	412.00	19,946
Aug	....	....	....	447.00	+ .40	575.00	419.30	9,034
Oct	....	....	....	452.70	+ .40	575.50	423.00	10,345
Dec	458.00	461.50	457.50	458.30	+ .40	514.50	428.00	12,041
Fb90	....	....	....	464.00	+ .50	516.00	439.70	4,272
Apr	....	....	....	469.80	+ .60	525.80	443.00	2,711
June	....	....	....	475.60	+ .70	497.00	447.00	2,219
Aug	....	....	....	481.60	+ .70	481.50	453.00	904

Est vol 50,000; vol Tues 38,543; open int 148,897, –3,776.

EXCHANGE ABBREVIATIONS
(for commodity futures and futures options)

CBT-Chicago Board of Trade; CME-Chicago Mercantile Exchange; CMX-Commodity Exchange, New York; CRCE-Chicago Rice & Cotton Exchange; CTN-New York Cotton Exchange; CSCE-Coffee, Sugar & Cocoa Exchange, New York; IPEL-International Petroleum Exchange of London; KC-Kansas City Board of Trade; MCE-MidAmerica Commodity Exchange; MPLS-Minneapolis Grain Exchange; NYM-New York Mercantile Exchange; PBOT-Philadelphia Board of Trade; WPG-Winnipeg Commodity Exchange.

PLATINUM (NYM)–50 troy oz.; $ per troy oz.

	Open	High	Low	Settle	Change	Lifetime High	Lifetime Low	Open Interest
Ja89	579.40	590.00	574.00	580.40	+ 2.20	646.00	459.00	13,455
Apr	579.00	587.00	573.50	578.10	+ 1.90	643.50	482.00	6,304
July	583.50	588.00	580.00	579.60	+ 2.40	640.00	501.00	1,254
Oct	579.00	579.00	577.50	582.10	+ 3.40	594.00	507.00	829

Est vol 9,344; vol Tues 4,313; open int 22,847, –91.

PALLADIUM (NYM) 100 troy oz.; $ per troy oz.

	Open	High	Low	Settle	Change	Lifetime High	Lifetime Low	Open Interest
Dec	127.25	129.50	127.00	127.40	+ .10	139.50	104.50	2,696
Mr89	125.50	127.00	125.50	125.65	+ .10	132.00	115.50	2,159
June	124.25	125.50	124.00	124.40	+ .10	131.00	114.00	1,247
Sept	....	....	....	123.40	+ .10	125.00	119.00	245

Est vol 1,076; vol Tues 918; open int 6,318, +118.

SILVER (CMX)–5,000 troy oz.; cents per troy oz.

	Open	High	Low	Settle	Change	Lifetime High	Lifetime Low	Open Interest
Nov	....	....	....	627.7	– 9.1	654.0	630.0	4
Dec	642.0	644.0	628.0	630.0	– 9.3	1082.0	606.0	42,349
Mr89	657.5	659.0	643.0	645.2	– 9.3	1073.0	631.0	15,706
May	665.5	668.5	655.0	655.3	– 9.3	948.0	645.0	4,451
July	677.0	677.0	663.0	665.8	– 9.3	985.0	654.0	7,820
Sept	687.0	687.0	687.0	676.0	– 9.3	861.0	660.0	6,087
Dec	704.0	705.5	689.0	691.5	– 9.3	886.0	680.0	5,610
Mr90	....	....	....	708.1	– 9.3	910.0	700.0	3,218
May	....	....	....	719.0	– 9.3	910.0	711.0	2,699
July	....	....	....	729.9	– 9.3	761.5	722.0	1,912

Est vol 18,000; vol Tues 13,692; open int 89,952, –1,095.

SILVER (CBT)–1,000 troy oz.; cents per troy oz.

	Open	High	Low	Settle	Change	Lifetime High	Lifetime Low	Open Interest
Nov	....	....	....	626.0	– 12.0	650.0	618.0	8
Dec	641.0	644.0	627.0	629.5	– 10.5	946.0	616.0	8,259
Fb89	651.0	655.0	638.0	640.0	– 10.5	840.0	627.0	[illegible]
Apr	660.0	665.0	650.0	650.5	– 10.5	855.0	640.0	511
June	670.0	675.0	659.0	660.0	– 11.5	865.0	650.0	1,216
Dec	703.0	707.0	692.5	692.5	– 10.5	735.0	675.0	[illegible]

Est vol 8,000; vol Tues 3,803; open int 11,519, –3,099.

CRUDE OIL, Light Sweet (NYM) 1,000 bbls.; $ per bbl.

	Open	High	Low	Settle	Change	Lifetime High	Lifetime Low	Open Interest
Dec	13.95	14.01	13.66	13.67	– .23	18.35	12.13	27,481
Ja89	13.83	13.90	13.53	13.55	– .24	18.20	12.20	77,696
Feb	13.72	13.82	13.37	13.41	– .28	18.10	12.30	42,875
Mar	13.78	13.86	13.43	13.43	– .32	18.05	12.45	23,247
Apr	13.84	13.88	13.48	13.45	– .32	18.25	12.60	11,549
May	13.86	13.86	13.48	13.47	– .32	17.82	12.70	[illegible]
June	13.88	13.92	13.50	13.49	– .32	16.80	12.85	5,196
July	13.90	13.95	13.60	13.51	– .32	17.60	12.90	[illegible]
Aug	13.95	13.95	13.60	13.53	– .32	16.40	13.00	[illegible]
Sept	14.00	14.00	13.75	13.55	– .32	14.90	13.08	[illegible]

Est vol 93,544; vol Tues 73,484; open int 196,115, –4,515.

HEATING OIL NO. 2 (NYM) 42,000 gal.; $ per gal.

	Open	High	Low	Settle	Change	Lifetime High	Lifetime Low	Open Interest
Dec	.4455	.4500	.4425	.4447	+ .0007	.5200	.3765	18,889
Ja89	.4425	.4455	.4385	.4410	+ .0008	.5150	.3825	27,118
Feb	.4335	.4350	.4285	.4299	– .0001	.5150	.3825	18,375
Mar	.4125	.4150	.4100	.4090	+ .0005	.5030	.3700	4,785
Apr	.3915	.3940	.3900	.3891	+ .0011	.5000	.3565	3,390
May	.3825	.3850	.3800	.3781	+ .0011	.4700	.3520	5,348
June	.3750	.3810	.3710	.3719	+ .0009	.4680	.3465	4,488
July	.3770	.3805	.3725	.3719	+ .0009	.4700	.3475	1,250
Aug	.3850	.3850	.3850	.3769	+ .0009	.4600	.3545	677
Sept	.3870	.3870	.3870	.3870	+ .0040	.4245	.3640	370
Oct	....	....	....	.3909	+ .0009	.4100	.3720	120
Dec	....	....	....	.4049	+ .0009	.4150	.3785	110

Est vol 25,729; vol Tues 20,899; open int 85,110, –1,178.

GASOLINE, Unleaded (NYM) 42,000 gal.; $ per gal.

	Open	High	Low	Settle	Change	Lifetime High	Lifetime Low	Open Interest
Dec	.4720	.4740	.4640	.4650	– .0046	.4880	.3600	12,349
Ja89	.4325	.4340	.4250	.4294	– .0005	.4640	.3465	13,283
Feb	.4175	.4215	.4145	.4168	+ .0022	.4630	.3490	10,436
Mar	.4210	.4240	.4190	.4196	+ .0026	.4680	.3590	6,380
Apr	.4240	.4280	.4240	.4240	+ .0030	.4735	.3680	4,178
May	.4315	.4325	.4300	.4280	+ .0030	.4495	.3740	2.157
June	.4300	.4320	.4280	.4265	+ .0030	.4350	.3850	2,259
July	.4270	.4300	.4250	.4235	+ .0030	.4300	.4050	100
Aug	.4250	.4250	.4250	.4205	+ .0030	.4250	.4200	120

Est vol 24,998; vol Tues 12,963; open int 51,358, +552.

GAS OIL (IPEL) 100 metric tons; $ per ton

	Open	High	Low	Settle	Change	Lifetime High	Lifetime Low	Open Interest
Dec	125.00	125.25	124.00	124.25	– 1.75	150.00	106.25	30,739
Ja89	123.25	124.00	122.50	123.00	– 1.00	149.00	107.25	30,126
Feb	122.00	122.50	121.25	121.75	– .75	138.75	108.00	4,151
Mar	117.75	118.50	118.00	118.25	....	129.50	106.00	2,044
Apr	114.25	115.50	113.50	114.75	+ .75	129.00	106.00	2,424
May	113.75	113.75	113.00	113.25	+ 1.25	125.00	108.00	1,677
June	111.25	113.00	112.00	112.50	+ 1.00	120.50	112.00	591

Actual Wed; vol 4,829; open int 71,752, n.a..

–WOOD–

LUMBER (CME)–150,000 bd. ft.; $ per 1,000 bd. ft.

	Open	High	Low	Settle	Change	Lifetime High	Lifetime Low	Open Interest
Jan	174.70	176.00	173.40	175.70	+ 1.10	187.60	160.00	3,054
Mr89	177.40	178.70	176.40	178.60	+ 1.20	185.50	171.00	1,305
May	179.40	180.40	178.50	180.40	+ 1.00	184.60	170.10	246
July	179.80	180.80	179.30	180.70	+ .80	184.50	175.10	250
Sept	180.00	181.40	179.90	181.40	+ .90	183.90	175.10	125

Est vol 1,084; vol Tues 1,074; open int 5,105, +25.

–OTHER COMMODITY FUTURES–

Settlement prices of selected contracts. Volume and open interest of all contract months.

Aluminum (CMX) 40,000 lbs.; cents per lb.
Dec 101.50 –2.00; Est. vol. 0; Open Int. 163

Cattle-Live (MCE) 20,000 lb. ¢ per lb.
Dec 73.25 –.10; Est. vol. 160; Open Int. 718

Corn (MCE) 1,000 bu.; cents per bu.
Dec 264¼ –1¾; Est. vol. 1,100; Open Int. 8,801

Gold (CBT) 100 troy oz., $ per troy oz.
Dec 425.50 ; Est. vol. 2,000; Open Int. 642

Gold (MCE) 33.2 fine troy oz.; $ per troy oz.
Dec 425.60 ; Est. vol. 150; Open Int. 203

Gold-Kilo (CBT) 32.15 troy oz.; $ per troy oz.
Dec 426.00 +.30; Est. vol. 300; Open Int. 758

Hogs-Live (MCE) 15,000 lb.; ¢ per lb.
Dec 41.35 +.30; Est. vol. 70; Open Int. 649

Propane (NYM) 42,000 gal.; ¢ per gal.
Dec 19.65 –.05; Est. vol. 258; Open Int. 1,282

Rice–Rough (CRCE) 2000 cwt; $ per cwt
Jan 7.110 +.050; Est. vol. 150; Open Int. 1,906

Silver (CBT) 5,000 troy oz., cents per troy oz.
Dec 629.5 –10.5; Est. vol. 50; Open Int. 89

Silver (MCE) 1,000 troy oz.; cents per troy oz.
Dec 630.0 –9.3; Est. vol. 50; Open Int. 714

Soybeans (MCE) 1,000 bu.; cents per bu.
Jan 758 ; Est. vol. 2,500; Open Int. 5,319

Soybean Meal (MCE) 20 tons; $ per ton
Dec 246.50 ; Est. vol. 20; Open Int. 584

Wheat (MCE) 1,000 bu.; cents per bu.
Dec 410¾ –3; Est. vol. 700; Open Int. 4,872

Exhibit 5.7:

Physical Futures Prices for Trading on November 16, 1988

New Financial Futures Contracts	Exchange (Year)
CBOE 50 Stock Index	CBOT (1988)
CBOE 250 Stock Index	CBOT (1988)
Nikkei 225 Stock Index	CME (1988)
Australian Dollar	MidAmerican (1988)
Tokyo Stock Price Index	CBOT (1988)
Long-Term Japanese Government Bonds	CBOT (1988)
Long-term British Government Gilts	CBOT (1988)
U.S. Federal Fund Rate Futures	CME (1988)

offered futures trading on U.S. Treasury bills. And stock index futures trading was initiated in 1982, with the Kansas City Board of Trade offering trading on the Value Line Composite Index. Today financial futures trading represents the majority of all futures trading. For example, futures trading on U.S. Treasury bonds totals over 40 million contracts annually and alone accounts for more than half of the annual volume at the CBOT. Futures trading on the SP500 is now over 20 million contracts annually, and represents the most liquid CME contract. Moreover, new financial futures contracts are being designed and implemented nearly every day. Exhibit 5.8 displays just some of these new contracts. Only time will tell whether these new financial futures prove to be popular.

Settlement futures prices for currencies, Treasuries, and indices are reported in Exhibit 5.9, for trading on November 16, 1988. These prices are reported in a similar manner as those for physical futures in Exhibit 5.7. For instance, the settlement futures price for British pounds, December delivery, was $1.8238/£1, up 2.2¢ from the previous trading day's settlement price. For the SP500, March 1989 delivery, the settlement futures price was 267.80. The day's trading range was 266.20 to 271.50. The settlement price for U.S. Treasury bond futures, March 1989 delivery, was 87–25, or $87,781.25.

Carrying Charges and Physical and Financial Futures

The most important distinction between physical and financial futures concerns *carrying charges,* the costs of carrying an asset forward in time. There are three such costs:

- *Storage costs.* These include warehousing and insuring the asset.
- *Transportation costs.* These are the costs of delivering the asset.
- *Financing costs.* Assets must be financed, and most futures traders pay

Exhibit 5.9:

Financial Futures Prices for Trading on November 16, 1988

TREASURY FUTURES

TREASURY BONDS (CBT)—$100,000; pts. 32nds of 100%

	Open	High	Low	Settle	Chg	Yield Settle	Yield Chg	Open Interest
Dec	88-31	89-08	88-03	88-05	− 26	9.316	− .098	312,034
Mr89	88-16	88-26	87-23	87-25	− 24	9.363	− .092	103,771
June	88-04	88-10	87-10	87-13	− 23	9.409	− .089	34,957
Sept	87-29	87-29	87-02	87-02	− 22	9.452	− .086	16,494
Dec	87-10	87-17	86-23	86-24	− 20	9.491	− .078	8,664
Mr90	87-01	87-07	86-15	86-15	− 18	9.526	− .070	6,355
June	86-15	86-18	86-06	86-06	− 16	9.562	− .063	751
Dec	85-22	85-30	85-20	85-20	− 12	9.634	− .048	171

Est vol 450,0000; vol Tues 304,310; op int 483,327, −4,250.

TREASURY BONDS (MCE)—$50,000; pts. 32nds of 100%

	Open	High	Low	Settle	Chg	Yield Settle	Yield Chg	Open Interest
Dec	88-29	89-09	88-03	88-05	− 25	9.316	+ .095	5,230
Mr89	88-15	88-24	87-23	87-25	− 23	9.363	+ .089	185

Est vol 7,900; vol Tues 3,828; open int 5,449, +42.

T-BONDS (LIFFE) U.S. $100,000; pts of 100%

	Open	High	Low	Settle	Chg			Open Interest
Dec	89-00	89-08	88-10	88-13	− 0-09	91-15	83-12	15,009
Mr89	88-17	88-17	87-29	87-31	− 0-07	88-20	87-29	160

Est vol 9,633; vol Tues 6,167; open int 15,169, −874.

TREASURY NOTES (CBT)—$100,000; pts. 32nds of 100%

	Open	High	Low	Settle	Chg	Yield Settle	Yield Chg	Open Interest
Dec	93-28	94-06	93-17	93-19	− 14	8.984	− .070	71,532
Mr89	93-28	93-30	93-11	93-13	− 13	9.014	− .065	21,348
June	93-18	93-18	93-06	93-07	− 14	9.045	− .071	393

Est vol 35,000; vol Tues 27,656; open int 93,338, −47.

5 YR TREAS NOTES (CBT) $100,000; pts. 32 of 100%

	Open	High	Low	Settle	Chg	Yield Settle	Yield Chg	Open Interest
Dec	96-31	97-05	96-19	96-20	− 11	8.85	+ .09	19,046
Mr89	96-255	97-01	96-15	96-16	− 12	8.88	+ .09	4,535

Est vol 3,604; vol Tues 3,701; open int 23,631, +385.

5 YR TREAS NOTES (FINEX) $100,000; pts. 32 of 100%

	Open	High	Low	Settle	Chg	Yield Settle	Yield Chg	Open Interest
Dec	96-265	96-31	96-165	96-17	−11.0	8.87	+ .08	10,210
Mr89	96-235	96-28	96-14	96-14	−11.0	8.90	+ .09	4,404
June	96-20	96-20	96-10	96-105	−11.0	8.93	+ .09	1,200

Est vol 2,400; vol Tues 2,844; open int 15,814, +267.

TREASURY BILLS (IMM)—$1 mil.; pts. of 100%

	Open	High	Low	Settle	Chg	Discount Settle	Discount Chg	Open Interest
Dec	92.17	92.20	92.07	92.12	− .06	7.88	+ .06	13,512
Mr89	92.43	92.43	92.30	92.34	− .08	7.66	+ .08	7,732
June	92.44	92.44	92.34	92.35	− .08	7.65	+ .08	1,498
Sept	92.39	92.40	92.32	92.35	− .06	7.65	+ .06	444
Dec	92.25	92.30	92.25	92.26	− .06	7.74	+ .06	243

Est vol 11,529; vol Tues 12,650; open int 23,500, −446.

EURODOLLAR (IMM)—$1 million; pts of 100%

	Open	High	Low	Settle	Chg	Yield Settle	Yield Chg	Open Interest
Dec	90.93	90.97	90.78	90.82	− .11	9.18	+ .11	151,997
Mr89	91.06	91.08	90.89	90.95	− .10	9.05	+ .10	161,946
June	91.05	91.08	90.91	90.94	− .10	9.06	+ .10	55,824
Sept	90.99	91.03	90.87	90.90	− .08	9.10	+ .08	31,679
Dec	90.88	90.90	90.76	90.79	− .08	9.21	+ .08	22,091
Mr90	90.90	90.93	90.80	90.82	− .07	9.18	+ .07	20,982
June	90.82	90.83	90.72	90.74	− .07	9.26	+ .07	18,853
Sept	90.74	90.75	90.64	90.66	− .07	9.34	+ .07	13,767
Dec	90.66	90.66	90.57	90.58	− .07	9.42	+ .07	12,856
Mr91	90.64	90.64	90.55	90.56	− .06	9.44	+ .06	8,924
June	90.57	90.57	90.48	90.49	− .06	9.51	+ .06	14,341
Sept	90.51	90.51	90.43	90.44	− .06	9.56	+ .06	6,591

Est vol 241,626; vol Tues 111,308; open int 519,851, +5,941.

EURODOLLAR (LIFFE)—$1 million; pts of 100%

	Open	High	Low	Settle	Change	Lifetime High	Lifetime Low	Open Interest
Dec	90.93	90.95	90.80	90.81	− .12	92.93	89.90	18,718
Mr89	91.05	91.07	90.91	90.92	− .13	92.33	90.68	11,032
June	91.07	91.07	90.92	90.93	− .12	92.10	90.54	4,302
Sept	91.01	91.02	90.88	90.88	− .12	91.44	90.08	1,498
Dec	90.88	90.88	90.83	90.77	− .12	91.30	90.29	382
Mar90		....	....	90.80	− .12	91.26	90.92	323

Est vol 12,470; vol Tues 7,515; open int 36,345, +505.

STERLING (LIFFE)—£500,000; pts of 100%

	Open	High	Low	Settle	Change	Lifetime High	Lifetime Low	Open Interest
Dec	87.73	87.77	87.66	87.66	− .07	91.45	87.54	25,919
Mr89	87.95	87.98	87.85	87.85	− .11	90.94	87.85	14,971
June	88.48	88.51	88.41	88.41	− .08	90.66	88.35	4,075
Sept	88.83	88.86	88.80	88.78	− .08	90.47	88.61	1,243
Dec	89.04	89.07	89.04	88.99	− .08	90.22	88.61	869
Mr90		....	....	89.05	− .07	89.98	88.63	356
June	89.24	89.24	89.24	89.18	− .05	89.70	88.65	281
Sept	89.24	89.24	89.24	89.18	− .05	89.44	89.24	105

Est vol 14,949; vol Tues 23,827; open int 47,819, +818.

LONG GILT (LIFFE)—£50,000; 32nds of 100%

	Open	High	Low	Settle	Change	Lifetime High	Lifetime Low	Open Interest
Dec	96-01	96-05	95-23	95-24	− 0-05	97-30	93-04	28,821
Mr89	96-17	96-17	96-07	96-06	− 0-04	98-05	96-07	4,536

Est vol 26,483; vol Tues 28,668; open int 33,357, +909.

—OTHER INTEREST RATE FUTURES—

Settlement prices of selected contracts. Volume and open intrest of all contract months.

Treasury Bills (MCE) $500,000; 100.00 yield
Dec 92.12 −.06; Est. vol. 25; Open Int. 39
Treasury Notes (MCE) $50,000; pts. 32nds of 100%
Dec 93-19 −11; Est. vol. 30; Open Int. 148

CBT—Chicago Board of Trade. FINEX—Financial Instrument Exchange, a division of the New York Cotton Exchange. IMM—International Monetary Market at Chicago Mercantile Exchange. LIFFE—London International Financial Futures Exchange. MCE—MidAmerica Commodity Exchange.

S&P 500 INDEX (CME) 500 times index

	Open	High	Low	Settle	Chg	High	Low	Open Interest
Dec	268.60	268.80	263.50	265.05	− 4.45	285.70	252.20	125,248
Mr89	271.50	271.50	266.20	267.80	− 4.45	288.50	253.90	12,164
June	273.55	273.55	268.90	270.45	− 4.40	291.20	263.80	386

Est vol 59,520; vol Tues 33,271; open int 137,801, −423.
Indx prelim High 268.41; Low 262.85 ; Close 263.82 −4.52

NYSE COMPOSITE INDEX (NYFE) 500 times index

	Open	High	Low	Settle	Chg	High	Low	Open Interest
Dec	151.35	151.40	148.45	149.35	− 2.30	160.75	137.95	5,856
Mr89	152.85	152.90	150.00	150.85	− 2.35	162.30	144.25	1,271
June	153.90	153.90	152.60	152.25	− 2.35	163.35	149.60	565
Sept	....	....	....	153.65	− 2.35	165.10	156.80	164

Est vol 8,153; vol Tues 4,263; open int 7,856, +418.
The index: High 151.36; Low 148.49; Close 148.96 −2.37

MAJOR MKT INDEX (CBT) $250 times index

	Open	High	Low	Settle	Chg	High	Low	Open Interest
Nov	406.50	406.70	396.00	399.30	− 7.50	428.60	388.90	3,807
Dec	407.80	407.80	397.30	400.55	− 7.45	429.60	390.50	1,695
Ja89	409.90	409.90	399.30	402.50	− 7.40	431.00	399.30	324

Est vol 13,000; vol Tues 3,512; open int 5,826, −125.
The index: High 406.87; Low 396.11; Close 398.21 −8.57

KC VALUE LINE INDEX (KC) 500 times index

	Open	High	Low	Settle	Chg	High	Low	Open Interest
Dec	234.30	234.50	230.80	232.50	− 2.20	255.40	230.80	1,519
Mr89	237.20	237.40	234.80	236.25	− 2.20	257.80	234.80	198

Est vol 250; vol Tues 233; open int 1,717, −43.
The index: High 237.21; Low 234.15; Close 234.47 −2.65

MUNI BOND INDEX(CBT)$1,000; times Bond Buyer MBI

	Open	High	Low	Settle	Chg	High	Low	Open Interest
Dec	90-13	90-20	89-29	89-30	− 15	92-02	80-16	12,774
Mr89	88-30	88-30	88-11	88-12	− 17	90-31	78-25	3,243
June	87-16	87-16	87-02	87-03	− 18	90-01	77-06	651
Sept	86-09	86-09	85-29	85-30	− 19	89-01	78-06	351
Dec	85-07	85-07	84-25	84-25	− 20	87-25	81-10	153

Est vol 3,000; vol Tues 4,228; open int 17,172, −21.
The index: Close 90-29; Yield 7.82.

CRB INDEX (NYFE) 500 times index

	Open	High	Low	Settle	Chg	High	Low	Open Interest
Dec	240.60	241.10	239.15	239.15	− 1.30	273.00	231.50	1,531
Mr89	239.45	239.45	238.00	237.75	− 1.00	269.00	233.35	710
May	238.20	238.25	238.00	236.75	− .85	242.75	233.00	269

Est vol 464; vol Tues417; open int 2,582, +9.
The index: High 241.94; Low 240.71; Close 240.71 −.51

U.S. DOLLAR INDEX (FINEX) 500 times USDX

	Open	High	Low	Settle	Chg	High	Low	Open Interest
Dec	91.66	91.90	90.77	90.78	− 1.03	99.75	88.40	4,296
Mr89	91.67	91.90	90.76	90.76	− 1.05	99.75	89.85	1,791

Est vol 2,500; vol Tues 729; open int 6,096, +45.
The index: High 91.78; Low 90.78; Close 90.83 −.97

—CURRENCY FUTURES—

JAPANESE YEN (IMM) 12.5 million yen; $ per yen (.00)

	Open	High	Low	Settle	Change	Lifetime High	Lifetime Low	Open Interest
Dec	.8156	.8208	.8143	.8205	+ .0064	.8530	.7115	46,936
Mr89	.8250	.8297	.8230	.8296	+ .0068	.8590	.7439	3,393
June	.8350	.8399	.8340	.8399	+ .0072	.8400	.7500	697
Sept	.8445	.8490	.8445	.8501	+ .0076	.8490	.7690	246

Est vol 45,934; vol Tues 24,165; open int 51,272, −2,692.

W. GERMAN MARK (IMM)—125,000 marks; $ per mark

	Open	High	Low	Settle	Change	Lifetime High	Lifetime Low	Open Interest
Dec	.5768	.5834	.5752	.5831	+ .0078	.6610	.5252	49,374
Mr89	.5829	.5890	.5800	.5887	+ .0079	.6240	.5304	3,278
June	.5900	.5950	.5900	.5950	+ .0082	.5950	.5434	204

Est vol 42,411; vol Tues 19,793; open int 52,856, −787.

CANADIAN DOLLAR (IMM)—100,000 dlrs.; $ per Can $

	Open	High	Low	Settle	Change	Lifetime High	Lifetime Low	Open Interest
Dec	.8101	.8139	.8093	.8115	+ .0027	.8340	.7390	13,915
Mr89	.8060	.8097	.8057	.8075	+ .0029	.8309	.7570	2,308
June	.8020	.8047	.8020	.8035	+ .0031	.8285	.7670	1,036

Est vol 7,727; vol Tues 5,324; open int 17,370, −183.

BRITISH POUND (IMM)—62,500 pds.; $ per pound

	Open	High	Low	Settle	Change	Lifetime High	Lifetime Low	Open Interest
Dec	1.8080	1.8244	1.8030	1.8238	+ .0220	1.9000	1.6394	18,097
Mr89	1.7970	1.8150	1.7906	1.8120	+ .0224	1.8150	1.6320	1,126

Est vol 11,900; vol Tues 7,153; open int 19,333, −433.

SWISS FRANC (IMM)—125,000 francs-$ per franc

	Open	High	Low	Settle	Change	Lifetime High	Lifetime Low	Open Interest
Dec	.6885	.6962	.6855	.6948	+ .0085	.8210	.6286	35,133
Mr89	.6956	.7040	.6935	.7026	+ .0088	.7735	.6360	1,497
June	.7070	.7118	.7025	.7110	+ .0090	.7118	.6450	116

Est vol 33,154; vol Tues 16,091; open int 36,751, −865.

AUSTRALIAN DOLLAR (IMM)—100,000 dlrs.; $ per A.$

	Open	High	Low	Settle	Change	Lifetime High	Lifetime Low	Open Interest
Dec	.8490	.8550	.8480	.8542	+ .0047	.8550	.7458	2,291

Est vol 303; vol Tues 326; open int 2,353, +93.

—OTHER CURRENCY FUTURES—

Settlement prices of selected contracts. Volume and open interest of all contract months.

British Pound (MCE) 12,500 pounds; $ per pound
Dec 1.8238 +.0220; Est. vol. 38; Open Int. 305
European Currency Unit (FINEX) 100,000 ECU
Dec 120.30 +1.33; Est. vol. 0; Open Int. 986
Japanese Yen (MCE) 6.25 million yen; $ per yen (.00)
Dec .8205 +.0064; Est. vol. 250; Open Int. 274
Swiss Franc (MCE) 62,500 francs; $ per franc
Dec .6948 +.0085; Est. vol. 350; Open Int. 268
West German Mark (MCE) 62,500 marks; $ per mark
Dec .5831 +.0078; Est. vol. 275; Open Int. 332

FINEX—Financial Instrument Exchange, a division of the New York Cotton Exchange. IMM—International Monetary Market at the Chicago Mercantile Exchange. MCE—MidAmerica Commodity Exchange.

the *repo rate* when financing an asset. This rate (discussed more in the next chapter) is usually slightly greater than the rate on U.S. Treasury bills.

There are more important differences in storage and transportation costs across physical and financial assets. Hence, these groups of assets can have different carrying charges. As you will learn in Chapter 6, carrying charges are important factors in determining futures prices.

Concerning storage costs, physical assets (e.g., corn) require costly warehousing, whereas financial securities (often deposited with banks approved by the futures exchange) require nominal warehousing costs. Also, financial securities normally yield cash flows while held in storage: stocks and stock indices pay dividends, foreign exchange can be used to buy interest-bearing foreign assets, and Treasury securities pay interest. Financial assets therefore often have a negative cost of storage and, possibly, an overall negative carrying charge.

Physical assets typically exhibit the greater transportation costs. For example, it can be costly to ship wheat from Nebraska to Chicago, but it costs almost nothing to wire transfer cash in order to settle an index futures contract.

FUTURES FUNDS

A *futures fund* represents a pool of shareholders' monies that are used, in part, to trade futures contracts. The advantage these funds offer is that they allow small public traders to participate in futures markets with reduced risk due to diversification and lower susceptibility to margin calls.

Each futures fund is overseen by a professional manager. On average, less than one-third of the fund's capital base is invested in futures; the remaining funds are held as cash and in money market assets.

Over 80 futures funds currently exist. The performances of these funds have varied widely. See S. Irwin and B. Brorsen (1985) (in "Selected References" at the end of the chapter) for a detailed analysis of futures funds.

SUMMARY

A futures contract is traded on an organized exchange and represents a contractual agreement to trade an underlying asset in the future at a predetermined futures price. The trading process involves clearinghouses, margin requirements, and daily resettlement, all of which help to assure market integrity. Both physical and financial futures contracts exist, and carrying charges differ dramatically between them. Carrying charges are the costs of carrying an underlying asset forward in time, including storage costs, transportation costs, and financing costs.

Listed futures trading has grown tremendously over the last decade, mostly in the area of financial futures contracts such as currency, interest rate, and stock index futures. We analyze each of these in subsequent chapters. In the next chapter we examine the determination of futures prices.

Selected References

Arrow, K. "Futures Markets: Some Theoretical Perspectives." *Journal of Futures Markets* 1 (Summer 1981): 107–116.

Carlton, D. "Futures Markets: Their Purpose, Their History, Their Successes and Failures." *Journal of Futures Markets* 4 (Fall 1984): 237–271.

Easterbrook, F. "Monopoly, Manipulation, and the Regulation of Futures Markets." *Journal of Business* 59 (1966): 103–127.

Edwards, F. "The Clearing Association in Futures Markets: Guarantor and Regulator." *Journal of Futures Markets* 3 (Winter 1983): 369–392.

Fischel, D. "Regulatory Conflict and Entry Regulation of New Futures Contracts." *Journal of Business* 59 (1986): 85–102.

Fishe, R., and L. Goldberg. "The Effects of Margins on Trading in Futures Markets." *Journal of Futures Markets* 6 (Summer 1986): 261–271.

Grossman, S. "An Analysis of the Role of 'Insider Trading' on Futures Markets." *Journal of Business* 59 (1986): 129–146.

Irwin, S., and B. Brorsen. "Public Futures Funds." *Journal of Futures Markets* 5 (1985): 463–485.

Kolb, R. *Understanding Futures Markets*. 2d ed. Glenview, Ill.: Scott, Foresman and Company, 1988.

Russo, T. *Regulation of the Commodities Futures and Options Markets*. New York: McGraw-Hill, 1983.

Silber, W. "Innovation, Competition and New Contract Design in Futures Markets." *Journal of Futures Markets* 1 (Summer 1981): 123–156.

Telser, L. "Margins and Futures Contract." *Journal of Futures Markets* 1 (Fall 1981): 225–253.

Questions and Problems

1. Describe the roles played by clearinghouses and margin deposits in ensuring contract performance.
2. How do physical and financial futures differ with respect to storage and transportation costs?
3. What are the two main differences between agricultural and metallurgical commodities?
4. Describe an initial margin, a maintenance margin, and a variation margin.

5. What are the three components of carrying charges?

6. What agencies are empowered to regulate futures trading?

7. From Exhibit 5.8, what was the settlement price of a NYSE Composite Index futures contract, with December delivery, on November 16, 1988? What was the closing price of the next deferred contract?

8. Describe how the vast majority of all futures contracts are closed out.

9. What is the major difference between a futures hedger and a futures speculator?

10. Describe the illegal trading activities known as frontrunning and bucket trading.

11. Assume that on Monday, March 1, you enter a futures contract to buy one CBOT March Treasury bond futures contract at the futures price of $98,156.25 (98 $^5/_{32}$). The initial margin is $2,500, and the maintenance margin is $2,000. For simplicity, you do not withdraw excess monies from your margin balance. All margin requirements are met with cash. You hold your long position through Friday, March 5. Then you sell the contract (a reversing trade) at the opening price of $98,125.00 (98 $^4/_{32}$) on Monday, March 8. Presented below is a schedule of assumed prices. Using Exhibit 5.3 as a guide, fill in the following information cells. Also, be sure to determine your gross profit on the entire transaction.

Trading Date	Settlement Price	Marked-to-the-Market	Other Entries	Account Balance
3/1	$98,000.00 (98 $^0/_{32}$)			
3/2	96,250.00 (96 $^8/_{32}$)			
3/3	96,750.00 (96 $^{24}/_{32}$)			
3/4	98,093.75 (98 $^3/_{32}$)			
3/5	98,937.50 (98 $^{30}/_{32}$)			
3/8	98,125.00 (98 $^4/_{32}$)			

6

FUTURES PRICING

This chapter concerns the determination of futures prices. Two related approaches are presented. The first focuses on the costs of carrying assets forward in time—the *carrying-charge theory* of futures prices. The second focuses on expectations about future spot prices—the *expectations approach*.

The carrying-charge theory basically treats the futures contract as a forward contract. As a result, the arbitrage strategies that determine the futures price are clear and straightforward. However, due to the daily resettlement of the futures contract, which is affected by nonconstant interest rates, the carrying-charge approach may not work. The expectations approach better recognizes the subtle differences between forward and futures contracts.

Before discussing these two approaches, however, it is useful to distinguish between price and value.

PRICE VERSUS VALUE

It is important to distinguish between price and value when dealing with forward and futures contracts. The forward or futures *price* is the price at which the contract parties agree to exchange the underlying asset in the future. As such, it simply represents an observable figure on a contract. It is not the contract's value. In general, the contract's *value* is determined by unanticipated changes in the asset's spot price, which in turn cause subsequent changes in forward and futures prices.

In this chapter we are vitally concerned with the determination of *prices*, that is, the method by which market participants determine the prices for trading assets in the future. Some statements about contract value are appropriate at this point in our discussion.

Contract Value at Inception

The value of a forward or futures contract is zero at the contract's inception. This follows from the fact that neither party to the contract pays or receives anything of monetary value. The long position (the buyer) does not pay for the contract, and the short position (the seller) does not receive any money for the contract. Indeed, with a forward contract no cash flow occurs until contract expiration, and the futures margin represents only a security deposit and not a contract "payment." Provided that the forward or futures price does not change, neither party can profit. Thus, the contract generates value only when prices subsequently change, and has no value when the contract is initially written.

Forward Contract Value at Expiration

At expiration, the forward contract calls for immediate delivery of the underlying asset. Thus, the forward price at contract expiration must be equal to the asset's spot price, ignoring delivery costs and multiple qualities of the deliverable asset. Since no cash flow has occurred prior to expiration, the value of the forward contract at expiration must equal the spot price at expiration minus the original forward price.

Forward Contract Value Prior to Expiration

Assuming that no default risk exists, the value of a forward contract prior to expiration is the difference between the new forward price and the original forward price, discounted at the risk-free rate of interest over the remaining time to contract expiration. To illustrate this, assume that you buy a forward contract today that has a forward price of $1.00 and expires in six months. Now suppose that in four months new forward contracts are available that expire at the same time (in two months) and are written at a forward price of $1.05. Assuming that the risk-free rate is 8 percent, the value of your forward contract is $0.004934:

$$\$0.04934 = (\$1.05 - \$1.00)e^{(2/12)(-.08)}$$

This value follows from arbitrage restrictions. When both forward contracts expire in two months, you can buy the underlying asset for $1.00 with the first contract and sell the asset for $1.05 with the second contract. Your proceeds are $0.05. Since no default risk is assumed to exist, and the forward prices are known, these proceeds are discounted at the risk-free rate to yield a present value of $0.04934. Any other contract value would result in riskless profit, ignoring market frictions.

Futures Contract Value

As noted above, the value of a futures contract is zero at the contract's inception. However, the contract's value is also zero each time the contract is marked-to-the-market. Suppose that you buy a futures contract. Its current value is zero. Later in the trading session, however, the futures price has increased. At this point you can profit by entering into a reversing trade. The contract has value. Once the trading session is over, however, the contract is marked-to-the-market, and any proceeds are credited to your margin account. Thus, the contract's value reverts to zero.

A futures contract's value reverts to zero each time the contract is marked-to-the-market.

CARRYING-CHARGE THEORY OF FUTURES PRICES

The carrying-charge theory of determining futures prices evolves from arbitrage restrictions relating to the costs of carrying an asset forward in time. Before explaining this approach further, it is wise to discuss the concepts of *carrying charges*, the *basis*, and *spreads*.

*The **carrying-charge theory** of determining futures prices evolves from arbitrage restrictions relating to the costs of carrying an asset forward in time.*

Carrying Charges

The three costs of carrying an asset forward in time, identified in Chapter 5, are storage costs, transportation costs, and financing costs. Let us consider the storage costs (SC), transportation costs (TC), and financing costs (FC) expressed as a percentage of an underlying asset's spot price:

(6.1) $$CC = SC + TC + FC,$$

where CC is the total percentage cost.

CC represents the total carrying charges particular to the underlying asset. Suppose that the asset in question exhibits storage costs equal to -1.5 percent of the spot price and transportation costs of 0.5 percent of the spot price. Recall from Chapter 5 that an asset can exhibit a negative cost of storage if it pays dividends or interest over the carrying period. Also, let the current *repo rate* be 10 percent. The repo rate is the interest rate on a *repurchase (repo) agreement* and often represents the cost of financing an asset faced by a futures trader, especially if the asset in question is a financial security. A repurchase agreement is an arrangement in which a security owner sells the security to a financial institution with the agreement to repurchase it, often just one day later (an overnight repo). The repo rate is relatively low, typically exceeding the rate on U.S. Treasury bills by a small amount. This is because anyone wanting to finance the security purchase can offer the security itself as collateral for the loan. Given $SC = -.015$, $TC = .005$, and $FC = .100$, the percentage carrying charges for the asset total 9 percent:

*The **repo rate** is the interest rate on repurchase agreements and often represents the cost of financing an asset faced by a futures trader.*

$$CC = -.015 + .005 + .100 = .090.$$

Thus, if the spot price is $100, and contract delivery occurs in one year, then, assuming continuous compounding, the futures price should be approximately $109.42:

$$\$109.42 = \$100e^{(.09)(1)}.$$

This futures price reflects the cost of carrying the asset to delivery.

The Basis

The **basis** is the difference between the spot price and the current futures price.

The *basis* is defined as the difference between the spot price and the futures price:

(6.2)   Basis = Spot Price − Futures Price.

Under the carrying-charge theory of futures prices, the basis represents the dollar cost of carrying an asset forward in time. For instance, in the above illustration the basis is −$9.42, representing the dollar cost of carrying the asset to delivery in one year.

There are a few important points to remember concerning the basis. First, the basis depends on the spot price of a commodity at a specific location. By the Law of One Price, an asset should not sell for different prices in two markets. However, because of frictions such as search and transportation costs the price of, say, corn may be different in Nebraska than in Pennsylvania. This difference likely arises because of the added transportation costs of shipping corn to Pennsylvania. Since the spot price of corn differs across these two locations, the basis will also differ according to location.

Second, the basis should converge toward zero as the delivery date approaches. This is evident from the fact that the futures and spot prices must be equal at delivery, ignoring transaction and transportation costs as well as different qualities of the deliverable asset. In Figure 6.1 the basis for the above asset, with spot price of $100 and one-year carrying costs of $9.42, is presented as a function of contract maturity. For simplicity, we assume that the spot price and *CC* remain constant through time. As the figure demonstrates, the basis converges to zero as the delivery date approaches. This reflects the smaller dollar costs of carrying an asset forward over a progressively shorter time period.

Of course, the spot price and carrying charges can vary over time, implying that the basis will not behave in reality as it does in Figure 6.1. As a vivid example, Figure 6.2 presents the December 1987 SP500 futures price (solid line) and the spot SP500 index (broken line), plotted by five-minute intervals around the time of the October 19, 1987, stock market crash. The basis (spot SP500 minus December 1987 SP500 futures) varies substantially over this extremely volatile market period. However, it should be noted that the basis was more stable than the spot *or* SP500 futures price. This is typical. While the futures price and spot

Maturity	Spot Price	Futures Price	Basis
1 Year	$100	$109.42	−$9.42
9 Months	100	106.98	− 6.98
6 Months	100	104.60	− 4.60
3 Months	100	102.28	− 2.28
1 Month	100	100.75	− 0.75
0	100	100.00	0.00

price may vary widely, the basis (spot minus futures) tends to be more stable because spot and futures prices are highly positively correlated. If the spot price falls, so too does the futures price, implying a comparatively stable basis. Indeed, under the carrying-charge theory, if CC is constant over time, then the spot and futures prices should be perfectly positively correlated. We will return to this point shortly.

Third, when referring to the basis we typically mean the difference between the spot price and the nearby futures price. However, a basis

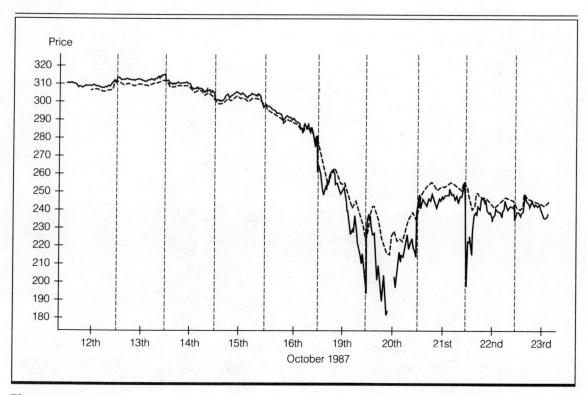

Figure 6.2:
October 1987 SP500 Spot-Futures Basis

exists for each delivery date. When measured in absolute value, the basis should be greater for more deferred contracts, reflecting the added dollar charges of carrying an asset forward over a progressively longer time period.

Spreads

The difference between two futures prices is often called a *spread*. If it entails two futures contracts written on the same underlying asset but exhibiting different delivery dates, it is an *intracommodity spread*. An *intercommodity spread*, in contrast, refers to the difference between the prices of futures contracts exhibiting the same maturity but different underlying assets.

For the purpose of determining futures prices, intracommodity spreads (also called *time spreads*) are important. The prices of nearby and more deferred futures contracts should be intimately related. Arbitrage restrictions ensure such relations. Under the carrying-charge theory, the time spread should reflect the different dollar costs of carrying an asset forward to different delivery dates. As a preview, consider the six-month and one-year futures prices provided in Figure 6.1. The spread, $4.82 = $109.42 − $104.60, merely reflects the six-month basis, $4.60, adjusted for continuous compounding:

$$\$4.82 = \$4.60e^{(.09)(.50)}.$$

Carrying Charges and Futures Prices

Armed with the above terminology and concepts, we are ready to demonstrate how futures prices are determined by arbitrage restrictions relating to carrying charges. To begin, suppose that a trader observes a spot asset price of $100, $CC = .09$, but a one-year futures price of $115. Recall that the futures price should be $109.42 to accurately reflect carrying costs. To exploit this situation, the trader can undertake the following transactions:

Today: Buy one unit of the asset for $100 in the spot market.
Arrange to carry the asset forward for one year at a cost of $9.42.
Short (sell) the one-year futures contract, thereby contracting to sell the asset in one year for $115.

In One Year: Remove the asset from storage and deliver it against the futures contract, collecting $115.

These transactions represent a winning arbitrage strategy, assuring proceeds of $5.58 in one year (per unit of the underlying asset). The transactions originally entered into assured the trader of the positive proceeds while requiring no investment. There is no investment because no cash outflow occurs at inception of the trading strategy. The trader borrowed the money required to purchase the asset and to carry it forward through time. The cost of borrowing the capital is already reflected in CC vis a vis the financing-cost component, FC.

The above transactions represent an example of what is commonly known as *cash-and-carry arbitrage*—a theoretically riskless transaction involving a long position in the spot asset and a short position in the futures contract that is held until contract delivery. This book will present numerous examples of cash-and-carry arbitrage designed to determine futures prices under the carrying charge approach.

As the trader executes the cash-and-carry strategy, the spot and futures prices, and perhaps the carrying charges, should change in such a way that arbitrage is no longer profitable. Exactly how prices and carrying charges will change is difficult to determine. In general, however, they should change to reflect the following condition:

(6.3) $$_T f_0 = S_0 e^{CC(T)},$$

where $_T f_0$ is the futures price for delivery in T years, and S_0 is the current spot price of the asset. For instance, if S_0 remains unchanged at $100, and CC remains unchanged at 9 percent, then the one-year futures price, $_1f_0$, should converge to $109.48:

$$\$109.48 = \$100e^{(.09)(1)}.$$

Now consider an observed futures price of, say, $105, in which case the futures price is below $109.48. To exploit this situation, the trader can undertake the following transactions:

Today: Short one unit of the asset, receiving $100.

Enter a long futures position to purchase the asset in one year for $105.

Invest the $100 short-sale proceeds for one year at 9 percent.

In One Year: Collect $109.42 on the investment: [$100e^{(.09)(1)}$].

Take delivery on the futures contract, paying $105 for the asset.

Return the asset (reverse the short position).

These transactions, which represent a type of reverse cash-and-carry arbitrage strategy, assure proceeds of $4.42 in one year (per unit of the underlying asset). Again, there is no initial investment, since no cash outflow occurred at the inception of the strategy. Also, recognize that the 9 percent return earned on the $100 investment consists of a 10 percent interest gain, a 1.5 percent loss, since the trader owes the asset owner all intervening dividend and interest payments under the short-sale agreement, and a 0.5 percent gain in transportation costs paid by the short futures trader.

Again, as the trader executes this strategy, S_0, $_1f_0$, and CC should change until arbitrage is precluded by the equality given by Equation 6.3. Whenever $_1f_0$ is above or below $109.42, therefore, an arbitrage opportunity exists.

Equation 6.3 is the carrying-charge theory of futures prices under perfect market conditions. It states that the futures price must equal the spot price plus the cost of carrying an asset forward to contract delivery.

For all intents and purposes, Equation 6.3 is the carrying-charge theory of futures prices (under perfect market conditions). This equation states that the futures price must equal the spot price plus the cost of carrying the asset forward to contract delivery. It follows from arbitrage restrictions. Also, notice from Equation 6.3 that the basis is given by $S_0 [e^{CC(T)} - 1]$:

$$\$9.42 = \$100[e^{(.09)(1)} - 1].$$

Exhibit 6.1 provides another, self-contained cash-and-carry arbitrage example.

Carrying Charges and Intracommodity Spreads

Arbitrage restrictions ensure close relations between the prices of nearby and more deferred futures contracts written on the same underlying asset. In fact, the more deferred futures price, $_df_0$, should be related to the nearby futures price, $_nf_0$, by the following equality:

A Self-Contained Illustration
of an Arbitrage Strategy Underlying the Carrying-Charge
Theory

Suppose you observe the following variables: $S_0 = \$10.00$, $_{.25}f_0 = \$11.00$, and $CC = .08$. To profit, you undertake the following transactions:

Today: Buy the spot asset for $10.00.
Arrange to carry it forward for three months at a cost of $0.20.
Sell (short) a three-month futures, contracting to deliver the asset for $11.00.

In 3 Months: Remove the asset from storage and deliver it against the futures contract, thereby collecting $11.00.

The profit from these transactions is $0.80 per unit of the underlying asset, ignoring market imperfections. If $S_0 = \$10.00$, and $CC = .08$, the futures price under the carrying-charge theory should be $10.20.

(6.4)
$$_d f_0 = {}_n f_0 e^{CC(T_d - T_n)},$$

where T_d and T_n refer to the maturities (expressed as a fraction of a year) of the deferred and nearby contracts, respectively.

For example, recall the six-month and one-year futures prices from Figure 6.1: $104.60 and $109.42. These prices are consistent with Equation 6.4:

$$\$109.42 = \$104.60 e^{(.09)(1.0 - 0.5)}.$$

From this equation, the intracommodity spread is $_n f_0 [e^{CC(T_d - T_n)} -1]$:

$$\$4.82 = \$104.60 [e^{(.09)(1.0 - 0.5)} - 1].$$

If the intracommodity spread is not consistent with the above expression, traders may engage in arbitrage strategies involving both futures contracts. For instance, suppose $_{.50}f_0 = \$104.60$, $CC = .09$, but $_1 f_0 = \$115.00$. This suggests that the nearby futures price is too low (an undervalued contract), the deferred futures price is too high (an overvalued contract), or both. To profit, the trader should implement the following transactions:

Today: Buy (long) the nearby (undervalued) contract expiring in six months.
Sell (short) the deferred (overvalued) contract expiring in one year.
Arrange to carry the asset from six months to one year.

In Six Months: Take delivery on the nearby futures contract, paying $104.60, and carry the asset forward for six months.

Exhibit 6.2:
A Self-Contained Illustration
of an Arbitrage Strategy Involving an Intracommodity
Spread

Suppose you observe the following variables: $_{.25}f_0 = \$5.00$, $_{.50}f_0 = \$5.25$, and $CC = .06$. To profit, you undertake the following transactions:

Today: Long the nearby contract expiring in 3 months.
Short the deferred contract expiring in 6 months.
Arrange to carry the asset from 3 to 6 months.

In 3 Months: Take delivery on the nearby contract, paying $5.00, and carry the asset forward for 3 months.

In 6 Months: Deliver the asset on the short position, collecting $5.25

These transactions provide a profit of $0.17 per unit of the underlying asset, ignoring market imperfections. If $_{.25}f_0 = \$5.00$, and $CC = .06$, then, according to the carrying-charge theory, $_{.50}f_0$ should equal $5.08.

In One Year: Deliver the asset on the short futures position, thereby collecting $115.
Pay the $109.42 owed [$104.60$e^{(.09)(.50)}$].

These transactions represent a profitable arbitrage strategy, assuring $5.58 in one year (per unit of the underlying asset). There is no investment because no cash outflow occurs at inception (today) or at the six-month mark. The investor borrowed the capital required to purchase the asset and to carry it forward from six months to one year. The cost of borrowing the capital is already reflected in CC through FC.

As traders execute the strategy, the futures prices, and perhaps CC, will change until Equation 6.4 prevails, that is, until arbitrage is precluded. By a similar argument, if $_1f_0$ is less than $109.42, then an arbitrage opportunity is presented. An analogous trading strategy would assure profit, so trading will be undertaken until Equation 6.4 prevails. Thus, this equation results from arbitrage restrictions and states that the deferred futures price must equal the nearby futures price plus the costs of carrying the asset from T_n to T_d. Exhibit 6.2 presents another, self-contained arbitrage example involving an intracommodity spread.

The deferred futures price must equal the nearby futures price plus the cost of carrying the asset from T_n to T_d.

Market Imperfections and Carrying-Charge Theory

Equation 6.3 reflects perfect market conditions. In real markets, however, frictions exist that render the equation somewhat inexact. Two of the most important frictions are transaction costs and restrictions on short selling, both of which tend to complicate arbitrage transactions and, in turn, weaken the validity of Equation 6.3.

Define τ as the dollar transaction costs associated with arbitrage trading. In order for arbitrage to be profitable, therefore, the proceeds from the arbitrage strategy must be sufficient to overcome τ. Thus, the spot-futures relation can deviate somewhat from the strict equality presented in Equation 6.3 and still preclude arbitrage. We can now adjust Equation 6.3 to reflect transaction costs:

(6.5) $$S_0 e^{CC(T)} - \tau \le {}_T f_0 \le S_0 e^{CC(T)} + \tau.$$

Equation 6.5 states that the futures price must be close to the spot price plus carrying charges; the futures price can deviate from $S_0 e^{CC(T)}$ by no more than τ.

To illustrate this, recall the above example in which a trader observes the following values: $S_0 = \$100$, $CC = .09$, and ${}_1 f_0 = \$115$. These values suggest an arbitrage opportunity since, by Equation 6.3, ${}_1 f_0$ should be \$109.42. The trader will engage in arbitrage provided that the associated transaction costs are less than \$5.58. If $\tau > \$5.58$, however, the trader will not engage in arbitrage, since the proceeds are insufficient to cover the transaction costs.

In actual markets, restrictions on short selling (discussed in Chapter 3) often exist. There it was stated that noninstitutional investors typically cannot use all of the funds from a short sale, since a broker may require a fraction of the proceeds to be deposited to insure against credit risk. Let us define g as the fraction of usable proceeds generated by a short sale. Also, remember from our discussion of Equation 6.2 that whenever ${}_T f_0 < S_0 e^{CC(T)}$, an arbitrage opportunity is present in which short selling is required. For instance, recall that when $S_0 = \$100$, $CC = .09$, and ${}_1 f_0 = \$105$, a trader can profit by short selling the underlying asset and entering into a long futures position. Recognizing this, we can adjust Equation 6.5 to reflect short selling restrictions:

(6.6) $$g[S_0 e^{CC(T)}] - \tau \le {}_T f_0 \le S_0 e^{CC(T)} + \tau.$$

Equation 6.6 represents the carrying-charge theory of futures prices in light of transaction costs and restrictions on the use of the proceeds from short selling. Thus, Equation 6.6 represents the carrying-charge theory after controlling for two important market imperfections. It should be kept in mind, however, that for large institutional investors, g is 100 percent and τ is very small. Hence, for these investors the futures price should remain very close to the spot price plus carrying charges.

Implicit Assumptions Underlying Carrying-Charge Theory

The carrying-charge theory invokes two important assumptions: (1) no default risk exists; and (2) carrying charges are constant over the life of the futures contract. These assumptions are implicit within the arbitrage trading strategies just discussed. For example, consider the strategy employed when $S_0 = \$100$, $CC = .09$, and ${}_1 f_0 = \$115$. Ignoring transaction costs, a profit of $5.58 could be attained by buying the asset and storing it for one year, and selling the one-year futures contract. However, this profit is certain only if (1) the long futures trader does not default on the contract, and (2) the carrying charges ($9.42) do not vary over the year.

It is reasonable to assume that the long futures trader does not default, since daily resettlement substantially reduces default risk, and the clearinghouse guarantees both sides of the contract. However, the assumption that carrying charges are constant is somewhat suspect. Although transportation costs are likely to be small and inflexible, both storage costs and financing costs are likely to vary over time. Storage costs can especially vary if the underlying asset is a financial security that pays dividends or interest. Such payments can vary intertemporally, causing the storage-cost component of CC to be nonconstant. Financing costs can change over time as well, because market rates of interest are time-varying. For instance, the overnight repo rate changes on a daily basis.

Since CC can vary over time, an arbitrager cannot be certain as to the actual carrying charges to be experienced over the life of the futures contract. For instance, if actual carrying charges incurred were greater than $9.42, the arbitrager's profit would be less than $5.58. Potentially, the arbitrager could even lose money because of time-varying carrying charges.

It is important to recognize the implications of the assumptions of no default risk and constant carrying charges that underlie the carrying-charge approach to determining futures prices. For instance, one implication of constant carrying charges is that spot and futures prices are perfectly positively correlated. In turn, this has implications for determining hedging strategies. We will return to this point in Chapter 7.

EXPECTATIONS APPROACH TO DETERMINING FUTURES PRICES

The costs of carrying an asset forward in time greatly influence the relations (1) between the futures price and the current spot price, and (2) among the asset's futures prices. However, because futures contracts entail the delivery of an asset at a future date, we should anticipate that futures prices are largely determined by the expectations of market players concerning the asset's spot price at delivery. The expectations approach of determining futures prices emphasizes the role of market expectations in generating futures prices. To fully comprehend this approach, it is important to be familiar with term structure theory, discussed below.

The **expectations approach** emphasizes the role of market expectations in generating futures prices.

Theories of Term Structure

The *term structure of interest rates* is the relation between the term to maturity and yield to maturity for bonds with different maturities but otherwise equivalent aspects, including risk. The observed yields are known as *spot interest rates*. Using these spot interest rates, it is possible to infer rates of interest that are expected to prevail in the future—that is, *forward rates of interest*. Thus, it is possible to infer forward interest rates from the term structure.

For instance, suppose that you observe the following spot rates on default-free, pure discount bonds:

Term to Maturity	Yield to Maturity
1 Year	.0800
2 Years	.0825
3 Years	.0860
4 Years	.0890

Since the rates are increasing, the term structure is said to be upward-sloping. To determine a forward interest rate, suppose that you purchase a two-year pure discount bond for $1.00. You will receive $1.1718 in two years, assuming annual compounding. Alternatively, you could purchase a one-year pure discount bond today and simultaneously enter into an agreement to purchase another one-year pure discount bond one year from today. The interest rate on the second bond is negotiated today. This represents the forward interest rate for year 2. Assuming that you and the bond issuer are indifferent between the one two-year bond and the two one-year bonds, the forward interest rate for year 2 can be determined by equating these two investment plans. The forward interest rate is 8.5 percent:

$$[(1.0825)^2/(1.0800)] - 1 = .085.$$

This is confirmed by recognizing that $1.1718 = $1(1.08)(1.085). Also, any other forward rate would result in arbitrage opportunities (under certain restrictive assumptions).

Using a similar approach, it is possible to determine the rest of the forward interest rates obtainable. For instance, the forward interest rate expected to prevail between years 2 and 3 is 9.3 percent:[1]

$$[(1.0860)^3/(1.0825)^2] - 1 = .093.$$

Term structures can assume a variety of shapes. For instance, Figure 6.3 shows how the term structure for high-grade corporate bonds varied

---

[1]In general, there are $N(N - 1)/2$ forward interest rates, where N is the number of bond maturities, and time intervals are annual.

Figure 6.3:
Term Structures, 1966-1982.

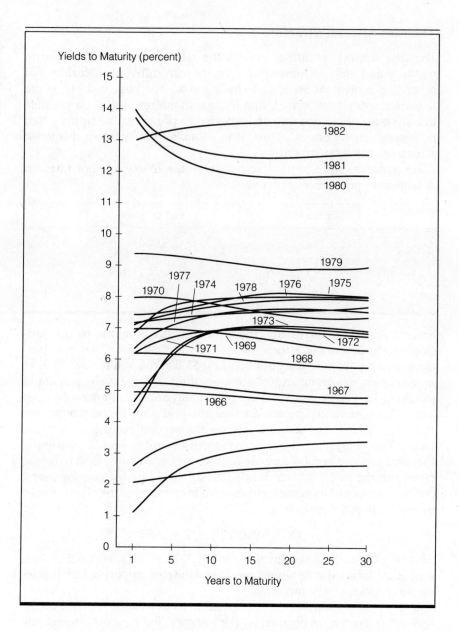

over the years 1966 through 1982. Economists have posited three theories purporting to explain why the term structure takes on various shapes: the expectations theory, the liquidity preference theory, and the market segmentation theory.

Expectations Theory If no market imperfections such as transaction costs exist, and investors are risk-neutral, then forward interest rates represent the market's expectations of actual future spot rates of interest. These assumptions underlie the *expectations theory*, which contends that the shape of the term structure indicates the expected direction of future interest rates.

In our earlier illustration, we assumed that the borrower and bond issuer were indifferent between the one two-year bond and the two one-year bonds. Thus, we assumed that individuals were risk-neutral; they were willing to engage in the two one-year bond strategy without fear that the actual interest rate one year hence would differ from 8.5 percent. In other words, their expectation of the forward interest rate prevailing in Year 2 must be 8.5 percent.

Liquidity-Preference Theory   Another theory of the term structure, the *liquidity-preference theory*, contends that the forward interest rate is a biased predictor of actual future rates of interest. Specifically, the forward rate overestimates the expected spot rate of interest because lenders (bond purchasers) prefer to maintain liquidity and hence prefer shorter-term bonds.

What motivates leaders to have a preference for shorter-term bonds, according to the liquidity-preference theory, is their risk averseness. Shorter-term bonds exhibit less interest rate risk than longer-term bonds. (Recall your knowledge of bond pricing from previous finance classes). Consequently, investors are willing to pay more for a shorter-term bond. This extra amount stems from their risk aversion and is known as the *liquidity premium*. Under the expectations theory, no such premium exists because investors are risk neutral. As we shall soon see, this difference comes into play when determining futures prices where investors may be either risk neutral or risk averse.

An implication of the liquidity-preference theory is that long-term interest rates must exceed short-term rates by the liquidity premium, which should itself increase with bond maturity. Empirical research concerning the existence of this premium has been mixed. Where it supports a premium, it suggests that the premium is small [cf. J. McCulloch (1975)]. Thus, if the term structure is observed to be upward-sloping, then future interest rates are probably expected to be higher; that is, the upward slope is not attributable solely to the time-increasing liquidity premium.

Market-Segmentation Theory   Also called the *preferred-habitat theory*, the *market-segmentation theory* contends that the term structure is determined by the interplay of supply and demand factors in different maturity segments of the credit market. As such, it is not stated in terms of forward interest rates or liquidity premiums. Rather, it simply states that the term structure prevailing at any point in time reflects the preferences of bond market participants, including commercial banks, life insurance companies, casualty insurers, and the like.

The preferences exhibited by these participants stem from their scope of operations and a desire to match the maturity structures of the asset

The **expectations theory** contends that the shape of the term structure indicates the expected direction of future interest rates.

The **liquidity-preference theory** contends that the forward rate overestimates the expected spot rate of interest.

The **market-segmentation theory** contends that the term structure is determined by the interplay of supply and demand factors in different maturity segments of the credit market.

and liability sides of their balance sheets in order to manage interest rate exposure. For instance, commercial banks prefer to invest in short-term bonds because their liabilities are also short-term (demand deposits and certificates of deposit). By conducting such matching, the commercial bank narrows the interest rate gap between its assets and liabilities. Because its assets and liabilities exhibit similar maturity structures, and thus interest rate sensitivities, the bank better manages to immunize itself against unanticipated interest rate changes. Life insurance companies, on the other hand, tend to purchase long-term bonds since their actuarial liabilities are longer-term.

The desires of these large institutional investors to participate in only certain segments of the maturity structure of credit markets is the basis for the market-segmentation theory. For instance, an upward-sloping term structure does not arise because of higher longer-term expected interest rates or liquidity premia per se; rather, it results from tighter monetary conditions in the long-term credit market than in the segmented, short-term credit market.

Forward Price under Risk Neutrality

Armed with a familiarity of the term-structure theories, we can now turn our attention toward the determination of futures prices using the expectations approach. We begin by examining forward prices and build toward determining futures prices. As is always the case with derivative securities, these prices follow from arbitrage restrictions.

Suppose that we are considering buying an asset in T years. Also suppose that the current yield to maturity on risk-free bonds is $_TY_0$ if these bonds exhibit a maturity of T years. Further, suppose that we purchase $(1 + {}_TY_0)$ forward contracts today, where each contract obligates us to buy one unit of the underlying asset at the forward price. Additionally, we buy $\$_TF_0$ of the risk-free bonds with T years to maturity, where $_TF_0$ is the forward price. Since the forward price is set so that the initial value of the forward contract is zero, our total initial investment must be $\$_TF_0$.

In T years the forward contracts expire, and their value is given by

(6.7) $$\$(1 + {}_TY_0)^T(\tilde{S}_T - {}_TF_0),$$

where $\tilde{S}_T$ is the asset's spot price at forward contract maturity. Of course, this price is currently unknown. The payoff from the bond investment is

(6.8) $$\$_TF_0(1 + {}_TY_0)^T.$$

Combining Equations 6.7 and 6.8 gives our total proceeds from the investment:

(6.9) $$\$(1 + {}_TY_0)^T(\tilde{S}_T - {}_TF_0) + {}_TF_0(1 + {}_TY_0)^T$$
$$= \$(1 + {}_TY_0)^T\tilde{S}_T.$$

Thus, we invest $\$_T F_0$ and receive $\$(1 + {_T}Y_0)^T \tilde{S}_T$. By arbitrage, it must therefore be true that the current forward price is equal to the present value of $\$(1 + {_T}Y_0)^T \tilde{S}_T$. Any other forward price would give rise to arbitrage opportunities (ignoring market imperfections).

To determine this present value, we discount the expected proceeds of the investment: $E[(1 + {_T}Y_0)^T \tilde{S}_T] = (1 + {_T}Y_0)^T E(\tilde{S}_T)$. We can discount at the risk-free rate if investors are risk neutral. In this case the present value is

(6.10)
$$\frac{(1 + {_T}Y_0)^T E(\tilde{S}_T)}{(1 + {_T}Y_0)^T} = E(\tilde{S}_T) = {_T}F_0.$$

In other words, ${_T}F_0$, the current forward price, is equal to the asset's expected spot price at contract expiration, $E(\tilde{S}_T)$, if investors are risk neutral.

The current forward price is equal to the asset's expected spot price at expiration if investors are risk neutral.

Equation 6.10 is a very powerful statement. It says that under risk neutrality (and ignoring market frictions such as transaction costs), the observed forward price represents the marketplace's expected spot price at contract expiration. Hence, if one wishes to obtain a market-determined forecast of the subsequent spot price, and is willing to live with the above assumptions of risk neutrality and perfect markets, then one need only observe the current forward price. The forward price is said to be an *unbiased predictor* of the future spot price under these assumptions.[2]

Forward Price under Risk Aversion

If market participants are now risk averse, we cannot determine forward prices by discounting expected payoffs at the risk-free rate of interest. Instead we must account for the risk associated with the initial investment.

In equilibrium, the market value of the initial investment must be such that the foregone utility associated with the investment is equal to the expected utility gained from the payoff:

(6.11)
$$U_0[{_T}F_0] = \sum_{i=1}^{n} h_i\{\tilde{U}_{T,i}[(1 + {_T}Y_0)^T \tilde{S}_{T,i}]\}.$$

In Equation 6.11, the term $U_0[{_T}F_0]$ represents the total utility lost by making the initial investment. U_0 denotes the utility associated with each dollar increase in our current consumption. Consequently, multiplying U_0 by our initial outlay, ${_T}F_0$, gives us the total loss in our current utility associated with making the investment.

---

[2]An unbiased predictor/estimator occurs if, and only if, the expected value of the estimator equals the actual value of the parameter being estimated.

The term $\tilde{U}_{T,i}$ denotes the utility associated with increasing our consumption by a dollar in the ith state of nature at contract expiration. This utility is currently unknown because the investment's payoff is currently uncertain. Given n possible states of nature, the right-hand side of Equation 6.11 gives the expected increase in utility from the investment.

Dividing both sides of Equation 6.11 by U_0 and taking expectations gives

(6.12) $$_TF_0 = (1 + {}_TY_0)^T E(\tilde{M}_{T,i}\,\tilde{S}_{T,i}),$$

where $\tilde{M}_{T,i} = \tilde{U}_{T,i}/U_0$. The term $\tilde{M}_{T,i}$ is the marginal rate of substitution of consumption at contract maturity for current consumption. For example, if $\tilde{M}_{T,i} = .75$, then we would be indifferent between \$1.00 of consumption at contract expiration in state i and \$0.75 of consumption now.

Consider the following well-known mathematical identity:

(6.13) $$E(AB) = E(A)E(B) + COV(A,B).$$

Applying this identity to Equation 6.12 gives

(6.14) $$_TF_0 = (1 + {}_TY_0)^T[E(\tilde{M}_T)E(\tilde{S}_T) + COV(\tilde{M}_T,\tilde{S}_T)],$$

where $E(\tilde{M}_T)$ is the expected marginal rate of substitution over all n states of nature. Intuitively, it is the expected value for the implicit rate of discount relating consumption now to consumption at contract expiration. Thus, it can be shown that

(6.15) $$E(\tilde{M}_T) = [(1 + {}_TY_0)^T]^{-1}.$$

Substituting Equation 6.15 into 6.14 gives

(6.16) $$_TF_0 = E(\tilde{S}_T) + (1 + {}_TY_0)^T COV(\tilde{M}_T,\tilde{S}_T).$$

Under risk aversion, the forward price is equal to the expected future spot price at contract expiration plus a hedging premium.

Equation 6.16 states that under risk aversion, the forward price is equal to the expected future spot price at contract expiration plus a *hedging premium* that is a function of $COV(\tilde{M}_T,\tilde{S}_T)$, the covariance between the marginal rate of substitution and the spot price at contract expiration.

Explaining the Hedging Premium Obviously, the hedging premium (also commonly referred to as a *risk premium*) arises because of the risk-averse nature of investors. To understand this more clearly, consider the fact that under risk neutrality, investors have linear utility functions and thus constant marginal rates of substitution. The consequence is that the covariance term in Equation 6.16 would be zero, and Equation 6.16 reduces to Equation 6.10. Therefore, we again obtain the result that under risk neutrality the current forward price equals the spot price expected to prevail at contract expiration.

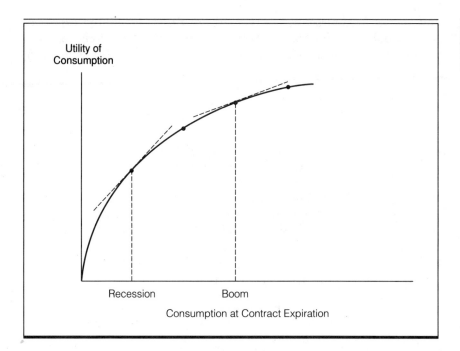

Figure 6.4:
A Representative Utility Function for a Risk-Averse Investor

Utility of Consumption

Recession

Boom

Consumption at Contract Expiration

A representative utility function (with respect to consumption) for a risk-averse investor is shown in Figure 6.4. As consumption increases, utility increases at a decreasing rate. This implies that the marginal rate of substitution (and the marginal utility of consumption) is greater when consumption is low (a recessionary state of nature) than when consumption is high (a boom state). This occurs if the level of consumption is greater in booms, which is very likely. The marginal utilities are given by the slopes of the utility function at different consumption levels.

Whether the covariance term $COV(\tilde{M}_T, \tilde{S}_T)$ is positive or negative depends both on the nature of the forward contract's underlying asset and the investor's overall portfolio from which wealth is drawn for consumption. For simplicity, assume that this portfolio consists strictly of one underlying asset and that this asset is "normal," meaning that its price increases (decreases) in boom (recessionary) states. To protect the portfolio's value, the investor seeks to short the forward contract; if a recessionary state occurs, and the asset's price declines, the loss on the long spot asset position will be offset (at least in part) by the gain on the short forward position. We can say that the hedger is *net short* in the forward market. Since the covariance term is clearly negative here (in a recession the asset's price falls, but the marginal rate of substitution is greater), the investor is willing to enter into the short forward position at a forward price that is less than his expected spot price at contract expiration. That is, $_TF_0 < E(\tilde{S}_T)$, since $COV(\tilde{M}_T, \tilde{S}_T) < 0$. In a sense, the investor must contract at a forward price that is below the expected future spot price in order to induce speculators to take long forward positions. The speculator in question is said to be *net long* in the forward market.

This argument, grounded in risk aversion and originally posited by J. Keynes (1930) and J. Hicks (1939), implies that the forward price is a biased predictor of the actual future spot price. When the forward price is below the expected future spot price, we say that *normal backwardation* occurs. The forward price can be expected to rise over the life of the contract (it must after all, equal the spot price at contract maturity) to compensate speculators for bearing risk. When the forward price is above the expected future spot price, then we say that *contango* occurs, perhaps because hedgers are net short or the underlying asset's price actually increases in recessionary states.

When the forward price is below the expected future spot price, we say that **normal backwardation** occurs.

When the forward price is above the expected future spot price, we say that **contango** occurs.

Futures Price under Risk Neutrality

To determine the futures price under risk neutrality, we must adjust our trading strategy to reflect the daily resettlement process present in the futures market. We now purchase one-day bonds and futures contracts, reinvesting the cash flows at the end of each trading session into new one-day bonds and purchasing futures contracts as their maturities unwind. Specifically, at the beginning of the initial trading day we buy an amount of bonds equal to the current futures price, $_Tf_0$. We then purchase $(1 + {}_1Y_0)$ futures contracts, where ${}_1Y_0$ is the current yield to maturity on a one-day riskless bond. At the end of the day the proceeds from the bond investment will be

$$(6.17) \qquad \$_Tf_0(1 + {}_1Y_0).$$

The amount credited (or debited) to our futures margin account will be

$$(6.18) \qquad \$(1 + {}_1Y_0)({}_{T-1}\tilde{f}_1 - {}_Tf_0),$$

where ${}_{T-1}\tilde{f}_1$ is the settlement futures price at the end of the day, which is currently unknown. Combining Equations 6.17 and 6.18 gives our total proceeds from the one-day investment:

$$(6.19) \qquad \$_Tf_0(1 + {}_1Y_0) + \$(1 + {}_1Y_0)({}_{T-1}\tilde{f}_1 - {}_Tf_0)$$
$$= \$(1 + {}_1Y_0)_{T-1}\tilde{f}_1.$$

In turn, these proceeds are reinvested in one-day bonds at the new, but is currently unknown, rate of ${}_1\tilde{Y}_1$. Also, we purchase more futures contracts. Hence, our proceeds at the end of the second day are

$$(6.20) \qquad \$(1 + {}_1Y_0)_{T-1}\tilde{f}_1(1 + {}_1\tilde{Y}_1) +$$
$$(1 + {}_1Y_0)(1 + {}_1\tilde{Y}_1)({}_{T-2}\tilde{f}_2 - {}_{T-1}\tilde{f}_1)$$
$$= \$(1 + {}_1Y_0)(1 + {}_1\tilde{Y}_1)_{T-2}\tilde{f}_2.$$

Continuing this process, and recognizing the emerging pattern of payoffs, at any day t the proceeds from our investment strategy will be

(6.21) $$\$(1 + {}_1Y_0)(1 + {}_1\tilde{Y}_1)(1 + {}_1\tilde{Y}_2) \ldots (1 + {}_1\tilde{Y}_t)_{T-t}\tilde{f}_t.$$

Finally, since at contract delivery the futures price must equal the prevailing spot price, $\tilde{S}_T$, we have proceeds at delivery of

(6.22) $$\$(1 + {}_1Y_0)(1 + {}_1\tilde{Y}_1)(1 + {}_1\tilde{Y}_2) \ldots (1 + {}_1\tilde{Y}_T)\tilde{S}_T.$$

Accordingly we invest $\$_T f_0$ and receive $\$\tilde{R}\tilde{S}_T$ at delivery, where $\tilde{R}$ is the product of 1 plus the one-day interest rates through delivery:

(6.23) $$\tilde{R} = (1 + {}_1Y_0)(1 + {}_1\tilde{Y}_1)(1 + {}_1\tilde{Y}_2) \ldots (1 + {}_1\tilde{Y}_T).$$

Therefore, in equilibrium and by arbitrage restrictions, it must be true that the current futures price is equal to the present value of $\tilde{R}\tilde{S}_T$.

In order to determine this present value, we discount the expected proceeds: $E(\tilde{R}\tilde{S}_T)$. We can discount at the risk-free rate if investors are risk neutral. Therefore,

(6.24) $$_T f_0 = E(\tilde{R}\tilde{S}_T)/(1 + {}_TY_0)^T.$$

Now recall from our discussion of term-structure theories that no liquidity premiums exist in the term structure under risk neutrality. Rather, when the expectations theory of the term structure applies, forward interest rates represent expectations of actual future spot rates of interest. Therefore, $(1 + {}_TY_0)^T = E(\tilde{R})$ when investors are risk neutral. The analysis of term-structure theory presented earlier was designed to drive home this important result. Using this result and the mathematical identity described by Equation 6.13, Equation 6.24 becomes[3]

(6.25) $$_T f_0 = E(\tilde{S}_T) + [COV(\tilde{R},\tilde{S}_T)/(1 + {}_TY_0)^T].$$

Equation 6.25 states that under risk neutrality, the futures price equals the spot price expected to prevail at contract delivery plus a *reinvestment rate premium* that depends on the covariance between $\tilde{R}$ and $\tilde{S}_T$. This additional term drives a wedge between the current forward and futures prices, and arises because of the different cash flow patterns exhibited by forward and futures contracts. Futures contracts are marked-to-the-market each trading day whereas forward contracts exhibit no cash flows until contract expiration.

Under risk neutrality, the futures price equals the spot price expected to prevail at contract delivery plus a reinvestment rate premium.

---

[3] $_T f_0 = E(\tilde{R}\tilde{S}_T)/(1 + {}_TY_0)^T$

$\quad = [E(\tilde{R})E(\tilde{S}_T) + COV(\tilde{R},\tilde{S}_T)]/(1 + {}_TY_0)^T$

$\quad = [(1 + {}_TY_0)^T E(\tilde{S}_T) + COV(\tilde{R},\tilde{S}_T)]/(1 + {}_TY_0)^T$

$\quad = E(\tilde{S}_T) + [COV(\tilde{R},\tilde{S}_T)/(1 + {}_TY_0)^T].$

However, the additional reinvestment rate premium also arises from the nonconstant behavior of interest rates. To comprehend this, suppose that rates and, thus, yields were constant. If this were so, then the covariance term, $COV(\tilde{R}, \tilde{S}_T)$, in Equation 6.25 would be zero, since $\tilde{R}$ would no longer be random. Hence the current futures price would equal $E(\tilde{S}_T)$, which is the current forward price under risk-neutrality. We conclude that the reinvestment rate premium arises because of (1) daily resettlement in the futures market, and (2) the nonconstant behavior of interest rates over time.

A Closer Look at the Reinvestment Rate Premium The sign and magnitude of the reinvestment rate premium depend on the covariance between the futures contract's underlying spot asset price and market interest rates. To illustrate this, suppose that you assume a long position in U.S. Treasury bill futures contracts. Clearly, $COV(\tilde{R}, \tilde{S}_T) < 0$; if interest rates rise, the price (value) of Treasury bills falls, and vice versa. Now suppose that on a given trading day, market interest rates fall, perhaps due to a relaxed monetary policy. Since rates fell, Treasury bill spot prices and thus their futures prices, rose. You experience a gain on your long futures position. However, if you wish to reinvest your day's margin credit, you must do so at the now lower market rates of interest. In a sense, your gain from the long Treasury bill futures position is somewhat offset by the lower reinvestment rate experienced. Such an offset would not occur in a forward market, since no cash flow occurs until contract expiration. As a consequence, you will demand a futures price that is below the forward price (the expected future spot price) to compensate you for your reinvestment loss. The opposite is true under positive covariance.

Futures Price under Risk Aversion

If market participants are now risk averse, we cannot determine futures prices by discounting expected payoffs at the risk-free rate of interest. We must account for the risk associated with the initial investment. We can expect that the futures price will change, much like the forward price changed when the assumption of risk neutrality was relaxed.

Invoking the same expected utility argument used for forward prices under risk aversion, the expected value of our futures investment strategy now is

(6.26) $$_Tf_0 = E(\tilde{M}_T\tilde{R}\tilde{S}_T).$$

By invoking the mathematical identity in Equation 6.13, we have

(6.27) $$_Tf_0 = E(\tilde{M}_T)E(\tilde{R}\tilde{S}_T) + COV[\tilde{M}_T, (\tilde{R}\tilde{S}_T)]$$
$$= E(\tilde{M}_T)[E(\tilde{R})E(\tilde{S}_T)] + COV(\tilde{R}, \tilde{S}_T)] + COV[\tilde{M}_T, (\tilde{R}\tilde{S}_T)].$$

Using Equation 6.15 gives

(6.28) $_Tf_0 = E(\tilde{S}_T)[E(\tilde{R})/(1 + {_TY_0})^T] + COV(\tilde{R},\tilde{S}_T)/(1 + {_TY_0})^T$
$$+ COV[\tilde{M}_T,(\tilde{R}\tilde{S}_T)].$$

Equation 6.28 states that under risk aversion, the current futures price differs from the spot price expected to prevail at contract delivery because of three premia: a term premium, a reinvestment rate premium, and a hedging premium.

The *term premium*, $E(\tilde{R})/(1 + {_TY_0})^T$, is constant across all futures contracts exhibiting the same maturity. It arises because of risk aversion. To understand this, recall that $(1 + {_TY_0})^T = E(\tilde{R})$ under risk neutrality, because no liquidity premiums exist in the term structure. Thus, the term premium is 1. In other words, it does not exist; ignoring the other premia, the futures price would equal the expected spot price (the forward price). However, presuming that investors are risk averse, that liquidity premiums exist, and that they are positive (the periodic rates of return on longer-term bonds are greater than those on shorter-term bonds), then $(1 + {_TY_0})^T > E(\tilde{R})$, and the term premium is less than 1. If liquidity premiums are negative, then $(1 + {_TY_0})^T < E(\tilde{R})$, and the term premium is greater than 1.

The *reinvestment rate premium*, $COV(\tilde{R},\tilde{S}_T)/(1 + {_TY_0})^T$, is associated with the daily resettlement process and the nonconstant behavior of interest rates. It is the same premium that appears in Equation 6.25.

The *hedging premium*, $COV[\tilde{M}_T,(\tilde{R}\tilde{S}_T)]$, derives from the relation between the futures payoff and the investor's marginal rate of substitution. It is analogous to the hedging premium appearing in Equation 6.16 for forward prices under risk aversion. Ignoring the term premium and reinvestment rate premium, futures prices can still deviate from the expected futures spot price due to the hedging premium. When this premium is negative, $_Tf_0 < E(\tilde{S}_T)$, we have a situation of normal backwardation in the futures market. A positive hedging premium implies a contango situation, again ignoring the other two premia.

Premia Signs for Selected Futures Contracts   Regarding futures contracts, this book will focus on interest rate, stock index, and foreign exchange futures (i.e., financial futures). It is therefore in our interest to discuss the expected signs of the premia relating to these underlying assets. The term premium is the same across all assets, but the signs of the reinvestment and hedging premiums are asset-dependent.

Exhibit 6.3 displays the "expected" signs. With respect to interest rate futures, we can safely state that the reinvestment rate premium is unambiguously negative. Rising interest rates imply lower Treasury security prices, and vice versa. Thus, $COV(\tilde{R},\tilde{S}_T) < 0$. We also conjecture that the hedging premium is positive. In boom states when the economy is hot and inflation and interest rates are high, Treasury security prices fall. So, too, does a risk-averse investor's marginal rate of substitution. Thus, $COV[\tilde{M}_T,(\tilde{R}\tilde{S}_T)] > 0$. Both premia should be larger (in absolute value) for longer-term Treasury securities, since these securities are

Under risk aversion, the futures price differs from the spot price expected to prevail at contract delivery because of three premia: a term premium, a reinvestment rate premium, and a hedging premium.

Exhibit 6.3:
Premia Signs for Financial Futures

Futures Contract	Sign of Reinvestment Premium	Sign of Hedging (Risk) Premium
Treasury Securities	−	+
Stock Indices	?	?
Foreign Exchange	?	?

more sensitive to interest rate changes than shorter-term Treasury instruments.

Concerning stock indices, the signs are ambiguous for both the reinvestment and hedging premia. There is a large body of empirical evidence that stock prices and interest rates are negatively correlated. But there is also a sizable body of well-performed empirical research suggesting that the relation is ambiguous or even positive. Thus, $COV(\tilde{R}, \tilde{S}_T) \gtreqless 0$. Also, one might argue that stock values decline in recessionary states, implying $COV[\tilde{M}_T, (\tilde{R}\tilde{S}_T)] < 0$. However, the stock market has a propensity to lead the economy; it is a leading economic indicator. Because of this, stock index levels may rise when marginal rates of substitution are high if an economic turnaround is anticipated. The sign of the hedging premium is therefore ambiguous.

Concerning foreign exchange, the signs of both premia are also ambiguous. Rising interest rates in the United States may attract foreign investment capital in the short run, thus strengthening the dollar's value (a decline in $\tilde{S}_T$, the dollar price per unit of foreign currency). This implies $COV(\tilde{R}, \tilde{S}_T) < 0$. However, rising interest rates are symptomatic of greater U.S. inflation, which, in the longer term, can depress the dollar's value, as foreigners are less willing to import more expensive U.S. goods and services. Thus, $COV(\tilde{R}, \tilde{S}_T) > 0$. The reinvestment rate premium is therefore ambiguous. With respect to the hedging premium, rising rates of interest suggest a domestic boom, implying $COV[\tilde{M}_T, (\tilde{R}\tilde{S}_T)] < 0$. However, the changing value of the dollar makes the sign of the hedging premium too difficult to call.

To conclude, with the exception of the reinvestment and hedging premia for futures contracts written on Treasury securities, the signs of these premia for financial futures are ambiguous. Complicating this matter is the fact that these premia can vary over time. Later in this chapter we will examine some empirical evidence on the subject.

CONTRASTING THE CARRYING-CHARGE AND EXPECTATIONS APPROACHES

The carrying-charge theory of determining futures prices is grounded in arbitrage restrictions relating to the costs of carrying an asset forward in time. The expectations approach to determining futures prices is grounded in arbitrage restrictions relating to the payoffs of investment strategies that involve the futures contract. Although both approaches seek to explain futures prices and are grounded in arbitrage restrictions, there are important differences between them. Some of these differences are rather obvious. For instance, as discussed earlier, the carrying-charge approach is equally applicable to both forward and futures contracts because it (implicitly) assumes constant carrying charges and risk neutrality. On the other hand, the expectations approach recognizes differences in forward and futures prices that are attributable to daily resettlement and nonconstant interest rates.

Another important but subtle difference between the two is that the carrying-charge approach basically treats the supply and demand conditions in the underlying asset market as constant over the contract's life. On the other hand, the expectations approach incorporates investor anticipation about changing market conditions. For this reason, the expectations approach can account for some seemingly unusual price behavior that, frankly, the carrying-charge theory cannot explain.

Let us consider two examples. First, consider an underlying asset that appears to exhibit an overall positive carrying charge but whose futures price is actually below its current spot price (a positive basis). Under the carrying-charge theory, this would suggest an exploitable arbitrage opportunity. However, suppose that the asset in question is in short supply. Present consumption is abnormally high relative to the supply of the asset, causing an unusually high spot price. If there is not an *expected* increase in future supply or decrease in future demand, then the futures price should be greater than the current spot price, since carrying charges are positive. However, suppose that there is an *expected* increase in asset supply or decrease in asset demand prior to contract delivery. This will tend to keep the futures price down and, quite possibly, lower than the current spot price. Thus, this apparent anomaly is attributable to expectations concerning supply and demand conditions in the spot market. The expectations approach recognizes this, whereas the carrying-charge theory does not.

When the basis is positive but carrying charges are positive, the basis is said to reflect a *convenience yield*—a premium earned by holders of the commodity due to temporarily increased (reduced) demand (supply). Under the arbitrage trading strategies surrounding the carrying-charge theory, the "apparent" arbitrage profit would be wrongly confused for the genuine convenience yield that results under the supply and demand expectations just described.

The **convenience yield** refers to a premium earned by holders of the commodity due to temporarily increased (reduced) demand (supply).

For our second example, consider the soybean futures prices appearing in Exhibit 6.4. These are actual settlement prices on the CBOT for contracts traded on March 1, 1989. Notice that whereas the July futures price is greater than the March and May prices, it is actually less than the August futures price. The carrying-charge theory would have a difficult time explaining this apparent anomaly. However, the price pattern is easily explained by the expectations approach. The market prices reflect

Delivery Month	Cents per Bushel
March	750½
May	761
July	770½
August	764½
September	743
November	731¼
January (1990)	738½
March	746

expectations of increased supply in August due to the harvest season. Once the harvest passes, the carrying-charge theory (cost-of-carry) will again tend to determine soybean futures prices.

EMPIRICAL EVIDENCE

In subsequent chapters we discuss empirical evidence relating to specific financial futures contracts. At this time, however, it is useful to briefly discuss some empirical evidence relating to the determination of futures prices. There is a large body of such evidence, so our analysis is clearly limited. It is merely intended to provide an introduction to the types of issues that are investigated by researchers. We divide the studies addressed into two (related) areas—those that investigate the relation between spot and futures (forward) prices, and those that test for the existence of premia.

Tests of the Relation between Spot and Futures (Forward) Prices

Most studies testing the relation between spot and futures (forward) prices examine whether futures (forward) prices are consistent with the carrying-charge approach. The studies test whether arbitrage opportunities are present, where such opportunities are given by deviations between observed prices and those predicted by the carrying-charge theory. Some of the best evidence in this area involves the testing of foreign exchange spot and forward prices. There is a large and active market in currency forward contracting. Also, the use of forward contracts eliminates the potential bias associated with term and reinvestment risk premia. Such premia should not exist for forward contracts, even under risk aversion. These studies, which include R. Aliber

(1973), W. Branson (1979), J. Frenkel and R. Levich (1977), and many others, generally support the carrying-charge theory. Currency forward prices are related to spot exchange rates such that arbitrage opportunities are not present after controlling for market imperfections such as transaction costs.

Studies involving other spot-asset markets also provide support for the carrying-charge approach. For instance, R. Rendleman and C. Carabini (1979) report that arbitrage profits from Treasury bill futures trading were generally insufficient to overcome the associated transaction costs. B. Cornell (1985) reports similar results for SP500 futures trading after a period of market seasoning.

Although most evidence upholds the carrying-charge approach, some well-performed studies do not. For example, R. Klemkosky and D. Lasser (1985) report rather sizable arbitrage opportunities involving the trading of Treasury bond futures. And E. Elton, M. Gruber, and J. Rentzler (1985) found that a sophisticated trading strategy involving Treasury bill futures was highly profitable. Thus, the evidence concerning the relation between spot and futures prices is mixed.

Tests for the Existence of Premia

Most of the studies attempting to detect the existence of premia in forward and futures prices are concerned with the existence of a hedging premium. Such an investigation can be difficult, since term and reinvestment rate premia may also exist, and because market imperfections can confound the empirical evidence. One of the most cited studies in this area is that of B. Cornell and M. Reinganum (1981). These authors examine the differences between currency forward and futures prices for contracts exhibiting the same maturities. They report no statistical or economic evidence of price differences between the two contracts. This implies that any hedging premium in foreign exchange markets is small.

However, others have reported a hedging premium for other spot assets. For example, E. Chang (1985) found that corn, soybean, and wheat futures all exhibited a statistically significant hedging premium. K. French (1983) found statistically significant differences between forward and futures prices for silver and copper. Thus, the evidence concerning the existence of a hedging premium is mixed. Also, J. Hill, T. Schneeweis, and R. Mayerson (1983) report evidence consistent with the existence of a small reinvestment rate premium in Treasury bond futures prices.

SUMMARY

One approach to the determination of futures prices is the carrying-charge theory, which holds that futures prices should equal spot prices plus the costs of carrying assets forward to delivery. Arbitrage restrictions ensure that futures prices should not deviate substantially from this sum. An important assumption underlying this theory is that carrying charges are constant. Without this assumption, the proceeds from arbitrage strategies are uncertain, implying that such strategies are not risk-free.

Another approach is the expectations theory, based on expectations concerning the future spot value of the underlying asset at contract delivery. It is grounded in arbitrage restrictions relating to the payoffs of investment strategies that involve futures contracts. This approach also emphasizes the role of risk aversion and uncertainty in determining futures prices. Under risk aversion and nonconstant interest rates, the futures price deviates from the expected future spot price because of three premia: a term premium related to liquidity premia in the term structure, a reinvestment rate premium stemming from the daily resettlement procedure, and a hedging premium that is a function of the covariance between spot prices and a risk-averse investor's marginal rate of substitution.

These two approaches show how futures prices, spot prices, forward prices, carrying charges, and investor expectations are interrelated. It is important to understand these interrelations and how futures prices are determined, since the proper employment of futures contracts depends largely on the futures price. In the next chapter we begin to examine the various uses of futures contracts.

Selected References

Aliber, R. "The Interest Rate Parity Theorem: A Reinterpretation." *Journal of Political Economy* 81 (December 1973): 1451–1459.

Branson, W. "The Minimum Covered Interest Differential Needed for International Arbitrage Activity." *Journal of Political Economy* (December 1979): 1029–1034.

Chang, E. "Returns to Speculators and the Theory of Normal Backwardation." *Journal of Finance* 40 (March 1985): 193–208.

Cornell, B. "Taxes and the Pricing of Stock Index Futures: Empirical Results." *Journal of Futures Markets* (1985): 89–101.

Cornell, B., and M. Reinganum. "Forward and Futures Prices: Evidence from the Forward Exchange Markets." *Journal of Finance* 41 (December 1981): 1035–1045.

Cox, J., J. Ingersoll, and S. Ross. "The Relation between Forward and Futures Prices." *Journal of Financial Economics* 10 (December 1981).

Dusak, K. "Futures Trading and Investor Returns: An Investigation of Commodity Risk Premiums." *Journal of Political Economy* 81 (December 1973): 1387–1406.

Elton, E., M. Gruber, and J. Rentzler. "Intra-Day Tests of the Efficiency of the Treasury Bill Futures Market." *Review of Economics and Statistics* (February 1984): 129–137.

French, K. "A Comparison of Future and Forward Prices." *Journal of Financial Economics* 12 (November 1983): 311–342.

Frenkel, J., and R. Levich. "Transaction Costs and Interest Arbitrage: Tranquil versus Turbulent Periods." *Journal of Political Economy* 85 (December 1977): 1209–1226.

Gray, R. "The Search for A Risk Premium." *Journal of Political Economy* 69 (June 1961): 250–260.

Harris, L. "The October 1987 S&P 500 Stock-Futures Basis." *Journal of Finance* 44 (March 1989): 77–99.

Hicks, J. *Value and Capital*. 2d ed. Oxford: Clarendon Press, 1939.

Hill, J., T. Schneeweis, and R. Mayerson. "An Analysis of the Impact of Market-To-Market in Hedging with Treasury Bond Futures." *Review of Research In Futures Markets* 2 (1983): 136–159.

Hodrick, R., and S. Srivastava. "The Covariation of Risk Premiums and Expected Future Exchange Rates." *Journal of International Money and Finance* 5 (March 1986): s5–s21.

Houthakker, H. "Can Speculators Forecast Prices?" *Review of Economics and Statistics* 39 (1957): 143–151.

Huang, R. "An Analysis of Intertemporal Pricing for Forward Foreign Exchange Contracts." *Journal of Finance* 44 (March 1989): 183–194.

Keynes, J. *A Treatise On Money*. London: Macmillan, 1930.

Klemkosky, R. and D. Lasser. "An Efficiency Analysis of the T-Bond Futures Market." *Journal Of Futures Markets* 5 (1985): 607–620.

McCulloch, J. "An Estimate of the Liquidity Premium." *Journal Of Political Economy* 93 (February 1985).

Rendleman, R. and C. Carabini. "The Efficiency of the Treasury Bill Futures Market." *Journal Of Finance* 34 (September 1979): 895–914.

Richard, S. and M. Sundaresan. "A Continuous Time Equilibrium Model of Forward Prices and Futures Prices in a Multigood Economy." *Journal Of Financial Economics* 10 (December 1981).

Tesler, L., "Futures Trading and the Storage of Cotton and Wheat." *Journal Of Political Economy* 66 (June 1958): 233–255.

Wood, J. "Do Yield Curves Normally Slope Up? The Term Structure of Interest Rates, 1862–1982." *Economic Perspectives*. Federal Reserve Bank of Chicago (July–August 1983).

Questions and Problems

1. What is the value of a futures contract at contract inception?

2. What is the value of a forward contract prior to expiration?

3. What is the repo rate?

4. Why does the basis tend to be more stable than either the spot or futures prices?

5. What is an intracommodity spread? An intercommodity spread?

6. Suppose that $S_0 = \$10$, $CC = .07$, and transaction costs and short-sale restrictions do not exist. Under the carrying-charge theory, what should be the price of a futures contract with six-month delivery?

7. Suppose that $S_0 = \$25$, $CC = .08$, and $_{.25}f_0 = \$27$. Describe the arbitrage strategy used to exploit this situation and the proceeds from the strategy.

8. Suppose that $_{.25}f_0 = \$2.00$ and $CC = .10$. Under the carrying-charge theory, what is the value of $_{.50}f_0$?

9. Suppose that $S_0 = \$1.00$, $CC = .10$, $\tau = \$0.05$, and $g = .50$. From Equation 6.6, what is the range of one-year futures prices that would preclude profitable arbitrage?

10. Define the term structure of interest rates.

11. Suppose you observe the following data on default-free, pure discount bonds:

Time to Maturity	Yield to Maturity
1 Year	.1000
2 Years	.1035
3 Years	.1075

Under the expectations theory, what is the implied two-year forward rate of interest?

12. What is the major difference between the expectations and liquidity preference theories of the term structure?

13. Under the expectations approach, what does the forward rate represent if investors are risk neutral?

14. If $COV(\tilde{M}_T, \tilde{S}_T) < 0$, then does the forward price overestimate or underestimate the expected spot price at delivery if investors are risk averse?

15. Define normal backwardation and contango.

16. Under what conditions does Equation 6.28 reduce to Equation 6.10?

17. Define the convenience yield.

18. How is the basis expected to change over the maturity of a futures contract?

19. Discuss some of the fundamental differences between the carrying-charge and expectations approaches to determining futures prices.

Self-Test Problems

ST-1. Suppose that a forward contract expires in one year and has a price of $10. The riskless rate of interest is 8 percent. It is now six months later, and new forward contracts, on the same underlying asset and exhibiting six-month maturities, are being written at a price of $12. What is the value of the original forward contract?

ST-2. If $S_0 = \$8$, $CC = .10$, $g = 1.00$, and $\tau = \$0.05$, what is the range of six-month futures prices that would preclude profitable arbitrage?

ST-3. Suppose that $S_0 = \$3$, $SC = -0.02$, $TC = .005$, $FC = .08$, and $_{.50}f_0 = \$3.20$. Under the carrying-charge theory, describe the arbitrage strategy used to exploit this situation and the proceeds from the strategy.

ST-4. Given $E(\tilde{S}_1) = \$1.00$, $E(\tilde{R}) = 1.14$, $_1Y_0 = 0.15$, $COV(\tilde{R},\tilde{S}_1) = 0.005$, and $COV[\tilde{M}_T, (\tilde{R}\tilde{S}_1)] = 0.003$, what is $_1f_0$ under the expectations approach?

ST-5. If $_{.50}f_0 = \$40$, $CC = .10$, and $_1f_0 = \$43$, describe the arbitrage strategy used to exploit this situation and the proceeds from this strategy.

Solutions to Self-Test Problems

ST-1. $(\$12.00 - \$10.00)e^{(.50)(-.08)} = \$1.92$.

ST-2. $1[\$8e^{(.10)(.5)} - \$.05] \leq {}_{.50}f_0 \leq \$8e^{(.10)(.5)} + \$.05$

$$\$8.36 \leq {}_{.50}f_0 \leq \$8.46.$$

ST-3. $CC = -.02 + .005 + .08 = 0.065$.

Therefore, $_{.50}f_0$ should equal 3.10: $\$3e^{(.065)(.5)}$ To arbitrage, undertake the following strategy:

Today: Buy the spot asset for $3.00.

           Arrange to carry it forward for six months at a cost of $0.10.

           Sell a six-month futures contract.

In Six Months: Remove the asset from storage and deliver it against the futures contract, collecting $3.20.

The proceeds are $0.10 per unit of the asset.

ST-4. $_1f_0 = \$1[1.14/(1.15)^1] + .005/(1.15)^1 + .003 = \$0.9986$.

ST-5. $_1f_0$ should equal 42.05: $\$40e^{(.10)(.05)}$.

To arbitrage, undertake the following strategy:

Today: Long the nearby contract expiring in six months.

           Short the deferred contract expiring in one year.

           Arrange to carry the asset from six months to one year.

In Six Months: Take delivery on the nearby contract, paying $40.00, and carry the asset forward for six months.

In One Year: Deliver the asset on the short position, collecting $43.00.

The proceeds are $0.95 per unit of the asset.

7

USING FUTURES CONTRACTS

There are three major uses of futures contracts. Foremost is to hedge risks associated with spot-asset positions, as mentioned in Chapter 4. Second is to speculate on forecasts of subsequent spot-price movements. By assuming positions in the futures contracts rather than in the spot asset itself, speculators can increase returns should their forecasts prove correct. Third, futures contracts can be used for price discovery, as suggested by the discussion of the expectations approach in Chapter 6.

This chapter addresses each of these three functions of futures contracts: hedging, speculating, and price discovery. In subsequent chapters, examples of each will be illustrated using specific futures contracts.

Futures contracts can be used for hedging, speculating, and price discovery.

HEDGING WITH FUTURES CONTRACTS

The most important role of futures contracts is that of risk reduction. For investors holding preexisting positions in the spot-asset market, futures contracts may be employed to reduce the disutility associated with future price uncertainty. When engaging in a futures contract in order to reduce risk in the spot position, the futures trader is said to establish a *hedge*. In this section we describe the various types of futures hedges and *hedge ratios* that you will encounter in this book.

Types of Hedges

There are three basic types of hedges: (1) a short hedge; (2) a long hedge (often called an anticipatory hedge); and (3) a cross hedge. In the most common of these, the *short hedge,* an investor who already owns a spot asset engages in a trade to sell its associated futures contract. For

*There are three types of futures hedges: a **short hedge**, a **long hedge**, and a **cross hedge**.*

example, an investor who holds one unit of the SP100 Stock Index sells one unit of the index short in the futures market. The investor has thereby contracted to sell the unit in the future for the existing futures price. This way he or she hedges against wealth loss due to subsequent stock market declines. Of course, the hedger also foregoes gains associated with unanticipated market upswings. But the utility gained from the hedge presumably was positive when initially established, because of investor uncertainty about the market and because of the investor's unique utility function. How long the hedge will be established depends largely on the individual investor. Whether a nearby or more deferred futures contract is utilized likely depends on (1) how long the investor believes that subsequent stock market movements will be ambiguous, and (2) whether or not the investor plans to sell the stock in the near future. For instance, if the investor intends to sell the index unit in three months in order to purchase another spot asset for investment or consumption, then a futures contract with delivery in three or more months will likely be employed for hedging purposes.

With an *anticipatory*, or *long hedge*, an investor protects against adverse price movements of an asset that will be purchased in the future. That is, the spot asset in question is not currently owned but is scheduled to be purchased or otherwise held at a later date. Consider a U.S.–based importer who contracts to purchase French-made goods. The payment for the goods will be made in francs and is scheduled to occur in six months. Since the spot dollar-franc exchange rate that will prevail in six months is currently unknown, the importer may wish to long a franc futures contract. Here the importer seeks to protect against an unanticipated depreciation in the dollar (a franc appreciation). Such a dollar depreciation would make the dollar cost of the import greater. By engaging in a long franc futures position, the investor locks into a dollar-franc exchange rate even though the francs will not be purchased for six months.

In the preceding examples, we conveniently assumed that the hedger's needs were perfectly matched with the institutional features of the various futures markets involved. Most important, the spot asset being hedged and the spot asset underlying the futures contract were identical. In certain hedging applications, however, a futures contract written on another underlying asset will have to be used. In this case, we are said to establish a *cross hedge*.[1]

In terms of financial futures, a cross hedge is most often invoked in the case of hedging corporate bond positions. There are no futures contracts written on corporate bonds. Instead, futures written on U.S. government securities (e.g., Treasury bond futures contracts) are used

---

[1]Note that a cross hedge may be a short hedge or an anticipatory hedge. The term merely refers to hedging a preexisting position in one particular asset with a futures contract written on another (presumably related) asset.

to immunize corporate bonds against adverse interest rate changes. Since corporate bonds and government bonds are presumably highly correlated, the cross hedge should be effective in reducing risk. Later, in Chapter 10, we will examine a cross hedge involving corporate bonds and Treasury bond futures contracts. Other cross-hedging examples will also be explored in later chapters.

It is important to recognize that a cross hedge will not likely be as effective as a *direct hedge*, one in which the underlying spot assets are identical. The reason for this will become apparent as our discussion continues.

Futures Hedge Ratios

Perhaps the most important and difficult decision for a hedger is the number of futures contracts to be bought or sold, that is, the *hedge ratio*. In general, the hedge ratio should be selected so as to minimize *basis risk*, a concept defined next.

Consider what happens when an investor uses a futures contract to hedge. For instance, consider a short hedge where the futures contract is sold at a price of $_Tf_0$. At time t, the hedge is lifted by selling the spot asset and buying the futures contract at the new price of $_Tf_t$ (a reversing trade). The profit from the short hedge is

(7.1)
$$Profit = (S_t - S_0) - (_Tf_t - _Tf_0)$$
$$= S_t - _Tf_t - (S_0 - _Tf_0),$$

where S_0 and S_t refer to the spot asset's price at time 0 (the hedge inception) and time t, respectively. Notice that we can write the profit as follows:

(7.2)
$$Profit = b_t - b_0,$$

where b_t and b_0 refer to the basis (the difference between the spot and futures prices) at time t and at time 0, respectively. Thus, the profit from the hedge is merely the change in the basis. In other words, when an investor uses a futures contract to hedge, the profit realized depends on how the *basis* changes. Without the hedge, the profit depends on how the *spot price* changes. As demonstrated in Chapter 6, however, the variability in the basis is typically much lower than that in the spot price. Recall that this result obtains because spot and futures prices tend to be highly correlated. Thus, we can conclude that the hedge position is typically much less risky than the unhedged position.

The uncertainty regarding how the basis will change over the life of the hedge is known as *basis risk*. Most hedging applications seek to

The uncertainty regarding how the basis will change over the life of the hedge is known as **basis risk**.

minimize it.[2] Return uncertainty is therefore minimized. There is no exact method of determining the optimal hedge ratio (the number of futures contracts traded) for minimizing basis risk before the hedge is lifted. However, there are several ways to estimate it, and several hedge ratios currently exist. In this book we will examine three of them: (1) the naive hedge ratio, (2) the minimum-variance hedge ratio, and (3) the price-sensitivity hedge ratio. With the *naive hedge ratio*, each unit in the spot market is hedged with a unit in the futures market. Our two hedging examples discussed earlier implicitly utilized this ratio. Simple in construction, the naive hedge ratio is also often effective and easy to implement. We will utilize this ratio when examining currency futures in the next chapter.

The three different hedge ratios employed in this book are the **naive hedge ratio**, the **minimum-variance hedge ratio**, and the **price-sensitivity hedge ratio**.

The *minimum-variance hedge ratio* is more complicated. Our hedging example illustrated in Chapter 4 introduced this ratio, and we will use it in Chapter 9, which deals with stock index futures contracts.

The *price-sensitivity hedge ratio* was specifically developed to be used in conjunction with interest rate futures contracts. In Chapter 10 we derive this more complex ratio and demonstrate its application. Although the derivation and applications of these ratios are deferred until later chapters, keep in mind that they are employed as a means to minimize basis risk.

A Hedging Summary

Ultimately, four questions are always faced by the hedger who employs futures contracts. (They were implicit in the hedging examples discussed earlier and will be more apparent in the detailed examples in subsequent chapters.)

First is the question of whether to be short or long. The answer is to choose the position that introduces negative correlation with the spot position. For example, if you are currently long the spot asset, then a short futures position is appropriate (and vice versa). This negative correlation reduces basis risk.

The second question faced by the hedger concerns which futures commodity to employ. In general, the hedger will choose a futures contract written on the same spot asset in question, since this will tend to maximize the correlation between the spot price and the futures price,

---

[2]In fact, all of the decisions faced by the hedger can be framed in terms of minimizing basis risk. Getting back to our discussion of cross hedging, we stated that a cross hedge will likely be less effective than a direct hedge. The reason for this is now obvious. The cross hedge will likely have more basis risk. Recall from Chapter 6 that the basis is more stable when the spot and futures prices are more highly correlated. With a cross hedge, the spot assets are different, implying less correlation between the spot asset held and the futures price than when a direct hedge can be obtained. In choosing the futures commodity to construct a cross hedge, the hedger will closely examine the correlation between the two spot assets in order to best reduce basis risk.

Micro versus Macro Hedging

Micro hedging refers to the hedging of individual transactions, whereas macro hedging refers to the hedging of all firm assets and liabilities as a group. An example of a micro hedge would be a paper-product manufacturer who employs a lumber futures contract to lock into subsequent lumber input costs of production. An example of a macro hedge would be a bank or other thrift institution that uses interest rate futures to equate the interest sensitivities of the asset and liability sides of its balance sheet (a process known as *managing the gap*).

It is generally difficult for a firm to determine its overall exposure. Because of this, firms employ macro hedging strategies far less often than micro applications. Besides, it is often senseless to continually engage in macro hedging—such hedging contradicts the fundamental purpose of operating the enterprise in the first place.

Most firms (and other investors) therefore commonly use micro hedging applications on an occasional basis. A firm typically hedges because of transitory uncertainty about the subsequent price of a particular asset. By using an appropriate futures hedging application, it can minimize the disutility associated with such temporary uncertainty. Profits can still be realized through other operations of the firm.

Because firms use micro hedging strategies more often, the hedging applications detailed in subsequent chapters will be of a micro nature.

---

thereby helping to reduce basis risk. If a futures contract is not written on the spot asset, then a cross hedge must be employed. Here the hedger will choose the futures commodity that is most highly correlated with the spot asset in question so as to minimize basis risk.

The third question concerns the maturity of the futures contract. In general, a futures contract with delivery occurring beyond the hedger's horizon will be selected; in this way the hedge does not have to be lifted prematurely. Also, to obtain the greatest reduction in basis risk, the hedger should hold the futures position until as close to expiration as possible so that the futures contract selected will be the one whose delivery occurs nearest to (but after) the hedger's horizon. Finally, if the horizon is so long that a sufficient futures maturity is unavailable, then the hedger should engage in a strategy called *rolling the hedge forward*. Here a more liquid, shorter-maturity futures contract is selected, and when it approaches its maturity, the futures position is closed out via a reversing trade, and a new position is established in a deferred contract. This procedure is repeated until the hedge is ultimately lifted.

The final question faced by a hedger entails the number of futures contracts to short or long—that is, the hedge ratio. In general, the ratio is selected so as to minimize basis risk. In subsequent chapters we will examine how to determine different hedge ratios.

SPECULATING WITH FUTURES CONTRACTS

Again, the major function of futures markets is to allow traders to reduce risk exposure. However, a side effect of futures trading is the

Gambler's Ruin and Futures Hedging

A hedger employing a futures contract must maintain a margin over the maturity of the hedge. An interesting question, therefore, is how much money the hedger requires in order to adequately maintain the margin for the entire hedging period. Clearly, the answer will depend largely on the volatility of the spot-asset price, since futures price changes are typically highly correlated with spot price changes. If volatility is high and the hedger's capital adequacy is low, then there will be a large probability of not meeting a margin call.

This consequence is analogous to the concept of *gambler's ruin,* a risk well recognized by sophisticated gamblers. For instance, a savvy gambler would never play at a $25 blackjack table if his "bank" is just $100 since, over dozens of hands, the probability of having several losing hands in a row is quite large. The probability of "tapping out" at a $25 table is much greater than that at a $5 table. To maximize his odds of winning, the gambler determines how large his "bank" must be in order to have sufficient "staying power." Similarly, a futures hedger should determine how much capital must be set aside so that the margin is always maintained and the hedge is not prematurely lifted.

Employing a simulation analysis, G. Gay, W. Hunter, and R. Kolb (1985) determined the probability of depleting different amounts of funds for futures hedges of varying lengths. As expected, they showed that the probability of ruin increases as the volatility of spot price changes increases, *ceretis paribus.*

As an illustration of their analysis, consider the figure below showing the probability of ruin for a silver futures contract where the standard deviation of daily futures price changes is $279 per contract. A larger pool of funds considerably reduces the inability to maintain the margin. For instance, for thirty-day hedges and a pool of just $250, the probability of ruin is over 80 percent. However, this probability is reduced to nearly zero if the initial capital pool is $4,000. The figure also shows, as expected, that the probability of ruin increases for a longer hedge length, *ceretis paribus.* Over longer periods of time the probability of large futures price changes is greater. Obviously, clearinghouses find this type of information useful for establishing margin requirements.

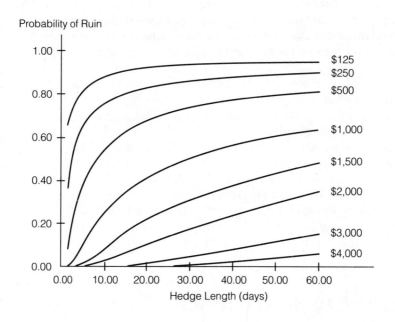

ability to engage in speculation about subsequent asset prices. *Speculation* is best viewed as a spillover of futures trading that can provide comparatively less risk-averse investors with the ability to enhance their percentage returns.

The major difference between a hedger and a speculator in the futures market is that the speculator (effectively) has no position in the spot asset. The speculator enters the futures market to willingly increase risk exposure, but in the hope of profiting on spot-price forecasts. Although risk is increased because of the leverage effect of futures trading described in earlier chapters, the speculator's utility can still be enhanced if the expected return is great. This was demonstrated in Chapter 4.

Does a speculator truly have no position in the spot asset? Technically, the answer to this question is no. A speculator who trades a currency futures contract will be affected by exchange rate movements through the everyday purchase of foreign goods and services. A speculator who trades an interest rate futures contract will be affected by interest rate changes through the purchase of adjustable-rate mortgages and the like. However, the speculator's preexisting risk exposure in the spot asset is typically very small, especially relative to the size of the futures contract. For instance, just one Treasury bill futures contract entails $1,000,000 face-value of Treasury bills. Clearly, it is unlikely that any individual entering the futures market will exhibit such a large degree of exposure. Thus, we can conclude that while a speculator faces a small and *indirect* risk in the spot market, for all intents and purposes his spot-asset position is zero. This contrasts sharply with the spot risk exposure of a hedger, which is large.

> **Speculation** is a spillover of futures trading that can provide comparatively less risk-averse investors with the ability to enhance their percentage returns.

Types of Speculators

There are three different types of futures speculators, depending on their holding horizons: (1) scalpers, (2) day traders, and (3) position traders. *Scalpers* have the shortest holding horizons, typically closing a position within a few minutes of initiation. In fact, W. Silber (1984) reported that futures scalpers averaged about seventy trades per day, and that an average open-to-close position lasted less than two minutes. Obviously, scalpers attempt to profit on short-term market movements through heavy-volume trading. They tend to trade on market emotion, sensing pressures to buy and sell by "reading" other traders. To do so, they must transact in the futures pits. Hence, a scalper is an exchange member or otherwise leases an exchange seat. This also helps to reduce transaction costs. Floor traders at the CME pay just 24¢ per round trip in most futures contracts, compared to a round-trip cost of about $30 for public futures traders. The many trades conducted by scalpers prevent the use of public orders, since the huge transaction costs of employing a broker would surely eliminate any profits. Finally, it can be argued that scalpers offer a valuable market service because their frequent trading enhances market liquidity.

> The three types of futures speculators are **scalpers**, **day traders**, and **position traders**.

The second type of futures speculator—the *day trader*—typically holds a futures position for a few hours, but never longer than one trading session. Thus, day traders open and close a futures position within the same trading day. Most often, a day trader attempts to profit from scheduled announcements such as money-supply announcements, trade-deficit announcements, and the like. Thus, the day trader opens a long or short futures position depending on his or her expectation of the announcement and its affect on the futures price, and enters a reversing trade later in the session and hopefully at a profit. Day traders may be exchange members or public traders.

The third type of futures speculator is the *position trader.* As you might expect by now, they have longer horizons, holding positions overnight and often as long as a few months. A position trader is typically exposed to greater risk because of the potentially large price swings that can occur over longer periods. Most of the speculative strategies detailed in subsequent chapters will involve position traders. They can assume one of two types of strategies, which are described next.

Speculative Strategies for Position Traders

pure speculative strategy
The trader assumes either a long or short position in a futures contract alone.

The first strategy that may be employed by a position trader is a *pure speculative strategy* (sometimes called an *outright* or *naked* position), in which the trader assumes either a long or short position in a futures contract alone. For example, a position trader who forecasts a general rise in equity values might assume a long position in a deferred stock index futures contract. If the forecast proves correct, then the percentage return to such a strategy can be quite lucrative.

However, if equity prices take a sharp decline unexpectedly, then the trader's loss on this outright position can be substantial. As usual, leverage offers both a large potential upside and downside. To reduce this exposure, more risk-averse position traders will engage in *futures spreads,* which entail assuming a position in two different futures contracts in order to control downside risk exposure. The positions are selected so that their returns are negatively correlated, implying that an unexpected loss in the focal futures position will be offset, at least in part, by a gain on the other futures position.

intracommodity futures spread
It consists of both a long and short position on the same futures commodity, but with different delivery dates.

For example, suppose that the speculator in the preceding example also assumed a short position in the nearby stock index futures contract. He or she now holds both a long and short position on the same futures commodity, but with different delivery dates. This is known as an *intracommodity futures spread.* If the forecast of a bullish stock market proves correct, there will be a gain on the long futures position. Moreover, the gain on this position should be greater than the corresponding loss on the short position, because the more deferred futures price will be more sensitive to stock market changes than the nearby futures price. Thus, the position trader profits. However, should the market decline, the gain on the short position would partially offset the unexpected loss on the focal, long futures position. This way the day trader is protected somewhat from downside loss. We can conclude that the intracommodity futures spread is less risky than a pure speculative position.

Another type of popular spread is the *intercommodity futures spread*, where a long and short position are undertaken in two different futures commodities having the same delivery date. For example, a position trader might assume a long position in a British pound futures contract with December delivery, while contemporaneously shorting a December Deutsche mark futures contract. Here the speculator is wagering that the dollar will depreciate relative to the pound, and will depreciate against the pound more than against the mark. If the forecast proves correct, the spread will be profitable; the gain on the long pound position will be greater than the loss on the short mark position. However, if the dollar should actually appreciate over the period, then the loss on the long position will be offset, all or in part, by the gain on the short position. Again, the intercommodity futures spread is less risky than an outright position.

Still other spreading strategies will be examined in subsequent chapters. However, these alternative spreads merely represent combinations of intra- and intercommodity futures spreads. The most important thing to recognize is that such spreads expose position traders to less risk than pure speculative strategies. Indeed, most position traders employ spreads rather than outright positions. Since spreads are less risky, the margins required for spreads by most clearinghouses are lower than for outright positions.

intercommodity futures spread
It consists of a long and short position in two different futures commodities having the same delivery date.

PRICE DISCOVERY

Price discovery represents the third major function of futures contracts. Equation 6.28 of Chapter 6 represented the equilibrium futures price under the expectations approach and under the assumptions of risk aversion and nonconstant interest rates. It was demonstrated that the futures price differed from the expected future spot price at contract delivery because of three premia: a term premium, a reinvestment rate premium, and a hedging premium. If each of these premia are small, or their net effect on the equilibrium futures price is small, then the futures price can be regarded as a consensus forecast by market traders of the subsequent spot price expected to prevail at contract delivery.

Empirical evidence does imply that the premia are small. For example, a well-cited study by B. Cornell and M. Reinganum (1981) reports that foreign exchange forward and futures prices are statistically and economically indistinguishable. From our discussion in Chapter 6, such similarity between forward and futures prices necessitates small premia.

The major results of Cornell and Reinganum are replicated in Exhibit 7.1. From Column 1, only two of the mean differences in forward and

Exhibit 7.1:
Currency Future versus
Forward Prices: Statistics
for Price Differentials

Currency	Maturity	(1) Mean (Fut-For)[c]	(2) t-statistic	(3) Mean (Ask-Bid)	(4) N
British Pound[a]	1	− 3.26	0.39	15.65	21
	2	− 13.91	− 1.48	15.24	21
	3	− 32.16[d]	− 4.05	19.83	21
	6	− 17.89	− 1.54	20.16	21
Canadian Dollar[a]	1	− 4.73[e]	− 2.59	4.18	21
	2	1.16	0.74	4.06	21
	3	0.51	0.57	4.72	21
	6	− 1.37	− 0.37	5.01	21
German Mark[a]	1	0.26	0.27	4.82	21
	2	1.31	1.15	5.00	21
	3	2.01	1.55	4.56	21
	6	0.34	0.19	5.42	21
Japanese Yen[b]	1	3.06	1.54	5.29	20
	2	− 1.91	− 1.24	6.79	17
	3	− 1.71	− 0.70	7.22	20
	6	− 4.17	− 0.95	10.79	17
Swiss Franc[a]	1	3.99	1.15	6.53	20
	2	− 0.47	− 0.23	6.35	21
	3	0.71	0.26	5.83	21
	6	2.16	1.04	7.89	20

[a]Each unit is $.0001
[b]Each unit is $.000001
[c]Forward price is equal to the observed bid price plus one-half the mean bid-ask spread.
[d]Significant at 1% level
[e]Significant at 5% level

futures prices are significantly different from zero for their sample: the three-month maturity for the British pound and the one-month maturity for the Canadian dollar. And even in these two cases the mean difference is less than twice the bid-ask spread in the forward market, implying an inability to conduct profitable arbitrage on average.

The evidence of small or nonexistent premia in equilibrium futures prices suggests that futures prices are reasonably unbiased estimates of actual future spot prices. In short, it is probably safe to say that futures prices accurately reflect the market's consensus forecast of spot prices expected to prevail at delivery. Using futures prices as predictors of subsequent spot prices therefore appears warranted.

However, the *usefulness* of forecasts based on futures prices also depends on two extraneous factors: (1) the actual need for future price information and (2) the accuracy and cost of alternative forecasting methods and services, especially when compared to forecasts based on futures prices.

The Need for Future Price Information

Individuals and corporations alike frequently require information about future spot prices for consumption and investment planning. As an example, consider a manufacturer of a line of paper goods who is currently developing a brochure for next year's product line. The brochure must contain item prices, implying that the manufacturer will need to estimate future production costs. Since lumber is a major input factor of production, the paper-line manufacturer requires an estimate of the future price of lumber to safely and competitively establish finished product prices. One way to obtain such an estimate, of course, is to employ observable futures prices for lumber. Thus, the manufacturer employs the futures price as a means for discovering information about subsequent spot prices. This helps to determine production costs and, in turn, the prices that will have to be charged for finished goods. Of course, at this point the manufacturer might strongly consider the use of the futures contract to ensure subsequent lumber costs via an anticipatory hedge.

Accuracy and Cost Issues

Unfortunately, researchers have documented that the forecasts from the futures market exhibit substantial errors. For instance, R. Kolb, G. Gay, and J. Jordan (1983) report that futures prices for a variety of underlying spot assets have large forecast errors, often exceeding 10 percent. In an examination of the accuracy of currency futures prices, R. Levich (1981) reports an average forecast error of nearly 15 percent. In an efficient market, such errors are undoubtedly caused by spot price changes associated with *unanticipated* informational events.[3]

These large errors cast doubt on the reliability of forecasts based on futures prices. However, a reasonable counter-argument for using futures is raised by the following question: "Do alternative forecasting techniques or services provide better estimates of future spot prices?" In general, the answer to this question is no. For example, R. Levich (1981) finds that only five of sixteen professional forecasting services outperformed the simple futures price when predicting the future spot exchange rates of four foreign currencies. Details of his findings are

---

[3]Such large errors also suggest that the bias issue associated with the hedging and other premia potentially contained in futures prices is of small consequence when extracting subsequent spot-price estimates.

presented in Chapter 8. This and similar evidence, combined with the relative expense of forecasting services and alternative forecasting techniques, suggests that futures prices are as good or better than any other demonstrated methods for predicting subsequent spot prices.

Futures provide a low-cost and comparatively accurate means of estimating subsequent spot prices.

SUMMARY

The three major functions of futures contracts are hedging, speculating, and price discovery. The four issues faced by futures hedgers are whether to go long or short, which futures commodity to employ, which delivery month to employ, and how many contracts to trade. Typically, the resolutions of these issues share a common origin—to minimize basis risk.

Speculators engage in futures trading to exploit forecasts of spot-price movements. By trading in the futures market, rather than the spot market itself, they can maximize the percentage returns to their forecasts (presuming they are correct). Pure speculation consists of assuming a sole position in a selected futures contract. However, to control risk somewhat, speculators often employ intra- or intercommodity futures spreads. Such spreads are less risky than pure speculation, since the returns to the focal futures position are offset, at least in part, by the returns to the other futures position.

As regards price discovery, manufacturers, investors, and consumers can utilize published futures prices in order to estimate subsequent spot-asset costs. Since futures prices are largely determined by investor expectations of future spot prices, a futures price may be regarded as the market's (approximate) consensus forecast of the spot price expected to prevail at contract expiration. Although the futures price may be a biased estimate due to premia associated with risk aversion and nonconstant interest rates, and although several studies document rather large forecasting errors for futures prices, these prices are useful for price discovery; alternative forecasting techniques have not demonstrated an ability to consistently outperform them, and such alternatives are typically more expensive.

In the next three chapters we focus on specific financial futures contracts and examine the three functions of futures markets in greater detail.

Selected References

Block, S., and T. Gallagher. "The Use of Interest Rate Futures and Options by Corporate Financial Managers." *Financial Management* 15 (August 1986):73–78.

Conroy, R., and R. Rendleman. "Pricing Commodities When Both Price and Output Are Uncertain." *Journal of Futures Markets* 3 (Winter 1983):439–450.

Cornell, B., and M. Reinganum. "Forward and Futures Prices: Evidence from the Foreign Exchange Markets." *Journal of Finance* 36 (December 1981):1035–1045.

Ederington, L. "The Hedging Performance of the New Futures Market." *Journal of Finance* 34 (March 1979):157–170.

Figlewski, S. "Hedging Performance and Basis Risk in Stock Index Futures." *Journal of Finance* 39 (July 1984):657–669.

Gay, G., W. Hunter, and R. Kolb. "Liquidity and Capital Requirements for Futures Market Hedges." *Review of Research in Futures Markets* 4 (1985):1–25.

Hill, J., and T. Schneeweis. "Risk Reduction Potential of Financial Futures for Corporate Bond Positions" in *Interest Rate Futures: Concepts and Issues*, ed. R. Kolb and G. Gay. Richmond, Vir.: R. F. Dame, 1982.

Johnson, L. "The Theory of Hedging and Speculating in Commodity Futures Markets." *Review of Economic Studies* 27 (October 1960):139–151.

Kolb, R., G. Gay, and J. Jordan. "Futures Prices and Expected Future Spot Prices." *Review of Research in Futures Markets* 2 (1983):110–123.

Levich, R. "Currency Forecasters Lose Their Way." *Euromoney* (August 1983):140–147.

McCabe, G., and C. Franckle. "The Effectiveness of Rolling the Hedge Forward in the Treasury Bill Futures Market." *Financial Management* 12 (Summer 1983):21–29.

Rose, L. "Commodity Money Management" in *Handbook of Futures Markets*, ed. P. Kaufman. New York: Wiley, 1984.

Silber, W. "Marketmaker Behavior in an Auction Market: An Analysis of Scalpers in Futures Markets." *Journal of Finance* 39 (September 1984):937–953.

Smith, C., and R. Stulz. "The Determinants of Firms' Hedging Policies." *Journal of Financial and Quantitative Analysis* 20 (December 1985):391–405.

Stulz, R. "Optimal Hedging Policies." *Journal of Financial and Quantitative Analysis* 19 (June 1984):127–140.

Tamarkin, R. *The New Gatsbys: Fortunes and Misfortunes of Commodity Traders.* New York: William Morrow and Company, Inc., 1985.

Questions and Problems

1. What are the three major functions of futures contracts? Of these, which is the primary function?

2. What factors must the futures hedger consider when choosing a hedging strategy? Explain how each decision is consistent with minimizing basis risk.

3. Explain the difference between a short hedge and a long hedge, and provide an example of each.

4. Define a cross hedge. When would a trader engage in one?

5. Define the hedge ratio. What three hedge ratios will we consider in subsequent chapters?

6. Why is basis risk less than the risk associated with an unhedged position? Be sure to discuss the issue of correlation among spot and futures prices when addressing this question.

7. Using the profit equation (Equation 7.2), explain why a growing (i.e., strengthening) basis benefits a short hedge and impairs a long hedge.

8. For each of the following hedge termination dates, identify the appropriate contract delivery to minimize basis risk. Assume that the delivery cycle is March, June, September, and December.

    a. February 2
    b. April 11
    c. October 19

9. What is the fundamental difference between a trader who employs futures for hedging and a trader who employs futures for speculation?

10. Why might a speculator engage in a futures contract rather than transacting in the spot market itself?

11. Why might a position trader engage in a futures spread rather than a pure speculative position? Explain your answer.

12. What is the difference between an intra- and intercommodity futures spread? Provide examples of each.

13. Why are margin requirements typically lower for spreaders than for pure speculators?

14. The existence of football games allows individuals to engage in betting. But, clearly, football games do not exist for the purposes of gambling. To this extent, how is a futures contract akin to a football game?

15. Under what conditions is it safe to state that futures prices represent the market's consensus forecast of subsequent spot prices?

16. Explain how a furniture manufacturer might employ lumber futures to forecast finished product prices.

17. Does empirical evidence generally find that futures prices are good predictors of subsequent spot prices? If not, does this necessarily imply an inefficient market? Why or why not?

18. Does empirical evidence generally find that futures prices are inferior predictors relative to alternative forecasting techniques and services?

8

CURRENCY FUTURES

A currency futures contract entails an obligation to trade a fixed number of units of foreign currency at a specified rate of exchange on a specified future delivery date. The first listed currency futures contracts began trading on the International Monetary Market division of the Chicago Mercantile Exchange on May 16, 1972. Since that time, volume in currency futures trading has grown substantially. This chapter begins with a description of current exchange rate regimes, followed by a description of the currency futures market and the determination of currency futures prices. Applications of hedging exchange rate risk and speculating on currency movements are presented. A summary of empirical evidence concerning currency futures is also provided.

A **currency futures contract** entails an obligation to trade a fixed number of units of foreign currency at a specified rate of exchange on a specified future delivery date.

CURRENT EXCHANGE RATE REGIMES

In order to settle international transactions of goods and services among international investors, multinational corporations, and foreign governments, the currency of one country often must be converted into the currency of another. The rate at which one currency can be currently converted into another is called the *spot exchange rate*. For instance, a U.S. dollar might be convertible into Swiss francs (SF) at the current exchange rate of $0.60/SF1. That is, it costs $0.60 to purchase one Swiss franc. Conversely, it costs SF1.67 (SF1/$0.60) to purchase one U.S. dollar.

In 1944 the allied nations of World War II signed the Bretton Woods Agreement in which each nation fixed its currency value in relation to the gold content of the U.S. dollar. For instance, originally it cost $35 and £17.5 to purchase an ounce of gold. Thus, the dollar-pound exchange rate was $2.00/£1. Foreign governments were obligated to maintain these rates within a very narrow range defined by *gold points*. They did so by buying and selling currencies through their central banks. Hence, exchange rates were, for all intents and purposes, fixed.

The integrity of the Bretton Woods Agreement ultimately depended on the true gold value of the U.S. dollar relative to that of the other participating currencies. In the late 1960s, however, the United States was experiencing a historically large international trade deficit brought on by record inflation. Because of increased inflation and interest rates, the dollar was losing value in the eyes of foreign trade partners.[1] In short, foreign nations felt that the dollar's value was being artificially maintained. Some countries (e.g., France) even threatened to convert their dollar holdings into gold. This was politically undesirable for the United States at the time, since the U.S.S.R. was a major gold-exporting nation.

Because of these pressures, the dollar was devalued by the U.S. government in 1971 and, contemporaneously, the dollar's convertibility into gold was suspended. The United States had gone off the gold standard established by the Bretton Woods Agreement and so the agreement itself had broken down. In late 1971 the Smithsonian Agreement attempted to resurrect the gold standard by allowing for a wider range of variation of exchange rates. However, this agreement was short-lived, and the fixed exchange rate regime was in disrepair by March of 1973.

After the breakdown of the Bretton Woods and Smithsonian agreements, participating nations were free to adopt a variety of exchange rate strategies, namely, the freely-floating, managed-floating, peg, and joint-floating strategies. Under a *freely-floating strategy*, a currency's value is free to vary according to supply and demand conditions in the foreign exchange market. Thus, an exchange rate is determined much the way the price of any commodity in a free competitive marketplace is determined.

Under a *managed-floating strategy*, the free movement offered by the free-float is tempered somewhat by government intervention. Most countries have adopted this strategy. The currency is allowed to vary with supply and demand forces, but through central bank intervention a nation may attempt to influence the rate of exchange. For instance, the U.S. Federal Reserve Bank attempted to depreciate the dollar several times during President Reagan's administration so as to improve the United States international trade deficit.

A number of smaller countries still employ a *peg strategy*. Here the currency is managed such that it is "pegged" (highly correlated) with another, often floating currency.

Finally, some nations participate in a *joint-float*. The best known example of this strategy involves the European Economic Community

---

[1]Later in this chapter, when we discuss interest rate parity, it will be apparent that higher domestic rates of inflation are associated with depreciation of domestic currencies.

Exhibit 8.1
Members of the European
Economic Community

Belgium (B)	Luxembourg (LUX)
Denmark (D)	Netherlands (N)
France (F)	Portugal (P)
Greece (GR)	Spain (SP)
Ireland (IR)	United Kingdom (UK)
Italy (IT)	West Germany (WGR)

Notes: Turkey applied to join the EEC in April 1987. Cyprus and Malta are expected to apply for membership.

(EEC). The twelve member nations that currently comprise the EEC, which include several major U.S. trading partners, are listed in Exhibit 8.1. Most member nations agree to maintain between-member exchange rates within 1.125 percent of established levels. However, the values of member currencies are free to float with nonmember currencies such as the U.S. dollar. The result is that the dollar tends to exhibit similar correlation with each member currency.[2] Because of the visual appearance of a time graph giving changes in the value of EEC currencies with respect to the dollar, this joint-float arrangement was often referred to as the "snake in the tunnel" prior to 1973. Since then, and because of the dollar's floating nature, the arrangement is sometimes called the "snake in the lake".

Exchange Rate Determination

Most countries can be described as operating under a managed-float exchange rate system whereby the exchange rate of two national currencies is determined by the interplay of supply and demand, with occasional "shocks" caused by central bank intervention. The demand for foreign exchange comes from governments attempting to devalue their currencies or, more generally, from international investors, multinationals, and governments who make payments to foreigners in foreign currencies. The transactions may involve the import of goods and services or the purchase of foreign securities. These are listed on the debit side of the domestic (U.S.) balance of payments. The supply of foreign currency derives from exporting goods and services and selling financial securities to foreigners or, on occasion, from a domestic

---

[2]This common correlation has important implications for currency futures trading. In particular, it facilitates cross-hedging strategies. Indeed, since the West German mark is the keystone currency within the EEC, mark futures (and options) tend to dominate currency futures (and options) trading. Traders must be careful when cross hedging EEC currencies, however, since on occasion member currencies are realigned. For instance, the Italian lira and French franc have been devalued several times since 1979.

Integration of the European Economic Community

With the removal of import tariffs in the late 1960s, and agreement on a common agricultural policy of price supports and production management, the nations comprising the European Economic Community (EEC) completed an important step toward the creation of a unified or Common Market. The total integration of EEC trading and markets is scheduled for completion in 1992, when the last of all non-tariff barriers are to be removed, including divergent national product standards, differential rates of value-added taxes and excise duties, and other barriers such as customs controls.

The collective thought among EEC nations is that integration will result in a united and strong Europe because of the economic gains, which will take two basic forms: (1) savings from unnecessary costs and lost opportunities associated with barriers and fragmented markets and (2) revenues from enhanced competitiveness in world markets and from synergies created by cooperative linkages.

Although full integration is not scheduled to occur until the end of 1992, nearly 150 acts to remove non-tariff barriers have been adopted and the expected effects of full integration are already being capitalized in financial markets. For instance, integration is resulting in higher correlations among member exchange rates as their economies become more interdependent. The exhibit on page 151 presents correlations

for rates of exchange among members for the two periods 1977–1982 and 1983–1988. The overall average correlations are 0.50 and 0.54, respectively, suggesting more common rate movements among EEC nations.

There are at least two consequences of this enhanced integration for U.S.–based foreign investors and multinationals who are considering hedging their exchange rate exposure. First, the effectiveness of cross hedging should be increased; as EEC-member currencies move more closely through time, the additional basis risk associated with cross hedging should be reduced. Thus, using a mark futures contract to hedge, say, a position in lira should be more effective as integration continues. Second, protectionism that may arise to help ensure smooth integration among members may actually increase the variability of member exchange rates relative to the dollar. EEC politicians and business leaders in many member nations feel that the early winners of 1992 may be the U.S. and Japanese multinationals with global marketing and manufacturing clout. As a result, signs are appearing that the EEC integration may be ushered in with broad European protectionism. If this occurs, and if it makes member currencies more volatile against the dollar, then U.S.–based foreign investors and multinationals may have to step up their overall hedging policies.

government's attempt to appreciate its currency by flooding the market with reserves of foreign exchange. These items are listed on the credit side of the balance of payments.

In Figure 8.1 the dollar-pound, that is $/£ (domestic-foreign), exchange rate is measured on the vertical axis, while the volume of pounds (foreign exchange) demanded and supplied is measured on the horizontal axis. The demand schedule, DD, is downward-sloping. A higher exchange rate makes imported U.K. goods more expensive to U.S. buyers since they need to pay more dollars to obtain pounds. Thus, the demand for imports, and, in turn, foreign exchange, is reduced. The supply schedule, SS, is upward-sloping for essentially the same reason. A higher exchange rate makes U.S. exports relatively cheaper to U.K. buyers, stimulating U.S. exports and in turn increasing the supply of pounds.

The equilibrium level of the rate of exchange, $S_0(\$/£)$, is determined by the intersection of the supply and demand schedules. Shifts of these

Correlation Coefficients Of Exchange Rates Across Member Nations											
	B	D	F	GR	IT	IR	LUX	N	P	SP	UK
D	.95 .99										
F	.89 .97	.90 .96									
GR	.77 .64	.77 .62	.84 .69								
IT	.92 .96	.91 .95	.94 .95	.83 .70							
IR	−.92 −.93	−.93 −.93	−.89 −.93	−.83 −.63	−.91 −.88						
LUX	.99 .99	.95 .99	.90 .97	.77 .64	.92 .97	−.92 −.93					
N	.94 .98	.95 .98	.91 .98	.78 .64	.92 .97	−.92 −.93	.94 .99				
P	.65 .89	.60 .89	.68 .88	.62 .56	.59 .86	−.64 −.86	.66 .90	.64 .88			
SP	.62 .77	.66 .73	.60 .77	.59 .55	.61 .78	−.61 −.69	.62 .77	.63 .78	.47 .79		
UK	.69 .66	.68 .64	.67 .70	.67 .63	.68 .62	−.76 −.79	.69 .66	.71 .68	.64 .60	.53 .61	
WGR	.94 .99	.94 .99	.92 .97	.80 .64	.92 .97	−.93 −.91	.94 .99	.98 .99	.66 .88	.63 .75	.72 .64

Notes: The top number in each cell is the correlation coefficient for the period 1977–1982, while the bottom number in each cell is that for the period 1983–1988. The overall average correlation coefficients for each subperiod are 0.4996 and 0.5383, respectively.

schedules result in exchange rate changes (i.e., new equilibria) and are caused by changes in domestic real income, prices, tastes, and various other factors. For example, a rapid growth in U.S. real income causes an increase in the demand for imports, thereby shifting the entire demand schedule rightward as given by $D'D'$ in Figure 8.2. The new equilibrium level of the exchange rate is at $S_1(\$/\pounds)$, indicating a U.S. dollar depreciation. As another example, higher U.K. inflation will encourage Britons to import more U.S. goods, thereby shifting the entire supply schedule rightward as given by $S'S'$ in Figure 8.3. The consequence is a U.S. dollar appreciation; the new equilibrium rate is $S_2(\$/\pounds)$.

Exchange Rate Risk

The factors underlying the supply and demand schedules include money supplies, real incomes, prices, inflation, interest rates, and the

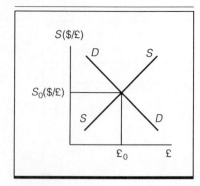

Figure 8.1
Equilibrium Dollar-Pound
Exchange Rate

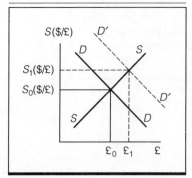

Figure 8.2
Dollar Depreciation

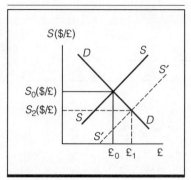

Figure 8.3
Dollar Appreciation

like. These determinants (and expectations concerning these determinants) change continually, forcing exchange rates to adjust continually to new equilibria.

Exhibit 8.2 gives foreign exchange rates quoted at 3 P.M. Eastern time by Bankers Trust Company and published by *The Wall Street Journal*. These are selling rates that apply to trading among banks in the amount of $1 million or more. The rates are wholesale prices, meaning that retail prices banks offer to customers on smaller amounts are usually more expensive. The first column in Exhibit 8.2 lists the name of the country and its currency, while the next four columns give the exchange rates for the two trading days preceding publication. Here rates are for Wednesday, March 1, 1989, and Tuesday, February 28, 1989, respectively. These exchange rates are given by two definitions: (1) "U.S. $ equivalent," which expresses the number of U.S. dollars required per unit of foreign currency; and (2) "currency per U.S. $," which is the units of foreign currency per U.S. dollar. These two definitions should be reciprocals. However, transaction costs or the markup between the buying and selling rates by banks may frustrate the reciprocity of the relationship.

Exhibit 8.2 shows that spot exchange rates change over time. For example, the $/£ rate changed from $1.7445 on Tuesday, February 28, to $1.7225 on Wednesday, March 1. This represents a 1.26 percent depreciation in the pound relative to the dollar. Other exchange rate changes are similarly interpreted. To provide a longer-term perspective on rate movements, Exhibit 8.3 portrays the value of the U.S. dollar relative to six major trading currencies for the period of 1976 through 1988. Since 1985 there has been a general depreciation in the dollar's value.

Fluctuations in exchange rates associated with the advent of the current floating-rate system have introduced *exchange rate risk* into international goods and security markets. This is the risk associated with uncertainty of future currency values. For instance, a U.S. multinational

Exchange rate risk is the risk associated with uncertainty of future currency values. Currency futures represent a vehicle for helping international investors manage their exchange rate risk.

Exhibit 8.2

Foreign Exchange Rates

EXCHANGE RATES

Wednesday, March 1, 1989

The New York foreign exchange selling rates below apply to trading among banks in amounts of $1 million and more, as quoted at 3 p.m. Eastern time by Bankers Trust Co. Retail transactions provide fewer units of foreign currency per dollar.

Country	U.S. $ equiv. Wed.	U.S. $ equiv. Tues.	Currency per U.S. $ Wed.	Currency per U.S. $ Tues.
Argentina (Austral) ...	.035984	035984	27.79	27.79
Australia (Dollar)	.8025	.8010	1.2461	1.2484
Austria (Schilling)	.07733	.07799	12.93	12.82
Bahrain (Dinar)	2.6525	2.6525	.37700	.37700
Belgium (Franc)				
Commercial rate	.02595	.02616	38.52	38.21
Financial rate	.02585	.02606	38.67	38.35
Brazil (Cruzado)	1.0101	1.0101	.99000	.99000
Britain (Pound)	1.7225	1.7445	.5805	.5732
30-Day Forward	1.7181	1.7400	.5820	.5747
90-Day Forward	1.7092	1.7318	.5850	.5774
180-Day Forward ...	1.6986	1.7207	.5887	.5811
Canada (Dollar)	.8345	.8340	1.1983	1.1990
30-Day Forward	.8333	.8329	1.2000	1.2006
90-Day Forward	.8307	.8304	1.2037	1.2042
180-Day Forward ...	.8268	.8266	1.2094	1.2097
Chile (Official rate) ...	.0040733	.0040733	245.50	245.50
China (Yuan)	.268622	.268622	3.7227	3.7227
Colombia (Peso)	.002919	.002919	342.50	342.50
Denmark (Krone)	.1398	.1408	7.1485	7.0985
Ecuador (Sucre)				
Floating rate	.001897	.001897	527.00	527.00
Finland (Markka)	.2327	.2343	4.2970	4.2665
France (Franc)	.1598	.1613	6.2555	6.1995
30-Day Forward	.1599	.1613	6.2521	6.1960
90-Day Forward	.1600	.1615	6.2467	6.1895
180-Day Forward ...	.1603	.1618	6.2375	6.1795
Greece (Drachma)	.006472	.006518	154.50	153.40
Hong Kong (Dollar) ...	.128205	.128196	7.8000	7.8005
India (Rupee)	.0653167	.0653167	15.31	15.31
Indonesia (Rupiah) ...	.0005777	.0005777	1731.00	1731.00
Ireland (Punt)	1.4715	1.4715	.6795	.6795
Israel (Shekel)	.5503	.5503	1.8170	1.8170
Italy (Lira)	.0007382	.0007447	1354.50	1342.75
Japan (Yen)	.007803	.007883	128.15	126.85
30-Day Forward	.007838	.007920	127.58	126.25
90-Day Forward	.007913	.007994	126.37	125.08
180-Day Forward ...	.008022	.008110	124.65	123.29
Jordan (Dinar)	1.8968	1.8968	.5272	.5272
Kuwait (Dinar)	3.4809	3.4809	.2872	.2872
Lebanon (Pound)	.002032	.002032	492.00	492.00
Malaysia (Ringgit)	.36516	.36569	2.7385	2.7345
Malta (Lira)	2.9806	2.9806	.3355	.3355
Mexico (Peso)				
Floating rate	.0004260	.0004260	2347.00	2347.00
Netherland (Guilder) .	.4820	.4858	2.0745	2.0584
New Zealand (Dollar) .	.6190	.6205	1.6155	1.6116
Norway (Krone)	.1485	.1494	6.7330	6.6925
Pakistan (Rupee)	.05208	.05208	19.20	19.20
Peru (Inti)	.0008123	.0008123	1231.00	1231.00
Philippines (Peso)	.048309	.048309	20.70	20.70
Portugal (Escudo)	.006654	.006654	150.28	150.28
Saudi Arabia (Riyal) ..	.2665	.2665	3.7510	3.7510
Singapore (Dollar)	.5174	.5175	1.9325	1.9320
South Africa (Rand)				
Commercial rate	.4032	.4032	2.4800	2.4800
Financial rate	.2513	.2525	3.9800	3.9600
South Korea (Won)	.0014858	.0014858	673.00	673.00
Spain (Peseta)	.008764	.008764	114.10	114.10
Sweden (Krona)	.1582	.1592	6.3180	6.2795
Switzerland (Franc) ...	.6369	.6425	1.5699	1.5562
30-Day Forward	.6392	.6449	1.5643	1.5504
90-Day Forward	.6435	.6492	1.5538	1.5402
180-Day Forward ...	.6502	.6562	1.5378	1.5239
Taiwan (Dollar)	.03603	.03603	27.75	27.75
Thailand (Baht)	.039525	.039525	25.30	25.30
Turkey (Lira)	.0005235	.0005235	1910.00	1910.00
United Arab (Dirham) .	.2722	.2722	3.6725	3.6725
Uruguay (New Peso)				
Financial	.002079	.002079	481.00	481.00
Venezuela (Bolivar)				
Floating rate	.02544	.02544	39.30	39.30
W. Germany (Mark) ..	.5442	.5486	1.8375	1.8225
30-Day Forward	.5457	.5502	1.8325	1.8174
90-Day Forward	.5486	.5533	1.8226	1.8079
180-Day Forward	.5577	.5578	1.7930	1.7925

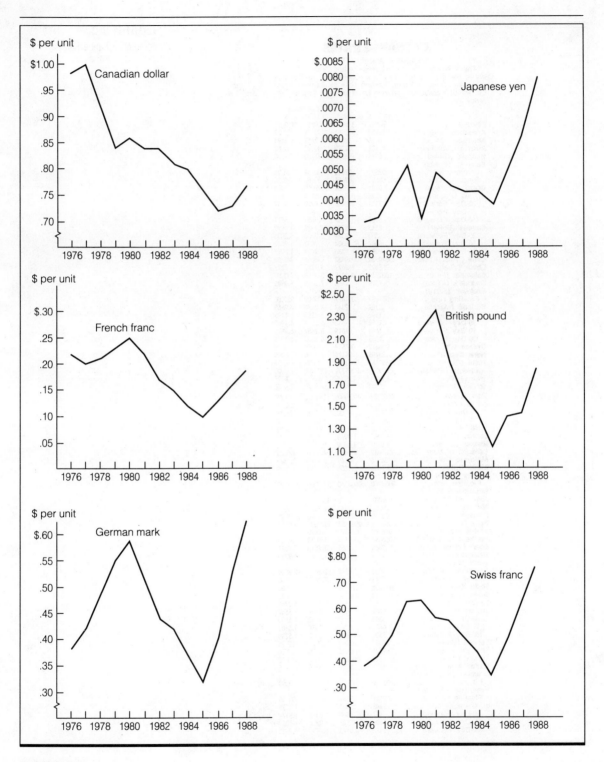

Exhibit 8.3
U.S. Dollar Value, 1976–1988

Standard Deviations of Exchange Rate Movements

J. Madura and E. Nosari (1984) analyze the standard deviations of eight foreign currencies using monthly data for the period of 1970 through 1983. The results of their analysis allow three noteworthy inferences: First, some currencies fluctuate more than others. For example, the West German mark exhibited a standard deviation for the entire period (3.97 percent) four times as great as that for the Canadian dollar (0.99 percent). Thus, an international investor need not be as concerned with hedging a position in Canadian dollars. Second, the variability of each currency was not stationary through time. For example, the mark's standard deviation during the 1973–1975 subperiod was substantially higher than in any other subperiod. Third, average volatility after the 1970–1972 subperiod was greater. Consequently, the advent of the floating exchange rate system in 1973 resulted in increased exchange rate risk.

	TIME PERIOD:				
Currency	1970–83	1970–72	1973–75	1976–79	1980–83
Belgian franc	3.09%	.88%	3.79%	3.13%	3.21%
British pound	2.47	1.31	1.96	2.31	3.42
Canadian dollar	.99	.73	.69	1.27	.99
Dutch guilder	3.03	.85	3.97	3.09	3.02
French franc	3.97	1.05	3.88	2.67	3.54
German mark	3.97	.75	7.54	1.72	2.90
Japanese yen	2.63	1.13	2.61	2.95	3.11
Swiss franc	3.18	1.02	4.64	2.65	3.20
Average	2.81	.99	3.64	2.47	2.92

corporation seeking to repatriate foreign currency at a future date is exposed to the risk of an unexpected U.S. dollar appreciation over the period. Such an appreciation would result in fewer dollars upon the repatriation of the foreign currency.

It is not a coincidence that currency futures trading began on the International Monetary Market division (IMM) of the Chicago Mercantile Exchange about the same time that exchange rates began to float. Currency futures represent a vehicle for helping international investors manage their exchange rate risk. With the introduction of floating rates, and thus increased exchange rate risk, there arose a demand for such a currency hedging instrument. Currency futures contracts were introduced to satisfy this demand. Later in this chapter we will illustrate a number of currency hedging applications.

Exhibit 8.4

Contract Specifications for IMM Currency Futures

Currency	Delivery Months	Contract Size	Minimum Price Fluctu- ation	Initial Margin	Maintenance Margin
Australian dollar	Jan/Mar/Apr June/July/ Sept/Oct/ Dec/Spot	AD100,000	$0.001/AD1	$2,000	$1,500
British pound	"	BP62,500	$0.005/BP1	$2,000	$1,500
Canadian dollar	"	CD100,000	$0.001/CD1	$ 900	$ 700
Deutsche mark	"	DM125,000	$0.0001/DM1	$2,000	$1,500
French franc	"	FF250,000	$0.00005/FF1	$2,000	$1,500
Japanese yen	"	JY12,500,000	$0.000001/JY1	$1,500	$1,000
Swiss franc	"	SF125,000	$0.0001/SF1	$2,000	$1,500
European unit currency	Mar/June/ Sept/Dec	ECU125,000	$0.001/ECU1	See	IMM

Notes: There are no daily price limits. The IMM removed daily price limits on currency futures in February, 1985. Trading hours are approximately 7:20 A.M. to 1:20 P.M. central time. Delivery takes place on the third Wednesday of the contract month. The last trading day is the second business day before delivery. The margin on spreads is zero. Hedge margins are usually less than the speculative margins shown here.

CURRENCY FUTURES MARKET

The IMM is the largest trader of listed currency futures contracts. Exhibit 8.4 provides contract sizes and other details. Presently futures trading is conducted on seven foreign currencies and the *European Currency Unit (ECU)*, which is a weighted-average index of the exchange rates of the nations comprising the European Economic Community. Exhibit 8.4 shows that contract sizes vary by underlying currency, as do margin requirements and minimum price fluctuations. There are currently no daily price limits on IMM currency futures.

IMM currency futures trading has grown substantially over the past decade, as shown by Figure 8.4. Over the period of 1977 through 1986, annual volume rose from 586,428 to 19,032,264 contracts. This represents a thirty-two-fold increase. Exhibit 8.5 presents trading volume by underlying currency for the year 1986. The mark leads all other currencies, with the pound, yen, and Swiss franc also exhibiting active volume. Futures on the French franc and ECU are inactive.

Exhibit 8.6 presents settlement prices for currency futures contracts traded on the IMM on March 1, 1989. Also presented are the day's high and low prices as well as other information, such as each

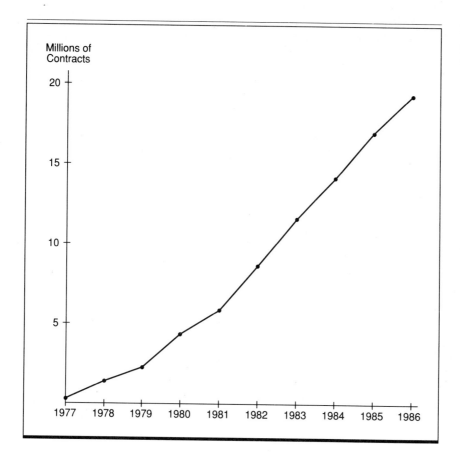

Figure 8.4:
Annual Trading Volume for
IMM Currency Futures

contract's daily volume and current open interest. For instance, the settlement price for Canadian dollar futures, September 1989 delivery, was $0.8270/CD1. Volume was 7,477 for all CD futures, and open interest was 30,683 contracts, down 366 contracts from the previous trading day.

Besides the IMM, currency futures are traded on a number of other organized exchanges worldwide. These include the Philadelphia Exchange, the Singapore International Monetary Exchange, the Sydney Futures Exchange, the London International Financial Futures Exchange (LIFFE), and several others. The LIFFE is the second largest trader of listed currency futures contracts.

The international nature of currency futures, combined with their trading on several overseas exchanges, has resulted in some unique market phenomena. For instance, the Philadelphia Exchange has recently begun evening trading of currency futures in an attempt to capture volume from overseas exchanges. The Chicago Mercantile Exchange will soon institute its after-hours electronic futures trading system called *Globex*, designed to capture business from Japanese and other Far East futures traders, including currency futures traders. British pound and Japanese yen futures contracts may be traded on the IMM and the position closed on the Singapore International Monetary Exchange. Finally, it is now possible to trade deutsche mark futures around-the-clock, since such futures are traded on several organized exchanges worldwide.

Exhibit 8.5:

Trading Volume by Currency, 1986

Currency	Contract Volume	Percent of Total Volume
British pound	2,701,330	14.19%
Canadian dollar	734,071	3.86
Deutsche mark	6,582,145	34.58
French franc	2,685	0.01
Japanese yen	3,969,777	20.86
Swiss franc	4,998,430	26.26
European currency unit	43,826	0.23

Note: The Australian dollar futures contract did not trade until 1987.

Exhibit 8.6:

Settlement Prices for IMM Currency Futures

FUTURES

	Open	High	Low	Settle	Change	Lifetime High	Lifetime Low	Open Interest
JAPANESE YEN (IMM) 12.5 million yen; $ per yen (.00)								
Mar	.7820	.7825	.7804	.7811	− .0086	.8590	.7439	43,395
June	.7934	.7939	.7917	.7926	− .0088	.8485	.7500	6,581
Sept	.8050	.8050	.8031	.8035	− .0089	.8580	.7690	599
Dec	.8188	.8188	.8130	.8142	− .0092	.8635	.7735	159

Est vol 31,125; vol Tues 24,230; open int 50,738, −1,326.

	Open	High	Low	Settle	Change	Lifetime High	Lifetime Low	Open Interest
W. GERMAN MARK (IMM) − 125,000 marks; $ per mark								
Mar	.5441	.5456	.5431	.5450	− .0046	.6240	.5304	61,979
June	.5485	.5502	.5475	.5498	− .0045	.5975	.5359	6,967
Sept	.5530	.5545	.5525	.5542	− .0045	.5977	.5411	441
Dec	....	....		.5588	− .0048	.5895	.5460	112

Est vol 30,217; vol Tues 25,465; open int 69,499, +894.

	Open	High	Low	Settle	Change	Lifetime High	Lifetime Low	Open Interest
CANADIAN DOLLAR (IMM) − 100,000 dirs.; $ per Can $								
Mar	.8352	.8363	.8320	.8343	+ .0012	.8476	.7570	22,884
June	.8314	.8321	.8280	.8303	+ .0012	.8433	.7670	6,901
Sept	.8275	.8285	.8260	.8270	+ .0012	.8385	.7990	624
Dec	.8250	.8250	.8250	.8239	+ .0012	.8370	.7920	231

Est vol 7,477; vol Tues 11,600; open int 30,683, −366.

	Open	High	Low	Settle	Change	Lifetime High	Lifetime Low	Open Interest
BRITISH POUND (IMM) − 62,500 pds.; $ per pound								
Mar	1.7270	1.7274	1.7172	1.7212	− .0202	1.8536	1.6320	22,152
June	1.7140	1.7140	1.7040	1.7076	− .0202	1.8370	1.6200	3,193

Est vol 12,498; vol Tues 11,543; open int 25,427, +1,143.

	Open	High	Low	Settle	Change	Lifetime High	Lifetime Low	Open Interest
SWISS FRANC (IMM) − 125,000 francs-$ per franc								
Mar	.6373	.6392	.6357	.6379	− .0063	.7735	.6260	27,472
June	.6448	.6461	.6427	.6448	− .0064	.7145	.6319	3,747
Sept	.6500	.6525	.6495	.6514	− .0064	.7210	.6380	404

Est vol 27,698; vol Tues 19,355; open int 31,709, +60.

	Open	High	Low	Settle	Change	Lifetime High	Lifetime Low	Open Interest
AUSTRALIAN DOLLAR (IMM) − 100,000 dirs.; $ per A.$								
Mar	.7995	.8020	.7967	.8004	+ .0024	.8880	.7630	2,757
June	.7865	.7895	.7850	.7875	+ .0022	.8725	.7800	711
Sept	....	....		.7765	+ .0022	.7819	.7750	187

Est vol 449; vol Tues 666; open int 3,655, −56.

Currency Futures and Forward Markets Compared

A large interbank market in currency forward contracting presently exists. According to most estimates, it is about twenty times larger than the IMM currency futures market as measured by the dollar amount of underlying currency traded. Like a futures contract, currency forward contracts represent obligations to trade foreign exchange at a specified price at a specified future date. However, the currency forward market offers private contracts that are tailored to the specific needs of clients. Large banks and private currency brokers network and trade electronically to meet the client's needs. For example, if a multinational corporation (MNC) requires a forward contract with a maturity of two or more years, it can obtain the contract through direct telephone negotiations with its bank (although the bank often requires compensating balances to insure the MNC's obligation).

Currency forward contracts are generally valued at $1 million or more of underlying foreign exchange in order to facilitate the transactions of large multinationals. In Exhibit 8.2 the *forward rates* presented for selected currencies are for forward contracts with thirty-, sixty-, or ninety-day maturities. For example, the thirty-day forward rate for British pounds was $1.7181 on Wednesday, March 1. This rate was lower than the current spot rate, $1.7225/£1, implying that the market anticipates the pound to depreciate against the dollar over the next thirty days. When this occurs we say that the foreign currency is selling at a *forward discount*. On the other hand, the thirty-day forward rate for Swiss francs, $0.6392/SF1, is greater than the spot rate, $0.6369/SF1, meaning that the foreign currency is selling at a *forward premium*. Since market forces determine forward rates, the market anticipates the Swiss franc to appreciate against the U.S. dollar over the period.

Currency futures contracts represent an institutionalized form of currency forward contracting. Although there are many similarities between the two contracts, important differences distinguish them. Exhibit 8.7 provides a comprehensive comparison of the interbank currency forward market and the IMM currency futures market. Note the following differences between the two markets:

- Qualified public speculation is encouraged for futures but not for forwards.
- Currency forward contracts are accessible only to large creditworthy customers that deal in foreign trade.
- Contract sizes and delivery dates are standardized for currency futures but are tailored for forward contracts.
- The majority of forward contracts are settled by delivery of the underlying currency, whereas the majority of futures contracts are settled through reversing trades.
- Currency futures trading entails posting margin and requires daily resettlement, whereas forward trading does not require a margin deposit and entails no cash flows until contract expiration.

Exhibit 8.7:

Differences between Currency
Forward and Futures Markets

	Forward	Futures
Size of Contract	Tailored to individual needs.	Standardized.
Delivery Date	Tailored to individual needs.	Standardized.
Participants	Banks, brokers, and multinational companies. Public speculation not encouraged.	Banks, brokers and multinational companies. Qualified public speculation encouraged.
Security Deposit	None as such, but compensating bank balances or lines of credit required.	Small security deposit required.
Clearing Operation	Handling contingent on individual banks and brokers. No separate clearinghouse function.	Handled by exchange clearinghouse. Daily settlements to the market price.
Marketplace	Over the telephone, worldwide.	Central exchange floor with worldwide communications.
Regulation	Self-regulating.	Commodity Futures Trading Commission; National Futures Association.
Liquidation	Most settled by actual delivery; some by offset, at a cost.	Most by offset; very few by delivery.
Transaction Costs	Set by "spread" between bank's buy and sell prices.	Negotiated brokerage fees, quoted for entry and exit.

Perhaps the most important difference between these markets is the fact that forward contracting entails no margin deposit. This is because very large, creditworthy investors participate in the market. Only such investors may participate because, with currency forwards, no cash flow occurs until contract delivery. Thus, investors must be creditworthy, since large exchange rate changes can take place over the entire life of the forward contract. This contrasts markedly with currency futures contracts, which are resettled each trading day. Because of that daily resettlement and the posting of margins, less creditworthy investors can participate in currency futures contracting.

Ultimately, the two contracts differ with respect to the timing of their cash flows. With futures, flows are daily, whereas with currency forwards no cash flow occurs until delivery. The differences in cash flows result in different market clienteles. This is the primary reason why the currency futures market can exist alongside the much larger currency forward market. This difference in cash flows also has consequences for currency forward versus futures pricing, which we investigate next.

DETERMINING THE CURRENCY FUTURES PRICE

Recall from Chapter 6 that futures prices can be determined by one of two related approaches. First, they can be determined from an application of the carrying-charge theory of futures prices. Second, futures prices arise from expectations concerning future asset values. In this part we discuss the application of both approaches to determining currency futures prices. We also compare the pricing of currency forward and futures contracts.

Interest Rate Parity (IRP)

Interest rate parity (IRP) is the theory that the currency futures price (i.e., future exchange rate) differs from the spot exchange rate by an amount that reflects the interest rate differential between two currencies. IRP represents the currency market's version of the carrying-charge theory of futures prices.

Recall from Chapter 6 the three costs of carrying an asset forward in time: storage costs, transportation costs, and financing costs. For currency, storage costs are nominal, and the foreign exchange can be used to purchase interest-bearing foreign assets. Thus, for currency, the storage costs, expressed as a fraction of the spot exchange rate, are $-r_f$, where r_f is the foreign rate of interest. Foreign exchange is said to exhibit a negative cost of storage. Also, transportation costs are nominal. It costs almost nothing to wire transfer foreign exchange in order to settle a futures contract. Letting the financing costs be represented by r, the applicable U.S. rate of interest, from Equation 6.1, we have:

(8.1)
$$CC = -r_f + 0 + r = r - r_f.$$

The cost of carrying foreign exchange forward in time is therefore the interest rate differential $r - r_f$. Using Equation 6.3, the carrying-charge model, we have

(8.2)
$$_T f_0 = S_0 e^{(r - r_f)T}.$$

Equation 8.2 states that the currency futures price, $_T f_0$, differs from the current spot exchange rate, S_0, by an amount that reflects the interest rate differential between the two currencies. This is the equation of interest rate parity. Thus, the IRP theorem is simply the foreign exchange market's version of the standard carrying-charge theory of futures prices. For currency, the basis is $e^{(r - r_f)T}$. If $r > r_f$, then $_T f_0 > S_0$, and the foreign currency is said to sell at a future premium. A premium currency exhibits an overall positive cost-of-carry. On the other hand, if $r < r_f$, then $_T f_0 < S_0$, and the foreign currency is said to sell at a future discount against the dollar. A discount currency exhibits an overall negative cost-of-carry. Finally, if $r = r_f$, then $_T f_0 = S_0$, and the foreign currency is said to sell at a future parity with the dollar.

Interest rate parity is the theory that the future exchange rate differs from the spot exchange rate by an amount that reflects the interest rate differential between two currencies. It represents the currency market's version of the carrying-charge theory of futures prices.

Covered Interest Arbitrage (CIA)

Recall from Chapter 6 that the carrying-charge model is derived from arbitrage restrictions present in well-functioning markets. *Covered interest arbitrage (CIA)* is the arbitrage trading strategy that ensures that interest rate parity holds. Thus, CIA is the currency market's version of the arbitrage strategy underlying the carrying-charge theory of futures prices. Indeed, CIA, developed by the famous economist John Maynard Keynes, is perhaps the earliest arbitrage trading strategy ever devised.

Suppose that you observe the following:

- The current spot rate is $1.75/£1.
- The futures price, with ninety days until delivery, is also $1.75/£1.
- The interest rate on a U.S. Treasury bill, with ninety days until maturity, is 8 percent.
- The interest rate on a U.K. Treasury bill, with ninety days until maturity, is 10 percent.

Since the spot and futures rates are equal, but the two interest rates on comparable-risk Treasury bills differ, there is a clear violation of IRP. To exploit this violation you would undertake one form of CIA. Specifically, you would

- Borrow, say, $1, at the rate of 8 percent for ninety days. Thus, you will owe $1.0202 in ninety days:

$$\$1 exp(.08)(.25) = \$1.0202.$$

- Convert the $1 into £0.5714, and invest this amount of pounds in U.K. Treasury bills, earning 10 percent for ninety days. Thus, you will have £0.5859 in ninety days:

$$£0.5714 exp(.10)(.25) = £0.5859.$$

- Enter into a short futures contract to sell £0.5859 in ninety days for $1.75/£1.

By delivering your £0.5859 in ninety days for $1.75/£1, you will have $1.0253. After repaying your dollar loan, $1.0202, you will be left with positive proceeds of $0.0051. These proceeds represent arbitrage profit in a frictionless market. In other words, ignoring transaction costs, taxes, restrictions on short selling, and the like, you have made money. Notice that this strategy is essentially one example of the cash-and-carry strategy described in Chapter 6.

As arbitragers conduct CIA, interest and exchange rates will be bid up or down until the violation no longer exists, that is, until IRP is restored. In this illustration, borrowing dollars in the United States will tend to exert upward pressure on U.S. interest rates; converting dollars to pounds will exert upward pressure on the spot exchange rate; purchasing U.K. Treasury bills will exert downward pressure on U.K. interest rates; and entering into a short futures contract will exert downward pressure on the futures price.

It is difficult to forecast the exact magnitude of each interest and exchange rate change. However, in frictionless markets the resulting rates due to arbitrage restrictions should be such that IRP holds. Finally, it is important to note that there are other forms of CIA. For instance, suppose that the interest rates in the above illustration were reversed such that $r = .10$, and $r_f = .08$. Then the appropriate trading strategy would involve borrowing pounds, investing in U.S. Treasury bills, and undertaking a long position in BP futures. This is an illustration of a reverse cash-and-carry strategy.

Assumptions Underlying IRP

A number of assumptions underlie the IRP theorem. First, it is assumed that no taxes or transaction costs exist. As discussed in Chapter 6, the effect of these market frictions is to create a band within which the carrying-charge model holds. Therefore, we have to anticipate that IRP holds only approximately in light of taxes and transaction costs. Second, the IRP theorem assumes that there are no restrictions on short selling. In the preceding illustration we were able to borrow dollars at the U.S. Treasury bill rate of 8 percent. In other words, we were able to short sell the U.S. Treasury bill; we reversed our short position when we repaid the dollar loan. Since short-selling restrictions exist in actual markets, as discussed in Chapter 6, then, again, IRP should only approximately hold. Third, it is assumed that the two financial assets involved exhibit the same risk. In the above illustration, U.S. and U.K. Treasury bills were used, since these instruments exhibit the same approximate risk class. If the two financial assets involved have different risks, then IRP may not hold, because investors will demand a risk premium on the higher-risk asset. For example, it may appear that a CIA opportunity exists if one utilizes BBB-rated U.S. corporate bonds and U.K. Treasury bonds. However, the "profits" from such an "arbitrage" may be nothing more than normal compensation for investing in the higher-risk corporate bonds.

Fourth, the IRP theorem assumes that securities are perfectly divisible. For instance, in the above illustration we were able to enter into a short BP futures contract to sell £0.5859. Therefore, to the extent that securities are indivisible, and we cannot fully hedge our currency position, IRP only approximately holds.[3] Finally, the IRP theorem assumes that interest rates are constant. This assumption is what allowed us to compute, with certainty, the amount of dollars owed and the amount of pounds received in the future in the above illustration. Without this critical assumption, our arbitrage trading strategy is not

---

[3]Actually, M. Klein (1973) shows that perfect security divisibility follows from the assumption of zero transaction costs.

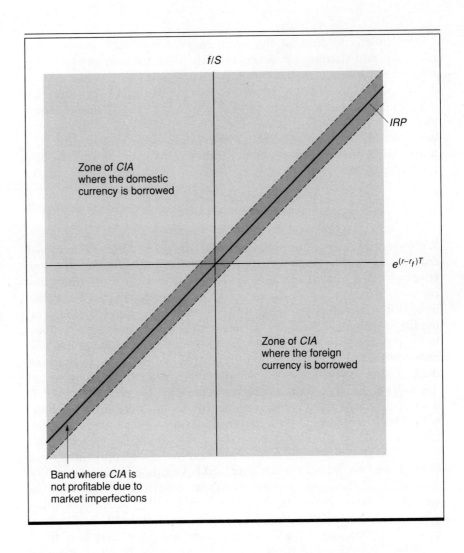

risk-free. For example, if interest rates were nonconstant, and the interest rate differential $r - r_f$ actually inverted over the ninety-day period, then our trading strategy might have resulted in losses.[4]

The overall effect of market frictions, such as taxes and transaction costs, restrictions on short selling, differences in security risks, imperfectly divisible securities, and nonconstant interest rates, is to cause IRP to be somewhat inexact. That is, Equation 8.2 holds only to an approximation. Figure 8.5 portrays the IRP band within which arbitrage is not profitable because of market imperfections.

---

[4]We will further discuss the critical assumption of constant interest rates in the next subsection, where we compare currency forward and futures prices.

Currency Forward and Futures Prices Compared

Currency forward and futures contracts are similar in many respects. Consequently, close relations must obtain between their prices if arbitrage opportunities are to be precluded. Differences in prices may arise, however, particularly because of their different cash flow patterns.

Recall that futures prices may be determined by expectations concerning future asset values. Using this approach, we can compare the pricing of currency forward and futures contracts. Specifically, recall from Equation 6.25 that under risk neutrality the futures price, $_Tf_0$, is given by

(8.3)
$$_Tf_0 = E(\tilde{S}_T) + \frac{COV(\tilde{R}, \tilde{S}_T)}{(1 + _TY_0)^T}.$$

In our present context, Equation 8.3 states that under risk neutrality the currency futures price is equal to the expected future spot exchange rate at contract delivery plus an additional term that depends on the covariance between $\tilde{R}$, the product of one-day interest rates, and $\tilde{S}_T$, the rate of exchange. Recall that this additional term represents a reinvestment rate premium that arises because of the daily resettlement procedure in futures markets.

Since no daily resettlement occurs in the currency forward market, however, currency forward prices should not exhibit a reinvestment rate premium. Thus, we can conclude that under risk neutrality the currency forward price, $_TF_0$, is

(8.4)
$$_TF_0 = E(\tilde{S}_T).$$

In other words, the forward rate represents an unbiased estimate of the actual future spot rate expected to prevail at contract delivery if investors are risk neutral. The difference between the currency futures and forward prices is the reinvestment rate premium, $COV(\tilde{R}, \tilde{S}_T)$, under risk neutrality.

The existence of daily resettlement in the futures market drives a wedge between currency forward and futures prices under risk neutrality. However, daily resettlement is only one necessary condition for price differences. Another is that interest rates be nonconstant over time. To illustrate this, suppose that interest rates are constant. The reinvestment rate premium will therefore be zero, since $COV(\tilde{R}, \tilde{S}_T)$ is zero.[5] Thus, the futures price will equal $E(\tilde{S}_T)$, which is the forward price under risk neutrality if interest rates are constant: $_Tf_0 \equiv _TF_0 = E(\tilde{S}_T)$ if $\bar{R}$. Recall that the IRP theorem assumes that interest rates are constant.

---

[5]The covariance of a constant, $\tilde{R}$, with any random variable, $\tilde{S}_T$, is zero. See Chapter 2.

The Interest rate parity (IRP) theorem applies to both currency forward and futures prices under risk neutrality.

Thus, we can conclude that the IRP theorem applies to both currency forward and futures prices under risk neutrality.[6]

Under risk aversion now, the futures price is given by the following (see Equation 6.28):

$$(8.5) \qquad _{T}f_0 = E(\tilde{S}_T)\frac{[E(\tilde{R})]}{[(1 + {}_TY_0)^T]} + \frac{COV(\tilde{R},\tilde{S}_T)}{(1 + {}_TY_0)^T} + COV(\tilde{M}_T,\tilde{R}\tilde{S}_T).$$

Recall that this equation states that the futures price differs from the expected spot exchange rate at contract delivery because of three premia: (1) a term premium association with liquidity premia in the term structure, (2) the reinvestment rate premium associated with daily resettlement, and (3) a hedging premium that derives from the relation between the futures payoff and an investor's marginal rate of substitution.

Since currency forwards do not entail daily resettlement, only a hedging premium applies to currency forwards under risk aversion. The currency forward price is[7]

$$(8.6) \qquad _{T}F_0 = E(\tilde{S}_T) + (1 + {}_TY_0)^T COV(\tilde{M}_T,\tilde{S}_T).$$

The difference between Equations 8.5 and 8.6 is the difference between currency futures and forward prices under risk aversion.

HEDGING WITH CURRENCY FUTURES

Currency futures can be used by international investors and multinational corporations to hedge *transaction exposure*—the degree to which the value of future cash transactions can be affected by exchange rate fluctuations. By providing an efficient means of hedging transaction exposure, currency futures promote international trade and enhance our social welfare.

Let us examine two hedging applications that entail currency futures contracts. The first is a long hedge (or anticipatory hedge) in which a U.S. importer contracts to take delivery of a foreign product in the future. Since payment for the import is made at the future delivery date and in the foreign currency, the importer will assume a long futures position in order to protect against an unexpected dollar

Transaction exposure represents the degree to which the value of future cash flows can be affected by exchange rate fluctuations.

---

[6]This illustrates the intimate relation between the two approaches to determining futures prices: the carrying-charge theory approach and the expectations approach. By invoking the assumptions of risk neutrality and constant interest rates, we see that the two approaches yield the same futures price.

[7]Under risk neutrality, investors have linear utility functions and therefore constant marginal rates of substitution. Hence, the covariance term $COV(\tilde{M}_T,\tilde{S}_T)$ in Equation 8.6 would be zero, and Equation 8.6 reduces to Equation 8.4. Again, under risk neutrality we see that the currency forward price is equal to $E(\tilde{S}_T)$.

depreciation. In the second hedging application, a U.S.–based multinational corporation undertakes a short hedge to protect against an unexpected depreciation in a foreign currency that is scheduled to be repatriated in the near future. This way the party in question minimizes its transaction exposure. The futures position is undertaken such that its returns are negatively correlated with the party's spot-currency position.

In the following two examples, we employ the *naive hedge ratio*. Recall from Chapter 7 that in this ratio, the hedger assumes a one-to-one correspondence between the spot and futures positions. That is, the number of units of foreign exchange underlying the futures contracts is approximately equal to the number of units of foreign exchange entailed in the preexisting spot position. Although the naive hedge ratio is simple in construction, it is generally effective in reducing exchange rate risk when applied to currency futures transactions, because spot and futures exchange rates are very highly correlated. In subsequent chapters dealing with stock index and interest rate futures contracts, we will employ more sophisticated hedge ratios in our hedging illustrations.

A Long Hedge

Assume that a U.S. watch retailer contracts on March 1 to take delivery of 1,000 Swiss watches, at SF375 each, on September 5. The importer must pay SF375,000 upon delivery and wants to immunize against an unexpected appreciation in the franc relative to the U.S. dollar. Such an appreciation in the franc would make the dollar cost of the watches greater. The current $/SF spot exchange rate is $0.6369/SF1 (see Exhibit 8.2).

Since francs will be paid in early September, the U.S. watch retailer uses the September SF futures contract. This contract is currently priced at $0.6514/SF1 (see Exhibit 8.6). At 125,000 francs per contract, the price of one contract is $81,425. The importer wants to hedge francs currently worth $238,837.50 (SF375,000 × $0.6369/SF1) with contracts priced at $81,425. The retailer decides to take a long position in three SF futures contracts with September delivery ($238,837.50/$81,425), in this way hedging each unit of foreign currency owed with a unit in the futures market. Thus, the importer is implicitly utilizing the naive hedge ratio.

Suppose that on September 5, the $/SF spot rate is $0.6600/SF1. This means the franc has appreciated, and the retailer must pay more for the watches: $0.6600/SF1 × SF375,000 = $247,500. Fortunately, however, the franc futures price has increased to $0.6750/SF1, or $84,375 per contract (assumed). The franc futures price increased because the spot price increased, and spot and futures prices are very highly positively correlated for foreign currencies.

The retailer enters a reversing trade on the three contracts, earning $8,850 [3 × ($84,375 − $81,425)]. The long futures position has therefore covered all of the additional cost of the watches ($247,500 − $238,837.50 = $8,662.50) due to the franc's appreciation. Also, the

March 1:	Spot rate is $0.6369/SF1.
	Cost of 1,000 watches is SF375,000.
	September SF futures price is $0.6514/SF1.
	Buy (long) three September SF futures contracts.
September 5:	Spot rate is $0.6600/SF (assumed).
	Cost of 1,000 watches is $247,500.
	September SF futures price is $0.6750/SF1 (assumed).
	Enter a reversing trade (sell three contracts).
Results:	Profit on watch import is −$8,662.50.
	Profit on futures transaction is $8,850.00
	Net profit is $187.50.

retailer has realized a profit of $187.50 ($8,850 − $8,662.50) on the entire transaction, which is summarized in Exhibit 8.8.

The degree of loss due to the franc's appreciation that is covered by the long futures position depends critically on the subsequent spot and futures rates realized on September 5. However, as long as the spot and futures rates move in the same direction, the long hedge will succeed in reducing at least part of the retailer's loss on the watch import.[8] The long position in the futures contract effectively introduces negative correlation with the preexisting spot position. If the franc had actually depreciated over the period, there would have been a loss on the long futures position that would have offset some or all of the gain on the watch import.

A Short Hedge

Assume that a U.S.–based multinational corporation (MNC) has a West German subsidiary expected to generate earnings of DM260,000 at the end of the operating quarter, March 31. The U.S. MNC wants to repatriate the marks at that time. The current spot rate (March 1) is $0.5442/DM1 (see Exhibit 8.2). The current June DM futures price is $0.5498/DM1 (see Exhibit 8.6). The U.S.–based MNC would like to hedge against an unexpected depreciation in the mark. It will use DM futures with June delivery, since this is the first active contract with delivery after March 31.

---

[8]Currency spot and futures price changes are very highly correlated. Most studies report correlation coefficients of 0.90 or higher. Also, according to IRP, we see that spot and futures prices are directly related: $\partial_T f_0 / \partial S_0 = e^{(r - r_f)T} > 0$.

Since there are DM125,000 per contract traded on the IMM, each contract's current price is $68,725. The MNC wants to hedge marks currently worth $141,492 ($0.5442/DM1 × DM260,000) with contracts priced at $68,725 each. The number of contracts is 2.06 ($141,492/$68,725). Given the inability to sell fractional shares of a futures contract, the MNC decides to take a short position in two June DM futures contracts. In this way, it nearly hedges each unit in the spot market (DM260,000) with one unit in the futures market (DM250,000).

Suppose that on March 31 the $/DM spot rate is $0.5400/DM1. The mark has therefore depreciated, and the U.S.–based MNC receives fewer dollars upon repatriation: $140,400 = $0.5400/DM1 × DM260,000. Fortunately, however, the June DM futures price also decreased to $0.5475/DM1, or $68,437.50 per contract (assumed). The U.S. firm enters a reversing trade and they realize a profit on the two contracts of $575 [−2 × ($68,437.50 − $68,725)]. Thus, the short futures position covered part of the loss (−$1,092 = $140,400 − $141,492) on the spot position due to the mark's unexpected depreciation. Exhibit 8.9 summarizes the transaction.

As with the long hedge just described, the short hedge was effective in protecting the MNC against loss due to unfavorable exchange rate movements. This is because the short hedge introduced negative correlation with the MNC's preexisting spot position. Although numerous other hedging applications could be provided here, each would work in this manner. That is, the currency hedger simply identifies an appropriate futures position that assures against extreme losses due to adverse currency fluctuations. This is accomplished by assuming a futures position whose returns offset that on the spot position.

Exhibit 8.9:
A Short Hedge

March 1:	Spot rate is $0.5442/DM1.
	Anticipate repatriating DM260,000 on March 31.
	June DM futures price is $0.5498/DM1.
	Short (sell) two June DM futures contracts.
March 31:	Spot rate is $0.5400/DM1 (assumed).
	Repatriate marks for $140,400.
	June DM futures price is $0.5475/DM1 (assumed).
	Enter a reversing trade (buy two contracts).
Results:	Profit on repatriation is -$1,092.
	Profit on futures transaction is $575.
	Net profit is −$517.

SPECULATING WITH CURRENCY FUTURES

The IMM encourages qualified public speculation involving currency futures, since such speculation is believed to result in increased market liquidity and rational pricing relations. Consider a simple speculative trade involving Canadian dollar futures. Suppose that the current (March 1) spot rate is $0.8345/CD1 (see Exhibit 8.2), and that the September CD futures price is $0.8270/CD1 (see Exhibit 8.6). If a speculator believes that the Canadian dollar will not depreciate to the degree implied by the futures price, then he will buy (long) the futures contract and subsequently undertake a reversing trade to close his naked position. To gain, the speculator must be able to reverse at a futures price, for September delivery, of $0.8270/CD1 or higher.

Figure 8.6 provides a contingency graph summarizing the speculator's position. In this example the speculator is a position trader who undertakes a naked futures position. If he is correct and can reverse at, say, a subsequent September CD futures price of $0.8400/CD1, then his proceeds are $0.0130/CD1, or $1,300 per contract. Of course, these proceeds must be sufficient to cover the transaction costs incurred—currently about $30.00 per futures contract at discount brokerage firms. Also, it is important to recognize that the $1,300 gain does not represent profit per se. Under risk aversion, the futures price includes a term premium, a reinvestment rate premium, and a hedging premium.

Recall from Chapter 7 that most futures speculators, who are position traders, tend to undertake intra- or intercommodity futures spreads, which are less risky than outright or pure speculative positions such as the one described in Figure 8.6. Following is an illustration of an intercommodity spread involving currency futures contracts—known as an *intercurrency spread*—to demonstrate a more complex speculative trade.

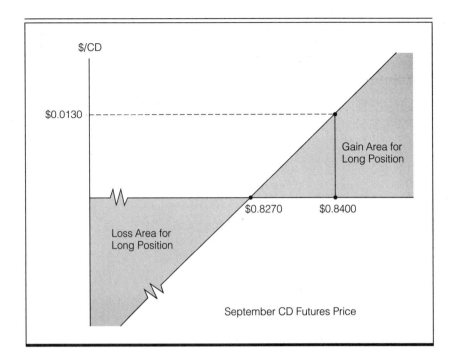

Intercurrency Spread

An intercurrency spread involves the purchase and sale of currency futures contracts with the same delivery dates but with two different underlying currencies. Suppose a position trader observes the following rates (see Exhibits 8.2 and 8.6):

	$/£	$/SF	Cross Rate (£/SF)
Spot:	1.7225	0.6369	0.3698
June Futures:	1.7076	0.6448	0.3776

The *cross rates* are generated by dividing $/SF by $/£. Further, suppose that the speculator feels that the pound will depreciate, relative to the franc, by less than that implied by the June futures cross rate, £0.3776/SF1. For instance, the speculator may feel that the pound will actually appreciate against the franc over the period.

The speculator can attempt to profit from this forecast through an intercurrency spread. Specifically, she will short the June SF futures and buy (long) the June BP futures. She must be careful to match the position sizes such that the numbers of pounds and francs are equal. If she can reverse these trades so that the futures price difference is greater than $1.0628 ($1.7076/£1 − $0.6448/SF1), then gains (ignoring taxes and transaction costs) are realized. For example, suppose that she can

Figure 8.7:
Contingency Graph for
Intercurrency Spread

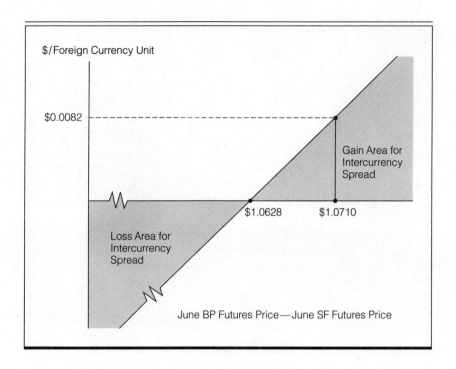

reverse at the following futures prices that exist sometime prior to June delivery: $1.7100/£1 and $0.6390/SF1. Consistent with her forecast, the pound did not depreciate greatly against the franc; so the new June futures cross rate is £0.3737/SF1. The resulting price difference is $1.0710 = $1.7100 − $0.6390, which is greater than $1.0628; thus, the speculator's gains are $0.0082 per unit of foreign currency. Figure 8.7 provides a contingency graph for this intercurrency spread. End-of-chapter problems illustrate other spreads entailing foreign exchange futures.

EMPIRICAL EVIDENCE ON CURRENCY FUTURES

This section summarizes a body of empirical evidence concerning currency futures contracts and markets. We are primarily interested in whether currency futures prices conform to the theoretical models discussed. Also, we are concerned with the hedging effectiveness of these instruments. The student is encouraged to examine the referenced articles.

Studies of Interest Rate Parity (IRP)

Empirical examinations of IRP have been conducted by R. Aliber (1973), W. Branson (1979), J. Frenkel and R. Levich (1977), and H. Stokes and

H. Neuburger (1979), among many others. These authors examined the relation between the *forward* rate premium (discount) and interest rate differentials. However, since currency forward and futures prices have been determined to be very similar (discussed later), their results apply to futures as well as forward contracts. Their results generally support IRP. While deviations from IRP are detected, they are not substantial enough to overcome the frictions involved in CIA, including taxes and transaction costs. Hence, it appears that the IRP theorem is descriptive of actual market rates of exchange.

Studies of Forward and Futures Price Differences

B. Cornell and M. Reinganum (1981) and H. Park and A. Chen (1985) examined the pricing of currency forward and futures contracts and reported no statistical or economic evidence of differences. This result implies that the term premium and reinvestment rate premium in Equation 8.5 are small.

T. Kolers and W. Simpson (1987) tested the relative forecasting accuracy of forward and futures contracts for five major foreign currencies. They found that forecast errors were statistically different, but had little economic significance. This result also implies that currency forward and futures prices are very similar.

Studies of Futures Prices as Predictors of Spot Exchange Rates

Recent studies by L. Hansen and R. Hodrick (1980), E. Fama (1984), and T. Chiang (1986) demonstrate the existence of a nonconstant hedging premium in several major foreign exchange markets. These authors examined forward rates, but presumably their analysis has implications for currency futures prices as well. Although they reported the existence of a hedging premium, this premium appears to be small. This implies that the modeling and incorporation of the premium into exchange rate forecasts will offer little improvement in predictive accuracy.

If the hedging premium is large and behaves systematically, professional forecasters should be able to model the premium and thus provide predictions superior to the simple forward or futures rate. *Euromoney* magazine conducted a survey of the accuracy of professional exchange rate forecasting services and the simple thirty-day forward rate. As Exhibit 8.10 shows, only five of the sixteen services surveyed had a smaller average forecast error than the forward rate. The best forecast service outperformed the forward rate by only 1 percent over the period.

The usefulness of currency forward and futures prices as predictors of subsequent spot rates depends on the accuracy and expense of alternative forecasting techniques. Viewed in this context, and given the results reported by *Euromoney*, the currency forward and futures prices appear

Exhibit 8.10:
Percentage Forecasting Errors for 16 Exchange Rate Forecasting Services and the 30-day Forward Rate

	$/JY	$/CD	$/£	$/DM	Average Error
1. Berkeley Consulting Group	7.4	1.2	15.1	29.1	13.2
2. European American Bank/Forex Research	3.5	1.2	17.2	31.2	13.2
3. Henley Centre/Manufacturers Hanover	7.4	6.0	11.5	28.3	13.3
4. Economic Models	8.3	4.5	14.1	28.7	13.9
5. Amex Bank	5.2	1.2	19.3	30.0	13.9
6. BI Metrics	—	1.2	10.9	32.9	15.0
7. Brown Brothers Harriman	9.6	4.5	16.7	30.4	15.3
8. Chemical Bank	7.4	6.0	18.3	31.2	15.7
9. Predex	12.3	3.6	18.3	29.1	15.8
10. Citibank	12.7	8.0	14.1	29.1	15.8
11. ContiCurrency	9.6	8.0	17.8	30.0	16.3
12. Phillips and Drew	12.7	8.0	17.8	29.1	16.9
13. Marine Midland	16.2	4.5	19.3	29.1	17.2
14. Data Resources	22.0	6.0	18.8	29.5	19.0
15. Harris Bank	12.3	8.0	25.6	33.3	19.8
16. Security Pacific	13.2	4.5	29.8	32.9	20.1
Forward Rate	4.0	6.0	18.8	28.3	14.2

to be attractive forecasting tools. However, several studies, including R. Meese and K. Rogoff (1983), R. Huang (1984), and T. Chiang (1986), report evidence of the current spot rate dominating the current forward rate in explaining movements of the future spot rate. The usefulness of currency forward and futures prices for price discovery therefore remains an open issue.

Studies of Hedging with Currency Futures

J. Hill and T. Schneeweis (1982) examined the effectiveness of currency futures contracts in reducing exchange rate risk. For four-week hedges, they found that futures reduced risk by more than 80 percent for most currencies tested. The effectiveness of shorter and longer hedges was considerably less, however. They also found that currency forward and futures hedges performed similarly for the British pound and Deutsche mark, but forward hedges were superior for the Japanese yen. R. Swanson and S. Caples (1987) report similar results for currency forward contracts.

SUMMARY

Currency futures contracts entail the obligation to trade underlying foreign exchange at a specified rate on a specified delivery date. These contracts have been traded since 1972 on the International Monetary Market (IMM) division of the Chicago Mercantile Exchange, the world's largest currency futures trader.

Currency futures are useful for helping international investors and multinational corporations hedge their exchange rate risk, which has magnified since the advent of the floating exchange rate system in 1973. These contracts can also be used to speculate on exchange rate movements and for future price discovery.

The currency futures market has grown substantially since its inception. The IMM presently trades over 20 million contracts per year. Still, the currency futures market is small when compared to the interbank forward market. Key distinctions between these markets include (1) their different cash flow patterns—the futures market requires daily resettlement—and (2) their different clienteles—the futures market encourages qualified speculation and offers trading to less creditworthy investors. This does not imply that the futures market is less safe or less efficient, however.

Interest rate parity (IRP) represents the currency market's version of the carrying-charge model. Covered interest arbitrage (CIA) ensures that this parity condition obtains. Most empirical evidence supports IRP, despite its assumption of constant interest rates. Under this assumption, currency forward and futures prices are equal, and equal the expected future spot exchange rate if investors are risk neutral. Under risk aversion, forward and futures prices should contain a hedging premium. Recent empirical evidence suggests that a hedging premium exists, but that it is small.

Selected References

Agmon, T., and Y. Amihud. "The Forward Exchange Rate and the Prediction of the Future Spot Rate." *Journal of Banking and Finance* (September 1981): 425–437.

Aliber, R. "The Interest Rate Parity Theorem: A Reinterpretation." *Journal of Political Economy* (December 1973): 1451–1459.

Branson, W. "The Minimum Covered Interest Differential Needed for International Arbitrage Activity." *Journal of Political Economy* (December 1979): 1029–1034.

Chiang, T. "On the Predictors of the Future Spot Rates—A Multi-Currency Analysis." *Financial Review* (February 1986), 69–83.

Chiang, T. "The Forward Rate as a Predictor of the Future Spot Rate—A Stochastic Coefficient Approach." *Journal of Money, Credit, and Banking* (May 1988): 212–232.

Cornell, B. "Spot Rates, Forward Rates, and Exchange Market Efficiency." *Journal of Financial Economics* (August 1977): 55–65.

Cornell, B., and M. Reinganum. "Forward and Futures Prices: Evidence from the Foreign Exchange Markets." *Journal of Finance* (December 1981): 1035–1045.

Edwards, S. "Exchange Rates and 'News': A Multi-Currency Approach." *Journal of International Money and Finance* (December 1982): 211–214.

Edwards, S. "Foreign Exchange Rates, Expectations and New Information." *Journal of Monetary Economics* (May 1983): 321–336.

Eun, C., and B. Resnick. "Exchange Rate Uncertainty, Forward Contracts, and International Portfolio Selection." *Journal of Finance* (March 1988): 197–215.

Fama, E. "Forward and Spot Exchange Rates." *Journal of Monetary Economics* (November 1984): 319–338.

Frenkel, J., and R. Levich. "Transaction Costs and Interest Arbitrage: Tranquil Versus Turbulent Periods." *Journal of Political Economy* (December 1977): 1209–1226.

Grammatikos, T. "Intervalling Effects and the Hedging Performance of Foreign Currency Futures." *Financial Review* (February 1986): 21–36.

Grammatikos, T., and A. Saunders. "Stability and the Hedging Performance of Foreign Currency Futures." *Journal of Futures Markets* (Fall 1983): 295–305.

Hansen, L., and R. Hodrick. "Forward Exchange Rates as Optimal Predictors of Future Spot Rates: An Econometric Analysis." *Journal of Political Economy* (October 1980): 829–853.

Hill, J., and T. Schneeweis. "The Hedging Effectiveness of Foreign Currency Futures." *Journal of Financial Research* (Spring 1982): 95–104.

Hodrick, R., and S. Srivastava. "An Investigation of Risk and Return in Forward Foreign Exchange." *Journal of International Money and Finance* (December 1984): 5–29.

Huang, R. "Some Alternative Tests of Forward Exchange Rates as Predictors of Future Spot Rates." *Journal of International Money and Finance* (August 1984): 153–178.

Klein, M. "The Economics of Security Divisibility and Financial Intermediation." *Journal of Finance* (September 1973): 923–931.

Kolers, T., and W. Simpson. "A Comparison of the Forecast Accuracy of the Futures and Forward Markets for Foreign Exchange." *Applied Economics* (July 1987): 961–967.

Kohlhagen, S. "The Performance of Foreign Exchange Markets: 1971–1974." *Journal of International Business Studies* (Fall 1985): 33–39.

Kohlhagen, S. "The Forward Rate as an Unbiased Predictor of the Future Spot Rate." *Columbia Journal of World Business* (Winter 1979): 77–85.

Madura, J., and E. Nosari. "Utilizing Currency Portfolios to Mitigate Exchange Rate Risk." *Columbia Journal of World Business* (Spring 1984): 96–99.

Meese, R., and K. Rogoff. "Empirical Exchange Rate Models of the Seventies: Do They Fit Out of Sample?": *Journal of International Economics* (February 1983): 3–24.

Panton, D., and M. Joy. "Empirical Evidence on International Monetary Market Currency Futures." *Journal of International Business Studies* (Fall 1978): 59–68.

Papdia, F. "Forward Exchange Rates as Predictors of Future Spot Rates and the Efficiency of the Foreign Exchange Market." *Journal of Banking and Finance* (June 1981): 217–240.

Park, H., and A. Chen. "Differences between Futures and Forward Prices: A Further Examination of the Marking-to-the-Market Effects." *Journal of Futures Markets* (Spring 1985): 77–88.

Stokes, H., and H. Neuburger. "Interest Arbitrage, Forward Speculation and the Determination of the Forward Exchange Rate." *Columbia Journal of World Business* (Winter 1979): 86–98.

Swanson, P., and S. Caples. "Hedging Foreign Exchange Risk Using Forward Exchange Markets: An Extension." *Journal of International Business Studies* (Spring 1987): 75–82.

Questions and Problems

1. Explain how interest rate parity is a special case of the more general carrying-charge model.

2. What are the assumptions that underlie the IRP theorem?

3. Under what conditions will Equation 8.5 collapse to Equation 8.3? Explain.

4. Under what conditions will Equation 8.5 collapse to Equation 8.4? Explain.

5. Assume that the covariance between the marginal rate of substitution and the exchange rate at delivery is positive. What is the current forward rate relative to the expected spot rate at delivery if investors are risk averse?

6. B. Cornell and M. Reinganum (1981) found that foreign exchange forward and futures prices are very similar. What does this suggest about the term premium and reinvestment rate premium in Equation 8.5?

7. How do currency forward and futures contracts differ with respect to cash flows? Contract settlement? Contract specifications such as size and maturity?

8. From Exhibit 8.6, what is the settlement price for a deutsche mark futures contract with September delivery? What is the settlement price of the nearby contract?

9. From Exhibit 8.4, why do you suppose that different currency futures contracts exhibit different margin requirements?

10. Suppose that a currency speculator believes that the U.K. central bank will soon begin to contract its money supply rapidly in order to slow its economy. What can the speculator do to exploit this belief?

11. Suppose that you observe the following variables:
Current Spot Rate: $1.50/£1
Current Futures Price: $1.45/£1
U.S. Treasury Bill Rate: 7%
U.K. Treasury Bill Rate: 11%
If the Treasury bills and futures contract all have six-month maturities, is there a violation of IRP? If so, how would you exploit this violation? What are the gains from your trading strategy? Do these gains necessarily represent arbitrage profits? If not, why?

12. Suppose that a U.S.–based multinational corporation with a British subsidiary decides that it will need to transfer £2 million from a bank account in

London to an account in New York. This transfer will be made early next June. Using the price information provided in Exhibits 8.2 and 8.6, how many June BP futures contracts should the MNC short (long)? Assume that a naive hedge ratio is used. What are the MNC's profit on the spot position, profit on the futures transaction, and net profit if the spot and June futures prices are $1.6720/£1 and $1.6640/£1, respectively, at the time the transfer is made?

Questions 13 through 15 refer to the following information:
On April 8, a U.S. furniture manufacturer contracts to purchase lumber from a Canadian exporter. The furniture manufacturer has agreed to pay CD3,650,000 upon delivery, which is scheduled for May 28. The current spot rate is $0.8220/CD1, and the June CD futures price is $0.8175/CD1. There are CD100,000 per futures contract.

13. How many June CD futures contracts should the importer short (long)? Assume a naive hedge ratio.

14. What is the importer's profit on the spot position if the spot rate prevailing on May 28 is $0.8382/CD1, and the new June CD futures price is $0.8340/CD1?

15. What is the importer's profit on the futures transaction, and what is the importer's overall net profit from the hedge?

16. Assume that a position trader forecasts an appreciation in the mark relative to the dollar. To profit, the trader undertakes the following intracurrency spread: long the June DM futures contract with current price $0.5498/DM1, and short the March DM futures contract with current price $0.5450/DM1. Suppose that in mid-March the trader decides to lift his spread by engaging in two reversing trades. If the new March and June DM futures prices are $0.5535/DM1 and $0.5625/DM1, respectively, what is the trader's profit per mark?

Self-Test Problems

Self-Test Problems 1 and 2 refer to the following information:

Current Spot Rate: $0.6000/SF1
Current Futures Price: $0.6200/SF1
U.S. Treasury Bill Rate: 7%
Swiss Treasury Bill Rate: 3%

ST-1. If the Treasury bills and futures contract all have six-month maturities, is there a violation of IRP?
ST-2. What are the gains from covered interest arbitrage if the assumptions underlying IRP hold?
Self-Test Problems 3 through 6 refer to the following information:
On January 8, a U.S. auto dealer agrees to purchase ten Mercedes at DM90,000 each. The dealer will take delivery on March 1. The dealer must pay DM900,000 upon delivery. The current (January 1) spot rate is $0.5800/DM1. The March DM futures price is currently $0.5950/DM1. There are DM125,000 per futures contract.
ST-3. How many March DM futures contracts should the U.S. auto dealer short (long)? Assume a naive hedge ratio.

ST-4. What is the dealer's profit on the spot position if the spot rate is $0.5990/DM1 and the March DM futures price is $0.6020/DM1 on March 1?

ST-5. What is the dealer's profit on the futures transaction?

ST-6. What is the dealer's net profit?

Solutions to Self-Test Problems

ST-1. $_{.50}f_0 = (0.6000)e^{(.07-.03)(.5)} = \$0.6121$. Violation.

ST-2. Borrow $0.6000 and convert to SF1.

You will owe $0.6214: $0.6000e^{(.07)(.5)}$

Invest SF1, and receive SF1.0151: $SF1e^{(.03)(.5)}$

Short SF1.0151, receiving $0.6294:

$$SF1.0151 \times \$0.6200/SF1.$$

Repay loan, earning $0.0080/SF1:

$$\$0.6294 - \$0.6214.$$

ST-3. Current value of marks is $522,000:

$$DM900,000 \times \$0.5800/DM1.$$

Current value of DM futures contract is $74,375:

$$DM125,000 \times \$0.5950/DM1.$$

Number of futures contracts to buy (long) is 7:

$$\$522,000/\$74,375.$$

ST-4. Profit on spot position is $-\$17,100$:

$$\$522,000 - (DM900,000 \times \$0.5990/DM1).$$

ST-5. Profit on futures transaction is $6,125:

$$(\$74,375 \times 7) - (-7 \times DM125,000 \times \$0.6020/DM1).$$

ST-6. Net profit is $-\$10,975$: $-\$17,100 + \$6,125$.

9

STOCK INDEX FUTURES

Stock index futures are cash-settled futures contracts written on indices of stock combinations. The first stock index futures contract was introduced on February 16, 1982, when the Kansas City Board of Trade began trading its Value Line Composite Index (VLCI) futures. In April of 1982, the CME began futures trading on the SP500 Stock Index. Currently, this is the most active index futures contract and represents the second most active of all futures contracts. In May of 1982, the New York Futures Exchange also introduced the trading of NYSE Composite Index futures, another highly successful contract. In the first year of trading, volume in all stock index futures was nearly 5 million contracts. Since that time annual trading volume has grown more than six-fold to over 30 million contracts. In fact, the dollar volume of underlying stocks traded in the index futures contracts actually exceeds the dollar volume of the stock market itself.

The popularity of stock index futures stems from the ability of traders to use these contracts to hedge stock positions, to speculate on general market swings, and to arbitrage the contracts against highly correlated stock portfolios. In this chapter we analyze this popular derivative security, describing the underlying stock indices and the specifications of the most actively traded stock index futures contracts. The determination of stock index futures prices is discussed, and applications of the contracts for hedging and speculating are presented. A body of empirical literature concerning these contracts is also summarized.

Stock index futures are cash-settled futures contracts written on indices of stock combinations.

STOCK MARKET INDICES

The four indices upon which futures contracts are actively traded are the SP500, the NYSE Composite Index, the Major Market Index (MMI) and the Value Line Composite Index (VLCI). Understanding how these indices are constructed is essential for determining their futures prices and for the proper application of their futures contracts for hedging and speculating.

Standard and Poor's 500 (SP500) Stock Index

The SP500 is made up of 400 industrial firms, 40 utilities, 20 transportation firms, and 40 financial institutions. The majority of these 500 stocks are listed on the NYSE. They are the stocks of some of the largest capitalized firms in the United States, and together these 500 stocks constitute about 75 percent of the total stock value of the NYSE. At any point in time t, the SP500 is constructed as follows:

$$(9.1) \qquad SP500_t = \frac{\sum_{j=1}^{500} n_{j,t} P_{j,t}}{\text{Base Value}} \times 10$$

where

$n_{j,t}$ = the number of shares outstanding for firm j at time t

$P_{j,t}$ = the share price for firm j at time t

Base Value = the average value of the index during the period 1941–1943, which was assigned an index value of 10.

This method of construction assigns a different weight to each stock, where the weight is proportional to the stock's total market value $(n_{j,t} P_{j,t})$. Thus, larger capitalized firms such as IBM represent greater shares of the SP500. Also, this method of construction ignores dividend payments, implying that the SP500 does not fully reflect the wealth received from actually holding the portfolio. The other indices to be discussed also omit dividends.

Figure 9.1 displays the sample path of the SP500 for the period of 1970 through mid-1987, when the index increased about three-fold. The absolute average daily change was about 1.38 points, or less than 0.75 percent of the average index level. This index is widely used to assess the performance of professional portfolio traders. It is a broad market index and is often used as the basis of many index funds. For these reasons, futures contracts written on the SP500 are actively traded.

New York Stock Exchange (NYSE) Composite Index

Like the SP500, the NYSE Composite Index is a value-weighted index where each stock is assigned a weight proportional to its total market value. Every stock listed on the NYSE (approximately 2,000) is used in this index's construction:

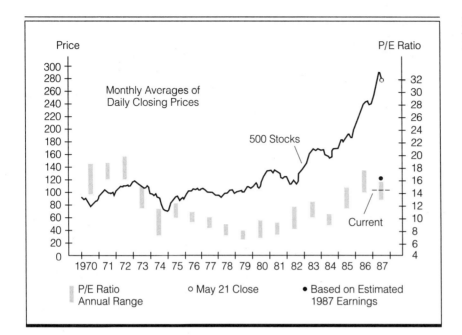

Price ... P/E Ratio

300
280
260
240
220
200
180
160
140
120
100
80
60
40
20
0

Monthly Averages of
Daily Closing Prices

500 Stocks

Current

32
30
28
26
24
22
20
18
16
14
12
10
8
6
4

1970 71 72 73 74 75 76 77 78 79 80 81 82 83 84 85 86 87

P/E Ratio   o May 21 Close   • Based on Estimated
Annual Range   1987 Earnings

$$
(9.2) \qquad \text{NYSE Composite Index} = \frac{\sum_{j=1}^{N} n_{j,t} P_{j,t}}{\text{Base Value}} \times 50,
$$

where N is the number of exchange-listed stocks, and "Base Value" is the original valuation of all shares as of December 31, 1965. Thus, the index had an initial value of 50.

Because the SP500 and NYSE Composite indices are both value-weighted and engage many of the same largest companies, they tend to be highly correlated.

Major Market Index (MMI)

Futures contracts on the Major Market Index (MMI) are traded on the Chicago Board of Trade (CBOT). Originally, the CBOT wanted to trade futures on the well-known Dow Jones Industrial Average (DJIA); however, such trading was prevented by legal restrictions. As an alternative, the CBOT created its own index upon which futures could be traded—the MMI.

The MMI is constructed to parallel the DJIA. Indeed, the two indexes exhibit a correlation coefficient of over 95 percent. Their samples paths are displayed in Figure 9.2 for a recent period. This high correlation makes the MMI futures contract an actively traded instrument; investors

Figure 9.2:
The MMI and DJIA,
1982–October, 1986

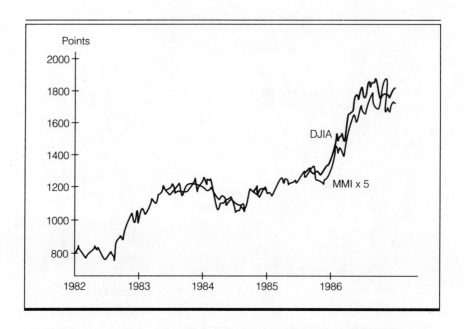

employ the contract to hedge and speculate the entire market as proxied by the well-known DJIA.

Like the DJIA, the MMI is a price-weighted index. Specifically, it is constructed as follows:

$$
\textbf{(9.3)} \qquad \mathrm{MMI}_t = \frac{\sum_{j=1}^{20} P_{j,t}}{\text{Divisor}}.
$$

Equation 9.3 indicates that the MMI is constructed using twenty stocks (many of which are the same as the thirty stocks underlying the DJIA), and that the MMI reflects only market prices rather than market values. The divisor term is necessitated by the occasional stock splits and stock dividends that affect share prices.[1]

Value Line Composite Index (VLCI)

The Value Line Composite Index (VLCI) is constructed using all NYSE-listed stocks as well as some AMEX and OTC stocks. Unlike the other

---

[1]Such a divisor is not needed by value-weighted indices such as the SP500 and NYSE Composite. Whereas stock splits and dividends affect price levels, they should not affect market values.

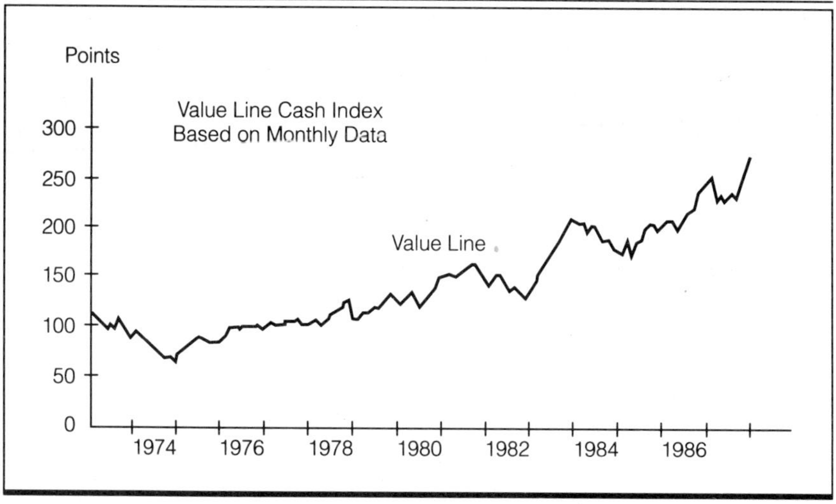

Figure 9.3:
The VLCI, 1974–1987

indices, the VLCI is geometrically averaged. Geometric averaging has the statistically attractive property that successive percentage changes in a component stock's price do not alter that stock's relative weight in the index.[2] Arithmetic averaging, on the other hand, causes the relative weight of a component stock to increase (decrease) as that stock appreciates (depreciates). The result is that a geometrically averaged index often exhibits less volatility than an otherwise similar but arithmetically averaged index.

The base value of the VLCI is 100, assigned on June 30, 1961. Given this, the index at any time t is computed as follows:

(9.4)
$$\text{VLCI}_t = \prod_{j=1}^{N} (P_{j,t}/P_{j,t-1})^{1/N} \times \text{VLCI}_{t-1},$$

where $\prod$ is a product operator. Figure 9.3 portrays the VLCI for the period of 1974 through 1987.

Unfortunately, geometric averaging makes arbitrage very impractical, because it is impossible to assemble a geometrically averaged spot portfolio; portfolios of different spot instruments (stocks) are arithmetic by definition.[3] Because of this, trading volume in VLCI futures has lagged the other, arithmetically averaged index futures contracts. This has been a problem for officials at the KCBT; the difficulties of replicat-

---

[2]This is why most government indices are geometrically averaged.
[3]Put another way, one cannot hold the logarithm of a stock.

A: Correlation Matrix

	SP500	NYSE	MMI	VLCI
SP500	1.000	0.974	0.942	0.875
NYSE		1.000	0.912	0.889
MMI			1.000	0.776
VLCI				1.000

B: Standard Deviations of Returns

Index	Annualized Standard Deviation
SP500	2.18
NYSE	2.06
MMI	2.25
VLCI	1.91

ing the index have resulted in comparatively low trading volume despite it being the first and the broadest index for futures contracts.

A Comparison of the Indices

The choice of the index futures contract for hedging will depend on the correlation between the underlying index and the asset (stock or stock portfolio) being hedged. In general, it is easier to hedge an asset with a higher correlated futures (i.e., lower basis risk). For speculation, the volatility of the index underlying the futures contract is particularly important.

Exhibit 9.1 presents a correlation matrix for the four indices for the year 1986. Also reported are the (annualized) standard deviations of returns for the indices. The SP500, NYSE Composite, and the MMI are all highly correlated. Reflecting its unique geometric averaging, the VLCI is less highly correlated with the other indices and exhibits a slightly lower standard deviation.

CONTRACT SPECIFICATIONS

The size of each stock index futures contract is some multiple of the underlying index.

Exhibit 9.2 provides contract specifications for the four stock index futures contracts. The size of each contract is some multiple of the underlying index. For the MMI, the contract multiple is $250. For the other three indices, the contract multiple is $500. So if you engage in,

Index	Contract Multiplier	Delivery Months	Initial Margin
MMI	$250	Monthly	$ 4,500
VLCI	$500	Mar/Jun/Sept/Dec	$ 4,500
SP500	$500	Mar/Jun/Sept/Dec	$10,000
NYSE	$500	Mar/Jun/Sept/Dec	$ 3,500

Exhibit 9.2:
Contract Specifications for Stock Index Futures Contracts

say, a long SP500 futures contract with futures price 300, and the day's settlement price is 302, then your margin account is credited by $1,000 upon marking-to-the-market.

Exhibit 9.2 also reveals that the MMI contract exhibits monthly settlement dates, while the other contracts have a March-June-September-December delivery cycle. Of course, actual delivery of the underlying index never occurs; instead each contract is *cash-settled*. The final settlement payment at contract expiration is determined uniquely with each contract. For instance, for the NYSE Composite futures contract, the final settlement value is determined by the difference between the daily settlement price on the last day of trading and the final value of the spot index on the last business day of the month. Of course, as with other futures contracts, positions in stock index futures are typically closed out via reversing trades rather than held to expiration.

As mentioned earlier, volume in index futures trading has grown substantially since the contract's inception in 1982 (Figure 9.4). Most of this growth can be attributable to one contract, namely, the SP500 futures contract traded on the CME. Today over 70 percent of all stock index futures trading volume is captured by the SP500 contract.

Exhibit 9.3 presents settlement futures prices for the four contracts for trading on March 1, 1989, showing that settlement futures prices were greater than the closing index level itself for all four contracts. Also, more deferred contracts had higher futures prices than the nearby contracts. Finally, Exhibit 9.3 reveals that volume and open interest for the SP500 contract were substantially greater than those for the other three contracts.

STOCK INDEX FUTURES PRICES

Both the expectations and carrying-charge approaches (discussed in Chapter 6) may be employed to determined stock index futures prices. In each case the analysis invokes a number of simplifying assumptions:

■ The stock index being hedged is identical to that underlying the futures contract.

Figure 9.4:
Growth in Stock Index
Futures Trading

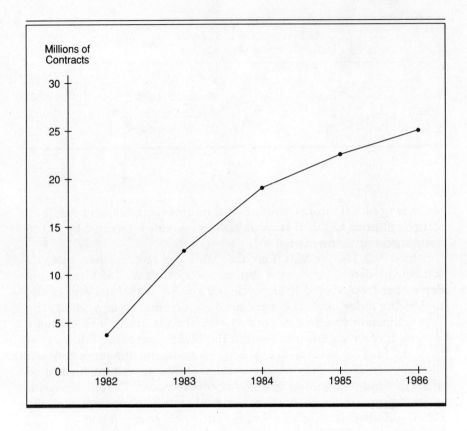

Exhibit 9.3:
Settlement Prices for
Stock Index Futures

FUTURES

S&P 500 INDEX (CME) 500 times index

	Open	High	Low	Settle	Chg	High	Low	Open Interest
Mar	290.60	291.75	286.90	288.20	− 1.45	302.64	253.90	102,690
June	294.40	295.50	290.60	291.85	− 1.50	306.20	263.80	31,914
Sept	298.80	299.30	294.80	295.60	− 1.85	309.70	271.50	779

Est vol 54,293; vol Tues 51,625; open int 135,398, +802.
Indx prelim High 290.28; Low 286.46; Close 287.11 −1.75

NYSE COMPOSITE INDEX (NYFE) 500 times index

	Open	High	Low	Settle	Chg	High	Low	Open Interest
Mar	163.40	163.90	161.20	161.85	− .95	169.80	144.25	6,074
June	165.25	165.85	163.15	163.80	− .90	·171.60	149.60	1,567
Sept	167.75	167.75	165.50	165.80	− .90	173.40	153.90	750
Dec	169.75	169.75	167.50	167.80	− .90	173.00	161.10	178

Est vol 9,006; vol Tues 7,055; open int 8,569, −27.
·The index: High 163.23; Low 161.45; Close 161.74 −.76

MAJOR MKT INDEX (CBT) $250 times index

	Open	High	Low	Settle	Chg	High	Low	Open Interest
Mar	445.00	447.00	439.10	440.65	− 2.80	468.20	404.60	3,812
Apr	449.35	449.60	442.00	443.60	− 2.75	467.25	440.50	330

Est vol 4,000; vol Tues 3,740; open int 4,190, +216.
The index: High 445.44; Low 438.35; Close 439.75 −2.85

KC VALUE LINE INDEX (KC) 500 times index

	Open	High	Low	Settle	Chg	High	Low	Open Interest
Mar	260.25	261.00	257.90	259.00	− .70	265.50	234.80	1,039
June	264.20	265.10	262.10	263.00	− .80	269.10	245.65	136

Est vol 175; vol Tues 139; open int 1,179, +3.
The index: High 259.91; Low 258.41; Close 258.61 −0.36

trading MMI futures claimed by officials at the CBOT. Although the MMI consists of just twenty stocks, it is highly correlated with the broader indices (see Exhibit 9.1). Still, the transaction costs and other difficulties associated with any index arbitrage are likely to frustrate the no-arbitrage condition underlying the carrying-charge model.

A Re-Examination of Stock Index Dividends

Exhibit 9.5 presents the daily dividend history of the SP500 for a representative quarter. Note that the actual dividend stream for a stock index is not continuous. Again, the assumption that the dividend stream can be represented by a continuous dividend yield (δ) is somewhat inexact. For this reason also, the carrying-charge model presented in Equation 9.8 will not hold exactly. Further, the expectations model presented in Equation 9.7 will be somewhat inexact due to the dividend assumption.

The Tax-Timing Option

Toward the end of a calendar year, a trader who has realized a paper loss on a stock may opt to sell the stock to reduce taxable income. On the other hand, a trader who realized a paper gain may choose to postpone a stock sale in order to push the associated tax liability into the next tax year. This is commonly known as the *tax-timing option*. With stock index futures, however, futures prices are marked-to-the-market at the end of the year for tax purposes. Hence, the futures contract exhibits no tax-timing option, as even paper gains or losses affect taxable income. Recognizing this, B. Cornell and K. French (1983) suggest that any resulting no-arbitrage pricing relation should reflect the differential role of the tax-timing option. Thus, the above models designed to yield stock index futures prices may be biased, since they omit consideration of the option.

In an empirical study, though, B. Cornell (1985) reports that the tax-timing option does not appear to influence stock index futures prices, likely because of the role played by large, tax-free institutional investors. For such investors the value of the tax-timing option on stock is zero.

PROGRAM TRADING

Equation 9.8, the carrying-charge model of stock index futures prices, results from the pressures of arbitrage strategies like those described in Exhibit 9.4. In order to properly execute the arbitrage transaction, traders must have *simultaneous* access to the futures price, the prices of the stocks making up the portfolio, their expected dividends, interest rates, and transaction costs. Further, traders must be able to transact quickly, so that prices do not change when they are applying the arbitrage strategy.

Exhibit 9.5:

SP500 Daily Dividend History, January–March 1983

January	Daily Dividend	February	Daily Dividend	March	Daily Dividend
1	-0-	1	$1,014,522,892	1	$ 475,481,425
2	-0-	2	620,986,860	2	233,877,935
3	-0-	3	706,450,730	3	211,252,855
4	244,450,655	4	1,083,636,845	4	226,646,535
5	84,333,375	5	760,013,549	5	46,388,835
6	-0-	6	-0-	6	-0-
7	-0-	7	-0-	7	-0-
8	-0-	8	302,863,260	8	221,314,295
9	-0-	9	77,539,835	9	456,911,665
10	-0-	10	79,395,850	10	12,290,885
11	125,031,970	11	493,953,535	11	160,487,000
12	14,781,315	12	-0-	12	132,207,945
13	-0-	13	-0-	13	-0-
14	77,423,915	14	-0-	14	-0-
15	1,493,800	15	-0-	15	93,392,590
16	-0-	16	147,042,660	16	24,396,600
17	-0-	17	175,652,290	17	-0-
18	110,004,260	18	229,103,802	18	77,890,880
19	56,192,560	19	33,335,295	19	-0-
20	-0-	20	-0-	20	-0-
21	-0-	21	-0-	21	-0-
22	36,231,630	22	243,098,250	22	1,156,973,290
23	-0-	23	388,689,790	23	-0-
24	-0-	24	100,333,870	24	106,333,017
25	122,280,645	25	59,752,500	25	79,197,416
26	299,047,115	26	59,209,980	26	64,933,420
27	6,999,970	27	-0-	27	-0-
28	11,502,180	28	-0-	28	-0-
29	78,875,975			29	14,167,000
30	-0-			30	236,973,080
31	-0-			31	23,754,500

Percentage of Total Dividend

January	1–15	4.6%	February	1–14	43.3%	March	1–15	18.9%
	16–31	6.1%		15–28	12.1%		16–31	15.0%
January	Total	10.7%	February	Total	55.4%	March	Total	33.9%

Despite these complexities, many large financial institutions execute arbitrage transactions, based on the carrying-charge model (Equation 9.8), involving billions of dollars each trading day. To manage the enormous data requirements involved in stock index futures arbitrage, these institutions employ computers. Real-time data from the money market, stock market, and futures market are continually fed into a computer that is programmed to detect arbitrage opportunities as given by violations of Equation 9.8. When a violation is detected, the arbitrage strategy is applied. In reality, most of these institutional arbitragers do not duplicate the index but instead purchase a smaller portfolio of stocks designed to be highly correlated with the index in question. Of course, this introduces some basis risk. The stock purchases are transacted quickly through the NYSE's computerized order-processing system known as *Designated Order Turnaround*. At contract expiration the institutions attempt to unwind their positions, selling their stocks at the closing price on the expiration date. This is accomplished by executing on-the-close orders, which instruct brokers to sell the stocks as near to closing as possible.[8]

Because these large financial institutions use computers for detecting arbitrage opportunities involving stock index futures contracts, this form of cash-and-carry arbitrage is often called *program trading*. Arguably, program trading represents the most efficient and state-of-the-art method of searching for profitable arbitrage opportunities. As such, it tends to ensure market efficiency by rapidly realigning prices so that they conform to rational pricing relations.

Program trading refers to the use of computers to monitor real-time data in order to detect profitable violations of cost-and-carry relations.

Program trading has been somewhat controversial, however, because of evidence that it results in increased market volatility about the time of contract expiration [see Stoll and Whaley (1986) in "Selected References"]. As many institutional investors engage in program trading, on-the-close orders to trade stocks near contract expiration hit the market contemporaneously. This can cause large stock price swings due to order imbalances. At one time such swings were especially pronounced during what was called the *triple witching hour*, the last hour of trading on dates when stock index futures, stock index options, and options on stock index futures all expired simultaneously. As a result, the CME altered its rules for expiration of the SP500 futures and futures options in June 1987.

Whether such expiration-based volatility is necessarily bad remains a debated issue. Clearly, market participants are generally averse to volatility. However, this temporary volatility may be viewed as nothing more than a minor spillover effect of program trading, which itself helps to ensure market efficiency, and thus benefits market participants. Besides, while evidence does exist documenting in-

---

[8]Of course, if stocks were originally sold short and index futures were purchased, an on-the-close order to purchase the stocks would have been executed.

creased volatility near contract expiration, other evidence indicates that the stock market is not more volatile, overall, since the inception of stock index futures trading in early 1982 [see Angrist (1987) in "Selected References"].

HEDGING WITH STOCK INDEX FUTURES

The fundamental economic rationale for the existence of stock index futures is that they allow equity investors to alter their risk-return profiles, thereby enhancing investor utility. As discussed in Chapters 2 and 3, a central tenet of modern portfolio theory is that diversification effectively eliminates unsystematic risk. With the introduction of stock index futures, however, equity investors can hedge against *systematic* risk. Indeed, the proper use of stock index futures contracts can eliminate nearly all systematic risk, thereby assuring diversified investors a riskless rate of return. Investors may find it desirable to reduce or eliminate systematic risk, and accept a lower or riskless return, during periods when the market is anticipated to be temporarily depressed or unusually volatile. An alternative strategy would be to liquidate stocks and reinvest in safer instruments such as U.S. Treasury bills. However, such a strategy can be unduly restrictive and entails huge transaction costs. Employing stock index futures can achieve the same goal at lower transaction costs.

In this section we describe how stock index futures can be used to reduce or eliminate systematic risk. We also describe how these derivative securities can be used to resolve conflicts between stock selectivity and market timing. We begin with an analysis of the *minimum-variance hedge ratio* for stock index futures, followed by examples of hedging applications.

Stock Index Futures Hedge

Suppose that an investor or equity portfolio manager holds an arbitrary stock portfolio whose current value is $V(0)$. Define N_S as the number of index units of value in the spot portfolio and N_f as the number of index units sold short in the futures market. Thus, $N_S = V(0)/I(0)$ and the hedge ratio, h, equals N_f/N_S. By varying h, the investor can obtain an entire set of portfolio risk-return combinations, yielding a wide range of choice for a given stock portfolio.

The expected rate of return on the hedged portfolio, $E[\tilde{R}(H)]$, is given by

(9.13) $$E[\tilde{R}(H)] = E[\tilde{R}(S)] - hE[\tilde{R}(f)],$$

where $E[\tilde{R}(S)]$ is the expected return on the stock portfolio. The negative sign in Equation 9.13 denotes that a short futures position has been undertaken. Using the concepts relating to portfolio return variance learned in Chapter 3, we can discover the variance of return for the hedged portfolio:

Expiration-Day Volatility

H. Stoll and R. Whaley (1986) investigated the volatility of the SP500 from 1983 to 1985, a period occurring shortly after the inception of SP500 futures trading on the Chicago Mercantile Exchange. These researchers compared volatility on contract-expiration days with that on non-expiration days. They found that expiration-day volatility was significantly greater. Further, most of this volatility difference was attributable to the last hour of expiration-day trading; the standard deviation of the SP500 during this hour was more than three times greater than the standard deviation of the SP500 for the last hour of trading on non-expiration days. Stoll and Whaley also documented that the mean return on the SP500 was significantly negative during the last hour of trading on expiration days. Finally, trading volume during this hour was about twice the level of trading volume for the corresponding hour on non-expiration days.

(9.14) $$VAR[\tilde{R}(H)] = VAR[\tilde{R}(S)] + h^2 VAR[\tilde{R}(f)] - 2hCOV[\tilde{R}(S),\tilde{R}(f)].$$

Figure 9.5 portrays the portfolio risk-return possibilities achieved for different values of h. The point where $h = 0$ corresponds to an unhedged position; and, thus, $E[\tilde{R}(H)] = E[\tilde{R}(S)]$ and $VAR[\tilde{R}(H)] = VAR[\tilde{R}(S)]$. Differentiating Equation 9.14 and solving for the minimum risk portfolio yields the following:[9]

(9.15) $$h = COV[\tilde{R}(S),\tilde{R}(f)]/VAR[\tilde{R}(f)].$$

Substituting $\tilde{R}(I) - r$ for $\tilde{R}(f)$ (see Equation 9.11a) in Equation 9.15 gives

(9.16) $$h = COV[\tilde{R}(S),\tilde{R}(I)]/VAR[\tilde{R}(I)] = \beta_S.$$

Equation 9.16 states that the minimum-variance hedge proportion is the stock portfolio's beta.[10] By selling β_S index units of futures against each unit in the portfolio, the investor hedges all market (i.e., systematic) risk. Unsystematic risk is diversified away via holding adequate numbers of stocks. Hence, the expected return on the fully hedged (zero-beta) portfolio must be the risk-free rate. This is labeled as r in Figure 9.5.

The hedge ratio given in Equation 9.16 is widely used in practice and will serve as the cornerstone of the hedging applications discussed below, despite two shortcomings. First, it assumes that the futures contract and the investor's equity portfolio are perfectly positively correlated. As discussed in footnote 6 of this chapter, a violation of this

The minimum-variance hedge proportion is the stock portfolio's beta.

---

[9] $\partial VAR[\tilde{R}(H)]/\partial h = 2hVAR[\tilde{R}(f)] - 2COV[\tilde{R}(S),\tilde{R}(f)]$. Setting this equal to zero (to determine an optimum) and solving for h gives Equation 9.15. A check of the second-order condition ensures that we have achieved a minimum.

[10] Actually, the minimum-variance hedge ratio is the stock portfolio's beta only if the index underlying the futures contract represents the market portfolio. However, since the indices underlying the traded futures contracts are broadly diversified, Equation 9.16 likely yields an accurate measure of the portfolio's beta.

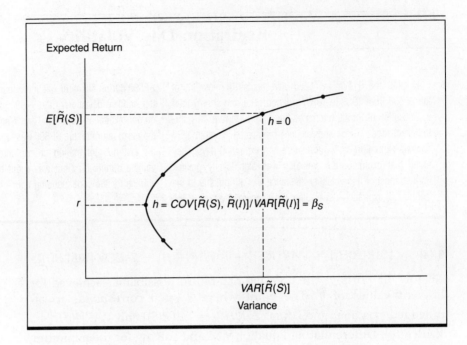

assumption introduces basis risk that can frustrate the effectiveness of the hedge. Second, it ignores dividends on the stock portfolio, since indices are measured without regard to dividend payments. For this reason also, the minimum-variance hedge may not completely eliminate risk.

A Hedging Example[11]

Suppose that a portfolio manager who oversees a $10 million stock portfolio feels that the outlook for the market is very uncertain. The manager decides to insulate the portfolio from adverse market swings by hedging with stock index futures over a one-year horizon. Assume that the capital asset pricing model (CAPM) holds:[12]

(9.17) $$E[\tilde{R}(S)] = r + \hat{\beta}_S\{E[\tilde{R}(M)] - r\},$$

where $E[\tilde{R}(M)]$ is the expected return on the market portfolio, and β_S is the stock portfolio's beta. Also assume that the characteristics of the portfolio and the market environment are as shown in the top portion of Exhibit 9.6.

---

[11]This hedging example is based largely on one presented by S. Figlewski and S. Kon (1982).

[12]Recall from your introductory finance course(s) that the CAPM represents an equilibrium model used to determine the expected return on a risky asset such as a stock. Appendix 9.A provides a refresher on the CAPM.

Part A of Exhibit 9.6 displays the transactions the manager must assume in order to achieve the minimum risk hedged position. The stock portfolio represents 40,000 index units ($10,000,000/250); since its beta is 0.70, the manager will write 28,000 units (40,000 × .70) in the futures market. Thus, the minimum-variance hedge proportion is .70, implying that the minimum-variance hedge ratio is 28,000 units. Of course, traded futures contracts will be written for quantities of more than one index unit. For example, if the standard contract entails a multiplier of $500, the manager will write 56 contracts (28,000/500).

Part B of Exhibit 9.6 demonstrates the overall return achieved by the manager if consensus expectations are fulfilled, and the market rises to 280 by year-end (recall Equation 9.7 for determining $_1f_0$). If the portfolio behaves as expected, its value increases by $960,000 in capital gains and $400,000 in dividend income. But covering the short futures position will result in a loss of $560,000 and an overall return of 8 percent, the riskless rate.

Instead, suppose that the market index drops 10 percent, meaning that the market's realized return including dividends is −6.0 percent for the year. The return on the portfolio, using the CAPM, is −1.8% [.08 + .70 (−.06 − .08)]; this is comprised of a 4 percent return from dividends and a capital loss of 5.8 percent. Part C of Exhibit 9.6 reveals, however, that the futures hedge will yield a profit of $980,000. Hence, the overall return is still 8 percent, the riskless rate. The long position in the stock portfolio and the short stock index futures position are negatively correlated.

This analysis shows that the manager was assured a risk-free return of 8 percent whether the index climbed by 12 percent or fell by 10 percent over the one-year period. Taking other possible market changes, we can show that the overall return is always 8 percent. The use of stock index futures, in conjunction with the minimum-variance hedge ratio, allowed the manager to fully immunize the stock portfolio. By artificially introducing negative correlation, the derivative security provided the manager with an effective and relatively low-cost way of altering risk-return outcomes, thereby enhancing utility.

A More Realistic Hedging Example

In the preceding example, the stock portfolio and stock index futures were perfectly positively correlated. Also, dividends were known and constant, and the portfolio's beta remained unchanged over the one-year period. So, too, did the risk-free rate of interest. Finally, the manager was able to write exactly 28,000 index units in the futures market; problems associated with imperfect security divisibility were ignored. Certainly, these assumptions are somewhat unrealistic. They were invoked to simplify the demonstration that the employment of stock index futures can dramatically alter the risk associated with holding a stock portfolio. Now we will demonstrate this concept using real price data for traded stocks and futures contracts. The example will

Exhibit 9.6:
Portfolio and Market Environment

Portfolio	Market
Value = $10 million	Riskless rate r = 8%
Beta = 0.70	$E[\tilde{R}(M)]$ = 16%
$E[\tilde{R}(S)]$ = 13.6%	Dividend = 4%
Dividend = 4%	Expected Capital Gain = 12%
Expected Capital Gain = 9.6%	$I(0)$ = 250
	$E[\tilde{I}(1)]$ = 280
	$_1f_0$ = 260

A: Initial Position, Index = 250

Stock	Futures
Total Expected Return = 13.6%	Write 28,000 units at 260
Dividend = 4.0%	
Capital Gains = 9.6%	

B: One Year Later, Index = 280

Stock	Futures
Total Realized Return = 13.6%	Cover Short Position at 280
Dividend = 4.0%	Loss = $560,000
Capital Gain = 9.6%	
Portfolio Value = $11,360,000	
Overall Return = $10,800,000 (8%) = r	

C: One Year Later, Index = 225

Stock	Futures
Total Realized Return = −1.8%	Cover Short Position at 225
Dividend = 4.0%	Profit = $980,000
Capital Gain = −5.8%	
Portfolio Value = $9,820,000	
Overall Return = $10,800,000 (8%) = r	

illustrate that while risk and wealth loss are not eliminated, spot portfolio losses are offset.

Exhibit 9.7 reports closing prices for eight actively traded stocks on March 1. Also reported is the settlement June SP500 futures price, 291.85. Individual stock betas, obtained from an investment advisory firm, are reported as well. Suppose that an investor owns a portfolio of

March 1st:

Stock	Price	Shares	Value	Weight	Beta
DuPont	$94.375	800	$ 75,500	.349	0.85
Enron	37.250	200	7,450	.034	0.70
Jamesway	11.125	200	2,225	.010	0.70
Motorola	42.125	600	25,275	.117	1.15
Navistar	6.125	400	2,450	.011	1.25
Pennzoil	80.875	600	48,525	.224	1.05
Polaroid	42.000	300	12,600	.058	1.10
Xerox	60.250	700	42,175	.195	.090
		Total Value	$216,200		

Portfolio Beta = (.349)(0.85) + (.034)(0.70) + ••• + (.195)(0.90) = 0.95
June SP500 futures price = 291.85
Futures price per contract = $145,925
Write one contract

May 31st:

Stock	Price	Value	Dividends
DuPont	$91.125	$72,900	$224
Enron	35.750	7,150	36
Jamesway	11.000	2,200	0
Motorola	39.875	23,925	180
Navistar	6.250	2,500	0
Pennzoil	80.875	48,525	0
Polaroid	41.250	12,375	0
Xerox	60.250	42,127	231
	Total Value	$211,750	Total Dividends $881

June SP500 futures price = 287.50
Futures price per contract = $143,750
Profit on stock portfolio = − $3,569
Profit on futures position = $2,175
Net profit = − $1,394

these stocks, comprised as shown in the exhibit. Since a portfolio's beta is given by a weighted average of the betas of the component stocks, the resulting portfolio beta is 0.95.

The investor is concerned about a possible market decline over the next several weeks. He intends on liquidating his stock portfolio on May 31 to transact a real estate deal, and he wants to employ the June SP500 futures contract to safeguard his wealth over the period. Since the current value of his portfolio is $216,200, he presently holds 740.79 index units ($216,200/291.85). Given a portfolio beta of 0.95, the investor should write 703.75 (740.79 × 0.95) index units in the futures market in order to fully hedge. Given a contract multiple of $500, he should write 1.41 (703.75/500) June SP500 futures contracts. Of course, writing 1.41 contracts is impossible; not being too risk averse, the investor decides to write just one contract.

The results of the investor's strategy are displayed in the lower half of Exhibit 9.7. Given the general market decline over the period, his loss on his stock portfolio was $3,569 after incorporating all dividend income earned over the period. However, the June SP500 settlement futures price on May 31 was 287.50, yielding a profit of $2,175 on the short futures position. Thus, his net profit on the hedge was −$1,394. The hedge was successful in offsetting, in part, the loss on the stock portfolio.

There are several reasons why the loss was not completely offset and, further, why the investor was not assured of a risk-free rate of return. Foremost, the investor was not fully hedged because he could not write 1.41 contracts. The indivisibility of futures contracts frustrated the hedging strategy. Other potential causes include nonstationary betas and an underdiversified stock portfolio. Still, the important point to recognize is that through the introduction of negative correlation, the hedge was largely successful in protecting the investor's wealth. Without hedging, his dollar loss would have been nearly three times greater.

Resolving Stock Selection and Market Timing Conflicts

Recall from Chapter 4 that derivative securities can enhance investor utility by expanding the investment opportunity set. We referred to this as *market completion*. Stock index futures can be used to clearly demonstrate this valuable property of derivative securities, because they can be employed to resolve conflicts that may arise between stock selection and market timing.

Stock index futures can be employed to resolve conflicts that may arise between stock selection and market timing.

A portfolio manager can earn excess returns by one of two means: superior stock selection or superior market timing. Stock index futures allow the manager to separate these activities, thereby resolving any conflicts between the two. For instance, suppose that a manager feels that the market will generally decline in the near future. However, she has also identified a number of undervalued, high-beta stocks. Holding such stocks presents a problem; any abnormal returns attributable to the stocks' undervaluation may be more than offset by their systematic price movements as the market declines. The manager, however, can still buy the stocks while hedging against market risk via shorting stock index futures. Similarly, she can buy undervalued, low-beta stocks when the forecast calls for a market rise by assuming a long position in the futures market. In this way, she does not forgo riding bulls wings by purchasing low-beta stocks.

Without the existence of stock index futures, it may be too difficult or costly to resolve the above conflicts. Thus, the existence of these contracts helps to complete the market, providing investors the ability to achieve risk-return combinations that are otherwise unattainable.[13]

SPECULATING WITH STOCK INDEX FUTURES

Besides hedging, stock index futures may be employed to speculate on subsequent movements in the equity market. Using stock index futures to speculate provides added leverage and entails lower transaction costs than undertaking similar speculation in the equity market itself.

Simple but rather risky speculation would entail trading a naked stock index futures contract. Position traders would assume a long position if their forecast called for a bullish stock market, while a short futures position would be undertaken to exploit a forecasted decline in general equity values. Speculators may opt to trade futures written on the broader indices—the VLCI and NYSE Composite—in order to more fully exploit their forecasts. This is because the broader indices contain the stocks of comparatively small firms, and empirical evidence indicates that smaller firms' stock prices tend to change more radically during general market swings. Thus, the VLCI and NYSE Composite may be expected to fluctuate more than the SP500 or MMI.

Less risky but nevertheless speculative strategies would entail spreads involving stock index futures. Let us consider examples of an intracommodity spread and an intercommodity spread.

Intracommodity Spread

Recall that, in general, an intracommodity futures spread involves the simultaneous trading of nearby and more deferred futures contracts written on the same underlying commodity. Opposite positions (long and short) are assumed so as to make the spread less risky than a naked futures position. Suppose that a position trader who is somewhat bullish decides to construct an intracommodity spread using the June and September SP500 futures contracts appearing in Exhibit 9.3. The settlement prices are 291.85 and 295.60, respectively. Since the speculator is bullish, a short position in the June contract and a long position in the more sensitive September contract are assumed. Since nearby and more deferred stock index futures prices tend to be so highly correlated,

---

[13]This completes our present discussion of hedging with stock index futures. In Chapter 20 we present a more complicated, dynamic hedging strategy involving these contracts. This strategy is one of the "portfolio insurance" techniques described in Chapter 20, most of which entail option contracts. Thus, we will postpone the discussion of this complicated strategy until after our analysis of option contracts.

Figure 9.6:
Profit Graph for an
Intracommodity Spread
Involving Stock Index Futures

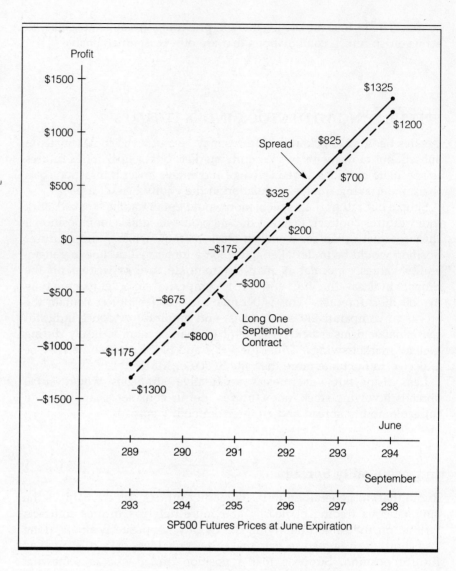

however, the speculator decides to long two of the September contracts. In this way, he hopes to generate more profit and assumes a bit more risk.

The speculator will have to reverse the spread prior to June expiration in order to avoid holding a naked position in the September contracts. Figure 9.6 presents the profit graph for the spread assuming various combinations of SP500 June and September futures prices occurring at June contract expiration. For instance, the gross profit realized is $825 if the resulting futures prices are 293 and 297, respectively, given a contract multiple of $500:

Short Position: $(-1) \times (293.00 - 291.85) \times (500) = -\$\ 575$

Long Position: $(2) \times (297.00 - 295.60) \times (500) = \underline{\quad 1,400}$

Total Profit $\quad \$\ 825$

In general, a profit will be realized if the speculator's forecast proves accurate. If the forecast is incorrect and the market declines, then engaging in the spread cushions the loss, since profits are realized on the short side of the spread. Indeed, losses are less under the spread than if a naked position had been assumed in one September contract, as represented by the broken line in Figure 9.6.

Intercommodity Spread

Recall from Chapter 7 that an intercommodity futures spread is constructed by assuming a long position in one particular contract while simultaneously taking a short position in a contract exhibiting the same expiration but different underlying commodity. For stock index futures, an intercommodity spread would be constructed by, say, shorting the June VLCI contract and buying the June SP500 contract appearing in Exhibit 9.3. The settlement prices are 263.00 and 291.85, respectively. A speculator might engage in such a spread if the forecast called for a short-term market decline; since the VLCI includes more small firm stocks than the SP500, the VLCI may be expected to decline more (in percentage terms) than the SP500. Thus, the above spread would prove profitable if the forecast is correct. Also, the spread is certainly less risky than assuming a short position in the June VLCI contract alone.

For illustrative purposes, suppose that the VLCI futures price declines 5 percent by June 1, while the SP500 futures price declines 3 percent. The VLCI futures price thus fell 13.15 points to 249.85, while the SP500 futures price dropped 8.75 points to 283.10. The position trader, whose forecast proved accurate, decides to abort the spread by engaging in reversing trades at the above futures prices. Ignoring transaction costs, the speculator's resulting profit is $2,200:

Short June VLCI: $(-1) \times (249.85 - 263.00) \times \$500 = \$6,575$

Long June SP500: $(1) \times (283.10 - 291.85) \times \$500 = \underline{-4,375}$

Total Profit $\quad \$2,200$

EMPIRICAL EVIDENCE ON STOCK INDEX FUTURES

Perhaps due to the relative newness of the market, few empirical studies concerning stock index futures contracts have been conducted. Below we summarize four studies that focus on pricing and market efficiency, and one study that examines hedging effectiveness.

The Cornell-French, Figlewski, Modest-Sundaresan, and Cornell Studies

B. Cornell and K. French (1983) and S. Figlewski (1984a) examined whether early futures prices on the SP500 and NYSE Composite indices conformed to the carrying charge model described by Equation 9.8. Both studies documented substantial mispricing. For instance, Figlewski reported that these indices traded at a future discount during the first year of trading when theory indicated that they should have traded at a premium. D. Modest and M. Sundaresan (1983) also reported early mispricing for two contracts studied, but concluded that arbitrage opportunities resulting from such mispricing were very sensitive to the assumption made regarding the use of short-sale proceeds. Finally, in a follow-up study, B. Cornell (1985a) found that SP500 futures mispricing had begun to disappear as the market seasoned. Thus, it appears as though the early mispricing may have represented a transitory phenomenon caused by unfamiliarity with a new market and institutional inertia in developing systems to exploit arbitrage opportunities. Such a seasoning pattern has been found for other newly created securities and unseasoned equity offerings.

The Figlewski Study

S. Figlewski (1984b) investigated the effectiveness of stock index futures hedges using data for the period of June 1982 through September 1983. He constructed one-week hedges using SP500 futures contracts and compared the volatilities of hedged and unhedged positions. Figlewski reported that, on an annual basis, the unhedged portfolio had a standard deviation of return that was four times greater. The annualized standard deviations for the hedged and unhedged positions were 18.9 percent and 4.6 percent, respectively. Figlewski also found that hedging effectiveness was sensitive to basis risk but not to dividend payments.

SUMMARY

Stock index futures contracts are popular because they help to enhance investor utility by providing an efficient and low-cost means of reducing the risk associated with equity positions. The contracts may also be employed to speculate on subsequent stock market changes.

By far, the most liquid index futures contract is written on the SP500. Both the expectations approach and carrying-charge model may be used to determine stock index futures prices. The difficulties of arbitraging an entire index tend to frustrate the cost-of-carry relation, however. Large financial institutions employ a technique known as program trading to engage in arbitrage transactions. It entails the use of real-time data to flag violations of the carrying charge model. While evidence exists that stock index futures were substantially mispriced in the early stages of trading, the mispricing has waned as the market has seasoned. Empirical evidence also suggests that stock index futures can substantially reduce the volatility associated with holding an equity portfolio.

Selected References

Angrist, S. "The Not So Awful Truth." *Forbes,* March 23, 1987.

Cornell, B. "Taxes and the Pricing of Stock Index Futures: Empirical Results." *Journal of Futures Markets* 5 (1985a): 89–101.

Cornell, B. "The Weekly Pattern in Stock Returns: Cash versus Futures: A Note." *Journal of Finance* 40 (June 1985b): 583–588.

Cornell, B., and K. French. "Taxes and the Pricing of Stock Index Futures." *Journal of Finance* 38 (June 1983): 675–694.

Dyl, E., and E. Maberly. "The Daily Distribution of Changes in the Price of Stock Index Futures." *Journal of Futures Markets* 6 (Winter 1986): 513–522.

Dyl, E., and E. Maberly. "The Weekly Pattern in Stock Index Futures: A Further Note." *Journal of Finance* 41, no. 5 (1986): 1149–1152.

Ehrhardt, M., and A. Tucker. "Pricing CRB Futures Contracts." *Journal of Financial Research* (forthcoming, 1990).

Eytan, T., and G. Harpaz. "The Pricing of Futures and Option Contracts on the Value Line Index." *Journal of Finance* 41 (September 1986): 843–855.

Eytan, T., G. Harpaz, and S. Krull. "The Pricing of Dollar Index Futures Contracts." *Journal of Futures Markets* 8 (April 1988): 127–139.

Figlewski, S. "Explaining the Early Discounts on Stock Index Futures: The Case for Disequilibrium." *Financial Analysts Journal* 40 (July–August 1984a): 43–47, 67.

Figlewski, S. "Hedging Performance and Basis Risk in Stock Index Futures." *Journal of Finance* 39 (July 1984b): 657–669.

Figlewski, S., and S. Kon. "Portfolio Management with Stock Index Futures." *Financial Analysts Journal* 38 (January–February 1982): 52–60.

Gastineau, G., and A. Madansky. "SP500 Stock Index Futures Evaluation Tables." *Financial Analysis Journal* 39 (November–December 1983): 68–76.

Grant, D. "How to Optimize with Stock Index Futures." *Journal of Portfolio Management* 8 (Spring 1982): 32–36.

Grant, D. "A Market Index Futures Contract and Portfolio Selection." *Journal of Economics and Business* 34 (1982): 387–390.

Gressis, N., G. Vlahos, and G. Philippatos. "A CAPM-based Analysis of Stock Index Futures." *Journal of Portfolio Management* 10 (Spring 1984): 47–52.

Hill, J. "Volatility and Correlation of Stock Indexes 1980–1986: Statistics and Charts" published by Kidder, Peabody and Co., 1987.

Marshall, J. "New Opportunities for the Whole-Market Investor." *Review of Business* 2 (Winter 1983).

Modest, D., and M. Sundaresan. "The Relationship between Spot and Futures Prices in Stock Index Futures Markets: Some Preliminary Evidence." *Journal of Futures Markets* 3 (1983): 15–41.

Santoni, G. *Has Programmed Trading Made Stocks More Volatile?* St. Louis: Federal Reserve Bank, May 1987.

Stoll, H., and R. Whaley. "Expiration Day Effects of Index Options and Futures," Salomon Brothers Center for the Study of Financial Institutions. Monograph Series in Finance and Economics, Monograph 1986–3.

Stoll, H., and R. Whaley. "Program Trading and Expiration Day Effects." *Financial Analysts Journal* 43 (March–April 1987): 16–23.

Weiner, N. "The Hedging Rationale for a Stock Index Futures Contract." *Journal of Futures Markets* 1, no. 1 (1981): 59–76.

Questions and Problems

1. Explain the differences between a value-weighted index, such as the SP500, and a price-weighted index, such as the MMI.

2. What are some of the advantages and disadvantages of constructing a geometrically averaged index?

3. Why do you suppose that the SP500 futures contract is so liquid while the VLCI futures contract is comparatively thinly traded?

4. From Exhibit 9.3, what was the March MMI settlement futures price? What was the contract's price?

5. Suppose that the beta coefficient for a stock portfolio was computed using regression analysis separately for three different market indices. In the first regression, when the SP500 is used, the resulting beta is 1.08 with an R^2 of 0.89. When the MMI is the explanatory variable, the regression yields a beta of 1.03 and an R^2 of 0.94. Finally, using the VLCI gives a beta of 1.17 and an R^2 of 0.82. Which futures contract would likely provide the most effective hedge, and why?

6. If the current index level is 290, has an expected return of 10 percent over the next six months, and exhibits a dividend yield of 2 percent, then what is the six-month futures price, assuming risk neutrality and ignoring daily resettlement?

7. If the current index level is 380, the dividend yield is 3.5 percent, and the three-month risk-free rate is 7 percent, then what is the three-month futures price under the carrying-charge approach?

8. Why might the cost-of-carry model be less descriptive for stock index futures than other futures contracts?

9. Given the following parameters, illustrate the resulting arbitrage profit (per index unit): $_1f_0 = 292$, $I(0) = 270$, $r = .10$, and $\delta = .04$. Assume a one-period arbitrage where dividends are paid at the end of the period.

10. Describe the concept known as program trading. Why might such trading increase market volatility about the time of contract expiration?

11. Assuming no basis risk exists, what is the minimum-variance hedge ratio? What would this ratio be if the stock portfolio being hedged were constructed exactly like the futures contract's underlying index?

12. Using the information provided at the top of Exhibit 9.6, how many index units must be written in the futures contract if the portfolio's beta was 0.90 rather than 0.70? Demonstrate how a risk-free rate of return is assured under the scenarios provided in both panels B and C.

13. Assume that you are currently managing the seven-stock portfolio described below. It is April 18, and you intend to sell your stock holdings on June 1. Anticipating a general market decline over the next six weeks, you decide to employ June SP500 futures contracts to fully hedge. The current futures price is 300, and none of the stocks is scheduled to pay a dividend prior to June 1. Determine the outcome of the hedge if the resulting futures price on June 1 is 294, and the resulting stock prices are as given below.

			Prices	
Stock	Shares	Beta	April 18	June 1
A	1,000	1.25	20.125	20.250
B	2,500	1.09	34.500	31.875
C	1,900	1.35	9.125	8.875
D	3,100	0.80	51.750	50.000
E	1,400	0.63	14.875	14.125
F	800	1.16	29.125	27.250

14. Describe how stock index futures can be employed to resolve conflicts between stock-selection and market-timing activities.

15. Why might a speculator opt to transact in the broader index futures if the forecast calls for large market swings?

16. Construct an intercommodity spread using the September SP500 and NYSE futures contracts appearing in Exhibit 9.3. Assume a short position in the SP500 contract. What is the profit outcome at contract expiration if the resulting futures prices are 287.11 (SP500) and 161.74 (NYSE)?

17. What were the likely causes of the stock index futures mispricing detected in the early stages of market trading?

18. Compare Equation 9.7, which is the index futures price under the expectations approach, with Equation 9.12, which is the index futures price under the carrying-charge approach. This comparison implies, of course, that the expected rate of return on a market index must be risk-free. Resolve this apparent paradox.

Self-Test Problems

Self-test Problems 1 through 6 refer to the following information:

			Share Prices		Sept. SP500 Futures	
Stock	Shares	Beta	Aug. 1	Sept. 1	Aug. 1	Sept. 1
A	900	1.25	8.750	9.250	225.15	232.50
B	700	0.80	21.250	22.000		
C	1,400	0.75	14.750	14.500		
D	2,000	0.95	35.500	36.250		
E	1,600	1.05	68.250	71.125		
F	300	1.45	19.750	20.000		
G	300	0.55	28.750	28.250		
H	1,100	1.80	26.250	26.750		
I	600	1.05	41.500	44.125		
J	800	0.95	38.000	40.500		

ST-1. Assume that you hold the above portfolio and that it is currently August 1. What is each stock's portfolio weight?

ST-2. What is the portfolio's beta?

ST-3. Assume that you want to fully hedge the portfolio. How many September SP500 futures contracts should you write?

ST-4. Assume that you liquidated your portfolio on September 1 at the given prices. Assume no dividends were paid over the period. What was the stock portfolio's profit?

ST-5. What was the profit on the futures position, given that the September SP500 futures price was 232.50 on September 1?

ST-6. What was the net profit from the hedge?

Solutions to Self-Test Problems

ST-1.

Stock	Value	Weight
A	$ 7,875[a]	0.0244[b]
B	14,875	0.0461
C	20,650	0.0641
D	71,000	0.2203
E	109,200	0.3388
F	5,925	0.0184
G	8,625	0.0267
H	28,875	0.0896
I	24,900	0.0772
J	30,400	0.0943
	$322,325 Total Value	

[a]E.g., $900 \times 8.750 = \$7,875$.
[b]E.g., $\$7,875/322,325 = .0244$.

ST-2. $\hat{\beta}_S = 0.0244(1.25) + 0.0461(0.80) + \quad = 1.0537.$

ST-3. $[\$322,325/(500 \times 225.15)] \times 1.0537 = 3.017.$
Therefore write three contracts.

ST-4. $(\$9.250 - 8.750)(900) + (22.00 - 21.250)(700) + \cdots + (40.500 - 38.000)(800) = \$10,775.$

ST-5. $(232.50 - 225.15) \times (-3) \times (\$500) = -\$11,025.$

ST-6. $\$10,775 - 11,025 = -\$250.$

Appendix 9.A

THE CAPITAL ASSET PRICING MODEL

The capital asset pricing model (CAPM) is an equilibrium model that purports to provide a linear relation between the expected return on a risky asset and the asset's risk, as measured by the covariability of the asset with the market portfolio. The most general form of the CAPM is derived under the following assumptions about investors and their opportunity set:

- Investors are risk-averse expected utility-of-wealth maximizers.
- Investors are price takers who exhibit homogeneous expectations about asset returns, which have a joint normal distribution.
- Investors may borrow or lend unlimited amounts at the risk-free rate of interest.
- Markets are perfect, with no taxes or transaction costs and with perfect security divisibility and no restrictions on short selling.

The figure below shows the expected return and standard deviation of the market portfolio, M, the risk-free asset, r, and a risky asset, i. The straight line connecting r and M is known as the *capital market line (CML)*. The equation for this line is

(9.A–1)
$$E[\tilde{R}(S)] = r + \sigma_S \frac{E[\tilde{R}(M)] - r}{\sigma_M},$$

where $E[\tilde{R}(S)]$ is the expected return on an asset (stock) portfolio, $E[\tilde{R}(M)]$ is the expected return on the market portfolio, σ_S is the standard deviation of returns on the asset portfolio, and σ_M is the standard deviation of returns on the market portfolio. The CML arises from a well-known result of optimal portfolio choice—namely, that if investors have homogeneous expectations, then they all have the same linear efficient set. The CML is this linear efficient set. In other words, it states that homogeneous investors faced with the same opportunity

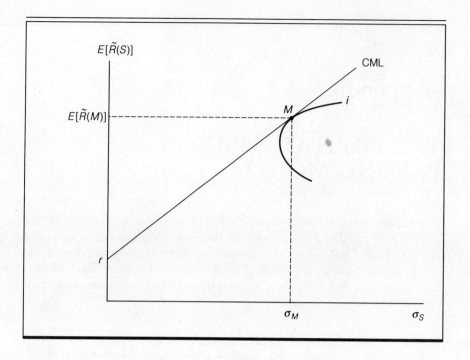

set will hold the same risky assets in the same proportions; only the weight in the risk-free asset will vary across investors with different degrees of risk aversion. If the opportunity set consists of *all* risky assets, then investors will hold a common fraction of the total market value of every risky asset in the economic system. This is called the *market portfolio*; it represents a type of ultimate market index.

In market equilibrium, the prices of all assets must adjust until all are held by investors such that there is no excess demand. As a consequence, in equilibrium the market portfolio will consist of all assets held in proportion to their value weights:

(9.A–2)
$$W_i = \frac{\text{Market Value of Asset } i}{\text{Market Value of All Assets}}.$$

A portfolio consisting of x percent invested in risky asset i and $(1 - x)$ percent in M will have the following mean and standard deviation:

(9.A–3)
$$E[\tilde{R}(S)] = xE[\tilde{R}(i)] + (1 - x)E[\tilde{R}(M)],$$

(9.A–4)
$$\sigma_S = [x^2\sigma_i^2 + (1 - x)^2\sigma_M^2 + 2x(1 - x)\sigma_{iM}]^{1/2},$$

where σ_i is the standard deviation of returns on i, and σ_{iM} is the covariance between i and M. The changes in the portfolio's mean and standard deviation with respect to x are determined as follows:

(9.A–5)
$$\partial E[\tilde{R}(S)]/\partial x = E[\tilde{R}(i)] - E[\tilde{R}(M)],$$

(9.A–6) $\quad \partial\sigma_S/\partial x = 1/2[x^2\sigma_i^2 - (1-x)^2\sigma_M^2 + 2x(1-x)\sigma_{iM}]^{-1/2}$
$$\times [2x\sigma_i^2 - 2\sigma_M^2 + 2x\sigma_M^2 + 2\sigma_{iM} - 4x\sigma_{iM}].$$

The market portfolio already has the value weight, W_i percent, invested in i. Thus, the percent x in Equations 9.A–5 and 9.A–6 represents excess demand. If these equations are investigated where $x = 0$, therefore, we can determine the slope of the risk-return trade-off evaluated at point M in market equilibrium:

(9.A–7) $\qquad \dfrac{\partial E[\tilde{R}(S)]/\partial x}{\partial\sigma_S/\partial x}\bigg|_{x=0} = \dfrac{E[\tilde{R}(i)] - E[\tilde{R}(M)]}{(\sigma_{iM} - \sigma_M^2)/\sigma_M}.$

This slope must be the same as the slope of the CML, or

$$\frac{E[\tilde{R}(i)] - E[\tilde{R}(M)]}{(\sigma_{iM} - \sigma_M^2)/\sigma_M} = \frac{E[\tilde{R}(M)] - r}{\sigma_M}.$$

Rearranging this expression yields

$$E[\tilde{R}(i)] = r + \sigma_{iM}/\sigma_M^2\{E[\tilde{R}(M)] - r\},$$

and recognizing that σ_{iM}/σ_M^2 is asset i's beta, $\hat{\beta}_i$, we have

(9.A–8) $\qquad\qquad E[\tilde{R}(i)] = r + \hat{\beta}_i\{E[\tilde{R}(M)] - r\}.$

Equation 9.A–8 is the CAPM. It states that the expected return on a risky asset is given by the risk-free rate plus a risk premium dependent on the asset's systematic movement with the market portfolio, $\hat{\beta}_i$. From Equation 9.A–8, it is obvious that a zero-beta asset is a risk-free asset whose expected return in equilibrium is r.

The CAPM is applicable to portfolios as well as individual assets. Since the expected return and beta of a portfolio are weighted averages of the expected returns and betas of the component assets, we have:

(9.A–9) $\qquad\qquad E[\tilde{R}(S)] = r + \hat{\beta}_S\{E[\tilde{R}(M)] - r\}.$

This is Equation 9.17 of Chapter 9.

INTEREST RATE FUTURES

Over the last decade, interest rates and bond returns have been substantially more volatile than in the past. For instance, during the late 1970s through 1987 the annualized monthly standard deviation of long-term corporate bond returns was approximately 11.7 percent. This compares with a yearly average of just 3.6 percent for the period of 1926 through 1973. Changes in monetary policy, the oil crises of the early 1970s, and other factors have contributed to this marked increase in risk associated with fixed-rate debt obligations.

Because of this increased risk, interest rate futures contracts were developed as a means to reduce volatility associated with holding spot positions in bonds and other interest-rate-sensitive securities. In this chapter we begin our analysis of interest rate futures contracts by examining the contract specifications of the four most important and liquid contracts. Next we explore the pricing of these contracts under the carrying-charge approach. Hedging applications are then provided, followed by some popular speculative strategies. Finally, a sizable body of empirical evidence concerning these contracts is summarized.

At this point you should be aware that interest rate futures represent a very important and useful derivative security. As evidence of this, Exhibit 10.1 shows that of the twelve most popular futures contracts for the trading year 1987, three are interest rate contracts: Treasury bond (T-bond), Eurodollar, and Treasury bill (T-bill) futures. Further, the CBOT's T-bond contract is by far the leading futures contract. Its annual volume during 1987 was nearly 67 million contracts, representing about 40% of the total contract volume reported. Given a contract size of $100,000, trading volume in 1987 entailed over $6.6 trillion! T-bond futures account for over half of all futures trading volume at the CBOT. The Eurodollar contract is the second most liquid contract, with over 20 million contracts traded. It represents the most popular interest rate futures contract corresponding to the short-term segment of the yield curve.

Contract	Volume
Treasury Bonds (CBOT)	66,841,474
Eurodollar (IMM)	20,416,216
SP500 (IOM)	19,044,673
Crude Oil (NYMEX)	14,581,614
Gold (Comex)	10,239,805
Soybeans (CBOT)	7,378,760
Corn (CBOT)	7,253,212
Deutsche Mark (IMM)	6,037,048
Japanese Yen (IMM)	5,358,556
Swiss Franc (IMM)	5,268,276
Treasury Notes (CBOT)	5,253,791
Live Cattle (CME)	5,229,294

CONTRACT SPECIFICATIONS

In this chapter we focus on the four most popular interest rate futures contracts: the T-bond and T-note contracts traded on the CBOT, and the Eurodollar and T-bill contracts traded on the IMM division of the CME.[1] Taken together, these contracts effectively span the entire yield curve, allowing traders to hedge underlying instruments with varying maturities. In this section we describe the various features particular to each of the four contracts.

Treasury Bill (T-Bill) Futures

United States T-bills are sold each week on an auction basis. The maturity on the newly auctioned bills is typically 91 days. They are sold at a discount from face value since no interest is paid over their maturity. The discount is quoted on a 360-day basis.

At the IMM, the futures contract allows delivery of a 90-, 91-, or 92-day T-bill, although the futures price is always based on a 90-day bill. For instance, suppose that a futures contract is priced such that the discount is 8.73. The IMM-quoted price is 100 − 8.73, or 91.27. This price corresponds to the March 1989 settlement price presented in part A of Exhibit 10.2. However, this price, which is called the *IMM Index*, is

---

[1] A fifth contract attaining some notoriety is the CBOT's Municipal Bond Index futures contract, which allows municipal bond holders to hedge their spot positions.

not the actual price at which the contract is traded. The true futures price (per $100) is given by the following expression:

(10.1) $\qquad f = 100 - (100 - \text{IMM Index})(90/360).$

For the March contract, $f = 97.8175$:

$$97.8175 = 100 - (100 - 91.27)(90/360).$$

Since a single futures contract entails $1 million face-value T-bills, the March contract price is $978,175.

The reason for quoting the IMM Index, rather than the true futures price, is as follows. Since a 90-day bill is assumed in the formula above, a one-basis-point change in the IMM Index corresponds to a $25 change in the futures price. For instance, if the IMM Index falls to 91.26, the new futures price will be $978,150. Hence, the conventions of assuming a 90-day bill and reporting the IMM Index allow traders to quickly assess the impact of changes in the index on wealth. This method of price quotation also ensures that the bid price is below the ask price, which is the usual relation for other futures contracts.

Contract specifications for T-bill futures are presented in part A of Exhibit 10.3. The expiration cycle is March-June-September-December, with trading ending according to a schedule established by officials at the IMM. The trading deadlines change over time so as to make newly issued T-bills immediately deliverable on the contract. Delivery can occur on any business day after the last trading day but must be before the end of the expiration month. The margin requirements shown in Exhibit 10.3 relate to pure speculators; hedgers and spreaders typically face lower margins.

Eurodollar Futures

The Eurodollar contract is the more liquid of the two actively traded futures contracts on money market instruments. A *Eurodollar* is a dollar-denominated deposit in a foreign bank or overseas branch of a U.S. bank. Thus, the underlying asset is a time deposit rather than a bond. The rate earned on such a deposit is variable and is called the London Interbank Offer Rate, or LIBOR for short. This rate is highly correlated with the U.S. Treasury bill rate, although the LIBOR is typically a bit greater due to the absence of deposit insurance and other risk factors related to overseas investment.

A **Eurodollar** is a dollar-denominated deposit in a foreign bank or overseas branch of a U.S. bank. The rate earned on such a deposit is variable and is called the London Interbank Offer Rate (LIBOR).

The futures contract is written on a three-month Eurodollar (LIBOR), and the futures price is quoted by the same IMM Index method used for the T-bill contract. Thus, the true Eurodollar futures price for the March 1989 contract appearing in part B of Exhibit 10.2 is 97.4325:

$$97.4325 = 100 - (100 - 89.73)(90/360).$$

Since the contract size is $1 million, the futures price is $974,325.

Exhibit 10.2:
Interest Rate Futures Prices

A: U.S. T-Bills

TREASURY BILLS (IMM)–$1 mil.; pts. of 100%

	Open	High	Low	Settle	Chg	Discount Settle	Chg	Open Interest
Mar	91.30	91.30	91.25	91.27	+ .02	8.73	– .02	8,565
June	90.94	90.96	90.87	90.89	– .02	9.11	+ .02	13,896
Sept	90.98	90.98	90.89	90.89	– .06	9.11	+ .06	2,309
Dec	91.08	91.10	91.01	91.04	– .04	8.96	+ .04	994
Mr90	91.39	91.39	91.38	91.42	– .02	8.58	+ .02	340

Est vol 8,717; vol Tues 8,529; open int 26,106, –291.

B: Eurodollars

EURODOLLAR (IMM)–$1 million; pts of 100%

	Open	High	Low	Settle	Chg	Yield Settle	Chg	Open Interest
Mar	89.77	89.78	89.73	89.73	....	10.27	....	143,656
June	89.52	89.53	89.40	89.41	– .06	10.59	+ .06	216,862
Sept	89.56	89.58	89.46	89.47	– .04	10.53	+ .04	124,529
Dec	89.69	89.72	89.62	89.62	– .02	10.38	+ .02	68,724
Mr90	90.00	90.07	89.97	89.97	....	10.03	....	39,435
June	90.21	90.26	90.18	90.18	+ .02	9.82	– .02	27,120
Sept	90.36	90.42	90.33	90.34	+ .03	9.66	– .03	23,075
Dec	90.37	90.42	90.32	90.34	+ .02	9.66	– .02	21,982
Mr91	90.49	90.50	90.40	90.44	– .02	9.56	+ .02	13,991
June	90.45	90.46	90.37	90.37	– .05	9.63	+ .05	10,922
Sept	90.46	90.47	90.35	90.37	– .06	9.63	+ .06	22,848
Dec	90.44	90.45	90.34	90.35	– .06	9.65	+ .06	9,177

Est vol 171,339; vol Tues 196,696; open int 135,398, +80

C: U.S. T-Notes

TREASURY NOTES (CBT)–$100,000; pts. 32nds of 100%

	Open	High	Low	Settle	Chg	Yield Settle	Chg	Open Interest
Mar	91-26	92-02	91-15	91-16	– 7	9.325	+ .036	34,524
June	92-01	92-07	91-20	91-20	– 9	9.305	+ .047	49,608
Sept	92-09	92-09	91-23	91-23	– 9	9.289	+ .046	549

Est vol 35,000; vol Tues 14,383; open int 84,681, +384.

D: U.S. T-Bonds

TREASURY BONDS (CBT)–$100,000; pts. 32nds of 100%

	Open	High	Low	Settle	Chg	Yield Settle	Chg	Open Interest
Mar	88-06	88-16	87-18	87-19	– 16	9.386	+ .062	118,746
June	88-09	88-18	87-20	87-22	– 16	9.374	+ .061	145,455
Sept	88-10	88-18	87-22	87-23	– 15	9.370	+ .057	21,673
Dec	88-11	88-18	87-23	87-23	– 15	9.370	+ .057	12,210
Mr90	88-10	88-18	87-21	87-21	– 15	9.378	+ .058	5,288
June	88-13	88-13	87-18	87-18	– 15	9.390	+ .058	2,750
Sept	87-21	87-21	87-14	87-14	– 15	9.405	+ .058	203
Dec	87-15	87-15	87-09	87-09	– 15	9.424	+ .058	274
Mr91	....	....	....	87-04	– 14	9.444	+ .054	98
June	87-17	87-21	86-31	86-31	– 13	9.463	+ .050	196

Est vol 340,000; vol Tues 333,891; op int 306,899, -4,903.

FINANCIAL FUTURES

A: 90-Day U.S. T-Bills (IMM)

Contract Size:	$1 million
Minimum Price Change:	One basis point ($25)
Daily Price Limit:	None
Delivery Months:	March, June, September, December
Trading Hours:	7:20 A.M.–2:00 P.M. central
Last Trading Day:	Varies
First Delivery Day:	Business day after last trading day
Margin:	$1,500 initial; $1,000 maintenance

B: Eurodollars (IMM)

Contract Size:	$1 million
Minimum Price Change:	One basis point ($25)
Daily Price Limit:	None
Delivery Months:	March, June, September, December
Trading Hours:	7:20 A.M.–2:00 P.M. central
Last Trading Day:	Second London business day before third Wednesday of the month
First Delivery Day:	Not applicable (cash settled)
Margin:	$1,500 initial; $1,000 maintenance

C: U.S. T-Notes (CBOT)

Contract Size:	$100,000
Minimum Price Change:	1/32 points ($31.25)
Daily Price Limit:	96/32 points ($3,000)
Delivery Months:	March, June, September, December
Trading Hours:	8:00 A.M.–2:00 P.M. central
Last Trading Day:	Business day prior to last seven days
First Delivery Day:	First business day of the month
Margin:	$4,000 initial; $3,000 maintenance

D: U.S. T-Bonds (CBOT)

Contract Size:	$100,000
Minimum Price Change:	1/32 points ($31.25)
Daily Price Limit:	96/32 points ($3,000)
Delivery Months:	March, June, September, December
Trading Hours:	8:00 A.M.–2:00 P.M. central
Last Trading Day:	Business day prior to last seven days
First Delivery Day:	First business day of the month
Margin:	$5,000 initial; $4,000 maintenance

The contract specifications for this instrument are reported in Part B of Exhibit 10.3. A major difference between the T-bill and Eurodollar contracts is that the latter, like a stock index futures contract, is cash-settled. This is because Eurodollar deposits are nontransferrable. The settlement price on the last trading day is the three-month LIBOR as determined by CME officials.[2]

Treasury Bond (T-Bond) Futures

Both T-note and T-bond futures contracts are traded on the CBOT and exhibit very similar specifications. The T-note contract entails Treasury instruments (notes) with maturities ranging from 6.5 to 10 years, while the T-bond contract entails instruments (bonds) with at least fifteen years until maturity or until their first permissible call date. Other than this maturity difference and a slight difference in margins (compare parts C and D of Exhibit 10.3), the two contracts are identical. Given this, and the tremendous liquidity of the T-bond contract, we will discuss T-bond futures only.

T-Bond Futures Price Quotations Prices for T-bonds are quoted in dollars and thirty-seconds of par value of $100. T-bond futures prices are quoted in the same manner. For example, the settlement March 1989 futures price reported in part D of Exhibit 10.2 is 87–19, or $87.59375. Since the contract size is $100,000, the contract price is $87,593.75. Prices quoted for T-note futures are similarly interpreted.

Delivery Process The delivery process for T-bond (and T-note) futures contracts is very complicated and gives rise to some unusual "options" that affect the futures price. Because of this, T-bond (and T-note) futures contracts are the most complex futures contracts traded today. In this section we describe the delivery process. The resulting "options" are discussed afterwards.

Delivery against the T-bond contract is initiated by the short trader and extends over three business days. On the first day, known as the *position day*, the short trader notifies the clearinghouse of the intention to deliver two business days later. Since the first business day of the delivery month is the earliest possible delivery day, the first position day permissible is actually two business days before the delivery month. Therefore, it falls in the month before the delivery month. As we shall see, the settlement price on the position day is instrumental in determining the obligations between the short party and the assigned long party.

---

[2]For the exact procedure used by CME officials, see Chicago Mercantile Exchange, "Inside Eurodollar Futures," p. 19.

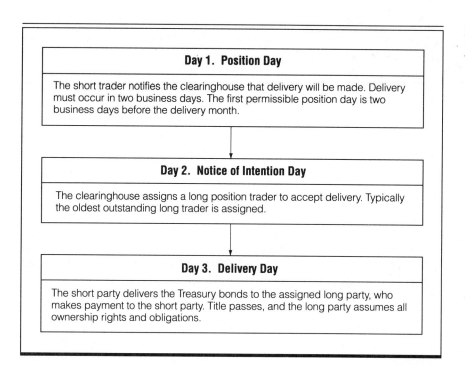

Figure 10.1:

Delivery Process for
T-bond Futures

Day 1. Position Day

The short trader notifies the clearinghouse that delivery will be made. Delivery must occur in two business days. The first permissible position day is two business days before the delivery month.

Day 2. Notice of Intention Day

The clearinghouse assigns a long position trader to accept delivery. Typically the oldest outstanding long trader is assigned.

Day 3. Delivery Day

The short party delivers the Treasury bonds to the assigned long party, who makes payment to the short party. Title passes, and the long party assumes all ownership rights and obligations.

The second day in the three-day sequence is known as the *notice-of-intention day*. On this day the clearinghouse assigns a long position holder to accept delivery. Usually the oldest long party outstanding is assigned. The clearinghouse thus serves in its role of matching parties to the contract while insuring both sides of the contract against default. The short trader is now obligated to deliver the Treasury bonds to the assigned long trader on the next business day.

The third day, when the bonds are delivered and title passes to the long trader, is called the *delivery day*. As part D of Exhibit 10.3 points out, the latest possible delivery (i.e., trading) day occurs on the business day prior to the last seven days of the delivery month. Figure 10.1 illustrates the delivery process for T-bond futures. The process is the same for T-note futures contracts.[3]

Wild-Card Option   On any permissible position day, the short trader can notify the clearinghouse of his or her intention to deliver until early that evening, after the spot and futures markets have closed. T-bond

---

[3]Of course, as with other contracts, delivery seldom occurs. Instead, reversing trades are employed to close out contract positions. Still, understanding the delivery process is important, since it is the possibility of delivery that is critical to determining the futures price.

futures cease trading at 3:00 P.M. Eastern time, while T-bonds are traded until 5:00 P.M. Eastern time. During this period of a few hours, information relevant to bond prices may be revealed. If the information causes bond prices to be depressed, then the short party may opt to notify the clearinghouse of delivery. Since the monetary amount charged to the assigned long party is largely determined by the settlement price on the position day, the short trader has a clear advantage. He or she can wait until the next business day to purchase the bonds more cheaply and deliver them at the (stale) higher settlement price.

In a very real sense, the short trader of a T-bond (or T-note) futures contract therefore owns an option that is exercisable during the delivery month. This option has come to be known as the *wild-card option*. It represents the opportunity that a short trader has to exploit information released after the market has closed. From the long party's view, the wild-card option represents an additional risk of engaging in a T-bond futures contract. Presumably, this risk is somehow reflected in the futures price. Thus, the unique delivery system just described gives rise to a valuable option that confounds the futures price; the futures price likely does not solely reflect the cost-of-carry or expectations concerning future spot prices. Indeed, the existence of the wild-card option should serve to *lower* the futures price in order to compensate the long party for added risk.

The **wild-card option** represents the opportunity that a short trader has to exploit information about bond prices after the futures market has closed. It represents an additional risk for long position holders in T-bond futures.

Delivery Option   An important determinant of any futures contract's success is the deliverable supply of the underlying asset. To ensure liquidity in the T-bond futures market, therefore, the CBOT allows delivery of T-bonds exhibiting a wide variety of coupon payments. Given the ample number of outstanding T-bonds with varying coupon rates and at least fifteen years to maturity or first call date, there are often thirty or more deliverable bonds for any given contract.

Because there are many T-bonds eligible for delivery, officials at the CBOT have designed a system to price all bonds on an equivalent coupon basis for the purpose of delivery. Specifically, the T-bond contract is built on the assumption that the underlying bond coupon is 8 percent, and a *conversion factor* (CF) is used to adjust the price paid by the long party to the short party upon delivery. The conversion factor is the price of a bond with a $1 face value, a coupon and maturity equal to that of the delivered bond, and an 8 percent yield. For the purpose of computing the conversion factor, *maturity* is defined as the bond's maturity on the first day of the delivery month. If the T-bond is callable, the first call date is used to define maturity.

The **conversion factor** (CF) is the price of a bond with $1 face value, a coupon and maturity equal to that of the delivered bond, and an 8 percent yield.

Conversion factors can be found by employing the following formulas:

(10.2a)
$$CF = \sum_{t=1}^{n} \frac{C_t}{(1.04)^t} + 1/1.04^n;$$

(10.2b)
$$CF = \frac{\displaystyle\sum_{t=1}^{n} \frac{C_t}{(1.04)^t} + \frac{1}{(1.04)^n} + C_t}{\sqrt{1.04}} - .5C_t,$$

where

C_t = the semiannual coupon payment (in dollars), assuming a $1 face-value bond, and

n = the number of full semiannual periods remaining until bond maturity (or first call date).

Equation 10.2a is used to compute conversion factors when n is an even integer, while Equation 10.2b is used when n is an odd integer.

Exhibit 10.4 presents the conversion factors for T-bonds eligible for delivery against various futures contracts as of February 6, 1987. Notice that CF varies directly with the coupon rate, and that it is closest to 1 when the deliverable bond's coupon rate is closest to 8 percent. To provide just one numerical example, consider the conversion factor for the 12 percent coupon T-bond, maturing on May 15, 2005, eligible for delivery against the March 1987 contract. The CF is 1.3782. With a $1 face value, the semiannual coupon would be $0.06. Since there are thirty-six full semiannual periods remaining until bond maturity,[4] using Equation 10.2a gives us a CF of 1.3782:

$$CF = \sum_{t=1}^{36} \frac{.06}{(1.04)^t} + 1/(1.04)^{36}$$
$$= 1.13449 + 0.24367$$
$$= 1.3782.$$

The amount the long party must pay to the short party for a particular deliverable bond is determined by multiplying the CF by the contract's settlement price on the position day, and then adding the accrued interest from the last coupon date until the delivery date. This amount is typically called the *invoice price*:

(10.3)
$$\textit{Invoice Price} = (CF)(SP) + AI_T,$$

where SP represents the contract settlement price on the position day and AI_T is the accrued interest.

The method the CBOT uses to determine conversion factors (Equations 10.2a and 10.2b) has two implicit assumptions: yields are 8 percent, and the term structure of interest rates is flat. However, we know that all yields are not 8 percent and that the term structure is virtually never flat (see Figure 6.3 of Chapter 6). As a result, the method employed gives

The **invoice price** is the amount the long party must pay to the short party for a particular deliverable bond.

---

[4]One in 1987, thirty-four in the years from November 15, 1987 to November 15, 2004, and one from November 15, 2004 to maturity on May 15, 2005.

Exhibit 10.4:
Conversion Factors for T-Bonds Eligible for Delivery as of February 6, 1987

Coupon Rate	Maturity	Amount ($ Billions)	Mar. '87	Jun. '87	Sep. '87	Dec. '87	Mar. '88	June. '88	Sep. '88	Dec. '88
7-1/4	May 15, 2016	18.01	.9159	.9159	.9163	.9163	.9167	.9167	.9171	.9171
7-1/2[a]	Nov. 15, 2016	18.51	.9437	.9436	.9439	.9439	.9442	.9441	.9445	.9444
7-7/8	Nov. 15, 2002–07	1.49	.9890	.9889	.9892	—	—	—	—	—
8-3/8	Aug. 15, 2003–08	2.10	1.0336	1.0335	1.0330	1.0330	1.0325	1.0324	—	—
8-3/4	Nov. 15, 2003–08	5.23	1.0681	1.0673	1.0670	1.0663	1.0660	1.0652	1.0648	—
9-1/8	May 15, 2004–09	4.60	1.1036	1.1026	1.1021	1.1011	1.1005	1.0995	1.0989	1.0979
9-1/4	Feb. 15, 2016	7.00	1.1396	1.1395	1.1390	1.1389	1.1383	1.1382	1.1376	1.1375
9-3/8	Feb. 15, 2006	4.75	1.1322	1.1316	1.1306	1.1300	1.1289	1.1283	1.1272	1.1266
9-7/8	Nov. 15, 2015	6.75	1.2093	1.2086	1.2083	1.2076	1.2073	1.2065	1.2062	1.2054
10	May 15, 2005–10	2.98	1.1891	1.1876	1.1866	1.1851	1.1841	1.1826	1.1815	1.1799
10-3/8	Nov. 15, 2004–09	4.20	1.2216	1.2199	1.2186	1.2168	1.2155	1.2136	1.2122	1.2103
10-3/8	Nov. 15, 2007–12	11.03	1.2374	1.2360	1.2350	1.2336	1.2326	1.2310	1.2300	1.2284
10-5/8	Aug. 15, 2015	6.50	1.2921	1.2916	1.2907	1.2902	1.2892	1.2887	1.2876	1.2871
10-3/4	Feb. 14, 2003	3.00	1.2436	1.2418	1.2396	1.2378	—	—	—	—
10-3/4	May 15, 2003	3.24	1.2458	1.2436	1.2418	1.2396	1.2378	—	—	—
10-3/4	Aug. 15, 2005	9.26	1.2614	1.2600	1.2581	1.2566	1.2546	1.2532	1.2511	1.2495
11-1/8	Aug. 15, 2003	3.50	1.2812	1.2793	1.2768	1.2748	1.2723	1.2702	—	—
11-1/4	Feb. 15, 2015	11.75	1.3599	1.3593	1.3581	1.3574	1.3561	1.3554	1.3541	1.3534
11-5/8	Nov. 15, 2002	2.75	1.3188	1.3158	1.3134	—	—	—	—	—
11-5/8	Nov. 15, 2004	4.01	1.3383	1.3357	1.3337	1.3311	1.3289	1.3262	1.3240	1.3211
11-3/4	Feb. 15, 2005–10	2.49	1.3520	1.3500	1.3473	1.3452	.13425	1.3403	1.3374	1.3351
11-3/4	Nov. 15, 2009–14	6.00	1.3885	1.3866	1.3853	1.3833	1.3820	1.3799	1.3785	1.3764
11-7/8	Nov. 15, 2003	7.26	1.3516	1.3487	1.3463	1.3433	1.3408	1.3376	1.3350	—
12	May 15, 2005	4.25	1.3782	1.3755	1.3733	1.3705	1.3682	1.3653	1.3630	1.3599
12	Aug. 15, 2008–13	14.75	1.4053	1.4037	1.4015	1.3999	1.3976	1.3959	1.3935	1.3917
12-3/8	May 15, 2004	3.75	1.4027	1.3996	1.3970	1.3937	1.3910	1.3876	1.3847	1.3812
12-1/2	Aug. 15, 2009–14	4.75	1.4640	1.4623	1.4601	1.4583	1.4560	1.4542	1.4517	1.4498
12-3/4	Nov. 15, 2005–10	4.73	1.4546	1.4516	1.4491	1.4459	1.4433	1.4400	1.4373	1.4339
13-1/4	May 15, 2009–14	5.00	1.5394	1.5368	1.5347	1.5320	1.5299	1.5270	1.5248	1.5219
13-3/4	Aug. 15, 2004	4.00	1.5327	1.5293	1.5252	1.5217	1.5175	1.5139	1.5095	1.5057
13-7/8	May 15, 2006–11	4.60	1.5689	1.5653	1.5623	1.5586	1.5554	1.5515	1.5483	1.5442
14	Nov. 15, 2006–11	4.90	1.5875	1.5840	1.5810	1.5773	1.5743	1.5705	1.5672	1.5633

[a]Most recently auctioned 30-year bond eligible for delivery.

rise to a pricing bias that will make one particular deliverable T-bond slightly less expensive than the rest of the eligible T-bonds. This unique bond is known as the *cheapest to deliver*. Obviously, the short position holder will find it advantageous to deliver this unique T-bond. Thus, the short player is said to hold a *delivery option* (also known as a *quality option* in the lingo of the futures market). In other words, the delivery option represents the opportunity that the short T-bond futures holder has to deliver the cheapest eligible bond; and this opportunity arises from violations of the assumptions underlying the CBOT's conversion system. A similar option is present for the CBOT's T-note futures contract.

The existence of the delivery option is well known by market participants. Indeed, many investment houses employ real-time data and computers to continually track the cheapest-to-delivery T-bond. The particular bond that is the cheapest may change over time as interest rates change.[5] As a result, the futures price at any given time tends to reflect this unique T-bond. Another implication is that the hedge ratio is influenced by this bond, since the futures price tracks the cheapest-to-deliver bond. Thus, the delivery option held by short traders has consequences for both the futures price and hedging.

> The **cheapest to deliver** is that particular deliverable T-bond that the futures price tends to reflect.

> The **delivery option** represents the opportunity that the short T-bond futures holder has to deliver the cheapest eligible bond.

FUTURES PRICES AND IMPLIED REPO RATES

Using the carrying-charge approach discussed in Chapter 6, the futures price may be determined by the current spot price plus the costs of carrying the asset forward to delivery. These costs entail storing, transporting, and financing the spot asset. The arbitrage strategy that underlies the carrying-charge approach is called *cash-and-carry arbitrage*. As discussed earlier, it involves the purchase of the spot asset and the sale of the futures contract. Since the asset's future sale price is assured if the futures position is held to expiration, the arbitrage strategy should produce a return that is just sufficient to cover the carrying charges. Otherwise riskless profits can be obtained, ignoring market imperfections such as transaction costs.

Interest rate futures involve no significant storage or transportation costs. Thus, under the carrying-charge approach, the only relevant cost is that associated with financing the purchase of the underlying security. Recall from Chapters 8 and 9 that the financing cost is the only relevant carrying cost applicable to currencies and stock indices as well. Currencies, stock indices, Eurodollars, and Treasury securities are all financial instruments. As such, they exhibit nominal storage and transportation costs that can be safely ignored.

---

[5]For reasons beyond the scope of this book, it can be demonstrated that the cheapest-to-deliver T-bond at any given point in time is the one eligible bond that has the lowest spot price in relation to its invoice value.

We can use this result to illustrate a useful technique for determining whether cash-and-carry arbitrage would be profitable. Specifically, we should be able to readily determine the financing cost implied from an observed financial futures price. Recall from Chapter 6 that the financing rate applicable to most futures traders is the repo rate. Thus, if the futures price implies a financing rate, call the *implied repo rate*, that differs markedly from the actual repo rate, a cash-and-carry arbitrage opportunity should be present.

In this section we describe how an implied repo rate can be determined from an observed futures price and the carrying charge model. We also show how discrepancies between the implied and actual repo rates can signal arbitrage opportunities. Before doing so, however, let us emphasize two points. First, the implied repo rate can be determined for any financial futures contract, not just interest rate futures. Second, differences between the implied repo rate and actual rate are used only as signals to flag profitable arbitrage opportunities. The strategy that will have to be employed to exploit the opportunity itself remains the cash-and-carry strategy described in Chapter 6. In one sense then, traders might choose to focus on the implied repo rate as a diagnostic test for arbitrage opportunities.

Implied Repo Rates and T-Bill Futures

T-bills are pure discount securities that have no explicit interest payments. As such, the difference between spot and futures T-bill prices should solely reflect the financing charge associated with purchasing the spot T-bill. Therefore, from our basic carrying-charge model (Equation 6.3), it follows that

(10.4) $$_T f_0 = S_0 (1 + r)^T,$$

where $_T f_0$ represents the T-bill futures price for delivery at time T, S_0 is the spot T-bill price, and r is the repo rate. Equation 10.4 assumes discrete compounding for convenience.

Notice from Equation 10.4 that if S_0 and $_T f_0$ are observable, then we can obtain the implied repo rate, $\hat{r}$:

(10.5) $$\hat{r} = (_T f_0 / S_0)^{1/T} - 1.$$

Clearly, the implied repo rate is that rate that makes the carrying-charge model hold exactly. In one sense, $\hat{r}$ is the cost of financing that produces no arbitrage profit. If the actual cost of financing the spot asset (i.e., the actual repo rate, r) is substantially less that the implied repo rate, $\hat{r}$, then cash-and-carry arbitrage may be profitable.

To illustrate how the implied repo rate can signal a profitable arbitrage opportunity, consider the following price information:

■ A T-bill maturing in thirty-three days has a discount rate of 5.75.

- A T-bill maturing in 124 days has a discount rate of 5.98.
- The nearby T-bill futures has an IMM Index of 94.20.

Recall that the discount for T-bills is quoted on a 360-day basis. Therefore, the T-bill maturing in 33 days has a price of 99.4729:

$$100 - 5.75(33/360) = 99.4729.$$

The return on the bill is 6.02 percent:

$$(100/99.4729)^{(365/33)} - 1 = .0602.$$

Similarly, the price of the T-bill maturing in 124 days is

$$100 - 5.98(124/360) = 97.9402.$$

Finally, the IMM Index of 94.20 implies a futures price of 98.55:

$$100 - 5.8(90/360) = 98.55.$$

If we buy the 124-day T-bill at 97.9402 and sell the futures contract at 98.55, we can sell the bill upon contract delivery and receive a price of 98.55. This is a cash-and-carry strategy. We are assured a return of 7.11 percent:

$$(98.55/97.9402)^{365/33} - 1 = .0711.$$

Notice that this is the same procedure for determining the implied repo rate (Equation 10.5). Indeed, 7.11 percent is the implied repo rate, $\hat{r}$, in this example. If the T-bill maturing in 124 days can be financed at a rate that is less than 7.11 percent, the cash-and-carry strategy provides a riskless arbitrage profit. This seems likely in our example, since the implied repo rate is more than 100 basis points above the return on a short-term Treasury bill (6.02 percent). Recall that the actual repo rate is typically only slightly greater than the rate on Treasury bills. Finally, since Eurodollars are also pure discount instruments, a similar procedure is used to determine the implied repo rate from Eurodollar futures prices.

Implied Repo Rates and T-Bond Futures

Determining the implied repo rate for a T-bond or T-note futures contract is more complex because we must account for the subtleties associated with the CBOT's unique delivery system. We illustrate the process here with T-bond futures. A similar procedure obtains for T-note futures.

Suppose that we have identified the cheapest-to-deliver T-bond. To buy the bond, we pay the spot price, S, plus any accrued interest since the last coupon payment, AI. Assume that we finance the purchase through the sale of a repo. Also, we simultaneously engage to write a T-bond futures contract expiring at T. If we hold the T-bond until expiration and make delivery, we receive the invoice price. This is a cash-and-carry strategy. By the carrying-charge theory, therefore, no arbitrage implies the following relation:

(10.6)
$$(CF)(SP) + AI_T = (S + AI)(1 + r)^T.$$

The left-hand side of Equation 10.6 is just the invoice price—that is, the amount we receive upon delivery of the bond (see Equation 10.3). The right-hand side is the amount paid for the bond, $S + AI$, compounded by the repo rate over the period T. Thus, Equation 10.6 is our no-arbitrage equilibrium condition; the amount we receive for the bond must be what we paid, plus the costs of carrying it to delivery.[6]

To obtain the implied repo rate, $\hat{r}$, we rearrange Equation 10.6:

(10.7)
$$\hat{r} = \left[\frac{(CF)(SP) + AI_T}{S + AI} \right]^{1/T} - 1.$$

If the T-bond can be financed at a rate less than $\hat{r}$, then a cash-and-carry arbitrage should prove profitable.

As a numerical example, consider the following variables:

CF	=	1.2610	S	=	124 12/32
SP	=	97.2500	AI	=	1.08
AI_T	=	3.70	T	=	.1479 (54 days)

From Equation 10.7, the implied repo rate is 4.82 percent:

$$\hat{r} = \left[\frac{(1.2610)(97.25) + 3.70}{124.375 + 1.08} \right]^{1/.1479} - 1 = .0482.$$

Since it is very unlikely that the bond can be financed in the actual repo market at a rate of less than 4.82 percent, a profitable arbitrage strategy is not present.

Notice that in the above example, we implicitly and quite unrealistically assumed that the invoice price was known. Of course, the invoice price is determined by the settlement price on the position day, which is currently unknown. In light of this, the trader must employ the current T-bond futures price to proxy for SP. Therefore, in the above example $SP = 97.25$ represents the current futures price.

HEDGING WITH INTEREST RATE FUTURES

In this section of the chapter, we examine a number of hedging applications entailing short- and long-term interest rate futures con-

---

[6]Equation 10.6 assumes that no coupon payment occurs between the time when the cash-and-carry position is assumed and the time when it is reversed at delivery. If a coupon is paid, it will serve to lower the arbitrager's financing cost. The effect on the implied repo rate should be small, however.

tracts. These applications certainly do not exhaust all of the hedging possibilities associated with interest rate futures. However, they illustrate fundamental hedging concepts that will serve as the basis of all hedging strategies involving interest rate futures.

The applications presented rely largely on a hedge ratio known as the *price-sensitivity hedge ratio*. This ratio, developed by R. Kolb and R. Chiang (1981), is designed exclusively to be used with interest rate futures contracts.

The **price-sensitivity hedge ratio** is designed to be used with interest rate futures contracts, and it insulates wealth from changes in interest rates.

Price-Sensitivity Hedge Ratio

The basic idea underlying the price-sensitivity hedge ratio is to determine a position in the interest rate futures contract where wealth is insulated from unanticipated changes in interest rates. To obtain this ratio, Kolb and Chiang assume that interest rate changes on all bonds result from a change in a single interest rate, r, which is the risk-free government bond rate. In other words, when r changes, so, too, do all other bond yields.

Define the following variables:

S = the price of the bond held in the spot market

f = the price of the interest rate futures contract

Y_S = the yield on the spot bond held

Y_f = the yield on the futures contract implied by f.

A hedged portfolio can be constructed by assuming a position in the futures contract along with the spot bond position held:

$$V = S + V_f N_f,$$

where V is the value of the hedged portfolio, V_f is the value of the futures contract, and N_f is the price-sensitivity hedge ratio. It is N_f that we wish to determine.

The change in V with respect to a change in r is determined by taking the total derivative, dV/dr. Since $dV_f/dr = df/dr$, we have

$$dV/dr = dS/dr + (df/dr)N_f.$$

To ensure that the hedged portfolio's value is insulated from changes in interest rates, we set the total derivative equal to zero. Since we do not know the derivatives dS/dr and df/dr, we employ the chain rule for differentiation:

$$dV/dr = \frac{dS}{dY_S} \times \frac{dY_S}{dr} + \frac{df}{dY_f} \times \frac{dY_f}{dr} \times N_f = 0.$$

Notice that his procedure introduces the yield changes, dY_S/dr and dY_f/dr, into the analysis. It is typically assumed that these yield changes are equal. Thus, substituting and solving for N_f gives us

(10.8)
$$N_f = -[(dS/dY_S)/(df/dY_f)].$$

The discrete version of Equation 10.8 is approximated by

(10.9) $$N_f = -[(\Delta S/\Delta Y_S)/(\Delta f/\Delta Y_f)].$$

Equation 10.9 is the price-sensitivity hedge ratio. Hedging applications follow in which it is useful to express N_f in terms of the *durations* of the bond and futures contract. Recall from your previous finance classes that *duration* is a measure of the sensitivity of a bond's price to interest rate changes. For our spot bond, it can be approximated as follows:

$$D_S \approx -[(\Delta S/S)(1 + Y_S)/\Delta Y_S],$$

where D_S represents duration. Similarly, for the futures contract duration is approximated by:[7]

$$D_f \approx -[(\Delta f/f)(1 + Y_f)/\Delta Y_f].$$

Letting $\Delta Y_f = \Delta Y_S$ and substituting in Equation 10.9 gives

(10.10) $$N_f = -[D_S S(1 + Y_f)/D_f f(1 + Y_S)].$$

The point of these equations is to show that the price-sensitivity hedge ratio can also be expressed in terms of duration.

Hedging a Commercial Paper Offering

We provide three hedging applications—two short hedges and one long hedge. The first example involves a forthcoming commercial paper issue. Large corporations continually borrow money in the short-term markets in order to meet their working capital requirements. Often these corporations choose to finance their short-term assets (e.g. inventory and accounts receivable) by issuing *commercial paper*, a short-term promissory note that, like Treasury bills, is sold at a discount and on a 360-day basis.

Suppose that it is March 1, and a corporate treasurer of a large, creditworthy firm decides to issue approximately $5 million of commercial paper. The issue will occur on June 1 and have a 180-day maturity. The treasurer is concerned about a general rise in interest rates over the next few months; such an increase would raise the firm's financing costs, since the paper would have to be issued at a higher rate (i.e., deeper discount). Thus, the treasurer wishes to hedge using short-term interest rate futures. She decides to employ the Eurodollar futures with June expiration. Since no futures on commercial paper exist, the treasurer is utilizing a *cross hedge*.

Exhibit 10.5 presents the results of the hedge. Since commercial paper and Eurodollars exhibit no coupon payments, their durations are their

---

[7]Actually, the duration of a futures contract refers to the duration of the bond underlying the contract as of the date of the contract's expiration.

maturities: 180 days and 90 days, respectively. Hence, $D_S/D_f = 2$. The variable S is the current (March 1) proceeds from the commercial paper, which are $4,773,000. This figure stems from an assumed current rate on 180-day commercial paper of 9.08 percent. Thus, the yield on commercial paper, Y_S, is now .0988. The futures price, f, is $973,525, based on an IMM Index of 89.41 (see Exhibit 10.2). The yield implied on 90-day Eurodollars, Y_f, is therefore .1149. With these numbers and Equation 10.10, the price-sensitivity hedge ratio is -9.95:

$$N_f = -2 \left(\frac{4,773,000}{973,525} \right) \left(\frac{1.1149}{1.0988} \right) = -9.95.$$

Hence, the corporate treasurer shorts 10 June Eurodollar contracts.

Assume that it is now June 1 and that (1) the firm can issue the paper at a discount rate of 10.12 percent; and (2) the June futures contract has an IMM Index of 88.64. Thus, interest rates have risen over the three-month period. The proceeds from the commercial paper issue are just $4,747,000. However, as Exhibit 10.5 shows, the firm realizes a $19,250 profit by reversing the short futures position. The effective proceeds from the paper issue are therefore $4,766,250, implying an effective financing rate of 10.20 percent. This is substantially lower than the rate that would have applied if no hedge had been employed: 11.10 percent.

The hedge proved successful since the commercial paper and Eurodollar rates moved together over the period. This is to be expected. Assuming a short position in the futures contract introduced negative

Exhibit 10.5:

Hedging a Commercial Paper Issue

March 1

Spot Market:
    Current 180-day commercial paper rate is 9.08
    Proceeds per $100: $100 - 9.08(180/360) = 95.46$
    Total proceeds = $4,773,000 = .9546 ($5,000,000)
    Yield: $(100/95.46)^{365/180} - 1 = .0988$
Futures Market:
    June Eurodollar IMM Index = 89.41
    Price per $100: $100 - 10.59(90/360) = 97.3525$
    Contract price = $973,525 = .973525 ($1,000,000)
    Implied yield = $(100/97.3525)^{365/90} - 1 = .1149$
    Short 10 contracts

June 1

Spot Market:
    Issue commercial paper at a discount of 10.12
    Proceeds per $100: $100 - 10.12(180/360) = 94.94$
    Total proceeds = $4,747,000 = .9494 ($5,000,000)
    Issue cost without hedge: $(100/94.94)^{365/180} - 1 = .1110$
Futures Market:
    Reverse short position at IMM Index = 88.64
    Price per $100: $100 - 11.36(90/360) = 97.1600$
    Contract price = $971,600
    Futures profit = $19,250 = (971,600 - 973,525)(-10)$
    Effective proceeds = $4,766,250 = 4,747,000 + 19,250
    Effective issuing cost: $(5,000,000/4,766,250)^{365/180} - 1 = .1020$

correlation that helped to reduce the interest rate risk associated with the future commercial paper offering. Obviously, similar hedging examples could be constructed to demonstrate this same principal, including a corporation about to issue a longer-term bond or a young married couple soon to obtain a home mortgage. Indeed, the interest rate uncertainty of any future borrowing strategies can be reduced by shorting the appropriate amount and type of interest rate futures contract.

Hedging a Long T-Bond Position

Suppose that it is currently March 1, and a pension fund manager holds $5 million face-value T-bonds with a coupon rate of 12 percent and a maturity of nearly 20 years. The bond is currently priced at 117 per $100 par value, and its yield is 10 percent. The bond's duration is 9.09 years.

Assume that the T-bonds must be sold on June 1 in order to meet scheduled pension payments. The manager is concerned about an unexpected increase in market interest rates during this period, since such an increase would reduce the market value of the bonds and might thus cause the fund to fail to meet its liability. Consequently, the manager seeks to employ the June T-bond futures contract in order to immunize against the adverse effects of interest rate changes. From Exhibit 10.2, the current June futures price is 87–22, or $87,687.50 per contract.

As discussed earlier in this chapter, the T-bond futures price tends to track the cheapest-to-deliver bond. Hence, the pension fund manager must identify this unique bond in order to determine the duration and implied yield on the June futures contract. Suppose that the manager identifies the cheapest-to-deliver as the T-bond with coupon 10 3/8s and maturity of about twenty-five years. If we assume that the futures contract expired on the first day of the delivery month, June 1, and given a futures price of 87–22, then the deliverable bond has a duration of 8.96 years and a yield of .1194.

With these figures, the price-sensitivity hedge ratio is −68.87:

$$N_f = -\left(\frac{9.09}{8.96}\right)\left(\frac{5,850,000}{87,687.50}\right)\left(\frac{1.1194}{1.1000}\right) = -68.87.$$

Thus, the fund manager will write sixty-nine T-bond futures contracts in order to immunize the current bond value of $5,850,000.[8] If interest rates rise unexpectedly, this short position should offset most, if not all, of the loss incurred on the long T-bond position.

Exhibit 10.6 illustrates this concept. Assuming that, on June 1, the bond price is down to 110–20, while the June futures price is down to 82–31, the pension manager sells the T-bonds for $5,531,250, sustaining a loss of $318,750. However, the profit on the short futures position is $4,718.75 per contract, or $325,593.75. Thus, the short hedge is sufficient to overcome all of the loss sustained in the spot position. Obviously, the same strategy applies to many other investors who hold fixed-income securities, including banks, mutual funds, insurance companies, and the like.

Hedging a Subsequent T-Bill Purchase

The preceding examples involved writing interest rate futures contracts in order to protect a spot position against unanticipated increases in market rates. However, interest rate futures can also be employed to ensure that capital will not be invested at a lower future rate. In other words, a long interest rate futures position can be used to hedge against falling interest rates.

Suppose that a corporate treasurer expects $1 million to be available for investment by May 19. It is now March 1, and the treasurer wishes to purchase 91-day T-bills at the weekly auction on May 18. In this way,

---

[8]Accrued interest is ignored since it is not subject to any uncertainty; the coupon rate on the bonds held is fixed at 12 percent.

Exhibit 10.6:

Hedging a Long T-bond

March 1

Spot Market:
   Current bond price is 117–00
   Current value of bonds held is $5,850,000
Futures Market:
   June T-bond futures price is 87–22
   Price per contract is $87,687.50
   Short 69 contracts

June 1

Spot Market:
   Sell T-bonds at 110–20
   Price per bond is $1,106.26
   Value of bond position is $5,531,250
Futures Market:
   Reverse short position at 82–31
   Price per contract is $82,968.75
   Profit on short position: $325,593.75 = (82,968.75 − 87,687.50)(− 69)
   Overall portfolio value: $5,856,843.75 = 5,531,250 + 325,593.75
   Overall profit = $6,843.75

the idle capital will earn interest until it is employed for longer-term investment opportunities, such as the purchase of plant and equipment. T-bills are presently sold at a discount of 8.60, and the treasurer feels that rates may be lower in the near term. Thus, he decides to assume a long position in the June T-bill futures contract. From Exhibit 10.2, the June T-bill IMM Index is 90.89. Since the durations, prices, and yields of the spot and futures contracts are very similar, the treasurer decides to assume a long position in one futures contract.[9]

Exhibit 10.7 presents the results of this hedging strategy under the following assumptions: (1) rates have declined, and the 91-day T-bill is purchased at a discount of 8.00 on May 18; and (2) the June IMM Index is now 92.10, implying a new futures price of $980,250 per contract. Since rates have fallen, the profit on the long futures contract, $3,025, has partially offset the cost associated with investing funds at a lower rate. By effectively reducing the T-bill cost by $3,025 to $976,753, the hedge raised the annualized yield to 9.89 percent. This is substantially greater than 8.54 percent, which is the yield that would have obtained if no hedge had been undertaken. Thus, the long hedge proves successful in protecting against a decline in market rates of interest. If rates had increased, the hedge would have unfortunately tempered the invest-

---

[9]The yield on the spot T-bill is .0922. The yield implied by the IMM Index is .0979. The spot T-bill price (per $100) is 97.8261, while the futures price (per $100) is 97.7225. Since the T-bill has a 91-day maturity, while the futures contract assumes a 90-day bill, both have durations of about .25 years. Thus, the price-sensitivity hedge ratio is nearly one contract.

March 1

Spot Market:
　91-day T-bills sell at a discount of 8.60
　Price per $100: $100 - 8.60(91/360) = 97.8261$
　Proceeds per $1 million: $978,261
　Yield: $(100/97.8261)^{365/91} - 1 = .0922$.
Futures Market:
　June T-bill IMM Index is 90.89
　Price per $100: $100 - 9.11(90/360) = 97.7225$
　Contract price: $977,225
　Implied yield: $(100/97.7225)^{365/90} - 1 = .0979$
　Buy one contract

May 18

Spot Market:
　91-day T-bills are purchased at a discount of 8.00
　Price per $100: $100 - 8.00(91/360) = 97.9778$
　Proceeds per $1 million: $979,778
　Yield: $(100/97.9778)^{365/91} - 1 = .0854$
Futures Market:
　Reverse long position at IMM Index of 92.10
　Price per $100: $100 - 7.90(90/360) = 98.025$
　Price per contract: $980,250
　Profit on futures position: $3,025 = (980,250 - 977,225)$
　Effective T-bill price: $976,753 = (979,778 - 3,025)$
　Effective yield: $(1,000,000/976,753)^{365/91} - 1 = .0989$

ment opportunity. But, of course, this is the implicit cost of hedging any spot position with a futures contract.

POPULAR SPECULATIVE STRATEGIES

Position traders can take outright positions in interest rate futures contracts to exploit forecasts of subsequent interest rate movements. For instance, a long position in a T-bill futures contract might be assumed if a speculator felt that short-term rates would soon decline. However, most speculators in the interest rate futures market employ spreads rather than outright contract positions. In this market, intracommodity spreads are generally used to speculate on the changing shape of the yield curve, while intercommodity spreads are generally used to speculate on changing yield spreads across different underlying instruments. In this section we provide some examples of these popular speculative strategies.

Intracommodity spreads are generally used to speculate on the changing shape of the yield curve, while intercommodity spreads are generally used to speculate on changing yield spreads across different underlying instruments.

A. Spot Rates

Time to Maturity	Rates
3 months	8.50%
6 months	9.50%
9 months	10.00%
12 months	10.50%

B. Futures Rates

Contract	Time to Expiration	IMM Index	Rates
June	3 months	89.49	10.51%
September	6 months	89.24	10.75%
December	9 months	88.83	11.17%

Intracommodity Spread

Exhibit 10.8 provides a series of spot and futures rates for U.S. Treasury bills assumed to exist on March 18. These rates imply a steep and upward-sloping yield curve, at least in the short-maturity segment of the market.

Now suppose that a position trader felt that, regardless of whether interest rates would rise or fall overall, the yield curve would flatten somewhat over the next few months. In this event, the yield spread between the various futures contracts would narrow. To exploit the forecast the speculator would therefore engage in a spread where a longer-maturity futures contract is purchased and a shorter-maturity contract is written. Specifically, assume the speculator takes a long position in the December contract while shorting the September T-bill contract.

Exhibit 10.9 presents the outcome of the spread if the yield curve indeed is less steep by August 15. On this date the speculator reverses the spread and, under the new assumed futures prices of 90.79 and 90.51 for the September and December contracts, earns a profit of $325 (13 basis points × $25 per basis point). Notice that the profit obtained because the December futures price movement was greater (in absolute terms); the longer-term futures price had to change by a greater amount, for a given change in the shorter-term futures price, if the upward-sloping yield curve became less steeply sloped.

This same type of intracommodity spread could have been applied to the T-note or T-bond futures market if the speculator anticipated a flatter yield curve in the middle- and longer-maturity segments of the market, respectively. More generally, we can state that an intracommodity instance, if we hold an equity portfolio whose capital value is 1,000 units of the SP500, then we short 1,000 units of the SP500 futures (or two SP500 futures contracts, since the contract multiple is $500).[6] The rate of return on our fully hedged portfolio, $R(H)$, is

(9.10)
$$R(H) = \tilde{R}(I) - \tilde{R}(f)$$
$$= \frac{\tilde{I}(1) - I(0)}{I(0)} + \delta - \frac{\tilde{I}(1) - {}_1f_0}{I(0)}$$
$$= \frac{{}_1f_0 - I(0)}{I(0)} + \delta.$$

Since all risk associated with the uncertain future value of the index, $\tilde{I}(1)$, has been hedged away, $R(H)$ is a riskless return. $R(H)$ must equal the rate of return on other types of riskless assets, or profitable arbitrage opportunities will be present. This implies a necessary, equilibrium relation between $\tilde{R}(I)$, the riskless rate r, and $\tilde{R}(f)$. Substituting r for $R(H)$ gives

(9.11a)
$$r = \tilde{R}(I) - \tilde{R}(f),$$

or

(9.11b)
$$r = \frac{{}_1f_0 - I(0)}{I(0)} + \delta.$$

Rearranging Equation 9.11b and solving for the futures price gives

(9.12)
$$ {}_1f_0 = I(0)[1 + r - \delta]. $$

Equation 9.12 is the one-period carrying-charge model for index futures prices. It represents the one-period analog of Equation 9.8. Thus, we have demonstrated the arbitrage argument underlying the carrying-charge approach of determining index futures prices. Of course Equations 9.8 and 9.12 will hold only approximately, given market imperfections such as transaction costs, restrictions on short selling, and the like.[7]

---

[6]Only a stock portfolio whose composition is identical to the index underlying the futures contract can be hedged perfectly with the contract. For all other portfolios, some amount of basis risk remains.

[7]When comparing Equation 9.7, the stock index futures price under the expectations approach, with Equation 9.8 or 9.12, the stock index futures price under the carrying-charge approach, we see that the two approaches yield equivalent price expressions only when $E[\tilde{R}(I)] = r$; that is, only when the expected return on the stock index equals the riskless rate of interest. At first, this seems unreasonable. However, recall that Equation 9.7 was derived under the explicit assumption of risk neutrality. Therefore, the two approaches are completely consistent, since all assets' expected returns are risk free when investors are risk neutral. If we relax this assumption, then, under the expectations approach, the index futures price will, in general, equal the expected value of the future index less a premium for risk:

$$ {}_Tf_0 = I(0)[1 + (E[\tilde{R}(I)] - risk\ premium) - \delta]. $$

Since $E[\tilde{R}(I)] - risk\ premium = r$, the seeming conflict between the two approaches is resolved.

Exhibit 9.4:

A Self-Contained Example of One-Period Stock Index Futures Arbitrage

Given:	$_1f_0 = I(0)[1 + r - \delta]$
	$_1f_0 = 325$
	$I(0) = 300$
	$r = .10$
	$\delta = .04$
Beginning-of-Period:	Write the futures contract.
	Borrow $300 at 10 percent.
	Buy the stock portfolio.
End-of-Period:	Sell the stock portfolio.
	Use the proceeds to reverse the short futures position, receiving $325.
	Collect dividends of $12.
	Repay principal and interest of $330.
Total Profit:	$7 (per index unit).

On the Ability to Arbitrage

The no-arbitrage condition underlying the carrying-charge approach of determining stock index futures prices depends critically on the ability of traders to create (nearly) perfect hedges. A futures price inconsistent with the carrying-charge model implies an exploitable arbitrage opportunity. To exploit the opportunity, however, the trader must create a hedged portfolio (as above). Exhibit 9.4 presents a one-period example of arbitrage involving stock index futures. Notice that this is a cash-and-carry arbitrage. Price pressure created from such arbitrage trading will serve to restore the cost-of-carry relation.

Clearly, replicating a position in the actual stock portfolio underlying the contract is difficult at best. Yet the arbitrage strategy relies on the trader's ability to do so, thereby creating the hedge. The vast numbers of stocks underlying many of the indices, and the tremendous transaction costs involved in trading such stocks, represent barriers to arbitrage that are difficult to overcome. In short, the ability of the arbitrager to exploit violations of the carrying-charge model is suspect because of the difficulties of assuming the stock portfolio and resulting hedge. For this reason, the cost-of-carry model is likely to be less accurate when applied to stock index futures than other contracts such as currency futures; it is easier to establish a hedge with single assets rather than whole indices. Indeed, researchers have documented substantial violations of the carrying-charge model when applied to stock index futures [see S. Figlewski (1984) in the end-of-chapter "Selected References"].

A viable solution to this problem is to create smaller portfolios that are highly correlated with the major indices. This would allow the arbitrager to create a sound hedge (i.e., one with little basis risk) while minimizing the transaction costs involved. Indeed, this is one of the advantages of

Equation 9.7 states that the current index futures price equals the current index value plus the expected index appreciation over the period. This equation represents the stock index futures price under the expectations approach and assuming risk neutrality and no daily resettlement. The expected *rate* of appreciation on the stock index is $E[\tilde{R}(I)] - \delta$, the expected index return less the dividend yield. This result obtains because, again, the stock index itself omits dividends. For the settlement prices reflected in Exhibit 9.3, where $_Tf_0 > I(0)$, the expectations approach implies that the expected rate of appreciation on the underlying index is positive, that is, $E[\tilde{R}(I)] > \delta$.

Of course, Equation 9.7 requires modification if we relax the assumptions of risk neutrality and no daily resettlement. As discussed in Chapter 6, the futures price should also reflect a term premium, a reinvestment rate premium, and a hedging premium if investors are risk averse, and if daily resettlement occurs under nonconstant interest rates. Thus, the observed differences between spot and future index prices in Exhibit 9.3 may not be solely attributable to the expected rate of appreciation on the index.

Carrying-Charge Approach

Recall that the carrying-charge theory of determining futures prices is grounded in arbitrage restrictions relating to the costs of carrying an asset forward in time. For stock indices, which are financial assets, storage costs and transportation costs are nominal and may be safely ignored. Of course, financing costs remain, and the index itself pays dividends over the carrying period. Thus, ignoring market imperfections such as transaction costs and restrictions on short selling, the carrying-charge model of futures prices given by Equation 6.3 implies:

$$(9.8) \qquad _Tf_0 = I(0)e^{(r - \delta)(T)},$$

where r represents the cost of financing the stock index.

Equation 9.8 represents the carrying-charge model for stock index futures. It states that the current index futures price for delivery in time T is equal to the current index level plus the costs of carrying the stock index through time. For the settlement futures prices reflected in Exhibit 9.3, the carrying-charge approach implies that $r > \delta$. This is consistent with observed dividend yields on major stock indices, which historically have been about 3 percent to 4 percent.

To illustrate the arbitrage argument underlying Equation 9.8, let us consider a one-period horizon where dividends are paid at the end of the period. Define the one-period "rate of return" on a long index futures position, $\tilde{R}(f)$, as follows:

$$(9.9) \qquad \tilde{R}(f) = [\tilde{I}(1) - _1f_0]/I(0).$$

Now consider a fully hedged equity portfolio constructed by shorting one "index unit" of the futures contract for each "index unit" held. For

- The stock index in question is arithmetically averaged.[4]
- Stock dividends are known with certainty.
- The dividend leakage exhibited by a stock index can be represented by a continuous stream determined by a constant *dividend yield*. This assumption is somewhat inconsistent with the actual dividend pattern exhibited by a stock index; stock indices truly have discrete dividend payouts that fluctuate through time because most stock dividends are clustered at certain calendar months and weekdays. However, it would be extremely difficult to determine index futures prices using day-to-day dividend figures. It is simpler to employ a dividend yield, which is defined as the dividends paid by all of the underlying stocks (properly weighted) divided by the current index level. Some investment services (e.g., *Value Line Options*) report periodic dividend yields on the major stock indices.[5]

Expectations Approach

Under risk neutrality and ignoring daily resettlement, the expectations approach argues that the current futures price represents an unbiased estimate of the spot price expected to prevail at contract delivery. For stock index futures, this implies that

(9.5)
$$_T f_0 = E[\tilde{I}(T)],$$

where $_T f_0$ is the current futures price for delivery at time T, and $E[\tilde{I}(T)]$ is the (unknown) stock index level expected to prevail at time T. We may express the expected return on the stock index as follows:

(9.6)
$$E[\tilde{R}(I)] = \frac{E[\tilde{I}(T)] - I(0)}{I(0)} + \delta,$$

where $E[\tilde{R}(I)]$ is the expected return on the stock index for the period, $I(0)$ is the current index level, and δ is the index's dividend yield. The dividend yield is known and constant, and it is treated separately since the stock index omits dividends; that is, the index is computed net of dividends as discussed above.

Substituting using Equation 9.5 and rearranging, Equation 9.6 becomes

(9.7)
$$_T f_0 = I(0)[1 + E[\tilde{R}(I)] - \delta].$$

---

[4]The determination of futures prices for geometrically averaged indices is more complicated. For a model to determine VLCI futures prices, see T. Eytan and G. Harpaz (1986). This complexity may be another cause for the relatively low volume in VLCI futures and is related to the inability to replicate the index (discussed above). For an analysis of futures contracts on other (non-stock) geometric indices, see T. Eytan, G. Harpaz, and S. Krull (1988) and M. Ehrhardt and A. Tucker (1990).

[5]For more on this topic, see the discussions in Chapters 11 and 18 regarding stock index options.

March 18:	Long one December T-bill futures at 88.83.
	Short one September T-bill futures at 89.24.
August 15:	Short one December T-bill futures at 90.51.
	Long one September T-bill futures at 90.79.
Profits:	December contract: $4,200 (168 basis points)
	September contract: $-$3,875 ($-$155 basis points)
	Total: $325 (13 basis points $\times$ $25)

March 18:	Write one December Eurodollar futures at 87.96.
	Buy one December T-bill futures at 88.83.
October 10:	Buy one December Eurodollar futures at 87.59.
	Write one December T-bill futures at 88.72.
Profits:	Eurodollar contract: $925 (37 basis points)
	T-bill contract: $-$275 ($-$11 basis points)
	Total: $650 (26 basis points $\times$ $25)

interest rate futures spread may be utilized to speculate on any fore-casted change in the shape of the yield curve; the speculator simply needs to design a spread that will profit from the forecasted change.

Intercommodity Spread

An intercommodity interest rate futures spread is used to speculate on changing yield spreads across different underlying instruments. One well-known yield spread, the *TED spread*, is the absolute yield spread between T-bills and Eurodollar deposits. By employing a spread entailing both T-bill and Eurodollar futures contracts of the same maturity, a position trader can wager on a forecasted change in the TED spread.

The **TED spread** is the absolute yield spread between T-bills and Eurodollar deposits.

For example, suppose that a position trader expects the TED spread to widen because Eurodollar deposits seem to be growing riskier, and he thinks this risk will soon be reflected in the LIBOR. To exploit this forecast, the speculator will write a Eurodollar futures contract and assume a long position in a T-bill futures contract with the same delivery date. Specifically, the speculator engages in the intercommodity spread described in the top half of Exhibit 10.10. If the forecast proves correct, and later, on October 10, the speculator can reverse the positions at the new IMM Index values shown, then a profit of $650 (twenty-six basis points at $25 per basis point) is realized. These new values imply that the TED spread widened. Under the old values of March 18 (87.96 and 88.83), the (implied) TED spread was 102 basis points:

$$\text{Implied T-bill yield: } 100 - 11.17(90/360) = 97.2075$$
$$(100/97.2075)^{365/90} - 1 = .1217$$
$$\text{Implied Eurodollar yield: } 100 - 12.04(90/360) = 96.9900$$
$$(100/96.9900)^{365/90} - 1 = .1319$$
$$\text{Implied TED spread: } |.1217 - .1319| = .0102.$$

Under the new values of October 10 (87.59 and 88.72), the (implied) TED spread is 133 basis points:

$$\text{Implied T-bill yield: } 100 - 11.28(90/360) = 97.1800$$
$$(100/97.1800)^{365/90} - 1 = .1230$$
$$\text{Implied Eurodollar yield: } 100 - 12.41(90/360) = 96.8975$$
$$(100/96.8975)^{365/90} - 1 = .1363$$
$$\text{Implied TED spread: } |.1230 - .1363| = .0133.$$

Of course, the speculator would have reversed the strategy if the forecast called for a narrowing of the TED spread.

The NOB

The *NOB* ("notes over bonds") refers to a popular speculative strategy involving the T-note and T-bond futures contracts traded on the CBOT. Since the T-bond contract is traded on a longer-term instrument (i.e., one with greater duration or interest rate sensitivity), a T-bond futures price will likely change by more than that of a T-note futures for a given change in market rates of interest. The NOB is an intercommodity spread designed to take advantage of expectations concerning changing market rates.

Suppose that you expect interest rates to decline in general. To profit from this expectation, you would buy T-bond futures and short T-note futures with the same delivery date. An equivalent decline in rates on both underlying Treasury securities will drive-up T-bond futures prices more than T-note futures prices. Thus, the NOB strategy should prove profitable, since the gain on the long position will be greater than the resulting loss on the short T-note position. An expectation of rising market rates will result in an opposite NOB spread, where bond futures are sold and note futures are bought.

Since the two underlying instruments have far different maturities, a NOB spread is somewhat like an intercommodity spread as well. It can therefore be employed to speculate on forecasted changes in the shape of the yield curve. For instance, suppose that you expect the (upward-sloping) yield curve to become flatter. This means you expect yields on longer-term T-bonds to fall (prices rise) relative to yields on shorter-term T-notes. As a consequence, you would assume a long position in T-bond futures while simultaneously taking a short position in T-note futures

The **NOB** is an intercommodity spread designed to take advantage of expectations concerning changing market rates of interest. It can also be used to speculate on forecasted changes in the shape of the yield curve.

with the same delivery date. The opposite NOB spread would be appropriate if the forecast called for the yield curve to become more steeply sloped. An example of this form of NOB spread is the subject of Problem 21 at the end of the chapter.

The Turtle

The *turtle* strategy entails a T-bill futures and two T-bond futures with different delivery dates. The idea is to exploit a misalignment in the futures prices. Based on the carrying-charge theory, the two T-bond futures prices should imply a yield that is (nearly) equivalent to that implied by a T-bill futures price, assuming the T-bill futures maturity is the same as the maturity difference among the two T-bond futures contracts. The turtle strategy can be employed to exploit violations of this illustration of the Law of One Price.

For instance, suppose that the yield implied from the two bond futures is 9 percent, while the yield implied by the T-bill futures is 9.5 percent. In other words, the T-bill futures price is too low relative to the T-bond futures prices. To exploit this, the speculator would engage in the following turtle strategy: long the T-bill futures contract, long the shorter-term T-bond futures contract, and short the long-term T-bond futures contract. That is, the speculator assumes a long position in the bill contract and an intracommodity spread in the bond contracts. Presuming the futures prices move in such a way as to restore parity among the implied yields, the turtle strategy will prove profitable. Indeed, the speculator's own trades will serve to "push" and "pull" the various futures prices so as to equate the implied yields.

One final caveat about the turtle strategy is that any misalignment between the implied yields may be due to the confounding price effects of the wild-card and delivery options present in the T-bond futures market. Recall that the CBOT's unique delivery system gives rise to these options. Thus, differences in the implied yields may represent only the value of these options. However, since the turtle strategy entails short *and* long positions in T-bond futures, much of this option value may be reduced or eliminated.

The **turtle** strategy entails a T-bill futures and two T-bond futures with different delivery dates. It is designed to exploit a misalignment in the futures prices.

EMPIRICAL EVIDENCE ON INTEREST RATE FUTURES

A substantial number of empirical studies regarding interest rate futures contracts have been conducted. In this section we summarize them, addressing the issues of hedging effectiveness, pricing and market efficiency, and the values of the wild-card and delivery options. Obviously, these issues are interrelated.

Hedging Effectiveness

Perhaps the earliest study investigating the hedging effectiveness of interest rate futures was that of L. Ederington (1979). Using weekly data for the period of 1976 through 1977, Ederington found that two-week hedges formed with T-bill futures contracts reduced risk by about 20 percent, as measured by the volatility of returns. For four-week hedges, the risk was reduced by about 75 percent.

Other authors report similar risk-reducing opportunities. A. Senchak and J. Easterwood (1983) examined the ability of T-bill futures to hedge the rates on CDs issued by commercial banks. Using three- and six-month hedges over the period 1976 to 1980, they found that a hedged position exhibited about one-third of the risk of an unhedged position.

J. Hill and T. Schneeweis (1982) examined the ability of T-bond futures to cross hedge corporate and utility bond positions. Using monthly data for 1977 through 1979, the authors reported that the T-bond hedges reduced risk by about 70 percent. Because of the nature of the cross hedge, effectiveness was not as substantial for lower-rated bonds. G. Gay, R. Kolb, and R. Chiang (1983) reported similar results for a sample of 250 corporate bonds for the period of 1979 through 1980. These authors also observed that hedges built on the price-sensitivity hedge ratio outperformed hedges based on more naive strategies.

Finally, D. Chance, W. Marr, and R. Thompson (1986) reported that hedges based on the price-sensitivity hedge ratio were successful in reducing the risk associated with shelf-registered corporate bond offerings by about 50 percent.

Pricing and Market Efficiency

R. Rendleman and C. Carabini (1979) examined the pricing and efficiency of T-bill futures contracts for the period of 1976 to 1978. Using the cost-of-carry model, they found that nearby futures were overpriced by nine basis points, while deferred T-bill futures were underpriced by twenty basis points on average. Based on this, Rendleman and Carabini applied arbitrage strategies involving the trading of spot T-bills and the futures contracts. They found the profits derived from the strategies to be insufficient to reject model specification and market efficiency after inclusion of transaction costs.

Using a similar data sample, A. Vignola and C. Dale (1980) also reported a small degree of mispricing based on the carrying-charge model. Specifically, they found that the model mispriced T-bill futures by an average of $85 per contract. B. Resnick (1984) and B. Resnick and E. Hennigar (1983) found a similar lack of profitable arbitrage opportunities in the T-bond futures market.

However, results reported by E. Elton, M. Gruber, and J. Rentzler (1984) challenge the efficiency of the interest rate futures market. These authors examined transactions data for the period of 1976 through 1982 and observed substantial profits from a *synthetic T-bill* strategy, in which a long position was assumed in a six-month T-bill and a short position in a T-bill futures contract expiring in three months. Actually, the example used earlier in this chapter to illustrate the implied repo rate concept involved the creation of a synthetic T-bill. Elton, Gruber, and Rentzler found that the differences between the synthetic and actual spot T-bill prices were sufficient to generate abnormally high profits after accounting for transaction costs.

Wild-Card and Delivery Options

Four widely cited studies exist on the wild-card and delivery options present in the T-note and T-bond futures markets. In a sophisticated attempt at quantifying the value of the wild-card option to the short position, A. Kane and A. Marcus (1986) found that the option's value was about one-fifth of a point. However, M. Arak and L. Goodman (1987) estimated the value to be substantially lower.

In two other studies, G. Gay and S. Manaster (1984, 1986) derived and investigated an optimal delivery policy for T-bond futures, discovering that actual delivery policies of market participants departed substantially from the optimal strategy. Gay and Manaster estimated that nearly $3 million per month in additional profits could have been earned by short traders who subscribed to the optimal delivery policy. Why short traders did not properly evaluate the delivery option remained unresolved.

SUMMARY

Interest rate futures represent the most actively traded futures contracts in U.S. markets. They were developed to reduce the risk associated with holding a spot position in bonds and other interest-rate-sensitive securities. A number of hedging applications are possible involving interest rate futures and based on the price-sensitivity hedge ratio. By assuming an appropriate position in an interest rate futures contract, hedgers can substantially reduce the disutility associated with interest rate risk. Several empirical studies have confirmed that interest rate futures substantially reduce risk when compared to unhedged positions.

The four major interest rate futures contracts—the T-bond and T-note contracts traded on the CBOT and the Eurodollar and T-bill contracts traded on the IMM division of the CME—span the entire yield curve. Because of the unique delivery system present at the CBOT for T-note and T-bond futures contracts, valuable options obtain for the short trader, specifically, the wild-card and delivery options. Their existence influences the futures price.

This chapter concludes our presentation of financial futures contracts and their applications. In Part 3 we focus our attention on option contracts. Like futures contracts, options are a popular derivative security that allow market investors to enhance their utility by expanding the investment opportunity set.

Selected References

Akemann, C. "Predicting Changes in T-Bond Futures Spreads Using Implied Yields from T-Bill Futures." *Journal of Futures Markets* 6 (Summer 1986): 223–230.

Arak, M., and L. Goodman. "Treasury Bond Futures: Valuing the Delivery Option." *Journal of Futures Markets* 7 (1987): 269–286.

Arak, M., L. Goodman, and S. Ross. "The Cheapest to Delivery Bond on the Treasury Bond Futures Contract." *Advances in Futures and Options Research* 1 (1986): 49–74.

Benninga, S., and M. Smirlock. "An Empirical Analysis of the Delivery Option, Marking to Market, and the Pricing of Treasury Bond Futures." *Journal of Futures Markets* 5 (Fall 1985): 361–374.

Block, S., and T. Gallagher. "The Use of Interest Rate Futures and Options by Corporate Financial Managers." *Financial Management* 15 (Autumn 1986): 73–78.

Capozza, D., and B. Cornell. "Treasury Bill Pricing in the Spot and Futures Markets," in *Interest Rate Futures: Concepts and Issues,* ed. G. Gay and R. Kolb. Richmond, Vir.: Robert F. Dame, Inc., 1982.

Chance, D. "A Semi-Strong Form Test of the Efficiency of the Treasury Bond Futures Market." *Journal of Futures Markets* 5 (Fall 1985): 385–405.

Chance, D., M. W. Marr, and G. R. Thompson. "Hedging Shelf Registrations." *Journal of Futures Markets* 6 (Spring 1986): 11–27.

Chiang, R., G. Gay, and R. Kolb. "Interest Rate Hedging: An Empirical Test of Alternative Strategies." *Journal of Financial Research* (Fall 1983): 187–197.

Ederington, L. "The Hedging Performance of the New Futures Market." *Journal of Finance* 34 (March 1979): 157–170.

Elton, E., M. Gruber, and J. Rentzler. "Intra-Day Tests of the Efficiency of the Treasury Bill Futures Market." *Review of Economics and Statistics* 66 (February 1984): 129–137.

Garbade, K., and W. Silber. "Futures Contracts on Commodities with Multiple Varieties: An Analysis of Premiums and Discounts." *Journal of Business* 56 (1983): 249–272.

Gay, G., and R. Kolb. "Immunizing Bond Portfolios with Interest Rate Futures." *Financial Management* 11 (1982): 81–89.

Gay, G., R. Kolb, and R. Chiang. "Interest Rate Hedging: An Empirical Test of Alternative Strategies." *Journal of Financial Research* 6 (Fall 1983): 187–197.

Gay, G., and S. Manaster. "The Quality Option Implicit in Futures Contracts." *Journal of Financial Economics* 13 (1984): 353–370.

Gay, G., and S. Manaster. "Implicit Delivery Options and Optional Delivery Strategies for Financial Futures Contracts." *Journal of Financial Economics* 15 (1986): 41–72.

Hegde, S., and B. Branch. "An Empirical Analysis of Arbitrage Opportunities in the Treasury Bill Futures Market." *Journal of Futures Markets* 5 (1985): 407–424.

Hegde, S., and B. McDonald. "On the Informational Role of Treasury Bill Futures." *Journal of Futures Markets* 6 (1986): 629–643.

Hill, J., and T. Schneewies. "Risk Reduction Potential of Financial Futures for Corporate Bond Positions" in *Interest Rate Futures: Concepts and Issues*, ed G. Gay and R. Kolb. Richmond, Vir.: Robert F. Dame, Inc., 1982.

Kane, A., and A. Marcus. "Valuation and Optimal Exercise of the Wild Card Option in the Treasury Bond Futures Market." *Journal of Finance* 41 (March 1986): 195–207.

Kawaller, I., and T. Koch. "Cash-and-Carry Trading and the Pricing of Treasury Bill Futures." *Journal of Futures Markets*

Klemkosky, R., and D. Lasser. "An Efficiency Analysis of the T-Bond Futures Market." 4 (Fall 1984): 115–123. *Journal of Futures Markets* 5 (1985): 607–620.

Kolb, R., and R. Chiang. "Improving Hedging Performance Using Interest Rate Futures." *Financial Management* 10 (Autumn 1981): 72–29.

Kolb, R., G. Gay, and J. Jordan. "Are There Arbitrage Opportunities in the Treasury-Bond Futures Market?" *Journal of Futures Markets*

Livingston, M. "The Cheapest Deliverable Bond for the CBT Treasury Bond Futures Contract." 2 (1983): 282–299. *Journal of Futures Markets* 3 (1984): 161–172.

McCabe, G., and C. Franckle. "The Effectiveness of Rolling the Hedge Forward in the Treasury Bill Futures Market." *Financial Management* 12 (1983): 21–29.

Meisner, J., and J. Labuszewski. "Treasury Bond Futures Delivery Bias." *Journal of Futures Markets* 4 (1984): 569–577.

Monroe, M., and R. Cohn. "The Relative Efficiency of the Gold and Treasury Bill Futures Markets." *Journal of Futures Markets* 6 (Fall 1986): 477–493.

Rendleman, R., and C. Carabini. "The Efficiency of the Treasury Bill Futures Market." *Journal of Finance* 44 (September 1979): 895–914.

Rentzler, J. "Trading Treasury Bond Spreads Against Treasury Bill Futures—A Model and Empirical Test of the Turtle Trade." *Journal of Futures Markets* 6 (1986): 41–61.

Resnick, B. "The Relationship between Futures Prices for U.S. Treasury Bonds." *Review of Research in Futures Markets* 3 (1984): 88–104.

Resnick, B., and E. Hennigar. "The Relation between Futures and Cash Prices for U.S. Treasury Bonds." *Review of Research in Futures Markets* 2 (1983): 282–299.

Senchak, A., and J. Easterwood. "Cross Hedging CD's with Treasury Bill Futures." *Journal of Futures Markets* 3 (1983): 429–438.

Toevs, A., and D. Jacob. "Futures and Alternative Hedge Methodologies." *Journal of Portfolio Management* (Spring 1986): 60–70.

Veit, T., and W. Reiff. "Commercial Banks and Interest Rate Futures: A Hedging Survey." *Journal of Futures Markets* 3 (1983): 283–293.

Vignola, A., and C. Dale. "The Efficiency of the Treasury Bill Futures Market: An Analysis of Alternative Specifications." *Journal of Financial Research* 3 (1980): 169–188.

Questions and Problems

1. The first interest rate futures contracts were traded on October 20, 1975. Why do you suppose that interest rate futures were not traded earlier? In other words, what factors existed in the 1970s that gave rise to the advent of interest rate futures?

2. Why might a trader be interested in a T-bill futures contract rather than a T-note or T-bond futures contract?

3. From Exhibit 10.2, the December 1989 T-bill and Eurodollar settlement IMM indices are 91.04 and 89.62, respectively. Given these, what are the actual settlement futures prices?

4. From Exhibit 10.2, what is the December 1989 T-bond settlement futures price?

5. Why is the LIBOR typically greater than the corresponding rate on U.S. Treasury bills?

6. Describe the three-day delivery process that exists for T-bond futures contracts traded on the CBOT.

7. Explain the concept of the wild-card option. How will this option likely affect the futures price?

8. From Exhibit 10.4, the conversion factor for the 9-7/8 coupon T-bond, maturing on November 15, 2015, and eligible for delivery against the March 1987 contract, is 1.2093. Show how this conversion factor is determined.

9. What is the cheapest-to-deliver bond, and why does the T-bond futures price tend to track this bond?

10. Suppose that you observe the following price information: (a) a T-bill maturing in 83 days has a discount rate of 5.19; (b) a T-bill maturing in 174 days has a discount rate of 5.35; and (c) the nearby T-bill futures has an IMM Index of 94.40. What is the implied repo rate? Will cash-and-carry arbitrage likely be profitable? Why or why not?

Questions 11 through 15 refer to the following information: Suppose that it is March 1, and a corporate treasurer decides that he will need to issue $2 million of commercial paper on June 1st. The paper will have a 180-day maturity and, concerned about the prospect of increasing interest rates, the treasurer decides to hedge the issue with the June T-bill contract. From Exhibit 10.2, the corresponding IMM Index is 90.89. Finally, assume that the current rate on 180-day commercial paper is 9.28 percent.

11. What are the current proceeds (March 1) from the commercial paper issue?

12. What is the current yield on commercial paper?

13. What is the actual futures price? What is the implied yield on 90-day T-bills from this price?

14. What is the price-sensitivity hedge ratio? To be fully hedged, how many contracts will the treasurer write?

15. Suppose that it is June 1, and that the following conditions hold: (1) the treasurer can issue the paper at a discount of 10.50 percent; and (2) the June T-bill futures contract has an IMM Index of 89.81. What are the effective proceeds from the commercial paper issue, and what is the effective financing rate? What financing rate would have applied if no hedge had been employed?

Questions 16 and 17 refer to the following information: Suppose that on August 27 a portfolio manager holds $2 million face-value T-bonds with a coupon of 11-7/8 maturing in nearly 19 years. The bonds currently sell at 101 per $100 par value, and the yield is 11.75 percent. The duration of the bonds is 7.83 years. The bonds must be sold on October 1st and, concerned about the prospect of rising interest rates, the manager decides to hedge using the December T-bond futures contract. The current futures price is 70–16. The cheapest-to-deliver bond, which this price is tracking, has a coupon of 10-3/8 and matures in 25 years. Its duration is therefore 7.20 years, and its yield is 14.91 percent.

16. How many December T-bond futures contracts will the manager write? In other words, what is the price-sensitivity hedge ratio?

17. Suppose that on October 1 the T-bond price is 97–12, and the December futures price is 67–28. What is the profit on the bond position? What is the profit on the futures position? What is the overall profit?

18. Are you more likely to use an intracommodity or intercommodity spread in order to speculate on changes in the shape of the yield curve?

19. From Exhibit 10.2, the September and December 1989 settlement T-bond futures prices are both 87–23. If a speculator felt that the yield curve would soon become more steeply sloped upward, describe the intracommodity spread she would likely take.

20. Suppose that on September 1 the new September and December T-bond futures prices are 88–02 and 88–19, respectively. If the speculator reverses the intracommodity spread, what are her gains (losses)?

21. Suppose that the current June T-note and T-bond futures prices are both 89–16. If you expect the yield curve to become more steeply sloped upward, describe the NOB spread that you would undertake. If in one month you reverse your NOB spread at the following futures prices, what is the profit (loss) realized?

	Futures Prices	
	Current	In One Month
June T-note	89–16	89–05
June T-bond	89–16	89–12

22. Suppose that the yield implied from the nearby and next deferred T-bond futures prices is 9.2 percent, while the yield implied by the nearby T-bill futures price is only 8.8 percent. Describe the turtle strategy you would use to exploit this situation.

Self-Test Problems

ST-1. Using the December T-bill and Eurodollar settlement futures prices appearing in Exhibit 10.2, construct an intercommodity spread based on the expectation that the TED spread will widen.

ST-2. Suppose that you reverse the spread on November 1st at the following futures prices:

December T-bill   90.93
December Eurodollar 89.55

What is the profit on your T-bill contract? On your Eurodollar contract? On your spread?

ST-3. What was the (implied) TED spread based on the March 1 futures prices?

ST-4. What is the new (implied) TED spread as of the November 1 futures prices? Did the TED spread widen as forecasted?

Solutions to Self-Test Problems

ST-1. March 1: Buy 1 December T-bill futures at 91.04.
                Write 1 December Eurodollar futures at 89.62.

ST-2. November 1: Write 1 December T-bill futures at 90.93.
                 Buy 1 December Eurodollar futures at 89.55.

Profit on T-bill contract:

$$-\$275\ (-11\text{ basis points})$$

Profit on Eurodollar contract:

$$\$175\ (7\text{ basis points})$$

Profit on spread:

$$-\$100\ (-4\text{ basis points}\times\$25)$$

ST-3. Implied T-bill yield:

$$100 - 8.96(90/360) = 97.7600$$
$$(100/97.7600)^{365/90} - 1$$
$$= .0962$$

Implied Eurodollar yield:

$$100 - 10.38(90/360) = 97.4050$$
$$(100/97.4050)^{365/90} - 1$$
$$= .1125$$

Implied TED spread:

$$|.0962 - .1125| = .0163$$

ST-4. Implied T-bill yield:

$$100 - 9.07(90/360) = 97.7325$$
$$(100/97.7325)^{365/90} - 1$$
$$= .0975$$

Implied Eurodollar yield:

$$100 - 10.45(90/360) = 97.3875$$
$$(100/97.3875)^{365/90} - 1$$
$$= .1133$$

Implied TED spread:

$$|.0975 - .1133| = .0158.$$

Therefore, the TED spread did not widen as forecasted.

Part Three

OPTIONS

This part of the book is designed to give you a working knowledge of what options are, how they are traded and valued, and how they can be employed to help manage risk. Chapter 11 describes the various options available and the markets on which they are traded. Chapters 12 through 14 are devoted to the valuation of option contracts. Here pricing boundaries are presented, followed by the binomial option-pricing model and the seminal European option-pricing model of Fisher Black and Myron Scholes. Then a discussion of early exercise and American options pricing is presented.

Chapter 15 concerns how to use options in speculative and hedging strategies. Chapters 16 through 19 are devoted to specific and popular options: stock options, currency options, stock index options, and futures options. Chapter 20 concludes this section with a discussion of portfolio insurance, which is the use of options, or the replication of option positions, to insure security portfolios against adverse price movements.

11

MARKETS AND INSTRUMENTS

We begin this chapter with a definition of options, followed by a presentation of the markets on which they are traded. The various option instruments are then discussed.

OPTIONS

An *option contract* conveys the right, but not the obligation, to purchase or sell a specified asset at a specified price on or before a specified date. The specified asset can be any one of many possible assets, including common stock, gold, foreign exchange, a stock market index, and the like. An option contract entails a specified amount of this asset. For instance, a standard stock option contract involves 100 shares of stock. The specified price is determined at contract inception and is known as the option's *exercise price* or *strike price*. Most options trading involves options where the underlying asset price is close to the exercise price. The specified date is the option's *expiration date* or *expiry date*. Often these dates are three, six, or nine months from the option's initial inception, although shorter and longer maturity options exist on many assets.

If the option buyer has the right to purchase the underlying asset, then the buyer holds a *call option*. For instance, the buyer may own an option to purchase (call) 100 shares of Ford stock, in three months, at an exercise price of $90 per share. Of course, whether the call option buyer exercises that right is contingent on the price of Ford stock at option expiration. He will exercise only if Ford stock is selling above $90 per share at contract expiration. For this reason, options are often called *contingent claims*. Alternatively, if the option buyer has the right to sell the underlying asset, then she is said to own a *put option*. For example,

An **option contract** conveys the right, but not the obligation, to purchase or sell a specified asset at a specified price on or before a specified date.

a put option buyer may have the right to sell (put) 100 shares of IBM, in three months, at an exercise price of $110 per share. Whether this right (option) is exercised or not is contingent on IBM's stock price in three months.

Besides the option buyer, an option contract involves a seller, or *option writer*. In the above example involving Ford stock, the call option writer agrees to sell the 100 shares, at $90 each, should the call option buyer exercise. For the IBM put option above, the writer agrees to buy the shares at $110 each. Of course, the option writer charges a price for selling the option. The determination of this price is the subject of Chapters 12 through 14.

Option contracts can be either European or American. With a *European option* the buyer may exercise only at expiration. With an *American option*, however, he may exercise prior to the option's maturity. Frequently it may be in the buyer's interest to exercise an option prematurely. In Chapter 14 we examine these conditions. Hence, an American option typically commands a greater price than an otherwise equivalent European option, since the buyer is paying a premium to be able to exercise prematurely. Quantifying this *early exercise premium* can be difficult. Chapter 14 concerns the valuation of American options. It is important to examine the valuation of American options, since the vast majority of all listed options are American rather than European.

A European option cannot be exercised prior to its maturity, whereas an American option may be exercised prematurely.

Like futures contracts (Part 2 of this book), options are derivative securities. That is, they are derived from some underlying asset, and their prices depend critically on the spot values of those assets. Other factors, such as interest rates, are also important determinants of option value. And options offer leverage; like futures, options generate large percentage returns for comparatively small percentage changes in the underlying asset's price. This leverage effect will be apparent in the pricing examples provided in subsequent chapters.

OPTION MARKETS

Option markets may be either organized or over-the-counter. An *organized market* is a physical place where standardized option contracts are traded. Contrastingly, an *over-the-counter market* offers private options that are tailored to the specific needs of the customer. Since these options are tailored, little secondary market trading takes place. Organized option exchanges evolved in response to the illiquidity of over-the-counter options. Today the vast majority of all options are listed. However, an active OTC stock option market still exists as well as a growing interbank market for European currency options. Here banks write tailored options on foreign exchange for their commercial customers.

The Chicago Board Options Exchange (CBOE) was the first option exchange to organize. It began trading on listed stock options in 1973 and is currently the largest organized options exchange in the world.

Exchange	Assets Underlying Options
American Exchange	Common stocks, the Major Market Stock Index, Computer Technology Index, Oil Index and the Institutional Index.
Chicago Board Options Exchange	Common stocks, U.S. Treasury bonds, 5-year U.S. Treasury note, and the SP100 and SP500 Stock Indexes.
International Options Corporation (Amsterdam, Montreal, Sydney and Vancouver)	Gold, silver, and platinum.
London Futures and Options Exchange	Common stocks, and the U.K. Financial Times Index.
New York Stock Exchange	Common stocks, and the NYSE Composite Stock Index.
Philadelphia Stock Exchange	Common stocks, the Value Line Stock Index, the National O-T-C Stock Index, Utilities Index, Gold/Silver Index, the Australian dollar, British pound, Canadian dollar, German mark, French franc, Japanese yen, Swiss franc, and the European Currency Unit.
Sydney Exchange	Common stocks.
Trans Canada (Montreal, Toronto, and Vancouver)	Common stocks, and Canadian Treasury bills and bonds.

Since 1973, listed option markets have developed throughout the free world, offering options on a wide variety of underlying assets. Exhibit 11.1 presents some of the largest organized markets and their option instruments.

Option Players

Ignoring transaction costs, options trading represents a *zero-sum game*. In other words, any profits (losses) experienced by option buyers are offset by the losses (profits) experienced by option writers. Once transaction costs are included, however, total options trading must be a less-than-zero-sum game. Still, options trading may result in utility gains through the transfer of risk between the market players. These players are option hedgers and speculators.

Hedgers If an option buyer or writer employs the option to reduce risk, then he is said to be a *hedger*. As we have seen in Part 2 of this book, futures contracts can be employed by hedgers to reduce risk. Unlike futures hedging, however, option hedging generally eliminates downside risk while allowing the hedger to capture any potential upside gain. Examples of option hedging are contained in subsequent chapters. For now, suffice it to say that options can facilitate the transfer of price uncertainty (risk), thus enhancing the utility of risk-averse hedgers.

Speculators If an option buyer or writer uses options primarily to profit, then he is a *speculator*. In principle, a speculator accepts the hedger's unwanted risk in order to generate profits. Examples of speculative trading strategies are presented in subsequent chapters. Since speculators are, by definition, less risk averse than hedgers— that is, the cost of risk to the speculator is comparatively less—then the transfer of risk from hedgers to speculators can result in net utility gains. Such potential gains are what underlie the very existence of options.

With futures contracts we saw that arbitrage plays an important role in determining prices. Arbitrage also largely determines option values. An option player who engages in arbitrage should be regarded as a type of speculator. The arbitrager engages in trading to exploit profit opportunities that are rarely risk-free.

The Clearing Corporation

An imperative part of any organized options market is its clearing corporation. For all U.S. option markets except those trading futures options, the *Options Clearing Corporation* (*OCC*) standardizes contracts and facilitates trading and option exercise. The OCC was formed in 1975 from the option clearinghouse of the CBOE. When an option trade is initiated, the OCC acts as a dealer creating two separate contracts: one option between the buyer and the OCC acting as a writer, and one option between the writer and the OCC acting as the buyer. The OCC in turn guarantees both sides of the contract. This procedure facilitates trading and promotes liquidity. For instance, the buyer can close a position by simply selling offsetting contracts (an *offset*), and the writer can buy into a previous position. Also, should the buyer decide to exercise the option, the OCC randomly selects a writer to accept exercise. This writer is said to be *assigned*.

The OCC recently created a subsidiary, the *Intermarket Clearing Corporation* (*ICC*), to facilitate the clearing of options on futures and options on indices. We discuss stock index options and futures options at great length in Chapters 18 and 19, respectively. Currently the ICC clears Eurodollar options and OTC stock index futures options traded on the Philadelphia Stock Exchange, as well as gold bullion options for the AMEX Commodities Corporation.

Margins

An option writer represents a source of credit risk to the OCC. For example, an uncovered call option writer (one who does not own the underlying asset) may have insufficient funds to purchase the underlying asset should the call buyer exercise. To insure itself, the OCC requires the writer to post *margin*, usually a cash margin. For covered option writing, this cash margin is often set equal to the current market price of the option plus a percentage of the underlying asset's value. This percentage varies as the option's price changes through time. Margins for uncovered options writing are greater due to the added risk involved. Also, margin requirements are more complicated when writing option combinations. Finally, the option buyer has no margin requirement; the most the buyer can lose is the original purchase price of the option, so the buyer does not represent a credit risk to the OCC.

Position and Exercise Limits

To also ensure contract performance, option exchanges impose limits as to the number of contracts that a trader can hold. For example, the Philadelphia Exchange presently imposes a *position limit* of 50,000 contracts for its listed currency options. Position limits are applied to "one side of the market." Purchased calls and written puts are considered one side of the market, because each contract's value increases (decreases) as the underlying asset's price increases (decreases). In other words, purchased calls and written puts are positively correlated. Also, written calls and purchased puts constitute one side of the market. Thus, a currency option trader who both writes calls and purchases puts on the same underlying currency is limited to a position of 50,000 contracts. Of course, different exchanges impose different position limits on different option contracts.

Exchanges sometimes impose *exercise limits* as well. An exercise limit represents the total number of option contracts that may be exercised within some specified period. It also serves to ensure contract performance.

Listing Requirements

Option exchanges specify requirements that an underlying asset must meet in order for its option to be listed for trading. These *listing requirements* vary across exchanges and types of underlying assets, but they typically concern the asset's trading volume, its price level, and other factors that are important in assuring the success of the option contract.

It is interesting to note that for stock options, the public firm's management has no say as to whether or not an option will be listed and traded on the stock. That decision is made by the exchange and its regulators. Some firms are opposed to options trading on their stocks. For instance, Golden Nugget unsuccessfully sued to prevent listing, claiming that options trading increased the volatility of underlying stock prices. However, most empirical evidence does not support this view.

Executing Trades

Option trades are executed in a similar manner across markets. To illustrate a trade, presume you (the client or principal) wanted to purchase an IBM call contract, with $115 exercise price and December expiration, *at market*. The option trades on the CBOE. By "at market" we mean that you are willing to buy at the best currently available price.

The process begins with a phone call to your agent (account executive or broker), who must trade through an exchange member. A member may be a *market maker* or *floor broker*. Typically, a floor broker's seat is financed by a trading firm, such as Prudential-Bache. Thus, calling an account executive or broker of a trading firm effectively gives you access to a floor broker. The price of an exchange seat varies, and does so directly with the level of trading volume. Recently an exchange seat at the CBOE costs about $375,000.

Your agent next places the order by booking and clocking it, and relaying it electronically to the firm's floor broker on the exchange. A floor broker executes trades for public clients and earns a flat salary or *commission* on each trade. Trading is conducted in a designated *pit* for the particular option involved. The floor broker then shouts a bid of, say, $3. This bid is countered by offers to sell from other traders on the exchange floor. The floor broker accepts the lowest counteroffer, say, $3.125, implying a contract price of $312.50 ($3.125 × 100 shares per option contract). The two traders match tickets, confirming the trade in pencil on slips of paper. The buying trader hands these slips of paper to an exchange official, who quickly checks them and passes them to an exchange employee who enters the trade information into the CBOE's computerized reporting system. This information is flashed on the trading floor screens and private wire service screens. Traders monitor these screens throughout the trading day. The time of the price agreement (trade) to the time the information is flashed is usually less than two minutes. The floor broker wires confirmation of the trade back to the agent, who then notifies you of your completed trade and its price. The entire execution process typically takes place in a few minutes, and the agent later forwards a written confirmation of the trade. You pay a commission charge to buy the option (and pay another should you later sell or exercise the option).

You must deposit the $312.50 with an OCC-member *clearing firm* by the next business morning. Typically, your broker or account executive handles this process, perhaps withdrawing funds from your established account. This money is credited to the option writer, who must post the appropriate initial margin by the same morning. When all of this occurs, the trade is cleared through the OCC-member clearing firm.

The counteroffer of $3.125 may have come from another floor broker serving as an agent for another client, or it may have been made by a market maker at the CBOE. *Market makers* are entrepreneurs who trade for themselves. Also, they are charged with the duty of satisfying a public order. That is, they must be willing to buy or sell an option when no other public trader (acting through a floor broker) is willing to transact. Thus, as the title suggests, the market maker ensures that a public order can be filled. However, their performance in fulfilling this duty has often been called into question.

A market maker earns a living by buying at one price and selling at another, higher price. This is accomplished by continuously quoting a bid price and an ask price on a particular option. The *bid price* is the maximum price that the market maker is willing to pay, while the *ask price* is the minimum price at which he will sell the option. The ask price is higher, of course, resulting in a *bid-ask spread*. Exchange regulation and market competition prevent this spread from being too large. Still, the bid-ask spread represents an important transaction cost for those who must transact with a market maker. Presently, an average spread at the CBOE is about one-eighth of a point (e.g., bid $3, ask $3.125). Individuals and institutional option traders can have immediate and continuous access to bid and ask prices via on-line private wire service screens.

Market makers are sometimes called *scalpers* or *position traders*, depending on their trading behavior. Scalpers trade actively in short-term positions on both sides of the market, while position traders take longer-term positions—perhaps for a few hours or entire trading session.

Types of Orders

Besides placing a *market order*—an order to trade at the best currently available price—you may have placed any of the following orders. These are essentially the same orders as those discussed in Chapter 5:

- *Limit order.* Stipulates a specific price at which you are willing to trade. It can be a *day order*, which is good only for the trading day on which it is placed, or an *open order*, which is good until canceled. At the CBOE, the Order Book Official (an exchange employee) is assigned the task of tracking and transacting all limit orders.

- *Fill-or-kill order.* Instructs the floor broker to fill the order immediately at a specified price. If the order cannot be filled quickly at this price, then it is canceled.

- *All-or-none order.* Allows the floor broker to fill part of the order at one specified price and part at another specified price.

- *On-the-open or on-the-close order.* Orders to trade only within a few minutes of opening or closing, respectively.

- *Stop order.* Triggers a transaction when prices hit a certain level. Unlike limit orders, they are used to protect against losses on existing positions.

Other Systems of Executing Trades

The CBOE trading system just described is called a *market maker system*. Some exchanges, namely the American and Philadelphia, use a slightly different system known as a *specialist system*. Here a specialist exists who must make the market and, additionally, transact limit orders. Thus, the specialist handles the tasks of both the market maker and Order Book Official. Also at the American and Philadelphia exchanges are *registered option traders* (*ROTs*) who can both trade for themselves or act as floor brokers. This is known as *dual trading*. At the CBOE, an individual can be both a market maker and floor broker, but not during the same trading session.

Transaction Costs

The following transaction costs are realized from options trading:

■ *Floor trading and clearing fees.* These are the small fees charged by the OCC, a clearing firm member, and the exchange itself. If the trade was executed through a broker, these fees are built into the broker's commission. Market makers pay these fees directly, so they are implicit in the bid-ask spread.

■ *Commissions on options.* A broker charges a commission to handle an order. Full-service brokers charge higher commissions than a discount broker. Presently the commission on an option trade, one-way, is about $30 for one contract at a discount brokerage.

■ *Commissions on spot assets.* Exercising an option implies the trading of the underlying spot asset. Thus, commissions may also have to be paid on the underlying asset.

■ *Bid-ask spreads.* When transacting with a market maker or specialist, a bid-ask spread is incurred. This represents a sizable transaction cost paid for obtaining trading immediacy. Studies have shown that the spread can be greater than 4 percent of the option's value.

Taxation

Determining the tax consequences of options trading can be complex. Below we provide a few generally applicable tax guides:

■ *Gains.* The realized gains from options trading are taxed at the ordinary personal income tax rate.

■ *Losses.* The realized losses are deductible by offsetting them against any other investment gains. If losses exceed gains, the excess up to $3,000 is deductible against ordinary income.

■ *Non-equity options.* Options on indices and foreign exchange, and other non-equity options, exhibit the following special tax consider-

Option Market Globalization

Option markets, like most securities markets, are moving toward globalization as investors recognize the interdependencies among national economies and demand more continuous access to financial markets. Technology advances are now facilitating the globalization of option markets by creating trading linkages. Perhaps the best example of this concerns the trading of gold options. Gold options were first traded by the European Options Exchange in Amsterdam in April 1981. Today gold options in Amsterdam, Montreal, Sydney, and Vancouver are interchangeable. These options have the same specifications and are cleared by the International Options Clearing Corporation, which is owned jointly by the four exchanges. Hence, a gold option purchased in Montreal may be sold in Amsterdam, Sydney or Vancouver. Given the time differences among these four cities, the daily trading of IOCC gold options totals 18.5 hours.

Another example concerns the trading of currency options. On September 16, 1987, the Philadelphia Exchange became the first U.S. securities market to initiate an evening trading session in foreign currency options in order to accommodate the developing needs of foreign exchange traders in Asia-Pacific time zones. Currently the night session accounts for over 10 percent of total trading volume.

---

ation: all *unrealized* gains are taxed at the ordinary income rate, and all *unrealized* losses are deductible as described above.

- *Commissions.* In general, brokerage commissions are tax deductible.
- *Wash sales.* Occurs when a trader sells a security at a loss and replaces it with the same security in order to realize a loss for tax purposes. Federal tax law does not allow the deduction on the original loss, however, when it determines that a wash sale has transpired.

Option Quotes

Exhibit 11.2 illustrates quotations for some common stock options listed on the CBOE, specifically, the closing-trade prices of various options traded on Wednesday, March 1, 1989. Closing prices are categorized by exercise price and expiration month. Also reported are the closing stock prices for the trading day.

To understand the exhibit, consider the first price entry for CBS: 9-⅝. This means that the last traded call price for CBS, with exercise price $160 and April expiration, was $9.625 per share, or $962.50 per contract. CBS's stock closed at $166.75 per share on March 1. Stock options traded on the CBOE expire on the Saturday following the third Friday of the expiration month. Thus, this American option on CBS expired on April 22, 1989.

Consider another example: the price entry for a Coke put option with exercise price $50 and March expiration. This option's closing price was 1-⅞, or $187.50 per contract. Coke's stock price closed at $48 per share.

Finally, Exhibit 11.2 reports total option volume for the trading day, as well as *open interest*. For stock call options, 235,605 contracts were traded

Exhibit 11.2:
Listed Options Quotations, March 1, 1989

CHICAGO BOARD

Option & NY Close	Strike Price	Calls—Last Mar	Calls—Last Apr	Calls—Last May	Puts—Last Mar	Puts—Last Apr	Puts—Last May
AlexAl	25	r	r	13/16	r	r	r
Amdahl	17 1/2	r	r	2	r	r	r
18 5/8	20	r	3/8	13/16	1 5/8	1 5/8	r
18 5/8	22 1/2	1/16	r	r	r	r	r
A E P	25	r	1 1/2	r	r	r	r
AlnGrp	70	1 7/8	2 13/16	3 1/2	7/8	r	r
Amoco	75	r	r	3 1/4	1/2	r	1 3/8
76 1/4	80	1/16	5/8	7/8	r	r	r
A M P	45	r	r	2 1/2	r	r	r
Anadrk	25	r	r	r	r	5/8	r
Baxter	15	s	s	3 3/4	s	s	r
18 5/8	17 1/2	1 1/4	r	1 13/16	1/16	3/16	r
18 5/8	20	1/16	5/16	9/16	1 3/8	1 1/2	1 5/8
18 5/8	22 1/2	r	r	3/16	r	r	r
Blk Dk	22 1/2	r	r	1 3/4	r	r	r
23 5/8	25	r	1/4	5/8	r	r	r
Boeing	55	r	s	r	r	s	3/8
62	60	2 3/4	3 3/4	4 1/2	7/16	1	1 1/2
62	65	5/16	1 1/16	1 9/16	3 1/8	3 3/8	r
62	70	s	s	1/2	s	s	r
Bois C	40	2	r	2 15/16	r	r	r
41 3/4	45	1/16	r	r	r	r	r
C B S	160	r	9 5/8	r	r	r	r
166 3/4	165	3 3/4	r	r	1 1/4	2 5/8	r
166 3/4	170	1	3 3/8	r	r	r	r
166 3/4	175	3/8	r	3 1/8	r	r	r
166 3/4	185	1/8	s	1 1/2	r	s	r
CapCit	350	r	s	r	1 3/4	s	r
358	360	r	r	r	4 3/4	r	r
358	370	r	r	8 3/4	13 1/8	r	r
358	380	r	2 1/2	5 1/8	r	r	r
Coke	40	r	s	8 7/8	r	s	1/16
48	45	3 3/8	3 5/8	4 1/2	1/8	3/16	1/2
48	50	3/8	7/8	1 5/8	1 7/8	r	2 7/8
48	55	r	1/8	r	r	r	r
CocaCE	17 1/2	r	r	3/8	r	r	r
Colgat	45	3/4	1 1/8	1 3/4	1	1 1/2	r
Cmw Ed	30	r	r	3 3/8	r	r	r
32 3/4	35	r	1/8	1/8	r	r	r
C Data	17 1/2	3 3/4	4 5/8	4 5/8	1/16	r	r
21 1/4	20	1 5/8	2 1/2	2 3/4	5/16	3/4	1
21 1/4	22 1/2	7/16	1 3/16	1 3/8	r	r	2 1/16
21 1/4	25	s	s	7/8	s	s	r
CornGl	27 1/2	s	s	6 3/4	s	s	r
32 3/4	30	r	r	3 7/8	r	r	r
32 3/4	32 1/2	r	s	2 1/4	r	s	r
32 3/4	35	3/8	r	r	2 1/2	r	2 1/2
32 3/4	37 1/2	r	s	5/16	r	s	r
32 3/4	40	r	r	3/16	r	r	r
Diebld	35	r	s	r	r	s	1/4
44 5/8	40	5	r	7	r	r	1 1/2
44 5/8	45	1 1/8	2 1/2	3	1 3/4	2 1/2	r
44 5/8	50	5/16	1 1/4	1 3/4	r	r	r
Edwrds	20	r	r	r	r	r	3/8
21 1/8	22 1/2	r	r	5/8	r	r	1 5/8
ForstL	20	s	s	7 3/8	s	s	r
26 7/8	30	1/4	5/8	1 3/16	r	r	r
FptMc	30	1 5/8	2 1/4	r	r	r	5/8
31 1/2	35	r	1/4	7/16	r	r	r
GnCine	25	r	1 1/8	1 5/8	r	r	r
Gn Dyn	50	1 1/4	r	2 1/2	1/2	r	1 1/4
50 3/8	55	r	3/16	r	r	r	r
Gdrich	50	2 1/8	2 3/4	r	1/2	r	1 3/4
50 3/4	55	3/16	5/8	1 1/4	3 1/4	r	r
50 3/4	60	1/16	s	3/8	r	s	r
		•	•	•			
Upjohn	25	5 3/4	6	6 1/4	r	1/16	3/16
30 1/2	30	1	1 9/16	2 1/2	1/4	3/4	1 5/16
30 1/2	35	1/16	1/4	3/4	r	4 1/2	4 3/8
WstPP	45	r	12 3/4	r	r	r	r
57 1/4	50	7 5/8	7 3/4	r	1/16	1/16	1/16
57 1/4	55	2 11/16	2 13/16	2 13/16	r	1/4	3/8
57 1/4	60	r	r	1/16	r	r	r
Weyerh	25	r	1 3/4	2 5/8	3/8	5/8	1 1/4
25 3/8	30	r	5/16	9/16	4 7/8	4 7/8	r
Winnbg	10	r	r	9/16	r	r	r
Xerox	55	7	7 3/8	r	1/16	r	r
60 3/8	60	1 5/8	2 3/4	r	7/8	1 7/8	2 1/2
60 3/8	65	1/4	1	2 1/2	r	5 1/4	r
60 3/8	70	1/8	7/16	1 5/8	9 1/2	r	r
Zayre	22 1/2	r	r	3 3/8	1/8	r	r
24 1/4	25	3/8	7/8	1 3/4	r	1 1/8	r

Total call vol 235,605 **Call open int** 2,883,747
Total put vol 194,080 **Put open int** 1,422,016

r-Not Traded. s-No Option.

CHICAGO BOARD

CALLS

		Sales	Last	Chg.	N.Y. Close
SP100	Mar275	38447	2 9-16	−1 3-16	272.29
SP100	Mar280	25979	7/8	− 3/4	272.29
SP100	Mar270	12491	5 3/8	− 1 3/8	272.29
SP100	Mar285	8556	.5-16	− 1/4	272.29
SP100	Apr285	4594	2 1/8	− 5/8	272.29

PUTS

		Sales	Last	Chg.	N.Y. Close
SP100	Mar275	36628	4 3/4	+ 1/4	272.29
SP100	Mar270	35700	2 1/2	......	272.29
SP100	Mar265	13112	1 5-16	− 1-16	272.29
SP100	Mar280	11369	8 1/4	+ 3/4	272.29
SP100	Apr275	5652	6 7/8	+ 1/4	272.29

PUTS

		Sales	Last	Chg.	N.Y. Close
TexEst	Apr50	1554	1 7/8	− 9-16	50 3/4
Panhdl	Apr22 1/2	754	3/4	− 1	22 3/4
BurlRs	Apr45	602	2 5/8	+ 3/4	45 3/4
TexEst	Jul50	568	2 3/4	− 3/8	50 3/4
BurlRs	Mar45	520	1 3/8	+ 1/2	45 3/4

PACIFIC

CALLS

		Sales	Last	Chg.	N.Y. Close
CircK	Apr12 1/2	4142	3 1/4	+ 7/8	15 1/4
CircK	Mar15	3857	3/4	+ 1/8	15 1/4
CircK	Apr15	3347	1 1/2	+ 1/4	15 1/4
PhilEl	Apr20	2781	1/4	− 1/8	19 1/8
HospCp	Apr45	2607	4 5/8	+ 3/8	48 3/4

PUTS

		Sales	Last	Chg.	N.Y. Close
CircK	Apr15	843	1 1/8	− 3/8	15 1/4
SmkB	Mar50	591	1 1/8	− 1/8	49 3/4
Lockhd	Apr45	489	1	+ 1/4	47 1/2
Compaq	Mar70	478	3 5/8	+ 1/4	66 3/4
Kinder	Apr7 1/2	467	1/4	− 1-16	8 3/8

AMERICAN

CALLS

		Sales	Last	Chg.	N.Y. Close
Dexter	Mar35	5980	2 7-16	+ 15-16	34 5/8
MMIdx	Mar450	4254	1 7/8	− 1 1/2	439.75
KimbCl	Apr60	3385	2 1/8	− 5-16	60 7/8
KimbCl	Jul60	3310	4 1/4	− 1/4	60 7/8
Dexter	Mar30	3101	5 1/8	+ 1 5/8	34 5/8

PUTS

		Sales	Last	Chg.	N.Y. Close
MMIdx	Mar440	3052	5 1/4	+ 1/8	439.75
MMIdx	Mar435	1907	3 1/2	......	439.75
MMIdx	Mar445	1762	7 7/8	+ 7/8	439.75
MMIdx	Mar430	1449	2 3/8	+ 1-16	439.75
MMIdx	Mar420	1219	15-16	− 1/8	439.75

NEW YORK

CALLS

		Sales	Last	Chg.	N.Y. Close
Emhart	Mar35	2910	5 1/4	− 1/2	40
Emhart	Apr40	1720	2 1/8	− 3/8	40
Emhart	Mar40	1295	15-16	− 9-16	40
Emhart	Apr35	782	5 7/8	− 1/2	40
Emhart	Jul45	540	5/8	− 5-16	40

PUTS

		Sales	Last	Chg.	N.Y. Close
Emhart	Mar35	1319	1/8	− 1-16	40
Emhart	Apr35	1200	3/8	− 1-16	40
Emhart	Apr40	1142	1 3/4	......	40
Maytag	Jul22 1/2	303	2 1/2	− 1/8	20 1/2
Maytag	Mar22 1/2	300	2	+ 1/8	20 1/2

PHILADELPHIA

CALLS

		Sales	Last	Chg.	N.Y. Close
BurlRs	Mar45	1569	2 5-16	−1 7-16	45 3/4
McDln	May17 1/2	1561	1/2	− 1/8	16 1/2
BurlRS	Mar50	1557	3/4	− 1/2	45 3/4
M C A	Aug50	1504	4 5/8	+ 1/4	49 3/8
G A F	Apr50	1502	2 5-16	+ 5-16	51 1/8

on the CBOE, while 194,080 put option contracts were traded. Open interest is simply the number of contracts currently outstanding. As Exhibit 11.2 shows, nearly 3 million call and 1.5 million put contracts were alive at the close of trading on March 1, 1989.

All organized option markets report their closing price quotations in a similar manner. Exhibit 11.3 presents quotations for some of the most actively traded options on U.S. markets for March 1, 1989. To take just one example, consider the GAF call option, with April expiration and $50 exercise price, traded on the Philadelphia Exchange. This call option had a closing price of 2-5/16 ($2.3125 per share), up 5/16 from the previous day's closing price of $2.00. There were 1,502 contracts traded. GAF closed at $51.125 (up $0.25 per share from its closing price on February 28, 1989). By the way, GAF was taken private in a leverage buyout by mid-March—the reason for the active option volume.

Market Regulation

The Securities and Exchange Commission (SEC) is the primary regulator of options trading, including the trading of options on individual common stocks, stock indices, and foreign exchange. The Commodity Futures Trading Commission (CFTC) is the primary regulator of all futures options. Also, the regulatory process consists of self-regulation by the exchanges and OCC, as well as regulation by the National Association of Securities Dealers (NASD), state authorities, and other agencies.

These regulatory agencies interact to assure contract performance and to preclude illegal and manipulative practices that might erode the credibility of the market and thus the confidence of the trading public. For instance, regulation seeks to ensure the competency of brokers and preclude abusive trading practices. These agencies also are empowered to review new contract proposals, listing requirements, position limits, and the like. Overall, the U.S. options industry has a good record of performance since the inception of listed options trading in 1973.

OPTION INSTRUMENTS

Options may be written on underlying assets exhibiting zero, discrete, or continuous leakages.

Options are currently traded on a variety of underlying assets, including stocks, stock indices, futures, and many others. These option instruments can be categorized as either options on futures or options on actuals. However, for the purpose of valuing options it is useful to categorize them according to the type of *leakage* exhibited by their underlying assets, that is, zero, discrete, or continuous. Since many securities that underlie option contracts pay dividends or interest, and since the prices of listed options are affected by these intervening capitalization changes, we say that the securities exhibit a *leakage*.

Zero-Leakage Option Instruments

Options written on assets paying no dividends or interest, and having no substantial storage costs or convenience yields, are *zero-leakage options*. For example, gold options fit this category. Gold clearly pays no dividends or interest. And the storage costs and convenience yield on gold are nominal; it costs about $0.06 a month to store an ounce of gold, and its convenience yield is less than $0.20 a month per ounce.

Stock options may also fit this category, depending on the firm's dividend pattern and the option's maturity. Some firms do not pay dividends, so they have zero-leakage stocks. Also, an option written on a dividend-paying stock may expire prior to the stock's next ex-dividend date. For all intents and purposes, this is a zero-leakage option.

Discrete-Leakage Option Instruments

If the underlying asset exhibits an intervening cash flow that is discontinuous, then the option is said to be a *discrete-leakage option*. One example is a typical stock option. The CBOE often trades over 400,000 stock options in a single session (see Exhibit 11.2). Researchers have reported that over 80 percent of these stock options exhibit at least one ex-dividend date prior to option expiration. Thus, the majority of stock options are written on stocks that pay a discrete dividend, that is, on stocks that exhibit a discrete leakage. Such a leakage is important to consider when valuing option contracts. For example, we will see that as the size of the dividend increases, so does the probability of prematurely exercising an American call stock option that is deeply in-the-money (Chapter 14).

Stock index options also fit this category. These are very popular options that help equity portfolio managers protect their portfolio's value. Two of the most popular U.S. stock index options are those traded on the SP100 and NYSE Composite Index. For instance, Exhibit 11.3 shows that at least 192,528 SP100 option contracts were traded on the CBOE on March 1, 1989.

Figure 11.1 displays the predicted dividend stream for the SP100 as of April 29, 1983. As this figure shows, the index exhibits a discrete dividend-payout pattern. Hence, even though the SP100 is an index of many individual stocks that pay different dividends throughout the year, the index itself exhibits a discontinuous leakage, since most stock dividends are clustered at certain calendar months and weekdays.

Continuous-Leakage Option Instruments

If the underlying asset exhibits a leakage which is continuous, then we have a *continuous-leakage option*. Two options fit this category: currency options and all futures options. Both of these are discussed at great length in Chapters 17 and 19, respectively. Foreign exchange can be used to purchase interest-bearing foreign assets, thus generating a continuous leakage determined by the foreign interest rate. A futures price exhibits a continuous leakage as the contract matures and the spot and futures prices converge.

Finally, please note that a zero-leakage option instrument may be thought of as a special case of a continuous-leakage option instrument, one in which the leakage rate is constant and zero.

OPTION FUNDS

A mutual fund represents a pool of shareholders' monies that is invested in financial securities, mostly stocks and bonds. Such funds are

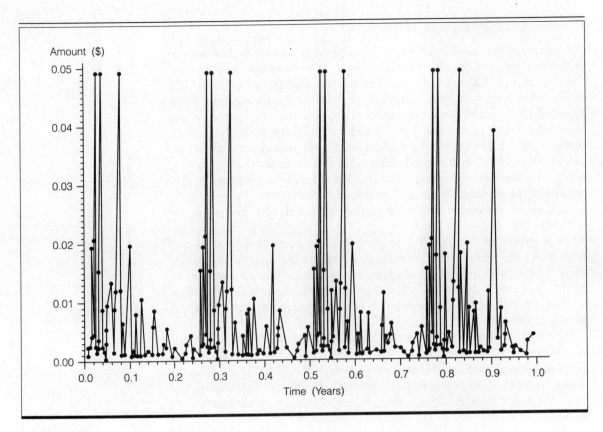

Figure 11.1:
SP100 Predicted Divided Stream

overseen by professional portfolio managers. One of the major services that these funds offer is diversification for the smaller investor.

Some of these mutual funds have specialized in writing call options against the stocks held. This procedure is known as *covered call writing* (discussed in Chapter 15). Funds that frequently engage in such writing are known as *option funds*. A few of the largest options funds are Dean Witter Option Income Funds; Kemper Option Income Fund; Putnam Options Income Trust II; and Shearson Lehman Option Income Fund.

An **option fund** is a mutual fund that specializes in writing call options against the stocks held.

SUMMARY

An option represents a contract giving the buyer the right to purchase or sell a specified asset at a specified exercise price on or before a specified expiration date. There are puts and calls, American and European options. The vast majority of options are American and are traded on organized option exchanges such as the CBOE. These exchanges are highly organized structures regulated by several bodies to ensure contract performance and trading purity. They are growing rapidly.

For the purpose of expediting options pricing, options are categorized here according to the type of leakage exhibited by their underlying assets. Such assets may have zero, discrete, or continuous leakages. We begin the topic of options pricing in the next chapter.

Selected References

Black, F. "Fact and Fantasy in the Use of Options." *Financial Analysts Journal* (July–August 1975).

Blomeyer, E. "An Analytic Approximation for the American Put Price for Options on Stocks with Dividends." *Journal Of Financial and Quantitative Analysis* 21 (June 1986):229–233.

Brennan, M. "The Cost of Convenience and the Pricing of Commodity Contingent Claims." Working paper, University of British Columbia, 1986.

Cox, J., and M. Rubenstein. *Option Markets.* Englewood Cliffs, N.J.: Prentice-Hall, 1985.

Goodman, L. "New Options Markets." *Federal Reserve Bank of New York, Quarterly Review* (August 1983).

Russo, T. *Regulation of the Commodities Futures and Options Markets.* New York: McGraw-Hill, 1983.

Smith, C. "Option Pricing: A Review." *Journal of Financial Economics* 3 (January–March 1976):1–51.

Stigler, G. "The Theory of Economic Regulation." *Bell Journal of Economics* (1971).

Questions and Problems

1. Distinguish between calls and puts, and between American and European options.

2. Explain the role played by the OCC in options trading.

3. Who are the major players in option markets, and what distinguishes these players?

4. What are some of the major organized option exchanges?

5. Distinguish between a floor broker and a market maker.

6. From Exhibit 11.2, what was the closing price of a Goodrich call option, with exercise price $55 and March expiration, on March 1, 1989? What was the value of the corresponding put option?

7. Describe a wash sale.

8. What are the three categories of options, as determined by the underlying asset's leakage? Provide examples of each.

9. Why is an option contract often referred to as a contingent claim?

10. If an American option sold for less than its European counterpart, could you create an arbitrage strategy that would profit? Demonstrate your strategy with assumed prices.

11. Under what conditions does options trading represent a zero-sum game?

12. Why doesn't an option buyer have to post margin with an OCC-member clearing firm?

13. How do position and exercise limits help to ensure contract performance?

BASIC OPTIONS PRICING

In this chapter we initiate the task of valuing option contracts. When an investor purchases an option she obtains something of value—namely the right to trade an underlying asset in the future for a specified exercise price. The option's price should accurately reflect the present value of this right.

We begin by presenting boundary conditions that govern an option's price. In other words, these are limits beyond which it should not stray. The process of arbitrage ensures that such boundaries are not violated in efficient markets. There are boundaries relating to European and American options, to calls and puts, to differential exercise prices and maturities, and others. We will show how arbitrage restrictions enforce each of these boundaries.

By focusing on boundary conditions we establish a range within which an option should be priced. We do not, however, determine the exact option price directly. Later in this chapter we present a simple model—the binomial option-pricing model—to determine option prices. Although the model has limitations, it provides insights into the process by which option prices are generated. In Chapter 13 we examine a more formidable option-pricing model.

BOUNDARIES FOR CALL OPTIONS

Minimum Value of American Call

An American call option should sell for at least zero or the difference between the underlying asset price and the exercise price, whichever is greater. That is:

(12.1)
$$C^A \geq MAX[0, S - X],$$

An American option should sell for at least zero or the difference between the underlying asset price and the exercise price, whichever is greater.

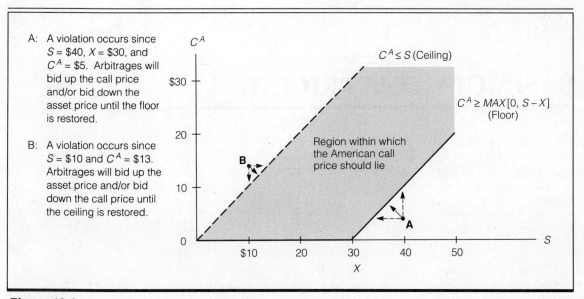

A: A violation occurs since $S = \$40$, $X = \$30$, and $C^A = \$5$. Arbitrages will bid up the call price and/or bid down the asset price until the floor is restored.

B: A violation occurs since $S = \$10$ and $C^A = \$13$. Arbitrages will bid up the asset price and/or bid down the call price until the ceiling is restored.

Figure 12.1:
Boundaries for American Call Options

where C^A is the price of an American call option, S is the underlying asset price, and X is the option's exercise price. This lower bound, or *floor*, is depicted by the bold line in Figure 12.1.

This boundary condition (Equation 12.1) follows from arbitrage restrictions. For example, suppose that $C^A = \$5$, $S = \$40$, and $X = \$30$ such that a violation of the boundary is observed. According to the equation, the American call should sell for at least $10 (per unit of the underlying asset). To exploit this violation, an arbitrager would (1) buy the option ($-\$5$), (2) immediately exercise it ($-\$30$), and (3) immediately sell the asset thus acquired ($+\$40$). Ignoring transaction costs, and assuming the trades can be executed rapidly, the riskless arbitrage profit earned is $5 (per unit of the underlying asset). As arbitragers engage in such trading, C^A should be bid up and S should be bid down until the inequality (Equation 12.1) is restored. This process is depicted graphically in Figure 12.1.

Minimum Value of European Call

For the American call, the arbitrage trading strategy that ensured the boundary (Equation 12.1) necessitated the immediate exercise of the call option (step 2 in the described procedure). This is acceptable for American options, which allow for premature exercise. However, European options do not; therefore, we cannot conclude that $C^E \geq MAX[0, S - X]$ where C^E is the European call price.

However, we can employ another arbitrage process to establish a lower bound for C^E. Suppose Portfolio A consists of the underlying

| Portfolio | Current Value | Payoffs at Option Expiration | |
		In-the-Money[a]	Out-of-the-Money[b]
A	S	S_T	S_T
B	$C^E + Xe^{-rT}$	$(S_T - X) + X = S_T$	X

[a]In-the-money means that the asset price at expiration, S_T, is greater than the exercise price, X.
[b]Out-of-the-money means that $S_T \leq X$.

asset, so its current value is S. Assume that this asset is a zero-leakage asset. Portfolio B consists of a European call written on the asset plus a risk-free, pure discount bond with face value X. Thus, Portfolio B has a current value of C^E plus Xe^{-rT}. Assume that the time until bond maturity, T, and the time until option maturity are the same.

The payoffs to these two portfolios at option maturity are shown in Exhibit 12.1. It is important to recognize that the payoff to Portfolio B is always at least as great, and potentially greater, than the payoff to Portfolio A. Thus investors will establish a price for Portfolio B that is at least as large as that for A:

(12.2a)
$$C^E + Xe^{-rT} \geq S.$$

Rearranging Equation 12.2a gives

(12.2b)
$$C^E \geq S - Xe^{-rT}.$$

Since an option always commands a nonnegative value, we can conclude that

(12.3)
$$C^E \geq MAX[0, S - Xe^{-rT}].$$

Boundary Equation 12.3 states that a European call option should sell for at least zero or the difference between the underlying asset price and the present value of the exercise price, whichever is greater.[1]

Arbitrage ensures the inequality (Equation 12.3). For example, suppose that $C^E = \$2$, $S = \$10$, and $Xe^{-rT} = \$7$ such that a violation is observed. According to Equation 12.3, C^E should be at least $3. To profit an arbitrager can (1) buy the call option ($-\$2$), (2) buy the risk-free, pure discount bond ($-\$7$), and (3) short sell the asset ($+\$10$). Proceeds are $1. At option maturity, the payoff is S_T if the option expires in-the-money. The arbitrager can reverse the short position in the asset. There

A European call option call should sell for at least zero or the difference between the underlying asset price and the present value of the exercise price, whichever is greater.

---

[1]Boundary Equation 12.3 is applicable to underlying assets that pay no dividends or interest; i.e. zero-leakage assets. We will adjust this boundary shortly to incorporate the effects of leakages.

is no loss. If the option expires out-of-the-money, the payoff is X. Since $X \geq S_T$, the arbitrager can reverse the short position in the asset and, again, there is no loss. Hence, the arbitrager never loses the initial $1 proceeds. As arbitragers execute the above trades, prices will be altered until Boundary Equation 12.3 is restored.

Leakages and Minimum Value of European Call If the underlying asset exhibits a leakage prior to option expiration, then the European call price should be at least zero, or the difference between the underlying asset price, adjusted for the present value of the leakage, and the present value of the exercise price—whichever is greater.

If the underlying asset exhibits a leakage prior to option expiration, then the European call price should be at least zero, or the difference between the underlying asset price, adjusted for the present value of the leakage, and the present value of the exercise price—whichever is greater.

For example, suppose that the underlying asset is a common stock that will pay a single, known dividend of D_t, where t denotes the time until the ex-dividend date and $t < T$. In this case, the minimum value of the European call is

(12.4a) $$C^E \geq MAX[0, S - D_t e^{-rt} - X e^{-rT}].$$

If there are a series of n discrete dividends prior to option expiration, then S should be reduced by the present value of each of the n discrete dividends. We discount at the risk-free rate since the dividends are assumed to be known. Finally, if the asset exhibits a constant continuous leakage (e.g., foreign exchange), then

(12.4b) $$C^E \geq MAX[0, S e^{-\delta T} - X e^{-rT}],$$

where δ is the constant proportional leakage factor.

Boundaries Equations 12.4a and 12.4b follow from arbitrage restrictions that are similar to the one underlying Boundary Equation 12.3. The intuition for the leakage adjustment is as follows. In the trading strategy underlying Equation 12.3, the arbitrager had to short sell the asset (step 3 above). Recall that when an asset is sold short, the short seller must pay the asset owner the value of each leakage paid by the asset over the period. Thus, adjusting S by subtracting the present value of the intervening leakages merely reflects the (present value) obligations of the arbitrager who short sells the asset. If the asset is a zero-leakage asset, there is no such obligation and Boundary Equation 12.3 applies.

Maximum Value of Call

The maximum value of a call option is the underlying asset's price. Obviously, no one would be willing to pay more for the right to buy an asset than the asset's price; a reasonable person would just buy the asset itself. However, this boundary condition also follows from arbitrage restrictions. For instance, suppose that you observe an American call price of $13 when the underlying asset's spot price is just $10. You could (1) buy the spot asset ($-$10$), and (2) write the call option ($+$13$). Your proceeds are $3 (per unit of the underlying asset). You can never lose these proceeds. If the option buyer ever exercises the option, you can simply turn over the asset. You hold a *covered call* position. As you execute these trades, C^A will be bid down and S will be bid up until the boundary is restored:

(12.5a) $$C^A \leq S.$$

The broken line in Figure 12.1 portrays this upper bound, or *ceiling*. The arbitrage strategy works for European calls as well. Thus:

(12.5b) $$C^E \leq S.$$

   At this point we can conclude that an American call price should be such that

(12.6) $$MAX[0, S - X] \leq C^A \leq S.$$

Equation 12.6 follows from combining Equations 12.1 and 12.5a. The shaded area in Figure 12.1 represents the range within which C^A should fall. For European calls we can conclude that

(12.7) $$MAX[0, S - PV_L - Xe^{-rT}] \leq C^E \leq S,$$

where PV_L denotes the present value of all intervening leakages exhibited by the spot asset over the option's life.

The Influence of Time to Maturity

Suppose there exist two American call options written on the same underlying asset and having the same exercise price but exhibiting two different expiration dates. Denote the time to maturity of the shorter term call option as T_1 and the time to maturity of the longer term call option as T_2. Thus, $T_2 > T_1$. By arbitrage, the price of a longer-term American call, $C^A(T_2)$, must be at least as great as the price of the corresponding shorter-term American call, $C^A(T_1)$:

The price of a longer-term American call must be at least as great as the price of the corresponding shorter-term American call.

(12.8) $$C^A(T_2) \geq C^A(T_1).$$

If $C^A(T_2) < C^A(T_1)$, an arbitrager could (1) buy $C^A(T_2)$ and (2) write $C^A(T_1)$. The positive proceeds can never be lost; if the buyer of the shorter-term call option should ever exercise, the arbitrager can cover the written call by exercising his own longer-term call option.

   Now suppose that the two options are European and, further, that the underlying asset is a zero-leakage asset. By arbitrage:

(12.9) $$C^E(T_2) \geq C^E(T_1).$$

If $C^E(T_2) < C^E(T_1)$, an arbitrager can (1) buy $C^E(T_2)$ and (2) write $C^E(T_1)$. The positive proceeds cannot be lost. Should the buyer of the shorter-term European call option exercise her option at its expiration, then she receives $S_1 - X$, where S_1 represents the asset's spot price at the maturity of the shorter term option. However, we know from Boundary Equation 12.3 that the value of the arbitrager's longer-term option should be, at that time, at least $S_1 - Xe^{-rT_2}$.[2] The arbitrager can sell her option and obtain at least $S_1 - Xe^{-rT_2}$. Therefore, she can cover the written call:

$$S_1 - Xe^{-rT_2} > S_1 - X.$$

The price of a longer-term European call written on a zero leakage asset must be at least as great as the price of an otherwise equivalent but shorter-term European call.

The arbitrager's original proceeds are intact. Thus, by arbitrage we can state that the price of a longer-term European call written on a zero-leakage asset must be at least as great as the price of an otherwise similar but shorter-term European call.

This same arbitrage argument can break down when the underlying asset exhibits a leakage. For instance, suppose that the asset in question has a continuous leakage at the rate δ. When the shorter-term option is exercised at its expiration, the minimum value of the arbitrager's longer-term option is $S_1 e^{-\delta T_2} - Xe^{-rT_2}$ (see Equation 12.4b). If δ is greater than r, however, then the arbitrager cannot cover the written call:

$$S_1 e^{-\delta T_2} - Xe^{-rT_2} < S_1 - X \text{ if } \delta > r.$$

The arbitrager's original proceeds do not remain intact. And if δ is sufficiently large, then the arbitrager could exhibit a net loss. Thus, there are conditions under which we cannot conclude that a longer-term European call option will have a greater price than a similar but shorter-term European call option. The conditions are (1) the underlying asset exhibits a leakage; and (2) the leakage is large.

As another example, suppose the underlying asset is a dividend-paying common stock. Specifically, at the end of the shorter-term option's life the stock will pay one known dividend at future time t, D_t, where $t < T_2$. From Equation 12.4a, the arbitrager can sell her option for (at least) $S_1 - D_t e^{-rt} - Xe^{-rT_2}$. However, this may be insufficient to cover the written call if the discrete dividend is large:

$$S_1 - D_1 e^{-rt} - Xe^{-rT_2} < S_1 - X \text{ if } D_t \text{ is large.}$$

The Influence of the Exercise Price

Suppose there exist two American call options having the same underlying asset and maturity but different exercise prices, X_2 and X_1, where

---

[2]The buyer of the shorter-term option exercised, so we know that $S_1 > X$. Therefore $C^E(T_2) \geq S_1 - Xe^{-rT_2}$.

		Payoffs at Option Expiration		
Portfolio	Current Value	$S_T < X_1$	$X_1 \leq S_T < X_2$	$S_T \geq X_2$
A	$C^E(X_1)$	0	$S_T \quad X_1$	$S_T - X_1$
	$-C^E(X_2)$	0	0	$-S_T + X_2$
		0	$S_T - X_1 > 0$	$X_2 - X_1 > 0$
B	$(X_2 - X_1)e^{-rT}$	$X_2 - X_1 > 0$	$X_2 - X_1 > 0$	$X_2 - X_1 > 0$

$X_2 > X_1$. The value of a lower exercise price call option must be at least as great as the value of the corresponding higher exercise price call option:

(12.10a)
$$C^A(X_1) \geq C^A(X_2).$$

Boundary Equation 12.10a follows from arbitrage restrictions. Suppose that $C^A(X_1) < C^A(X_2)$. An arbitrager can (1) buy $C^A(X_1)$ and (2) write $C^A(X_2)$. The positive proceeds cannot be lost. If the buyer of the written option should exercise, the arbitrager is out $S - X_2$. However, the arbitrager could always exercise his own option, generating $S - X_1$, and cover the written option: $S - X_1 - (S - X_2) = X_2 - X_1 > 0$. Such trading will eventually restore the inequality (Equation 12.10a). This process works for European calls as well:

(12.10b)
$$C^E(X_1) \geq C^E(X_2).$$

Establishing Limits on These Price Differences From Equations 12.10a and 12.10b we know that the value of a lower exercise price call option must be at least as great as the value of a corresponding but higher exercise price call option. But how large can this price difference be? The answer, as usual, lies in arbitrage restrictions.

Suppose that we construct two portfolios: Portfolio A consists of a purchased European call with exercise price X_1 and a written European call with exercise price X_2. Portfolio B consists of a risk-free, pure discount bond with face value $(X_2 - X_1)$. Exhibit 12.2 displays the values of A and B at option expiration. It is important to recognize that the value of Portfolio B is never less, and is sometimes greater, than that of Portfolio A. Thus, investors will always pay at least as much for B as they pay for A:

The difference between the prices of two European calls that differ only by their exercise prices must be less than or equal to the present value of the exercise price difference.

(12.11)
$$(X_2 - X_1)e^{-rT} \geq C^E(X_1) - C^E(X_2).$$

Equation 12.11 states that the difference in the prices of two European calls that differ only by their exercise prices must be less than or equal to the present value of the exercise price difference.

For American options we must recognize that the written call option (with higher exercise price X_2) can be exercised prematurely. Suppose that the written call is exercised at time t^*, an instant of time after the portfolios were originally formed. The value of Portfolio A is now $X_2 - X_1$.[3] These proceeds can be invested in a risk-free asset, earning $(X_2 - X_1)e^{r(T - t^*)}$. This exceeds Portfolio B's payoff $(X_2 - X_1)$. Hence, Portfolio B will not always outperform Portfolio A when options are American.

However, suppose that we originally formed Portfolio B by purchasing risk-free, pure discount bonds with face value $(X_2 - X_1)e^{rT}$. In this case Portfolio B's payoff will always be at least as great as that of Portfolio A. We can conclude that

$$(12.12) \qquad X_2 - X_1 \geq C^A(X_1) - C^A(X_2).$$

The difference between the prices of two American calls that differ only by exercise price cannot exceed the exercise price difference.

Equation 12.12 states that the difference in the prices of two American calls that differ only by exercise price cannot exceed the exercise price difference.

American versus European Calls

Suppose there exist two call options that are exactly the same in every aspect, except that one is American and one is European. You might expect the American call to command a greater price since it conveys the privilege to exercise prematurely:

$$(12.13) \qquad C^A \geq C^E.$$

However, Boundary Equation 12.13 follows from arbitrage restrictions as well. Suppose that $C^A = \$3$, and $C^E = \$4$. An arbitrager can profit by (1) purchasing C^A ($-\$3$) and (2) writing C^E ($+\$4$). The $1 proceeds (per unit of the underlying asset) cannot be lost. The European option cannot be exercised until its maturity. At that time, however, $C^A = C^E$ since both options have no remaining life. Thus, holding the American option until expiration assures the arbitrager of riskless profit. An American call option should sell for at least as much as its European counterpart.

An American call option should sell for at least as much as its European counterpart.

BOUNDARIES FOR PUT OPTIONS

Minimum Value of American Put

An American put option should sell for at least zero or the difference between the exercise price and the underlying asset price, whichever is greater.

An American put option should sell for at least zero or the difference between the exercise price and the underlying asset price, whichever is greater:

---

[3]The written call must be in-the-money if it is rationally exercised. That is, $S_{t^*} > X_2$. Exercising the purchased American call with exercise price X_1 causes the payoff to Portfolio A at time t^* to be $X_2 - X_1$.

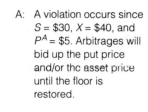

A: A violation occurs since S = \$30, X = \$40, and P^A = \$5. Arbitrages will bid up the put price and/or the asset price until the floor is restored.

B: A violation occurs since X = \$40, and P^A = \$45. Arbitrages will bid down the put price until the ceiling is restored.

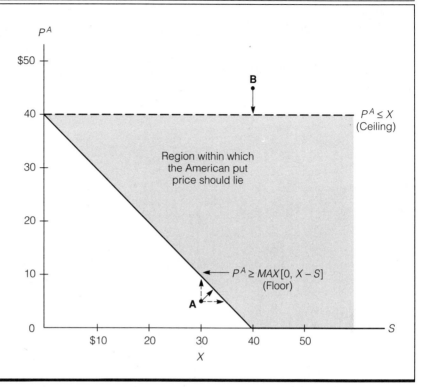

Figure 12.2:
Boundaries for American Put Options

(12.14) $$P^A \geq MAX[0, X - S],$$

where P^A denotes the American put price. The lower boundary, or *floor*, is depicted by the bold line in Figure 12.2. It follows from arbitrage restrictions. Suppose, for example, that P^A = \$5, S = \$30, and X = \$40 such that a violation of Equation 12.14 occurs. To exploit this, an arbitrager will (1) buy the put (−\$5), (2) buy the asset (−\$30), and (3) immediately exercise the put, thereby selling the asset for the exercise price (+\$40). Ignoring transaction costs, and assuming the trades can be executed rapidly, the riskless arbitrage profit earned is \$5 (per unit of the underlying asset). As arbitragers engage in such trading the put price and asset price will be bid up until Boundary Equation 12.14 is restored.

Minimum Value of European Put

The price of a European put written on a zero-leakage asset must be at least zero or the present value of the exercise price less the asset price, whichever is greater:

The price of a European put written on a zero-leakage asset must be at least zero or the present value of the exercise price less the asset price, whichever is greater.

(12.15) $$P^E \geq MAX[0, Xe^{-rT} - S],$$

where P^E denotes the European put price.

		Payoffs at Option Expiration	
Portfolio	Current Value	In-the-Money[a]	Out-of-the-Money[b]
A	S	S_T	S_T
B	$Xe^{-rT} - P^E$	$X - (X - S_T) = S_T$	X

[a]*In-the-money* means that the asset price at expiration, S_T, is less than the exercise price, *X*.
[b]*Out-of-the-money* means that $S_T \geq X$.

Boundary Equation 12.15 is analogous to Boundary Equation 12.3 for European calls written on zero-leakage assets. Again consider the case of two portfolios, where *A* consists of the underlying asset in question and *B* consists of a written European put and a purchased risk-free, pure discount bond with a face value *X*. This bond matures at *T*, the put's expiration. The payoffs to the two portfolios are presented in Exhibit 12.3. Since Portfolio *A*'s payoff is always at least as great as that of *B*, investors will pay as much or more for *A* than *B*:

(12.16) $$S \geq Xe^{-rT} - P^E.$$

Rearranging Equation 12.16 and noting that P^E must be nonnegative gives us Boundary Equation 12.15.

Leakages and Minimum Value of European Put   Recall that the floor for a European call changed when the asset paid interest or dividends (compare Equation 12.3 with Equation 12.4a or 12.4b). It is easily demonstrated than an analogous adjustment will occur for European puts written on discrete or continuous leakage assets:

(12.17a) $$P^E \geq MAX[0, Xe^{-rT} - (S - D_t e^{-rt})],$$

(12.17b) $$P^E \geq MAX[0, Xe^{-rT} - Se^{-\delta T}].$$

Maximum Value of Put Option

An American put should sell for no more than its exercise price:

An American put should sell for no more than its exercise price.

(12.18a) $$P^A \leq X.$$

Boundary Equation 12.18a, which is depicted by the broken line in Figure 12.2, follows from arbitrage restrictions. For instance, suppose that $P^A = \$45$ while $X = \$40$. An arbitrager can write the put, collecting $45. If the written option is ever exercised, the most the arbitrager is out is the exercise price, $40. This is because the asset price cannot fall below zero. The put writer's *limited liability* is *X*. As the arbitrager writes the put, its price is bid down until Boundary Equation 12.18a is restored.

The same arbitrage strategy holds for European puts, so

(12.18b) $P^E \leq X.$

However, we can establish a more restrictive upper bound for European puts, namely

(12.19) $P^E \leq Xe^{-rT}.$

If $P^E > Xe^{-rT}$, an arbitrager can write the put and place the proceeds in a risk-free, pure discount bond maturing at T. The bond's payoff will be more than X at expiration; therefore, the arbitrager can cover the European put even if $S_T = \$0$. Boundary Equation 12.19 states that a European put price cannot exceed the discounted exercise price.

A European put price cannot exceed the discounted exercise price.

At this point we can conclude that an American put price should be such that

(12.20) $MAX[0, X - S] \leq P^A \leq X.$

Equation 12.20 follows from combining Equations 12.14 and 12.18a. The shaded area in Figure 12.2 represents the range within which P^A should fall. For European puts we can conclude that

(12.21) $MAX[0, Xe^{-rT} - (S - PV_L)] \leq P^E \leq Xe^{-rT}.$

The Influence of Time to Maturity

Suppose there exist two American put options written on the same underlying asset and having the same exercise price but exhibiting two different maturities, T_2 and T_1, where $T_2 > T_1$. By arbitrage, the price of a longer-term American put, $P^A(T_2)$, must be at least as great as that of the corresponding shorter-term American put, $P^A(T_1)$:

The price of a longer-term American put must be at least as great as that of the corresponding shorter-term American put.

(12.22) $P^A(T_2) \geq P^A(T_1).$

If $P^A(T_2) < P^A(T_1)$, an arbitrager could (1) buy $P^A(T_2)$ and (2) write $P^A(T_1)$. The positive proceeds cannot be lost; if the written put is exercised, the arbitrager can cover it by exercising her own longer-term put option.

For European puts, however, we cannot determine unambiguously whether or not a longer-term option exhibits a greater price than its shorter-term counterpart. For instance, consider two European puts, $P^E(T_2)$ and $P^E(T_1)$, written on a zero-leakage asset. If $P^E(T_1)$ is exercised at its maturity, the arbitrager's longer-term put will be worth at least $Xe^{-rT_2} - S_1$.[4] However, this is insufficient to cover the written put exercised:

$$Xe^{-rT_2} - S_1 < X - S_1.$$

---

[4]The buyer of the shorter-term put exercised, so we know that $S_1 < X$. Therefore, by Equation 12.15, $P^E(T_2) \geq Xe^{-rT_2} - S_1$.

This ambiguity persists if the underlying asset exhibits a leakage:

$$Xe^{-rT_2} - (S_1 - PV_L) \le X - S_1.$$

However, note that the larger the leakage, the more likely is the success of the arbitrage strategy.

The Influence of the Exercise Price

Suppose there exist corresponding American puts having two different exercise prices, X_2 and X_1, where $X_2 > X_1$. The value of a higher-exercise-price put must be at least as great as the value of the corresponding lower-exercise-price put:

(12.23a) $$P^A(X_2) \ge P^A(X_1).$$

Boundary Equation 12.23a follows from arbitrage restrictions. If $P^A(X_2) < P^A(X_1)$, an arbitrager can (1) buy $P^A(X_2)$ and (2) write $P^A(X_1)$. The proceeds received cannot be lost. If the written put is ever exercised, the arbitrager is out $X_1 - S$. However, the arbitrager could always exercise his own option, generating $X_2 - S$, and cover the written put:

$$X_2 - S - (X_1 - S) = X_2 - X_1 > 0.$$

Such trading will serve to restore Boundary Equation 12.23a. This trading strategy works for European puts as well:

(12.23b) $$P^E(X_2) \ge P^E(X_1).$$

Establishing Limits on These Price Differences Recall Equations 12.11 and 12.12. These establish value limits on the price difference between call options exhibiting different exercise prices. They follow from an arbitrage trading strategy involving call options and risk-free, pure discount bonds. Using an analogous strategy for puts, it is easily demonstrated that

(12.24) $$(X_2 - X_1)e^{-rT} \ge P^E(X_2) - P^E(X_1),$$

(12.25) $$(X_2 - X_1) \ge P^A(X_2) - P^A(X_1).$$

Equation 12.24 states that the difference between the prices of two corresponding European put options having different exercise prices must not exceed the present value of the exercise-price difference. Equation 12.25 states that the difference between the prices of two corresponding American put options having different exercise prices must not exceed the exercise-price difference.

American versus European Puts

An American put will be at least as valuable as its European counterpart:

(12.26)
$$P^A \geq P^E.$$

If $P^A < P^E$, an arbitrager can profit by (1) buying P^A and (2) writing P^E. The value of the written European put at its expiration must be identical to the value of the purchased American put. Hence, holding the American put until expiration assures the arbitrager of riskless profit.

PUT-CALL PARITY

The previous boundary conditions dealt with calls or puts. None of them dealt with corresponding calls and puts—that is, calls and puts exhibiting the same underlying asset, exercise price, and maturity. We now investigate a condition developed by H. Stoll (1969) and known as *put-call parity* that relates corresponding European calls and puts. It follows from an elegant arbitrage strategy.

For zero-leakage assets, put-call parity is given by

(12.27a)
$$C^E = P^E + S - Xe^{-rT}.$$

Equation 12.27a states that the price of a European call is equal to the price of its corresponding put plus the spot asset price less the discounted exercise price. Thus, if we know P^E, we can easily determine C^E, and vice versa.

To illustrate why Equation 12.27a must obtain, suppose that we select parameter values that result in a violation of put-call parity: $C^E = \$1$, $P^E = \$7$, $S = \$35$, $X = \$40$, $T = .50$ (180 days), and $r = .10$. Thus, we have

$$C^E = \$1 < P^E + S - Xe^{-rT} = \$7 + 35 - 40e^{-.10(.50)} = \$3.95.$$

To exploit this violation, an arbitrager undertakes the following steps: (1) buy C^E ($-\$1$); (2) write P^E ($+\$7$); (3) short sell the asset ($+\$35$); and (4) invest the net proceeds ($\$41$) in a risk-free, pure discount bond with maturity $T = .50$, the same common maturity of the two European options.[5] In six months, therefore, the arbitrager receives $\$43.10$: $\$41e^{.10(.50)}$. To complete the strategy, the arbitrager must now reverse her short position, returning the borrowed asset. Suppose that the asset's spot price at option expiration is $\$40$ ($S_T = \$40$). Both the call and put options expire worthless. The arbitrager can reverse her short position at $\$40$, thus earning $\$3.10$: $\$43.10 - \$40.00$. Now suppose that $S_T < \$40$,

---

[5]The arbitrager purchases a risk-free bond to ensure that her strategy is riskless.

say, $35. In this case the put buyer exercises, and the arbitrager therefore buys the asset at the common exercise price of $40. Consequently, the arbitrager can still reverse her short position at $40, earning $3.10. The call expires worthless. Finally, suppose that $S_T > \$40$, say, $50. In this case the put is worthless, and the arbitrager can exercise her call, buying the asset for the common exercise price of $40. Again, she can reverse the short asset position for $40 and earn $3.10. Thus, no matter what S_T is, the arbitrager is assured of a riskless profit of $3.10 (per unit of the underlying asset). Her trading strategy will be executed, exerting price pressure, until put-call parity is restored.

What if a violation occurs such that $C^E > P^E + S - Xe^{-rT}$? To exploit this violation (where the inequality is now reversed), an arbitrager simply reverses the above trading strategy. Suppose that C^E is now $5 such that

$$C^E = \$5 > P^E + S - Xe^{-rT} = \$7 + 35 - 40e^{-.10(.50)} = \$3.95.$$

To profit, an arbitrager (1) writes C^E ($+\$5$); (2) buys P^E ($-\$7$); (3) buys the underlying asset ($-\$35$); and (4) borrows the money required ($37) at the risk-free rate of .10 for six-months.[6] Therefore, he owes $38.90 in six months. Suppose that $S_T = \$40$. The arbitrager now owns an asset worth $40, and both options expire worthless. He can sell the asset and repay the loan (i.e., reverse his short position in the risk-free asset), profiting $1.10: $40 − $38.90. Now suppose that $S_T = \$35$. The call expires worthless, and the arbitrager can exercise his put, selling the asset for $40. Again he earns $1.10. Finally, if $S_T = \$50$, the put expires worthless, and the written call will be exercised. The arbitrager sells the asset for the exercise price of $40 and again earns $1.10. Thus, no matter if the asset price goes up or down over the period, the arbitrager is assured of a riskless profit of $1.10 (per unit of the underlying asset). His trading will eventually restore put-call parity.

If the underlying asset exhibits a leakage, then we must adjust Equality Equation 12.27a to reflect this leakage:

(12.27b) $$C^E = P^E + (S - PV_L) - Xe^{-rT}.$$

For instance, if the underlying asset is a stock that will pay a known dividend, D_t, where $t < T$, then

(12.27c) $$C^E = P^E + (S - D_t e^{-rt}) - Xe^{-rT}.$$

If the asset exhibits a continuous leakage at the rate δ, then

(12.27d) $$C^E = P^E + Se^{-\delta T} - Xe^{-rT}.$$

Obviously, we must adjust for the leakage to reflect all of the relevant cash flows over the period. For instance, in the original arbitrage stra-

---

[6]Thus, we assume that the arbitrager can sell/issue risk-free bonds. In other words, he can short sell the risk-free asset.

Find the Boundary Violations

Suppose that you observe the following contemporaneous European option prices where the underlying asset exhibits no leakages and has a current price of $10. Assuming that there are no transaction costs or restrictions on short selling, the risk-free interest rate is 8 percent, and trades can be conducted at prevailing prices, identify the seven exploitable arbitrage opportunities.

Calls			Puts		
Exercise Price	Time to Expiration[a]	Call Price[b]	Exercise Price	Time to Expiration	Put Price
$ 8.00	30 Days	$2.10	$ 8.00	30 Days	$0.05
$ 8.50	30 Days	$1.60	$ 8.50	30 Days	$0.10
$ 9.00	90 Days	$1.25	$ 9.00	90 Days	$0.08
$ 9.50	90 Days	$1.35	$ 9.50	90 Days	$0.20
$10.00	120 Days	$1.07	$10.00	120 Days	$0.80
$10.50	120 Days	$1.13	$10.50	120 Days	$1.35
$11.00	30 Days	$0.17	$11.00	30 Days	$1.09
$11.00	60 Days	$0.12	$11.00	60 Days	$0.98
$12.00	60 Days	$0.06	$12.00	60 Days	$1.91

[a]Assume a 360-day year.
[b]Round-up all prices to the nearest whole penny.

ANSWERS:
1. Violation of put-call parity for $X = \$8.50$, $T = 30$ days.
2. Violation of $(X_2 - X_1)e^{-rT} \geq C^E(X_1) - C^E(X_2)$ for 30-day calls.
3. Violation of $C^E(X_1) \geq C^E(X_2)$ for 90-day calls.
4. Violation of put-call parity for $X = \$9.50$, $T = 90$ days.
5. Violation of $(X_2 - X_1)e^{-rT} \geq P^E(X_2) - P^E(X_1)$ for 120-day puts.
6. Violation of $C^E(X_1) \geq C^E(X_2)$ for 120-day calls.
7. Violation of $C^E(T_2) \geq C^E(T_1)$ for $X = \$11.00$ calls.

tegy, the arbitrager sold short the asset and was consequently obligated to pay all intervening dividends and interest to the asset owner.

Does put-call parity obtain for American options? Strictly speaking, the answer is no. This is because the written American option in the above strategies could be exercised prematurely, making the arbitrager's proceeds uncertain. However, empirical evidence does suggest that corresponding American puts and calls exhibit prices that do not deviate substantially from put-call parity. The reason for this will become clear when we address the issue of American options pricing in Chapter 14.

Exhibit 12.4:

Summary of Boundary Conditions

A: Call Options	
(12.6)	$MAX[0, S - X] \leq C^A \leq S$
(12.7)	$MAX[0, S - PV_L - Xe^{-rT}] \leq C^E \leq S$
(12.8)	$C^A(T_2) \leq C^A(T_1), T_2 > T_1$
(12.11)	$(X_2 - X_1)e^{-rT} \geq C^E(X_1) - C^E(X_2), X_2 > X_1$
(12.12)	$X_2 - X_1 \geq C^A(X_1) - C^A(X_2), X_2 > X_1$
(12.13)	$C^A \geq C^E$

B: Put Options	
(12.20)	$MAX[0, X - S] \leq P^A \leq X$
(12.21)	$MAX[0, Xe^{-rT} - (S - PV_L)] \leq P^E \leq Xe^{-rT}$
(12.22)	$P^A(T_2) \geq P^A(T_1), T_2 > T_1$
(12.24)	$(X_2 - X_1)e^{-rT} \geq P^E(X_2) - P^E(X_1), X_2 > X_1$
(12.25)	$(X_2 - X_1) \geq P^A(X_2) - P^A(X_1), X_2 > X_1$
(12.26)	$P^A \geq P^E$

C: Put-Call Parity	
(12.27a)	$C^E = P^E + S - Xe^{-rT}$
(12.27b)	$C^E = P^E + (S - PV_L) - Xe^{-rT}$

SUMMARY OF BOUNDARY CONDITIONS

For future reference, the boundary conditions presented thus far have been summarized in Exhibit 12.4. It is important to remember that these conditions were derived from arbitrage applications in markets where no imperfections exist. The effects of imperfections such as transaction costs and restrictions on short selling are described below. Shortly thereafter, we present a simple model to determine exact option prices, which, of course, conform to these boundary conditions.

TRANSACTION COSTS AND RESTRICTIONS ON SHORT SELLING

All of the arbitrage trading strategies discussed here involve transaction costs, and some entail the short selling of a spot asset. Consequently, the existence of transaction costs and restrictions on short selling will cause each of the boundaries discussed to be somewhat inexact. In order for a boundary violation to imply a profitable arbitrage opportunity in actual markets, the violation must be sufficiently large to overcome the frictions faced by market traders. The relevant, least-cost traders are typically exchange members. Numerous empirical studies have examined whether option markets exhibit unexploited arbitrage opportunities based on boundary violations where the arbitrager in question is an exchange member. The overwhelming majority of these studies finds no truly unexploited opportunities and thus supports market efficiency. We briefly summarize a few of these studies next.

EMPIRICAL EVIDENCE ON OPTIONS MARKETS

Klemkosky and Resnick Study

R. Klemkosky and B. Resnick (1980) used transactions data for CBOE stock options for the period of July 1977 through June 1978 in order to investigate put-call parity. The authors concluded that profits from observed violations would be eliminated after accounting for bid-ask spreads and a short execution delay. Thus, their results can be interpreted as supporting the efficiency of the CBOE on an *ex ante* basis.

Bhattacharya Study

M. Bhattacharya (1983) used transactions data for CBOE stock options for the period of August 1976 through June 1977 in order to test a series of boundary conditions. He concluded that virtually all of the violations observed for the thousands of boundary tests conducted would be unprofitable after controlling for transaction costs. His evidence supports CBOE efficiency.

Bodurtha and Courtadon Study

J. Bodurtha and G. Courtadon (1986) used transactions data for currency options traded on the Philadelphia Stock Exchange for the period of February 1983 to September 1984 and examined a battery of arbitrage boundaries. The authors found strong support for the premise that currency option prices conform to boundary conditions.

Ball and Torous Study

C. Ball and W. Torous (1986) used closing futures option prices and corresponding settlement futures prices to test boundaries applicable to options written on futures contracts. For the most part, such boundaries were analogous to those examined in this chapter. Their data pertained to three underlying futures contracts—on the deutsche mark, gold, and sugar—for the period of January 1983 to June 1984. Their results provide little evidence to support the possibility of riskless arbitrage opportunities in futures option markets.

THE BINOMIAL OPTION-PRICING MODEL (BOPM)

Previously in this chapter we were concerned with establishing boundaries governing an option's price. Also, through put-call parity we established how a European call (put) option could be valued given its corresponding European put (call) option. We did not, however, determine an exact option price directly.

The binomial option-
pricing model assumes that
the underlying asset price obeys
a binomial generating process.

The binomial option-pricing model (BOPM), developed independently by J. Cox, S. Ross, and M. Rubinstein (1979) and R. Rendleman and B. Bartter (1979), assumes that the underlying asset price obeys a *binomial generating process*. This means that in any single period of time, the asset price can either go up or down, possibly at different rates. The BOPM is often called a *two-state model*, reflecting the two possible states of the asset's future price. Obviously, in reality an asset's price can assume more than two possible outcomes. However, the BOPM is useful as a pedagogical tool since it demonstrates the process by which option prices are generated. Also, it can be shown that the model will, in a multi-period world, converge to the Black-Scholes model, the preeminent options-pricing model that is presented in the next chapter. Understanding the BOPM will therefore help you understand the Black-Scholes model. And despite its limitations, the BOPM can be used to price American options, the subject of Chapter 14.

The One-Period BOPM

Let us begin our explanation of the BOPM by assuming a one-period world in which, therefore, the option's maturity represents one time period. If the option expires in three months, then the one period is three months. If it expires in nine months, then the one period is nine months, and so on. Suppose that an asset currently worth $10 can increase in value by 20 percent or can decrease by 15 percent over the one time period. Let the probability of an increase be 50 percent, and assume that the risk-free rate of interest is 10 percent. Hence, the asset price follows a binomial generating process as shown in part A of Figure 12.3, where

S = $10.00, the asset's current price

p = .50, the probability of an increase in asset price

$(1 + r)$ = 1.10; that is, 1 plus the risk-free rate of interest

u = 1.20, the multiplicative upward movement in the asset price, and

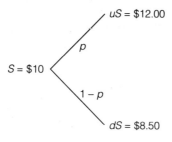

A. Spot Price Dynamics

$S = \$10$

p

$uS = \$12.00$

$1 - p$

$dS = \$8.50$

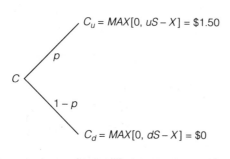

B. Call Price Dynamics

C

p

$C_u = MAX[0, uS - X] = \$1.50$

$1 - p$

$C_d = MAX[0, dS - X] = \$0$

$d = 0.85$, the multiplicative downward movement in the asset price.[7]

Now suppose that we want to determine the value of a call option written on this asset. Let the option's exercise price be $10.50. Given the above generating process, the option has a 50 percent chance of exhibiting a value of $1.50 at expiration, and a 50 percent chance of having zero value at expiration. These two payoffs are illustrated in part B of Figure 12.3. To determine the option's value, we construct a riskless hedged portfolio consisting of one unit of the asset and h units of the call option written against the asset. The variable h represents our *hedge ratio*. Part A of Figure 12.4 presents the two possible payoffs to the hedged portfolio. If we equate these two, then the end-of-period payoff will be certain, and the hedged portfolio will be risk-free. Equating the payoffs in Figure 12.4 gives

(12.28)
$$uS - hC_u = dS - hC_d.$$

---

[7]In order for the derivation of the BOPM to obtain, it is required that $d < (1 + r) < u$. Also, d must be less than 1 to preclude a negative asset price in a multi-period world.

A. Two Possible Payoffs

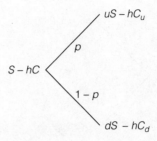

B. Equating Two Possible Payoffs

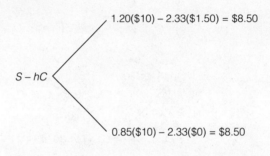

Solving Equation 12.28 for h gives

(12.29) $$h = S(u - d)/(C_u - C_d).$$

In our problem, $h = 2.33$:

$$h = \$10(1.20 - 0.85)/(\$1.50 - 0).$$

Thus, the riskless hedged portfolio will consist of one long unit of the underlying asset and 2.33 written call options. Such a combination will insure an end-of-period payoff of $8.50, regardless of whether S goes up or down. See part B of Figure 12.4.

Since the hedged portfolio is riskless, our initial portfolio investment must earn the risk-free rate of return over the period in order to preclude arbitrage. Thus, we have[8]

(12.30a) $$(1 + r)(S - hC) = uS - hC_u,$$

---

[8]Since the value of the hedged portfolio is the same regardless of whether S goes up or down, we can equate $(1 + r)(S - hC)$ to $uS - hC_u$ or to $dS - hC_d$ and obtain the same result.

or

(12.30b) $C = S[(1 + r) - u] + hC_u/h(1 + r).$

Substituting Equation 12.29 for h and rearranging algebraically gives

(12.31) $C = qC_u + (1 - q)C_d/(1 + r),$

where

$$q = [(1 + r) - d]/(u - d)$$

and

$$(1 - q) = [u - (1 + r)]/(u - d).$$

Equation 12.31 is the one-period BOPM for calls. The formula gives the call price as determined by the parameters C_u, C_d, q, and r. C_u and C_d are in turn determined by the parameters S, X, u, and d, and q is determined by r, u, and d. Thus, the parameters that affect a call option's price are the spot-asset price (S), the option's exercise price (X), the risk-free rate of interest (r), and u and d, which define the spot-asset prices possible at option expiration.[9]

Returning to our numerical example, the price of the call option is $0.974:

$$\$0.974 = \left[\left(\frac{1.10 - .85}{1.20 - .85} \right)\$1.50 + \left(\frac{1.20 - 1.10}{1.20 - .85} \right)\$0 \right]/(1.10).$$

We can confirm that this is the correct call price by assuring that our initial investment in the hedged portfolio earns the riskless rate. If $C = \$0.974$, our initial investment is $7.73:

$$\$7.73 = S - hC = \$10 - (2.33)(\$0.974).$$

Since we are guaranteed an end-of-period payoff of $8.50, our return is 10 percent, the risk-free rate of interest:

$$(\$8.50 - \$7.73)/(\$7.73) = .10.$$

Using a similar hedging strategy, the one-period BOPM for puts can be given by

(12.32) $P = qP_u + (1 - q)P_d/(1 + r).$

In our example, where $S = \$10$, $X = \$10.50$, $u = 1.20$, $d = 0.85$, $p = 0.50$, and $r = .10$, $P_u = \$0$ and $P_d = \$2.00$, so that $P = \$0.519$.

---

[9] Besides understanding the parameters that affect the call option price, it is useful to note the parameters that do not. Specifically, notice that p and $(1 - p)$ do not enter Pricing Equation 12.31. Thus, the equation contains no parameters that are affected by the risk preferences of investors. This leads to what has been called *risk-neutral options pricing*. All that is required for determining the option's price is that investors prefer more wealth to less such that arbitrage opportunities are eliminated.

An Example of Arbitrage   Suppose that the call option just discussed is priced at $1.25, that is, overpriced. We should be able to exploit this mispricing by buying one unit of the underlying asset at $10.00 and writing 2.33 calls.[10] Our initial investment is thus $7.09. If the asset price goes up or down, we receive a certain $8.50 at the end of the period. Our return is therefore 20 percent, which is twice the risk-free rate. Obviously, a riskless portfolio that earns twice the risk-free rate will lure arbitragers. Their trading should bid up S and/or bid down C until equilibrium is restored. For instance, if the asset price remains at $10.00, C should be bid down to $0.974. Similar arbitrage strategies work for underpriced calls and mispriced puts.

The *n*-Period BOPM

The BOPM assumption that an asset price can have only two possible outcomes may be realistic for some lotteries but not for most assets. Their prices represent continuous random variables, whereas a binomial generating process is applicable to discrete random variables. This would seem to suggest that the BOPM is quite limited in its application. However, now consider a world in which there are two states, but many time periods. That is, the option's maturity would be made up of thousands and thousands of small time periods. In this case the underlying asset price could take on thousands of different values at option maturity. And even if this maturity were just one day (or one hour, or one minute), the potential price outcomes would be in the thousands (or millions, or billions). In short, the resulting distribution of price outcomes would begin to appear continuous, like a tree diagram eventually appears to be continuous. This being the case, the BOPM should be very accurate when applied to continuous random variables if we allow the number of time periods to be very large.

Let us begin by extending the model to two time periods (see Figure 12.5). Assume that 1 plus the two-period risk-free rate is $(1 + r)^2$. To solve for C_u and C_d, which are the values of the one-period options initially traded at the end of the first period, we simply apply Pricing Equation 12.31, the one-period call BOPM:

(12.33a) $$C_u = [qC_{uu} + (1 - q)C_{ud}]/(1 + r)$$

(12.33b) $$C_d = [qC_{du} + (1 - q)C_{dd}]/(1 + r),$$

where C_{uu}, C_{du}, and C_{dd} are the three possible call prices at the end of two periods. These are

$$C_{uu} = MAX[0, u^2 S - X];$$

---

[10]Obviously, in reality we cannot write 2.33 call options. However, we could easily buy 100 units of the spot asset and write 233 calls and thus achieve the same percentage return.

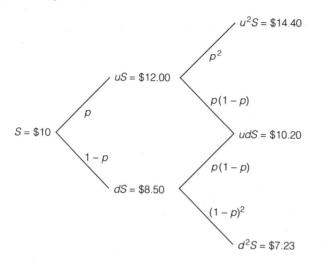

A. Spot Price Dynamics

$$u^2S = \$14.40$$

$$p^2$$

$$uS = \$12.00$$

$$p(1 - p)$$

$$p$$

$$S = \$10$$

$$udS = \$10.20$$

$$1 - p$$

$$p(1 - p)$$

$$dS = \$8.50$$

$$(1 - p)^2$$

$$d^2S = \$7.23$$

Figure 12.5:
Two-Period Binomial
Generating Process

B. Call Price Dynamics

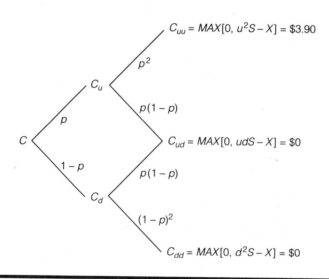

$$C_{uu} = MAX[0, u^2S - X] = \$3.90$$

$$p^2$$

$$C_u$$

$$p(1 - p)$$

$$p$$

$$C$$

$$C_{ud} = MAX[0, udS - X] = \$0$$

$$1 - p$$

$$p(1 - p)$$

$$C_d$$

$$(1 - p)^2$$

$$C_{dd} = MAX[0, d^2S - X] = \$0$$

$$C_{ud} = MAX[0, udS - X];$$
$$C_{dd} = MAX[0, d^2S - X].$$

As we did earlier, we can now construct a riskless hedged portfolio and determine the current value of the two-period call option:

(12.34a) $\qquad C = [qC_u + (1 - q)C_d]/(1 + r).$

Substituting Equations 12.33a and 12.33b into Equation 12.34a gives

(12.34b) $C = [q^2 C_{uu} + 2q(1 - q)C_{ud} + (1 - q)^2 C_{dd}]/(1 + r)^2.$

The call option's value is $1.644:[11]

$$\$1.644 = \left[\left(\frac{1.10 - .85}{1.20 - .85} \right)^2 \$3.90 + \$0 + \$0 \right]/(1.10)^2.$$

Equation 12.34b results from applying the one-period BOPM twice. When we reapply the process in an iterative way, the n-period generalization becomes

(12.35) $C = \sum_{j=0}^{n} \left\{ \frac{n!}{(n - j)!j!} q^j (1 - q)^{n-j} MAX[0, u^j d^{n-j} S - X] \right\} \div (1 + r)^n,$

where j is the number of upward price movements ($j = 0, 1, \ldots, n$). Equation 12.35 is the generalized BOPM, as applied to call options. In words, it states that the value of a call is the sum of the probabilities of each final call outcome multiplied by the value of that outcome and discounted at the risk-free rate for all n time periods. For put options, the generalized BOPM is

(12.36) $P = \sum_{j=0}^{n} \left\{ \frac{n!}{(n - j)!j!} q^j (1 - q)^{n-j} MAX[0, X - u^j d^{n-j} S] \div (1 + r)^n \right\}.$

A Numerical Example Recall that our one-period put was valued at $0.519. Let us now apply Equation 12.36, the generalized BOPM for puts, to determine/check this value.

For $j = 0$:

$$\frac{\frac{1!}{1!0!} \left(\frac{1.10 - .85}{1.20 - .85} \right)^0 \left(\frac{1.20 - 1.10}{1.20 - 0.85} \right)^1 MAX[0, 10.50 - (1.2)^0 (.85)^1 10]}{(1.10)} = \$0.519$$

For $j = 1$:

$$\frac{\frac{1!}{0!1!} \left(\frac{1.10 - .85}{1.20 - .85} \right)^1 \left(\frac{1.20 - 1.10}{1.20 - 0.85} \right)^0 MAX[0, 10.50 - (1.2)^1 (.85)^0 10]}{(1.10)} = \$0$$

Summing gives us $0.519.

Although the process of applying the generalized BOPM seems tedious, the model is easily programmable and can be run on any micro computer, and for small n, on many hand-held programmable calculators.

---

[11]By increasing the option's maturity from one period to two periods, we increased its value from $0.974 to $1.644. This suggests that option value is directly related to maturity. Maturity is a determinant of option value.

SUMMARY

Numerous boundary conditions, which define ranges within which option prices should lie, follow from arbitrage restrictions. Most empirical studies find that market prices conform to these boundaries after imperfections such as transaction costs, restrictions on short selling, and execution delays are controlled for.

The binomial option-pricing model (BOPM) shows that the determinants of an option's price are the underlying asset's price, the exercise price, the option's maturity, the riskless rate of interest, and asset volatility. Using these determinants, the option's price can be calculated without regard to investors' risk preferences. The BOPM will be used again in Chapter 14 to help determine the prices of American options.

Selected References

Ball, C., and W. Torous. "Futures Options and the Volatility of Future Prices." *Journal of Finance* 41 (September 1986): 857–870.

Bhattacharya, M. "Transaction Data Tests of Efficiency of the Chicago Board Options Exchange." *Journal of Financial Economics* 12 (1983): 161–185.

Bodurtha, J., and G. Courtadon. "Efficiency Tests of the Foreign Currency Options Market." *Journal of Finance* 41 (March 1986): 151–162.

Cox, J., S. Ross, and M. Rubinstein. "Option Pricing: A Simplified Approach." *Journal of Financial Economics* 7 (September 1979): 229–263.

Finnerty, J. "The CBOE and Market Efficiency." *Journal of Financial and Quantitative Analysis* 13 (March 1978): 29–38.

Galai, D. "Empirical Tests of Boundary Conditions for CBOE Options." *Journal of Financial Economics* 6 (1978): 187–211.

Gould, J., and D. Galai. "Transaction Costs and the Relationship between Put and Call Prices." *Journal of Financial Economics* 1 (1974): 105–129.

Hsia, C. "On Binomial Option Pricing." *Journal of Financial Research* 6 (Spring 1983): 41–50.

Klemkosky, R., and B. Resnick. "An *Ex Ante* Analysis of Put-Call Parity." *Journal of Financial Economics* 8 (1980): 363–378.

Merton, R. "Theory of Rational Option Pricing." *Bell Journal of Economics* 4 (Spring 1973): 141–183.

Rendleman, R., and B. Bartter. "Two-State Option Pricing." *Journal of Finance* 34 (December 1979): 1093–1110.

Stoll, H. "The Relationship between Put and Call Option Prices." *Journal of Finance* 24 (May 1969): 319–332.

Smith, C. "Option Pricing: A Review." *Journal of Financial Economics* 3 (1976): 3–51.

Questions and Problems

1. Suppose that $S = \$50$, $X = \$50$, $T = .50$, $r = .10$, and the underlying asset exhibits no leakages. If $C^E = \$3$, what is the value of the corresponding European put?

2. Why does the put sell for less than the call, even though both options are currently exactly at-the-money ($S = X$)?

3. Suppose that $S = \$10$, $X = \$9$, $T = .25$, $r = .08$, $\delta = .03$, $C^E = \$1.50$, and $P^E = \$0.75$. Ignoring market imperfections, is there a violation of put-call parity for this continuous-leakage asset? If so, how would you exploit this violation, and what is your resulting profit?

4. Suppose that $C^A = \$4$, $S = \$90$, and $X = \$83$. How would you exploit this situation?

5. Suppose that $C^E = \$2$, $S = \$35$, $X = \$33$, $T = .40$, $r = .10$, $D_t = \$0.50$, and $t = .25$. Is there a boundary violation and, if so, how would you exploit it?

6. Suppose that a longer-term European put option exhibited a lower price than an otherwise equivalent but shorter-term European put option. Does this represent an exploitable arbitrage opportunity? Why or why not?

7. Let $S = \$25$, $X = \$22$, and $r = .10$. If in each of two periods the asset price can go up 15 percent or down 15 percent, what is the current price of its call option?

8. Demonstrate why Boundary Equation 12.24 obtains. (Hint: Use portfolios analogous to those in Exhibit 12.2.)

9. Under what conditions will a longer-term European call option have a lower price than an otherwise identical but shorter-term European call option?

10. Suppose that you observe the following contemporaneous American option prices where the underlying asset exhibits a continuous leakage of $\delta = .03$ and a current price of $100. Assuming that $r = .07$, and that there are no market imperfections, identify five exploitable arbitrage opportunities.

Calls			Puts		
X	T	C^A	X	T	P^A
$ 97	.25	$3.12	$ 97	.25	$0.15
98	.25	2.50	98	.25	0.12
99	.50	2.22	99	.50	0.75
100	.50	1.10	100	.50	1.95
100	.75	0.85	100	.75	1.80
102	.25	0.60	102	.25	2.09
103	.25	0.08	103	.25	2.55

11. Use the generalized BOPM to value a call option given the following parameters: $S = \$50$, $X = \$50$, $n = 3$, $u = 1.10$, $d = .90$, and $r = .06$.

Problems 12 through 16 refer to the following information: In a one-period, two-state world, an asset with a current price of $50 can either rise in value by 20 percent or fall by 20 percent. The risk-free rate of interest is 8 percent. A call option written on the asset has an exercise price of $49.

12. Determine the two possible call prices at expiration.

13. What is the call option's current price?

14. Determine the hedge ratio, h.

15. Show how the hedged portfolio earns the riskless rate over the single period.

16. If the observed market price is $3, how would you exploit this mispricing, and what would be the return to your hedged portfolio?

Self-Test Problems

ST-1 through ST-5 utilize the following information:
In a one-period, two-state world, an asset with current price $100 can either rise in value by 20 percent or fall by 20 percent. The risk-free rate of interest is 8 percent. A put option written on the asset has an exercise price of $98.

ST-1. Determine the two possible put prices at expiration.

ST-2. What is the put option's current price?

ST-3. Determine the hedge ratio, h.

ST-4. Show how the hedged portfolio earns the riskless rate over the single period.

ST-5. If the observed market price is $4, how would you exploit this mispricing, and what would be the return to your hedged portfolio?

Solutions To Self-Test Problems

ST-1. $P_u = MAX[0, 98 - 120] = \$0.$

$P_d = MAX[0, 98 - 80] = \$18.$

ST-2. $P = \left[\left(\dfrac{1.08 - .80}{1.20 - .80} \right)\$0 + \left(\dfrac{1.20 - 1.08}{1.20 - 0.80} \right)\$18 \right] / (1.08) = \$5.00.$

ST-3. To hedge a long spot asset, you buy a put. A long position in an asset and its put are negatively correlated. Therefore,

$$uS + hP_u = dS + hP_d,$$

or

$$h = (dS - uS)/(P_u + P_d)$$
$$= (80 - 120)/(0 - 18) = 2.22.$$

ST-4. Investment: $S + hP = 100 + (2.22)(5) = \$111.11.$

Payoff: $uS + hP_u = 120 + (2.22)(0) = \$120$
$$= dS + hP_d = 80 + (2.22)(19).$$

Return: $(120 - 111.11)/(111.11) = .08 = r.$

ST-5. The put is underpriced. You want to buy it. To hedge, you also buy the spot asset. You have a covered put.

Investment: $S + hP = 100 + (2.22)(4) = \$108.88.$
Payoff: $120.
Return: $(120 - 108.88)/(108.88) = .102 > r.$

13

THE BLACK-SCHOLES MODEL

In 1973 F. Black and M. Scholes developed a formula to value European options written on zero-leakage assets. Widely known as the *Black-Scholes model*, it has become the preeminent options-pricing model. Moreover, numerous researchers have extended its basic framework in order to value options written on assets exhibiting leakages and American options.

Black and Scholes derived their model by constructing a riskless hedged portfolio consisting of nondividend-paying common stock and European options. By continuously rebalancing the hedged portfolio so that it remained risk-free, they were able to solve for the option's value using continuous-time mathematics. Unfortunately, such mathematics, and thus the model's derivation, are beyond the scope of this book. For those familiar with continuous-time mathematics, Appendix 13.A provides the Black-Scholes derivation.

Another useful way to derive their model is by extending the binomial option-pricing model (BOPM) to an infinite number of time periods. Indeed, the *Black-Scholes model* is the continuous-time analogue of the BOPM, which is a discrete-time model. In other words, the BOPM contains the Black-Scholes formula as a limiting case. Appendix 13.B loosely develops the Black-Scholes model by extending the BOPM.

Since the model's derivation is taken pretty much for granted here, this chapter focuses on model application and empirical evidence. We begin with its application to zero-leakage assets. After that, we consider the valuation of European options written on both discrete- and continuous-leakage assets. A discussion on exploiting mispriced options follows. Finally, a summary of empirical evidence regarding the model's accuracy is presented.

> The **Black-Scholes model** is the continuous-time analogue of the binomial option-pricing model.

MODEL FOR ZERO-LEAKAGE ASSETS

Black and Scholes originally developed their model for European options written on zero-leakage assets. The assumptions employed in their development were

- There are perfect markets with no taxes, no transaction costs, perfect security divisibility, and no restrictions on short selling.
- Interest rates are constant over the option's life.
- The underlying asset pays no intervening dividends or interest over the option's life; it is a zero-leakage asset.
- Options are European.
- The distribution of possible asset prices at the end of any finite interval is lognormal, implying that percentage price changes over the interval are normally distributed with constant variance.

Given these assumptions, the resulting model for call options is

(13.1) $$C^E = SN(d_1) - Xe^{-rT}N(d_1 - \sigma\sqrt{T}),$$

where

$$d_1 = \frac{ln(S/X) + [r + (\sigma^2/2)]T}{\sigma\sqrt{T}}$$

S = the underlying asset's spot price.

X = the option's exercise price.

T = the option's maturity expressed as a fraction of a year.

r = the risk-free rate of interest.

σ^2 = the instantaneous variance of the annual return on a holding of the underlying asset.

$N(\cdot)$ = the standard normal cumulative probability distribution.

Equation 13.1 states that the European call price, C^E, is a function of five determinants: the asset price S, the exercise price X, the option's maturity T, the riskless rate of interest r, and the asset's volatility as captured by σ^2, the asset's annualized return variance. Recall from Chapter 12 that these are the same determinants underlying the option's price as given by the BOPM. Shortly we will investigate how changes in these variables affect option value.

A Numerical Example

Although Equation 13.1 appears rather forbidding, its application is really quite simple. It can even be applied on many hand-held calculators. Suppose that we want to value a European call where S = 17.50, X = 17.00, r = $.08$, T = $.25$, and σ^2 = $.10$. The first step is to compute the probabilities $N(d_1)$ and $N(d_1 - \sigma\sqrt{T})$. These are probability terms

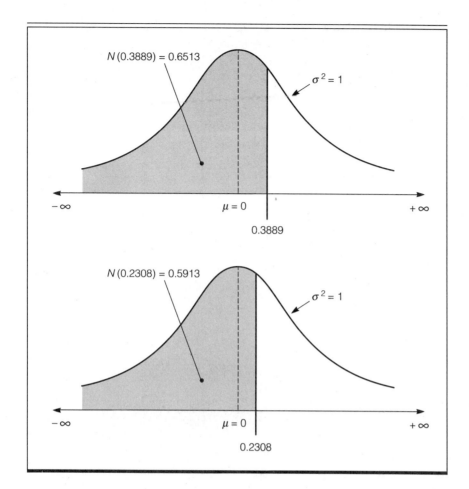

and must lie between zero and 1. The terms d_1 and $d_1 - \sigma\sqrt{T}$ represent the upper limits of integration of the standard normal probability distribution function. They are given by

$$d_1 = \frac{ln(\$17.50/\$17.00) + [.08 + (.10/2)](.25)}{\sqrt{.10}\sqrt{.25}} = 0.3889;$$

$$d_1 - \sigma\sqrt{T} = 0.3889 - \sqrt{.10}\sqrt{.25} = 0.2308.$$

Thus, we are looking for the areas under the standard normal curve from $-\infty$ to 0.3889 and from $-\infty$ to 0.2308. These are illustrated by the shaded areas in Figure 13.1.

We obtain $N(0.3889)$ and $N(0.2308)$ by employing Exhibit 13.1 and interpolating: $N(0.3889) = 0.6513$, and $N(0.2308) = 0.5913$. Notice that the probability 0.6513 is fairly high. It can be easily demonstrated that $N(d_1)$ is the probability that the call option will expire in-the-money. Hence, this option's probability of being exercised at expiration is currently over 65 percent. We expect a high probability here, since this option is currently in-the-money ($S > X$).

$N(d_1)$ is the probability that the call option will expire in-the-money.

		Values for d and $N(d)$			
d	$N(d)$	d	$N(d)$	d	$N(d)$
		−1.00	.1587	1.00	.8413
−2.95	.0016	−.95	.1711	1.05	.8531
−2.90	.0019	−.90	.1841	1.10	.8643
−2.85	.0022	−.85	.1977	1.15	.8749
−2.80	.0026	−.80	.2119	1.20	.8849
−2.75	.0030	−.75	.2266	1.25	.8944
−2.70	.0035	−.70	.2420	1.30	.9032
−2.65	.0040	−.65	.2578	1.35	.9115
−2.60	.0047	−.60	.2743	1.40	.9192
−2.55	.0054	−.55	.2912	1.45	.9265
−2.50	.0062	−.50	.3085	1.50	.9332
−2.45	.0071	−.45	.3264	1.55	.9394
−2.40	.0082	−.40	.3446	1.60	.9452
−2.35	.0094	−.35	.3632	1.65	.9505
−2.30	.0107	−.30	.3821	1.70	.9554
−2.25	.0122	−.25	.4013	1.75	.9599
−2.20	.0139	−.20	.4207	1.80	.9641
−2.15	.0158	−.15	.4404	1.85	.9678
−2.10	.0179	−.10	.4602	1.90	.9713
−2.05	.0202	−.05	.4801	1.95	.9744
−2.00	.0228	.00	.5000	2.00	.9773
−1.95	.0256	.05	.5199	2.05	.9798
−1.90	.0287	.10	.5398	2.10	.9821
−1.85	.0322	.15	.5596	2.15	.9842
−1.80	.0359	.20	.5793	2.20	.9861
−1.75	.0401	.25	.5987	2.25	.9878
−1.70	.0446	.30	.6179	2.30	.9893
−1.65	.0495	.35	.6368	2.35	.9906
−1.60	.0548	.40	.6554	2.40	.9918
−1.55	.0606	.45	.6736	2.45	.9929
−1.50	.0668	.50	.6915	2.50	.9938
−1.45	.0735	.55	.7088	2.55	.9946
−1.40	.0808	.60	.7257	2.60	.9953
−1.35	.0885	.65	.7422	2.65	.9960
−1.30	.0968	.70	.7580	2.70	.9965
−1.25	.1057	.75	.7734	2.75	.9970
−1.20	.1151	.80	.7881	2.80	.9974
−1.15	.1251	.85	.8023	2.85	.9978
−1.10	.1357	.90	.8159	2.90	.9981
−1.05	.1469	.95	.8289	2.95	.9984

Given $N(d_1)$ and $N(d_1 - \sigma\sqrt{T})$, the next step to compute this option's price is to simply employ Equation 13.1:

$$C^E = \$17.50(0.6513) - \$17.00e^{-.08(.25)}(0.5913)$$
$$= \$11.40 - \$9.85 = \$1.55.$$

The call option's price is $1.55 (per unit of the underlying asset). Notice that this price conforms with the applicable boundary conditions presented for European calls in Chapter 12. The $1.55 price is above the floor of $MAX[0,\$17.50 - \$17.00e^{-(.08)(.25)}]$ and below the ceiling of $17.50.

Value of a Corresponding Put

Suppose that we want to value a corresponding put option. Since the options are European, we can use Equation 12.27a, which is put-call parity for zero-leakage assets:

$$P^E = C^E - S + Xe^{-rT} = \$1.55 - \$17.50 + 17.00e^{-.08(.25)} = \$0.71.$$

Alternatively, we could obtain P^E directly through an application of the Black-Scholes model for zero-leakage European puts:

(13.2) $$P^E = e^{-rT}X[1 - N(d_1 - \sigma\sqrt{T})] - S[1 - N(d_1)].$$

We have

$$P^E = e^{-.08(.25)}\$17.00[1 - 0.5913] - \$17.50[1 - 0.6513] = \$0.71.$$

Here $[1 - N(d_1)]$, or 0.3487, represents the probability that the put will expire in-the-money. The probability is low, reflecting the fact that $X < S$.

[marginal note: $[1 - N(d_1)]$ represents the probability that the put will expire in-the-money.]

DETERMINANTS AFFECTING OPTION PRICES

We now wish to analyze the effects on option prices of changes in the determinants S, X, r, T, and σ^2. To do so, we will take the partial derivative of the option price with respect to each determinant. This will tell us the effect on option price of an infinitesimally small change in that unique determinant while holding all other determinants constant. Such an analysis is typically called *comparative statics*.

Comparative Statics for Calls

We begin our analysis with call options. The partial derivatives are[1]

(13.3a) $$\partial C^E/\partial S = N(d_1) > 0;$$

---

[1]The partial derivatives can be found in C. Smith (1976).

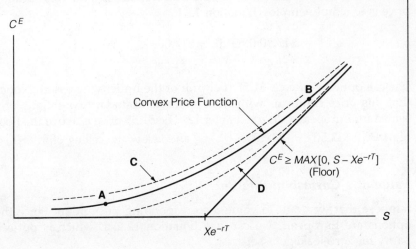

A: Deeply out-of-the-money; C^E asymptotically approaches zero as S is lowered.

B: Deeply in-the-money; C^E asymptotically approaches $S - Xe^{-rT}$ as S is increased.

C: An upward shift in the function caused by a larger r, σ^2, or T.

D: A downward shift in the function caused by a smaller r, σ^2, or T.

Figure 13.2:
European Call Option Value

$$(13.3b) \qquad \partial C^E/\partial X = -e^{-rT}N(d_1 - \sigma\sqrt{T}) < 0;$$

$$(13.3c) \qquad \partial C^E/\partial r = XTN(d_1 - \sigma\sqrt{T})e^{-rT} > 0;$$

$$(13.3d) \qquad \partial C^E/\partial\sigma^2 = Xe^{-rT}N(d_1 - \sigma\sqrt{T})\sqrt{T}/2\sigma > 0;$$

$$(13.3e) \qquad \partial C^E/\partial T = Xe^{-rT}[(\sigma/2\sqrt{T})N(d_1 - \sigma\sqrt{T})$$
$$+ rN(d_1 - \sigma\sqrt{T})] > 0.$$

The price of a European call option is directly related to S, r, σ^2, and T, and is inversely related to X.

Equation 13.3a states that C^E and S are directly related. In other words, an increase in S results in an increase in C^E. Figure 13.2 portrays how C^E changes with S while other determinants and held constant. The function in Figure 13.2 is convex. This follows from the fact that C^E approaches zero as S is lowered, and C^E approaches $S - Xe^{-rT}$ as S increases. To see this more clearly, let's employ Equation 13.1. As $S \to 0$, the probability of expiring in-the-money goes to zero; that is, $N(\cdot) \to 0$. Therefore, from Equation 13.1, C^E must approach zero: $C^E \to S(0) - Xe^{-rT}(0)$. On the other hand, as $S \to \infty$, the probability of expiring in-the-money goes to 1; that is, $N(\cdot) \to 1$. From Equation 13.1, C^E must approach $S - Xe^{-rT}$: $C^E \to S(1) - Xe^{-rT}(1)$. The convex function in Figure 13.2 is consistent with such "tail" behavior.

In common option-market lingo, the change in an option's value for a unit change in S is called the option's *delta*. Here delta is $N(d_1)$. In our previous illustration where $N(d_1) = 0.6513$, we can anticipate a change of about 65¢ in C^E for a $1 change in S.

Equation 13.3b states that C^E and X are inversely related. We already saw this in Chapter 12. A European call option with a higher exercise price can sell for no more, and typically less, than an otherwise equivalent option having a lower exercise price.

Power-Series Approach for Obtaining $N(d_1)$ and $N(d_1 - \sqrt{T})$

It is important to obtain accurate values of the probability terms $N(d_1)$ and $N(d_1 - \sigma\sqrt{T})$ because any inaccuracy here will be magnified when pricing the option. This follows because the option price is multiplicative in $N(d_1)$ and $N(d_1 - \sigma\sqrt{T})$. For instance, examine Equation 13.1, where $S = \$17.50$. If there is an error in $N(d_1)$, this error is multiplied by S; that is, it is magnified seventeen and one-half times!

To obtain accurate probability terms, it is important to interpolate when using a standard normal probability table such as Exhibit 13.1. Such tables exist to ease computation since the standard normal probability distribution function is not integrable.

An alternative approach to obtaining standard normal probabilities is to use power-series functions. Not only can such functions provide highly accurate standard normal probability values, they are also conducive for programming purposes. A power-series function that works well for most options is

$$N(x) = 1 - 1/2[1 + a_1x + a_2x^2 + a_3x^3 + a_4x^4]^{-4},$$

where $a_1 = 0.196854$, $a_2 = 0.115194$, $a_3 = 0.000344$, and

$a_4 = 0.019527$.

For example, consider the computation of $N(0.3889)$:

$$N(0.3889) = 1 - 1/2[1 + (0.196854)(0.3889) + (0.115194)(0.3889)^2 + (0.000344)(0.3889)^3 + (0.019527)(0.3889)^4]^{-4} = 0.6515.$$

The resulting probability, 0.6515, is very close to that obtained by interpolation (0.6513). For $N(0.2308)$ the power-series approximation gives a probability of 0.5912, which again is very close to that obtained by interpolation (0.5913).

When x is less than zero and we wish to make use of the above power-series function, we must invoke the fact that the standard normal curve is symmetric about its mean. In other words, if $x < 0$, we must obtain the corresponding probability by symmetry. Suppose that $x = -0.2552$. Here we must first compute the probability associated with $x = +0.2552$, then subtract this value from 1.0. Using the power-series approximation, we see that $N(+0.2552) = 0.6007$. Therefore, $N(-.2552) = 1.0 - 0.6007$, or 0.3993.

Equation 13.3c states that C^E and r are directly related. As the interest rate increases, the financing cost of purchasing an asset also increases. Options are leveraged instruments, allowing an investor to lay claim to the underlying asset without paying its full purchase price S. This option feature implies that option value increases with r.

Equation 13.3d states that C^E and σ^2 are directly related. An option buyer prefers a more volatile underlying asset. This is because the buyer can never lose more than the call option's original price if S should fall, but may realize large profits if S should climb. The asymmetry implies that option value increases with σ^2. The change in option value for a unit change in σ^2 is called the option's *lambda*.

Finally, Equation 13.3e states that C^E and T are directly related. As the call option's maturity is increased, there is an increasing probability of a large change in S. This is desirable, since the option buyer exhibits a large profit potential with a limited loss potential. Time also compounds the interest rate effect described above. An option's *theta* represents its change in value for a unit change in T.

In Figure 13.2, the effects of changes in r, σ^2, and T are illustrated by shifts of the convex price function. A larger r, σ^2, or T will cause an upward shift of the function. In other words, a call option where r, σ^2, or T is greater will command a higher price than an otherwise similar call

Example A				Example D	
S	C^E	P^E	σ^2	C^E	P^E
$15.00	$0.37	$2.03	0.05	$1.26	$0.42
17.50	1.55	0.71	0.10	1.55	0.71
20.00	3.51	0.17	0.15	1.79	0.95

Example B				Example E	
X	C^E	P^E	T	C^E	P^E
$14.00	$3.84	$0.63	.10	$1.18	$0.34
17.00	1.55	0.71	.25	1.55	0.71
19.00	0.66	1.78	.50	1.98	1.14

Example C		
r	C^E	P^E
.05	$1.54	$0.70
.08	1.55	0.71
.13	1.56	0.72

Note: For all examples, the base values of the parameters are S = $17.50, X = $17.00, r = .08, σ^2 = .10, and T = .25. Prices are reported per unit of the underlying asset.

option where r, σ^2, or T is lower. A smaller r, σ^2, or T will cause a downward shift of the function.

Exhibit 13.2 further illustrates the above relations. Here different call prices, obtained using Equation 13.1, are presented for various values of the five determinants. Example A shows that C^E increases in S. Example B shows that C^E decreases in X. The remaining examples show that C^E increases in r, σ^2, and T.

Comparative Statics for Puts

The price of a European put option is directly related to X, r, σ^2, and T, and is inversely related to S.

Taking the appropriate partial derivatives for put options, it is easily demonstrated that P^E is directly related to X, r, σ^2, and T, and is inversely related to S. Figure 13.3 illustrates these relations. As S increases (decreases) the put price approaches zero (Xe^{-rT}), giving the function a convex shape. This can be confirmed using Equation 13.2. As S increases, $[1 - N(\cdot)] \to 0$, so P^E approaches zero: $P^E \to e^{-rT}X[0] - S[0]$. As S decreases toward zero, $[1 - N(\cdot)] \to 1$, so P^E approaches Xe^{-rT}: $P^E \to e^{-rT}X[1] - 0[1]$. An increase in r, σ^2, or T is denoted by an upward shift of the convex function. Increased volatility and maturity

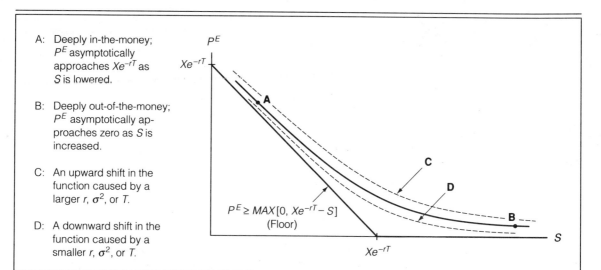

A: Deeply in-the-money; P^E asymptotically approaches Xe^{-rT} as S is lowered.

B: Deeply out-of-the-money; P^E asymptotically approaches zero as S is increased.

C: An upward shift in the function caused by a larger r, σ^2, or T.

D: A downward shift in the function caused by a smaller r, σ^2, or T.

$P^E \geq MAX[0, Xe^{-rT} - S]$
(Floor)

Figure 13.3:
European Put Option Value

benefit the put buyer because of his limited loss potential. Higher interest rates make the put option more valuable due to its leverage feature. A decrease in r, σ^2, or T is denoted by a downward shift of the convex function.

Exhibit 13.2 further illustrates these relationships. In the third column of each example, different European put prices, obtained from put-call parity and the corresponding call prices in Column 2, are presented for various values of the five determinants. Example A shows that P^E decreases in S. Example B shows that P^E increases in X. The remaining examples show that P^E increases in r, σ^2, and T.

ESTIMATING VOLATILITY

Of the five determinants of option prices, only one is not readily observable: the annualized return variance, σ^2. The variables T and X are specified by the option contract, S is merely the underlying asset's current price, and r is easily proxied by, say, the yield on a U.S. Treasury bill whose maturity aligns closest to that of the option contract. Besides a T-bill yield, r may be proxied by other money market yields, such as that for top-quality commercial paper. The interest rate used should have a duration as close as possible to the time until option expiration. Example C of Exhibit 13.2 demostrates that the option price is not overly sensitive to the interest rate specification.

It is imperative to obtain an accurate measure of the unknown variance in order to properly price the option. This is because the Black-Scholes model is very sensitive to the volatility estimate, as can be

It is imperative to obtain an accurate measure of the unknown variance in order to properly price an option.

Exhibit 13.3:
Historic Return Series

Week[a]	Asset Price	Asset Return
t-11	$18.25	------
t-10	18.75	0.0274
t-9	19.00	0.0133
t-8	18.75	−0.0132
t-7	18.00	−0.0400
t-6	17.75	−0.0138
t-5	18.00	0.0141
t-4	18.25	0.0138
t-3	18.25	0.0000
t-2	17.75	−0.0274
t-1	17.50	−0.0141

[a]t represents the time of option valuation.
The mean weekly return is −0.0040.
The weekly return variance is 0.00045.
The annualized return variance is 0.0234.

confirmed by examining Example D of Exhibit 13.2. Increasing σ^2 from .05 to .15 increased the put's value by over 225 percent ($0.95/0.42). Below we discuss the two popular methods of estimating σ^2.

Historical Method

The first method to estimate σ^2 is based on a series of past asset returns. For instance, suppose that an investor observes the weekly prices and returns shown in Exhibit 13.3 for some underlying asset. The investor can obtain the variance of these weekly returns. In this case, the weekly return variance is .00045. Recall that the volatility input required by the Black-Scholes model is an annualized return variance. Obviously, an annual variance measure will be greater than a weekly variance measure since asset prices tend to fluctuate more over longer intervals. To obtain an annualized return variance measure, the investor simply multiplies .00045 by 52. The resulting σ^2 estimate is .0234.[2]

If daily returns were observed, the investor should multiply the daily return variance by 365; if monthly measures were observed, then multiply by 12, and so on. Also, the investor should employ the most recent data available, since the Black-Scholes model assumes that σ^2 will

---

[2]This technique assumes that successive changes in asset prices are uncorrelated and that asset values continue to fluctuate on nontrading days.

remain constant over the option's life. Presumably, the more recent the data, the better the estimate will be.

How long should the historic return series be? This is always a bothersome issue. A larger sample will provide a more accurate estimate of the true population variance. However, the deeper one samples into the past, the more likely it is that the underlying asset's basic makeup will have changed. For instance, a corporation could have been far different with respect to its product offerings or management two years ago than it is today. Industry competition or regulation may have changed as well. In light of this, one should obtain as long a time series of returns as possible to estimate σ^2, provided one is confident that the underlying asset's nature remains intact.[3]

Implied Method

The second and more practiced method of estimating volatility is to impute σ^2 from a similar option's price. For example, suppose that we want to price an IBM call option with exercise price $120 and thirty-day maturity. IBM will not pay a dividend over the next thirty days. Suppose further that we can observe the current price of an IBM call option with thirty-day maturity but exercise price $125. This corresponding option must have the same maturity. Using this observed price and Equation 13.1, we can impute σ^2. That is, we can use the observed price and the model to solve for the unknown variance, the *implied variance*, which equates the model price and the observed market price. Thus, this implied variance represents the option market's assessment of the annualized return variance on IBM stock over the next thirty days, provided that Equation 13.1 holds. We can now use this implied volatility to price our focal option.

Imputing σ^2 requires computer routines since an iterative procedure is used. One has to try alternative values of σ^2 until the model and observed prices are nearly equal. This is similar to how a bond's yield to maturity can be obtained through trial and error. Several studies have found that implied volatilities are superior predictors of actual future volatilities than are historically estimated volatilities [see Latané and Rendleman (1976) in "Selected References" at end of chapter]. Inher-

The **implied variance** is the variance that equates the model price and the observed market price.

---

[3]Statistical techniques from time-series analysis, often called *Box-Jenkins analysis*, can be used to improve the historically estimated volatility input. Time-series analysis enters the past values of the underlying asset's price movements into an equation in a weighted form. The weights are determined by tendencies or patterns in the movement of the volatility. For instance, the volatility may change systematically with the level of the asset's price. Time-series analysis may be employed to detect and incorporate such tendencies in order to provide improved volatility forecasts based on historical data.

Algorithm to Generate Implied Volatilities

Step 1: Define p as the observed market price of the option and m_i as the model-determined price.

Step 2: $i = 1$.

Step 3: Calculate m_i using an initial node of $\sigma_i = .20$.

Step 4: If $|m_i - p| < .001$, $\sigma = \sigma_i$, and stop;
If $m_i < p$, $\sigma_{i+1} = \sigma_i + .10$;
If $m_i > p$, $\sigma_{i+1} = MAX[\sigma_i - .10, \sigma_i/2]$.

Step 5: $i = i + 1$.

Step 6: Calculate m_i using new σ_i.

Step 7: If $|m_i - p| < .001$, $\sigma = \sigma_i$, and stop.

Step 8: If $m_i = m_{i-1}$, then go to Step 4.

Step 9: $\Delta = [(p - m_i)/(m_i - m_{i-1})](\sigma_i - \sigma_{i-1})$.

Step 10: If $m_i < p$, $\sigma_{i+1} = MIN[\sigma_i + \Delta, \sigma_i + .10]$;
If $m_i > p$, $\sigma_{i+1} = MAX[\sigma_i + \Delta, \sigma_i - .10, \sigma_i/2]$.

Step 11: Return to Step 5.

---

ently, implied σ^2s are superior, since they reflect current market prices and expectations, whereas historic σ^2s do not.[4,5]

THE BLACK-SCHOLES MODEL FOR DISCRETE LEAKAGE ASSETS

Any leakage exhibited by an underlying asset should result in a reduction of asset price. In the Black-Scholes world, the reduction should equal the amount of the leakage per asset unit. For example, a stock that sells for $50 just prior to the ex-dividend instant should sell for $49 just after if the dividend per share is $1. Since the asset's price is affected by the leakage, so, too, should the option's price, provided the option is not "leakage protected." Some over-the-counter stock options are dividend protected because, by contractual agreement, the exercise price is reduced by the amount of any dividend per share paid on the underlying stock. However, listed options offer no such protection. Because of this, the original Black-Scholes model requires some modification.

Let us begin with discrete-leakage assets. Suppose that an asset pays a discrete leakage, D_t, occurring at time $t < T$. If we assume that the

---

[4]Even though implied volatilities are superior, they are likely biased estimates when employed to price the focal option. This is because unbiasedness is not preserved under nonlinear transformations.

[5]Different options having the same maturity and written on the same underlying asset may have different implied volatilities. There are weighting techniques to combine the implied volatilities from various option prices to obtain a single, representative estimate of the true volatility. However, studies have documented that simply deriving the implied volatility from the option that is closest at-the-money is often best.

discrete leakage is known with certainty, then we can adjust the current asset price by subtracting the discrete leakage discounted by the risk-free rate. Specifically, let

(13.4)
$$S_D = S - D_t e^{-rt},$$

where S_D represents the current asset price adjusted for the intervening discrete leakage paid prior to option expiration. By substituting S_D everywhere for S in the original Black-Scholes model, we account for the discrete leakage and its effect on option value.

A Numerical Example

Suppose that a stock has a current price of $17.50 and will pay a dividend of $1.00 per share in 60 days. What is the value of a European call option written on this stock if $X = \$17.00$, $T = .25$, $r = .08$, and $\sigma^2 = .10$?

Since the stock pays a dividend prior to option expiration, Equation 13.1 becomes

(13.5)
$$C^E = S_D N(d_2) - Xe^{-rT} N(d_2 - \sigma\sqrt{T}),$$

where

$$d_2 = \frac{ln(S_D/X) + [r + (\sigma^2/2)]T}{\sigma\sqrt{T}}.$$

Here $S_D = \$17.50 - 1.00e^{-.08(.1666)} = \$16.513$.

Also, d_2 and $d_2 - \sigma\sqrt{T}$ are .0217 and $-.1364$, respectively:

$$d_2 = \frac{ln(\$16.513/17.00) + [.08 + (.10/2)](.25)}{\sqrt{.10}\sqrt{.25}} = .0217$$

$$d_2 - \sigma\sqrt{T} = .0217 - \sqrt{.10}\sqrt{.25} = -.1364.$$

Using Exhibit 13.1 and interpolating, $N(.0217) = .5086$, and $N(-.1364) = .4458$. Therefore, the option's price is $0.97:

$$C^E = \$16.513(.5086) - \$17.00e^{-.08(.25)}(.4458) = \$0.97.$$

Notice that the effect of the dividend payment was to lower the call option's price. Recall that without the payment the option's value was $1.55. The leakage tends to lower the call's value through lowering S. The greater the discrete leakage, the lower is C^E. Also, if multiple dividends were paid over the stock option's life, then S_D would equal S minus the present value of all such dividends.

The effect of a dividend payment is to lower a call option's price. The opposite is true for puts.

To obtain the corresponding European put option value, we use put-call parity as given by Equation 12.27c:

$$P^E = \$0.97 - 16.513 + 17.00e^{-.08(.25)} = \$1.12.$$

Notice that the effect of the dividend payment was to raise the put option's price. Recall that without the payment, the put's value was $0.71. The leakage raises P^E through lowering S.

BLACK-SCHOLES MODEL FOR CONTINUOUS-LEAKAGE ASSETS

For a continuous-leakage asset, we adjust S as follows:

$$\textbf{(13.6)} \qquad S_\delta = Se^{-\delta T}.$$

Here δ represents a constant yield. In other words, Equation 13.6 states that the leakage is continuous and, further, that the leakage paid at any instant is a constant percentage of the asset's price. This constant percentage is δ.

Given Equation 13.6, the Black-Scholes model becomes

$$\textbf{(13.7a)} \qquad C^E = S_\delta N(d_3) - Xe^{-rT}N(d_3 - \sigma\sqrt{T}),$$

where

$$d_3 = \frac{ln(S_\delta/X) + [r + (\sigma^2/2)]T}{\sigma\sqrt{T}}.$$

An equivalent expression is

$$\textbf{(13.7b)} \qquad C^E = S_\delta N(d_4) - Xe^{-rT}N(d_4 - \sigma\sqrt{T}),$$

where

$$d_4 = \frac{ln(S/X) + [r - \delta + (\sigma^2/2)]T}{\sigma\sqrt{T}}.$$

A Numerical Example

Suppose that an asset has a current price of $17.50 and exhibits a constant, continuous-leakage rate of 3 percent. That is, $S = \$17.50$, and $\delta = .03$. What is C^E if $X = \$17.00$, $T = .25$, $r = .08$, and $\sigma^2 = .10$? The answer is $1.51:

$$S_\delta = \$17.50e^{-.03(.25)} = \$17.37.$$

$$d_3 = \frac{ln(\$17.37/17.00) + [.08 + (.10/2)](.25)}{\sqrt{.10}\sqrt{.25}} = .3417.$$

$$d_3 - \sqrt{.10}\sqrt{.25} = .1836.$$

$$N(.3417) = .6366.$$

$$N(.1836) = .5728.$$

$$C^E = \$17.37(.6366) - 17.00e^{-.08(.25)}(.5728) = \$1.51.$$

Notice that the continuous leakage lowered the call's value; $\partial C^E/\partial\delta < 0$. The opposite is true for puts; $\partial P^E/\partial\delta > 0$. To obtain the corresponding European put price, we use put-call parity as given by Equation 12.27d:

The effect of a continuous leakage is to lower a call option's price. The opposite is true for puts.

$$P^E = \$1.51 - 17.37 + 17.00e^{-.08(.25)} = \$0.80.$$

EMPIRICAL EVIDENCE ON BLACK-SCHOLES MODEL

Many studies have investigated the accuracy of the Black-Scholes model, especially when applied to stock options. Although the evidence generally suggests that the model performs well, systematic mispricing patterns are detected. Two of the most referenced studies reporting such patterns are those by J. Macbeth and L. Merville (1979) and M. Rubinstein (1985).

Macbeth and Merville examined the prices of six actively traded stock options for the year 1976. Using implied volatility estimates, they reported that the Black-Scholes model underpriced in-the-money call options and overpriced out-of-the-money calls. Also, the degree of mispricing increased directly with the extent to which the option was in- or out-of-the-money. Mispricing further increased as time to option maturity decreased.

Rubinstein (1985) took a somewhat different approach. Using stock option data for the two-year period of August 1976 through August 1978, he investigated the patterns of volatilities implied from the Black-Scholes model and call options exhibiting different maturities and S/X ratios. If the model had been unbiased, there would have been no discernable patterns. However, Rubinstein found that out-of-the-money calls had higher implied volatilities as maturity decreased, whereas the opposite was observed for at-the-money calls over the first sample year. During this year he also observed higher implied volatilities for lower exercise price options. This reversed in the second sample year, suggesting that the mispricing pattern itself was not stationary.

Other researchers found similar mispricing patterns when the Black-Scholes model was applied to options written on assets other than common stock. For instance, J. Bodurtha and G. Courtadon (1987) reported a definite time-to-maturity bias when the model was applied to listed currency options. As maturity increased, the mispricing of in-the-money and at-the-money currency options decreased, while the underpricing of out-of-the-money currency options first decreased, then increased slightly.

Given such systematic pricing biases, researchers have attempted to develop alternative option-valuation models that exhibit better pricing fit. In general, these alternative models are derived from relaxing one or more of the assumptions underlying the Black-Scholes model. For instance, there are alternative models that allow for nonconstant interest rates, nonconstant return variances, and different distributional forms for asset returns. Such models are more complex than the scope of this book,[6] but we can state that they do not correct all of the mispricing exhibited by the Black-Scholes model. Indeed, many of these alternatives have been demonstrated empirically to be no more accurate than the simpler Black-Scholes model. For example, Rubinstein found that five alternative models cannot explain all of the Black-Scholes stock option biases all of the time. And C. Ball and W. Torous (1985) found no operationally significant differences between the Black-Scholes model prices of listed stock options and model prices provided by the *jump model* of R. Merton (1976), which assumes that underlying asset returns exhibit discrete, step-like jumps, perhaps caused by important informational events.

EXPLOITING MISPRICED OPTIONS

In Chapter 12 we demonstrated how to risklessly profit from violations of boundary conditions that govern option prices. Now that we have a model to determine precise option values, however, we need to consider the process of riskless arbitrage from nonboundary-violation mispricings. In this section we demonstrate how to exploit situations where actual option prices deviate from predicted (i.e., model) prices. The process entails frequent rebalancing of the option and underlying asset positions.

Suppose that an investor feels that a particular option is currently overpriced, so he decides to write the option, obtaining a price above its fair market value. However, the written option's price may increase later in time, so much so that the investor exhibits a loss even though he was correct about the initial mispricing. How can the investor protect against this possibility and still exploit the mispricing opportunity?

The answer is to take an offsetting position in the underlying asset. For example, suppose that the option in question is a call written on a nondividend-paying stock. Further, suppose that a $1 change in the price of this stock will cause the call option to change in value by about $0.75. Therefore, if the investor assumes a long position in seventy-five shares of stock for each call *contract* written, he will be insulated from short-term movements in the stock price. A $1 increase in the stock's price would result in a $75 loss on the short option position ($1 × .75 × −100), but such a loss would be entirely offset by the long stock position

---

[6]See J. Hull, *Options, Futures, And Other Derivative Securities* (Englewood Cliffs, N.J.: Prentice-Hall, 1989), chapter 12, for a presentation of many of these alternative models.

($1 × 75). Thus, if the stock and the option are held in the appropriate proportions, their price movements will counterbalance such that the investor's total position will be unchanged. The investor will ultimately profit from the movement of the option's price toward its fair value, while being insulated from the effects of spot price changes.

The ratio of the number of shares of stocks required to be held per option is called the *hedge ratio*. In the above example the hedge ratio that fully immunized the investor from movements in the stock's price was −.75. The minus sign denotes that the option and stock were held in opposite positions (short and long) such that their payoffs were negatively correlated.

Recall from Equation 13.3a that the derivative of C^E with respect to S is $N(d_1)$. In other words, the change in the call option's price for a small change in the price of a nondividend-paying stock is equal to the term $N(d_1)$, known as the option's *delta*. For our call option above, therefore, $N(d_1) = .75$. Thus, we can conclude that the hedge ratio that fully immunizes the investor is given by $-N(d_1)$. Denoting this hedge ratio by the parameter h, we have

(13.8) $$h = -N(d_1).$$

By employing this hedge ratio, the investor is insulated from short-term movements in the underlying stock price.

> The hedge ratio is given by $-N(d_1)$. It is the ratio of the number of shares of stocks required to be held per option in order to insulate an investor from risk associated with subsequent stock price movements.

An Illustration

Recall our earlier example where $S = \$17.50$, $X = \$17.00$, $r = .08$, $T = .25$, and $\sigma^2 = .10$. The resulting European call price was $1.55, and $N(d_1)$ was equal to 0.6513. Thus, a $1 change in the price of this nondividend-paying stock would result in an approximate change of $0.65 in the price of the call.

Suppose that an investor believes that this call is currently overpriced. Perhaps she feels that the true annualized variance of this stock's returns is less than 10 percent. She can write this option contract and fully hedge by assuming a long position in sixty-five shares of the underlying stock. In other words, the hedge ratio is −.65. If the stock's price appreciates to $18.50, the option price will increase to $2.20 ($1.55 + 0.65). As a result, the long stock position will appreciate by $65, the short option position will depreciate by $65, and the investor's net position change will be zero. Ultimately, the investor profits if her assessment that the call option is overvalued proves correct. For instance, if the stock price remained unchanged, but the call price declined due to the market's reassessment of its fair value, the investor profits.

More on Hedging

For an overpriced call option, an investor can form a riskless hedged portfolio by purchasing $N(d_1)$ shares of stock for each option unit written. For an underpriced call, the investor assumes a short position of $N(d_1)$ stock shares. However, the number of stocks held long or short cannot remain intact for long intervals and still insulate the investor. This is because the hedge ratio, h, will change through time as the stock price changes and as the option's maturity unwinds. Equation 13.3a proves this.

As a consequence, the investor who wishes to remain fully hedged must continual update his portfolio positions such that his net exposure is zero. In theory, he must readjust his position in the options or, more likely, in the stocks, on a continuous basis in order to remain fully hedged. But, of course, such continual rebalancing is not practical. The costs of continually monitoring the hedge and the costs of engaging in frequent security transactions would be prohibitive. Therefore, the investor tends to rebalance his hedged portfolio at discrete intervals, occurring when the stock price changes substantially or when the time to option expiration declines substantially. The use of discrete rebalancing results in risk being introduced into the position. In other words, the investor is no longer fully hedged. He must decide how often to rebalance by trading off this exposure against the above costs of rebalancing.

Another issue regarding the hedging process concerns the hedge ratio itself. Like any partial derivative, the hedge ratio is a local measure; utilizing it will immunize the investor only if the stock price moves by small amounts. Otherwise, the hedge is not riskless. The investor cannot expect to be fully immunized if the stock price jumps suddenly by several points due to an important informational event, such as a takeover bid.[7]

Finally, please realize that the hedge ratio is equal to $-N(d_1)$ only if the option in question is a call written on a nondividend-paying stock. In general, the hedge ratio is given by the negative of the partial derivative of the option's price with respect to the underlying asset's price.

SUMMARY

The Black-Scholes option-pricing model is a continuous-time model derived from arbitrage restrictions. The binomial option-pricing model (BOPM) contains the Black-Scholes model as a limiting case. The model is applicable to European options. Presuming the underlying asset exhibits no leakages, the model has five determinants: the asset's price, the

---

[7]If asset returns exhibit jumps, fully hedged portfolios are impossible. The stock market crashes of October 19, 1987, and October 13, 1989, seem to support the existence of such jumps. Derivative securities that can hedge against these extremely large price changes may therefore be necessary.

option's exercise price, the option's maturity, the risk-free rate of interest, and the underlying asset's annual return variance. Call prices are directly related to all of these determinants except the exercise price. Put prices are directly related to all of these determinants except the asset's price.

The key variable to determining an option's value is the underlying asset's return volatility. It is the only unobservable model parameter, and option prices are sensitive to this input. When investors disagree on the value of an option, it is probably because they have different estimates of the asset's return variance. The two popular methods of obtaining return variance are (1) the historic method, in which past price data are used to compute a return variance estimate, and (2) the implied method, in which variance is determined by equating the model price and the market price of a corresponding option having a different exercise price. Empirical evidence suggests that the implied method is superior, since it incorporates current market information and expectations.

The Black-Scholes model is easily adjusted for application to discrete- or continuous-leakage assets. Call prices are inversely related to the size of the intervening leakage, while put prices are directly related.

The negative of the partial derivative of an option's price with respect to the underlying asset's price represents a hedge ratio that, if continually maintained, allows an investor to insulate an option position from small changes in the asset's spot price. An investor can employ this ratio to profit from observed option mispricings.

Empirical studies reveal that the Black-Scholes model exhibits systematic mispricing patterns. This probably should be expected. Any model designed to tackle such a difficult valuation problem will likely have some shortcomings. Further, alternative and more complex models have generally failed to provide substantial pricing improvement beyond that exhibited by the Black-Scholes model. This suggests that much of the mispricing bias observed may be attributable to sampling error or to factors other than model misspecification. In light of this, the Black-Scholes model and its application represent a reasonable approach to valuing European option contracts.

Selected References

Ball, C., and W. Torous. "On Jumps in Common Stock Prices and Their Impact on Call Pricing." *Journal of Finance* 40 (1985): 155–173.

Beckers, S. "Standard Deviations Implied in Option Prices as Predictors of Future Stock Price Variability." *Journal of Banking and Finance* 5 (September 1981): 363–382.

Brenner, M., and M. Subrahmanyam, "A Simple Formula to Compute the Implied Standard Deviation," *Financial Analysts Journal* 44 (September–October 1988): 80–83.

Black, F. "Fact and Fantasy in the Use of Options." *Financial Analysts Journal* 31 (July–August 1975): 36–41, 61–72.

Black, F., and M. Scholes. "The Valuation of Option Contracts and a Test of Market Efficiency." *Journal of Finance* 27 (May 1972): 399–418.

Black, F., and M. Scholes. "The Pricing of Options and Corporate Liabilities." *Journal of Political Economy* 81 (May–June 1973): 637–659.

Bodurtha, J., and G. Courtadon. "Tests of an American Option Pricing Model on the Foreign Currency Options Market." *Journal of Financial and Quantitative Analysis* 22 (June 1987): 153–167.

Chiras, D., and S. Manaster. "The Information Content of Option Prices and a Test of Market Efficiency." *Journal of Financial Economics* 6 (1978): 213–234.

Cox, S., S. Ross, and M. Rubinstein. "Option Pricing: A Simplified Approach." *Journal of Financial Economics* (September 1979): 229–263.

Cox, J., and M. Rubinstein. "A Survey of Alternative Option Pricing Models" in *Option Pricing*, ed. M. Brenner. Lexington, Mass.: Heath: 1983.

Feller, N. *An Introduction to Probability Theory and Its Applications*, vol. 1, 3d ed. John Wiley and Sons, New York, 1968.

Gultekin, N., R. Rogalski, and S. Tinic. "Option Pricing Model Estimates: Some Empirical Results." *Financial Management* 11 (Spring 1982): 58–69.

Itô, K. "On Stochastic Differential Equations." Memiore, *American Mathematical Society* 4 (December 1951): 1–51.

Latané, H., and R. Rendleman. "Standard Deviations of Stock Price Ratios Implied in Option Prices." *Journal of Finance* 31 (May 1976): 369–382.

Macbeth, J., and L. Merville. "An Empirical Examination of the Black-Scholes Call Option Pricing Model." *Journal of Finance* 34 (December 1979): 1173–1186.

Merton, R. "Option Pricing When Underlying Stock Returns Are Discontinuous." *Journal of Financial Economics* 3 (January–February 1976): 125–144.

Rao, R. "Modern Option Pricing Models: A Dichotemous Classification." *Journal of Financial Research* 4 (Spring 1981): 33–44.

Rubinstein, M. "Nonparametric Tests of Alternative Option Pricing Models Using All Reported Trades and Quotes on the 30 Most Active CBOE Option Classes From August 23, 1976 Through August 31, 1978." *Journal of Finance* 40 (June 1985): 455–480.

Sinkey, J., and J. Miles. "The Use of Warrants in the Bail Out of First Pennsylvania Bank: An Application of Option Pricing." *Financial Management* 11 (1982): 27–32.

Smith, C. "Option Pricing: A Review." *Journal of Financial Economics* 3 (January–March 1976): 3–51.

Trennelpohl, G. "A Comparison of Listed Option Premiums and Black-Scholes Model Prices: 1973–1979." *Journal of Financial Research* (Spring 1981): 11–20.

Questions and Problems

1. What are the assumptions underlying the Black-Scholes option-pricing model?

2. Contrast the Black-Scholes model with the binomial option pricing model.

3. What are the five determinants underlying the original Black-Scholes model? How are the values of call and put options related to these determinants?

4. How do call and put values react to intervening leakages exhibited by the underlying asset?

5. What are the two popular methods of estimating return variance?

6. Why is the Black-Scholes model so popular, given that researchers have reported systematic mispricing biases when applying the model to real-world data?

7. Suppose that you observe the following series of daily asset prices. What is the asset's annualized return variance?

Day	Price	Day	Price	Day	Price
-15	$8.250	-10	$8.375	-5	$8.875
-14	8.250	-9	8.375	-4	8.750
-13	8.000	-8	8.375	-3	8.750
-12	8.125	-7	8.500	-2	8.875
-11	8.250	-6	8.625	-1	9.000

8. Suppose that you observe the following parameters for an option written on a zero-leakage asset: $S = \$40$, $X = \$40$, $T = .25$, $r = .10$, and $C^E = \$3.56$. What is this option's implied volatility? Use the Black-Scholes model.

9. What is the value of C^E for a zero-leakage asset where $S = \$10$, $X = \$11$, $r = .08$, $T = .50$, and $\sigma^2 = .12$? What is the value of the corresponding put?

10. What is the value of C^E for a discrete-leakage asset where $S = \$25$, $X = \$23$, $r = .08$, $T = .50$, $\sigma^2 = .15$, and $D_t = \$1.75$ where $t = .25$? What is the value of the corresponding put?

11. What is the value of C^E for a continuous-leakage asset where $S = \$2.50$, $X = \$2.40$, $r = .10$, $T = .35$, $\sigma^2 = .09$, and $\delta = .04$? What is the value of the corresponding put?

12. Define an option's delta, theta, and lambda.

13. Determine C^E for a nondividend-paying stock, given the following parameters: $S = \$30$, $X = \$31$, $T = .50$, $r = .08$, and $\sigma^2 = .20$.

14. In Problem 13, what is the applicable hedge ratio, h? Interpret this ratio.

15. Suppose that an investor felt that the option in Problem 13 was overvalued. Describe the hedged portfolio she would construct to be fully insulated from movements in S.

16. Why would maintaining this position for long periods not fully immunize the investor?

17. What factors likely influence the investor's decision concerning rebalancing the portfolio?

18. Why is a hedged portfolio like the one discussed not risk-free when large changes in the underlying asset's price occur?

Self-Test Problems

ST-1. Determine C^E and P^E given the following parameters: $S = \$15$, $X = \$17$, $T = .25$, $r = .10$, and $\sigma^2 = .20$.

ST-2. Given these parameters, what are $\partial C^E/\partial S$, $\partial C^E/\partial X$, $\partial C^E/\partial r$, $\partial C^E/\partial \sigma^2$, and $\partial C^E/\partial T$?

ST-3. Determine C^E and P^E given the following parameters: $S = \$15$, $X = \$17$, $T = .25$, $r = .10$, $\sigma^2 = .20$, and $\delta = .05$.

ST-4. Determine P^E directly, using Equation 13.2 and the following parameters: $S = \$30$, $X = \$34$, $T = .50$, $r = .12$, and $\sigma^2 = .18$.

Solutions to Self-Test Problems

ST-1. $d_1 = [ln(15/17) + [.10 + (.20/2)](.25)]/(.20)^{1/2}(.25)^{1/2} = -.3361.$

$d_1 - \sigma\sqrt{T} = -.3361 - (.20)^{1/2}(.25)^{1/2} = -.5597.$

$N(-.3361) = .3685; N(-.5597) = .2897.$

$C^E = \$15(.3685) - 17e^{-.10(.25)}(.2897) = \$0.72.$

$P^E = \$0.72 - 15 + 17e^{-.10(.25)} = \$2.30.$

ST-2. $\partial C^E/\partial S = .3685.$

$\partial C^E/\partial X = -e^{-.10(.25)}(.2897) = -.2825.$

$\partial C^E/\partial r = 17(.25)(.2897)e^{-.10(.25)} = 1.2008.$

$\partial C^E/\partial \sigma^2 = 17e^{-.10(.25)}(.2897)(\sqrt{.25})/2\sqrt{.20} = 2.6851.$

$\partial C^E/\partial T = 17e^{-.10(.25)}[(\sqrt{.20}/2\sqrt{.25})(.2897) + .10(.2897)] = 2.6284.$

ST-3. $S_\delta = \$15e^{-.05(.25)} = \$14.814.$

$d_3 = [ln(14.814/17) + [.10 + (.20/2)](.25)]/(.20)^{1/2}(.25)^{1/2} = -.3920.$

$d_3 - \sigma\sqrt{T} = -.3920 - (.20)^{1/2}(.25)^{1/2} = -.6156.$

$N(-.3920) = .3476; N(-.6156) = .2692.$

$C^E = \$14.814(.3476) - 17e^{-.10(.25)}(.2692) = \$0.69.$

$P^E = \$0.69 - 14.814 + 17e^{-.10(.25)} = \$2.46.$

ST-4. $d_1 = [ln(30/34) + [.12 + (.18/2)](.50)]/(.18)^{1/2}(.50)^{1/2} = -.0672.$

$d_1 - \sigma\sqrt{T} = -.0672 - (.18)1/2(.50)^{1/2} = -.3672.$

$N(-.0672) = .4733; N(-.3672) = .3568.$

$P^E = \$34e^{-.12(.50)}[1 - .3568] - 30[1 - .4733] = \$4.79.$

Appendix 13.A

DERIVATION OF THE BLACK-SCHOLES MODEL USING CONTINUOUS-TIME CALCULUS

F. Black and M. Scholes (1973) assume that asset returns are lognormally distributed with constant mean and variance:

(13.A–1) $$d\tilde{S}/S = \mu dt + \sigma d\tilde{Z},$$

where

μ = the asset's instantaneous expected rate of return.

σ = the instantaneous standard deviation of the rate of return.

dt = a small increment of time.

$d\tilde{Z}$ = a standard Wiener process increment.

Applying Itô's (1951) lemma to Equation 13.A-1, we can express the change in the call option price by the following stochastic differential equation:

(13.A–2) $$d\tilde{C}^E = (\partial C^E/\partial S)d\tilde{S} + (\partial C^E/\partial t)dt + 1/2(\partial^2 C^E/\partial S^2)\sigma^2 S^2 dt.$$

Note that the only stochastic term in the expression for $d\tilde{C}^E$ is $d\tilde{S}$.

Next form a hedged portfolio, V_H, consisting of N_S units of the asset and N_{C^E} units of the call option:

(13.A–3) $$V_H = N_S S + N_{C^E} C^E.$$

The change in the value of this hedged portfolio is the total derivative of Equation 13.A-3:

(13.A–4) $$d\tilde{V}_H = N_S d\tilde{S} + N_{C^E} d\tilde{C}^E.$$

Substituting Equation 13.A-2 into Equation 13.A-4 gives

(13.A–5) $$d\tilde{V}_H = N_S d\tilde{S} + N_{C^E}[(\partial C^E/\partial S)d\tilde{S} + (\partial C^E/\partial t)dt$$
$$+ 1/2(\partial^2 C^E/\partial S^2)\sigma^2 S^2 dt].$$

Notice that $d\tilde{V}_H$ is stochastic. However, by properly selecting N_S and N_{C^E}, we can eliminate the stochastic element $d\tilde{S}$. In equilibrium the now riskless hedged portfolio should earn the risk-free rate, r:

(13.A–6) $$dV_H/V_H = rdt.$$

To eliminate $d\tilde{S}$, we set N_S and N_{C^E} equal to

(13.A–7)
$$N_S = 1, \, N_{C^E} = -1/(\partial C^E/\partial S).$$

Substituting Equations 13.A-6 and 13.A-7 into Equation 13.A-5 gives

(13.A–8)
$$(\partial C^E/\partial t) = rV_H(-\partial C^E/\partial S) - 1/2(\partial^2 C^E/\partial S^2 2)\sigma^2 S^2.$$

Substituting Equation 13.A-3 for V_H and using Equation 13.A-7 gives

(13.A–9)
$$\partial C^E/\partial t = rC^E - rS(\partial C^E/\partial S) - 1/2(\partial^2 C^E/\partial S^2)\sigma^2 S^2.$$

Equation 13.A-9 is a nonstochastic partial differential equation for the value of an option. This partial differential equation may be solved subject to the following two boundary conditions:

(13.A–10)
$$C^E(S,X,T = 0) = MAX[0, S - X],$$
$$C^E(S = 0, X, T) = 0.$$

The solution to Equation 13.A-9 subject to Equation 13.A-10 is the Black-Scholes option-pricing model:

(13.A–11)
$$C^E = SN(d_1) - e^{-rT}XN(d_1 - \sigma\sqrt{T}),$$

where

$$d_1 = \frac{ln(S/X) + [r + (\sigma^2/2)]T}{\sigma\sqrt{T}}.$$

Appendix 13.B

DERIVATION OF THE BLACK-SCHOLES MODEL BY EXTENSION OF THE BINOMIAL OPTION-PRICING MODEL

Rewrite the generalized binomial option-pricing model (BOPM) for calls, which is Equation 12.35 from Chapter 12:

(13.B–1)
$$C^E = \left\{ \sum_{j=0}^{n} \left(\frac{n!}{(n-j)!j!} \right) q^j (1-q)^{n-j} MAX[0, u^j d^{n-j} S - X] \right\} \div (1+r)^n.$$

Define x as a positive integer that bounds the states of nature in which $S > X$ at expiration. Thus, we can rewrite Equation 13.B-1 as follows:

(13.B–2) $C^E = \left\{ \sum\limits_{j=x}^{n} \left(\dfrac{n!}{(n-j)!j!} \right) q^j (1-q)^{n-j} [u^j d^{n-j} S - X] \right\} \div (1+r)^n.$

Next rewrite Equation 13.B-2 as follows, separating it into two parts:

(13.B–3) $C^E = S \left[\sum\limits_{j=x}^{n} \left(\dfrac{n!}{(n-j)!j!} \right) q^j (1-q)^{n-j} \dfrac{u^j d^{n-j}}{(1+r)^n} \right] -$

$\qquad\qquad (1+r)^{-n} X \left[\sum\limits_{j=x}^{n} \dfrac{n!}{(n-j)!j!} q^2 (1-q)^{n-j} \right].$

The complementary binomial distribution function is

(13.B–4) $B(j \geq x | n, q) = \sum\limits_{j=x}^{n} \left(\dfrac{n!}{(n-j)!j!} \right) q^j (1-q)^{n-j}.$

In words, it provides the probability that the sum of j random variables, each of which can take the value 1 with probability q and the value 0 with probability $(1 - q)$, will be greater or equal to x. Substituting Equation 13.B-4 into Equation 13.B-3 gives

(13.B–5) $C^E = S \left[\sum\limits_{j=x}^{n} \left(\dfrac{n!}{(n-j)!j!} \right) q^j (1-q)^{n-j} \dfrac{u^j d^{n-j}}{(1+r)^n} \right] -$

$\qquad\qquad (1+r)^{-n} X B(j \geq x | n, q).$

Next define q' and $1 - q'$ as follows:

(13.B–6) $q' = [uq/(1+r)], \; 1 - q' = [d(1-q)/(1+r)].$

Therefore, we have

$$q^j (1-q)^{n-j} [(u^j d^{n-j})/(1+r)^n]$$
$$= [uq/(1+r)]^j [d(1-q)/(1+r)]^{n-j}$$
$$= (q')^j (1-q')^{n-j},$$

and the bracketed expression in Equation 13.B-5 must become $B(j \geq x | n, q')$. Thus, Equation 13.B-5 becomes

(13.B–7) $C^E = SB(j \geq x | n, q') - (1+r)^{-n} X B(j \geq x | n, q).$

In the limit as $n \to \infty$, J. Cox, S. Ross, and M. Rubinstein (1979) have proven that

$$B(j \geq x | n, q') \to N(d_1), \; B(j \geq x | n, q) \to N(d_1 - \sigma \sqrt{T}).$$

Also, a well-known result from financial math is that $(1 + r)^{-n} \to e^{-rT}$ when $n \to \infty$. Therefore, as $n \to \infty$, Equation 13.B-7 becomes

(13.B–8) $C^E = SN(d_1) - e^{-rT} X N(d_1 - \sigma \sqrt{T}),$

which is the Black-Scholes model. Hence, the two-state binomial option-pricing model converges to the Black-Scholes model when n becomes large.

14

AMERICAN OPTIONS PRICING

The Black-Scholes option-pricing model is applicable to European options. However, most listed options are American, allowing for premature exercise. Under certain conditions it is optimal for an option holder to exercise prior to expiration. Since American options can facilitate early exercise they typically command a greater price than otherwise equivalent but European options. The difference between the prices of corresponding American and European options is called the *early-exercise premium*.

The purpose of this chapter is to first identify those conditions under which premature exercise is optimal and, second, to present procedures for valuing American options. These procedures can be complex, often representing extensions of the Black-Scholes model to incorporate the early-exercise privilege.

The **early-exercise premium** represents the value associated with the early-exercise privilege offered by American options.

CONDITIONS UNDER WHICH EARLY EXERCISE IS OPTIMAL

Zero-Leakage Puts

We are interested in identifying the conditions under which early exercise is optimal. To ease exposition, let us begin with put options written on zero-leakage assets. Recall Equation 13.2 for determining the value of such a European put:

$$P^E = e^{-rT}X[1 - N(d_1 - \sigma\sqrt{T})] - S[1 - N(d_1)].$$

If the underlying asset's price, S, declines substantially, then the probability terms $N(\cdot)$ approach zero such that

$$P^E \rightarrow e^{-rT}X - S.$$

Under this condition the put option is deeply in-the-money, and its current market value will be less than its *exercisable proceeds*, which are $X - S$:

$$P^E \rightarrow e^{-rT}X - S < X - S.$$

Thus, it would be optimal to prematurely exercise this option. It is worth more "dead" than "alive."

The logic behind this decision is simple. By continuing to hold the option, the investor forgos the interest that could be earned on the exercisable proceeds. At a sufficiently low underlying asset price, this forgone interest will be greater than any possible further gain on holding the put option. For instance, if $S = 0$, then the put can never command a greater value in the future. The option holder should clearly exercise and reap the interest income. More generally, we can state that there exists a *critical asset price* below which the early exercise of a zero-leakage put option is optimal. At this critical asset price the current market value of the option is just equal to its exercisable proceeds. Below it, the put is worth more dead than alive.

If the underlying asset price should fall sufficiently such that early exercise is optimal, the holder of an American put can exhaust his exercise privilege and exploit the situation. However, a European option holder cannot. It is for this reason that the American option commands a higher price. The condition for premature exercise of a zero-leakage put to occur is a substantial decline in S. Since this is clearly possible, option buyers are willing to pay more for an American option.

How much more will the American option sell for? In other words, what is the value of the early-exercise privilege? The procedures presented later in this chapter attempt to quantify the premium associated with this privilege. For now, however, suffice it to say the more likely it is that the critical asset price will be achieved, the greater the early-exercise premium will be. For zero-leakage puts, the likelihood that S will fall below the critical asset price increases as the ratio S/X declines. In other words, the more in-the-money the put is, the greater should be its early-exercise premium. Also, this premium should increase with T. The longer the option's maturity is, the greater the probability of a large price decline in the underlying asset. Finally, the early-exercise premium should increase with r. Higher rates of interest make the opportunity cost of not exercising (i.e. foregone dollar interest) greater. This is evident by recognizing that $e^{-rT}X - S$ will be lower for higher r. Thus, we can conclude that for zero-leakage puts the early-exercise premium increases in X, T, and r, and decreases in S.

Discrete-Leakage Puts

Recall Equation 12.27c, which is put-call parity for discrete-leakage options:

$$C^E = P^E + (S - D_t e^{-rt}) - Xe^{-rT}.$$

If S declines substantially, then C^E approaches zero. Recognizing this, and rearranging algebraically, we have

$$P^E \rightarrow Xe^{-rT} - (S - D_t e^{-rt}) < X - S$$

if D_t is small. Accordingly, it may be optimal to prematurely exercise a discrete-leakage put option. The necessary conditions are that (1) as for zero-leakage puts, the option must be deeply in-the-money, and (2) the intervening discrete leakage(s) must be small.

This implies that the early-exercise premium for discrete leakage puts decreases in D_t. The reasoning is simple. Exercising the put means that the holder is selling the underlying asset (for the exercise price). By doing so, she gives up her asset ownership and the right to any future capital payments on the asset. For instance, if the asset is a common stock, the exercising party forgos future dividend payments. The larger these payments are, the more costly it is (in a present-value sense) to exercise the option. A larger discrete leakage therefore seems to lower the critical asset price for the put option. This reduces the probability of premature exercise.

Continuous-Leakage Puts

Recall Equation 12.27d, which is put-call parity for continuous-leakage options:

$$C^E = P^E + Se^{-\delta T} - Xe^{-rT}.$$

If S declines substantially, then C^E approaches zero. Recognizing this, and rearranging algebraically, we have

$$P^E \rightarrow Xe^{-rT} - Se^{-\delta T}.$$

This value may be less than the put option's exercisable proceeds if δ is less than or equal to r:

$$P^E \rightarrow Xe^{-rT} - Se^{-\delta T} < X - S$$

if $\delta \leq r$. For this reason, it may be optimal to prematurely exercise a continuous-leakage put option. The necessary conditions for optimal early exercise are (1) the option must be deeply in-the-money, and (2) the constant, continuous leakage rate, δ, must be no greater than r. The early-exercise premium for continuous-leakage puts declines in δ for essentially the same reason that the early-exercise premium declines in D_t for discrete-leakage puts.

Zero-Leakage Calls

It is never optimal to prematurely exercise a call option written on a zero-leakage asset. Thus $C^E \equiv C^A$ for zero-leakage calls. To understand this, recall Equation 13.1:

It is never optimal to prematurely exercise a call option written on a zero-leakage asset.

$$C^E = SN(d_1) - Xe^{-rT}N(d_1 - \sigma\sqrt{T}).$$

If $S >>> X$ such that C^E is deeply in-the-money, then

$$C^E \to S - Xe^{-rT}.$$

However, this value can never be less than the call option's exercisable proceeds:

$$C^E \to S - Xe^{-rT} > S - X.$$

So it is never optimal to prematurely exercise a zero-leakage call option. For this reason, Equation 13.1 is applicable to American zero-leakage calls as well as their European counterparts.

Discrete-Leakage Calls

Recall Equation 13.5 for valuing discrete-leakage European calls:

$$C^E = S_D N(d_2) - Xe^{-rT} N(d_2 - \sigma\sqrt{T}).$$

If this option were deeply in-the-money due to a substantial increase in S, then $N(\cdot) \to 1$, and we have

$$C^E \to S_D - Xe^{-rT} = S - D_t e^{-rt} - Xe^{-rT}.$$

This value can be less than the option's exercisable proceeds if D_t is large:

$$C^E \to S - D_t e^{-rt} - Xe^{-rT} < S - X$$

if D_t is large. Thus, it may be optimal to prematurely exercise a discrete-leakage call. The conditions required are that (1) the option must be deeply in-the-money, and (2) that the discrete leakage(s) must be large.

The reasoning is as follows. The call option will not likely accrue much more value. The probability terms $N(\cdot)$ are already near 1. Recall from Exhibit 13.2 that the call value is rapidly and asymptotically approaching $S - Xe^{-rT}$. We can say that the option's *time value*, which is the difference between its current price and its minimum value, is nearly zero. On the other hand, exercising the option would give the holder ownership of the underlying asset and, thus, the right to its discrete payouts. Hence it may be optimal to exercise, thereby forgoing the option's negligible time value and reaping the discrete leakage(s). To optimize completely, the call owner should wait to exercise until the instant before the discrete leakage occurs. This way the holder gains the leakage and fully exploits the option's available time value.

The condition that the discrete leakage must be large implies that the call option's early-exercise premium increases in D_t. A greater discrete leakage *increases* the probability of early exercise for calls by lowering the critical asset price *above* which early exercise is optimal. As expected, this

There exists a critical asset price above which the early exercise of a discrete- or continuous-leakage call option is optimal. The more likely it is that the critical asset price will be achieved, the greater the early-exercise premium will be.

An option's **time value** is the difference between its current price and its minimum value.

is the opposite result of that observed for discrete-leakage puts. Also, the call's early-exercise premium should increase in S, T, and r, and decrease in X.

Continuous-Leakage Calls

Recall Equation 13.7a for valuing continuous-leakage European calls:

$$C^E = S_\delta N(d_3) - Xe^{-rT}N(d_3 - \sigma\sqrt{T}).$$

If such an option were deeply in-the-money due to a substantial increase in S, than $N(\cdot) \to 1$, and we have

$$C^E \to S_\delta - Xe^{-rT} = Se^{-\delta T} - Xe^{-rT}.$$

This value can be less than the option's exercisable proceeds if δ is greater than or equal to r:

$$C^E \to Se^{-\delta T} - Xe^{-rT} < S - X$$

if $\delta \geq r$. Thus, it may be optimal to prematurely exercise a continuous-leakage call option. The conditions needed are that (1) the option must be deeply in-the-money, and (2) the constant, continuous leakage rate, δ, must be no less than r. This latter condition implies that the call's early-exercise premium increases in δ.

Summary of Early-Exercise Conditions

This section demonstrated that it may be optimal to prematurely exercise *any* put option. Also, it may be optimal to prematurely exercise call options if the underlying asset exhibits an intervening leakage. For all puts, a necessary condition for premature exercise is that the option be deeply in-the-money. If the underlying asset pays a discrete leakage, then the leakage must be small. If a continuous-leakage occurs, then the leakage rate must be no greater than the riskless rate of interest. For discrete- or continuous-leakage calls, the option must be deeply in-the-money for premature exercise to occur. Further, if a discrete leakage occurs, it must be large. For a continuous-leakage call, the leakage rate must be no less than the riskless rate of interest. It is never optimal to prematurely exercise an American call written on a zero-leakage asset. For pricing purposes we can treat such a call as if it were European.

For puts, the probability of premature exercise increases in X, T, and r, and decreases in S and the size of any intervening leakage. In turn, this implies that the early-exercise premium increases in X, T, and r, and decreases in S, D_t, and δ. For discrete- or continuous-leakage calls, the probability of premature exercise and the early exercise premium increase in S, T, and r, and decrease in X, D_t, and δ. It is interesting to note that these are the same relations that hold for a European option's price. For instance, we saw in Chapter 13 that P^E increases in X, T, and r, and decreases in S, D_t, and δ. It follows that these same relations occur, because the early-exercise feature is itself a type of option. Anything that tends to increase the probability that the option will expire in-the-money also generally tends to enhance its early exercise premium.[1]

AN ILLUSTRATION OF THE EARLY-EXERCISE PREMIUM USING THE BOPM

Let us use a two-period BOPM and a zero-leakage put to illustrate the early-exercise premium. To provide a concrete example, we employ the following parameters: $u = 1.25$, $d = .50$, $r = .10$, $X = \$40$, and $S = \$40$. Figure 14.1 provides the two-period binomial generating process. At the end of the second period, the asset price may be \$62.50, \$25.00, or \$10.00. The corresponding values of the put are \$0, \$15.00, and \$30.00, respectively.

If the option in question is European, then it must be held until expiration, and its value is given by a straightforward application of Equation 12.36. The European put's value, P^E, is \$4.96:

For $j = 0$:

$$\frac{\frac{2!}{2!0!}\left(\frac{1.10 - .50}{1.25 - .50}\right)^0 \left(\frac{1.25 - 1.10}{1.25 - .50}\right)^2 MAX[0, 40 - (1.25)^0(.50)^2 40]}{(1.10)^2} = \$0.99$$

For $j = 1$:

$$\frac{\frac{2!}{1!1!}\left(\frac{1.10 - .50}{1.25 - .50}\right)^1 \left(\frac{1.25 - 1.10}{1.25 - .50}\right)^1 MAX[0, 40 - (1.25)^1(.50)^1 40]}{(1.10)^2} = \$3.97$$

For $j = 2$:

$$\frac{\frac{2!}{0!2!}\left(\frac{1.10 - .50}{1.25 - .50}\right)^2 \left(\frac{1.25 - 1.10}{1.25 - .50}\right)^0 MAX[0, 40 - (1.25)^2(.50)^0 40]}{(1.10)^2} = \$0.00$$

Total = \$4.96

---

[1]The only possible exception is the annual return variance, σ^2. The early-exercise premium may actually decrease in σ^2 if the option is already deeply in-the-money. This is because the underlying asset's price is already near the critical value for premature exercise to occur (i.e., it is already in one tail of the distribution). When this occurs, increased volatility actually reduces the likelihood of early exercise, because it increases the probability of a spot-price change *away* from the critical value. The underlying spot price lies in an asymmetric position within its distribution function.

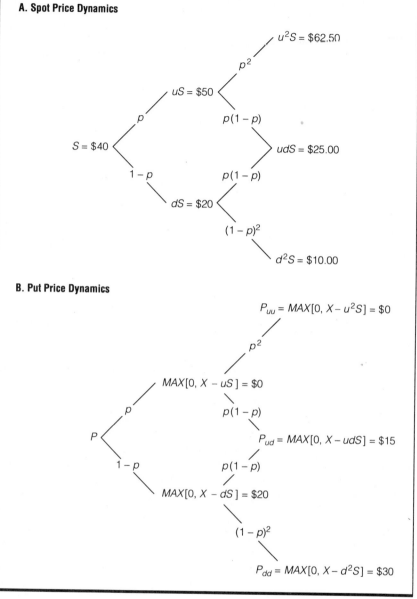

A. Spot Price Dynamics

$u^2S = \$62.50$

p^2

$uS = \$50$

p

$p(1-p)$

$S = \$40$

$udS = \$25.00$

$1-p$

$p(1-p)$

$dS = \$20$

$(1-p)^2$

$d^2S = \$10.00$

B. Put Price Dynamics

$P_{uu} = MAX[0, X - u^2S] = \$0$

p^2

$MAX[0, X - uS] = \$0$

p

$p(1-p)$

$P_{ud} = MAX[0, X - udS] = \$15$

P

$p(1-p)$

$1-p$

$MAX[0, X - dS] = \$20$

$(1-p)^2$

$P_{dd} = MAX[0, X - d^2S] = \$30$

Figure 14.1:
Two-Period Binomial
Generating Process

For an American put, however, the problem is complicated by the fact that the put option holder has the ability to prematurely exercise at the end of the first period. To determine if this will occur, we must first compute the put values at the end of the first period, P_u and P_d. Applying the one-period BOPM, we have

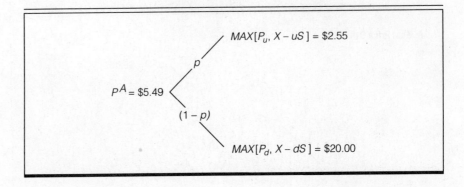

$$P_u = [qP_{uu} + (1 - q)P_{ud}] \div (1 + r)$$

$$= \left[\left(\frac{1.10 - .50}{1.25 - .50} \right)(\$0) + \left(\frac{1.25 - 1.10}{1.25 - .50} \right)(\$14) \right] \div (1.10)$$

$$= \$2.55;$$

$$P_d = [qP_{ud} + (1 - q)P_{dd}] \div (1 + r)$$

$$= \left[\left(\frac{1.10 - .50}{1.25 - .50} \right)(\$14) + \left(\frac{1.25 - 1.10}{1.25 - .50} \right)(\$30) \right] \div (1.10)$$

$$= \$15.64.$$

We now compare these values to the option's exercisable proceeds. If the asset price falls to $dS = \$20$ at the end of the first period, the put holder will exercise prematurely. The option's market price is $15.64, but its exercisable proceeds are $X - dS$, or $20.00. Thus, there is a good chance that the option will be exercised at the end of the first period.

The opportunity offered by an American put option to exercise early should, in this case, cause it to have a substantially greater price than its counterpart European option. Indeed, in our illustration the American option should command a price of $5.49:

$$P^A = [qP_u + (1 - q)(X - dS)] \div (1 + r)$$

$$= \left[\left(\frac{1.10 - .50}{1.25 - .50} \right)(\$2.55) + \left(\frac{1.25 - 1.10}{1.25 - .50} \right)(\$20) \right] \div (1.10)$$

$$= \$5.49.$$

This is portrayed in Figure 14.2.

The American put price, $5.49, exceeds the counterpart European put price, $4.96, by nearly 11 percent. In actual option markets the early-exercise premium is typically much lower, though still substantial enough that incorporating it enhances the accuracy of the Black-Scholes model. For instance, studies by R. Whaley (1982) and S. Sterk (1982) report that an American stock option-pricing model outperformed a European counterpart when valuing CBOE-traded stock options. In the next two sections we present some American option-pricing techniques.

PRICING AMERICAN OPTIONS WITH THE BOPM

As suggested by the above illustration, the BOPM is capable of valuing American options. The trick is to start at option expiration (time T) and work backward through the tree diagram to detect early-exercise opportunities. This is what we did in our earlier illustration; for the two-period put we had to check whether early exercise was optimal at the end of the first period. This procedure, sometimes referred to as *dynamic programming*, can be illustrated by using two examples: a zero-leakage American put and a continuous-leakage American call.

> The binomial option-pricing model (BOPM) is capable of valuing any American option.

Valuing American Zero-Leakage Put

Consider a four-month American put option written on a nondividend-paying stock where $S = \$25$, $X = \$25$, $r = 10$ percent, and $\sigma^2 = .16$. Suppose that we divide the option's life into four one-month intervals ($= 0.0833$ years) in order to construct a binomial tree. To value the option properly, we must choose values of u, d, and p that give correct values for the mean and variance of the change in the stock price over the interval $\Delta t = 0.0833$. S. Cox, S. Ross, and M. Rubinstein (1979) prove that for zero-leakage assets,

$$p = (a - d)/(u - d)$$
$$u = e^{\sigma\sqrt{\Delta t}}$$
$$d = e^{-\sigma\sqrt{\Delta t}}$$
$$a = e^{r\Delta t}.$$

Thus, in our example, $u = 1.1224$, $d = 0.8909$, $a = 1.0084$, and $p = 0.5076$.

Figure 14.3 shows the binomial tree. There are two numbers at each node. The top number shows the stock price at the node, while the bottom number shows the value of the option. Computations are illustrated using the nodes labeled A and B. At A, if the option is exercised immediately, it is worth $\$25 - 22.27 = \$2.73$. If the put is not exercised, it is worth $\$2.52$:

$$(\$0 \times 0.5076 + \$5.16 \times 0.4924)e^{-.10(.0833)} = \$2.52.$$

We discount at the risk-free rate since, as demonstrated in Chapter 12, investor risk preferences do not affect option value. Thus we are free to assume risk neutrality.

Since at Node A, the option's exercisable proceeds, $\$2.73$, are greater than $\$2.52$, the option should be exercised. The value of the option at Node A is therefore $\$2.73$. At Node B, the exercisable proceeds are $\$25 - 22.27 = \$2.73$. This is less than the option's market value, or $\$3.19$:

$$(\$1.33 \times 0.5076 + \$5.16 \times 0.4924)e^{-.10(.0833)} = \$3.19.$$

Figure 14.3:

Binomial Tree Diagram for Zero-Leakage Put

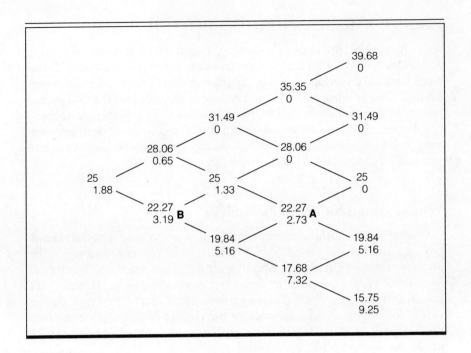

Hence, the put should not be exercised at Node B.

By working backward through the entire tree, we obtain an option price of $1.88. This price reflects the premium associated with the privilege to exercise the American option at nodes such as A. We can obtain a more accurate American option value by allowing for a much smaller value of Δt.

Valuing American Continuous-Leakage Call

The BOPM can also readily price American options written on continuous-leakage assets, such as foreign exchange. The procedure is the same as that described above for zero-leakage assets, except that $a = e^{(r-\delta)\Delta t}$, where δ is the continuous-leakage rate.

Consider a four-month American call on a British pound where

$$S = \$1.50/£1, \ X = \$1.50/£1, \ r = .08, \ r_f = .12, \text{ and } \sigma^2 = .16.$$

Here the foreign riskless rate of interest, $r_f = .12$, represents the continuous-leakage rate δ. Again dividing the option's maturity into four one-month intervals, we have $u = 1.1224$, $d = .8909$, $a = .9967$, and $p = 0.4569$. The resulting binomial tree is presented in Figure 14.4. Working backward as we did before, we obtain the American currency call option price of $0.121/£1.

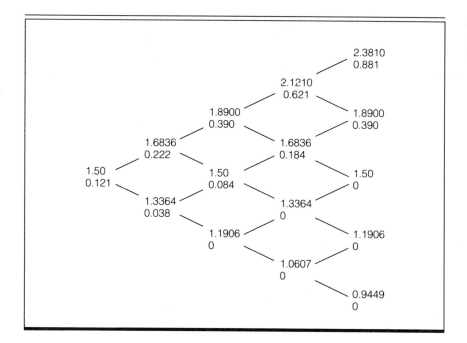

Figure 14.4:
Binomial Tree Diagram for Continuous-Leakage Call

OTHER AMERICAN OPTION PRICING METHODS

While the BOPM is capable of valuing any American option, the procedure required can be tedious. In this section we examine other American valuation methods that are more rapid. Often these alternative methods represent analytic approximations that are highly accurate and much more efficient than the dynamic programming procedure just described. However, let the reader be advised that the material presented in this section is more advanced.

Discrete-Leakage Calls

As an exact procedure for pricing European options, the Black-Scholes model often is said to give "closed-form solutions." In a series of papers, R. Roll (1977), R. Geske (1979), and R. Whaley (1981) developed a likewise exact procedure for valuing American call options written on discrete-leakage assets. For an asset exhibiting a single leakage D_t, their model is

The **Roll-Geske-Whaley model** is an exact procedure for valuing American call options written on discrete-leakage assets.

(14.1)
$$C^A = (S - D_t e^{-rt})N(d_5) + (S - D_t e^{-rt})M(d_6, -d_5; -\sqrt{t/T})$$
$$- Xe^{-rT}M(d_6 - \sigma\sqrt{t}, -d_5 + \sigma\sqrt{t}; -\sqrt{t/T})$$
$$- (X - D_t)e^{-rt}N(-d_5 + \sigma\sqrt{t}),$$

where

$$d_5 = \frac{ln[(S - D_t e^{-rt})/X] + (r + (\sigma^2/2))T}{\sigma\sqrt{T}}$$

$$d_6 = \frac{ln[(S - D_t e^{-rt})/\bar{S}] + (r + (\sigma^2/2))t}{\sigma\sqrt{t}}.$$

The function $M(a,b;\rho)$ represents the cumulative probability in a standardized bivariate normal distribution that the first variable is less than a and the second variable is less than b, where ρ represents the correlation between the two.[2] The variable $\bar{S}$ is the solution to the following equation:

$$C^E(\bar{S},t) = \bar{S} + D_t - X,$$

where $C^E(\bar{S},t)$ is the Black-Scholes call option price for underlying asset price $\bar{S}$ and maturity t. In other words, $\bar{S}$ represents the critical asset price above which early exercise is optimal. If premature exercise is never optimal, then $\bar{S} = \infty$, $d_5 = \infty$, $d_5 - \sigma\sqrt{t} = \infty$, and Equation 14.1 reduces to Equation 13.5, which is the Black-Scholes model for discrete-leakage European calls.

If several discrete leakages occur over the option's life, then premature exercise is typically optimal only on the last leakage date (if at all).[3] To account for multiple leakages, therefore, Equation 14.1 must be adjusted by (1) reducing S by the present value of all leakages except the last, and (2) setting D_t equal to this final leakage, where t now represents the time until the last leakage occurs.

The application of Equation 14.1 is complex but is amenable to computerization. In a well-cited study, however, R. Whaley (1982) reports that Equation 14.1 performs only slightly better than a far simpler approximation, posited by F. Black (1975), when applied to CBOE-listed stock options. Black suggests calculating a series of European call prices—one for each maturity given by the discrete-leakage dates and one for the option's overall maturity. Once this series of prices is obtained, the American price is established to be the greatest price in the series. For instance, if the asset in question is a common stock having two ex-dividend dates prior to option expiration, the American price is given by the greatest of three European prices—one with a maturity given by the first ex-dividend date, one with a maturity given by the second ex-dividend date, and one with a maturity given by option's expiration date.

Black's approximation is useful for valuing American stock options.

---

[2] See Z. Drezner (1978) for a discussion of the standardized bivariate normal distribution. Drezner also presents a simple approximation to accurately calculate bivariate normal probabilities.

[3] See J. Hull, *Options, Futures, And Other Derivative Securities* (Englewood Cliffs, N.J.: Prentice-Hall, 1989), chapter 5, for a proof.

Although Black's method is only an approximation, whereas Equation 14.1 is an exact procedure (Black's method assumes that the probability of premature exercise at each leakage date is one), Whaley finds that Black's method is accurate empirically. Using over 15,000 stock option trades, Whaley reports mean pricing errors of 1.08 percent and 1.48 percent, respectively, for Equation 14.1 and the Black approximation. Since the difference in mean errors is well within a stock option's typical bid-ask spread, Whaley concludes that the simpler Black approximation is useful for pricing American stock options.

A Numerical Illustration of Black's Approximation Suppose that a stock has a current price of $17.50 and will pay a dividend of $1.00 per share in 60 days. What is the value of an American call option written on this stock if (1) Black's approximation is used, and (2) the other parameters are $X = \$17.00$, $T = .25$, $r = .08$, and $\sigma^2 = .10$?

Recall that this is the same option used to illustrate Equation 13.5 of Chapter 13. $C^E(T=.25)$ equaled $0.97. Using Equation 13.1 to compute $C^E(t=.167)$, we found that the European option price associated with the leakage date is $0.84. (Try computing this yourself; recognize that if early exercise occurs at the instant before the leakage payout, Equation 13.1 is applicable, since no intervening leakages happen prior to this first and only leakage date.) Therefore, the American option price is the greater of $0.97 and $0.84, or $0.97.

Continuous-Leakage Calls

Unfortunately, there exists no exact procedure to price continuous-leakage American call options.[4] Instead, numerical procedures or analytic approximations must be used. A very accurate analytic approximation has been developed by G. Barone-Adesi and R. Whaley (1987) to solve this problem. Their pricing formula is

(14.2)
$$C^A = \begin{cases} C^E + A_2(S/\bar{S})^{q_2} & \text{if } S < \bar{S} \\ S - X & \text{if } S \geq \bar{S}, \end{cases}$$

where

$$A_2 = (\bar{S}/q_2)\{1 - e^{-\delta T}N[d_7(S)]\}$$
$$d_7 = [ln(\bar{S}/X) + [r - \delta + (\sigma^2/2)]T]/(\sigma\sqrt{T})$$
$$q_2 = .50[-(\beta - 1) + \sqrt{(\beta - 1)^2 + (4\alpha/h)}]$$

The **Barone-Adesi and Whaley quadratic approximation** is very accurate for pricing American options written on continuous-leakage assets. It can also be used safely to price zero-leakage American puts.

---

[4]This is because an additional boundary condition associated with the continuous early-exercise privilege precludes the solution of the partial differential equation underlying the Black-Scholes model.

$$\beta = [2(r - \delta)]/\sigma^2$$

$$\alpha = (2r)/\sigma^2$$

$$h = 1 - e^{-rT}.$$

In Equation 14.2, $\bar{S}$ refers to the critical asset price above which premature exercise should occur. $\bar{S}$ is determined iteratively by solving the equation,

$$\bar{S} - X = C^E(\bar{S}) + \{1 - e^{-\delta T}N[d_7(\bar{S})]\}\bar{S}/q_2.$$

Barone-Adesi and Whaley provide a rapidly converging algorithm to solve this equation.

In words, Equation 14.2 states that if the asset's current price is below $\bar{S}$, then the American call value is given by the corresponding European value plus the early-exercise premium, as approximated by the quadratic term $A_2(S/\bar{S})^{q_2}$. Above $\bar{S}$, the value of the American continuous-leakage call is its exercisable proceeds, $S - X$.

Exhibit 14.1 gives the prices of various continuous-leakage American calls as computed by Barone-Adesi and Whaley's approximation. Also reported are the corresponding European call values. Thus, the differences between these corresponding prices represent the early exercise premia. From Column 3 of Exhibit 14.1, we see that the premium increases with S, T, and δ. This is consistent with our earlier discussion in this chapter concerning the determinants of the premium. The exhibit also shows that the premium can be large, as much as 12 percent of the European option's value in this simulation. If the parameter values used are reflective of actual market conditions, this result suggests that it is important to account for the premium in order to accurately value the American option. Finally, notice that δ is always set greater than (or equal to) r in the simulation. Recall that this is a necessary condition for early exercise of American continuous-leakage calls.

Although the Barone-Adesi-Whaley formula appears complex at first, its application is not difficult and can be performed on a personal computer.

Continuous- and Zero-Leakage Puts

While discussing the approximation of Barone-Adesi and Whaley, we might as well consider the valuation of continuous- and zero-leakage American puts, since they, too, can be accurately and efficiently priced this way. For continuous-leakage American puts, the formula is

(14.3)
$$P^A = \begin{cases} P^E + A_1(S/\bar{S})^{q_1} & \text{if } S > \bar{S} \\ X - S & \text{if } S \le \bar{S}, \end{cases}$$

where

Option Parameters	S	(1) American Option Price[a]	(2) European Option Price[b]	(3) Early-Exercise Premium (Percent)	
$r = .08, T = .25$	$ 80	$ 0.03	$ 0.03	$0.00	(0.00%)
$\sigma = .20, \delta = .12$	90	0.59	0.57	0.02	(3.51)
$X = \$100$	100	3.52	3.42	0.10	(2.92)
	110	10.31	9.85	0.46	(4.67)
	120	20.00	18.62	1.38	(7.41)
$r = .12, T = .25$	80	0.03	0.03	0.00	(0.00)
$\sigma = .20, \delta = .16$	90	0.59	0.56	0.03	(5.36)
$X = \$100$	100	3.51	3.39	0.12	(3.54)
	110	10.29	9.75	0.54	(5.54)
	120	20.00	18.43	1.57	(8.52)
$r = .08, T = .25$	80	1.07	1.05	0.02	(1.90)
$\sigma = .40, \delta = .12$	90	3.28	3.23	0.05	(1.55)
$X = \$100$	100	7.41	7.29	0.12	(1.65)
	110	13.50	13.25	0.25	(1.89)
	120	21.23	20.73	0.50	(2.41)
$r = .08, T = .50$	80	0.23	0.21	0.02	(9.52)
$\sigma = .20, \delta = .12$	90	1.39	1.31	0.08	(6.11)
$X = \$100$	100	4.72	4.46	0.26	(5.83)
	110	10.96	10.16	0.80	(7.87)
	120	20.00	17.85	2.15	(12.04)

Exhibit 14.1:
Prices and Early Exercise Premia for American Call Options Written on Continuous-Leakage Assets

[a]Given by Equation 14.2.
[b]Given by Equation 13.7a.

$$A_1 = -(\bar{S}/q_1)\{1 - e^{-\delta T}N[-d_7(\bar{S})]\}$$

$$q_1 = .50[-(1 - \beta) - \sqrt{(\beta - 1)^2 + (4\alpha/h)]}$$

and where all other parameters are defined as before. Here $\bar{S}$ represents the critical asset price below which the put should be exercised prematurely. It is determined iteratively by solving the following equation, for which Barone-Adesi and Whaley provide a rapidly converging algorithm:

$$X - \bar{S} = P^E(\bar{S}) - \{1 - e^{-\delta T}N[-d_7(\bar{S})]\}\bar{S}/q_1.$$

Exhibit 14.2 gives the prices of various continuous-leakage American puts as computed by Equation 14.3. Also reported are the corresponding European option values and the resulting early exercise premia. Here δ is set to be less than r. The premia increase in T and decrease in S and δ.

Exhibit 14.2:

Prices and Early Exercise Premia for American Put Options Written on Continuous-Leakage Assets

Option Parameters	S	(1) American Option Price[a]	(2) European Option Price[b]	(3) Early-Exercise Premium (Percent)	
$r = .08, T = .25$	$ 80	$20.00	$18.87	$1.13	(6.00%)
$\sigma = .20, \delta = .04$	90	10.18	9.76	0.42	(4.30)
$X = \$100$	100	3.54	3.46	0.08	(2.31)
	110	0.80	0.78	0.02	(2.56)
	120	0.12	0.11	0.01	(9.09)
$r = .12, T = .25$	80	20.00	18.68	1.32	(7.07)
$\delta = .20, \sigma = .08$	90	10.16	9.67	0.49	(5.07)
$X = \$100$	100	3.53	3.42	0.11	(3.22)
	110	0.79	0.77	0.02	(2.60)
	120	0.12	0.11	0.01	(9.09)
$r = .08, T = .25$	80	20.53	20.11	0.42	(2.09)
$\sigma = .40, \delta = .04$	90	12.93	12.74	0.19	(1.49)
$X = \$100$	100	7.46	7.36	0.10	(1.36)
	110	3.96	3.91	0.05	(1.28)
	120	1.95	1.93	0.02	(1.04)
$r = .08, T = .50$	80	20.00	18.08	1.92	(10.62)
$\sigma = .20, \delta = .04$	90	10.71	10.04	0.67	(6.67)
$X = \$100$	100	4.77	4.55	0.22	(4.84)
	110	1.76	1.68	0.08	(4.76)
	120	0.55	0.51	0.04	(7.84)

[a]As given by Equation 14.3.
[b]As given by Equations 13.7a and 12.27d.

Again, this is consistent with our prior discussion concerning the determinants of the early-exercise premium for continuous-leakage puts. Finally, notice that the premium can be as large as 10 percent in our simulation, suggesting that its incorporation can be vital to accurately determining the American option's value.

Equation 14.3 is applicable to continuous-leakage American puts. Since zero-leakage American puts are just a special case of continuous-leakage American puts where $\delta = 0$, the equation can also be used to price zero-leakage American puts by setting $\delta = 0$ everywhere.

Discrete-Leakage Puts

The remaining American option-valuation problem concerns discrete-leakage puts. Like continuous-leakage American calls and continuous- and zero-leakage American puts, there exists no exact procedure for determining American discrete-leakage put prices. Furthermore, the valuation of discrete-leakage American puts represents the most tedious and complex American option-valuation problem presented here.

R. Geske and H. Johnson (1984) provide an accurate method to approximate the value of any American put option. Their approximation, known as the *compound-option approach*, involves (1) assuming that premature exercise can occur only at discrete points over the option's life and then (2) extrapolating to value an option that can be exercised at any instant. For discrete-leakage puts, it is reasonable to assume that exercise will not occur for any period just prior to a leakage date, since the option holder can wait and reap the intervening leakage. Recognizing this, and employing a modification of the Roll-Geske-Whaley model discussed above, Geske and Johnson are able to accurately approximate the value of a discrete-leakage American put. Unfortunately, their procedure requires multivariate normal density functions and is well beyond the intended scope of this book. For details concerning the compound-option approximation, see Geske and Johnson (1984) in "Selected References."

Geske and Johnson's **compound-option model** can be used to value American put stock options.

EMPIRICAL EVIDENCE ON AMERICAN OPTIONS PRICING

Several empirical studies have investigated the accuracy of American option-pricing models, especially in light of their European counterparts. Overall, the evidence suggests that the American models slightly outperform the European models when applied to listed options that allow for early exercise. This implies that market participants assign a small but discernable premium to the early-exercise privilege. Below we briefly summarize a few of these studies.

The Whaley, Sterk, and Blomeyer-Klemkosky Studies

R. Whaley (1982) used over 15,000 reported prices for CBOE-listed stock options to test the American model of Roll-Geske-Whaley and its European counterpart. On average, the two models produced pricing errors of 1.08 percent and 2.15 percent, respectively. This result suggests that the American model slightly outperforms its European counterpart, probably because of the early-exercise premium traders assigned to CBOE stock options. Most stocks upon which options are traded pay regularly scheduled dividends. A study by W. Sterk (1982) reports similar findings.

However, these pricing errors are smaller than a typical bid-ask spread on the CBOE for the period, suggesting that the pricing difference may not be economically significant. Also, a study by E. Blomeyer and R. Klemkosky (1983) reports no observable difference between these same two models when employing transaction prices from the CBOE.

The Shastri-Tandon, and Whaley Studies

Using a simulation analysis, K. Shastri and K. Tandon (1986) investigated an American model and its European counterpart when applied to futures options. Recall from Chapter 11 that futures options represent a type of continuous-leakage option. They reported small but discernable pricing differences, especially for puts. As anticipated, these differences—representing early-exercise premia—increase with the extent to which the futures options are in-the-money. If the parameters underlying their simulation analysis are reflective of actual market conditions, then the results of Shastri and Tandon suggest that American futures options should command a small early-exercise premium. It would be better to employ an American model (such as Barone-Adesi and Whaley's quadratic approximation) to price American futures options, especially those deeply in-the-money.

Also using a simulation analysis, R. Whaley (1986) reported that the early-exercise privilege of American futures options contributes meaningfully to the value of in-the-money SP500 futures option contracts. Using his quadratic approximation developed with Barone-Adesi, Whaley then proceeded to test the American model using SP500 futures options traded on the Chicago Mercantile Exchange for the calendar year 1983. His major results were that (1) a moneyness and a maturity bias appear for the American model; (2) standard deviations implied from SP500 call futures options are on average lower than those implied from puts (a disturbing anomaly); and (3) a hedging strategy generated abnormal returns for the period *after* adjusting for transaction costs. Thus, Whaley's results refute the joint hypothesis that the American model is correct and the SP500 futures options market is efficient.

The Shastri-Tandon, and Bodurtha-Courtadon Studies

Using a very similar simulation experiment, K. Shastri and K. Tandon (1986) found that the early-exercise privilege of American currency options can be meaningful for in-the-money calls and most puts. However, using a large sample of actual transactions data for PHLX-traded currency options, J. Bodurtha and G. Courtadon (1987) did not find a statistically significant difference in the average pricing errors of American and European currency option-valuation models. For instance, they reported average errors of about 7 percent for both models when applied to currency call options. This result suggests that the early-exercise premium assigned to American currency options is negligible, and/or the models are too noisy to detect the premium.

The Hilliard-Tucker Study

Exploiting the only situation in the history of U.S. option markets in which American and European options on the same underlying asset are traded side by side on the same exchange, J. Hilliard and A. Tucker (1989) were able to quantify what the market determines to be the early-exercise premium on American option contracts. Specifically, they employed transactions data for PHLX-traded currency options for a twenty-month period. Their sample contained over 5,000 corresponding American and European options that traded less than five minutes apart. The differences in the observed prices for these corresponding pairs provided direct measures of the market-assigned early-exercise premia. They found that the market assigns, on average, a premium of about 1.5 percent to American currency options. This average premium is statistically significant. Further, they found that the behavior of the premia was consistent with the comparative statics implied by the pricing models. For instance, the premium for American currency calls appeared to increase with the option's maturity and degree to which it was in-the-money.

SUMMARY

The early-exercise privilege offered by American options is perhaps best thought of as an option itself—its value being determined by the very same factors that influence the value of the option's European component.

Except for zero-leakage calls, it may be optimal to prematurely exercise any American option. As a consequence, option buyers are typically willing to pay a premium for American options relative to their European counterparts. Empirical evidence generally suggests that an early-exercise premium exists for listed American options but represents just a small fraction of the option's total value.

However, it is still important to quantify and incorporate this premium in order to accurately price the option. The BOPM is capable of this task. For discrete-leakage calls an exact procedure exists for determining option value. For continuous-leakage calls and all puts, analytic approximations are possible (representing more advanced material). The reader is encouraged to see the original works, referenced within, for more details.

Selected References

Barone-Adesi, G., and R. Whaley. "Efficient Analytic Approximation of American Option Values." *Journal of Finance* 42 (June 1987): 301–320.

Black, F. "Fact and Fantasy in the Use of Options." *Financial Analysts Journal* 31 (July–August 1975): 61–72.

Blomeyer, E., and R. Klemkosky. "Tests of Market Efficiency of American Call Options" in *Option Pricing*, ed. Menachem Brenner, Lexington, Mass.: Heath, 1983.

Bodurtha, J., and G. Courtadon. "Tests of An American Option Pricing Model on the Foreign Currency Option Market." *Journal of Financial and Quantitative Analysis* 22 (June 1987): 153–167.

Boyle, P. "Options: A Monte Carlo Approach." *Journal of Financial Economics* 4 (1977): 323–338.

Boyle, P. "A Lattice Framework for Option Pricing with Two State Variables." *Journal of Financial and Quantitative Analysis* 23 (March 1988): 1–12.

Brennan, M., and E. Schwartz. "The Valuation of American Put Options." *Journal of Finance* 32 (May 1977): 449–462.

Cox, J., S. Ross, and M. Rubinstein. "Option Pricing: A Simplified Approach." *Journal of Financial Economics* 7 (1979): 229–264.

Drezner, Z. "Computation of the Bivariate Normal Integral." *Mathematics of Computation* 31 (January 1978): 227–279.

Geske, R. "A Note on An Analytic Formula for Unprotected American Call Options on Stocks with Known Dividends." *Journal of Financial Economics* 7 (December 1979): 375–380.

Geske, R., and H. Johnson. "The American Put Valued Analytically." *Journal of Finance* 39 (December 1984): 1511–1524.

Geske, R., and K. Shastri. "Valuation by Approximation: A Comparison of Alternative Valuation Techniques." *Journal of Financial and Quantitative Analysis* 20 (March 1985): 45–71.

Hilliard, J., and A. Tucker. "Market-Determined Premia for American Currency Spot Options." Working paper, Temple University, 1989.

Hull, J., and A. White. "The Use of the Control Variate Technique in Option Pricing." *Journal of Financial and Quantitative Analysis* 23 (1988): 237–256.

Johnson, H. "An Analytic Approximation to the American Put Price." *Journal of Financial and Quantitative Analysis* 18 (March 1983): 141–148.

Macmillan, L. "Analytic Approximation for the American Put Option." *Advances in Futures and Option Research* 1 (1986): 119–139.

Rendleman, R., and B. Bartter. "Two-State Option Pricing." *Journal of Finance* 34 (1979): 1093–1110.

Roll, R. "An Analytic Valuation Formula for Unprotected American Call Options on Stocks with Known Dividends." *Journal of Financial Economics* 5 (November 1977): 251–258.

Schwartz, E. "The Valuation of Warrants: Implementing a New Approach." *Journal of Financial Economics* 4 (1977): 79–94.

Shastri, K., and K. Tandon. "Options on Futures Contracts: A Comparison of European and American Pricing Models." *Journal of Futures Markets* 6 (1986): 593–618.

Shastri, K., and K. Tandon. "On the Use of European Models to Price American Options on Foreign Currency." *Journal of Futures Markets* 6 (1986): 93–108.

Sterk, W. "Tests of Two Models for Valuing Call Options on Stocks with Dividends." *Journal of Finance* 37 (December 1982): 88–99.

Whaley, R. "On the Valuation of American Call Options on Stocks with Known Dividends." *Journal of Financial Economics* 9 (June 1981): 207–212.

Whaley, R. "Valuation of American Call Options on Dividend Paying Stocks: Empirical Tests." *Journal of Financial Economics* 10 (March 1982): 29–58.

Whaley, R. "Valuation of American Futures Options: Theory and Empirical Tests." *Journal of Finance* 41 (1986): 127–150.

Questions and Problems

1. Under what conditions might it be optimal to prematurely exercise an American call option written on a discrete-leakage asset?

2. Why is it optimal to exercise the above option just prior to the leakage date, assuming that early exercise will occur?

3. Name the two conditions under which it might be optimal to prematurely exercise an American call option written on a continuous-leakage asset.

4. What are the determinants of the value of the early-exercise privilege for American calls written on continuous-leakage assets?

5. Under what conditions might it be optimal to prematurely exercise an American put option written on a zero-leakage asset?

6. Using the two-period binomial option-pricing model, determine the values of a European zero-leakage put and its counterpart American zero-leakage put given the following parameter values: $u = 1.2$, $d = 0.6$, $r = .10$, $X = \$50$, and $S = \$50$.

7. Under what conditions might it be optimal to prematurely exercise an American put written on a discrete-leakage asset?

8. What are the determinants of the value of the early-exercise privilege for American puts written on discrete-leakage assets?

9. Name the two conditions under which the holder of an American continuous-leakage put option might exercise prematurely.

10. Suppose that a stock has a current price of $40 per share and will pay a dividend of $3 per share at times $t_1 = .25$ and $t_2 = .50$. Using Black's approximating method, what is the value of an American call option written on this stock given the following parameters: $X = \$35$, $T = .70$, $r = .12$, and $\sigma^2 = .20$?

11. Match the following models/approximations to the appropriate options:

    1. American zero-leakage calls
    2. American discrete-leakage calls
    3. American continuous-leakage calls
    4. American zero-leakage puts
    5. American discrete-leakage puts
    6. American continuous-leakage puts

    a. Black's approximation
    b. Barone-Adesi and Whaley's approximation
    c. Geske and Johnson's approximation
    d. Black-Scholes model
    e. Roll-Geske-Whaley model

12. Consider a five-month American put option written on a nondividend-paying common stock where $S = \$30$, $X = \$30$, $r = .08$, and $\sigma^2 = .16$. Using one-month intervals, what is this option's price? At what nodes will it be optimal to prematurely exercise this call option?

13. Consider a five-month American put option written on a foreign currency where $S = \$1.00$, $X = \$1.02$, $r = .08$, $r_f = .05$, and $\sigma^2 = .09$. Using one-month intervals, what is this option's price? What is the option's early-exercise premium? (Hint: Compute its European value as you go along.)

Self-Test Problems

ST-1. Determine the value of a five-month American put option written on a nondividend-paying common stock where $S = \$40$, $X = \$41$, $r = .10$, $\sigma^2 = .09$, and $\Delta t = .0833$.

ST-2. Determine this option's early-exercise premium.

Solutions to Self-Test Problems

ST-1.

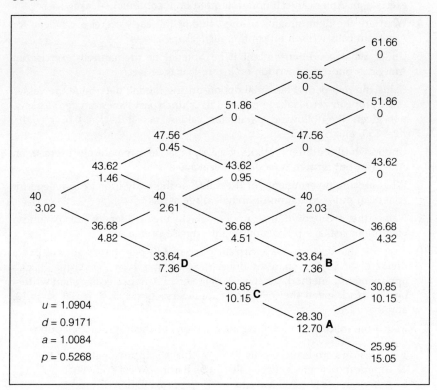

$u = 1.0904$	
$d = 0.9171$	
$a = 1.0084$	
$p = 0.5268$	

ST-2. In the solution to Problem ST–1, early exercise should occur at the nodes labeled A, B, C, and D. Precluding early exercise at these nodes, the European option value is $2.85. Thus, the early-exercise premium is $0.17 per underlying stock.

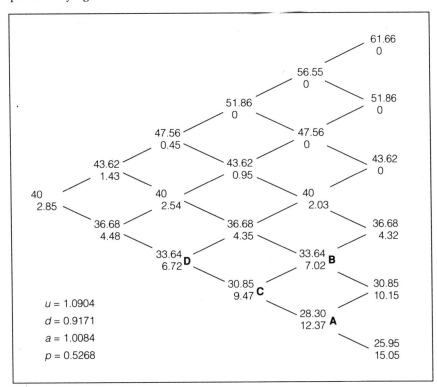

15

USING OPTION CONTRACTS

This chapter describes how option contracts can be used for hedging a preexisting risk in the spot market, and for speculating on subsequent spot price movements. Under hedging, we describe various strategies including fiduciary call writing, covered call writing, and protective put buying. We also describe how options can be combined to create synthetic futures contracts. Under speculating, we begin with simple strategies and then consider more advanced speculative strategies involving spreads, straddles, and other option combinations.

The strategies described in this chapter are popular among risk managers and investors. However, many more strategies involving option contracts may be designed and implemented. Our purpose here is not to exhaustively detail all possible strategies but rather to familiarize you with some of the most practiced strategies and with how strategies can be constructed in general.

Obviously, the existence of market imperfections such as transaction costs will tend to make the realized payoffs somewhat different from those determined here. This difference should be small, however, and does not significantly alter the fundamental strategy and its effect on investor wealth and utility. Also, to simplify the analysis, we will focus on European options, which cannot be exercised prematurely. Leakages are also ignored. However, the strategies described can be adjusted for premature exercise as well as intervening leakages—albeit some more readily than others.

HEDGING WITH OPTIONS

Perhaps the greatest social welfare provided by option contracts is that they allow individuals to reduce the risk associated with preexisting positions in underlying spot assets. In this section we present some very popular and powerful hedging strategies that employ option contracts in conjunction with spot-asset positions.

Fiduciary Call Writing

Fiduciary call writing entails writing call options against an asset already held. By writing a call on the asset, the investor can reduce or eliminate downside risk. This is because any loss incurred on the asset due a price decline will be offset, at least in part, by the premium received on the written call option. The two positions—long the underlying asset and short the call option—are negatively correlated.

Consider a combination of one written call option and h units of the underlying asset. The value of this portfolio is given by

$$V = hS + C,$$

where S and C represent the current prices of the asset and call option, respectively. To fully hedge, we must determine the value of the *hedge ratio, h*, that will immunize V against any changes in the asset's value, S. Taking the total derivative of V with respect to S we have

$$dV/dS = h + dC/dS.$$

To make the portfolio's value, V, unaffected by changes in S, we set dV/dS equal to zero. Solving for h yields

$$h = -dC/dS.$$

Thus, the hedge ratio is the negative of the derivative of the call price with respect to the underlying asset's price. From the Black-Scholes model and Equation 13.3a, we discover this derivative is equal to $N(d_1)$, assuming a zero-leakage asset. Thus, the hedge ratio is equal to $-N(d_1)$. This is the same result found in Chapter 13.

The probability $N(d_1)$ lies between 0 and 1, implying that the number of units of the asset owned for each written call is between 0 and 1. The hedged portfolio will therefore entail more calls than units of the underlying asset. This result obtains because the (dollar) change in a call option's price will be less than a given (dollar) change in S.

A Numerical Example Suppose that a call option currently exhibits a delta of 0.60. In other words, the derivative of the call's price with respect to S is 0.60. To fully hedge, the owner of the underlying asset would write 100 calls for every 60 units of the asset held. For each $1 change in S, the call's price should change by (about) $0.60. Thus, if the asset's price decreases (immediately) by $1.00, the $60.00 loss on the long spot-asset position (60 units) will be fully offset by the $60.00 gain on the short call-option position ($0.60 × 100). The investor could buy 100 call options at the now lower price, thereby reversing her short option position and gaining $60.00 on the option trades. She is now net zero in options. Because of the offsetting nature of the positions under the fiduciary call writing strategy, this strategy is often referred to as *delta-neutral hedging*.

Covered Call Writing

In the above illustration, the change in asset price will cause the hedge ratio to change. Further, the hedge ratio will change with time as the option contract unwinds (see Equation 13.3a). This implies that in order to remain fully hedged the investor must (in theory) continuously rebalance her asset-option portfolio. As a practical matter and in light of transaction costs, continuous rebalancing is undesirable.

A real-world alternative, however, is a simple strategy known as *covered call writing*, wherein a hedger simply writes one call option for each unit of the asset held. Thus, if the number of asset units remains unchanged over the option's life, rebalancing will not occur. Covered call writing may be considered a more realistic and practical hedging strategy than fiduciary call writing, which necessitates continuous rebalancing. Of course, it will not fully protect the investor the way fiduciary call writing does. Instead, the payoffs to the portfolio will vary according to the resulting asset price.

In **covered call writing,** the hedger simply writes one call option for each unit of the asset held.

A Numerical Example Suppose that an investor owns 100 units of an asset valued at $100 per unit. Further, he writes 100 call options on the asset, where each option has an exercise price of $95 and a sixty-day expiration. Presume that the option price is $7. Figure 15.1 presents the resulting profit possibilities to the investor for different values of the spot-asset price at option expiration. If the resulting asset price at expiration, S_T, is above the exercise price of $95, the hedger's profit is $200. For instance, if $S_T = \$104$, the hedger earns $400 on his long spot position [($104 − 100) × 100] and loses $200 on his short option position [($104 − 95) × (−$100) + $7 × 100]. If the resulting asset price, S_T, is below the exercise price, the hedger's profit is less than $200. At $S_T = \$93 = S - C$, representing the hedger's initial investment, a zero profit results. Below $S_T = \$93$, losses are incurred. The maximum possible loss is −$9,300, occurring when $S_T = \$0$. However, this loss is still less than that incurred if no option position were undertaken (−$10,000). Further, a profit occurs when $S_T > S - C$. If no options were employed, profit would occur only if $S_T > S$.

In general, the hedger's profit per unit of the spot asset is given by the following expression:

$$S_T - S - MAX[0, S_T - X] + C.$$

This expression obtains if the written call is held to expiration, which it must if it is European and should if it is American and the underlying asset exhibits no leakages.

Figure 15.1:
Profits for a Covered Call Strategy

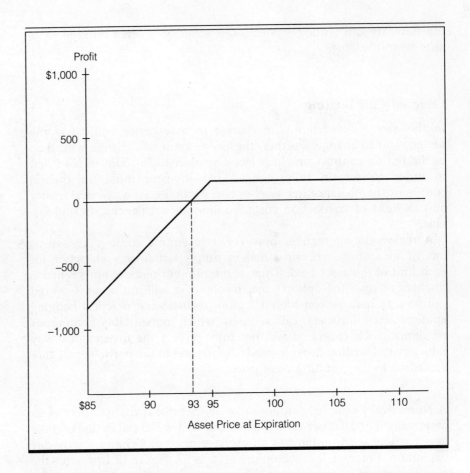

Selecting an Exercise Price The premium received from covered call writing serves to moderate the potential loss on a long asset position. Because of its easy implementation, covered call writing is popular among professional option traders and institutional investors. When writing calls, these traders must choose an exercise price. Implementing a covered call strategy at a lower exercise price tends to reduce downside loss potential, but also diminishes the upside gain potential. On the other hand, implementing a covered call strategy at a higher exercise price will achieve more upside potential but offers less downside protection. This is illustrated in Figure 15.2 for our $100 spot asset described above. With options having an exercise price of $100 and market price of $3, the maximum profit potential is greater ($300), but the potential loss is more substantial (−$9,700). Also, the breakeven point for the $100 exercise-price strategy is associated with a greater spot price at expiration ($97). Thus, writing the higher exercise-price option represents the more aggressive covered call strategy. Ultimately, the choice of exercise price will depend on the writer's degree of risk aversion and forecast of the future spot price.

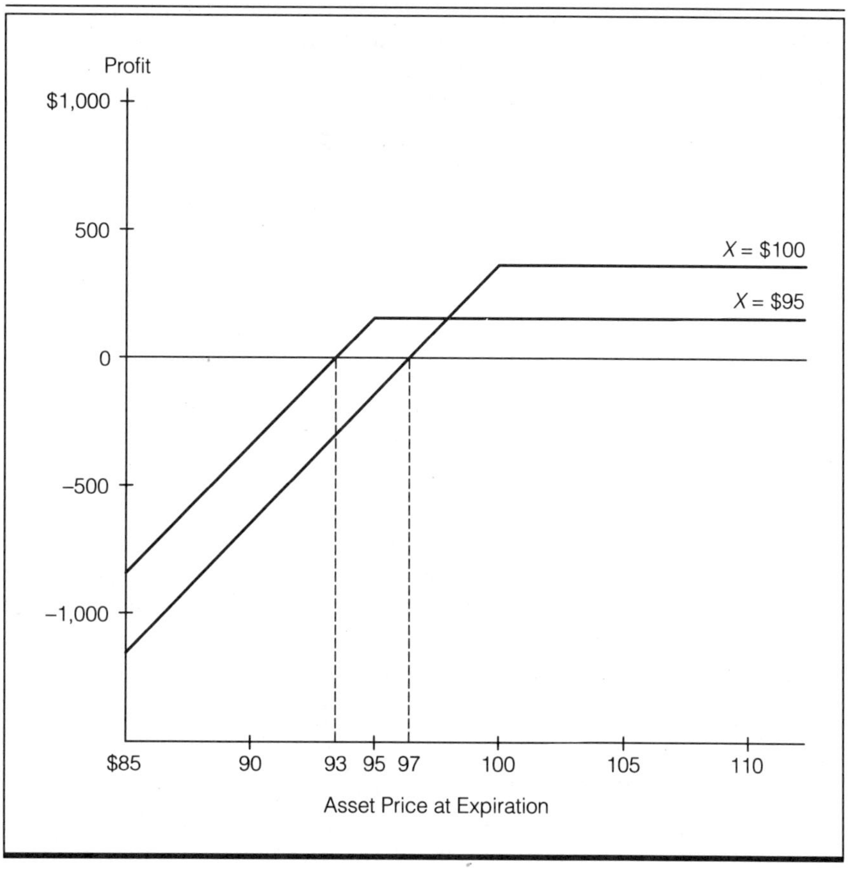

Figure 15.2:
Profits for Covered Call Strategies with Two Different Exercise Prices

Selecting an Option Maturity   When implementing a covered call strategy, traders must also choose an option maturity. Writing longer term calls will generate more revenue, since longer-term options generally command a greater price. However, a longer maturity tends to increase the probability of a change in asset price, which could prove harmful to the hedger. Ultimately, the option's price should accurately reflect the probability of a change in the underlying asset's price, so there is no particular advantage to writing shorter- or longer-term options. With this in mind, the hedger should originally seek to write options whose maturities correspond to the length of the holding period expected in the spot asset.

Synthetic Puts

Covered call writing entails writing one call for each unit of the asset held. But what if we sought to hedge a short position in the underlying asset? Obviously we could lower risk by contracting to buy call options.

If the asset price should rise, the loss on our short position would be offset, at least in part, by the gain on our long option position. The two positions are negatively correlated.

A strategy of buying one call option for each unit of an asset sold short is known as a *synthetic-put strategy*. The name derives from the fact that the payoff to such a strategy resembles the payoff to a put option. To see this, recall put-call parity (for a zero-leakage asset) from Chapter 12:

$$C = P + S - Xe^{-rT}.$$

In a synthetic-put strategy, we short the spot asset and buy call options:

$$C - S.$$

Utilizing these two expressions, we see that

$$C - S = P - Xe^{-rT}.$$

In other words, the investment in a synthetic put and an actual put differ only by Xe^{-rT}, which is the price of a risk-free, pure discount bond. Thus, the payoffs to a synthetic put and an actual put differ only by the interest earned on a pure discount bond. A simple arbitrage strategy, known as a *reversal*, ensures this relation.

A Numerical Example   Suppose an investor assumes a short position for one month in an asset whose current price is $50.00. The size of the short position is 100 units of the asset. To hedge, the investor purchases 100 call options with maturity of one month and exercise price $52.00. The price of each call is $0.40. Figure 15.3 portrays the different profit outcomes possible from the synthetic-put strategy. The maximum possible loss is $240.00, occurring when $S_T > \$52.00$. The breakeven point occurs at $S_T = \$49.60$, or $S - C$. The maximum possible profit is $4,960.00, occurring when $S_T = \$0$. In general, the profit per unit of asset is given by

$$S - S_T + MAX[0, S_T - X] - C.$$

Of course, the investor can purchase lower exercise-price calls to gain more protection, at a higher price, against downside loss in the short asset position.

Protective Put Buying

Another popular way that an investor can protect a long asset position is through purchasing put options on the asset. With this strategy, known as *protective put buying*, the risk associated with a price decline is tempered by the long put position, which increases in value as the spot-asset price falls. The two positions—long the asset and long the put option—are negatively correlated.

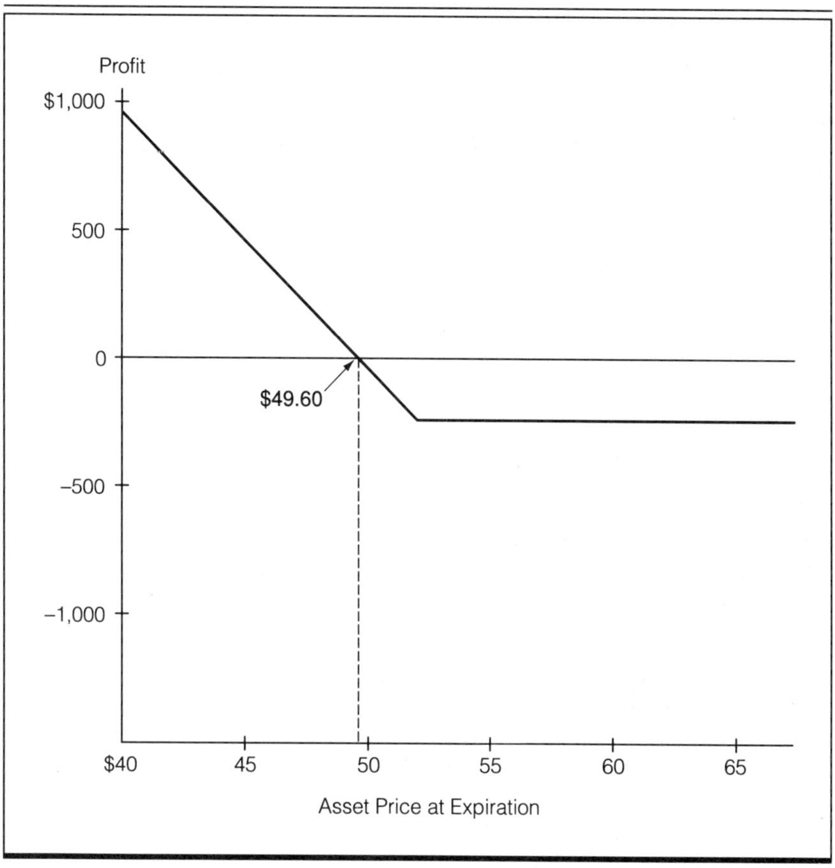

Figure 15.3:
Profits for a Synthetic-Put
Strategy

By fully exploiting this negative correlation through continuous rebalancing, it is possible to completely hedge via protective put buying. However, the transaction costs and persistent monitoring costs associated with continuous rebalancing are so large as to make such a strategy very impractical. Instead, traders often purchase one put option for every unit of the underlying asset held. The payoff associated with such a one-to-one strategy resembles the payoff to a call option. For this reason, the protective put strategy is also called a *synthetic-call strategy*. Combining put-call parity and the protective put, $P + S$, we see that the investment in a protective put/synthetic call differs from the investment in an actual call by just Xe^{-rT}:

$$P + S = C + Xe^{-rT}.$$

Thus, the payoffs to a protective put strategy must closely resemble those of an ordinary call option in order to prevent arbitrage. The simple arbitrage strategy that relates a synthetic call and an actual call is known as a *conversion*.

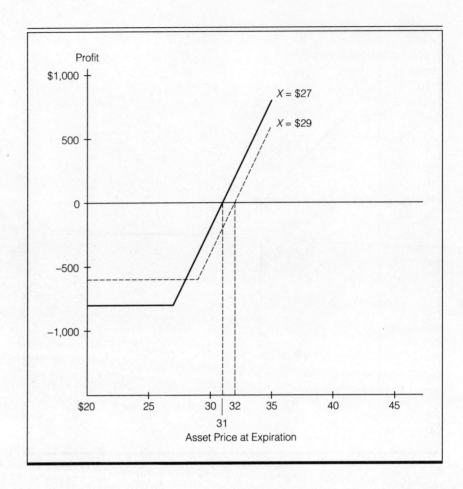

The profit from a protective put strategy, per unit of the underlying asset, is given by the following expression:

$$S_T - S + MAX[0, X - S_T] - P,$$

where P refers to the price of the put option. As a numerical illustration, suppose that you currently hold 200 units of an asset worth $30 per unit and purchase 200 put options with an exercise price of $27 and nine months to expiration. The put options sell for $1 each. Presumably you have chosen nine-month puts to correspond to the anticipated holding period in the underlying spot asset. The solid line in Figure 15.4 represents the profit associated with this protective put strategy. Profits are realized whenever S_T is above $31, the breakeven point $(P + S)$ representing your initial investment. The maximum possible loss is $800, occurring whenever $S_T < $27. Obviously, this maximum loss is nowhere near the loss potential had no put options been purchased $(-\$6,000)$. The profit potential is unlimited, reflecting the unlimited potential of the underlying asset's value.

Selecting An Exercise Price   Although all options and other derivative securities can be employed to offer insurance-like protection, the protective put strategy may illustrate this best. This strategy provides insurance against downside price risk. If the spot price declines, the put option (i.e., insurance claim) is exercised. If the spot price does not decline, the put is allowed to expire (i.e., no claim is filed) and the cost of the put (i.e., the insurance premium) is sunk.

Choosing an exercise price for the protective put strategy is analogous to choosing a deductible on any insurance contract. By purchasing a higher exercise-price put, the hedger obtains more protection against downside price risk. For instance, in the above illustration an exercise price of $29 would have reduced the maximum loss from $800 to $600, presuming the new put sold for $2. (See the broken line in Figure 15.4.) However, with each consecutively higher exercise price, a hedger pays more for the put options (here $2). In other words, the greater the insurance (the lower the deductible), the greater is the insurance premium. Ultimately, the choice of an exercise price for the protective put strategy depends on the hedger's willingness to trade off risk reduction and the cost of the coverage. This is true for virtually any decision regarding insurance; different individuals will contract for different deductibles and levels of coverage given their associated costs.

Combining Short Assets and Written Puts

We have considered combining long asset positions with written calls and purchased puts, and short asset positions with purchased calls. The remaining hedging strategy entails combining a short asset position with written puts. Should the spot asset appreciate, the loss on the short asset position will be somewhat offset from the premium realized by writing the put options. Thus, the two positions are negatively correlated. And, as before, altering the exercise price on the written puts will change the potential profit outcome.

Assuming a one-to-one correspondence between the underlying asset and the associated puts, by put-call parity it may be demonstrated that the payoff to the short asset/short put strategy is similar to that of a written call option:

$$-S - P = -C - Xe^{-rT}.$$

Thus, the combination of a short asset and written put forms a *synthetic short call*.

The combination of a short asset and written put forms a **synthetic short call**.

Creating Synthetic Futures Contracts

Part 1 of this book repeatedly demonstrated how futures contracts could be used to hedge. Ignoring the effects of daily resettlement, options can

Synthetic futures con-
tracts can be constructed
through the trading of option
contracts.

be combined to create *synthetic futures contracts*. Thus, certain option combinations can be employed to hedge risk in much the same way that a futures contract can be used for hedging. (Understanding how futures contracts can be created through option combinations will also help the reader understand the complex hedging strategy known as *portfolio insurance* that is presented in Chapter 20.)

A combination of options that consists of a written European call and a purchased European put, with the same exercise prices and expirations, behaves in a manner identical to a short position in a futures contract. A long position in a synthetic futures contract is created by purchasing European calls and writing corresponding puts.

As an example, suppose that a U.S.–based multinational corporation that will receive DM625,000 in September purchases ten September DM put-option contracts with an exercise price of $0.56/DM, and simultaneously writes ten corresponding call-option contracts. Each European option contract entails DM62,500. The result is that the multinational corporation can always sell its deutsche marks at $0.56/DM, regardless of how the $/DM exchange rate moves from now until the September contract expiration. Thus, the multinational has created a short position in synthetic DM futures.

Because synthetic futures can be created by option combinations, close pricing relations should be observed between options and actual futures. Arbitrage restrictions should ensure that the payoffs obtained from actual and synthetic futures strategies are nearly identical. Small differences may arise due to market imperfections.

In general, the prices of the corresponding options and the actual futures price should conform to the following relation, which is often called *put-call-futures parity:*

Put-call-futures parity
follows from arbitrage restrictions and relates the prices of
traded option and futures contracts.

(15.1)
$$|P^E - C^E| = |X - {}_Tf_0|e^{-rT}.$$

Equation 15.1 follows from arbitrage restrictions. For instance, a risk-free portfolio can be constructed by combining a short futures contract and a long synthetic-futures contract. The long synthetic futures requires buying a call and writing a corresponding put. The current value of this portfolio and its payoff at expiration are shown in Exhibit 15.1. Since the payoff is ${}_Tf_0 - X$ regardless of the value of S_T, the portfolio's current worth must be the present value of ${}_Tf_0 - X$, where the discounting factor is the riskless rate of interest. In equilibrium, we therefore have

$$C^E - P^E = ({}_Tf_0 - X)e^{-rT},$$

which conforms to Equation 15.1. For a hedged portfolio consisting of a long futures contract and a short synthetic-futures contract, we have

$$P^E - C^E = (X - {}_Tf_0)e^{-rT}.$$

The ability to create a futures contract through option combinations may suggest that actual futures are redundant instruments—a type of

Position	Current Value	Payoffs at Expiration	
		$S_T \leq X$	$S_T > X$
Short Futures	0	$_Tf_0 - S_T$	$_Tf_0 - S_T$
Long Call	C^E	0	$S_T - X$
Short Put	$-P^E$	$-(X - S_T)$	0
	$C^E - P^E$	$_Tf_0 - X$	$_Tf_0 - X$

Exhibit 15.1:
A Riskless Portfolio Consisting of a Short Futures Contract and a Long Synthetic-Futures Contract

financial "excess." However, actual futures trading entails lower transaction costs than option combinations, so they offer less costly risk protection than synthetic futures, implying that the actuals are not redundant instruments. By the way, a synthetic option cannot be created by combining futures contracts.

SIMPLE SPECULATIVE STRATEGIES

In the previous section we described how options could be combined with spot-asset positions in order to reduce downside risk. The fundamental idea was to assume an option position whose returns were negatively correlated with those on the spot-asset position. Also, we described how options could be combined to replicate futures positions. Thus, to the extent that futures may be used to hedge risk, so, too, can option combinations that result in synthetic-futures positions.

Besides hedging, options are often employed to speculate on subsequent changes in the prices of spot assets. In this section we present some very simple speculative strategies that involve options trading. In the next section we consider more advanced speculative strategies.

Simple Strategies for Expected Spot-Price Appreciation

If a speculator forecasts an increase in the value of a spot asset, she could simply assume a long position in that asset. However, to profit, the speculator could instead purchase a call option written on the asset. By doing so, she increases *financial leverage*, meaning that the percentage return on the call option will be greater than the percentage return on the spot asset should its price increase (and vice versa). By varying the exercise price on the call option purchase, the speculator changes her degree of leverage. For instance, deeply out-of-the-money options offer the greatest leverage; their prices increase more, in percentage terms, than the prices of at- or in-the-money calls should the spot price increase. Also, by purchasing the call, the speculator's maximum potential loss is limited to the amount of the call premium. By simply assuming a long position in the spot asset, her potential dollar loss is greater.

Besides purchasing a call, the speculator may choose to write a put option on the asset. Here she will reap the full put option premium should the spot price increase as forecasted. If the spot price falls, her liability is limited to the put option's exercise price.

Figure 15.5 provides profit graphs for all three positions: long the spot asset, long the call option, and short the put option. In each case, the speculator will profit if the forecast of increased spot-asset value proves correct.

Simple Strategies for Expected Spot-Price Depreciation

If a speculator forecasts a decrease in the value of a spot asset, he may either (1) short the asset, (2) purchase a put option, or (3) write a call option. Transacting in options will provide more leverage, and this leverage can be altered by varying the exercise price. Figure 15.6 provides profit graphs for all three positions. In each, the speculator will profit if the forecast of decreased spot-asset value proves correct.

ADVANCED SPECULATIVE STRATEGIES

Advanced speculative strategies generally involve option combinations. Two or more different options are combined in order to allow small profits to be earned if forecasts prove correct, but also to limit the

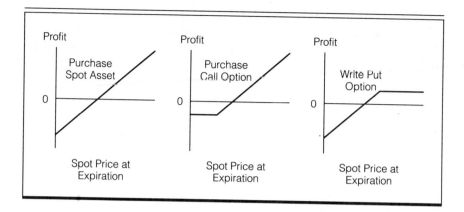

Figure 15.5:
Profit Graphs for Expected Spot-Price Appreciation

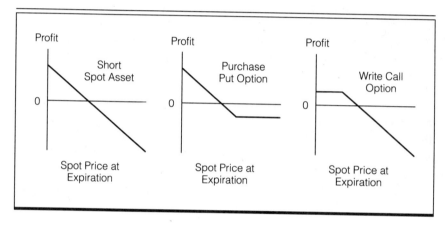

Figure 15.6:
Profit Graphs for Expected Spot-Price Depreciation

amount of risk entailed. Risk is lower than that associated with lone option positions, because with option combinations, the loss on one option may be somewhat offset by the gain on the other(s). Thus, option combinations can represent less risky speculative positions than the simple speculative strategies described above. This does not mean that option combinations are not speculative in nature. No position is held in the spot asset, so the options are not being employed to offset preexisting risk in spot markets. Rather, the option combinations described below represent less risky speculative positions than the naked option strategies described in the previous section.

The option combinations of spreads, straddles, straps, and strips represent the most popular speculative combinations utilized by professional option traders.

Money Spreads

An option spread involves the purchase of one option and the sale of another. One type of spread is a *money spread*, which entails two options

A **bull money spread** is constructed by buying an option with a lower exercise price and writing an otherwise identical option with a higher exercise price. A **bear money spread** is engineered in the opposite manner.

that differ only in exercise price, that is, in the degree to which they are in- or out-of-the-money (hence the term "money spread"). A *bull money spread* is constructed by buying an option with a lower exercise price and writing an otherwise identical option with a higher exercise price. A *bear money spread* entails purchasing a higher exercise price option and writing a corresponding option having a lower exercise price.

Illustration of a Bull Money Spread   A bull money spread may be used by a speculator who forecasts an appreciation of the underlying spot asset. The speculator is said to be "bullish" on the spot asset. Suppose this asset has a current price of $50. Also, a call option written on this asset and exhibiting a $47 exercise price currently sells for $4.00. A corresponding call option having an exercise price of $52 currently sells for $1. Figure 15.7 portrays the profits to a bull money spread involving these two option contracts. The maximum loss that may occur is $3 (per option), which is the difference between the two option premiums. This occurs whenever S_T is less than $47. The maximum gain is $2 (per option), which occurs for any expiration asset price above $52. This maximum gain is given by the difference in exercise prices ($5) less the absolute net premium ($3). The breakeven point is associated with an expiration spot price of $50, or $47 − (1 − 4). In other words, the breakeven point is given by the exercise price of the long option less the net premium.

Figure 15.7:
Profit Graph for a Bull Money Spread

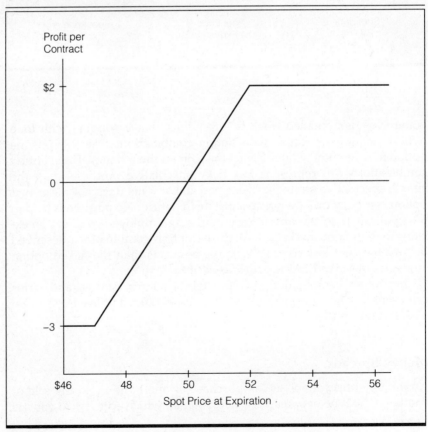

In order for this bull money spread to be profitable, S_T must be greater than $50. That is, the spot asset must appreciate as forecasted by the speculator. But why not just purchase a lone call option to profit? This could be done, but the risk exposure would be greater than that of the bull money spread. For instance, purchasing the $47 exercise-price call alone subjects the speculator to a potential loss of $4 per option. Writing a put would be even riskier. The bull money spread instead offers the speculator a modest profit should the asset appreciate while at the same time providing limited risk exposure should the forecast be incorrect.[1]

Illustration of a Bear Money Spread Recall that a bear money spread entails buying a higher exercise-price option and selling a lower exercise-price option. This strategy may be employed if the forecast calls for a depreciation of the spot asset. The speculator is said to be "bearish" on the asset.

Let us illustrate a bear money spread while using put options. Suppose that we have a $50 spot asset, a put with an exercise price of $47 that currently sells for $1, and another put with an exercise price of $52 that now sells for $4. Figure 15.8 portrays the profits to a bear money

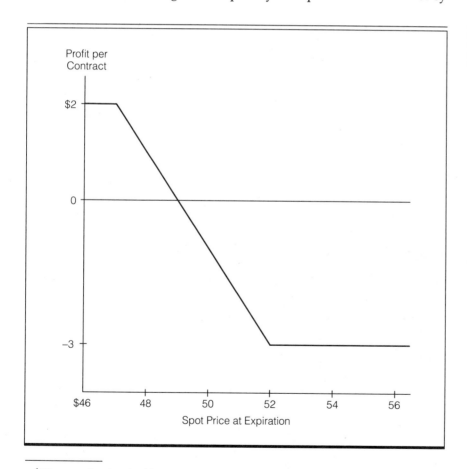

Figure 15.8:
Profit Graph for a Bear Money Spread

---

[1]Of course, buying the $52 exercise-price call subjects the speculator to a maximum loss of just $1 per option, but the breakeven point for profitability climbs to $53 from $50.

spread involving these two put options. In order for the speculator to profit, the spot price at expiration must be less than $49. In other words, profit will be realized if the asset depreciates as forecasted.

Butterfly Spreads

A **butterfly spread** represents a combination of a bull money spread and a bear money spread. It is used to speculate on a forecast of spot-price stability.

A *butterfly spread* represents a combination of a bull money spread and a bear money spread. It is utilized by speculators who anticipate little change in the value of the underlying spot asset. As an example, suppose that a speculator buys one $25 exercise-price call option, writes two $20 exercise-price calls, and buys one $15 exercise-price call on an asset currently worth $20:

Option Position	Option Price	Investment
Long One Call, $X = \$25$	$1	+ $1
Short Two Calls, $X = \$20$	$3	− 6
Long One Call, $X = \$15$	$6	+ 6
	Total Investment	+ $1

The total investment in the butterfly spread is $1, given the assumed option prices above. Notice that calls with three different exercise prices were used to construct the butterfly spread. However, this is really nothing more than a combination of a bull money spread (long one call with $X = \$15$, and short one call with $X = \$20$) and bear money spread (long one call with $X = \$25$, and short one call with $X = \$20$).

Figure 15.9 displays the potential profit outcomes for the butterfly spread at option expiration. For values of S_T less than $15, a loss of $1 (the initial investment) is incurred. Here the values of the long option positions are exactly offset by the liabilities on the two written options. For $S_T > \$25$ all options expire worthless, so again the initial investment is lost. However, profits will be realized if the resulting spot price at option expiration lies between $16 and $24. Thus, if the spot asset's value does not change much, as forecasted, the speculator will profit from the butterfly-spread strategy. In essence, the speculator is wagering that the asset's volatility is less than that implied by the option prices, as determined by other market players. The maximum profit obtains when $S_T = S = \$20$.

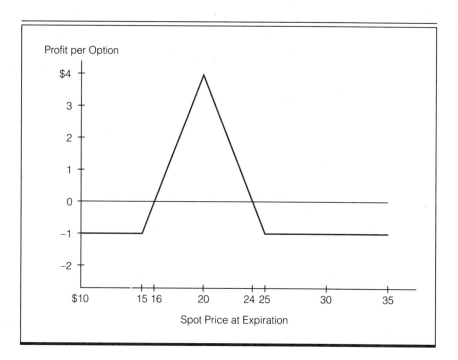

Calendar Spreads

Whereas a money spread involves options with the same maturity but different exercise prices, a *calendar spread* entails options with the same exercise price but different maturities. Specifically, a calendar spread is created by writing a shorter maturity option and purchasing an otherwise equivalent but longer maturity option. Like a butterfly spread, a speculator will engage in a calendar spread if the forecast calls for a stable spot-asset price.

A **calendar spread** is created by writing a shorter maturity option and purchasing an otherwise equivalent but longer-term option. A reverse calendar spread is engineered in the opposite manner.

Suppose that a speculator creates a calendar spread by writing a September call and buying a December call. Both options have the same intrinsic value, $MAX[0, S - X]$. The December option commands a greater price, however, reflecting its greater time value. Upon expiration of the September call, the speculator must close out the calendar spread by now writing the December call. At this time the September call has no more time value. Thus, the speculator who wrote the September call realized all of the shorter-term option's time value. Also, the December call's intrinsic value remains about the same because of the spot-price stability. It has lost some time value, but likely not as much as that of the September call. Consequently, the speculator will profit, because the time value reaped on the September call was greater than the time value lost on the December call. The speculator could have profited by simply writing the September call, but engaging in the spread was less risky. If the asset in question appreciated greatly, contrary to the forecast of spot-price stability, the gains on the long December call would have helped offset the losses on the short September call.

Now consider a *reverse calendar spread*, which is formed by purchasing the shorter-term option and writing the corresponding longer-term option. A speculator might engage in this strategy if the forecast calls for an unstable spot price. If the asset price changed dramatically, up or down, there would be little time value remaining to be purchased upon reversing the longer-term position. Recall that at extreme asset prices, the option's price rapidly and asymptotically approaches its intrinsic value (see Figure 13.2). Thus, the speculator profits because he receives more money from writing the longer-term option than he spent purchasing the shorter term option, and both options command about the same price at expiration of the shorter-term option.

Illustration of a Reverse Calendar Spread Suppose an investor perceives an asset with current price of $60 to be extremely volatile over the next few months. He cannot determine with confidence whether the spot price will increase or decrease, but he is certain that asset volatility is greater than that reflected in current market prices. Perhaps the asset in question is being challenged by a rival technology that is still unproven. A critical test of this new technology, scheduled to occur over the next few months, will likely determine if the focal asset will become obsolete or will retain its market share and thus appreciate due to unrealized expectations about the effects of the new technology.

The speculator can wager on this uncertainty by engaging in a reverse calendar spread. Specifically, presume the speculator purchases a September call with exercise price of $58 while writing a December call with exercise price of $58. The prices of the September and December calls are $3 and $4, respectively. Thus, the initial proceeds to the speculator are $1 (per option). Now suppose that the new technology is proven successful, and therefore the focal asset's price declines markedly. At September maturity, the purchased September call expires worthless. However, the written December call is also deeply out-of-the-money, likely commanding a price of nearly zero. The speculator can therefore buy a December call, thereby closing out the reverse calendar spread, and pocket nearly all of the initial proceeds of $1. The spot asset's extreme price movement made the spread profitable.

A **straddle** consists of two options, one a call and the other a corresponding put. It is used to speculate on a forecast of excessive spot-price variability. A reverse straddle is created by writing the call and corresponding put.

Straddles

Spreads involve buying one option and selling another option. Since both options are calls (or puts), the long-short position results in less risk than a simple naked position. With a *straddle*, a speculator *buys* two options, one a call and the other a corresponding put. Thus, a straddle represents a long-long position, but risk is still controlled somewhat because calls and puts are negatively correlated.

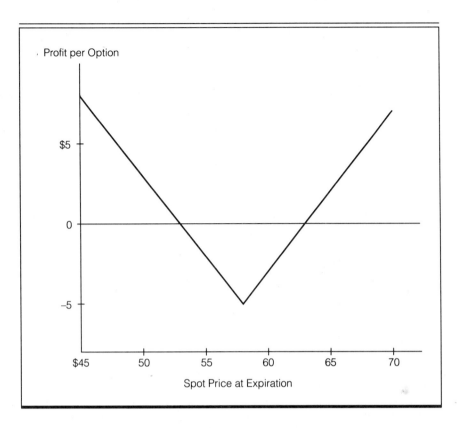

Like a reverse calendar spread, a straddle is assumed by a speculator who perceives the spot asset to be more volatile than do other market participants. Consider the earlier mentioned asset selling for $60. Suppose that a speculator forms a straddle on this asset by purchasing the September call ($X = \$58$) for $3 while simultaneously purchasing a September put ($X = \$58$) for $2. Thus, the investment in the straddle is $5. Figure 15.10 presents the profits associated with this straddle for different spot prices at September expiration. The profit graph takes on a V shape. If the resulting spot price, S_T, is less than $53 or greater than $63, the speculator profits. The spot price must change substantially in order for the straddle to be successful.

A *reverse straddle*, also called a *short straddle*, is constructed by writing both a call and its corresponding put. Like a calendar spread, a reverse straddle is undertaken in anticipation of spot-price stability. If the spot price moves within a narrow range, the speculator who assumes a reverse straddle position will profit. As expected, the profit graph for a reverse straddle is represented by an inverted V shape.

Straps

A *strap* is a combination of two long calls and a long corresponding put. As such, it represents a slight variation of a straddle. With a straddle,

A **strap** is a combination of two long calls and a long corresponding put.

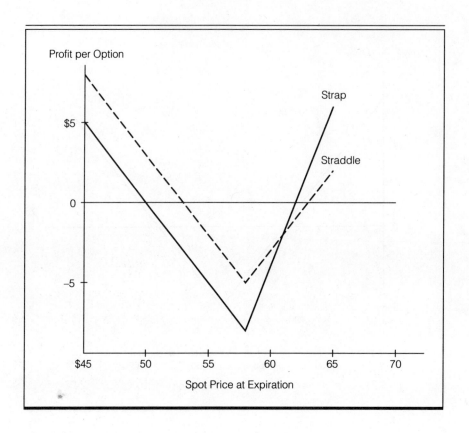

Profit per Option

Strap

$5

Straddle

0

−5

$45   50   55   60   65   70

Spot Price at Expiration

the speculator is wagering on a large spot-price change that may occur in either direction. With a strap, she is somewhat more bullish on the asset, purchasing two calls for each put option bought.

Figure 15.11 portrays the profit graph for a strap constructed by purchasing two September calls ($X = \$58$) for $3 each while simultaneously buying one September put ($X = \$58$) for $2. Thus, the investment in the strap is $8. The profit graph takes on a tilted V shape. When compared to the straddle (broken line), we see that the strap offers relatively more profit should the spot price appreciate dramatically, while yielding less profit should the spot price at expiration be low. The two breakeven points for the strap occur at $S_T = \$50$ and $S_T = \$62$. In general, the first breakeven point occurs at $S_T = X - P - 2C$, while the second occurs at $S_T = X + C + (P/2)$.

Strips

A **strip** is a combination of two long puts and one long corresponding call.

A *strip* is a combination of two long puts and one long corresponding call. As such, it represents a variation of a straddle where the speculator is somewhat more bearish than bullish on the spot asset. Figure 15.12 presents the profit graph for a strip constructed by purchasing two of

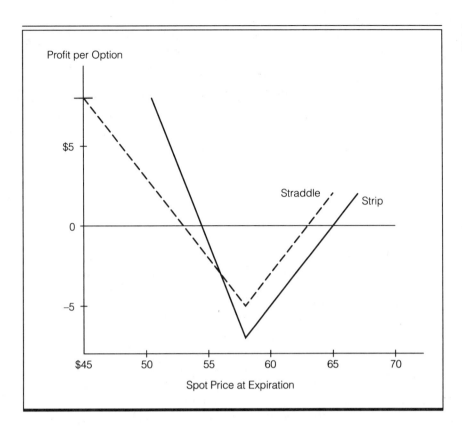

Profit per Option

$5

0

−5

Straddle

Strip

$45   50   55   60   65   70

Spot Price at Expiration

our same September puts and one of our same September calls. The investment in the strip is $7. Again, the profit graph takes on a tilted V shape, with more profit potential than a straddle should the spot price decline substantially. The two breakeven points for the strip occur at $S_T = \$54.50$ and $S_T = \$65.00$. In general, the first breakeven point for the strip occurs at $S_T = X - P - (C/2)$, while the second occurs at $S_T = X + C + 2P$.

EMPIRICAL EVIDENCE ON OPTIONS FOR HEDGING AND SPECULATING

Surprisingly little empirical evidence concerning the use of options for hedging or speculating currently exists. A study by R. Grube, D. Panton, and J. Terrell (1979) found that portfolios of as few as five stocks combined with written calls exhibit no more risk than much larger plain-stock portfolios. Thus, covered call writing appears to provide substantial risk reduction. Another study, by J. Yates and R. Kopprasch (1980), found that a portfolio index of stock and written calls provided better performance than the SP500.

Two studies have also focused on speculative strategies entailing option combinations such as bull and bear money spreads and calendar spreads, one by M. Gombola, R. Roenfeldt, and P. Cooley (1978) and another by R. Billingsley and D. Chance (1985). Both reported that such combinations do not yield abnormal profit opportunities or generally outperform simpler option strategies after accounting for commissions and other costs. Obviously, commission costs are rather high for spreads and other advanced option strategies since multiple option transactions are involved.

SUMMARY

Options can be employed to hedge risk or to speculate on subsequent spot-price changes. With respect to hedging, they can be combined with preexisting spot-asset positions to reduce downside risk. The fundamental idea is to assume an option position whose returns are negatively correlated with those on the spot position. Long spot positions can be combined with written calls or purchased puts, while short spot positions can be combined with long calls or short puts. The degree of risk exposure can be managed by altering the exercise price or massaging the frequency by which the option position is updated.

In principle, an option position can be continuously rebalanced such that the resulting spot-option portfolio is risk-free. In light of real-world restrictions on such a strategy, however, simpler and discretely rebalanced positions are typically assumed that help prevent downside risk. Different hedgers exhibiting different degrees of risk aversion can employ various spot-option combinations, exercise prices, and rebalancing intervals to maximize their own unique utility functions.

Concerning speculation, simple option strategies and advanced strategies involving option combinations exist. The simple strategies entail naked positions, buying or writing lone calls or puts to exploit spot-price forecasts. Such strategies can be very risky. Popular option combinations are spreads, straddles, straps, and strips. While still speculative in nature, these combinations are typically safer than assuming a naked position, since the combined options are themselves negatively correlated.

In this chapter we abstracted from the effects of transaction costs, intervening leakages, and premature option exercise. When practicing the above strategies, hedgers and speculators must recognize and account for such complicating effects. For example, a covered call writing strategy entailing American options exposes the hedger to the possibility of premature exercise if the asset in question exhibits intervening leakages, thus aborting the planned holding horizon of the underlying spot asset. As another example, transaction costs will effectively expand the range of expiration spot prices beyond which a straddle is profitable. In subsequent chapters we present numerous examples of hedging and speculating with option contracts.

Selected References

Billingsley, R., and D. Chance. "Options Market Efficiency and the Box Spread Strategy." *Financial Review* 20 (November 1985):287–301.

Dawson, F. "Risks and Returns in Continuous Option Writing." *Journal of Portfolio Management* 5 (Winter 1979):58–63.

Frankfurter, G., R. Stevenson, and A. Young. "Option Spreading: Theory and Illustration." *Journal of Portfolio Management* 5 (Summer 1979):59–63.

Gladstein, M., R. Merton, and M. Scholes. "The Returns and Risks of Alternative Put Options Portfolio Investment Strategies." *Journal of Business* (January 1982).

Grube, R., D. Panton, and J. Terrell. "Risks and Rewards in Covered Call Positions." *Journal of Portfolio Management* 5 (Winter 1979):64–68.

Gombola, M., R. Roenfeldt, and P. Cooley. "Spreading Strategies in CBOE Options: Evidence on Market Performance." *Journal of Financial Research* 1 (Winter 1978):35–44.

Merton, R., M. Scholes, and M. Gladstein. "A Simulation of Returns and Risk of Alternative Option Portfolio Investment Strategies." 51 *Journal of Business* (April 1978).

Mueller, P. "Covered Call Options: An Alternative Investment Strategy." *Financial Management* 10 (Winter 1981):64–71.

Pounds, H. "Covered Call Option Writing: Strategies and Results." *Journal of Portfolio Management* 5 (Winter 1978):31–42.

Pozen, R. "The Purchase of Protective Puts by Financial Institutions." *Financial Analysts Journal* 34 (July–August 1978):47–60.

Ritchken, P., and H. Salkin. "Safety-First Selection Techniques for Option Spreads." *Journal of Portfolio Management* 9 (1981):61–67.

Slivka, R. "Call Option Spreading." *Journal of Portfolio Management* 7 (Spring 1981):71–76.

Welch, W. *Strategies for Put and Call Option Trading.* Cambridge, Mass.: Winthrop Publishers, 1982.

Yates, J., and R. Kopprasch. "Writing Covered Call Options: Profits and Risks." *Journal of Portfolio Management* 6 (Fall 1980):74–80.

Questions and Problems

1. Explain how a short spot-asset position can be protected using options.
2. Explain how a long spot-asset position can be protected using options.
3. Explain how a protective-put buying strategy is analogous to purchasing insurance on the underlying asset.
4. How is the choice of exercise price on a protective-put buying strategy akin to a deductible decision on any insurance policy?

5. Explain how the strategy of purchasing one call for each unit of an asset sold short is like creating a synthetic put.

6. Explain how the combination of a short spot position and written puts is like creating a synthetic short call option.

7. How can you create a synthetic short futures position with futures price $X through combining option contracts? How would a synthetic long futures position be engineered?

8. Why might a speculator employ spreads or other option combinations rather than naked option positions?

9. What strategies might a speculator employ if his forecast called for unprecedented spot-asset volatility?

10. What strategies might a speculator employ if her forecast suggested spot-price stability in the near term?

11. Explain the differences between a strap and a straddle as well as a strip and a straddle. When is a speculator likely to use one over the other?

12. Explain how a butterfly spread represents a combination of a bull money spread and a bear money spread.

13. How do calendar spreads differ from money spreads?

The remaining problems refer to the following European option-price information. Assume that the underlying asset is a zero-leakage asset with current spot price of $120.

Exercise Price	Calls			Puts		
	MAR	APR	JUN	MAR	APR	JUN
$120	2⅛	4⅛	7⅛	1¾	2¹³⁄₁₆	4⅜
125	⁷⁄₁₆	1⅞	4⅝	5¼	5¾	7
130	¹⁄₁₆	¹¹⁄₁₆	2¾	10¼	10⅛	10¼

14. Suppose that an investor owns 100 units of the spot asset and writes 100 APR $120 calls. Determine the hedger's profits for spot prices at expiration of $110, $115, $120, $125, and $130. Determine the profits if the APR $125 calls were written instead.

15. Suppose that another investor is short 100 units of the spot asset and purchases 100 JUN $125 calls. Determine his profits for the same expiration spot prices.

16. Suppose another investor owns 200 units of the spot asset and decides to purchase 200 JUN $120 puts. What are her profits for the same expiration spot prices? What are her profits if the JUN $125 puts are purchased instead?

17. Suppose yet another investor is short 300 units of the spot asset and writes 300 MAR $125 puts. Determine his profits for the same expiration spot prices.

18. Construct a bear money spread using JUN $120 and $125 calls. What does the profit graph look like for this spread, assuming the options are held to expiration? Identify the breakeven expiration spot price and the profit range as well.

19. Construct a butterfly spread using APR $120, $125, and $130 calls. What does the profit graph look like for this spread, assuming the options are held to expiration? Identify the two breakeven spot prices.

20. Construct a short strip using JUN $125 options. Present the profit graph assuming options are held to their maturity, and identify the breakeven spot prices.

21. Construct a long strap using the MAR $130 options. Determine the strap's profit graph at option expiration. What are the breakeven expiration spot prices and the minimum and maximum profits?

22. Construct a long straddle using the same MAR $130 options. Determine the profit graph, and identify the breakeven expiration spot prices.

Self-Test Problems

Self-test Problems 1 through 6 refer to the following European option-price information. Assume that the underlying asset is a zero-leakage asset with current spot price of $84.50.

Exercise Price	Calls			Puts		
	MAR	APR	JUN	MAR	APR	JUN
$80	4⅞	6¼	7⅛	⅜	¹⁵⁄₁₆	2
85	1⁷⁄₁₆	3⅛	3⅞	1¾	2½	4
90	¼	1⅛	2	5⅝	5⅞	7

ST-1. What are the breakeven expiration spot prices for a long strip constructed using APR $80 options?

ST-2. Construct a bull money spread using MAR $80 and $85 calls. Determine the breakeven expiration spot price.

ST-3. Construct a reverse straddle using JUN $85 options. Present the profit graph at option expiration. Label the breakeven points.

ST-4. Construct a profit diagram comparing a long spot position with a covered call position. Use the APR $85 calls and expiration spot prices ranging from $75 to $95.

ST-5. Construct a profit diagram comparing a long spot position with a protective put position. Use the APR $85 puts and the same expiration spot prices.

ST-6. Construct a profit diagram comparing a short spot position with a short spot/written put position. Use the JUN $80 puts and the same expiration spot prices.

Solutions to Self-Test Problems

ST-1. First breakeven point:
$$\$80 - (^{15}\!/_{16}) - [(6\tfrac{1}{4})/2] = \$75^{15}\!/_{16}.$$
Second breakeven point:
$$\$80 + 6\tfrac{1}{4} + 2(^{15}\!/_{16}) = \$88\tfrac{1}{8}.$$

ST-2. Breakeven point:
$$\$80 - (1^{7}\!/_{16} - 4\tfrac{7}{8}) = \$83^{7}\!/_{16}.$$

ST-3.

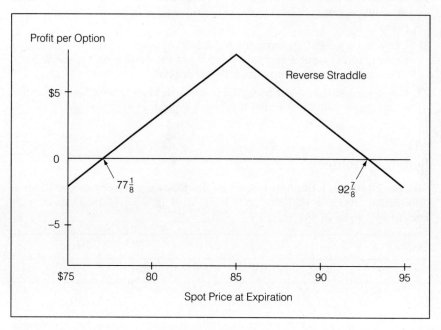

ST-4.

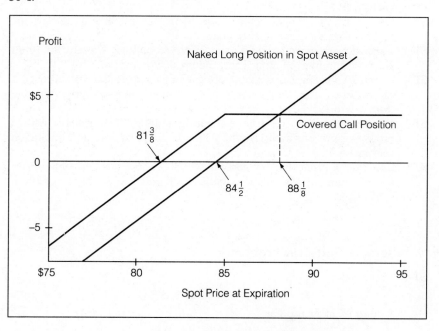

ST-5.

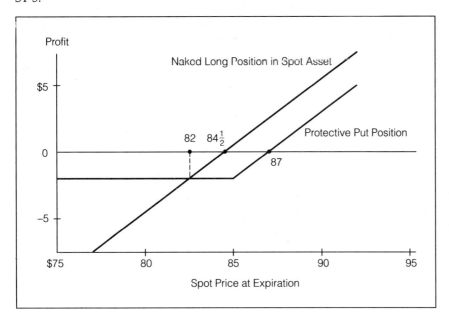

ST-6.

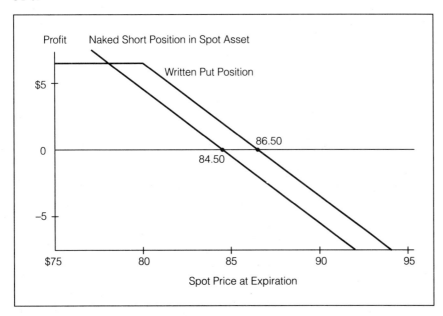

16

STOCK OPTIONS

The first listed option contracts were offered by the Chicago Board Options Exchange (CBOE) in 1973 and were traded on common stock. Today the CBOE transacts nearly 300,000 contracts per day, plus, stock options are traded on other U.S. exchanges and exchanges worldwide. Their volume still exceeds that of any other underlying instrument.

In this chapter the markets for stock options are described, followed by valuation issues. Examples of hedging and speculating with stock options are provided, along with a summary of empirical evidence on the subject.

STOCK-OPTION MARKETS

In the United States, listed stock options are traded on the CBOE, the American Stock Exchange (AMEX), the Philadelphia Stock Exchange (PHLX), the Pacific Stock Exchange (PSE), and the New York Stock Exchange (NYSE). The CBOE is the leading trader of stock options, accounting for nearly one-half of the annual contract volume. The AMEX is second. Figure 16.1 presents the share of stock-option volume for each exchange for the calendar year of 1986. Note that in that year the CBOE captured 46 percent of the entire market, trading about 65 million contracts.

Exhibit 16.1 presents closing prices for two selected stock-option contracts for a recent trading day: IBM stock options traded on the CBOE and Compaq Computer stock options traded on the PSE on March 1, 1989. Each stock-option contract entails 100 shares (a *round lot*) of the underlying stock. The closing stock prices for IBM and Compaq (organized in 1982 to produce IBM-compatible portable computers) were $119-7/8 and $66-3/4, respectively, on March 1. As the exhibit demonstrates, stock-option prices increase with maturity, and call (put) prices

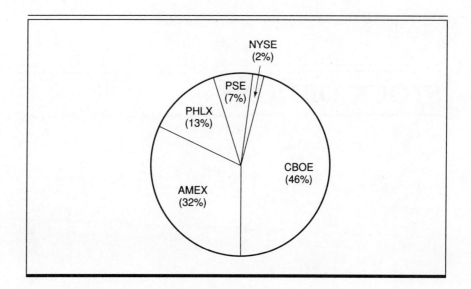

increase (decrease) with the ratio S/X. Also, options that are deeply in- or out-of-the-money often are unavailable or not traded. Most volume is concentrated in the at-the-money contracts, where S/X is close to unity.

E. Blomeyer (1986) reports that over 80 percent of all CBOE-listed stock options are traded on firms scheduled to pay at least one dividend prior to option expiration. In the over-the-counter (OTC) stock-options market (the predecessor of the CBOE), options were dividend-protected, meaning that the exercise price was reduced by the per-share dividend. With listed stock options, however, such adjustments would result in nonstandardized exercise prices. Consequently, exchanges such as the CBOE do not adjust exercise prices when cash dividends are paid; that is, listed stock options are not dividend-protected. As we saw in Chapters 13 and 14, this rule affects the valuation of listed stock options. The prices reported in Exhibit 16.1 already reflect anticipated dividend payments. To help clarify stock-option valuation, we next discuss dividend-payment procedures.

Listed stock options are not dividend-protected.

DIVIDEND-PAYMENT PROCEDURES

Firms normally pay dividends on a quarterly basis. If a firm's regular quarterly dividend is $0.70 per share, its annual dividend is $2.80. Dividends (and ex-dividend dates) are available in *Moody's Dividend Record*. Also, various investment advisory services, such as *Value Line*, regularly provide forecasts of firm earnings and dividends. Future short-term dividend payments usually can be predicted with great accuracy. This is because most firms tend to smooth their dividend

Option and NY Close	Strike Price	Calls - Last			Puts - Last		
		Mar	Apr	May	Mar	Apr	May
IBM	105	s	r	s	s	1/4	s
119-7/8	110	s	12	15-1/4	s	9/16	1-3/8
119-7/8	115	s	7-1/2	10	s	1-3/16	2-1/2
119-7/8	120	2-1/8	4-1/8	7-1/8	1-3/4	2-13/16	4-3/8
119-7/8	125	7/16	1-7/8	4-5/8	5-1/4	5-3/4	7
119-7/8	130	1/16	11/16	2-3/4	10-1/4	10-1/8	10-1/4
119-7/8	135	1/16	1/4	1-5/8	r	15-1/8	r
Compaq	50	s	r	r	s	3/16	r
66-3/4	55	r	14	r	r	5/16	1
66-3/4	60	r	8-1/2	10-1/2	1/4	3/4	1-7/8
66-3/4	65	3-1/8	5-1/4	7-3/4	7/8	2-3/8	3-7/8
66-3/4	70	9/16	2-3/8	5-3/8	3 3/8	4-7/8	6-3/8
66-3/4	75	1/8	1	3-2/4	r	r	8-1/8
66-3/4	80	1/16	1/2	2-1/4	r	r	r

r = Not traded
s = No option

payments over time. Even though earnings represent the major determinant of a firm's ability to pay dividends, dividends per share are almost always less volatile than earnings per share. Firms tend to smooth their dividend payments for two reason: First, some stockholders use dividends for current consumption and thus prefer a more stable dividend policy. Second, frequent dividend changes typically lead to greater market uncertainty about the firm's future investment opportunities and earning power; investors will tend to assign a lower value to firms with greater operating uncertainty, as reflected (i.e., signaled) in a fluctuating dividend policy.

The actual dividend-payout procedure is as follows:

- *Declaration date.* On this date the firm's directors declare the regular dividend, when it will be paid, and the holder-of-record date. For instance, the directors may announce on February 15 that a $0.70 per share dividend will be paid on April 2 to shareholders of record as of March 10.

- *Holder-of-record date.* On March 10 the firm closes its stock-transfer books and creates a listing of all shareholders as of this date. Notification of a stock transfer occurring before March 10 but received after this date does not entitle the new owner to the April 2 dividend. The previous holder-of-record retains the dividend right.

- *Ex-dividend date.* The ex-dividend date occurs four trading days prior to the holder-of-record date. Here the ex-dividend date is March 6 (assuming March 6 through March 10 represent trading days). On the ex-dividend date the right to the declared dividend leaves the stock. Thus, even if the firm is notified by March 10 of a transfer that occurred on March 6 or later, the seller retains the right to the April 2 dividend. For all intents and purposes, the ex-dividend date therefore represents the leakage date when valuing a stock option.

> The ex-dividend date represents the leakage date when valuing a stock option.

- *Payment date.* The firm mails the dividend checks to the appropriate parties. Here checks are mailed April 2. Barring anything highly unusual, the check is for $0.70 per share, the dividend declared on February 15.

VALUING EUROPEAN STOCK OPTIONS

> In the perfect market world of Black and Scholes, the stock-price should fall by the amount of the per-share dividend on the ex-dividend date.

In the perfect market world of Black-Scholes, where no frictions such as taxes exist, the stock price should fall by the amount of the per-share dividend on the ex-dividend date.[1] To value a European call stock option, therefore, we employ Equation 13.5, where D_t is the dividend

---

[1]With no market imperfections, a simple arbitrage strategy ensures that the share price drop and dividend per share are equivalent. Empirical research, however, has found that the share price decline on the ex-dividend date is on average less than the per-share dividend. Most researchers have attributed this result to the existence of personal income tax payable on dividend income. For a discussion, see E. Elton and M. Gruber (1970) in "Selected References."

per share and t represents the time until the ex-dividend date. The corresponding European put stock-option value follows from put-call parity, as given by Equation 12.27c.

As an illustration, suppose that we wish to value a European call option where $S = \$40$, $X = \$38$, $D_t = \$0.70$, $t = .15$, $T = .25$, $r = .08$, and $\sigma^2 = .15$.[2] Thus, we want to value an option written on a stock exhibiting one ex-dividend date prior to option expiration. Failure to account for this dividend leakage will cause us to overvalue the call stock option, since the effect of the dividend is to reduce the share price.

To begin, let us rewrite Equation 13.5 as below:

$$C^E = S_D N(d_2) - Xe^{-rT}N(d_2 - \sigma\sqrt{T}),$$

where

$$S_D = S - D_t e^{-rt}$$

$$d_2 = \frac{ln(S_D/X) + [r + (\sigma^2/2)]T}{\sigma\sqrt{T}}.$$

In our illustration, $S_D = \$39.31$:

$$S_D = \$40 - .70e^{-.08(.15)} = \$39.31.$$

Of course, S_D represents the current stock price less the present value of the dividend paid. We discount at the risk-free rate of interest since, by assumption, the dividend is known with certainty. This is not an unreasonable assumption given the smooth dividend policies exhibited by most corporations.

Continuing the example, the upper limits of integration d_2 and $d_2 - \sigma\sqrt{T}$ are .3751 and .1815, respectively:

$$d_2 = \frac{ln(39.31/38) + [.08 + (.15/2)](.25)}{\sqrt{.15}\sqrt{.25}} = .3751:$$

$$d_2 - \sigma\sqrt{T} = .3751 - \sqrt{.15}\sqrt{.25} = .1815.$$

Using Exhibit 13.1 and interpolating, we have:

$$N(.3751) = .6461; \ N(.1815) = .5720.$$

Notice that the probability that this call option will expire in-the-money is currently 64.61 percent, reflecting the fact that $S_D/X > 1$. The resulting option value is $4.0926 per stock share, or $409.26 per contract.

$$C^E = 39.31(.6461) - 38e^{-.08(.25)}(.5720) = 4.0926.$$

---

[2]Recall that all of these variables are readily observable except σ^2. Volatility can be estimated using historical data or the implied method discussed in Chapter 13.

The corresponding put value is $2.0301 per stock share, as given by Equation 12.27c:

$$P^E = 4.0926 - 39.31 + 38e^{-.08(.25)} = \$2.0301.$$

The above illustration involved a stock option with one ex-dividend date prior to expiration. For two or more ex-dividend dates prior to option expiration, simply adjust S_D to reflect the present value of all dividend payouts:

$$S_D = S - D_1 e^{-rt_1} - D_2 e^{-rt_2} - \ldots - D_n e^{-rt_n}.$$

Of course, if the underlying stock exhibits no ex-dividend date prior to option expiration, then $S_D = S$ and the original Black-Scholes model holds.

VALUING AMERICAN STOCK OPTIONS

Listed stock options are typically American, allowing for premature exercise. Recall from Chapter 14 that it may be optimal to prematurely exercise American call or put options written on assets exhibiting discrete leakages, such as common stock. The conditions that give rise to optimal early exercise are: (1) the option must be deeply in-the-money; and (2) for calls (puts), the discrete leakage must be large (small).

In Chapter 14 we discussed an exact procedure applicable to the problem of pricing American call stock options. This was the Roll-Geske-Whaley model. Unfortunately, the application of this model is beyond the intended scope of this book.[3] Also, analytic approximations applicable for pricing American put stock options, such as Geske and Johnson's compound-option approach, also discussed in Chapter 14, are beyond the scope of this book. The interested reader is encouraged to review these articles and models directly.

The magnitude of the early-exercise premia associated with American stock options is revealed in Figure 16.2, which summarizes the results of a simulation analysis comparing the model prices of counterpart European and American put stock options. The European prices are obtained from the Black-Scholes model, while the American prices are obtained from the Geske and Johnson analytic approximation. These put options have maturities ranging from one to nine months and are in-the-money, with a stock price of $40 and an exercise price of $45. The cash dividends are $1, and the stock goes ex-dividend in one-half, three and one-half, and six and one-half months. Also, $r = .10$, and $\sigma = .30$.

---

[3]Recall, however, that R. Whaley (1982) reports that the simpler Black (1975) approximation appears to work well for pricing American call stock options. See Chapter 14 for a discussion of Black's procedure.

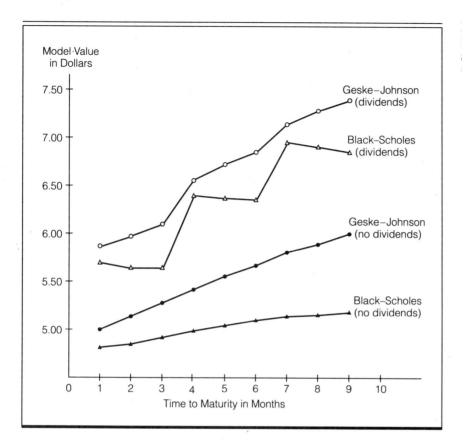

Figure 16.2:
Model Values for American and European Put Stock Options

The top two plots in Figure 16.2 suggest that the early-exercise premium can be substantial for in-the-money American put stock options. Thus, incorporating this premium is likely important for accurately valuing American stock options, particularly those in-the-money. Indeed, using transaction data for four actively traded put stock options, E. Blomeyer and H. Johnson (1988) report that the Geske and Johnson model values are significantly closer to market prices than the Black-Scholes model values. The bottom two plots in Figure 16.2 suggest that the early-exercise premium can also be substantial for in-the-money put options written on nondividend-paying stocks.

HEDGING WITH STOCK OPTIONS

A long stock position can be hedged by writing call stock options or purchasing put options. Short positions in a stock may be hedged by

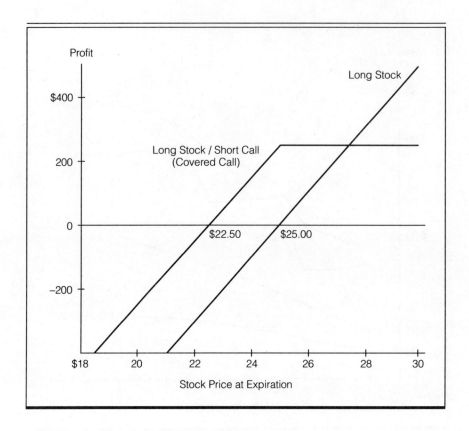

writing put options or purchasing calls. As an illustration, Figure 16.3 presents the profit graphs for a long stock position and a long stock/short call position. A round lot of stock is purchased for $25 per share, and in the covered call strategy the investor writes one call option contract with an exercise price of $25 and six-month maturity. The price of the call is $2.50 per share (by assumption). The profit graphs in Figure 16.3 reflect maintaining the positions until option expiration. As the figure demonstrates, the long stock/short call strategy is less risky than merely purchasing the stock itself. Should the stock price depreciate over the six-month period, the premium received for writing the call option contract ($250) partially offsets the loss on the long stock position. The two positions—long the stock and short the call option— are negatively correlated. The investor gives up significant upside potential to help preserve capital in the event of a stock price decline. The degree of exposure can be managed by altering the exercise price.

Figure 16.4 presents the profit graphs for a long stock position and a long stock/long put position. In this illustration, the protective put strategy entails buying one put contract with an exercise price of $25 and six-month maturity for $2 per share. As the figure demonstrates, the long stock/long put strategy is substantially less risky than the long

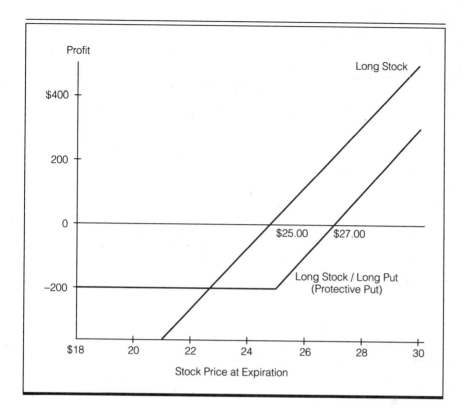

Figure 16.4:
Profit Graphs for a Long
Stock Position and Long
Stock/Long Put Position

stock position. If the stock price declines, the protective put strategy insures a maximum loss of $200. Also, this strategy allows the investor to profit from substantial increases in the stock price. Altering the exercise price changes the degree of risk exposure, with higher-exercise-price puts providing less exposure (but at a greater price). Constructing analogous profit graphs involving short stock positions is left as an end-of-chapter exercise.

SPECULATING WITH STOCK OPTIONS

Stock options can be employed to speculate on subsequent stock price movements. Indeed, a trader who possesses superior information about a particular stock will likely transact in the options market first in order to maximize the returns to the information; the leverage offered by stock options provides a greater profit opportunity for traders wagering on a "sure thing." Speculators can undertake naked option positions, which may be very risky, or they can utilize option combinations such as money spreads and straddles to exploit their stock price forecasts. These different strategies were described in Chapter 15.

Puttable Stock

In 1984 drapery maker Arley Merchandise Corporation undertook an initial public offering of $6 million worth of a new type of security known as *puttable stock*. This security allowed investors to sell their stock back to Arley at the original issue price of $8 per share after two years. Thus, the corporation guaranteed to support a stated floor value (i.e., exercise price) of the stock for the new shareholders.

In 1985 Chris Anderson, managing director at Drexel Burnham Lambert and the security's creator, marketed $85 million of puttable stock for Gearhart Industries. Gearhart sold units consisting of five shares of common stock and five rights to sell these shares back to the issuer for a guaranteed price of $14.68 per share in June 1986, the first put window. The exercise price of the puttable stock rose each year for the next four years at nearly 10 percent per annum, and Gearhart was obligated to honor up to 20 percent of the offering's rights every year. Smith Barney and Prudential Bache have underwritten similar puttable stock offerings for companies such as Conquest Exploration. These offerings are also known as *shareholder-protection rights* or *price-protection rights*.

Since puttable stock contains a built-in put option written by the issuer, the stock already offers investors self-contained protection from downside price risk. The profit graph for such a security should appear like that of a stock/protective put combination. In an analysis of puttable stock, A. Tucker (1990) concludes that this new hybrid security may become popular for companies going public. An initial public offering of puttable stock would convey a more favorable signal of the firm's future investment opportunities than the issuance of plain common stock. This is because the issuance of puttable stock offers a guaranteed floor value for the investor, and thereby imposes a potential cost on the firm's insider-owners should the stock price depreciate. Hence, the issuance of puttable stock may result in less of the share-value dilution associated with most common stock offerings.

As an illustration of a speculative strategy involving stock options, suppose that we construct a bear money spread using the March 120 and 125 calls on IBM stock listed in Exhibit 16.1. Recall that a bear money spread is used to speculate on a price depreciation and is constructed by purchasing a high exercise-price call and simultaneously writing a corresponding but low exercise-price call. Here the proceeds from undertaking a bear money spread are $168.75:

$$\text{Write One IBM March 120 Call: } + \$212.50$$
$$\text{Purchase One IBM March 125 Call: } - \underline{\quad 43.75}$$
$$\text{Total } + \$168.75$$

Figure 16.5 presents the profit graph for the spread at option expiration. The breakeven expiration stock price is $121 11/16 [$120 + 2 1/8 − 7/16]. At any IBM price below this, the bear spread proves profitable. The maximum profit is $168.75, occurring when both options expire out-of-the-money ($S_T \leq \$120$). The maximum loss is $331.25 [$120 − 125 + 2 1/8 − 7/16], occurring whenever $S_T \geq \$125$. Thus, the bear money spread is profitable if the forecast of an IBM stock price depreciation proves correct. Also, the bear money spread exhibits limited downside risk, whereas simply writing the March 120 call does not (see the broken line in Figure 16.5).

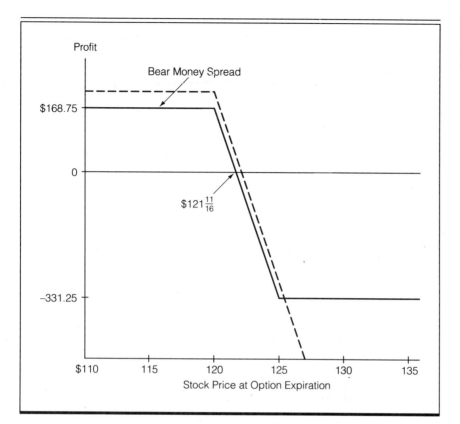

EMPIRICAL EVIDENCE ON STOCK OPTIONS

The year 1973 was a threshold one for options; the CBOE initiated organized stock options trading, and F. Black and M. Scholes published their seminal article on options valuation. R. Merton, also at M.I.T. at the time, published an important paper concerning options pricing as well. Since that time, dozens of empirical studies have been published regarding stock-options valuation and the efficiency of the organized stock-options market. Here we summarize just a handful of the most cited studies.

Galai Study

D. Galai (1977) tested the Black-Scholes model using CBOE stock options traded between April 1973 and November 1973. He constructed hedged portfolios consisting of the underlying stock and an opposite position in the option. When a mispricing signal was observed, under-valued options were bought, and overvalued options were sold at the end of each day. Also, the hedged position was reestablished by trading the underlying stock. Galai found that all excess returns from the trading strategy were completely eliminated after imposing transaction costs of just 1 percent. Spreading strategies also tested yielded similar results. These results led Galai to conclude that the market was efficient and that the Black-Scholes model was fairly accurate for valuing exchange-traded stock options.

Klemkosky and Resnick Study

R. Klemkosky and B. Resnick (1979) tested the efficiency of the CBOE by examining over 600 pairs of corresponding call and put options for violations of put-call parity. The data covered July 1977 through June 1978, a period occurring just after the introduction of put options trading. The call, put, and underlying stock all had to be traded within one minute of each other to ensure price synchronization. Klemkosky and Resnick reported that less than 7 percent of the observed violations were profitable after imposing a minimum $60 transaction cost. As a result, the authors concluded that the CBOE appeared to operate efficiently for the period tested.

MacBeth and Merville Studies

In two studies, J. MacBeth and L. Merville (1979, 1980) tested the accuracy of the Black-Scholes model as applied to actively traded options written on six large corporations. Their data were daily closing prices for the year 1976 for call options on AT&T, Avon, Exxon, IBM, Kodak, and Xerox. Using implied volatility measures, MacBeth and Merville found that the Black-Scholes model exhibited systematic mispricing biases. Specifically, they reported that (1) the model underprices in-the-money options and overprices out-of-the-money options; (2) the degree of underpricing (overpricing) increases with the extent to which the options are in-the-money (out-of-the-money); and (3) the model largely overprices out-of-the-money options exhibiting maturities of less than three months. Also, in their 1980 study MacBeth and Merville found that a model allowing for nonconstant return variance slightly outperformed the Black-Scholes model. This alternative model, known as the *constant-elasticity-of-variance* model, was more general in that it allowed return variance to change with the stock price level; MacBeth and Merville had detected a discernable pattern of higher volatility for lower priced stocks. Together, these results suggested that while the Black-Scholes model was reasonably descriptive of actual market prices, it could be improved.

Bhattacharya Study

M. Bhattacharya (1983) conducted an important test of the efficiency of the CBOE, using transaction data to detect violations of rational pricing

Black-Scholes Pricing Biases

Recall from Chapter 13 that the Black-Scholes model assumes that the underlying stock's price follows a lognormal distribution. Researchers have documented systematic mispricing biases when applying the model to real-world data, implying that this assumption may be violated in actual stock markets.

The figures below show four ways in which the actual stock price distribution may deviate from the assumed lognormal distribution. For instance, in Part A both tails are fatter than that predicted by the lognormal distribution, while in Part D both tails are thinner than predicted. In Parts B and C one tail is fatter and the other is thinner.

R. Jarrow and A. Rudd (1982) describe the resulting Black-Scholes mispricing biases associated with each of the deviations from lognormality presented by the figures. Listed below each figure are these biases. For example, consider a put option that is substantially out-of-the-money. It has positive value only if there is a large decrease in the stock price. The put option's value therefore depends only on the left tail of the distribution. The fatter this left tail is, the more valuable the option is. As a consequence, the Black-Scholes model will tend to underprice this out-of-the-money put option in the situations shown in Parts A and B, and overprice it in C and D.

—— Lognormal Distribution
---- True Distribution

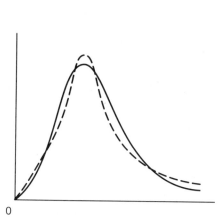

A: Black-Scholes model underprices in-the-money and out-of-the-money calls and puts.

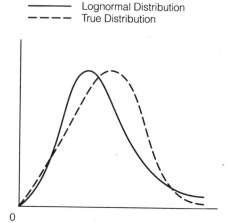

B: Black-Scholes model underprices in-the-money calls and out-of-the-money puts, and overprices out-of-the-money calls and in-the-money puts.

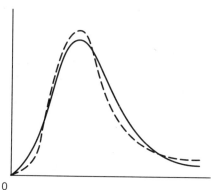

C: Black-Scholes model underprices in-the-money puts and out-of-the-money calls, and overprices in-the-money calls and out-of-the-money puts.

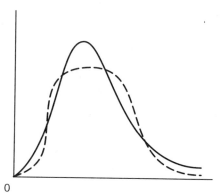

D: Black-Scholes model overprices in-the-money and out-of-the-money calls and puts.

bounds applicable to stock options. His tests closely approximated actual market conditions since they incorporated transaction costs, trading delays, and ensured synchronization of option and underlying stock prices. After testing thousands of trades for 706 option series on fifty-eight underlying stocks for the period of August 1976 through June 1977, Bhattacharya found that the small and relatively infrequent profits due to market violations disappeared when transaction costs were taken into account. Thus, his results supported the efficiency of the CBOE for the sample period.

Rubinstein Study

Also employing synchronous transaction data from the CBOE, M. Rubinstein (1985) examined the pattern of implied standard deviations generated from market prices and the Black-Scholes model. If the model is unbiased, there should be no discernable pattern across S/X ratios or option maturities. However, Rubinstein observed systematic changes in implied volatility patterns, suggesting that the Black-Scholes model is a biased predictor of actual market prices. Still, he found the patterns to be unstable over time and generally inconsistent with several alternative models as well, including the constant-elasticity-of-variance model tested by MacBeth and Merville. Indeed, none of the alternative models were superior to the Black-Scholes model in both time periods tested, August 1976 through October 1977 and November 1977 through August 1978.

Blomeyer and Johnson Study

E. Blomeyer and H. Johnson (1988) conducted an *ex post* performance test comparing the accuracy of an American model to a European model for valuing listed put stock options. Specifically, the Geske and Johnson American put-valuation model discussed in Chapter 14 was compared with the Black-Scholes European put model. Using all transactions occurring during the months of June through August 1978 on the CBOE for Avon, Kodak, GM, and Honeywell, the authors found that both models on average undervalued put options. However, the Geske and Johnson values were significantly closer to market prices than were the Black-Scholes model values. Incorporating the early-exercise premium when valuing traded put options therefore appeared to be important.

SUMMARY

The CBOE began listed call options trading on common stocks in April 1973. In June 1977 the exchange introduced standardized put options on common stocks. Currently, listed stock options are traded on five U.S. exchanges, and annual volume is over 200 million contracts.

Stock options can be used to hedge risk and to speculate on subsequent stock price changes. The majority of stocks upon which listed options are traded exhibit quarterly dividend payments. To price European stock options, therefore, we employ the Black-Scholes model adjusted for discrete leakages. The stock's ex-dividend date represents the leakage date when valuing the option contract. American stock options typically command a greater price than their European counterparts because of their early-exercise feature. It may be optimal to prematurely exercise a put stock option as well as a call option, provided the stock underlying the call exhibits an ex-dividend date prior to option expiration.

A large body of empirical evidence regarding stock options presently exists and, in general, supports market efficiency and the importance of incorporating the early-exercise premium in valuing listed American stock options. Studies also find that the Black-Scholes model systematically misprices listed stock options, but that alternative models do not provide substantial pricing improvement.

Selected References

Beckers, S. "The Constant Elasticity of Variance Model and Its Implications for Option Pricing." *Journal of Finance* 35 (June 1980): 661–673.

Bhattacharya, M. "Empirical Properties of the Black-Scholes Formula Under Ideal Conditions." *Journal of Financial and Quantitative Analysis* 15 (December 1980): 1081–1106.

Bhattacharya, M. "Transaction Data Tests of Efficiency of the CBOE." *Journal of Financial Economics* 12 (1983): 161–186.

Black, F. "Fact and Fantasy in the Use of Options." *Financial Analysts Journal* 31 (July–August 1975): 36–41, 61–72.

Black, F., and M. Scholes. "The Valuation of Option Contracts and a Test of Market Efficiency." *Journal of Finance* 27 (May 1972): 399–418.

Black, F., and M. Scholes. "The Pricing of Options and Corporate Liabilities." *Journal of Political Economy* 81 (May–June 1973): 637–659.

Blomeyer, E. "An Analytic Approximation for the American Put Price for Options on Stocks with Dividends." *Journal of Financial and Quantitative Analysis* 21 (June 1986): 229–233.

Blomeyer, E., and H. Johnson. "An Empirical Examination of the Pricing of American Put Options." *Journal of Financial and Quantitative Analysis* 23 (March 1988): 13–22.

Elton, E., and M. Gruber. "Marginal Stockholder Tax Rates and the Clientele Effect." *Review of Economics and Statistics* 52 (February 1970): 68–74.

Finnerty, J. "The Chicago Board Options Exchange and Market Efficiency." *Journal of Financial and Quantitative Analysis* 13 (March 1978): 29–38.

Galai, D. "Tests of Market Efficiency of the Chicago Board Options Exchange." *Journal of Business* 50 (April 1977): 167–197.

Geske, R. "A Note on an Analytical Valuation Formula for Unprotected American Call Options on Stocks with Known Dividends." *Journal of Financial Economics* 7 (December 1979): 375–380.

Geske, R., and H. Johnson. "The American Put Option Valued Analytically." *Journal of Finance* 39 (December 1984): 1511–1524.

Jarrow, R., and A. Rudd. "Approximate Option Valuation for Arbitrary Stochastic Processes." *Journal of Financial Economics* 10 (November 1982): 347–369.

Klemkosky, R., and B. Resnick. "Put-Call Parity and Market Efficiency." *Journal of Finance* 34 (December 1979): 1141–1155.

MacBeth, J., and L. Merville. "An Empirical Examination of the Black-Scholes Call Option Pricing Model." *Journal of Finance* 34 (December 1979): 1173–1186.

MacBeth, J., and L. Merville. "Tests of the Black-Scholes and Cox Call Option Valuation Models." *Journal of Finance* 35 (May 1980): 285–300.

Merton, R. "The Theory of Rational Options Pricing." *Bell Journal of Economics* 4 (Spring 1973): 141–183.

Roll, R. "An Analytic Valuation Formula for Unprotected American Call Options on Stocks with Known Dividends." *Journal of Financial Economics* 5 (November 1977): 251–258.

Rubinstein, M. "Nonparametric Tests of Alternative Option Pricing Models Using all Reported Trades and Quotes on the 30 Most Active CBOE Option Classes from August 23, 1976 Through August 31, 1978." *Journal of Finance* 40 (June 1985): 455–480.

Tucker, A. "Puttable Stock: Valuation and Use." *Advances in Futures and Options Research* (forthcoming, 1990).

Whaley, R. "On the Valuation of American Call Options on Stocks with Known Dividends." *Journal of Financial Economics* 9 (June 1981): 207–212.

Whaley, R. "Valuation of American Call Options on Dividend Paying Stocks: Empirical Tests." *Journal of Financial Economics* 10 (March 1982): 29–58.

Questions and Problems

1. From Exhibit 16.1, what was the closing price of a Compaq April 70 call contract? What was the price of the corresponding put?

2. Explain the concept of the ex-dividend date. Why does this date represent the leakage date when valuing a stock option?

3. What is the value of a European stock call option where $S = \$20$, $X = \$21$, $D_t = \$0.50$, $t = .20$, $T = .35$, $r = .10$, and $\sigma = .10$?

4. What is the value of a corresponding put option?

5. Suppose you undertake a short position in one round lot of a stock currently worth $25 per share. You are considering buying a call option with three-month maturity and exercise price of $25 for $1.75 per share. Draw the profit graphs for the short stock and short stock/long call positions at option expiration. Use expiration stock prices ranging from $20 to $30.

6. Now suppose that you are considering writing a put option on the stock with three-month maturity and exercise price of $26. The put's price is $2.25 per share. Draw the profit graphs for the short stock and short stock/short put positions at option expiration.

7. Using the Compaq March 65 and 70 calls listed in Exhibit 16.1, create a bull money spread, and draw the profit graph for expiration stock prices ranging from $55 to $85.

8. Using the IBM March 120 options listed in Exhibit 16.1, create a strap, and draw the profit graph for expiration stock prices ranging from $110 to $130.

9. Why do corporations tend to smooth their dividend payments? What implications does such a policy have for dividend prediction and the pricing of stock options?

10. If the stock price decline exceeds the dividend per share on the ex-dividend date, what is the arbitrage opportunity available in the Black-Scholes world? Provide an example of your arbitrage strategy.

11. Describe the conditions under which it may be optimal to prematurely exercise an American stock call option.

12. From Figure 16.2, why do the Geske-Johnson model values tend to be greater than the corresponding Black-Scholes model values?

13. What is the value of a European stock call option where S = $30, X = $28, D_t = $025, t = .10, T = .25, r = .06, and σ = .15?

14. Determine the value of the corresponding put using put-call parity.

Self-Test Problems

ST-1. Determine the value of a European call option where S = $100, X = $97, D_t = $1.75, t = .0833, T = .25, r = .10, and σ = .15.

ST-2. What is the value of a corresponding put option?

ST-3. Using Black's approximation, what would be the value of the above call option if it were American?

ST-4. Using the above European call and put options, create a straddle, and draw the profit graph for expiration stock prices ranging from $85 to $110.

Solutions to Self-Test Problems

ST-1. $S_D = \$100 - 1.75e^{-.10(.0833)} = \$98.26.$

$$d_2 = \frac{ln(98.26/97) + [.10 + (.15^2/2)](.25)}{.15\sqrt{.25}}$$

$$= .5429.$$

$$d_2 - .15\sqrt{.25} = .4679.$$

$$N(.5429) = .7063; N(.4679) = .6800.$$
$$C^E = 98.26(.7063) - 97e^{-.10(.25)}(.6800)$$
$$= \$5.07.$$

ST-2. $P^E = 5.07 - 98.26 + 97e^{-.10(.25)} = \$1.42.$

ST-3. $d_1 = \dfrac{ln(100/97) + [.10 + (.15^2/2)](.0833)}{.15\sqrt{.0833}}$
$$= .9176.$$
$$d_1 - .15\sqrt{.0833} = .8743.$$
$$N(.9176) = .8205; N(.8743) = .8089.$$
$$C^E(t = .0833) = 100(.8205) - 97e^{-.10(.0833)}(.8089)$$
$$= \$4.24.$$
$$C^E = MAX[\$4.24, \$5.07] = \$5.07.$$

ST-4.
Put Purchase:	$142.00
Call Purchase:	507.00
Total	$649.00

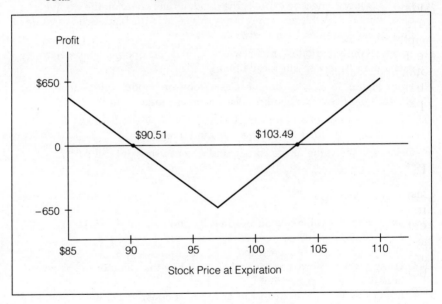

17

CURRENCY OPTIONS

Beginning in December 1982, the Philadelphia Exchange (PHLX) began trading American options on British pounds. Since that time the currency-options market has exhibited tremendous growth. In this chapter we analyze currency options, beginning with a description of the market, followed by pricing issues. We examine how currency options can be used to hedge exchange exposure. A discussion of the interbank currency options market also is provided, along with other topics.

LISTED CURRENCY-OPTIONS MARKET

Presently, the PHLX offers American options trading on seven foreign currencies: the Australian dollar (AD), the British pound (BP), the Deutsche mark (DM), the French franc (FF), the Japanese yen (JY), and the Swiss franc (SF). The PHLX also provides side-by-side trading of European options on these seven currencies ever since it took over the CBOE's currency-option operations on August 27, 1987. Prior to this date the CBOE traded European currency options, but volume and open interest were comparatively low. Over the 487 days during which European currency options were traded on the CBOE, 825,870 contracts were executed. This compares with 22,566,852 American contracts traded on the PHLX during this same period. The PHLX also trades options on the European Currency Unit (ECU), which is a weighted-average index of exchange rates for the member nations that comprise the European Economic Community. However, trading volume has been very low for ECU options.

The PHLX began the trading of American currency options in December 1982, when listed options on the BP were first offered. By February 1983, the PHLX was trading options on the BP, CD, DM, JY, and SF.

Exhibit 17.1:

Contract Specifications for PHLX-Traded Currency Options

Currency	Symbols[a]	Exercise-Price Intervals	Underlying Units	Premium Quotations
Australian Dollar	CAD XAD	$0.0100	50,000	Cents per unit
British Pound	CBP XBP	$0.0250	31,250	Cents per unit
Canadian Dollar	CCD XCD	$0.0100	50,000	Cents per unit
Deutsche Mark	CDM XDM	$0.0100	62,500	Cents per unit
French Franc	CFF XFF	$0.0050	125,000	Tenths of a cent per unit
Japanese Yen	CJY XJY	$0.0001	6,250,000	Hundredths of a cent per unit
Swiss Franc	CSF XSF	$0.0100	62,500	Cents per unit
ECU	ECU	$0.0200	62,500	Cents per unit

Note: For all contracts: (1) expiration months are March, June, September, and December, plus two additional near-term months; (2) the expiration date is the Saturday before the third Wednesday of the expiration month; (3) the expiration settlement date is the third Wednesday of the month; (4) the margin for an uncovered writer is the option premium plus 4 percent of the underlying contract value less the out-of-the-money amount if any, to a minimum of the option premium plus 3/4 percent of the underlying contract value, which equals the spot price times the number of units per contract; (5) the position limit is 50,000 contracts; (6) the delivery method requires the call buyer (seller) to deliver dollars (foreign currency) to an OCC domestic (foreign) bank account; the opposite is the case for puts.
[a]C = European options, X = American options. Only American ECU options are traded.

Exhibit 17.1 presents the contract specifications for the seven individual currency options now traded on the PHLX. All are cleared and guaranteed by the Options Clearing Corporation (OCC). Also, if an option is exercised, then traders must deposit currency to OCC bank accounts.

The volume of listed currency options trading has grown tremendously since the inception of trading, as Figure 17.1 shows. For the period of 1983 through 1988, annual volume has increased more than twenty-five-fold. The most traded contracts are those on the DM and JY, accounting for approximately 60 percent of all trading volume, as evidenced by Figure 17.2. On one recent record-setting day (July 15, 1987), the PHLX traded nearly 114,000 contracts, representing over $4.5 billion in underlying currency value. JY put options totaled 65,216 on this day alone, when the U.S. trade deficit figures were announced and the July options were one day away from expiration.

Growth in currency options trading is also exemplified by the recent advent of evening and early-morning trading sessions. On September 16, 1987, the PHLX initiated an evening trading session (6:00 to 10:00 P.M., EST) in order to accommodate market participants in Asia-Pacific time zones. On January 20, 1989, the PHLX extended its morning trading session, pushing the opening time back to 4:30 A.M., EST, in order to accommodate market participants in West European time zones. With these extended sessions, the PHLX now trades currency options fourteen

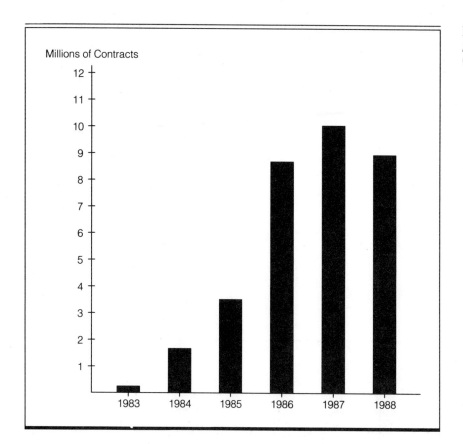

Figure 17.1:
Annual Trading Volume for
Currency Options

hours each trading day. Figure 17.3 (page 393) shows evening-session volume as a percentage of total volume for a recent time period.

Price Quotes

Exhibit 17.2 (page 394) illustrates closing price quotations for PHLX-traded currency options for trading on March 1, 1989. Also reported are the closing interbank spot exchange rates as well as daily trading volume and open interest. For example, the closing (2:30 P.M., EST) interbank $/£ spot rate was $1.7229/£1. Total volume was 51,104 contracts, and open interest on March 1 was 680,191 contracts.

To understand the exhibit, consider the first price entry for Australian dollars: 1.10. This means that the last traded American put option on the AD, with exercise price $0.77/AD1 and June expiration, was 1.10 cents per AD ($0.011/AD1). Since there are AD50,000 per contract, this option contract had a closing price of $550 ($0.011 × 50,000). Since currency options on the PHLX expire on the Saturday before the third Wednesday

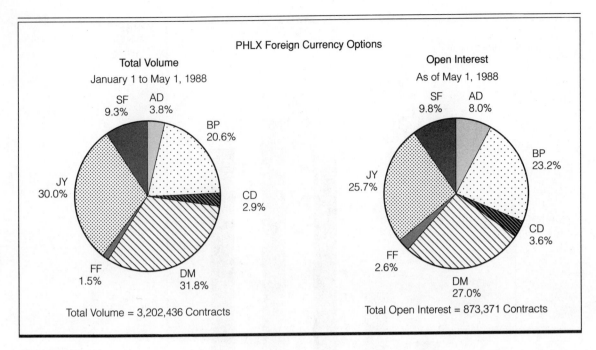

Figure 17.2:
Relative Currency Option Volume and Open Interest

of the contract month, this option expired on June 17, 1989. The other prices reported in Exhibit 17.2 should be similarly interpreted.

EUROPEAN CURRENCY CALL OPTIONS PRICING

Recall from Chapter 11 that currency options represent a type of continuous-leakage option. Here the riskless hedged portfolio underlying the Black and Scholes model is formed by taking a long position in the underlying currency and a short position in the call option. This currency can be used to purchase interest-bearing foreign assets exhibiting the same maturity as the currency option. In order to maintain the risk-free nature of the hedged portfolio, however, these interest-bearing foreign assets must be riskless. Thus, the option holder is assumed to earn the foreign risk-free rate of interest over the option's life. This risk-free rate is assumed to be constant, and is denoted by r_f.

Given that the underlying currency produces a constant continuous leakage, we can use Equation 13.7b to value European currency call options. Here δ is replaced by r_f, the foreign riskless rate of interest:

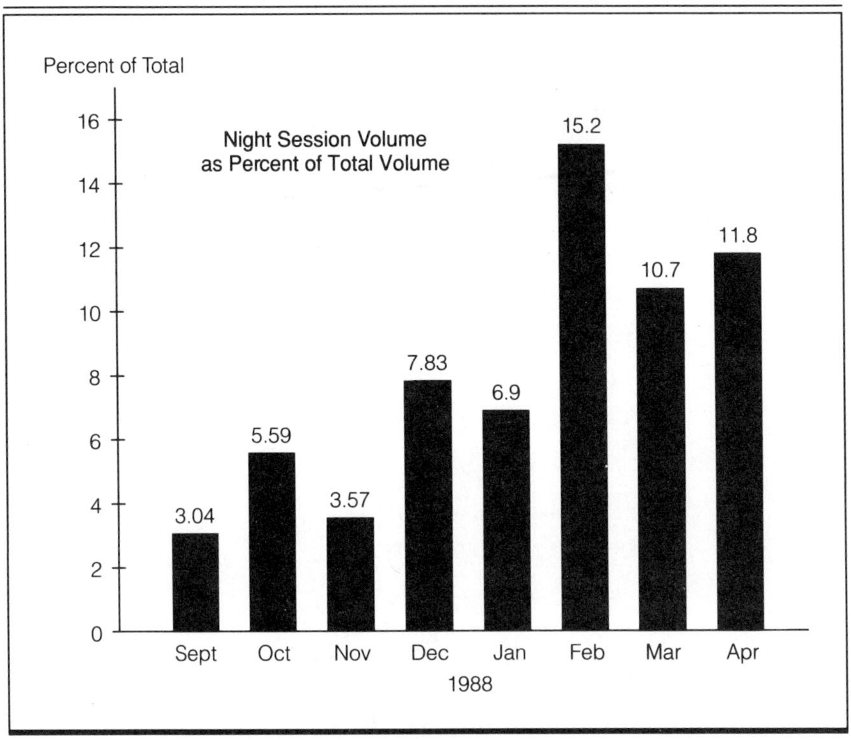

Figure 17.3:
Currency Option
Evening-Session Volume

Percent of Total

Night Session Volume
as Percent of Total Volume

1988

(17.1)
$$C^E = e^{-r_f T}SN(d) - e^{-rT}XN(d - \sigma\sqrt{T}),$$

where

$$d = \{[ln(S/X) + (r - r_f + (\sigma^2/2))T]/\sigma\sqrt{T}\},$$

S = the spot exchange rate,

X = the exercise price,

r = the U.S. riskless rate of interest,

r_f = the foreign riskless rate of interest,

σ = the instantaneous variance of the returns on holding the foreign currency,

T = the option's maturity expressed as a fraction of a year, and

$N(\cdot)$ = the standard normal cumulative distribution function.

Equation 17.1 yields the value of a European currency call option, denoted C^E, provided that the assumptions underlying the Black-Scholes model are reasonably descriptive of actual market conditions.

Exhibit 17.2:
Price Quotes for PHLX Currency Options

OPTIONS
PHILADELPHIA EXCHANGE

Option & Underlying	Strike Price	Calls—Last			Puts—Last		
		Mar	Apr	Jun	Mar	Apr	Jun
50,000 Australian Dollars-cents per unit.							
ADollr	...77	r	r	r	r	r	1.10
80.23	...78	r	r	r	r	0.82	r
80.23	...79	r	r	r	0.31	r	r
80.23	..80	r	1.57	r	0.69	1.70	2.65
80.23	...81	0.36	r	r	r	r	r
80.23	...82	0.23	r	1.00	1.96	r	r
80.23	...84	0.03	0.23	r	r	r	r
80.23	...85	r	r	r	4.84	r	r
80.23	...87	r	r	r	6.84	r	r
50,000 Australian Dollars-European Style.							
80.23	...80	r	r	r	r	1.52	r
80.23	...82	r	r	r	r	2.82	r
31,250 British Pounds-cents per unit.							
BPound	167½	r	r	r	0.15	0.95	r
172.29	.170	r	3.75	r	0.44	r	3.10
172.29	172½	1.05	r	3.35	1.34	3.10	4.75
172.29	.175	0.33	1.25	r	3.10	4.50	5.85
172.29	177½	0.13	0.65	1.83	5.40	r	r
172.29	182½	r	0.30	r	r	r	r
31,250 British Pounds-European Style.							
172.29	172½	r	r	3.10	r	r	r
50,000 Canadian Dollars-cents per unit.							
CDollr	.81½	r	r	r	r	r	0.44
83.53	...83	r	r	r	0.16	0.53	r
83.53	.83½	0.18	r	r	r	0.64	r
83.53	...84	0.08	0.36	r	r	1.10	r
83.53	.84½	0.04	r	0.46	r	r	r
83.53	...85	0.01	0.16	r	r	1.68	r
62,500 West German Marks-cents per unit.							
DMark	.. 50	r	r	r	r	r	0.06
54.41	...52	r	r	r	r	r	0.30
54.41	...53	r	r	r	0.02	0.22	r
54.41	...54	0.64	1.09	1.72	0.18	0.50	0.89
54.41	...55	0.15	0.63	1.20	0.68	1.07	r
54.41	...56	0.03	0.30	0.78	r	r	r
54.41	...57	0.01	0.13	r	r	r	r
54.41	...58	r	r	0.32	r	r	r
250,000 French Francs-10ths of a cent per unit.							
FFranc	..16	1.02	2.30	r	r	2.30	r
6,250,000 Japanese Yen-100ths of a cent per unit.							
JYen	...74	r	r	r	r	r	0.18
77.99	...76	r	r	r	r	0.22	r
77.99	...77	r	r	r	0.13	0.41	0.70
77.99	...78	0.51	r	r	0.42	0.75	r
77.99	...79	0.14	0.78	r	1.00	1.27	r
77.99	...80	0.04	0.42	r	r	r	2.11
77.99	...81	0.02	0.23	r	2.98	r	r
77.99	...83	r	0.06	r	r	r	r
62,500 Swiss Francs-cents per unit.							
SFranc	..60	r	r	r	r	r	0.21
63.65	...61	r	r	r	0.02	r	r
63.65	...63	0.90	r	2.30	0.16	0.60	r
63.65	...64	0.33	0.96	r	0.54	0.96	1.38
63.65	...65	0.08	r	1.26	r	r	r
63.65	...68	r	r	0.42	4.27	r	r
63.65	...69	r	r	0.27	r	r	r
63.65	...70	r	r	0.16	r	r	r
62,500 Swiss Francs-European Style.							
63.65	...63	0.94	r	r	r	r	r
63.65	...64	0.37	r	r	0.56	r	r

Total call vol.	27,295	Call open int.	326,410
Total put vol.	23,809	Put open int.	353,781

r—Not traded. s—No option offered.
Last is premium (purchase price).

Input Parameters

The parameters required by Pricing Equation 17.1 are S, X, T, r, r_f, and σ. Of course, S, X, T, r, and r_f are readily observable, while σ must be estimated. Recall from Chapter 13 that σ can be estimated by two methods: (1) using historical data, or (2) inputing σ from a similar option with the same maturity but different exercise price. Exhibit 17.3 provides

Currency	Standard Deviation	Interest Rate
British Pound	0.1153	9.57%
Deutsche Mark	0.1109	3.77
Japanese Yen	0.1163	3.50
Swiss Franc	0.1449	1.71
U.S. Dollar	N.A.	7.27

Exhibit 17.3:
Historical σ, r, and r_f Parameters

historically estimated σ parameters for the four major currencies upon which most options are traded: BP, DM, JY, and SF. These estimates are based on daily currency returns for the calendar year 1988. Recall that each σ represents an annualized measure of volatility. Also reported in Exhibit 17.3 are average annual risk-free interest rates for 1988.

An Illustration Of European Call Currency Options Pricing

To illustrate Pricing Equation 17.1, suppose we value the European British pound call option, with exercise price of \$1.7250/£1 and June expiration, reported in Exhibit 17.2. This option had a closing price of \$0.031/£1, with 108 days until expiration (March 1 to June 17, 1989). For S we can use the closing exchange rate, \$1.7229, reported in Exhibit 17.2. We will use the historical σ, r, and r_f measures given in Exhibit 17.3. Thus, we have

$$S = \$1.7229$$
$$X = \$1.7250$$
$$T = 0.2959 (= 108/365)$$
$$\sigma = 0.1153$$
$$r = 0.0727$$
$$r_f = 0.0957.$$

To price this option, we first compute the upper limits of integration:

$$d = \frac{ln(1.7229/1.7250) + (.0727 - .0957) + (.1153^2/2))(.2959)}{(0.1153)(.2959)^{1/2}}$$

$$= -.0966;$$

$$d - \sigma\sqrt{T} = -.0966 - (0.1153)(.2959)^{1/2} = -.1593.$$

Notice that these limits are slightly negative since this option is slightly out-of-the-money.

Next we must compute the probability terms. Recall that we can employ Exhibit 13.1 to compute these probabilities. They are $N(-.0966) = .4616$ and $N(-.1593) = .4367$. Notice that the probability that this option will expire in-the-money is currently .4616. It is less than 50 percent, since the option is currently out-of-the-money. Given these terms, its value is

$$C^E = e^{-.0957(.2959)}1.7229(.4616) -$$
$$e^{-.0727(.2959)}1.7250(.4367) = \$0.036/£1.$$

Since there are 31,250 pounds per contract, this contract has a model price of $1,125 ($0.036 × 31,250).

Pricing Error The difference between the model and market prices is $.005 ($.036 − $.031). This represents an error of about 16 percent, which indicates that the model price is surprisingly accurate given the crudeness of the input parameters. Other sources of error (other than model misspecification) include

- *Stale volatility and interest rate estimates.* Recall that these historical estimates were based on 1988 data, whereas the option trade occurred in March 1989. A trader will use more current data when generating prices.
- *Non-synchronous exchange rates and reported market prices.* Error may have been introduced if the option trade occurred prior to the 2:30 P.M., reported exchange rate. For instance, if the trade actually occurred at 2:00 P.M., when the rate of exchange was, say, $1.7215, then the lower reported market price simply reflects a lower exchange rate at the true time of trade.

PRICING EUROPEAN CURRENCY PUT OPTIONS

Recall that Equation 12.27d represents put-call parity for European options where the underlying asset exhibits a constant continuous leakage, δ. This parity condition follows from arbitrage restrictions. Replacing δ by r_f in Equation 12.27d yields the put-call parity model for European currency options:

(17.2) $$P^E = C^E + Xe^{-rT} - Se^{-r_fT},$$

where P^E is the value of the corresponding European put. In the above example involving the British pound call option, the value of the corresponding put option would be $0.049/£1:

$$P^E = \$0.036 + (1.7250)e^{-.0727(.2959)} - (1.7229)e^{-.0957(.2959)}$$
$$= \$0.049/£1.$$

Here the corresponding put option exhibits a greater price ($0.049 > $0.036) since the put is relatively in-the-money ($X > S$, or $1.7250 > $1.7229).

Alternatively, the price of the put option could have been obtained directly by the following formula:

(17.3) $P^E = e^{-rT}X[1 - N(d - \sigma\sqrt{T})] - e^{-r_fT}S[1 - N(d)].$

To verify the equivalence of Equations 17.2 and 17.3, simply compute P^E using 17.3:

$$P^E = e^{-.0727(.2959)}1.7250(1 - .4367) - e^{-.0957(.2959)}1.7229(1 - .4616)$$
$$= \$0.049/\pounds1.$$

VALUING AMERICAN CURRENCY OPTIONS

Under certain conditions it may be optimal to prematurely exercise a currency option. Thus, American currency options, which allow such early exercise, ought to command some premium over their corresponding European counterparts. Suppose that we observe a deeply in-the-money call option such that the probability terms $N(\cdot)$ approach 1. Then the value of the currency call option approaches $Se^{-r_fT} - Xe^{-rT}$. You can verify this using Equation 17.1. Notice that this value, $Se^{-r_fT} - Xe^{-rT}$, can be less than the option's exercisable proceeds, $S - X$, if $r_f > r$. In other words, it may be in the option buyer's best interest to prematurely exercise a deeply in-the-money call option written on a discount currency. We can say that there exists a critical exchange rate above which the option is worth more dead than alive.

The opposite is true for puts. That is, a deeply in-the-money put written on a premium currency ($r_f < r$) may be exercised prematurely. Here $N(\cdot)$ approach zero, so the put's value approaches $e^{-rT}X - e^{-r_fT}S$; this value can be less than $X - S$ if $r_f < r$. We say that there exists a critical exchange rate below which the put option is worth more dead than alive.

Exhibit 17.4 illustrates the price differences between corresponding American and European currency call options resulting from a simulation analysis involving Equation 17.1 and a counterpart American model.[1] The purpose of this exhibit is to give you a feel for the magnitudes of the early-exercise premia for representative currency call options. The exhibit reveals that the premia increase with S/X, T, σ, and r_f. The largest premium is \$0.00314, which represents about 8.5 percent of the price of the European option. Exhibit 17.4 reveals that American currency options command an early-exercise premium.

An example of this can be seen in Exhibit 17.2. Recall the European British pound call option with exercise price of \$1.7250 and June 1989 expiration. This option had a closing price of \$0.0310/£1. In Exhibit 17.2,

---

[1]The American model is an adaptation of the Barone-Adesi and Whaley (1987) model and is described in Appendix 17.A. The BOPM could also be used to price American currency options.

Exhibit 17.4:
Early-Exercise Premia for American Currency Call Options

$r - r_f$	$C^A - C^E$	S	$C^A - C^E$
.04	0.000	.54	0.314
.02	0.000	.50	0.033
−.02	0.033	.46	0.001

T	$C_A - C_E$	σ	$C^A - C^E$
30	0.007	.10	0.033
120	0.033	.20	0.038
210	0.066	.30	0.046

Note: For each section, the base values of the parameters are S = $0.50, X = $0.50, T = 120 days, σ = .10, r = .08, and r_f = .10. The European option prices, C^E, are given by Equation 17.1, while the American option prices, C^A, are given by the model described in Appendix 17.A. All differences in model prices are reported in U.S. cents per unit of foreign exchange.

the closing price of a corresponding American British pound call option also is reported: $0.0335/£1. Hence, assuming these two options traded at about the same clock time, the early-exercise premium is $0.0025 ($0.0335 − $0.0310), which represents about 8.1 percent of the European option's value ($0.0025/$0.0310).

HEDGING WITH CURRENCY OPTIONS

Although currency options can be used to speculate on exchange rate movements, their primary economic purpose is to help safeguard overseas investors and multinational corporations from exchange rate risk. They accomplish this by introducing negative correlation. An illustration involving currency puts follows.

Using Currency Puts to Protect an Overseas Bid[2]

Suppose a U.S. manufacturer wishes to bid on a contract allowing it to export some product to a Swiss retailer. The firm must bid in Swiss francs. It is now March, and the contract will be awarded in June. The firm has calculated that it will require $1,000,000 in revenue, after the francs are repatriated to dollars, in order to meet its profit goal.

---

[2]The hedging strategy provided in this section is based on an illustration found in G. Feiger and B. Jacquillat, "Currency Option Bonds, Puts and Calls on Spot Exchange, and the Hedging of Contingent Foreign Earnings," *Journal of Finance* 5 (December 1979): 1129–1139.

Since December 1982 the Philadelphia Exchange (PHLX) has provided American options trading on foreign exchange. Since August 1987, it also has provided European options trading on foreign exchange. The Chicago Board Options Exchange (CBOE) offered European currency option trading from September 1985 through early August 1987. Together these two markets provide the only contemporaneous and sustained trading of both American and European options on the same underlying instrument in the history of U.S. security markets.

A. Tucker (1989) (see "Selected References") exploited this situation to quantify what the market determines to be the early-exercise premia for corresponding American currency options. He analyzed over 48,000 pairs of American and European options exhibiting the same underlying currency, maturity, and exercise price. On average, these pairs traded less than ten minutes apart. By comparing the price differences for them, Tucker was able to quantify the early-exercise premia paid by currency option buyers.

Tucker found that the market assigns a significant premium to American currency options. For calls, the average premium is 1.62 percent of the European option's value, while for puts it is 1.54 percent. The average percentage premium for each currency are as follows:

Currency	Calls	Puts
British Pound	2.90%	0.43%
Canadian Dollar	2.88	0.59
Deutsche Mark	1.94	1.60
Japanese Yen	0.77	1.26
Swiss Franc	1.01	2.51

Since the company will submit a bid in a foreign currency, it is exposed to fluctuations in exchange rates before knowing whether its bid has been accepted. It does not want to hedge this exposure using currency futures since, if its bid is rejected, it faces exchange rate losses that will not be offset (because no business follows). Consequently, the firm may employ currency options to hedge its exposure. Such options are effective immunization tools when international trade agreements are contingent, as in the submission of contract bids in a foreign currency. Here the U.S. firm can use different SF put options to create different bids and to protect its revenue target against adverse currency movements.

In March, suppose the following price quotes exist (see Exhibit 17.2, in fact):

Exercise Prices	Prices of June SF Puts
$0.60/SF1	$.0021/SF1
$0.64/SF1	$.0138/SF1

Various bids can be determined by subtracting the option price from the exercise price and then dividing this rate into the target revenue figure, $1,000,000. This results in the bid for the project. The number of option contracts required to hedge the bid is obtained by dividing the bid by the

A	B	C	D	E	F
Exercise Price	Option Price	Effective Exchange Rate [A − B]	Rounded Projected Bid in Francs [$1,000,000/C]	Number of Contracts [D/62,500]	Premium [B × E × 62,500]
$0.60	$0.0021	$0.5979	SF1,672,520	27	$ 3,543.75
$0.64	$0.0138	$0.6262	SF1,596,934	26	$22,425.00

Exhibit 17.5:
Contract Bids

number of currency units per option contract (62,500). The total cost of hedging is determined by multiplying the option price (per SF) by the value of the bid. Exhibit 17.5 presents the bids that are associated with the two exercise prices: SF1,672,520 and SF1,596,934.

In Exhibit 17.5, note that the U.S. firm's bid is inversely related to the exercise price. That is, the higher bid (SF1,672,520) corresponds to the lower exercise-price option ($X = \$0.60$). However, the lower bid results in the higher total cost of hedging ($22,425). These relations reveal the truly insurance-like nature of option contracts. The lower bid results in a higher total premium cost because it costs more to obtain the higher effective exchange rate; hence the more insurance, the higher the premium.

Exhibit 17.6 presents the revenue outcomes for two assumed spot rates at option expiration: $0.59/SF1 and $0.65/SF1. Buying the $0.64 exercise-price put options represents the more conservative strategy. The U.S. firm buys more insurance and can make a lower bid. As a result, it is more likely to win the contract from the Swiss retailer. If the U.S. firm gets the contract, it meets its $1,000,000 revenue target, regardless of the spot rate at expiration. This is attributable to the fact that the options introduce negative correlation, providing an insurable floor against exchange exposure. Here if the dollar appreciates ($0.59/SF1), the firm receives fewer repatriated dollars; however, the firm is compensated by the profit on the option contracts ($58,825). Thus the two positions—long on Swiss francs and long on put options—are negatively correlated. If the bid is rejected, then the firm's revenue is simply the gain or loss on the puts: $58,825.00 or −$22,425.00. Again, it is important to recognize that the potential loss is limited here, and is more limited than if the U.S. firm engaged in currency futures trading.

The more aggressive strategy for the U.S. firm is to buy the $0.60 exercise-price puts. The bid here is higher and thus more likely to be rejected. However, a successful bid combined with a dollar depreciation can result in more revenue ($1,083,594.25). Ultimately, the choice of option depends on how aggressively the U.S. firm pursues the contract, as well as its forecast of the $/SF exchange rate.

	1	2	3	4	5
					Revenue
	Assumed Future Spot Rates	Final Option Values	Initial Option Values	Bid Rejected [2 − 3]	Accepted Bid [Bid × (1) + (2) − (3)]
Conservative Strategy:					
Buy $0.64 Puts	(A) $0.59	$81,250[a]	$22,425.00	$58,825.00	$1,001,016.06
Bid SF1,596,934	(B) $0.65	0		($22,425.00)	$1,015,582.10
Premium = $22,425					
Aggressive Strategy:					
Buy $0.60 Puts	(A) $0.59	$16,875[b]	$3,543.75	$13,331.25	$1,000,118.05
Bid SF1,672,520	(B) $0.65	0		($3,543.75)	$1,083,594.25
Premium = $3,543.75					

[a]($0.64 − 0.59) × 62,500 × 26.
[b]($0.60 − 0.59) × 62,500 × 27.

Exhibit 17.6:
Revenue Outcomes

Future versus Options The above example utilizing SF put options demonstrates an important distinction between futures contracts and options contracts. Namely, futures represent contractual claims, whereas options represent contingent claims that do not have to be exercised. Specifically, suppose that the U.S. firm (naively) entered into a futures contract, with June expiration, to sell francs. If the firm lost the bid, and the dollar depreciated greatly, then the firm would lose money on its short futures position. Since the firm does not receive francs, it effectively holds a naked futures position. And since, in theory, the franc could appreciate without bound, the firm's potential losses are unlimited. The use of put options, however, insures a limited downside loss for the firm. For instance, if the aggressive strategy were undertaken and the firm's bid rejected, its losses would be at most $3,543.75, the initial premium.

Figure 17.4 portrays the different revenue distributions from using option and futures contracts here. The use of options effectively truncates the distribution such that losses are limited, whereas the use of futures does not. Stated simply, options represent the superior hedging vehicle in this case, since the trade agreement itself is contingent on the resolution of the bidding process.

SPECULATING WITH CURRENCY OPTIONS

To complement the example just provided of using currency options to hedge, we now offer a currency option strategy that is speculative in

Figure 17.4:
Revenue Distributions for Naked Futures and Options Positions

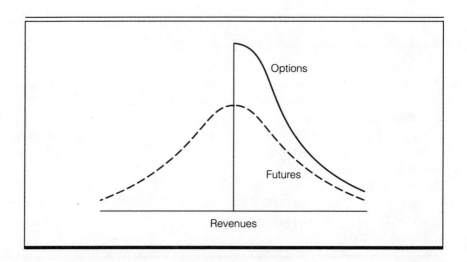

nature—specifically, a butterfly spread involving deutsche mark options. Obviously, many more speculation and hedging strategies could be discussed.

A Butterfly Spread with Mark Options

Exhibit 17.2 reports closing prices for American mark call options, with April expiration, for various exercise prices. For instance, for exercise prices $0.54, $0.55 and $0.56, the April calls prices are $1.09, $0.63, and $0.30, respectively. The closing spot rate is $0.5441. We can use these three options to construct a butterfly spread. Recall from Chapter 15 that a butterfly spread is constructed by combining call options written on the same asset and with the same expiration, but with three different exercise prices. A speculator might employ a butterfly spread if he feels that the mark's volatility is less than that implied by current option prices.

Suppose the speculator creates the following butterfly spread:

	Price
Purchase 1 DM April Call, X = $0.54	$-$0.0109
Sell 2 DM April Calls, X = $0.55	$+$0.0063 \times 2
Purchase 1 DM April Call, X = $0.56	$-$0.0030
	$-$0.0013

The total cost of this combination is $0.0013/DM1.

Figure 17.5 displays the value of this spread at option expiration under various spot exchange rates. If the spot rate is less than $0.54 at expiration, then none of the calls are exercised. The value of the spread is zero, and the speculator loses $0.0013/DM1. At spot rates greater than $0.56, the value of the spread is also zero; the gains from the two long

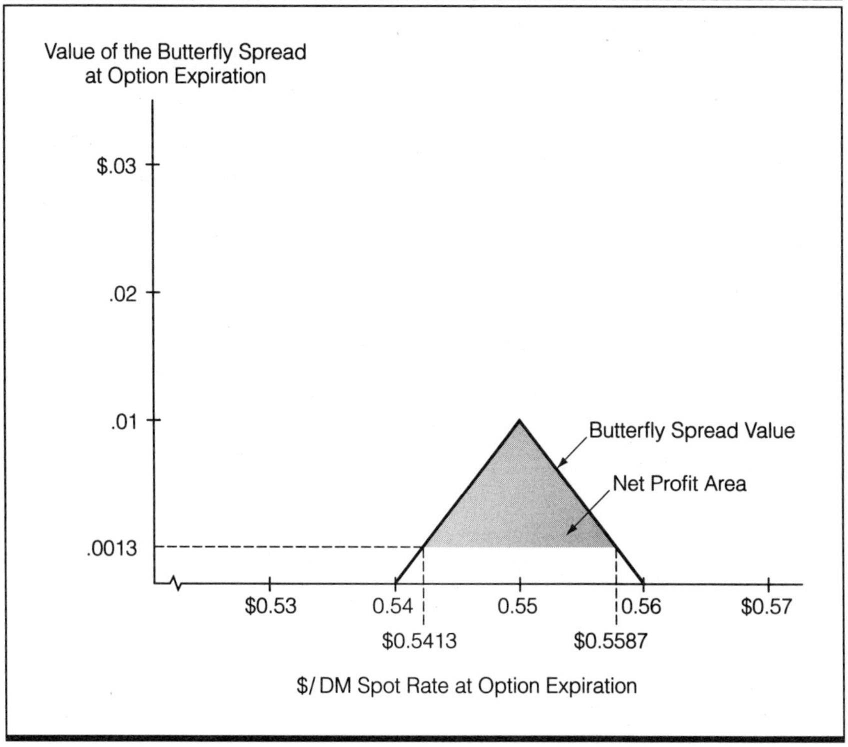

Figure 17.5:
Butterfly Spread for Mark Options

Value of the Butterfly Spread at Option Expiration

Butterfly Spread Value

Net Profit Area

$/ DM Spot Rate at Option Expiration

option positions are offset by the losses experienced on the two written options. The butterfly spread exhibits positive value at expiration for spot rates between $0.54 and $0.56, with the maximum spread value of $0.01 occurring at $0.55/DM1.

The speculator's net profit (ignoring transaction costs and taxes) from the spread is positive only when the resulting spot rate at expiration lies between $0.5413 and $0.5587. Thus, the speculator profits only if the future spot rate remains near the current spot rate of $0.5441 —in other words, if the $/DM exchange rate remains very stable until option expiration.

INTERBANK CURRENCY-OPTIONS MARKET

A sizable interbank market for European currency options presently exists, centered in London and New York. It exhibits open interest yearly tenfold that of PHLX-listed currency options. Over-the-counter (OTC) options traded on the interbank market differ substantially from listed currency options, in that they are:

■ Much larger, typically involving $1,000,000 or more of foreign currency.

- European, whereas most listed-options trading involves American currency options.
- Available for a wider variety of foreign currencies, including many South American currencies.
- Tailored to the specific needs of the client; and consequently, there is little secondary trading in them.

Commercial banks, investment banks, and brokerages write OTC options for clients, often multinational firms. To offset their exposure, these banks and brokerages often trade currency options listed on the PHLX. Also, many banks rely on currency option brokers, like Bierbaum-Martin and Exco International, to help manage exposure.

Some Unique OTC Currency Options

A niche in the market has been carved out by interbank currency-option traders, who create tailor-made (and often complex) options by trading standardized options and repackaging them to the client's specifications. For example, Citibank and Salomon Brothers both offer a popular instrument known as a *range-forward* that is a combination of a purchased currency put and a written currency call such that a zero price results at the contract inception. Here the buyer (an exporter holding foreign currency) and the bank agree on two exchange rates, S_1 and S_2, at inception. At contract maturity, the bank will purchase the currency at S_1 if the current spot rate is less than S_1, or at S_2 if the spot rate is greater than S_2. At any rate between S_1 and S_2, the currency is purchased at the current spot rate. From a simple application of put-call parity, S_1 and S_2 can be set such that no money changes hands at contract inception.

A **range-forward** contract is a combination of a purchased currency put and a written currency call such that a zero price results at the contract inception.

Another example of a unique OTC option is the *bounded-payoff put*, which is a currency put option where the payoff is limited. Figure 17.6 displays its contingency graph. If at maturity the spot rate lies between the exercise price X and the limit B, the payoff is that of a regular put $(X - S)$. If the spot rate lies below B, however, the payoff is bounded at $X - B$. Clearly, this option should command a lower price than a corresponding ordinary put. The bounded-payoff put may be attractive to a corporate treasurer who anticipates a modest decline in the exchange rate.

Other unique options are offered by banks and brokerages, including currency cylinder options, proportional-coverage puts, and the like. Each of these unique instruments may be thought of as financially engineered, replicable by combinations of instruments traded on organized markets.

A **bounded-payoff put** is a currency put option where the payoff is limited to less than the exercise price.

FUTURES-STYLE OPTIONS

American futures-style options on foreign exchange are currently traded on the London International Financial Futures Exchange (LIFFE). These options are unique in that both the option buyer and seller post margin representing a small fraction of the option's value, and each trading day the loser must post additional capital. In other words, the traders engage in a type of futures contract that is written on the currency option. Each day the contract is marked-to-the-market. Cash flows occur daily, whereas the buyer of an ordinary currency option has no further cash flow until the option is sold or exercised. Unlike a mere futures contract, however, the buyer of an American futures-style option can exercise the option. Thus, this unique instrument is somewhat like an ordinary currency option and somewhat like a futures contract. It conveys the same rights and obligations as an ordinary currency option, but exhibits cash flows like a futures contract. The daily resettlement procedure allows players to engage in currency option trading while posting only a fraction of the contract's value.

American futures-style currency options represent a type of futures contract that is written on a currency option.

EMPIRICAL EVIDENCE ON CURRENCY OPTIONS

As the market and popularity of currency options expand, so, too, does the body of empirical evidence concerning these derivative securities. Most empirical studies concern (1) the efficiency of the currency-options market, and (2) the accuracy of currency-option pricing models. Some of this empirical evidence is summarized below.

Market Efficiency

J. Bodurtha and G. Courtadon (1986), K. Shastri and K. Tandon (1986), and A. Tucker (1985), among others, have conducted extensive arbitrage

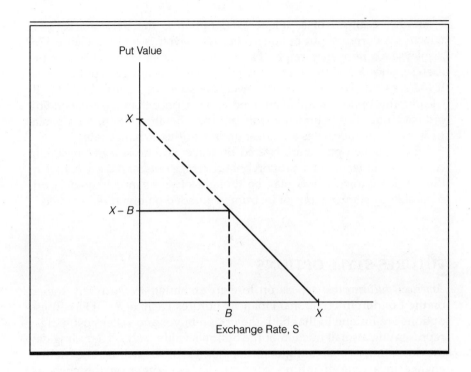

tests of currency-options market efficiency. They employ synchronous transaction data (the underlying exchange rate is recorded at the time of the currency-option trade) to investigate violations of pricing bounds such as those discussed in Chapter 12. They incorporate the effects of trading frictions, such as transaction costs and execution lags, into their analyses. An efficient market should not exhibit violations of rational pricing bounds after controlling for such frictions. Each study supports the efficiency of the currency-options market, as very few unexploited arbitrage opportunities remained after trading frictions were incorporated. Currency-option prices appear to be efficiently determined down to the level of transaction costs.

Model Accuracy

J. Bodurtha and G. Courtadon (1987) report that a Black-Scholes type of currency-option model, such as Equation 17.1, exhibits a definite time-to-maturity bias. As maturity increases, overpricing of the in-the-money and at-the-money currency options decreases, while the model's underpricing of out-of-the-money options first decreases, then increases slightly. K. Shastri and K. Wethyavivorn (1987) and others have documented similar model mispricing, although no one has demonstrated an ability to exploit this mispricing and generate abnormal economic returns.

Several researchers have developed alternative currency-option models that relax one or more of the assumptions underlying the Black-Scholes framework in order to better proxy market prices. For instance, models exist that allow for nonconstant interest rates or for exchange rate distributions that are not lognormal. Such models do appear to offer greater pricing accuracy, although their complexity often makes their implementation difficult and costly. A description of some of the alternative models follows:

- *J. Hilliard, et al. (1989).* These authors derive a model that incorporates both nonconstant U.S. and foreign interest rates. The model exhibits, on average, a pricing error about 15 percent lower than that exhibited by a Black-Scholes constant-interest-rate model.
- *A. Tucker (1990).* This author derives a model that incorporates random jumps in exchange rate changes. Such jumps may be associated with realignment activities by central banks or the European Economic Community. Tucker finds that such a model can reduce pricing errors up to 50 percent.
- *E. Borensztein and M. Dooley (1987).* These authors report that a currency option formula built on a pure jump process for exchange rate movements eliminates the pricing bias observed for out-of-the-money options.

SUMMARY

American and European options on foreign exchange are traded on both listed and OTC markets. Volume and open interest in these instruments have shown tremendous growth. Although these options can be used to speculate on exchange rate movements, they exist primarily to help investors and multinational companies immunize against exchange exposure. Currency options are particularly useful when international trade agreements are contingent, as in the submission of a contract bid in a foreign currency.

Over-the-counter (OTC) currency options offered by some banks and brokerages exhibit unique properties tailored to the client's specifications. For instance, some of these options offer bounded payoffs. Since they are unique, these options are not actively traded. Futures-style currency options represent another unusual form of currency options.

Currency options may be regarded as a type of continuous-leakage option, where the constant continuous leakage is represented by the foreign risk-free rate of interest. American currency options may be exercised prematurely, and these options appear to command a slight early-exercise premium. The empirical evidence regarding currency options supports market efficiency. Recent evidence suggests that more elaborate valuation models can offer improved pricing accuracy.

Selected References

Barone, Adesi, G., and R. Whaley. "Efficient Analytic Approximation of American Option Values." *Journal of Finance* 42 (June 1987): 301–320.

Bodurtha, J., and G. Courtadon. "Efficiency Tests of the Foreign Currency Options Market." *Journal of Finance* 41 (March 1986): 151–162.

Bodurtha, J., and G. Courtadon. "Tests of An American Option Pricing Model on the Foreign Currency Options Market." *Journal of Financial and Quantitative Analysis* 22 (June 1987): 153–167.

Borensztein, E., and M. Dooley. "Options of Foreign Exchange and Exchange Rate Expectations." *International Monetary Fund Staff Papers* 34 (December 1987): 643–680.

Briys, E., and M. Crouhy. "Creating and Pricing Hybrid Foreign Currency Options." *Financial Management* 17 (Winter 1988): 59–65.

Feiger, G., and B. Jacquillat. "Currency Option Bonds, Puts and Calls on Spot Exchange, and the Hedging of Contingent Foreign Earnings." *Journal of Finance* 5 (December 1979): 1129–1139.

Gendreau, B. "New Markets in Foreign Currency Options." *Business Review* (July–August 1984): 3–12.

Hilliard, J., J. Madura, and A. Tucker. "Currency Option Pricing with Stochastic Domestic and Foreign Interest Rates." Working paper. University of Tennessee, 1989.

Hsieh, D. "A Model of Foreign Currency Options with Random Interest Rates." Working paper. University of Chicago, 1988.

Jorion, P., and N. Stoughton. "The Valuation of the Early Exercise Premium in the Foreign Currency Options Market" in *Recent Developments in International Banking and Finance,* ed. S. Khoury and A. Ghosh.: Lexington Books, 1988.

Madura, J., and T. Veit. "Use of Currency Options in International Cash Management." *Journal of Cash Management* (January–February 1986): 42–48.

McCulloch, H. "Foreign Currency Option Pricing with Log-Stable Uncertainty" in *Recent Developments in International Banking and Finance,* ed. S. Khoury and A. Ghosh.: Lexington Books, 1987.

Peterson, D., and A. Tucker. "Implied Spot Rates as Predictors of Currency Returns: A Note." *Journal of Finance* 43 (March 1988): 247–258.

Shastri, K., and K. Tandon. "Arbitrage Tests of the Efficiency of the Foreign Currency Options Market." *Journal of International Money and Finance* 4 (December 1985): 455–468.

Shastri, K., and K. Wethyavivorn. "The Valuation of Currency Options for Alternative Stochastic Processes." *Journal of Financial Research* 10 (Winter 1987): 283–293.

Tucker, A., "Empirical Tests of the Efficiency of the Currency Option Market." *Journal of Financial Research* 7 (Winter 1986): 275–285.

Tucker, A. "Market-Determined Premia for American Currency Spot Options." Working paper. Temple University, 1989.

Tucker, A. "Exchange Rate Jumps and Currency Options Pricing" in *Recent Developments in International Banking and Finance,* ed. S. Khoury and R. Haugen. Lexington Books, forthcoming 1990.

Questions and Problems

1. From Exhibit 17.2, what was the closing price of a Swiss franc put option, American style, with exercise price of $0.64 and March expiration? What was the closing price of its counterpart European option?

2. Using the above Swiss franc options, construct a trading strategy that would yield riskless profits, assuming no frictions such as transaction costs. (Hint: Recall the analysis of counterpart European and American options from Chapter 11.)

3. From Exhibit 17.2, observe the closing prices of (1) the Swiss franc March call with exercise price of $0.64, European style; and (2) its corresponding put option. Are these prices likely consistent with put-call parity? (Hint: Use the parameters given in Exhibit 17.3.) If not, then what are some potential causes for this violation?

4. Why are currency options considered to be continuous-leakage options?

5. Suppose you obtained the following current data in order to price a European deutsche mark option: $S = \$0.5450$, $X = \$0.5800$, $T = .25$, $\sigma = .11$, $r = .09$, and $r_f = .04$. Use Equation 17.1 to price the call option. Is it likely that this option will be exercised prematurely?

6. From the previous problem, what is the value of the corresponding European put option?

7. Suppose you make a bet with a foreigner and, if you win, you will be paid in the foreign currency. How can you use currency options to immunize against your exchange exposure? Why wouldn't you use currency futures?

8. Name two conditions under which it might be optimal to prematurely exercise an American currency put option.

9. What is an American futures-style currency option?

10. From Exhibits 17.5 and 17.6, what are the potential revenue outcomes of the conservative strategy if the spot rate at option expiration is $0.63/SF1?

11. Foreign exchange rates are reciprocals. For instance, $\$1.67/£1 = £0.60/\$1$. This implies that a currency call option on a foreign currency can be priced as a currency put option on the domestic currency. Demonstrate this using Equations 17.1 and 17.3 and the following parameters: $S = \$1.67/£1$, $X = \$1.67/£1$, $\sigma = .10$, $r = .08$, $r_f = .12$, and $T = .50$.

12. Using the March DM call options with exercise prices of $0.54/DM1 and $0.55/DM1 appearing in Exhibit 17.2, construct a bull money spread. Draw a profit graph for expiration spot exchange rates ranging from $0.50/DM1 to $0.60/DM1.

13. Using the March SF options with exercise price of $0.63/SF1 appearing in Exhibit 17.2, construct a straddle. Draw a profit graph for expiration spot exchange rates ranging from $0.58/SF1 to $0.68/SF1.

14. Consider a three-month American call option on a British pound where $S = \$1.70$, $X = \$1.70$, $r = .06$, $r_f = .09$, and $\sigma = .30$. Dividing the option's maturity into three one-month periods for the purpose of constructing a binomial tree, use the BOPM to determine the option's value.

Self-Test Problems

Questions ST-1 through ST-7 refer to the following information:

$$S = \$0.50/DM1 \qquad r = .08$$
$$X = \$0.48/DM1 \qquad r_f = .03$$
$$T = 0.25 \qquad n = 62{,}500, \text{ the number of deutsche}$$
$$\sigma = 0.15 \qquad \text{marks per contract.}$$

ST-1. What is the value of the European call option?

ST-2. What is the value of the corresponding European put option?

ST-3. Suppose a U.S. exporter were employing this put option to hedge a contract bid in marks. For simplicity, assume that the contract decision, mark payment, and option expiration are contemporaneous. If the U.S. firm's target revenue figure is $1,000,000, then what will be its bid in marks?

ST-4. How many put option contracts must the firm buy to fully immunize itself against exchange exposure?

ST-5. What is the insurance premium?

ST-6. What is the firm's revenue if the bid fails and the spot rate at option expiration is $0.49/DM1?

ST-7. What is the firm's revenue if the bid is successful and the spot rate at option expiration is $0.51/DM1?

Solutions to Self-Test Problems

ST-1. $d = \{ln(.50/.48) + [.08 - .03 + (.15)^2/2](.25)\}/(.15)(\sqrt{.25}) = .7485.$

$$d - (.15)(\sqrt{.25}) = .7485 - .075 = .6735.$$

$$N(.7485) = .7729; N(.6735) = .7496.$$

$$C^E = e^{-.03(.25)}0.50(.7729) -$$

$$e^{-.08(.25)}\, 0.48(.7496) = \$0.0308/DM1.$$

ST-2. $P^E = .0308 + e^{-.08(.25)}0.48 - e^{-.03(.25)}0.50 = \$0.0050/DM1.$

ST-3. Effective exchange rate: $\$0.48 - .005 = \$0.475.$
Project bid: $\$1{,}000{,}000/0.475 = DM2{,}105{,}263.$

ST-4. Number of contracts: DM2,105,263/62,500 = 33.68, or 34.

ST-5. Premium: $\$0.005 \times 34 \times 62{,}500 = \$10{,}625.00.$

ST-6. Revenue: ($10,625.00); the options expire worthless.

ST-7. Revenue: $\$0.51/DM1 \times DM2{,}105{,}263 - \$10{,}625 = \$1{,}063{,}059.$

Appendix 17.A

AN AMERICAN CURRENCY OPTIONS PRICING MODEL

G. Barone-Adesi and R. Whaley (1987) provide a very accurate approximation to price American options written on assets that exhibit continuous leakages. The model is advanced, as it is designed to quantify the early-exercise premium associated with the American feature. This appendix adapts their model, which was provided earlier in Chapter 14, so that it is applicable to American currency options.

For call currency options the model is

(17.A–1) $$C^A = C^E + A_2(S/\bar{S})^{q_2}$$

where $S < \bar{S}$, and

$$C^A = S - X$$

where $S \geq \bar{S}$, and where

$$A_2 = (\bar{S}/q_2)\{1 - e^{-r_f T}N\{d_2(\bar{S})\}\}$$
$$d_2(\bar{S}) = \{[ln(\bar{S}/X) + (r - r_f + (\sigma^2/2))T]/\sigma\sqrt{T}\}$$
$$q_2 = (1 + \sqrt{1 + 4K})/2$$
$$K = 2r/[\sigma^2(1 - e^{-rt})]$$

$\bar{S}$ = the critical exchange rate above which the American currency option should be exercised immediately.

$\bar{S}$ can be solved iteratively by solving

(17.A–2) $$\bar{S} - X = C^E = \{1 - e^{-r_f T}N[d_2(\bar{S})]\}\bar{S}/q_2.$$

Equation 17.A.1 states that if the exchange rate is below $\bar{S}$, then the American call value C^A is equal to the European value (see Equation 17.1), plus the early-exercise premium as approximated by the quadratic term $A_2(S/\bar{S})^{q_2}$. Above $\bar{S}$, the option should be exercised, and thus the value of C^A is its exercisable proceeds, $S - X$.

Similarly, the value of an American currency put option, P^A, is well approximated by the following formula:

(17.A–3) $$P^A = P^E + A_1(S/\bar{S})^{q_1}$$

where $S \geq \bar{S}$, and

$$P^A = X - S$$

where $S \leq \bar{S}$, and where

$$A_1 = -(\bar{S}/q_1)\{1 - e^{-r_f T}N[-d_2(\bar{S})]\}$$
$$q_1 = (1 - \sqrt{1 + 4K})/2.$$

Here $\bar{S}$ represents the critical exchange rate below which the American currency put option should be exercised immediately. $\bar{S}$ now is determined iteratively by solving

(17.A–4) $\qquad X - \bar{S} = P^E - \{1 - e^{-r_f T}N[-d_2(\bar{S})]\}\bar{S}/q_1.$

See G. Barone-Adesi and R. Whaley (1987) in "Selected References" for details.

18

STOCK INDEX OPTIONS

On March 11, 1983, the CBOE began trading listed options on the Standard and Poor's 100 Stock Index. This represented the first stock index option ever offered. The contract, typically referred to by its ticker symbol, OEX, proved highly successful. Current annual volume in the OEX exceeds 125 million contracts. It is the most traded contract on the CBOE, with annual volume actually exceeding the combined volume of all CBOE-listed stock options.

The tremendous success of the OEX quickly led to the development and trading of stock index options on the other organized exchanges. Highly successful contracts include the Major Market Index (MMI) (first traded on the AMEX less than two months after the inception of the SP100 option) and the NYSE Composite Index (traded on the NYSE). Taken together, annual trading volume in all stock index options represents about three-fourths of the combined annual trading volume of all listed stock options.

In this chapter we describe the various stock index options traded, their unique features, and the reason for their popularity. We also examine the pricing of index options, how they can be employed to hedge or speculate, and the empirical evidence concerning these options.

STOCK INDEX OPTIONS MARKETS AND INSTRUMENTS

Exhibit 18.1 describes the various index options now offered on organized exchanges. The contracts can be categorized as belonging to one of two groups: broad market indices or more specialized industry indices. Options on broad market indices are those written on the SP100, SP500, Major Market Index (MMI), Value Line Index, National OTC Index, and the NYSE Composite Index. Options on industry indices include those written on the Computer Technology Index, the

Stock index options are written on broad market indices or more specialized industry indices.

Exhibit 18.1:

Currently Traded Index Options

A: Broad Market Indices

Index	Exchange	Description
SP100	CBOE	100 stocks weighted by market value
SP500	CBOE	500 stocks weighted by market value; European
Major Market Index	AMEX	20 blue-chip stocks weighted by price; highly correlated with SP100 and SP500
Value Line Index	PHLX	1,700 stocks equally weighted and geometrically averaged
National OTC Index	PHLX	100 OTC stocks weighted by market value
NYSE Composite	NYSE	All NYSE stocks weighted by market value

B: Industry Indices

Index	Exchange	Description
Computer Technology Index	AMEX	30 computer stocks weighted by market value
Oil Index	AMEX	15 oil stocks weighted by market value
Institutional Index	AMEX	75 stocks held widely by institutions and weighted by market value; European
Gold/Silver Index	PHLX	7 mining stocks weighted by market value
Utilities Index	PHLX	20 electric utility stocks weighted by market value
Financial News Composite Index	PSE	30 blue-chip stocks weighted by price; European

Gold/Silver Index, the Utilities Index, and others. These specialized index options were developed to attract traders who analyzed specific industries. However, volume in these contracts has been insignificant—disappointingly so for the exchanges. For this reason, we will concentrate on the broader market options such as the OEX.

These broader index options are popular for two reasons. First, many individual investors prefer to analyze the market as a whole rather than focusing on selected stocks. There are nearly 600 individual stock options now traded on organized exchanges. Rather than trading a basket of such options, investors who want to trade the entire market can transact in index options such as the OEX. Second, many institutional investors, including mutual funds and pension funds, hold stock portfolios that are highly correlated with broad market indices. These institutional investors can employ index options to help manage the portfolio's risk. For instance, many option funds (discussed in Chapter 11) specialize in writing index call options against their stock portfolios.

Unique Features

Index options exhibit some unique features that differentiate their trading from that of individual stock options. These features are

- *A contract multiple.* The size of an index option contract is defined as some multiple of the underlying index. For instance, the OEX has a multiple of 100, meaning that the option contract buyer actually purchases 100 options.
- *Cash settlement.* When an index option is exercised, the writer pays the buyer cash equal to the contract multiple times the difference between the index level and exercise price. For example, if a put index option is exercised where the contract multiple is 100, the index level is 300, and the exercise price is $310, then the assigned writer pays the put buyer $1,000 [100 × ($310 − 300)]. We cannot determine if the put buyer made a profit here, since we do not know what he or she originally paid for the option. Later in this chapter we analyze the valuation of index options.
- *End-of-day exercise.* When an index option is exercised, the index value occurring at market closing is used to determine the cash settlement. Therefore, traders find it optimal to wait until the end of the trading session to exercise; it is possible to order the exercise of an in-the-money index option during the day only to find at the close that it is out-of-the-money.
- *Expiration cycle.* Some of the most liquid index options have frequent expiration cycles. For instance, the OEX has a cycle consisting of the current month plus the next three consecutive months. This reflects its popularity among traders.
- *Taxation.* Stock index options have a different tax status than ordinary stock options. Specifically, at the end of the calendar year all realized and unrealized gains are taxed as ordinary income. Also, all losses—both realized and unrealized—are deductible by offsetting them against any other investment gains.

Index Option Quotes

Exhibit 18.2 presents closing index option prices for selected contracts for trading on March 1, 1989. These prices are interpreted the way those

INDEX TRADING

Wednesday, March 1, 1989

OPTIONS

Chicago Board

S&P 100 INDEX

Strike Price	Calls—Last Mar	Calls—Last Apr	Calls—Last May	Puts—Last Mar	Puts—Last Apr	Puts—Last May
230	46¼	....	....	1/16	....	....
235	....	....	....	1/16	....	....
240	....	....	38	1/16	½	⅞
245	....	....	....	⅛	⅝	1¼
250	23½	....	....	3/16	1	1 11/16
255	21½	....	....	⅜	1 7/16	2½
260	13½	17	....	11/16	2 3/16	3⅜
265	9¼	12¾	....	1 5/16	3¼	4¾
270	5⅜	9⅛	12¾	2½	4¾	6¼
275	2 9/16	6¼	8	4¾	6⅞	8¼
280	⅞	3¾	5½	8¼	9⅝	11½
285	5/16	2⅛	3½	13	13¼	14½
290	1/16	1⅛	2 11/16	18	18	17
295	1/16	9/16	1 9/16	....	20¾	20¼
300	1/16	¼	1	....	....	....

Total call volume 108,668 Total call open int. 349,889
Total put volume 134,091 Total put open int. 427,928
The index: High 275.59; Low 271.42; Close 272.29, −1.75.

S&P 500 INDEX

Strike Price	Calls—Last Mar	Calls—Last Apr	Calls—Last Jun	Puts—Last Mar	Puts—Last Apr	Puts—Last Jun
175	....	....	....	....	....	1/16
200	....	....	....	....	....	⅛
245	42⅛	....	....	....	....	....
250	....	....	....	....	....	1
255	....	....	....	⅛	....	....
260	....	....	....	....	....	2 3/16
265	24⅝	....	....	¼	....	2 13/16
270	19⅞	....	....	7/16	1 5/16	3⅛
275	....	....	....	⅜	1⅞	3½
280	8⅝	....	....	1⅜	2½	5¾
285	5⅛	9½	....	2½	3¾	6
290	2 7/16	6⅛	10⅝	4⅝	7¼	9¼
295	¾	4	....	8⅞	9⅜	11⅝
300	¼	2⅞	....	....	....	14⅜
305	⅛	1 11/16	....	15½	....	14½
310	1/16	....	3⅛	19¼	....	19¾
315	....	7/16	....	....	....	....
325	....	....	⅞	....	....	....

Total call volume 7,636 Total call open int. 244,434
Total put volume 1,055 Total put open int. 236,517
The index: High 290.28; Low 286.46; Close 287.11, −1.75.

Philadelphia Exchange

GOLD/SILVER INDEX

Strike Price	Calls—Last Mar	Calls—Last Apr	Calls—Last May	Puts—Last Mar	Puts—Last Apr	Puts—Last May
95	5¼	....	....	1	....	....
100	2⅛	....	....	¾	....	....

Total call volume 15 Total call open int. 414
Total put volume 19 Total put open int. 319
The index: High 100.32; Low 98.41; Close 98.67, −2.07.

VALUE LINE INDEX OPTIONS

Strike Price	Calls—Last Mar	Calls—Last Apr	Calls—Last May	Puts—Last Mar	Puts—Last Apr	Puts—Last May
255	5¾	....	....	1½	....	....
260	2⅞	....	....	....	....	....
265	⅜	....	....	....	....	....

Total call volume 40 Total call open int. 651
Total put volume 17 Total put open int. 1,233
The index: High 259.91; Low 258.41; Close 258.62, −0.35.

NATIONAL O-T-C INDEX

Strike Price	Calls—Last Mar	Calls—Last Apr	Calls—Last May	Puts—Last Mar	Puts—Last Apr	Puts—Last May
255	....	....	....	⅛	....	....

Total call volume 0 Total call open int. 95
Total put volume 10 Total put open int. 13
The index: High 277.62; Low 274.92; Close 275.33, −0.15.

UTILITIES INDEX

180	7¼	....	....	....	....	....
195	....	⅜	....	....	....	....

Total call volume 250 Total call open int. 3,101
Total put volume 0 Total put open int. 2,903
The index: High 188.28; Low 186.42; Close 186.42, −1.40.

American Exchange

MAJOR MARKET INDEX

Strike Price	Calls—Last Mar	Calls—Last Apr	Calls—Last May	Puts—Last Mar	Puts—Last Apr	Puts—Last May
390	....	....	....	1/16	....	....
395	⅛	....	....	⅛	....	....
400	....	....	....	3/16	....	....
410	31	....	....	5/16	....	....
415	....	35⅜	....	⅝	2¼	....
420	24½	....	....	15/16	3	....
425	17⅜	....	....	1 7/16	4¼	5⅛
430	13	....	....	2⅜	5¼	6⅛
435	9⅜	....	20¾	3½	7	7⅜
440	6⅜	12⅛	....	5¼	8⅞	12⅛
445	3⅝	9⅝	15¼	7⅞	11⅛	13⅞
450	1⅞	6¾	11	11½	13½	15⅛
455	13/16	5	9⅝	15¼	13	....
460	7/16	3½	5⅞	19⅞	16⅛	....
465	¼	2 13/16	5	....	20¼	....
470	⅛	2	....	....	24½	....
475	1/16	1¾	2⅝	....	27⅞	....
480	1/16	11/16	1⅞	....	....	....
485	....	7/16	1 5/16	....	....	....
490	....	½	1⅛	....	....	....

Total call volume 18,631 Total call open int. 80,456
Total put volume 13,638 Total put open int. 54,650
The index: High 445.44; Low 438.35; Close 439.75, −2.85.

COMPUTER TECHNOLOGY INDEX

Strike Price	Calls—Last Mar	Calls—Last Apr	Calls—Last May	Puts—Last Mar	Puts—Last Apr	Puts—Last May
110	....	....	....	2⅞	....	....
115	⅛	....	....	....	....	....

Total call volume 2 Total call open int. 93
Total put volume 60 Total put open int. 12
The index: High 109.61; Low 107.21; Close 107.65, −1.15.

OIL INDEX

Strike Price	Calls—Last Mar	Calls—Last Apr	Calls—Last May	Puts—Last Mar	Puts—Last Apr	Puts—Last May
165	....	26¾	....	....	⅛	....
190	2 7/16	....	....	....	....	....

Total call volume 28 Total call open int. 521
Total put volume 12 Total put open int. 304
The index: High 190.70; Low 188.79; Close 189.27, −0.15.

INSTITUTIONAL INDEX

Strike Price	Calls—Last Mar	Calls—Last Apr	Calls—Last May	Puts—Last Mar	Puts—Last Apr	Puts—Last May
250	....	....	....	1/16	....	....
270	....	....	....	½	....	....
275	....	....	....	....	1 15/16	....
280	....	....	....	1½	....	....
290	2 1/16	....	....	....	....	....
295	1	....	....	8	....	....
300	7/16	....	....	....	....	....
305	3/16	....	....	....	....	....

Total call volume 400 Total call open int. 35,078
Total put volume 112 Total put open int. 39,073
The index: High 288.68; Low 284.83; Close 285.67, −1.50.

N.Y. Stock Exchange

NYSE INDEX OPTIONS

Strike Price	Calls—Last Mar	Calls—Last Apr	Calls—Last Jun	Puts—Last Mar	Puts—Last Apr	Puts—Last Jun
145	....	....	....	1/16	5/16	..
150	....	....	....	⅛	....	....
155	....	....	....	⅜	1 1/16	....
157½	6	....	....	11/16	....	....
160	3	5	....	1⅜	2⅝	3
165	9/16	2 9/16	....	4⅛	5	....
170	1/16	15/16	....	7⅛	....	....
175	....	5/16	....	....	....	....

Total call volume 1,515. Total call open int. 11,950.
Total put volume 1,008. Total put open int. 7,712.
The index: High 163.23; Low 161.45; Close 161.74, −0.75.

Pacific Exchange

FINANCIAL NEWS COMPOSITE INDEX

Strike Price	Calls—Last Mar	Calls—Last Apr	Calls—Last Jun	Puts—Last Mar	Puts—Last Apr	Puts—Last Jun
160	44⅝	....	....	....	....	....
170	34½	....	39⅝	....	....	5/16
175	29⅝	....	....	....	....	....
180	....	....	....	....	....	13/16
185	20⅞	....	....	....	....	....
190	17¼	....	....	¼	....	....
195	....	....	....	⅜	....	....
200	5⅝	....	....	1⅛	....	....
205	2½	6½	....	2⅝	4⅛	....
210	⅝	2 13/16	....	5⅞	....	....
215	....	1½	....	10¾	10⅛	....
220	1/16	....	....	....	....	....
230	....	....	....	25	....	....

Total call volume 753 Total call open int. 2,845
Total put volume 709 Total put open int. 5,141
The index: High 207.10; Low 203.84; Close 204.45, −1.34.

Exhibit 18.2:
Index Option Prices for March 1, 1989

How the SP100, SP500, NYSE Composite, and IMM Indices are Constructed

The SP100 and SP500 are value-weighted indices of stocks traded on the New York Stock Exchange. To compute the SP500, first multiply the share price of each component stock by that stock's number of shares outstanding. This gives the stock's market value. Next, these market values are summed across all of the 500 stocks, and the sum is divided by index's base-period level. This level is the average value of the index during 1941 to 1943. Lastly, the quotient is multiplied by 10:

$$\text{SP500}_t = \sum_{i=1}^{500} n_{i,t} P_{i,t} / \text{Base-Period Level} \times 10,$$

where $n_{i,t}$ is the number of shares outstanding, and $P_{i,t}$ is the price per share for stock i at time t. The SP100 is constructed in a similar manner.

The NYSE Composite Index is also a value-weighted index. It uses all of the stocks listed on the NYSE, has a base period of December 31, 1965, and employs a multiple of 50 rather than 10. The SP100, SP500, and NYSE Composite are all highly correlated with each other.

The MMI is based on twenty industrial stocks and uses a price-weighted scheme:

$$\text{MMI}_t = \sum_{i=1}^{20} P_{i,t} / \text{Adjustment Factor},$$

where the adjustment factor is necessitated because of occasional stock splits and stock substitutions. The SP100, SP500, and NYSE Composite indices are robust to stock splits (and dividends) because they are value-weighted indices, and a split should not alter the firm's market value.

of individual stock options are. For example, the closing price of the SP100 March 270 call contract was 5-3/8 on March 1, or $537.50. The corresponding put price was $250.00. The SP100 closed at 272.29, down 1.75 points. As suggested by the volume and open interest figures appearing below each contract, options written on the SP100, SP500, MMI, and NYSE Composite are liquid, whereas the remaining index options are thinly traded.

VALUING STOCK INDEX OPTIONS

In Chapter 11 we argued that the dividend stream exhibited by a stock index was discontinuous because most stock dividends are clustered at certain calendar months and weekdays (see Figure 11.1). Thus, it is more exact to classify a stock index as a discrete-leakage asset than a continuous-leakage asset. However, it would be very impractical to obtain accurate day-to-day dividend figures for all of the stocks underlying the index and to value the index option as a discrete-leakage contract. Instead, a more practical and reasonably accurate approach is to obtain a *dividend yield* on the underlying index and to value the index option as a continuous-leakage contract. Obtaining an estimate of the *dividend yield* exhibited by stock indices is crucial for their pricing.

An individual stock's dividend yield is given by the dividend per share divided by the current price per share. Thus, the discrete dollar dividend is reported as a percentage (i.e., a continuous rate) of the underlying stock price. If the stock price is relatively stable, the dividend yield will exhibit little variability, since most firms tend to smooth their dividend payments through time. For a stock index, the dividend yield is expressed as the dividends paid by all of the underlying stocks (properly weighted) divided by the current index level. Thus, an index's dividend yield represents the dividend leakage as a continuous rate, enabling the index option to be valued by the Black-Scholes model, modified for a continuous leakage.

> A **stock index dividend yield** is expressed as the dividends paid by all of the underlying stocks, properly weighted, divided by the current index level.

The weighting scheme used to construct the index's dividend yield depends on how the index itself is constructed. Recall that the most liquid index options are those written on the SP100, SP500, MMI, and NYSE Composite. Of these, three are constructed by weighting each stock's dividend by the stock's market value. For the MMI, the yield is obtained by weighting each dividend by the stock's market price.

Constructing a dividend yield for a stock index can be a nuisance. Fortunately, some investment services calculate and report dividend yields for the major stock indices. For instance, *Value Line Options* reports yields on a weekly basis. Figure 18.1 presents the dividend yield for the SP500 for a recent time period. The average yield is about 3.1 percent. The dividend yields on the other major stock indices are similar since the largest capitalized stocks appear in all of the indices. For comparative purposes, Figure 18.1 also portrays the yield on long-term bonds for the same period.

Valuing European Index Options

To value European index options let us begin by rewriting Equation 13.7a, which is the Black-Scholes model for continuous-leakage assets:

$$C^E = S_\delta N(d_3) - Xe^{-rT}N(d_3 - \sigma\sqrt{T}),$$

where

$$S_\delta = Se^{-\delta T}$$

$$d_3 = \frac{ln(S_\delta/X) + [r + (\sigma^2/2)]T}{\sigma\sqrt{T}}.$$

For stock index options, S represents the current index level, δ represents the index's dividend yield, and σ^2 represents the variability of returns on holding the index.

As an illustration, suppose that we want to value a European call option written on a stock index where $S = 300$, $X = 297$, $T = .20$,

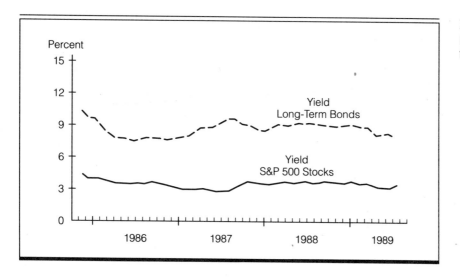

Figure 18.1:
Dividend Yields
for the SP500

$\delta = .04$, $r = .08$, and $\sigma^2 = .003$. Of these parameters, only σ^2 is not readily observable. It may be estimated using historic stock index price series or by the implied method described in Chapter 13. Obviously, the return variance for a stock index will be lower than that for an individual stock due to diversification effects (see Chapter 3). With these inputs, the call's price is $633.80 per contract, assuming a contract multiple of 100:

$$S_\delta = 300e^{-.04(.20)} = 297.61;$$

$$d_3 = \frac{ln(297.61/297) + [.08 + (.003/2)](.20)}{\sqrt{.003}\sqrt{.20}} = .7492;$$

$$d_3 - \sqrt{.003}\sqrt{.20} = .7247;$$

$$N(.7492) = .7732; N(.7247) = .7656;$$

$$C^E = 297.61(.7732) - 297e^{-.08(.20)}(.7656) = \$6.3380.$$

To obtain the corresponding put option's value, we employ put-call parity as given by Equation 12.27d:

$$P^E = 6.3380 - 297.61 + 297e^{-.08(.20)} = \$1.0138,$$

or $101.38 per index option contract.

Valuing American Index Options

The majority of stock index options are American. The exceptions are those written on the SP500, the Institutional Index, and the Financial News Composite Index (see Exhibit 18.1). Under certain conditions it

Under certain conditions it may be optimal to prematurely exercise American index options.

may be optimal to prematurely exercise American index options. Specifically, a call index option may be exercised prematurely if it is deeply in-the-money and the dividend yield is greater than or equal to the risk-free interest rate. The option's market price may in this case be less than its exercisable proceeds. However, since the inception of index options trading, the typical dividend yield has been about one-half the risk-free rate of interest, making early exercise typically undesirable, since the amount of the dividend captured by exercising does not exceed the forgone interest on the exercise price. For American put index options, the conditions needed for optimal premature exercise are $X >>> S$ and $r \geq \delta$. That is, the put must be deeply in-the-money and the index's dividend yield must be less than the risk-free rate.

Because it may be optimal to prematurely exercise an American index option, the American option should command a slightly greater price than its European counterpart. The price difference represents a premium associated with the early-exercise privilege offered by American stock index options. Exhibit 18.3 reports the results of a simulation analysis of the early-exercise premium for American put index options. Reported are the European index option prices, their counterpart American prices, and the resulting early-exercise premia. The American put prices are obtained using the quadratic approximation of Barone-Adesi and Whaley, discussed in Chapter 14. Recall that this approximation is applicable to American options written on continuous-leakage assets. As discussed in Chapter 14, the BOPM could also be used to value American stock index options.

The results of the simulation suggest that the early-exercise premium can be substantial for in-the-money index put options. Thus, it may be important to incorporate the premium associated with the early-exercise privilege offered by stock index put options, especially those that are in-the-money.

Exhibit 18.3:
Early Exercise Premia for American Put Index Options

Index Level	European Price	American Price	Early-Exercise Premium
292	$718.84	$735.46	$16.62
295	521.93	529.67	7.74
297	409.88	413.83	3.95
300	270.17	271.39	1.22
303	169.90	170.16	0.26
305	116.79	116.79	0.00
307	80.51	80.51	0.00

Note: The simulation parameter values are $X = 300$, $T = .25$, $\delta = .05$, $\sigma^2 = .004$, and $r = .08$. The contract multiple is 100.

How One Investor Hit It Rich with Stock Index Put Options

Soon after graduating from SUNY-Binghamton in 1981, where he studied math and economics, Jeffrey Yass formed an "investment club" with five young partners also schooled there. The six friends shared a penchant for gambling and other ventures entailing probability theory. They called their club RAMJAC, after the fictitious international conglomerate in Kurt Vonnegut's novel, *Jailbird*. In the novel, RAMJAC schemed to take over everything in the world and to redistribute wealth through peaceful economic revolution. At first, the club's activities mainly involved high-stakes poker, thoroughbred racing, and the like. For instance, in 1985 Mr. Yass and his partners collected $752,778 at a jai alai fronton in Miami after betting $524,288 on every possible combination in a "Pick-Six" jackpot, which requires bettors to select the winners in six straight matches.

During this time, Mr. Yass also began trading stock options and, with the backing of a well-known Wall Street trader, Israel Englander, he became a member of the Philadelphia Stock Exchange. Here he worked as a market maker and later as a specialist trading options. He was making tremendous money in the bull market of the mid-1980s, and soon RAMJAC had

moved its headquarters to Philadelphia. With the new location came a new same—Susquehanna Investment Group. The partners began expanding operations as a fast-growing trading firm that soon specialized in stock index arbitrage.

In the stock market crash of October 1987, Susquehanna was holding a sizable position in SP100 put options. With the market drop came a nearly ten-fold increase in the value of the put options. According to records filed with the SEC, the payoff for Susquehanna was more than $10 million on October 19th alone. In 1987, though it had been in business only eight months, Susquehanna made nearly $18 million in profits and compensation for Mr. Yass and his five partners.

Today, Susquehanna has offices in four cities, over 100 employees, and owns seats at seven different exchanges. When the NYSE recently disclosed its most active program traders, Susquehanna was first, conducting more index arbitrage than Morgan Stanley, Merrill Lynch, Kidder Peabody, and Bear Sterns. Mr. Yass is currently the youngest governor at the Philadelphia Stock Exchange (PHLX). When recently asked about him, Arnie Staloff, president of the PHLX, responded: "Money to Mr. Yass is just a way to keep score."

HEDGING WITH STOCK INDEX OPTIONS

Index options can be employed to hedge entire stock portfolios against downside price risk. As an illustration, suppose an option fund that holds an equity portfolio mimicking the SP100 writes the SP100 April 275 calls appearing in Exhibit 18.2. The fund's market value is $25 million, or about 91,800 units of the SP100 ($25 million ÷ 272.29). Since the option contract multiple is 100, the fund's management decides to write 918 contracts. The proceeds from writing these contracts are $573,750 ($6 1/4 × 100 × 918).

Figure 18.2 presents the profit graph for the long-index/short-call hedging strategy at option expiration (solid line). Also presented is the profit graph for the long-index (i.e., unhedged) position (broken line). As the figure demonstrates, the covered call position is less risky. The losses on the stock portfolio are offset in part by the option premium should the index level fall. For the covered call strategy, the breakeven expiration index level is 266.04, whereas it is 272.29 for the unhedged long-index position.

Index options can be employed to hedge entire stock portfolios against downside price risk.

Figure 18.2:
Profit Graph for a
Long-Index / Short-Index Call
Hedge

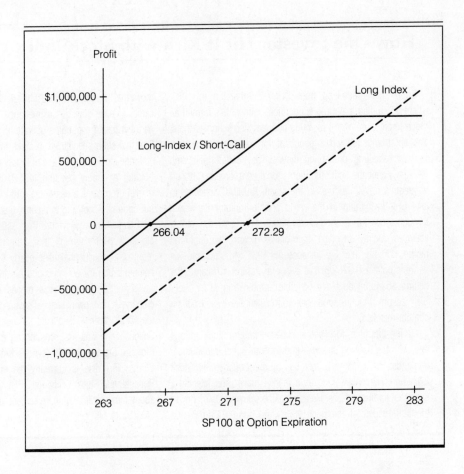

As another hedging example, Figure 18.3 presents the profit graph for an index fund purporting to mimic the SP100. The fund's management had purchased the SP100 April 275 puts appearing in Exhibit 18.2. Assuming 918 put contracts were purchased, the figure demonstrates that the protective put strategy is much less risky than an unhedged position. In the event of a market decline, the protective put strategy assures the fund of a loss no greater than $382,309.[1]

SPECULATING WITH STOCK INDEX OPTIONS

The two ways of profiting in the stock market are (1) detecting mispriced stocks and (2) accurately forecasting swings in the entire market. For

---

[1] $-\$382{,}309 = [(275 - 272.29/272.29)(\$25{,}000{,}000)] - (\$6\ 7/8 \times 100 \times 918)$. For simplicity, we assume that the purchase of the puts does not reduce the investment in the stock portfolio.

422   PART 3   OPTIONS

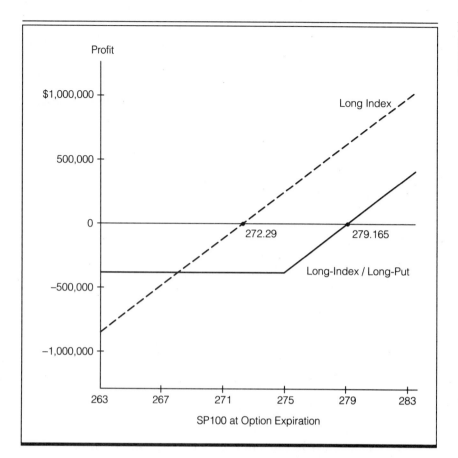

Profit

$1,000,000

500,000

0

272.29   279.165

Long Index

Long-Index / Long-Put

−500,000

−1,000,000

263   267   271   275   279   283

SP100 at Option Expiration

traders who like to track the market as a whole, index options provide an attractive means for speculation. To illustrate, let us create a bull money spread using the SP100 April 270 and 275 calls appearing in Exhibit 18.2. Recall that a bull money spread is used to speculate on a price appreciation, and is constructed by purchasing a lower exercise-price call while writing a higher-exercise price call. Here the initial cost of the bull money spread is $287.50:

For traders who track the entire market, index options provide an attractive means for speculation.

Buy SP100 April 270 Call: − $912.50
Write SP100 April 275 Call: +   625.00
Total − $287.50

Figure 18.4 presents the profit graph for our bull money spread at option expiration. As the figure demonstrates, the spread is profitable if the resulting index level is greater than 272.875 (270 + 9-1/8 − 6-1/4).

Figure 18.4:
Profit Graph for a Bull
Money Spread Utilizing Stock
Index Call Options

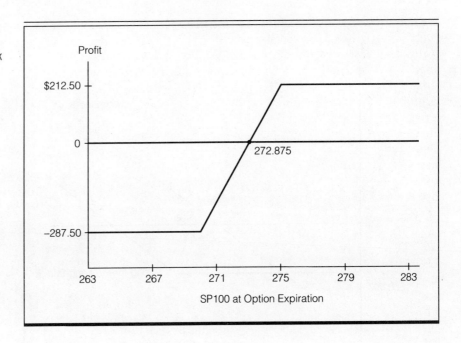

EMPIRICAL EVIDENCE ON STOCK INDEX OPTIONS

Given the popularity and huge daily trading volume of stock index options, surprisingly little empirical evidence exists regarding them. Indeed, at the time of this writing just three empirical studies exist—J. Evnine and A. Rudd (1985) and D. Chance (1986, 1987). We summarize these studies below.

Evnine and Rudd Study

Evnine and Rudd employed transaction data for SP100 and MMI options traded from June 26, 1984, to August 30, 1984, to test the efficiency of the index options market and to investigate the pricing of index options. Using 1,798 trades, they reported a substantial number of violations of arbitrage restrictions and substantial options mispricing when using a binomial pricing model (BOPM). These results suggested that the market was inefficient to some degree. However, this conclusion was tentative for several reasons discussed by the authors. First, much of the inefficiency may have been induced by the inability of investors to arbitrage the index options at low risk. Since there is no simple arbitrage between the option and underlying index, as there is with individual stock options, arbitrage forces are likely not as powerful with index

Since there is no simple arbitrage between the option and underlying index, as there is with individual stock options, arbitrage forces are likely not as powerful with index options.

options.[2] Second, many of the violations were clustered around the first week of August of 1984, when the market had a rapid upswing. Arbitragers may not have been able to exploit violations in such a "fast" market. Also, data nonsynchronization problems may have been exacerbated during this week. With respect to the mispricing observed, errors may have been introduced by the complex dividend-adjustment procedure used by the authors. Finally, it is doubtful whether the MMI meets the pricing assumptions of lognormality and constant variance. Since the MMI is a price-weighted average, a large return on any one asset in one period will cause a change in the composition of the index over the succeeding period; thus, the MMI will likely show nonstationary return variance, introducing a pricing bias.

Chance Studies

D. Chance (1986, 1987) employed closing-price data for SP100 options traded during the first four months of 1984 in order to conduct several empirical tests, including (1) an investigation of the pattern of volatilities implied across moneyness and maturities using an adaptation of the Black-Scholes model, (2) an investigation of the pricing accuracy of this model, and (3) an investigation of put-call parity. Consistent with earlier empirical evidence regarding individual stock options, Chance reports discernable patterns of implied volatilities and systematic pricing biases that together imply that the Black-Scholes adaptation is somewhat misspecified. The author also reports many violations of put-call parity. However, after accounting for bid-ask spreads, other transaction costs, and frictions associated with arbitrage involving an entire stock index, Chance concludes that the market appears to be efficient, as the detected mispricing is insufficient to yield abnormal profits.

SUMMARY

Stock index options have been traded on organized exchanges since early 1983 and have exhibited tremendous volume growth ever since. This popularity stems from the ability of traders to hedge entire stock portfolios or to speculate on broad market swings by employing index options such as the OEX.

---

[2]Soon this may no longer be the case. On June 1, 1989, the NYSE approved the trading of stock baskets, enabling investors to buy or sell an entire portfolio of stocks in one trade. The device is known as the Exchange Stock Portfolio, and its construction is similar to that of the SP500. Unlike other stock index products, stocks in the portfolio actually would be delivered to the buyers. The product's trading is pending approval by the SEC. Such a product may be employed to better arbitrage apparent violations of pricing bounds applicable to current stock index options.

The dividend stream for an index is far more complex than that for an individual stock. A practical way to value index options is to treat the dividend payout as a continuous stream represented by a dividend yield. In this way, European index options may be priced using the Black-Scholes model adjusted for continuous leakages, while American index options may be priced using extant methods such as the Barone-Adesi and Whaley quadratic approximation. The early empirical evidence regarding stock index options suggests substantial model mispricing. However, alternative and more complex valuations models have not been tested empirically.

Selected References

Baily, W., and R. Stulz. "The Pricing of Stock Index Options in a General Equilibrium Model." *Journal of Financial and Quantitative Analysis* 24 (March 1989): 1–12.

Barone-Adesi, G., and R. Whaley. "Efficient Analytic Approximation of American Option Values." *Journal of Finance* 42 (June 1987): 301–320.

Chance, D. "Empirical Tests of the Pricing of Index Call Options." *Advances in Futures and Options Research* 1 (1986): 141–166.

Chance, D. "Parity Tests of Index Options." *Advances in Futures Options Research* 2 (1987): 47–64.

Evnine, J., and A. Rudd. "Index Options: The Early Evidence." *Journal of Finance* 40 (July 1985): 743–756.

Eytan, T. and G. Harpaz, "The Pricing of Futures and Options Contracts on the Value Line Index." *Journal of Finance* 41 (September 1986): 843–855.

Merton, R. "Theory of Rational Option Pricing." *Bell Journal of Economics* 4 (Spring 1973): 141–183.

Questions and Problems

1. How do index options differ from ordinary stock options? Be sure to discuss concepts such as cash settlement.

2. Why is it rather foolish to order the exercise of an index option during a trading session?

3. From Exhibit 18.2, what was the closing price of a SP500 March 290 call? What was the closing price of the corresponding put option?

4. Why is it convenient to express the dividend payout exhibited by a stock index in the form of a dividend yield?

5. Demonstrate the conditions under which early exercise of an index call option may be optimal. Why is it unlikely that index calls will be exercised prematurely?

6. What is the value of a European call index option given the following parameter values: $S = 280$, $X = 280$, $\delta = .04$, $T = .15$, $\sigma^2 = .002$, and $r = .10$? What is the value of a corresponding put option?

7. Using the SP100 April 270 and 275 calls appearing in Exhibit 18.2, construct a bear money spread and present the profit graph for expiration index levels ranging from 260 to 285.

8. Suppose that you observe a violation of a floor condition for an American call index option. Why would it be difficult to risklessly exploit this violation?

9. What is the value of a European call index option where $S = 300$, $X = 300$, $T = .30$, $\delta = .04$, $\sigma^2 = .005$, and $r = .07$?

10. Using the above call option, present a profit graph at option expiration for a covered call strategy. Assume that your portfolio mimics the underlying index and that the portfolio's current worth is $1.5 million, or 5,000 index units.

11. Consider a five-month American put option on a stock index where $S = 300$, $X = 305$, $r = .08$, $\delta = .03$, and $\sigma^2 = .003$. Divide the option's maturity into five one-month periods for the purpose of constructing a lattice. What is the option's price using the BOPM?

Self-Test Problems

ST-1. Determine the value of a European call index option where $S = 290$, $X = 288$, $T = .25$, $\delta = .05$, $\sigma^2 = .003$, and $r = .09$.

ST-2. Determine the value of a corresponding put index option.

ST-3. Using these two options, present a profit graph for a strap at option expiration. Assume that the contract multiple is 100 and let the expiration index level range from 270 to 300.

Solutions to Self-Test Problems

ST-1. $S_\delta = 290e^{-.05(.25)} = 286.398$.

$$d_3 = \frac{ln(286.398/288) + [.09 + (.003/2)](.25)}{\sqrt{.003}\sqrt{.25}}$$

$$= .6315.$$

$$d_3 - \sqrt{.003}\sqrt{.25} = .6042.$$

$$N(.6315) = .7361; N(.6042) = .7271.$$

$$C^E = 286.398(.7361) - 288e^{-.09(.25)}(.7271)$$

$$= \$6.0718.$$

ST-2. $P^E = 6.0718 - 286.398 + 288e^{-.09(.25)}$

$$= \$1.2662.$$

ST-3. Strap:

$$2 \text{ Calls: } \$1,214.36$$
$$\underline{1 \text{ Put: } \quad 126.62}$$
$$\text{Total } \$1,340.98$$

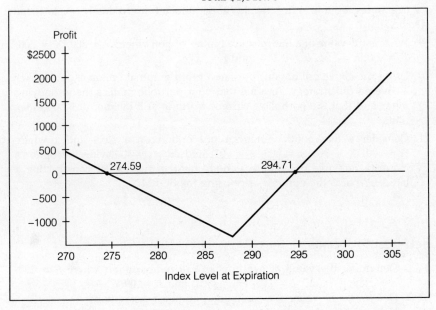

19

FUTURES OPTIONS

In 1982 the Commodity Futures Trading Commission approved the experimental trading of options written on futures contracts. Each futures exchange was allowed to offer one futures option contract. This experiment proved so successful that futures options were authorized for permanent trading in early 1987. Since that time, futures options trading has grown substantially with options on financial futures leading the way.

In this chapter we describe futures options, explaining how they differ from regular spot options, and their markets and valuation procedures. Examples of hedging and speculating with futures options are provided, along with a summary of empirical evidence. Overall, you will find that futures options really are not much different from regular spot options. Because of this, the pricing of the two should be closely related to prevent arbitrage opportunities.

OPTIONS ON FUTURES VERSUS OPTIONS ON SPOTS

In this book we have already considered futures contracts and option contracts written on spot assets. To ease exposition, suppose that this spot asset is a British pound. With a spot option the owner has the right to trade British pounds in the future for a specified exercise price. Exercise of a spot call or put option entails the transfer of actual pounds. However, with a futures option, the underlying asset is a *futures contract* written on British pounds. If the owner of a BP futures call option exercises, she assumes a long position in the futures market with a futures price equal to the exercise price. For a BP futures put option, the exerciser assumes a short BP futures position. Immediately upon exercise, the futures contract, which typically expires after the futures option, is marked-to-the-market. Additionally, the exerciser and new holder of a futures contract must post the regular futures margin.

As an illustration of this process, suppose that a BP call futures option with exercise price of $1.70/BP is exercised at option expiration. At this time the relevant futures price is $1.75/BP. Thus the option is in-the-money, a requirement for rational exercise. If there are BP62,500 per futures contract, then the call option writer owes the exercising party $3,125 [($1.75 − 1.70) × 62,500]. A payment of this amount is made immediately from the writer to the option buyer; thus, the newly created futures contract is immediately marked-to-the-market. The exerciser assumes a long position in the yet-to-mature BP futures contract, while the option writer is assigned the short side of the BP futures contract. Both parties must therefore post the normal futures margin requirements. From this point on, the two parties engage in a regular futures contract. Each is free to continue to hold his respective position or relinquish it via a reversing trade.

Hence, the major difference between a spot option and a futures option is that with the former, exercise entails trading of the actual spot asset, while with the latter, exercise entails assuming a position in a futures contract written on the spot asset. In the above example we cannot determine if the BP futures call option buyer profited overall, since we do not know the original premium paid for the option contract. Later in this chapter we analyze the valuation of futures options.

If options on the spot had existed prior to the introduction of options on the future in 1982, then what marginal benefits do futures options provide? How can futures options compete side by side with their counterpart spot options? The answer to these questions appears to be three-fold. First, some have argued that futures options are popular because they have less severe capital requirements than spot options. To exercise a spot option, the exerciser must have sufficient capital to cover the entire exercise price. With a futures option, however, option exercise entails only the futures margin to be posted. This difference may be important for traders with limited capital.

Second, futures options may overcome liquidity problems associated with shortages of the spot asset. For instance, suppose that a unique asset is the subject of a traded spot option. Since there is a fixed supply of this unique asset, there exists a limit on the deliverable supply of the asset against which a regular spot option is written. With a futures option, however, additional supplies of the deliverable asset can be freely created—traders can write and contract in more futures contracts. This implies that futures options may overcome problems associated with shortages of the actual spot asset.

Third, futures options may provide competitive advantages in the form of lower transaction costs to futures floor traders. Prior to the introduction of futures options traded on listed futures exchanges, futures floor traders seeking to contract in related options had to transact in spot options like any other public trader. The spot options, if they existed, were traded on the floors of other exchanges. With the

The major difference between a spot option and a futures option is that with the former, exercise entails trading of the actual spot asset, whereas with the latter, exercise entails assuming a position in a futures contract written on the spot asset.

introduction of futures options came the side-by-side trading of futures and their options on the same exchange floor. This offered futures traders the ability to transact in options at a lower cost. Traders may seek to transact in futures options for hedging or speculation. At futures exchanges, the pits for futures contracts and their options are typically side by side, which can facilitate hedging and speculation, and enhance market efficiency.

For the above reasons, options on futures offer some advantages over spot options trading (although spot options exhibit other comparative advantages). Thus, futures options are not a financial "excess," and the trading of futures options appears to be here to stay. In the next section we describe the markets for listed futures options.

FUTURES OPTIONS MARKETS AND INSTRUMENTS

Futures options are traded on a number of underlying assets, including Treasury bonds and notes, currencies, stock indexes, gold and other precious metals, and a variety of agricultural commodities such as wheat, soybeans, and coffee. Options on futures typically exhibit the same contract months, position limits, trading hours, and other specifications as their underlying futures contracts. As stated previously, however, expiration of the options usually occurs earlier—often about one to two weeks before the futures contract. For instance, BP futures options traded on the Chicago Mercantile Exchange expire nine calendar days earlier than their underlying BP futures.

Exhibit 19.1 presents some of the more liquid futures options, providing details concerning exercise-price intervals and other contract specifications. The markets represented in this exhibit are U.S.–based. Similar information is provided in Exhibit 19.2 for futures options listed on overseas exchanges. As these exhibits demonstrate, futures options are now traded on a wide variety of underlying assets despite the instrument's recent introduction. Virtually any spot asset on which futures contracts are traded is a candidate for futures options trading.

Besides contract development, volume in futures options trading has shown remarkable growth. In the years 1983 through 1986 annual trading volume in all U.S. futures options increased nearly six-fold, to 30 million contracts. Most of this volume growth has been concentrated in financial futures options, with the CME offering successful contracts on the SP500 and several major trading currencies, and the CBOT offering successful contracts on U.S. Treasury notes and bonds. Figure 19.1 portrays the composition of futures options volume for U.S. markets for the year 1986. On the overseas exchanges, futures options on gold, currencies, Treasury securities, and stock indexes have also exhibited the greatest liquidity.

The trading of futures options is conducted—and prices are reported—in a manner analogous to the trading of spot options. Exhibit

Exhibit 19.1:

Contract Specifications for Selected U.S. Futures Options

Underlying Futures Contracts	Contract Sizes	Exercise-Price Intervals	Minimum Price Fluctuations	Exchanges[a]
U.S. Treasury Bonds	$100,000	2 pt.	1/64 pt.	CBOT
U.S. Treasury Notes	$100,000	2 pt.	1/64 pt.	CBOT
Soybeans	5,000 bu.	25¢	1/8¢/bu.	CBOT
Corn	5,000 bu.	10¢	1/8¢/bu.	CBOT
SP500 Stock Index	500 × SP500	5 pt.	0.05 pt.	CME
British Pound	BP62,500	2-1/2¢	.05¢/BP	CME
Live Cattle	40,000 lb.	2¢	.025¢/lb.	CME
Live Hogs	30,000 lb.	2¢	.025¢/lb.	CME
Cocoa	10 metric tons	$100	$1/metric ton	CSCE
Gold	100 troy oz.	10¢/oz.	10¢/oz.	CMX
Wheat (Hard Red Winter)	5,000 bu.	10¢	1/8¢/bu.	KCBT
Wheat (Soft Winter)	1,000 bu.	10¢	1/8¢/bu.	MCE
Wheat (Spring)	5,000 bu.	10¢	1/8¢/bu.	MGE
Cotton No. 2	50,000 lb.	1¢	1/100¢/bu.	NYCE
Orange Juice	15,000 lb.	2-1/2¢	5/100¢/lb.	NYCE
NYSE Composite Index	500 × NYSE	2 pt.	0.05 pt.	NYFE
Crude Oil (Light Sweet)	1,000 barrels	$1/barrel	1¢/barrel	NYME

[a]CBOT = Chicago Board of Trade
CME = Chicago Mercantile Exchange and associate divisions
CSCE = Coffee, Sugar and Cocoa Exchange
CMX = Commodity Exchange Inc.
KCBT = Kansas City Board of Trade
MCE = MidAmerica Commodity Exchange
MGE = Minneapolis Grain Exchange
NYCE = New York Cotton Exchange and associated divisions
NYFE = New York Futures Exchange
NYME = New York Mercantile Exchange

19.3 (on page 435) presents settlement futures option prices for selected contracts. Interpreting these like those of any spot option, we see, for example, that the closing British pound call futures option price, for March delivery and exercise price of $1.675/BP, was $0.0462/BP on March 1, 1989, or $2,887.50 per contract. The corresponding put futures option closed at just $0.0002/BP, or $12.50 per contract.

VALUING EUROPEAN FUTURES OPTIONS

Futures contracts do not pay dividends or interest per se. However, the futures price does exhibit a continuous leakage as the contract matures and the spot and futures prices converge. The resettlement (marking-

Underlying Futures Contracts	Contract Sizes	Exercise-Price Intervals	Minimum Price Fluctuations	Exchanges[a]
Gold	20 oz.	$20/oz.	10¢/oz.	WCE
Coffee	50 60-kg. bags	Cz$100/bag	Cz$1/bag	BMF
Gas Oil	100 metric tons	$5/ton	$0.05/ton	IPE
Cocoa No. 6	10 metric tons	£50/ton	£1/ton	FOX
EEC Wheat	100 metric tons	£1/ton	5 pence/ton	LGFM
3-Month Eurodollar	$1,000,000	.25 pt.	1 basis pt.	LIFFE
Financial Times 100	£25 × FTSE	2-1/2 pt.	0.01 pt.	LIFFE
Lead	25 metric tons	£20/$20	25 pence/ton	LME
Potatoes (Main crop)	40 metric tons	£5	10 pence/ton	LPFM
French Gov. Nat'l. Bond	500,000 FRF	2%	0.01%	MATIF
Eurodollar	$1,000,000	25 pt.	0.01 pt.	SIMEX
10-Year Treasury Bonds	AD100,000	0.25%	0.01 pt.	SFE

[a]WCE = Winnepeg Commodity Exchange
BMF   = Bolsa Mercantil & de Futuros
IPE   = International Petroleum Exchange
FOX   = London Futures and Options Exchange
LGFM = London Grain Futures Market
LIFFE = London International Financial Futures Exchange
LME   = London Metal Exchange
LPFM = London Potato Futures Market
MATIF = Marche A Terme des Instruments Financiers de Paris
SIMEX = Singapore International Monetary Exchange
SFE   = Sydney Futures Exchange Ltd.

to-the-market) on a futures contract means that there is a series of cash flows associated with a position in the futures market. These resettlement cash flows may be represented as a continuous leakage when valuing futures options. Recognizing this, F. Black (1976) developed a variation of his earlier Black-Scholes model to price all European futures options. For calls, the Black model is

(19.1)
$$C_f^E = e^{-rT}[fN(d_8) - XN(d_8 - \sigma_f\sqrt{T})],$$

where

$$d_8 = \frac{ln(f/X) + (\sigma_f^2/2)T}{\sigma_f\sqrt{T}}.$$

In Equation 19.1, f refers to the current underlying futures price and σ_f^2 refers to the annualized variance of futures price change relatives (i.e., futures "returns"). Also, notice that the expression for d_8 does not include r, the riskless rate of interest. This is because r represents the opportunity cost of funds invested in the underlying asset; however, no investment is required to assume a futures position.

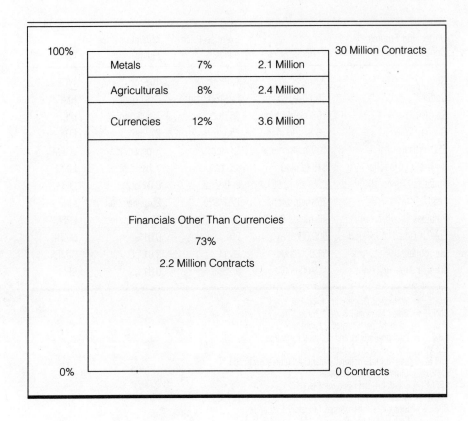

One of the most interesting aspects of Black's model is that it yields an identical price as that for a corresponding European spot option if the options and futures contracts all expire simultaneously. This result is rather obvious when one considers that the spot and futures prices are identical at contract expiration and that early exercise is prohibited when the options are European.[1]

A Numerical Example

Suppose that we wish to price a European call BP futures option with exercise price of $1.675/BP and three-month maturity. The current BP futures price underlying the option is $1.710/BP, and the relevant risk-free interest rate is 8 percent ($r = .08$). Also, the annualized variance of futures returns is 0.15. This measure can be obtained by sampling recent BP futures price changes, or by imputing σ_f^2 from a similar option with three-month maturity but different exercise price. In

---

[1]Another implicit condition for this result to obtain is that the variance of spot and futures returns are equal, which they will be under the assumptions employed by the Black-Scholes framework. We will return to this point later in the chapter.

FUTURES OPTIONS

T-BONDS (CBT) $100,000; points and 64ths of 100%

Strike	Calls–Last			Puts–Last		
Price	Jun-c	Sep-c	Dec-c	Jun-p	Sep-p	Dec-p
84	4-05	....	....	0-32	1-08	....
86	2-39	3-20	....	0-63	1-47	2-22
88	1-30	2-17	2-52	1-51	2-39	3-12
90	0-47	1-30	2-01	3-03	3-48	....
92	0-22	0-60	1-32	4-39	5-09	....
94	0-10	0-37	1-00	6-27	....	....

Est. vol. 68,000, Tues vol. 37,899 calls, 27,689 puts
Open interest Tues; 150,963 calls, 169,606 puts

T-NOTES (CBT) $100,000; points and 64ths of 100%

Strike	Calls–Last			Puts–Last		
Price	Jun-c	Sep-c	Dec-c	Jun-p	Sep-p	Dec-p
89	....	....	....	0-24	0-53	....
90	2-13	....	....	0-38	....	....
91	1-35	....	....	0-59	....	....
92	1-00	1-40	....	1-23	1-57	....
93	0-38	....	....	1-61	2-28	....
94	0-23	0-54	....	2-44	3-04	....

Est. vol. 2,000, Tues vol. 2,488 calls, 817 puts
Open interest Tues; 13,879 calls, 15,229 puts

S&P 500 STOCK INDEX (CME) $500 times premium

Strike	Calls–Settle			Puts–Settle		
Price	Mar-c	Apr-c	Jn-c	Mar-p	Apr-p	Jun-p
280	9.35	14.55	16.95	1.15	2.85	5.45
285	5.50	10.85	13.55	2.30	4.05	6.90
290	2.65	7.60	10.60	4.45	5.75	8.75
295	1.00	4.95	7.95	7.80	8.05	11.00
300	0.25	3.00	5.80	12.00	11.00	13.75
305	0.05	1.70	4.10	16.80	....	16.85

Est. vol. 4,279; Tues vol. 1,617 calls; 2,019 puts
Open interest Tues; 23,119 calls; 24,002 puts

NYSE COMPOSITE INDEX (NYFE) $500 times premium

158	4.50	7.40	8.20	0.75	1.65	2.50
160	3.00	5.95	6.85	1.20	2.20	3.15
162	1.80	4.65	5.60	2.00	2.90	3.90
164	0.95	3.50	4.45	3.10	3.75	4.75
166	0.40	2.50	3.45	4.60	4.75	5.70
168	0.15	1.70	2.60	6.35	5.95	6.85

Est. vol. 145, Tues vol. 36 calls, 80 puts
Open interest Tues 721 calls, 1,331 puts

GOLD (CMX) 100 troy ounces; dollars per troy ounce

Strike	Calls–Last			Puts–Last		
Price	Apr-c	Jun-c	Aug-c	Apr-p	Jun-p	Aug-p
370	17.50	25.00	31.50	0.40	3.30	4.90
380	8.60	17.80	25.00	1.50	5.90	7.50
390	2.30	11.70	18.40	5.20	9.50	11.00
400	0.50	7.00	13.00	13.40	14.60	15.20
410	0.20	4.30	9.60	23.10	21.90	21.80
420	0.10	2.50	6.80	33.00	29.90	28.50

Est. vol. 6,800, Tues vol. 1,911 calls, 2,005 puts
Open interest Tues; 58,300 calls, 38,938 puts

BRITISH POUND (IMM) 62,500 pounds; cents per pound

Strike	Calls–Settle			Puts–Settle		
Price	Mar-c	Jun-c	Sep-c	Mar-p	Jun-p	Sep-p
1675	4.62	....	....	0.02	2.44	....
1700	2.20	4.20	....	0.10	3.46	5.36
1725	0.42	3.04	4.10	0.80	4.78	6.72
1750	0.02	2.16	....	2.90	6.32	8.24
1775	0.004	1.48	....	5.40	8.06	9.94
1800	0.004	1.02	1.92	7.90	10.04	11.78

Est. vol. 2,733, Tues vol. 301 calls, 1,377 puts
Open interest Tues; 11,496 calls, 12,621 puts

CORN (CBT) 5,000 bu.; cents per bu.

Strike	Calls–Settle			Puts–Settle		
Price	May-c	Jly-c	Sep-c	May-p	Jly-p	Sep-p
260	19½	26½	28	1¾	6	15
270	11¾	20½	23	4¼	9	19½
280	6¾	15	19½	9	13¾	25
290	3⅝	11	16¼	16	19¾	32½
300	1¾	8	12¾	23¼	26½	....
310	⅞	6	10½	32¼	34	....

Est. vol. 4,000, Tues vol. 2,246 calls, 1,422 puts
Open interest Tues 47,201 calls, 28,723 puts

SOYBEANS (CBT) 5,000 bu.; cents per bu.

Strike	Calls–Settle			Puts–Settle		
Price	May-c	Jly-c	Aug-c	May-p	Jly-p	Aug-p
700	64½	81½	....	4½	12½	....
725	45	64	74	9½	19½	....
750	30	50½	62	18⅝	30	47½
775	19½	40	51	32½	44½	....
800	12½	31½	43	50½	60½	....
825	8¼	25	36	70½	77½	....

Est. vol. 7,500, Tues vol. 4,499 calls, 2,230 puts
Open interest Tues 56,482 calls, 19,444 puts

COCOA (CSCE) 10 metric tons; cents per ton

Strike	Calls–Settle			Puts–Settle		
Price	May-c	Jly-c	Se-c	May-p	Jly-p	Sep-p
1200	232	204	....	9	13	33
1300	146	129	124	23	38	43
1400	76	83	88	55	75	107
1500	37	45	44	113	148	163
1600	15	23	33	192	232	252
1700	9	16	25	286	325	....

Est. vol. 568; Tues vol. 523 calls; 58 puts
Open interest Tues; 9,031 calls; 7,306 puts

CRUDE OIL (NYM) 1,000 bbls.; $ per bbl.

Strike	Calls–Settle			Puts–Settle		
Price	Apr-c	May-c	Jn-c	Apr-p	May-p	Jun-p
16	2.28	1.91	1.76	0.01	0.14	0.33
17	1.30	1.13	1.09	0.03	0.35	0.65
18	0.45	0.55	0.62	0.17	0.76	1.16
19	0.08	0.22	0.31	0.80	1.42	....
20	0.01	0.07	0.16	1.72	2.26	....
21	0.01	....	....	....	....	....

Est. vol. 18,253; Tues vol. 8,533 calls; 13,840 puts
Open interest Tues; 102,398 calls; 135,460 puts

CATTLE-LIVE (CME) 40,000 lbs.; cents per lb.

Strike	Calls–Settle			Puts–Settle		
Price	Apr-c	Jun-c	Aug-c	Apr-p	Jun-p	Aug-p
74	3.42	1.87	1.30	0.15	1.47	2.85
76	1.75	1.00	0.70	0.47	2.60	4.20
78	0.67	0.50	0.35	1.40	4.02	....
80	0.20	0.22	0.17	2.92	....	....
82	0.05	0.07	....	4.77	....	....
84	0.02	0.05	....	....	....	....

Est. vol. 4,321, Tues vol. 1,523 calls, 1,242 puts
Open interest Tues; 31,770 calls, 32,465 puts

HOGS–LIVE (CME) 30,000 lbs.; cents per lb.

Strike	Calls–Settle			Puts–Settle		
Price	Apr-c	Jun-c	Jly-c	Apr-p	Jun-p	Jly-p
40	4.42	....	....	0.07	0.05	....
42	2.55	....	....	0.20	0.15	0.25
44	1.05	....	....	0.70	0.35	0.60
46	0.30	3.55	3.70	1.95	0.75	1.10
48	0.05	2.30	2.50	3.70	1.45	1.90
50	0.02	1.37	1.45	....	2.50	2.85

Est. vol. 542, Tues vol. 200 calls, 72 puts
Open interest Tues; 5,960 calls, 5,085 puts

Exhibit 19.3:

Settlement Futures Options
Prices for Selected Contracts

other words, we can obtain σ_f^2 by the same two methods used to obtain σ_S^2 (the spot asset's volatility), as discussed in Chapter 13.

To price this futures option, we first compute the upper limits of integration:

$$d_8 = \{[ln(1.710/1.675) + (.15/2)(.25)]/\sqrt{.15}\sqrt{.25}\}$$
$$= 0.2036;$$
$$d_8 - \sqrt{.15}\sqrt{.25} = 0.0110.$$

Using Exhibit 13.1 and interpolating, we find that the associated standard normal probabilities are

$$N(.2036) = .5807; N(.0100) = .5040.$$

Thus, the BP futures option price is $0.1459/BP:

$$C_f^E = e^{-.08(.25)}[1.710(.5807) - 1.675(.5040)]$$
$$= \$0.1459/BP.$$

The value of the corresponding European put BP futures option can be obtained from the following expression:

(19.2) $$C_f^E = P_f^E - e^{-rT}(X - f).$$

Equation 19.2 represents put-call parity for European futures options; it follows from arbitrage restrictions similar to those underlying spot put-call parity, as described in Chapter 12. For our illustration, the corresponding put value is $0.1116/BP:

$$P_f^E = .1459 + e^{-.08(.25)}(1.675 - 1.710) = \$0.1116/\text{BP}.$$

Alternatively, P_f^E could have been obtained directly from the following pricing equation:

(19.3) $$P_f^E = e^{-rT}[X(1 - N(d_8 - \sigma\sqrt{T})) - f(1 - N(d_8))].$$

VALUING AMERICAN FUTURES OPTIONS

Without exception, all U.S.–listed futures options are American, capable of being exercised prematurely. The necessary condition for optimal early exercise is that the futures option be sufficiently in-the-money; for calls (puts), the underlying futures price must be greater than (less than) a critical futures price.

To see this more clearly, reexamine Equation 19.1, where $f \to \infty$ such that $N(\cdot) \to 1$:

$$C_f^E \to e^{-rT}[f - X].$$

This expression, representing the market price of the call futures option, may be less than the option's exercisable proceeds:

$$C_f^E \to e^{-rT}[f - X] < f - X.$$

Thus, it may be optimal to prematurely exercise an in-the-money futures call option. Allowing $f \to 0$, and using Equation 19.3, we see that it may be optimal to prematurely exercise an in-the-money American put futures option as well:

$$P_f^E \to e^{-rT}[X - f] < X - f.$$

Because it may be optimal to prematurely exercise an American futures option, investors are willing to pay more for American futures options relative to their European counterparts. This price difference represents the American option's early exercise premium. To correctly price American futures options, we must incorporate this premium.

The analytic approximation of G. Barone-Adesi and R. Whaley (1986), as described in Chapter 14, may be used to price American futures options. To apply the model here, one must substitute the risk-free rate of interest, r, for δ, and f for S:

$$(19.4) \qquad C_f^A = \begin{cases} C_f^E + A_2(f/\bar{f})^{q_2} & \text{if } f < \bar{f}, \\ f - x & \text{if } f \geq \bar{f} \end{cases}$$

where

$$A_2 = (\bar{f}/q_2)\{1 - e^{-rT}N[d_9(\bar{f})]\}$$

$$d_9 = \frac{ln(f/X) + (\sigma_f^2/2)T}{\sigma_f\sqrt{T}}$$

$$q_2 = .50\{-(\beta - 1) + \sqrt{(\beta - 1)^2 + (4\alpha/h)]}$$

$$\beta = 2/\sigma_f^2$$

$$\alpha = 2r/\sigma_f^2$$

$$h = 1 - e^{-rT}.$$

In Equation 19.4, $\bar{f}$ refers to the critical futures price above which premature exercise should occur; $\bar{f}$ is determined iteratively by solving the equation

$$\bar{f} - X = C_f^E(\bar{f}) + \{1 - e^{-rT}N[d_9(\bar{f})]\}\bar{f}/q_2.$$

The Barone-Adesi and Whaley analytic approximation for American put options is similarly altered to price American put futures options.

Exhibit 19.4 presents the results of a simulation analysis of the early-exercise premia associated with American futures options. Reported are the prices of corresponding European and American futures options, as well as the early-exercise premia for various parameter values. The European prices are given by Equations 19.1 and 19.3, while the American prices are given by Barone-Adesi and Whaley's analytic approximation. As discussed in Chapter 14, the BOPM could also be used to value American futures options. The results of the simulation suggest that for call options, the early-exercise premium increases in f/X, r, and T. For puts, the premium increases in X/f, r, and T. The average percentage premium is 1.82 percent of the European option's price. Overall, the results suggest that it is important to incorporate the early-exercise premium when valuing American futures options, especially for deeply in-the-money options.

BOUNDARIES FOR AMERICAN FUTURES OPTIONS

Since listed futures options are strictly American, we now provide boundary conditions applicable to American futures option prices.

	Call Options			Put Options		
Futures Price	European Price	American Price	Early-Exercise Premium	European Price	American Price	Early-Exercise Premium
Futures Options Parameters: $r = .08$, $T = .25$, $\sigma_f = .15$, $X = \$100$						
80	0.0027	0.0029	0.0002	19.6067	20.0000	0.3933
90	0.2529	0.2547	0.0018	10.0549	10.1506	0.0957
100	2.9321	2.9458	0.0137	2.9321	2.9458	0.0137
110	10.1752	10.2627	0.0875	0.3732	0.3756	0.0024
120	19.6239	20.0000	0.3761	0.0199	0.0204	0.0005
Futures Options Parameters: $r = .12$, $T = .25$, $\sigma_f = .15$, $X = \$100$						
80	0.0027	0.0030	0.0003	19.4116	20.0000	0.5884
90	0.2504	0.2533	0.0029	9.9549	10.1153	0.1605
100	2.9029	2.9257	0.0228	2.9029	2.9257	0.0228
110	10.0740	10.2205	0.1465	0.3695	0.3734	0.0039
120	19.4286	20.0000	0.5714	0.0197	0.0205	0.0008
Futures Options Parameters: $r = .08$, $T = .25$, $\sigma_f = .30$, $X = \$100$						
80	0.3956	0.3986	0.0030	19.9996	20.2032	0.2036
90	1.9817	1.9913	0.0096	11.7837	11.8543	0.0707
100	5.8604	5.8878	0.0274	5.8604	5.8878	0.0274
110	12.2527	12.3237	0.0710	2.4507	2.4624	0.0116
120	20.4776	20.6470	0.1694	0.8737	0.8790	0.0053
Futures Options Parameters: $r = .08$, $T = .50$, $\sigma_f = .15$, $X = \$100$						
80	0.0583	0.0603	0.0020	19.2740	20.0000	0.7260
90	0.8150	0.8256	0.0106	10.4229	10.6004	0.1815
100	4.0637	4.1099	0.0463	4.0637	4.1099	0.0463
110	10.6831	10.8584	0.1753	1.0752	1.0887	0.0134
120	19.4105	20.0018	0.5913	0.1947	0.1991	0.0043

Exhibit 19.4:
Simulation of Early-Exercise Premia for American Futures Options

These bounds follow from arbitrage restrictions similar to those discussed in Chapter 12. For proofs of these conditions, see K. Ramaswamy and S. Sundaresan (1985) and C. Ball and W. Torous (1986).

Conditions Applicable to Calls

Upper and lower bounds for American call futures options are

$$f(t_0,\tau) \geq C_f^A(t_0,T) \geq MAX[0,f(t_0,\tau) - X],$$

where

$f(t_0,\tau) =$ the price at time t_0 of the underlying futures contract maturing at time $\tau > t_0$;

$$C_f^A(t_0, T) = \text{the price at time } t_0 \text{ of the American call futures}$$
$$\text{option maturing at time } T, \text{ where } t_0 < T \le \tau.$$

Conditions Applicable to Puts

Upper and lower bounds for American put features options are

$$X \ge P_f^A(t_0, T) \ge MAX[0, X - f(t_0, \tau)],$$

where

$$P_f^A(t_0, T) = \text{the price at time } t_0 \text{ of the American put futures option}$$
$$\text{maturing at time } T, \text{ where } t_0 < T \le \tau.$$

Parity Conditions

Two put-call parity conditions govern American futures options. The first is an upper parity condition given by

$$C_f^A(t_0, T) \le P_f^A(t_0, T) + f(t_0, \tau) - Xe^{-rT}.$$

The second is a lower parity condition given by[2]

$$C_f^A(t_0, T) \ge P_f^A(t_0, T) + f(t_0, \tau) - X.$$

ARBITRAGING AMERICAN SPOT AND FUTURES OPTIONS

Options on the spot and options on futures are closely related, so their prices must be closely related in order to prevent risk-free arbitrage.

Options on the spot and options on futures are closely related, so their prices must be closely related in order to prevent risk-free arbitrage. For example, earlier in this chapter we found that European spot and futures options had the same price if the options and underlying futures contract all exhibited the same expiration. Any violation of this equality would give rise to arbitrage opportunities, ignoring market imperfections. For instance, if one observed that the European spot option's price was less than that of the corresponding futures option, buying the spot option and writing the futures option would assure a riskless profit. Holding the spot option to maturity assures a profit, since the spot option's price must be equal to that of the written futures option at expiration.

American spot and futures options prices should also be closely related, although perhaps not equal, due to the possibility of early

---

[2]Whereas the previous boundary conditions are valid regardless of the dynamics of $f(t_0, \tau)$ and r, this second parity condition requires the restriction that r is constant. See C. Ball and W. Torous (1986).

exercise. M. Brenner, G. Courtadon, and M. Subrahmanyam (1985) and J. Ogden and A. Tucker (1988) investigate the relative prices of corresponding American spot and futures options, and obtain the following results: (1) for zero-leakage spot assets, the American futures option value should always be greater than that of the corresponding American spot option; (2) for discrete-leakage spot assets, the American futures option price will typically be greater, but the American spot option price could be greater, depending on the size of the intervening discrete leakage; and (3) for continuous-leakage spot assets, the American spot or futures option price may be greater, depending on the magnitude of the proportional leakage rate.

To illustrate these results, let us consider the relative valuation of American currency spot and futures options. Recall that currency represents a type of continuous-leakage asset. Assume that the options and futures contracts all expire at the same time, and the volatilities of spot and futures price change relatives are equal. This will occur under the assumptions of the Black-Scholes framework; Appendix 19.A offers a formal proof. Also, it is assumed that interest rates are constant and that interest rate parity holds continuously. Under these conditions, an American spot call (put) currency option should have a greater (lower) price than the corresponding American futures call (put) currency option if the underlying currency sells at a forward discount against the dollar: $C^A > C_f^A$ and $P^A < P_f^A$ if $r < r_f$. The opposite obtains for a premium foreign currency: $C^A < C_f^A$ and $P^A > P_f^A$ if $r > r_f$. Thus, the relative valuation of American currency spot and futures options depends critically on the size of r_f. The above conditions hold because of the arbitrage restrictions described next.

Strategies for Currency Calls

Suppose that $C^A < C_f^A$ for a discount currency such that a violation occurs. The arbitrage strategy used to exploit this violation is (1) purchase the spot call option, (2) write the futures call option, and (3) invest the proceeds in a domestic risk-free asset maturing at T. If the written futures call option is not exercised prematurely, then holding the spot call option until expiration provides a profit of $(C_f^A - C^A)e^{rT}$:

	Payoff at T	
	$f = S \leq X$	$f = S > X$
Purchase C^A	$-C^A e^{rT}$	$-C^A e^{rT} + (S - X)$
Write C_f^A	$C_f^A e^{rT}$	$C_f^A e^{rT} - (f - X)$
Total	$(C_f^A - C^A)e^{rT} > 0$	$(C_f^A - C^A)e^{rT} > 0$

Note that $f = S$ at T, and that the riskless profit earned is the same regardless of whether the options expire in- or out-of-the-money. Similarly, if $C^A > C_f^A$ for a premium currency such that a violation occurs, then (1) writing the spot call option, (2) purchasing the futures call option, and (3) investing the proceeds in a riskless domestic asset provides a riskless profit of $(C^A - C_f^A)e^{rT}$, assuming the written spot call option is not exercised prematurely.

Now assume $C^A < C_f^A$ for a discount currency, but the written futures call option is exercised prematurely at time $t < T$. The first trading strategy mentioned above provides a profit of $(C_f^A - C^A)e^{rt} + (S - f)$ at t:

	Payoff at t
Purchase C^A	$-C^A e^{rt} + (S - X)$
Write C_f^A	$C_f^A e^{rt} - (f - X)$
Total	$(C_f^A - C^A)e^{rt} + (S - f) > 0$

Note that the spot call option can be exercised to yield $S - X$, that both options must be in-the-money at t for premature exercise to occur, and that $S > f$ at t by interest rate parity and the assumption of constant interest rates r and r_f. Similarly, if $C^A > C_f^A$ for a premium currency, and the written spot call option is exercised early, then the second trading strategy presented above provides a riskless profit of $(C^A - C_f^A)e^{rt} + (f - S)$ at t.

Strategies for Currency Puts

Suppose that $P^A > P_f^A$ for a discount currency such that a violation occurs. The trading strategy used to exploit this violation is (1) write the spot put option, (2) purchase the futures put option, and (3) invest the proceeds in a risk-free domestic asset maturing at T. If the written spot put option is not exercised prematurely, then holding the futures put option until expiration provides a profit of $(P^A - P_f^A)e^{rT}$:

	Payoff At T	
	$f = S < X$	$f = S \geq X$
Write P^A	$P^A e^{rT} - (X - S)$	$P^A e^{rT}$
Purchase P_f^A	$-P_f^A e^{rT} + (X - f)$	$-P_f^A e^{rT}$
Total	$(P^A - P_f^A)e^{rT} > 0$	$(P^A - P_f^A)e^{rT} > 0$

Note that $f = S$ at T, and that the riskless profit is the same regardless of whether the options expire in- or out-of-the-money. Similarly, if $P^A < P_f^A$ for a premium currency such that a violation occurs, then (1) purchasing the spot put option, (2) writing the futures put option, and (3) investing the proceeds in a riskless U.S. asset provides a profit of $(P_f^A - P^A)e^{rT}$, assuming the written futures put option is not exercised prematurely.

If the written spot put option in the first trading strategy on page 442 is exercised early, at time t, the riskless profit is $(P^A - P_f^A)e^{rt} + (S - f)$ at t. If the written futures put option in the second trading strategy is exercised early, the profit is $(P_f^A - P^A)e^{rt} + (f - S)$. (Problem number 5 at the end of the chapter invites the reader to demonstrate such profits.)

HEDGING WITH FUTURES OPTIONS

Like spot options, futures options may be used to immunize a pre-existing spot-asset position against downside risk. As an illustration, suppose that a Swiss industrial concern has made a tender offer for a U.S. electrical equipment manufacturer with 2 million shares of common stock outstanding. The initial offer was for $25 a share, but a bidding war with a U.S. rival has broken out. The Swiss firm expects to have to raise its offer to $30 a share in order to succeed in its takeover attempt. During the interim period, it expects a modest decline in U.S. interest rates to strengthen the franc's value relative to the dollar and thus lower the price of the acquisition. The Swiss firm suspects a possibility, however, that a U.S. recovery might overheat, causing a run-up in U.S. interest rates and a drop in the franc's value, lowering the profitability of the takeover.

The acquisition is not expected to be profitable if the Swiss firm raises its bid to $30 per share and the franc subsequently depreciates by 5 percent. The firm decides that it can tolerate a one-in-a-hundred chance that this will occur. In order to maintain a tolerable risk level, it must offset the foreign exchange losses associated with declines in franc value of as much as 6.6 percent.

The firm's exposure to foreign exchange risk can be controlled by adjusting the deadline by which shares must be tendered. However, the interval necessary to lower the probability of a 6.6 percent decline in the franc to 1:100 is estimated to be too short, thereby severely jeopardizing the tender offer's acceptance. The firm could short Swiss franc futures, but such a strategy has three shortcomings. First, the firm may not end up being the high bidder, thereby not incurring a dollar-denominated liability. As a result, the futures position would not be covered and would yield net losses if the dollar depreciated. Second, if the bid is accepted and the dollar depreciates as forecasted, futures losses would offset the reduction of the purchase price in francs and thereby lower the acquisition's profitability. Third, managing the cash flows associated with the futures position can be difficult.

An alternative strategy that overcomes these problems is to purchase franc put futures options. With put options on Swiss franc futures, the firm can defer selling franc futures until it actually has a dollar-denominated liability. If the bid is accepted, the firm will exercise its options and assume a short franc futures position, thereby protecting its

Like spot options, futures options may be used to immunize a pre-existing spot-asset position against downside price risk.

exposure to a franc depreciation. Should the firm not be the high bidder, holding naked put futures options is less risky than holding a naked short futures position. Finally, the cash-flow management difficulties associated with a futures position and daily resettlement are not incurred with futures options.

To flesh out our illustration, suppose that the spot exchange rate is $0.4587/SF and that the breakeven exchange rate is $0.4358/SF [(1 − .05)$0.4587]. A 6.6 percent drop would lower the spot rate to $0.4284/SF and raise the acquisition's cost to SF2,367,130 above the breakeven cost:

$$SF2,367,130 = \frac{\$60,000,000}{\$0.4284/SF} - \frac{\$60,000,000}{(1 - .05)\$0.4587/SF}.$$

The breakeven cost represents 1,101 Swiss franc futures contracts:

$$1,101 = \frac{\$60,000,000}{(1 - .05)\$0.4587/SF} \div SF125,000 \text{ per contract.}$$

Assume that the price of a put option contract on Swiss franc futures with exercise price $0.4500/SF and thirty days until expiration is $325.00. The option position costs SF780,085:

$$SF780,085 = \frac{\$325 \text{ per contract} \times 1,101 \text{ contracts}}{\$0.4587/SF},$$

and generates profits if the futures price falls below $0.4474/SF [$0.4500 − ($325 ÷ SF125,000)]. The cost of the position is equivalent to an insurance premium. The difference between the purchase price at the breakeven exchange rate and the purchase price at the current rate [SF134,108,180.6 − SF130,804,447.4 = SF3,303,733] is equivalent to an insurance deductible.

Each $0.001 decline in the futures price below $0.4474/SF yields an additional profit of $13,762 [$0.0001 × SF125,000 × 1,101 contracts]. Therefore, the protection offered by the options can be determined by solving the following equation:

$$\frac{[x + (\$0.4474 - 0.4358)]\$13,762}{.0001} = \frac{\$60,000,000}{\$0.4358 - x} - \frac{\$60,000,000}{\$0.4358},$$

where x denotes the drop in the value of the franc below the breakeven exchange rate. The left-hand side represents the option profits, while the right-hand side represents the increase in the acquisition's cost over the breakeven cost. By solving the equation, we find that the spot exchange rate must drop at least 6.9 percent (from the current rate) to $0.4272/SF before the option profits fail to offset the increase in the acquisition's cost over the breakeven cost. Thus, the position in SF futures put options ensures the firm of maintaining its tolerable risk level. The difference between the purchase price at an exchange rate of $0.4272/SF and the purchase price at the breakeven exchange rate [SF140,449,438 − SF134,108,180 = SF6,341,258] is equivalent to the maximum payout on an insurance policy.

SPECULATING WITH FUTURES OPTIONS

Like spot options, futures options can be used to speculate on subsequent price changes. With futures options a speculator is wagering on a change in a *futures* price, but of course changes in futures prices are largely dictated by changes in the underlying spot-asset price. Many illustrations of how futures options can be used to speculate are possible. Such strategies are completely analogous to those for spot options presented in Chapter 15. We will consider just one example here—using SP500 futures options to create a straddle.

Like spot options, futures options can be used to speculate on subsequent price changes.

Suppose that a speculator feels that future stock market activity will be very volatile. A straddle formed with SP500 futures options can be used to capitalize on this high volatility. The straddle is constructed by purchasing a call SP500 futures option and simultaneously buying a corresponding put SP500 futures option. These option contracts are traded on the Chicago Mercantile Exchange, and each contract entails 500 times the SP500 Stock Index. Figure 19.2 presents the profit graph at option expiration, assuming the following price information (see Exhibit 19.3):

Purchase SP500 Futures April 290 Call:	$3,800
Purchase SP500 Futures April 290 Put:	2,875
Total Straddle Investment:	$6,675

Should the underlying SP500 futures price be 290 at option expiration, neither option expires in-the-money, and the speculator loses $6,675, the initial investment. However, should the resulting futures price be below 276.65 or above 303.35, the speculator will exhibit a net profit. Therefore, much like a straddle created with spot options, the speculator profits if the underlying futures price deviates greatly in either direction.

EMPIRICAL EVIDENCE ON FUTURES OPTIONS

Because futures options are a relatively new derivative security, only a few empirical studies concerning these instruments now exist. Below we briefly discuss these studies.

Jordan-Seale and Ogden-Tucker Studies

J. Jordan and W. Seale (1986) and J. Ogden and A. Tucker (1987) investigated the efficiency of selected futures options markets by determining whether violations of rational pricing bounds went unexploited. Jordan and Seale focused on U.S. Treasury bond futures options traded on the CBOE, while Ogden and Tucker analyzed options written on British pound, Deutsche mark, and Swiss franc futures traded on the

Figure 19.2:
Profit Graph for a Straddle Constructed with SP500 Futures Options

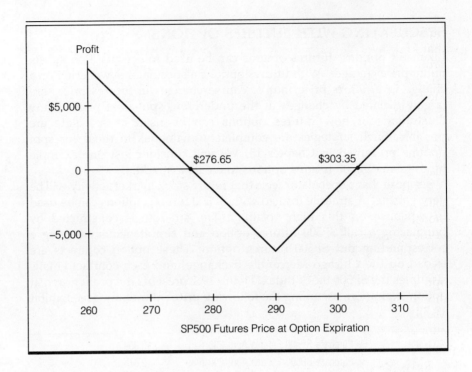

CME. Each study employed thousands of transactions but found almost no violations after controlling for relevant transaction costs and small execution delays. Thus, the results uphold the efficiency of these futures options markets.

Merville-Overdahl and Whaley Studies

L. Merville and J. Overdahl (1986) tested the accuracy of Black's model to price call options written on U.S. Treasury bond futures. They found that Black's model exhibited systematic mispricing patterns, generally overpricing at-the-money and out-of-the-money options while underpricing in-the-money options. The authors suggested that the observed patterns are consistent with nonconstant volatility of futures price change relatives. A modified pricing model designed to capture such nonconstant volatility proved to be slightly more accurate.

R. Whaley (1986) employed nearly 30,000 transactions on SP500 futures options to test the accuracy of his quadratic approximation developed with G. Barone-Adesi. Recall that this approximation incorporates the premium associated with the early exercise feature offered by listed American futures options. Whaley found several mispricing patterns, including underpricing of out-of-the-money calls and overpricing of in-the-money calls; underpricing of shorter-term options and overpricing of longer-term options; and underpricing of in-the-money puts and overpricing of out-of-the-money puts. Also, Whaley reported that an implemented hedging strategy appeared to provide abnormal profits, even after controlling for transaction costs faced by floor traders. His results tend to refute the joint hypothesis of market efficiency and model specification, at least for the sample period.

Baily Study

Black's model assumes constant interest rates. K. Ramaswamy and S. Sundaresan (1985) developed an alternative futures option-pricing model that allows for nonconstant interest rates. They contend that a constant-rate model can misprice futures options if the interest rate fluctuates significantly or if the underlying spot asset is correlated with the interest rate.

W. Baily (1987) compared the nonconstant-rate model of Ramaswamy and Sundaresan to the constant-rate model when pricing gold futures options traded on the New York Commodity Exchange. He found that the nonconstant-rate model was a superior predictor of market prices. Measured in absolute-value terms, the errors from the Ramaswamy and Sundaresan model were smaller by an average of $43 per contract for calls and $96 per contract for puts.

SUMMARY

Futures options differ from spot options in that the former are written on futures contracts, which typically expire after the option, so a holder of a call (put) futures option who exercises assumes a long (short) position in the underlying futures contract, with all of the rights and obligations associated with that position. The futures option writer is assigned the opposite position.

F. Black developed a variation of his earlier Black-Scholes model to value European futures options. The analytic approximation of G. Barone-Adesi and R. Whaley may be used in the valuation of American futures options. Options on futures and options on the spot asset are closely related. Consequently, their prices must be closely related in order the preclude riskless arbitrage. Futures options can be used to hedge risk and to speculate on subsequent price changes in a manner analogous to that of spot options.

Options on futures are a relatively new derivative security. Their trading volume is strong and growing, however. Potential advantages of trading futures options include less severe capital requirements and lower transaction costs.

Selected References

Baily, W. "An Empirical Investigation of the Market for Comex Gold Futures Options." *Journal of Finance* 42 (December 1987): 1187–1194.

Ball, C., and W. Torous. "Futures Options and the Volatility of Futures Prices." *Journal of Finance* 41 (September 1986): 857–870.

Barone-Adesi, G., and R. Whaley. "Efficient Analytic Approximation of American Option Values." *Journal of Finance* 42 (June 1987): 301–320.

Black, F. "The Pricing of Commodity Contracts." *Journal of Financial Economics* 4 (January–March 1976): 167–179.

Brenner, M., G. Courtadon, and M. Subrahmanyam. "Options on the Spot and Options on Futures." *Journal of Finance* 40 (December 1985): 1303–1317.

Itô, K. "On Stochastic Differential Equations." *Memoirs, American Mathematical Society* 4 (December 1951): 1–51.

Jordan, J., and W. Seale. "Transactions Data Tests of Minimum Prices and Put-Call Parity for Treasury Bond Futures Options." *Advances in Futures and Options Research* 1 (1986): 63–87.

Merton, R. "Theory of Rational Option Pricing." *Bell Journal of Economics* 4 (Spring 1973): 141–183.

Merville, L., and J. Overdahl. "An Empirical Examination of the T-Bond Futures (Call) Option Market under Conditions of Constant and Changing Variance Rates." *Advances in Futures and Option Research* 1 (1986): 89–118.

Ogden, J., and A. Tucker. "Empirical Tests of the Efficiency of the Currency Futures Options Market." *Journal of Futures Markets* 7 (December 1987): 695–703.

Ogden, J., and A. Tucker. "The Relative Valuation of American Currency Spot and Futures Options: Theory and Empirical Tests." *Journal of Financial and Quantitative Analysis* 23 (December 1988): 351–368.

Patell, J., and M. Wolfson. "Anticipated Information Releases Reflected in Call Option Prices." *Journal of Accounting and Economics* 1 (1979): 117–140.

Ramaswamy, K., and S. Sundaresan. "The Valuation of Options on Futures Contracts." *Journal of Finance* 40 (December 1985): 1319–1340.

Samuelson, P. "Proof That Properly Anticipated Prices Fluctuate Randomly." *Industrial Management Review* 6 (Spring 1965): 41–49.

Sinquefield, J. "Understanding Options on Futures." *Mortgage Banking* (July 1982): 35–40.

Whaley, R. "Valuation of American Futures Options: Theory and Empirical Tests." *Journal of Finance* 41 (March 1986): 127–150.

Wolf, A. "Fundamentals of Commodity Options on Futures." *Journal of Futures Markets* 2 (1982): 391–408.

Questions and Problems

1. What are some potential advantages in trading futures options not found in spot options trading?

2. From Exhibit 19.3, what was the closing price of gold futures April 390 calls? What was the closing price of the corresponding put option?

3. Explain why a European futures option should exhibit the same price as a corresponding European spot option if the options and futures contracts have the same expiration. Provide an example of a violation of this condition and the resulting arbitrage strategy.

4. What is the price of a European call futures option given the following parameters: $f = \$10$, $X = \$9$, $T = .50$, $\sigma_f = .10$, and $r = .08$? What is the price of a corresponding European put futures option?

5. Suppose that $P^A > P_f^A$ for a discount currency. Demonstrate the arbitrage profit if the written spot put option is exercised early at time $t < T$. Also, demonstrate the arbitrage profit given $P^A < P_f^A$ for a premium currency if the written futures put option is exercised prematurely at t.

6. Under what conditions may it be optimal to prematurely exercise an American call (put) futures option? Demonstrate your answers.

7. Suppose that $f(t_0, \tau) = \$3$, and $C_f^A(t_0, T) = \$4$. How would you exploit this arbitrage opportunity?

8. Suppose that $P_f^A(t_0, T) < MAX[0, X - f(t_0, \tau)]$. How would you exploit this arbitrage opportunity?

9. What are the determinants of the early-exercise premium on American call (put) futures options? How is the premium related to these determinants?

10. Using the BP futures options with March expiration and exercise price of $1.75/BP from Exhibit 19.3, create a reverse straddle. Draw a profit graph for this reverse straddle at option expiration. What are the associated breakeven futures prices?

11. How can a long futures position be protected with futures options? A short futures position?

12. Using the SP500 futures options with March expiration and exercise price of 295 from Exhibit 19.3, present a profit graph for a strap at option expiration. Remember that the contract multiple is $500, and let the expiration futures prices range from $275 to $315.

13. Consider a four-month American put option on an index futures contract where the current futures price is $300, the exercise price is $300, the risk-free rate of interest is 10 percent, and the volatility of the futures returns (σ_f^2) is .009. Divide the time-to-option-maturity into four one-month periods in order to construct a binomial tree. Using the BOPM, what is the option's value? (Hint: Since a futures contract is like an asset exhibiting a continuous leakage at the rate r, $a = 1$.)

Self-Test Problems

ST-1. What is the price of a European call futures option given the following parameter values: $f = \$20$, $X = \$20$, $T = .25$, $\sigma_f = .15$, and $r = .10$?

ST-2. From Problem ST-1, what is the price of the corresponding put option?

ST-3. Determine the price of a European put futures option directly, given the following parameters: $f = \$8$, $X = \$8.50$, $T = .35$, $\sigma_f = .20$, and $r = .08$.

ST-4. Suppose you engage in a long futures position where $f = \$50$. The futures contract entails 100 units of the underlying spot asset. At the same time, you purchase a put option on this futures contract where $P_f = \$1$ and $X = \$50$. For simplicity, assume that the put option and futures contract exhibit the same expiration. Draw a profit graph contrasting this strategy and an uncovered long futures position for expiration futures prices ranging from $35 to $60.

Solutions to Self-Test Problems

ST-1. $d_8 = [ln(20/20) + ((.15^2/2)(.25)]/(.15)(.25)^{1/2} = .0375.$

$d_8 - (.15)(.25)^{1/2} = -.0375.$

$N(.0375) = .5149; N(-.0375) = .4851.$

$C_f^E = e^{-.10(.25)}[20(.5149) - 20(.4851)] = \$0.5813.$

ST-2. $P_f^E = 0.5813 + e^{-.10(.25)}[20 - 20] = \$0.5813.$

ST-3. $d_8 = [ln(8/8.50) + ((.20)^2/2)(.35)]/(.20)(.35)^{1/2} = -.4532.$

$d_8 - (.20)(.35)^{1/2} = -.5715.$

$N(-.4532) = .3253; N(-.5715)$
$\qquad\qquad = .2839.$

$P_f^E = e^{-.08(.35)}[8.50(1 - .2839) - 8.00(1 - .3253)] = \$0.6702.$

ST-4.

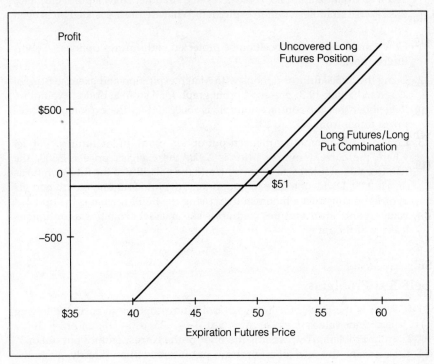

Appendix 19.A

PROOF THAT THE INSTANTANEOUS VOLATILITIES OF SPOT AND FUTURES PRICE CHANGES ARE EQUAL UNDER THE BLACK-SCHOLES FRAMEWORK

Define the instantaneous spot price change relative by the following standard Itô process:

(19.A–1)
$$d\tilde{S} = \mu S dt + \sigma S d\tilde{Z}.$$

Also, let the associated futures price be given by the following cost-of-carry model:

(19.A–2)
$$f = Se^{CC(T)},$$

where CC is assumed constant. From Itô's lemma:

(19.A–3)
$$df̃ = [(\partial f/\partial S)\mu S + (\partial f/\partial t) + 1/2(\partial^2 f/\partial S^2)\sigma^2 S^2]dt$$
$$+ (\partial f/\partial S)\sigma S d\tilde{Z},$$

where $\partial f/\partial S = e^{CC(T)}$, $\partial f/\partial t = -(CC)Se^{CC(T)}$, and $\partial^2 f/\partial S^2 = 0$.

Substituting for the partial derivatives yields

(19.A–4)
$$df̃ = [e^{CC(T)}\mu S - (CC)Se^{CC(T)}]dt + e^{CC(T)}\sigma S d\tilde{Z}$$
$$= (\mu - CC)fdt + \sigma f d\tilde{Z}.$$

Thus, the instantaneous volatility of spot price changes, σ, equals that of futures price changes, σ. The instantaneous drifts differ by the cost-of-carry, CC, since spot and futures prices must converge over time.

SP500 is 280 and the portfolio is worth $560,000, or 2,000 units of the index. Assume that it is currently mid-November and that the December 280 SP500 put contract, which currently sells for $1,250, expires in one month. Further assume that the option is European and that the one-month risk-free rate of interest is 0.0085. Finally, assume that the annualized return variance of the SP500 is .015.

The manager seeks to insure the portfolio by purchasing the December puts. Purchasing four contracts would reduce the investment in the stock portfolio by $5,000. Thus the stock portfolio now contains (approximately) 1,982.14 units of the SP500 index, and the manager holds four put contracts entailing 2,000 index units. Of course, if the stocks and put contracts were perfectly divisible, the manager could assume a one-to-one correspondence between the portfolio index units held and the number of index units underlying the put contracts.

If the resulting SP500 index level is at or above the exercise price of 280 at contract expiration, then the options expire worthless. For instance, if the expiration SP500 is 310, the puts are not exercised, and the resulting portfolio value is $614,463.40 [1,982.14 units $\times$ 310]. Here the opportunity cost of undertaking the insurance is $5,536.60, since a 100% investment in the stock portfolio would have yielded a value of $620,000 [2,000 units $\times$ 3100]. This $5,536.60 cost represents about 1 percent of the portfolio's original value, implying 99 percent *upside capture*—the percentage of the uninsured appreciation in an up market that is captured by the insured portfolio.

On the other hand, if the expiration SP500 is below 280, the put contracts are exercised, and the proceeds are used to offset losses in the equity position. For example, if the SP500 is 250 at option expiration, the resulting insured portfolio value is $555,535:

$$(1,982.14 \times 250) + (280 - 250)(2,000).$$

Of course, an uninsured portfolio's value would have been just $500,000 [2,000 units $\times$ 250]. In general, the minimum insured level of the portfolio is $555,000, occurring when the expiration SP500 level is exactly 280 [1,982.14 $\times$ 280 = $555,000].[3]

The above illustration of portfolio insurance employing index put options should be somewhat familiar to you. It is analogous to the hedging strategy described in Chapter 18 and illustrated in Figure 18.2. The simple idea behind the strategy is that the purchase of put options introduces negative correlation and, as a result, guarantees a certain minimum future value for the portfolio.

Upside capture represents the percentage of uninsured appreciation in an up market that is captured by the insured portfolio.

---

[3]If stocks and put contracts were perfectly divisible such that a one-to-one correspondence were attainable, then the minimum insured level of the portfolio, V_{MIN}, would be given by the following expression: $V_{MIN} = XV/(S + P)$, where X is the option's exercise price, V is the original value of the portfolio, S is the original level of the stock index, and P is the per index unit price of the put option. The guaranteed percentage return on the insured portfolio must be less than the risk-free rate to prevent arbitrage. One cannot insure a minimum return on a risky portfolio that is greater than the riskless rate of interest.

Stock–Treasury Bill Insurance

The stock-put insurance technique described above appears to be simple to implement and effective in insuring investor wealth. As discussed in the introduction to this chapter, however, the technique is not widely used in practice, because put options with the appropriate terms are not traded on organized exchanges. Recognizing this, H. Leland (1980) sought to obtain portfolio insurance through trading other securities. The initial technique he proposed involved the use of Treasury bills as follows:

Define TB as the current price of a $10,000-face value Treasury bill that expires in one-month. Since the one-month risk-free rate is 0.0085, TB should be $9,915.72:

$$\$9,915.72 = \$10,000(1.0085)^{-1}.$$

To ensure that the portfolio attains the same minimum value that can be achieved with the put options, $555,000, the manager needs to purchase 55.5 T-bills ($555,000 ÷ 10,000). Given the inability to purchase fractional amounts of the security, the manager chooses to buy 56 T-bills. Thus, the investment in the equity portfolio must be reduced by $555,280.32 [56 × $9,915.72], leaving just $4,719.68 in equities (or 16.856 index units).

As before, suppose that the resulting SP500 index level is either 310 or 250 in one month. The resulting insured portfolio values are $565,225.36 and $564,214.00, respectively:

$$\$565,255.36 = (16.856 \times 310) + (56 \times 10,000),$$
$$\$564,214.00 = (16.856 \times 250) + (56 \times 10,000).$$

Each of these values exceeds $555,000. Indeed, the stock–Treasury bill insurance technique must provide a minimum value of $560,000, since the lowest the SP500 index could fall to is zero.[4] Thus, it provides the same coverage as the stock-put insurance technique.

Figure 20.1 portrays the resulting portfolio values for various levels of the SP500 at the end of the one-month holding period. For SP500 levels above 280, the stock–Treasury bill portfolio's value increases at a slower rate than the stock-put portfolio's value. This is because the former has less upside capture. The upside capture for the stock-put portfolio was about 99 percent, whereas it is about 90 percent for the stock–Treasury bill portfolio:

$$1 - [(\$620,000 - 565,225.36) / (\$560,000)].$$

---

[4]Do not be fooled into believing that the stock–Treasury bill insurance technique is superior because its guaranteed minimum portfolio value ($560,000) is greater than that provided by the stock-put insurance technique ($555,000). This difference arises only because of the rounding assumed when undertaking contract positions. Indeed, each insurance technique examined can be demonstrated to provide exactly the same minimum insured value if all securities are perfectly divisible.

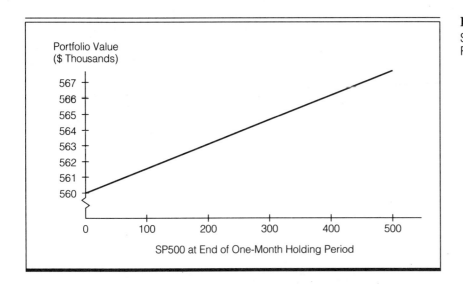

Figure 20.1:
Stock–Treasury Bill Insured
Portfolio Values

Portfolio Value
($ Thousands)

567
566
565
564
563
562
561
560

0   100   200   300   400   500

SP500 at End of One-Month Holding Period

Call–Treasury Bill Insurance

Recall from Chapter 15 that a protective put strategy can be replicated by a combination of a call option and a pure discount, default-free bond. This result obtained from an application of put-call parity. With this in mind, we should be able to replicate the above insurance techniques by assuming positions in T-bills and stock index call options.

In our example, call–Treasury bill insurance is obtained by purchasing the same number of T-bills, 56, and employing the remaining $4,719.68 in portfolio wealth to purchase index call options. By put-call parity, the price of a corresponding December 280 SP500 call option is $4.86 per index unit:[5]

$$C = \$2.50 - 280(1.0085)^{-1} + 280 = \$4.86.$$

Thus, the manager is able to purchase 971.13 call index units ($4,719.68/4.86), which at a multiplier of 500 represents 1.942 call contracts. To simplify the analysis, we allow the manager to purchase fractional index call option contracts.

As before, we suppose that the expiration SP500 index level is either 310 or 250. The resulting call–Treasury bill portfolio values are $589,130 and $560,000, respectively:

$$\$589,130 = (310 - 280)(1.942)(\$500) + 56(\$10,000),$$

$$\$560,000 = 56(\$10,000).$$

---

[5]Recall that the options are assumed to be European. Further, an implicit assumption here is that no dividends are paid on the index's underlying stocks over the one-month holding period.

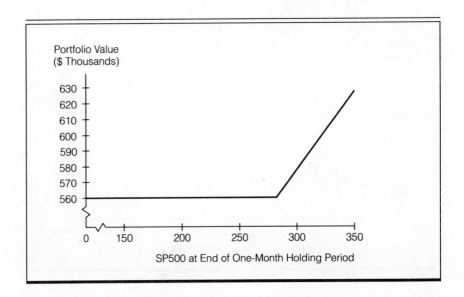

Further, the minimum insured portfolio value is $560,000, since the call options are not exercised for expiration index levels below the 280 exercise price. Thus, the call–Treasury bill insurance technique provides similar results as the above stock-put and stock–Treasury bill techniques.

Figure 20.2 portrays the values of the call–Treasury bill portfolio for different expiration index levels. Notice that the graph is similar to that of a protective put strategy. (For instance, compare Figure 20.2 with Figure 18.2, which portrays profits from a protective put involving SP100 index options.) For the call–Treasury bill strategy, the upside capture is about 95 percent.[6]

$$1 - [(\$620,000 - 589,130)/(\$560,000)].$$

Dynamic Hedging

As discussed earlier, the stock-put insurance technique suffers from the inability to obtain traded index put options exhibiting the desired terms.

---

[6]It is instructive to note that the upside capture on the call–Treasury bill insurance technique would be exactly the same as that on the stock-put technique if all securities were perfectly divisible. Specifically, 55.5 T-bills would be purchased, leaving $7,677.54 in portfolio wealth to purchase 1,991.26 call index units. At an expiration index value of 310, the call–Treasury bill portfolio would be worth $614,737.80, implying an upside capture of 99 percent. This is the same upside capture as that for the stock-put insurance technique and affirms the fact that the stock-put insurance technique can be replicated by a combination of index call options and T-bills.

Tailored portfolio insurance may be attained by contracting with investment banking outfits to purchase customized index options, but such contracts would likely be expensive.

The alternative insurance techniques described above that employ T-bills also have shortcomings, the primary one being that they require portfolio managers to trade tremendous numbers of individual stocks, creating prohibitive transaction costs. Furthermore, not all institutional managers can use these techniques, as someone must hold the stocks.

Because of these problems, M. Rubinstein (1985) sought a technique that replicated the desirable properties of stock-put insurance while reducing stock trading and the associated transaction costs of the stock–Treasury bill and call–Treasury bill techniques. The method he developed entails the trading of stock index futures contracts and is typically referred to as *dynamic hedging*; it replicates the behavior of a stock-put insured portfolio by continually adjusting a portfolio of stocks and index futures contracts. Because it does so with comparatively lower transaction costs, it has become the most popular form of portfolio insurance among institutional managers. Leland, O'Brien, Rubinstein Associates, Inc. (among others) has been successful in marketing this type of portfolio insurance to pension-fund managers especially. In this section we examine this popular insurance technique.

Dynamic hedging is an insurance technique that replicates the behavior of a stock-put insured portfolio by continually adjusting a portfolio of stocks and index futures contracts.

Dynamic hedging with stock index futures entails writing a number of futures contracts in such a way that the portfolio achieves the same price action as a stock-put insured portfolio. In the appendix to this chapter, a procedure is described for determining the number of index futures contract required. Defining this number by N_f, we have

(20.1) $$N_f = [(V/S + P)(1 + dP/dS) - (V/S)]e^{-rT}.$$

The term N_f is called the *dynamic-hedge ratio*. Notice that the portfolio manager must continuously adjust this ratio, since the variables in Equation 20.1 will change over time as the index varies and the futures contract unwinds.

Getting back to our example, the dynamic hedge ratio is[7]

$$N_f = \left[\left(\frac{560,000}{280 + 2.50} \right)(1 - .394) - \left(\frac{560,000}{280} \right) \right](.9915) = -791.94.$$

Since the index futures multiple is 500, the manager requires -1.584 contracts $[-791.94/500]$. The cost of a futures contract is zero at contract inception. Thus, the dynamic-hedging technique entails holding

---

[7]The derivative dP/dS is $-.394$ for our put option. Since no dividends are assumed to be paid over the one-month holding period, $dP/dS = N(d_1) - 1$. [See Chapter 13.]

$560,000 in stock (2,000 index units) and writing 1.584 index futures contracts exhibiting a one-month maturity. The futures price should be 282.38.[8]

To illustrate how this stock-futures portfolio achieves the same price action as a stock-put insured portfolio, let us assume that the derivatives dP/dS and df/dS accurately portray the changes in the option and futures prices, respectively, for a discrete one-point change in the SP500. In other words, a one-point decline in the index will cause the put option price to change by 39.4 cents and the index futures price to change by $-\$1.0085$. For our earlier stock-put insured portfolio, where the manager held 1.982.14 index units in stock and four index put options contracts, the resulting value change is $-\$1,194.14$ for a one-point decline in the index:

Stock:	1,982.14 units $\times$ $-\$1$ =	$-\$1,982.14$
Options:	4 contracts $\times$ 500 $\times$ $(-\$1)$ $\times$ $(-.394)$ =	788.00
Total:		$-\$1,194.14$

For the stock-futures portfolio, the resulting value change is

Stock:	2,000 units $\times$ $-\$1$ =	$-\$2,000.00$
Futures:	-1.584 contracts $\times$ 500 $\times$ $(-\$1)$ $\times$ (1.0085) =	798.73
Total:		$-\$1,201.27$

The difference between the two outcomes is nominal and attributable to rounding error. Hence, the two techniques appear to achieve the same price action. Had the index increased by one point, then both insured portfolios would have risen by about $1,200 in value. We can conclude that dynamic hedging effectively replicates the protection offered by stock-put insurance.

Some Issues Regarding Dynamic Hedging It would appear that dynamic hedging is a nearly cost-free technique, since the cost of a futures contract at contract inception is zero, and the transaction costs of futures trading are smaller when compared to those of trading stocks, options, and T-bills. Indeed, such low (direct) transaction costs are what attract portfolio managers to insure with this technique rather than with, say, the stock–Treasury bill technique described above. However, dynamic hedging still carries with it the important opportunity cost associated with bull market swings. And from the portfolio manager's perspective, this opportunity cost is its most important potential draw-

---

[8]The index futures price of 282.38 obtains because we have a one month period, and no dividends occur over the period. By the cost-of-carry model, we have

$$f = S(1 + r) = 280(1.0085) = 282.38.$$

Notice that $df/dS = (1 + r)$, or 1.0085.

back. The portfolio does not gain as much when the short index futures position is assumed and the market rises as when no futures position is assumed and the market rises. Writing the futures contract introduces negative correlation that helps to insure a minimum future value for the portfolio, but along with this insured value comes the potential for losing some gains in a bull market. Hence, the apparent low cost of the technique can be misleading. Like the other techniques described above, dynamic hedging has an upside capture that is less than 100 percent.

Another important issue concerns rebalancing. Dynamic hedging requires continuous trading to adjust the hedge ratio and thereby guarantee a specific future portfolio value. This will become more evident when we explore a multi-period setting later. However, continuous trading clearly is impossible. Frequent rebalancing entails large monitoring and trading costs, but less frequent rebalancing can jeopardize the future insured value of the portfolio. The portfolio manager must decide how often to rebalance in light of these trade-offs.

A closely related issue is the sensitivity of the portfolio's value to changes in the market index. The above derivatives provide only approximate changes for the option and futures prices as the market varies. When big market movements occur, these approximations are poor.[9] This implies that in fast-moving markets, dynamic hedging may be ineffective.

Finally, it should be obvious that the manager needs to write fewer futures contracts to achieve the insured value when stock prices climb, and similarly must write more and more futures contracts as stock prices fall. Hence, it is often said that with dynamic hedging one buys index futures when stocks are high and sells them when stocks are low. In other words, one "buys high and sells low". This would be an unfortunate strategy to earn profits, but it is sensible when insuring a position against losses should a market downturn occur. Some have argued, however, that such a strategy can serve to exacerbate downturns in the market. Indeed, a presidential commission reported publicly that dynamic hedging, in conjunction with index arbitrage activities, may have fueled the stock market crash of October 19, 1987. For more on this, see the feature on "Portfolio Insurance and Its Role in the October 1987 and October 1989 Market Crashes."

A UNIFIED ANALYSIS OF PORTFOLIO INSURANCE

In this section we provide a unified analysis of portfolio insurance, based on the binomial generating process and permitting us to extend the discussion of portfolio insurance to a multi-period setting. This

---

[9]Recall that partial derivatives are local measures only.

Portfolio Insurance and Its Role in the October 1987 and October 1989 Market Crashes

The Brady Commission, appointed by President Ronald Reagan to study the causes of the October 1987 stock market crash, concluded that dynamic hedging, in conjunction with stock index arbitrage, exacerbated the precipitous decline in equity values on October 19. Specifically, the commission reported that the initial market decline was a result of changes in a number of fundamental macroeconomic indicators, including domestic and international trade deficits, and other factors such as proposed legislation to make corporate takeovers more difficult and costly. This initial market decline in turn triggered a wave of index futures selling by institutional portfolio insurers. Portfolio managers sold over $4 billion worth of index futures contracts on October 19 alone.

The commission suggested that the selling of vast amounts of index futures caused a disparity between futures and stock prices that resulted in over $1.7 billion worth of index arbitrage trading. Program traders, through the Designated Order Turnaround (DOT) system of the NYSE, sold the stocks and bought the futures. Such stock selling was concluded to have fueled the market's decline.

Presumably, the activities of portfolio insurers and index arbitragers would tend to counteract and not exacerbate the initial market decline. However, recall that portfolio insurance is ineffective during fast-moving markets. Trading delays due to unprecedented volume also drove a wedge between the activities of portfolio insurers and program traders. Further complicating matters was the fact that NYSE officials stopped members from using the DOT system to engage in index arbitrage on October 20. The commission concluded that this action effectively segmented the trading activities of portfolio insurers and

(continued)

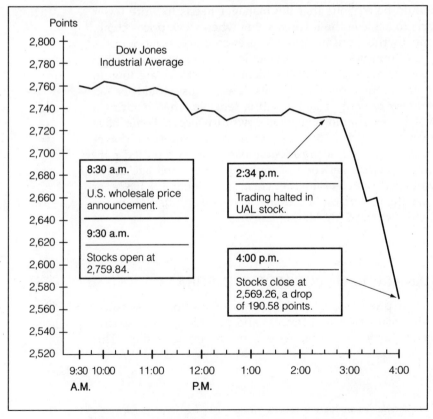

extension provides more insight and detail, especially with respect to the dynamic nature of the insurance techniques.

Underlying Portfolio Dynamics

The assumed prices of the underlying portfolio in the insurance program are presented in Figure 20.3. The figure is known as a tree diagram, or lattice, and depicts a three-period, two-state process where the (multiplicative) upward movement is 1.2 times the current portfolio value and the (multiplicative) downward movement is 1/1.2. The original portfolio value is assumed to be $100. Thus, after one period its value may be $120 or $83.33, and so on. This is the same binomial generating process used by J. Cox, S. Ross, and M. Rubinstein (1979) and R. Rendleman and B. Bartter (1979). Recall from Chapter 12 that

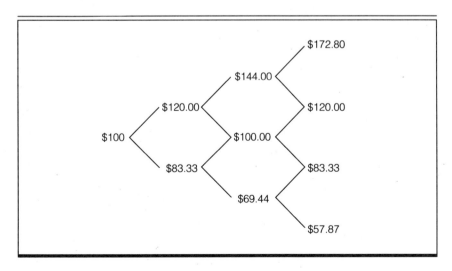

Figure 20.3:
Underlying Portfolio Price Dynamics

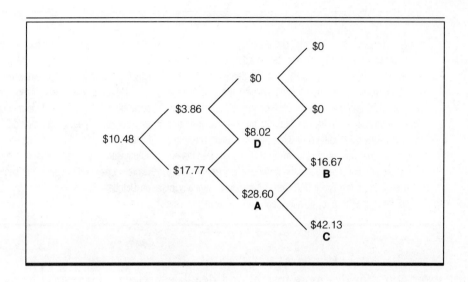

these authors developed a discrete-time version of the Black-Scholes model known as the binomial option-pricing model (BOPM). The price dynamics shown in Figure 20.3 will be used here to demonstrate the stock-put and dynamic-hedging portfolio insurance techniques in a multi-period world.

Option Prices and Dynamics

Assuming a one-period risk-free rate of 2 percent and an exercise price of $100, Figure 20.4 depicts the index put-option price dynamics corresponding to the portfolio price dynamics presented in Figure 20.3. These European put-option prices are produced by the BOPM, where the probability of an upward movement in the portfolio's value, p, is assumed to be .5093.

As an example of how these option prices are computed, consider the price of $28.60 identified by Node A in Figure 20.4. The associated option prices at Nodes B and C are known, since, at option expiration, the put's value must be $MAX[0,X - S_T]$. For Node B, the put's price is $MAX[0,\$100-83.33]$ or $16.67, while for Node C, the put's price is $MAX[0,\$100 - 57.897]$ or $42.13. The price at Node A is determined as a weighted average of the known prices, discounted for one period at the risk-free rate:

$$\$28.60 = [(.5093)(\$16.67) + (.4907)(\$42.13)](1.02)^{-1}.$$

By using this valuation procedure in a recursive manner, the current put-option price eventually will be attained. In our example, this price is $10.48.

```
                                              $172.80
                                     $144.00
                           $123.86            $120.00
                 $110.48            $108.02
                           $101.10            $100.00
                                      $98.04
                                        A
                                              $100.00
```

Stock-Put Portfolio Insurance

As before, let us begin by demonstrating the stock-put insurance technique under the assumption that such a technique is feasible. Suppose that the above three-period European index put option was available with an exercise price of $100.00. The option is assumed to correspond to the portfolio insurer's horizon and target insured value. Thus, the manager can simply purchase the option for $10.48 and be fully insured.[10]

Figure 20.5 depicts the dynamics of the stock-put insured portfolio. The values presented are simply the sums of the underlying portfolio values (Figure 20.3) and the put values (Figure 20.4) for each corresponding node. For example, at Node A, the insured portfolio's value is $69.44 + $28.60, or $98.04. As the figure demonstrates, the expiration portfolio value is always at least $100.00. Therefore, if an index put option with the appropriate terms is available, the manager can insure a future portfolio value of $100.00.

Before considering dynamic hedging with index futures contracts, it is instructive to now mention that a combination of a $100 face-value, pure discount, riskless asset and an index call option with exercise price of $100 will achieve the same price action as that depicted in Figure 20.5. The current prices of the riskless asset and call option are $94.23 and

---

[10]For simplicity, assume that the manager has $110.48 and wishes to insure for $100.00. Later we show how the manager can insure at the same level of initial capital with associated reductions in upside capture.

Figure 20.6:
Index Futures
Price Dynamics

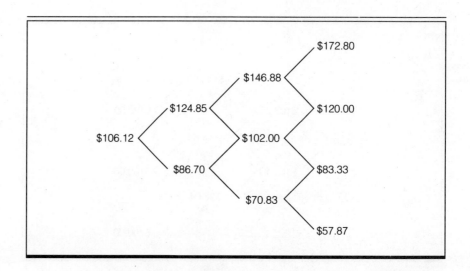

$16.25, respectively.[11] Thus, $110.48 again is required to insure a future portfolio value of $100.00. As before, the call–Treasury bill insurance technique can be used to replicate the stock-put technique. Similarly, it is easy to demonstrate how the stock–Treasury bill technique also achieves the same price action. In this case, the manager would initially purchase .5138 $100-face value T-bills maturing in three periods and invest the remaining $62.06 in the stock portfolio. Through reallocating the stock and T-bills each period in the prescribed manner, the manager can obtain the same terminal portfolio values as those appearing in Figure 20.5.

Application of Dynamic Hedging

We are now ready to demonstrate the mechanics of the dynamic-hedging insurance strategy given our three-period setting. Under the assumptions of constant interest rates and no intervening stock dividends, Figure 20.6 portrays the index futures prices as given by the cost-of-carry model. For example, the current (time 0) index futures price is $106.12, or $100(1.02)^3$. Note that the expiration futures prices are the same as the expiration index values depicted in Figure 20.3. As always, the spot and futures prices converge at contract expiration.

---

[11]The current price of the pure discount, risk-free asset is given by

$$\$94.23 = \$100(1.02)^{-3}.$$

The current price of the European index call option is obtained from put-call parity:

$$\$16.25 = \$10.48 - \$100(1.02)^{-3} + \$100.$$

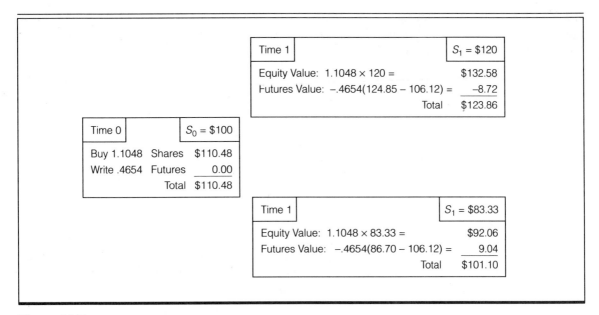

Figure 20.7:
Stock-Futures
Price Dynamics

In the dynamic-hedging technique, the portfolio insurer must determine the number of index futures contracts to write at the beginning of each period. For the index put option employed here, $dP/dS = -.389$ at time 0. Thus, the initial dynamic-hedge ratio, obtained from Equation 20.1, is $-.4654$:

$$N_f = [(110.48/100 + 10.48)(1 - .389) - (110.48/100)](1.02)^{-3}$$

$$= -.4654.$$

The portfolio insurer should initially write .4654 index futures contracts exhibiting a three-period maturity.

Figure 20.7 presents the initial stock-futures portfolio and its resulting values at the end of the first period (time 1). The initial portfolio contains $110.48 in stock, since the value of the futures contract is zero at time 0. At the end of the period, the insured portfolio's value is either $123.86 or $101.10, depending on the resulting index value. Notice that these portfolio values, $123.86 and $101.10, are exactly the same as those for the stock-put insured portfolio appearing in Figure 20.5. Thus, the initial stock-futures position, based on the dynamic-hedge ratio as given by Equation 20.1, was successful in replicating the price action of the stock-put insured portfolio over the first period. Of course, now the manager must readjust the stock-futures portfolio based on the new dynamic-hedge ratio calculated at the beginning of period 2. The ratio

Exercise Price	Put Price	n^a	Total Cost[b]
$100	$10.48	1.0000	$110.48
105	12.80	0.9524	107.43
110	16.38	0.9090	105.79
119	19.41	0.8403	100.34
120	19.64	0.8333	99.70

[a]$n = \$100 \div$ Exercise Price.
[b]Total Cost $= n(\$100 +$ Put Price$)$.

will clearly change, since the variables S and T have changed. However, by computing the new hedge ratios at the start of each period and dynamically hedging, the manager can insure a payoff profile at expiration equivalent to that in Figure 20.5.

Dynamic Hedging with Longer-Term Horizons

Generally, a portfolio manager's holding horizon will be longer than the maturity of a liquid index futures contract. In this case the manager can employ a series of shorter-term futures contracts. For example, suppose that the above three-period setting corresponds to three six-month intervals, implying a horizon of 1.5 years for the manager. Here the manager can go about insuring the portfolio while using three consecutive six-month index futures and the very same procedure just described.

Dynamic Hedging with a Fixed-Capital Constraint

In the above analysis we conveniently assumed that the manager had capital of $110.48 to insure for $100.00. But what if the manager had less than $110.48 or desired to insure for more than $100.00? In this section we describe how the manager must alter his or her actions in the case where insurance of $100 is desired but a capital constraint of $100 is imposed. The ultimate result is that the insurance costs more in the sense that the upside capture is reduced. Although we limit the analysis to the stock-put insurance technique, the resulting price dynamics can be replicated through dynamic hedging as well.

Time 0 index put-option prices for various exercise prices are reported in Exhibit 20.1. These prices are computed using the same procedure portrayed in Figure 20.4. The exhibit also provides the corresponding value of n, where n is defined as the target insurance floor ($100) divided by the option's exercise price. In the last column of the exhibit, the total costs of buying n shares and n puts are provided.

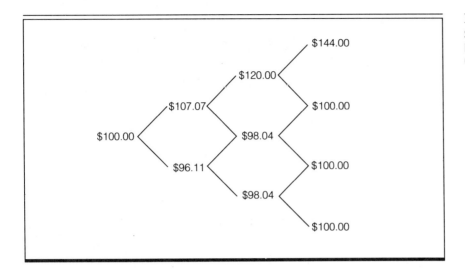

Figure 20.8:
Stock-Put Insured Portfolio
Dynamics with $100 Capital
Constraint Imposed

The portfolio insurer must select the associated option such that the total cost figure is $100, the capital constraint. This requires an exercise price somewhere between $119 and $120. To simplify the analysis, assume that the manager employs the $120 exercise-price puts and thus holds .8333 shares ($83.33) and .8333 puts ($16.37), yielding an approximate expenditure of $100.[12]

The stock-put insured price dynamics are illustrated in Figure 20.8 for the above portfolio. Again, these dynamics could be replicated by trading index futures contracts. We see that the portfolio will attain a value of at least $100 at option expiration, so the insurance strategy is successful. However, the upside capture has been reduced, since higher exercise-price puts had to be employed. From Figure 20.5, recall that the stock-put insured portfolio value was $172.80, for a resulting index value of $172.80, when the $100 exercise-price puts were used and the amount of original capital was $110.48. In Figure 20.8, however, the corresponding stock-put insured portfolio value is just $144.00. You can see that the upside capture has been reduced to .8333 ($144.00/$172.80). This loss in upside capture is attributable to employing $120 exercise-price puts due to the $100 capital constraint imposed. As before, the loss in upside capture represents an important cost of any portfolio insurance technique.

The loss in upside capture represents an important cost of any portfolio-insurance technique.

---

[12]This example illustrates why index options with fixed exercise prices may be undesirable even if they are long term. The portfolio insurer may still prefer dynamic hedging because of the ability to refine the target insurance floor.

SUMMARY

The most straightforward form of portfolio insurance entails the purchase of long-term European index put options. Since such options are not listed, however, alternative paths to portfolio insurance have been developed, the most popular being dynamic hedging, which involves the continual trading of stock index futures such that a synthetic stock-put insured portfolio is maintained. Other strategies entailing the trading of index call options and Treasury bills can also replicate the payoffs of a stock-put insured portfolio.

Portfolio insurance may be regarded as a form of hedging for investors holding well-diversified equity portfolios. Users of portfolio insurance tend to be institutional managers such as pension and mutual-fund managers. Because of the complex nature of this special hedging strategy, we have devoted an entire chapter to portfolio insurance. However, for the purpose of understanding how portfolio insurance "fits" into the broader realm of derivative securities and their analysis, it is best to think of portfolio insurance as simply one more hedging application.

Finally, it should be mentioned that the trading of longer-term European index options may become a reality in the near future. If so, use of the dynamic-hedging technique may decline considerably.

Selected References

Asay, M., and C. Edeslburg. "Can a Dynamic Strategy Replicate the Returns of an Option?" *Journal of Futures Markets* 6 (Spring 1986): 63–70.

Benninga, A., and M. Blume. "On the Optimality of Portfolio Insurance." *Journal of Finance* 40 (December 1985): 1341–1352.

Cox, J., S. Ross, and M. Rubinstein. "Option Pricing: A Simplified Approach." *Journal of Financial Economics* 7 (September 1979): 229–263.

Etzioni, E. "Rebalance Disciplines for Portfolio Insurance." *Journal of Portfolio Management* 13 (Fall 1986): 59–62.

Gatto, M., R. Geske, R. Litzenberger, and H. Sosin. "Mutual Fund Insurance." *Journal of Financial Economics* 8 (September 1980): 283–317.

Hill, J., A. Jain, and R. Wood. "Portfolio Insurance: Volatility Risk and Futures Mispricing." *Journal of Portfolio Management* (Winter 1988): 23–29.

Leland, H. "Who Should Buy Portfolio Insurance?" *Journal of Finance* 35 (May 1980): 581–594.

Leland, H. "Option Pricing and Replication with Transaction Costs." *Journal of Finance* 40 (December 1985): 1283–1301.

O'Brien, T. "The Mechanics of Portfolio Insurance." *Journal of Portfolio Management* (Spring 1988): 40–47.

Pozen, R. "The Purchase of Protective Puts by Financial Institutions." *Financial Analysts Journal* 34 (July/August 1978): 47–60.

Rendleman, R., and B. Bartter. "Two-State Option Pricing." *Journal of Finance* 34 (December 1979): 1093–1110.

Rendleman, R., and R. McEnally. "Assessing the Costs of Portfolio Insurance." *Financial Analysts Journal* 43 (May–June 1987): 27–37.

Rubinstein, M. "Alternative Paths to Portfolio Insurance." *Financial Analysts Journal* 41 (July–August 1985): 42–52.

Rubinstein, M., and H. Leland. "Replicating Options with Positions in Stock and Cash." *Financial Analysts Journal* 37 (July–August 1981): 63–71.

Singleton, C., and R. Grieves. "Synthetic Puts and Portfolio Insurance Strategies." *Journal of Portfolio Management* 10 (Spring 1984): 63–69.

Wallace, A. "Marketing a 'Miracle' Model." *Institutional Investor* 16 (September 1982): 101–106.

Questions and Problems

1. Why has the use of index put options to insure equity portfolios not been a popular technique among institutional portfolio managers?

2. What constitutes the major cost of any portfolio-insurance technique?

3. The guaranteed percentage return on an insured portfolio must be bounded above by what rate of return?

4. What are some of the shortcomings of the stock–Treasury bill and call–Treasury bill insurance techniques?

5. What are some of the comparative advantages offered by the dynamic-hedging insurance technique? Describe this technique and why it is dynamic in nature.

6. What factors are likely considered by portfolio managers when deciding how often to rebalance under the dynamic-hedging technique?

7. Why might dynamic hedging not be effective in a fast-moving market environment?

8. In Figure 20.4, describe how the price of $8.02 appearing in Node D is determined.

9. From Exhibit 20.1, use a lattice to show how the price of $12.80 was determined for the $105 exercise-price put option.

   Problems 10 through 19 refer to the following information: You are a portfolio manager who oversees a small index fund designed to mirror the SP100. The current SP100 is 215.00, and the portfolio is worth $15,050,000. Thus, assuming the portfolio is fully funded, you are managing 70,000 index units. Assume that it is mid-November and that the December 215 SP100 put contract, which expires in one month, currently sells for $1,125 (or $2.25 per underlying index unit). This option is European and the one-month risk-free rate of interest is 0.0085. Finally, assume that all securities are perfectly divisible and that the annualized return variance of the SP100 is 0.015.

10. In the stock-put insurance technique, how many units of the index and put contracts will you hold to insure an expiration portfolio value of $15,050,000?

11. What is the resulting insured portfolio value if the expiration SP100 level is 200?

12. What is the resulting insured portfolio value if the expiration SP100 level is 240? What is the portfolio's upside capture?

13. Under a stock–Treasury bill insurance technique, how many one-month $10,000-face value T-bills must you purchase to insure the same minimum value as in the above stock-put insurance technique? What is the current price of the T-bill, and how many index units will you hold in your equity portfolio?

14. Assuming that the SP100 is 240 in one month, what is the upside capture for the stock–Treasury bill insurance strategy?

15. Assuming no dividends occur on the underlying stocks during the one-month period, what is the current price of a corresponding index call option?

16. Under the call–Treasury bill technique, how many call option contracts will be purchased?

17. Employing a contingency graph, illustrate the resulting call–Treasury bill insured portfolio values at option expiration. At an expiration index level of 240, what is this strategy's upside capture?

18. Under the dynamic-hedging technique, what is the initial dynamic hedge ratio, N_f? What is the initial futures price?

19. Given a one-point decline in the SP100, how does the stock-futures insured portfolio value change? How does this change compare with the change in the stock-put insured portfolio?

20. Why do you suppose that long-term European index options with small exercise-price intervals are not listed on organized exchanges?

Self-Test Problems

ST-1. Given a starting stock price of $50, a multiplicative upward jump of 1.20, and a multiplicative downward jump of 0.85, use a lattice to show the stock price dynamics over a three-period horizon.

ST-2. If the one-period interest rate is .01, and the European put option's exercise price is $50, use a lattice to demonstrate the index put option's price dynamics. Assume the option expires in three periods and that the probability of an upward jump, p, is 0.52.

ST-3. Assuming a capital constraint of $54.391, use a lattice to demonstrate the dynamics of a stock-put insured portfolio designed to insure an expiration value of $50.

Solutions to Self-Test Problems

ST-1.

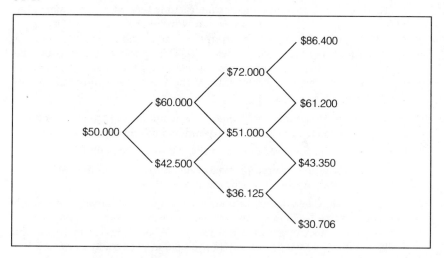

ST-2. Example:

(A) $\$12.593 = [(6.650)(.52) + (19.294)(.49)](1.01)^{-1}$.

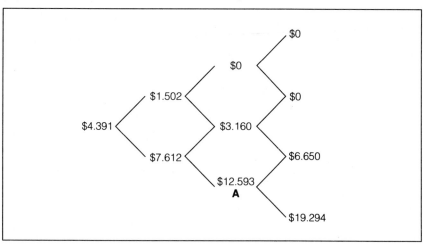

ST-3. Example:

(A) $\$36.125 + \$12.593 = \$48.718$.

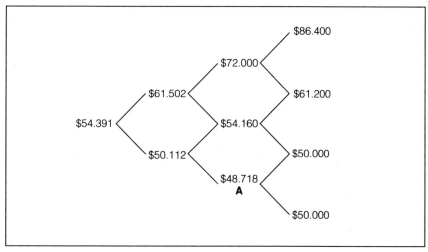

Appendix 20.A

DERIVATION OF THE DYNAMIC-HEDGE RATIO

Assume that we construct a portfolio consisting of N_S shares of stock and N_f futures contracts. Since the initial value of the futures contracts must be zero, the initial value of the portfolio, V, is given by the investment in stocks:

(20.A–1) $$V = N_S S.$$

The change in the value of the portfolio for a small change in S is given by

(20.A–2) $$dV/dS = N_S + N_f(df/dS),$$

where df/dS represents the change in the futures price for the small change in S. If no dividends are paid on the stock, then the futures price is determined by the following cost-of-carry model:

(20.A–3) $$f = Se^{rT}.$$

Thus:

(20.A–4) $$df/dS = e^{rT}.$$

Substituting Equation 20.A-4 into Equation 20.A-2, and recognizing that $N_S = V/S$ gives:

(20.A–5) $$dV/dS = V/S + N_f e^{rT}.$$

Equation 20.A-5 expresses the change in portfolio value with respect to a small change in S in terms of N_f, the number of futures contracts.

Now consider a stock-put insured portfolio where all securities are perfectly divisible, so there is an equal number of stocks and puts, and, by definition, the portfolio's value is

(20.A–6) $$V = N(S + P),$$

where N is the number of stocks and puts and P is the put price per share of stock. The change in the portfolio's value with respect to a small change in S is given by

(20.A–7) $$dV/dS = N + N(dP/dS) = N(1 + dP/dS).$$

Using Equation 20.A-6, Equation 20.A-7 can be rewritten as follows:

(20.A–8) $$dV/dS = [(V/S + P)(1 + dP/dS)].$$

In the dynamic-hedging strategy, the objective is to continually maintain a specified number of futures contracts, N_f, such that the stock-futures insured portfolio achieves the same price action as the stock-put insured portfolio. This is accomplished by setting the two derivatives, Equations 20.A-5 and 20.A-8, equal to one another. By doing so, we equate the changes in the two portfolios' values for a given small change in S. Equating Equations 20.A-5 and 20.A-8 thus gives us the following expression:

(20.A–9) $$V/S + N_f e^{rT} = [(V/S + P)(1 + dP/dS)].$$

Solving for N_f gives

(20.A–10) $$N_f = [(V/S + P)(1 + dP/dS) - (V/S)]e^{-rT}.$$

This is Equation 20.1 of Chapter 20.

Appendix 20.B

PRIMES AND SCORES

In a recent development in the derivative securities market, a trust is established that purchases common stock and in turn issues units, each containing a *prime* and a *score*. The prime component receives all dividend payments and any stock appreciation up to a termination value. The score component receives any stock appreciation beyond the termination value. This termination value is therefore akin to an option's exercise price. The trust therefore effectively separates each stock's cash flow into a dividend-based component (the prime) and an option-based component (the score).

The trust exhibits a maturity of five years, after which the units are reconverted to the underlying stock. The prime, score, and unit for each trust are traded separately on the American Stock Exchange. The termination price, which is set at trust inception, is commonly 20 to 25 percent above the original stock price. It is called a *termination price*, since the trust cannot accept further shares if the stock price exceeds the termination price.

Since the trust has a five-year life, the creation of the score component represents a long-term European option on the underlying stock.[1] Thus, the score component can potentially offer the kind of portfolio insurance currently attainable only through dynamic hedging. Indeed, since the score component can provide long-term insurance while avoiding the large transaction costs of dynamic hedging, the joint value of the prime and score can actually exceed the value of the underlying common stock.

This is what was found in an empirical study of primes and scores conducted by R. Jarrow and M. O'Hara (1989).[2] Analyzing five trusts created before June 1987, Jarrow and O'Hara reported that the combined prime and score prices exceeded the price of the underlying stock, often by a considerable amount and beyond the required transaction costs of arbitrage. Presumably, if the combined prime and score price is greater, then arbitragers will buy the stock and sell (write) the prime and score. Jarrow and O'Hara conclude that the apparent overpricing of primes and scores is attributable to the unique ability of the score component to avoid the transaction costs of dynamic hedging. Their results are intriguing, since they suggest that it may be possible to create value simply by splitting a security into different parts.

Whether the prime and score market will grow remains to be seen. At the time of this writing, only 28 trusts exist. Further, a recent tax ruling has apparently hurt this market. Specifically, a March 1986 amendment to Treasury Regulation Section 301.7701-4(c) classifies such a trust as an association taxable as a corporation. This effectively subjects holders in the trust to an added taxation of dividend income at the personal level.

---

[1]To demonstrate this more formally, define the following variables: T = the maturity of the trust; X = the termination price; S_t = the current stock price; P_t = the current prime price; and K_t = the current score price. Since the prime receives all-dividends, the score may be viewed as a long-term European call option on the stock with exercise price X and maturity T. At maturity, the score price is $K_T = MAX[S_T - X, 0]$, while the prime price is $P_T = MIN[S_T - X]$.

[2]See R. Jarrow and M. O'Hara, "Primes and Scores: An Essay on Market Imperfection," *Journal of Finance* 44 (December 1989).

Part Four

SWAPS

Although the best-known derivative securities are futures and options, swaps, which first appeared in the early 1980s, are rapidly gaining prestige. Several large commercial and investment banking firms have become active intermediaries in swap markets. Several forms of swaps exist, the most common being currency and interest rate swaps, which facilitate risk reallocation similar to that offered by currency and interest rate futures. Swaps offer other potential benefits as well. In this part we analyze the emerging markets for currency and interest rate swaps, emphasizing the latter due to its larger size.

CURRENCY AND INTEREST RATE SWAPS

A *currency swap* allows two firms to exchange currencies at recurrent intervals and is usually used in conjunction with debt issues. For instance, each of two firms may issue fixed-rate debt in a unique currency, then swap the proceeds of the issues and assume each other's obligation to pay principal and interest payments. This swap of currencies can allow each firm to make payments without exposure to exchange rate risk.

An *interest rate swap* occurs when a firm that has issued one form of debt agrees to swap interest payments with another firm that has issued a different form of debt denominated in the same currency. For instance, a firm that issued floating-rate dollar-denominated debt agrees in a swap to make fixed-rate payments to another firm that issued dollar-denominated fixed-rate debt. In return, the second firm makes floating-rate payments to the first. Such a swap may result in net interest savings and represents an efficient vehicle for transferring interest rate risk from one party to another.

The markets for both currency and interest rate swaps have grown substantially during the 1980s. For instance, although the first interest rate swaps appeared in 1982, U.S.–dollar interest rate swaps exhibited a volume estimated at $541 billion in 1987 alone. In this chapter we analyze these emerging derivative securities, undertaking the following investigative issues: What are swaps and how did they evolve? What benefits do swaps provide? How are swap pricing schedules determined? How are swaps related to other securities, including forward contracts and default-free loans? And what lies in the future for this emerging market?

A **currency swap** allows two firms to exchange currencies at recurrent intervals and is usually used in conjunction with debt issues.

An **interest rate swap** occurs when a firm that has issued one form of debt agrees to swap interest rate payments with another firm that has issued a different form of debt denominated in the same currency.

CURRENCY SWAPS

A standard currency swap entails the exchange of debt denominated in one currency for debt denominated in another currency. For example,

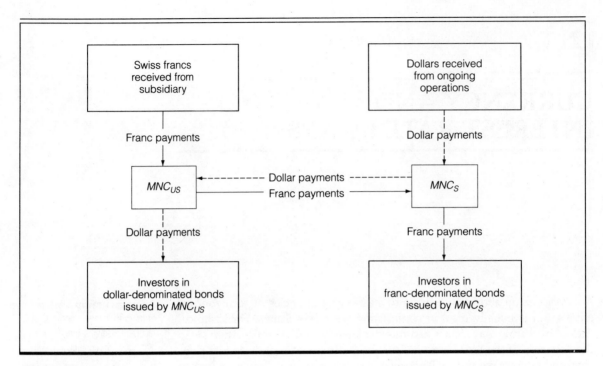

Figure 21–1:
A Currency Swap

suppose a U.S. multinational corporation, MNC_{US}, desires to issue a Swiss franc–denominated bond, since it can make payments with franc inflows generated by a Swiss subsidiary. Also suppose there exists a Swiss multinational, MNC_S, that seeks to issue dollar-denominated debt. MNC_{US} could issue dollar debt while MNC_S issues franc debt. MNC_{US} could then provide franc payments, both principal and interest, to MNC_S in exchange for dollar payments. This swap of currencies allows the two multinationals to make payments to their respective debtholders without having to repatriate foreign exchange. For instance, MNC_{US} does not need to convert francs into dollars. Thus, the two multinationals have reduced their exchange exposure. Figure 21.1 illustrates this currency swap.

Currency swaps evolved from back-to-back loans and parallel loans, which came into popularity in Britain in the 1970s as a means of circumventing foreign exchange controls implemented to prevent the outflow of British capital. The controls were usually in the form of taxes imposed on foreign transactions. *Back-to-back loans* were made between two national firms, each making the other a loan in its

A **back-to-back loan** occurs between two national firms, each making the other a loan in its respective currency.

A Currency Swap between IBM and the World Bank

International Business Machines (IBM) and the World Bank engaged in the first-ever currency swap in August 1981. IBM exhibited outstanding debt in both West German marks and Swiss francs. The debt was fixed-rate. The dollar had greatly appreciated against both foreign currencies earlier in the year, and the management of IBM wanted to swap its foreign obligations for dollar obligations in order to reap the resultant gain on its liabilities. To do so, IBM engaged in a swap with the World Bank, arranged by Salomon Brothers. The World Bank issued two dollar Eurobonds, one with the same maturity as IBM's mark debt, and one with the same maturity as IBM's franc debt. The World Bank paid all principal and periodic interest obligations on IBM's debt and, in return, IBM paid the World Bank's dollar obligations. This transaction created an entirely new financial instrument, the currency swap.

respective currency. *Parallel loans* were made by one multinational to another multinational's subsidiary; here each multinational made the loan in its respective currency, and each subsidiary was located in the other's country. For instance, MNC_{US} might loan dollars to a British multinational's U.S. subsidiary, while the British multinational, MNC_{UK}, loans pounds to the U.S. multinational's subsidiary located in Britain. The principal and periodic interest payments on these loans were structured to coincide, and since the loans were repaid with foreign revenues from ongoing operations, the tax on currency translations was avoided. The British multinational did not need to convert pounds into dollars.

Note that such loans achieved the basic structure of a currency swap, which minimizes the multinationals' exposure to exchange rate risk. Figure 21.2 illustrates the swap for the parallel loan, from which today's currency swaps evolved.[1]

A **parallel loan** occurs when each multinational makes a loan to the other's subsidiary. Each multinational makes the loan in its respective currency, and each subsidiary is located in the other's country.

Rationales for Existence of Currency Swaps

Since foreign exchange controls are generally not applied by today's governments, why do currency swaps still exist? Two (related) reasons are generally agreed upon: The first is exchange rate risk reallocation, as exemplified by the swap arrangements just described. The second is regulatory barriers to capital flows. For instance, in the first currency swap described here, MNC_{US} desired to issue Swiss franc–denominated debt. Instead of issuing such debt directly, it issued dollar-denominated

---

[1]The parallel-loan agreement often contained an embedded futures contract. Should one currency have depreciated greatly relative to the other during the loan period, the lender of the devalued currency had to increase its loan to offset its gain.

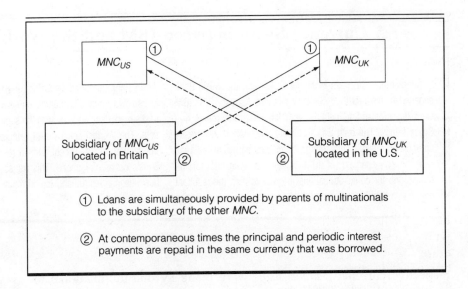

① Loans are simultaneously provided by parents of multinationals to the subsidiary of the other *MNC*.

② At contemporaneous times the principal and periodic interest payments are repaid in the same currency that was borrowed.

debt and engaged in a currency swap with MNC_S in order to reduce exchange exposure. Perhaps MNC_{US} was precluded from issuing franc debt directly. That is, the inability to issue debt in Switzerland, representing a barrier to capital flow, resulted in the swap arrangement. Thus, by engaging in the swap, the U.S. multinational circumvented the capital-flow barrier. Also, MNC_{US} may have preferred to issue dollar-denominated debt because it is better known in the United States than in Switzerland. If issuing dollar-denominated debt reduces financing costs, the swap arrangement is attractive. This same argument holds from the viewpoint of MNC_S.[2] By being used this way to overcome barriers to international capital movements, currency swaps have played an important role in integrating the world's capital markets.

INTEREST RATE SWAPS

Interest rate swaps evolved in the early 1980s as a special case of a currency swap in which all payments are made in the same currency. In the classical example of an interest rate swap, borrowers who are creditworthy, with a cost advantage in both the fixed-rate and floating-rate debt markets, but exhibit a comparative advantage in the fixed-rate market, may borrow in that market and swap the fixed interest pay-

---

[2]Recognize that not being well-known in Switzerland really represents a form of capital-flow barrier faced by MNC_{US}. Further, the foreign exchange controls originally implemented by the British government represent a form of capital-flow barrier.

	Firm A	Firm B	Differential
Fixed:	9.5%	10.2%	70 bps
Floating:	LIBOR + 15 bps	LIBOR + 30 bps	15 bps
		Net Differential	55 bps

Note: The differential represents the relative credit risk premium. The relative credit risk premium for A for fixed-rate debt (70 bps) is greater than its relative credit risk premium for floating-rate debt (15 bps).
bps = basis points

ments for floating payments with another, less creditworthy borrower who issues floating-rate debt. Interest payments, but not the principal, are swapped, and payments are conditional in that if one party defaults, the other is absolved of its obligation. Since the principal is not swapped, we say that it is *notional*. The gains from this swap are allocated between the two parties and, typically, a financial intermediary who facilitates the swap.[3]

The parameters provided in Exhibit 21.1 may be used to illustrate a traditional interest rate swap. Firm A can issue U.S. dollar-denominated fixed-rate debt at 9.5 percent or floating-rate debt at LIBOR plus 15 basis points (bps).[4] Firm B, which is less creditworthy, can issue dollar-denominated fixed-rate debt of the same maturity at 10.2 percent or floating-rate debt at LIBOR plus 30 bps. The difference in the credit risk premiums in the fixed and floating debt markets are 70 bps and 15 bps, respectively. Hence, the difference in the fixed market is greater than the difference in the floating market; firm A has a credit advantage in both markets, but a *comparative advantage* in the fixed market. The net difference in Exhibit 21.1, 55 bps, represents the gain from the swap, which is distributed among the two firms and the swap intermediary.

Assume that firm A issues fixed-rate debt at 9.5 percent and firm B issues floating-rate debt at LIBOR plus 30 bps. In the swap, firm A pays the intermediary a floating rate of LIBOR plus 5 bps, and the interme-

---

[3]Swaps are not standardized contracts traded on organized exchanges. Commercial or investment banks acting as brokers facilitate the swap, often guaranteeing both sides of the contract. These banks maintain carefully guarded lists of debt issuers who may be potential parties to a swap. Also, banks will serve as a party to the swap, warehousing it until they can off-load it.

[4]LIBOR is an acronym for the London Interbank Offer Rate, which is the interest rate earned on Eurodollar deposits. Eurodollar deposits are dollar-denominated deposits in European banks or a European branch of an American bank. The LIBOR is a variable rate, and it is typically used to establish the coupon payments on floating-rate Eurobonds, which are bonds underwritten by international syndicates and sold outside the country of the currency that denominated the bonds. Here, firm A can issue Eurobonds denominated in U.S. dollars but sold outside the United States at LIBOR plus 15 bps. The growth of interest rate swaps is linked to the increasing growth of the Eurobond market. For more on this, see D. Kidwell, W. Marr, and R. Thompson (1985).

Figure 21.3:
An Interest Rate Swap

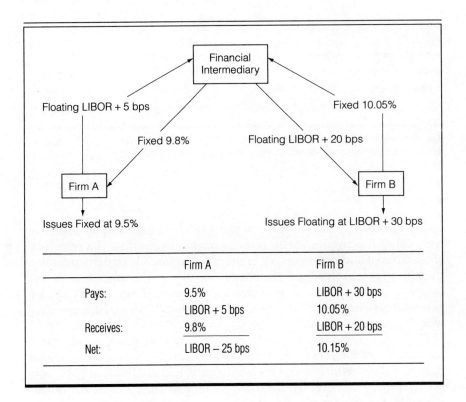

	Firm A	Firm B
Pays:	9.5%	LIBOR + 30 bps
	LIBOR + 5 bps	10.05%
Receives:	9.8%	LIBOR + 20 bps
Net:	LIBOR − 25 bps	10.15%

diary pays firm A a fixed rate of 9.8 percent.[5] Firm B pays the intermediary a fixed rate of 10.05 percent and in return receives a floating rate of LIBOR plus 20 bps from the intermediary. The net payments to the two firms are shown in Figure 21.3.

The result of the swap is that firm A has effectively issued floating-rate debt at LIBOR minus 25 bps, saving 40 bps from issuing floating debt directly. Firm B has effectively issued fixed-rate debt at 10.15 percent, saving 5 bps from issuing fixed debt directly. The intermediary reaps 10 bps: +25 bps on the fixed-rate debt and −15 bps on the floating-rate debt. Hence, the total gain from the swap to all parties is 55 bps.[6]

Rationales for Existence of Interest Rate Swaps

Currently some debate revolves around the issue of why interest rate swaps exist and what benefits they provide. In the classical example of

---

[5]In practice, these payments would be netted. Also, assume (for simplicity only) that all payments are made contemporaneously.

[6]The market for swaps has grown more competitive. As a result, the spreads earned by swap intermediaries have declined. Today a spread of about 5 to 10 bps earned by the intermediary is common.

an interest rate swap, the swap itself results from a credit-market comparative advantage. Firm A's comparative advantage in the fixed-rate debt market results in "gains from trade" similar to those gains arising from any specialization of trade arrangement.

This rationale has been criticized on two accounts, however. First, it is unusual that the creditworthy firm (A) should exhibit a relative credit risk premium on floating debt (15 bps) that is lower than its premium on fixed debt (70 bps). Presumably, the lower-rated firm (B) should face a higher premium on floating-rate debt since it has less ability to meet debt obligations should interest rates rise. Some have argued that this apparent underpricing of floating-rate credit risk may be the result of embedded option values. Specifically, the apparent savings from borrowing at a fixed rate via a swap may be attributable to a lost *prepayment option* that firm B would normally have if it issued fixed debt directly. This prepayment option is the call provision evident in the vast majority of standard corporate bonds. Therefore, in our example, firm B can borrow at a fixed rate more cheaply by swapping from floating because the borrowing-floating/swap-to-fixed alternative does not include the interest rate (i.e., prepayment) option contained in the borrow-fixed alternative. Firm B has effectively sold an interest rate option, since interest rate swaps normally do not contain such an option. The apparent gains from trade therefore may not be genuine; they derive from a forgone option. The premium from this sold option is shared by the two firms and the intermediary.

The second criticism of the gains-from-trade argument is as follows: If the gains from trade were genuine, then in an efficient credit market, they would not persist since arbitragers would rapidly exploit them. The comparative-advantage rationale neglects arbitrage. With no barriers to capital flows, this rationale cannot obtain, as arbitrage eliminates any potential gains. Thus, the comparative-advantage argument cannot explain the persistent growth of the interest rate swap market, if credit markets operate efficiently.

These two criticisms make it apparent that superficial interest rate savings may not be motivating interest rate swaps. So why are these swaps still so popular?

Another viable rationale focuses on the management of interest rate exposure. For example, a savings and loan or other thrift may employ an interest rate swap to help manage the gap between its asset and liability maturities. As an alternative to offering adjustable-rate mortgages, or selling mortgages and reinvesting the proceeds in shorter-term assets, the thrift may engage in swaps to help reduce its interest rate exposure. By properly engaging in an interest rate swap, the thrift can convert its fixed-rate assets to floating-rate assets, convert its floating-rate liabilities to fixed-rate liabilities, or both. Thrifts and insurance companies are active participants in the interest rate swap market.

Further, these swaps may exist because of their usefulness in creating new financial instruments. Prior to the introduction of interest rate swaps, when the only instruments available to borrowers were long-term fixed-rate, long-term floating-rate, and short-term debt, there was no instrument that allowed a firm to achieve a fixed base-interest rate and a floating credit spread. A combination of short-term funding and a swap in which the borrower receives floating and pays fixed, however, achieves a fixed base and floating spread. A firm that anticipates an improved credit rating may employ this combination. Thus, interest rate swaps allow issuers to separate interest rate risk and credit risk, and hedge the target amount of each. They therefore provide for more complete markets.

As another example of a synthetic instrument created by interest rate swaps, consider the combination of a fixed-rate loan and interest rate swap where the firm pays fixed. This combination produces a reverse floating-rate loan. If interest rates rise, then the coupon payments on the loan actually fall.

SWAP INTERMEDIARIES

Investment banks, commercial banks, and independent brokers and dealers facilitate swap transactions. In the early days of the swap market, these intermediaries would act as brokers. That is, they would simply serve as an agent in matching the swap parties. For this service the intermediary would charge a commission. Also, since the intermediary merely served as a broker, it exhibited no risk exposure.

Today, however, most intermediaries in the swap market act as dealers. Serving thus as a counterparty to the swap, they are consequently exposed to exchange rate, interest rate, or default risks. To limit these risks, the intermediary typically engages in an offsetting swap (also known as a *matched swap*), thereby laying-off its swap risk. Like a futures clearinghouse, by engaging in a matched swap, the intermediary assumes a position of net zero in the market. Here the intermediary profits from the basis-point spread (as illustrated in Figure 21.3), and may charge each client a front-end fee as well.

A swap intermediary typically engages in a **matched swap** to lay-off its swap risk.

What if the intermediary has trouble finding a swap counterparty? How can the intermediary protect itself during the interim period? The answer is that the intermediary must use the short-term debt market. For example, suppose that a client issues $10 million of floating-rate debt and then swaps this debt for fixed-rate debt with the intermediary. Ideally, the intermediary would like to swap with another client— serving as a counterparty—who seeks to issue fixed-rate debt and exchange it for floating. If such a counterparty cannot be found quickly, however, the intermediary will likely seek to short $10 million of longer-term fixed debt and employ the proceeds to purchase $10 million of T-bills. The intermediary is then paying a fixed rate and receiving a floating rate (i.e., the T-bill rate). Since the T-bill and LIBOR rates are highly correlated, however, the intermediary is hedging its interest rate risk. The intermediary will roll over its T-bill position until a counterparty can be found.

INDICATION PRICING SCHEDULES

Intermediaries who facilitate swap transactions regularly quote swap prices through the use of *indication pricing schedules*. Exhibit 21.2 provides such a schedule for interest rate swaps. The schedule was obtained from a leading swap dealer. It assumes semiannual rates and *bullet transactions*, meaning that the loan principal is repaid in full at maturity. For example, a T-bill represents a type of bullet transaction.

Swap prices are quoted by intermediaries through **indication pricing schedules**.

Notice two important aspects of this typical pricing schedule. First, there is a spread between the situations where the intermediary pays a fixed rate and where it receives a fixed rate. For example, the spread for a maturity of five years is 25 basis points. The intermediary's revenue ultimately stems from this spread. Second, no floating rates appear in the schedule. When this occurs, the floating side is assumed to be the six-month LIBOR flat.

Suppose that a U.S. company decides to issue $10 million of five-year debt, at par, which is nonamortizing (a bullet transaction) and exhibits a semiannual coupon payment of 9.50 percent. The company then approaches our intermediary to arrange a swap in which the intermediary pays a fixed rate and receives a floating rate. In other words, the U.S. company seeks to swap its fixed-rate debt for floating. Since the intermediary will pay fixed and receive floating, it will pay 9.17 percent (five-year TN rate + 31 bps) and receive six-month LIBOR flat. The intermediary will then seek a counterparty to offset this swap transaction. For the U.S. company, the resulting debt cost is approximately LIBOR + 0.33 percent (9.50% + LIBOR − 9.17%).[7] Presumably, this cost is lower than what the firm could have obtained by issuing floating-rate debt directly.

Exhibit 21.3 provides a typical indication price schedule for a fixed-for-floating rate currency swap entailing the British pound and U.S. dollar. Notice that prices are expressed as a midrate, with the intermediary adding or deducting basis points depending on whether it receives or pays a fixed rate. Here the spread is 10 bps, representing the source of revenues for the currency-swap intermediary.

Suppose that a British firm seeks to convert £10,000,000 three-year semiannual fixed-rate debt into floating-rate dollar-denominated debt. The intermediary will exchange dollars for pounds at the prevailing spot exchange rate, which is $1.60/£1 (assumed). Thus, the intermediary will receive £10,000,000 and pay $16,000,000. The principals will be exchanged in three years at the same initial spot rate of $1.60/£1. These principals are assumed to be bullet transactions.

---

[7]Actually, a slight adjustment has to be made to reflect the fact that the six-month LIBOR is quoted on a 360-day year basis, whereas bond yields assume a 365-day year. Since the LIBOR and coupon rates are both semiannual here, the adjustment is simply LIBOR + 0.33%(360/365) = LIBOR + 0.3255%.

Exhibit 21.2:
Indication Pricing Schedule for Interest Rate Swap Transactions

Maturity (Years)	Intermediary Pays Fixed Rate	Intermediary Receives Fixed Rate	U.S. Treasury Note Rate
2	2-yr. TN sa + 19 bps	2-yr. TN sa + 41 bps	8.50%
3	3-yr. TN sa + 23 bps	3-yr. TN sa + 49 bps	8.67
4	4-yr. TN sa + 26 bps	4-yr. TN sa + 54 bps	8.79
5	5-yr. TN sa + 31 bps	5-yr. TN sa + 56 bps	8.86
6	6-yr. TN sa + 35 bps	6-yr. TN sa + 63 bps	8.91
7	7-yr. TN sa + 40 bps	7-yr. TN sa + 69 bps	8.95

TN sa = *Treasury note rate* semiannually
bps = basis points

Exhibit 21.3:
Indication Price Schedule for British Pound/U.S. Dollar Swaps

Maturity (Years)	Midrate[a]
2	6.05%sa
3	6.27
4	6.44
5	6.58
6	6.68
7	6.75

[a]Deduct 5 bps if the intermediary is paying a fixed rate, and add 5 bps if it is receiving a fixed rate.
sa = semiannually

Since the intermediary is paying a fixed rate, the applicable rate is 6.22 percent semiannually (sa): 6.27% sa midrate − 5 bps. Thus, the British firm pays the swap intermediary the six-month LIBOR on a principal of $16,000,000, and the intermediary pays the British firm 6.22 percent sa on a principal of £10,000,000. Presumably, the British firm would have had to pay more to issue floating-rate dollar-denominated debt directly, or perhaps it was precluded from issuing such debt at all because of capital-flow barriers. Meanwhile, the intermediary will search for a swap counterparty to eliminate its exchange rate risk. Ideally, the counterparty would seek to exchange $16,000,000 three-year floating-rate debt for fixed-rate debt denominated in British pounds. Depending on market conditions, the intermediary may have to move its midrates or spread in order to attract such a counterparty. Like any security, the price of a swap depends on supply and demand forces in the marketplace.

SWAPS AS A PORTFOLIO OF FORWARD CONTRACTS

It is interesting to relate swaps to other securities, including other derivative securities. For example, a traditional swap can be expressed as a portfolio of forward contracts. Consider the interest rate swap shown in Figure 21.3.[8] Suppose that this swap is based on the six-month LIBOR such that interest payments are exchanged every six months. One party simply sends a check covering the difference between the fixed and floating payments to the other. However, with a swap, the rate that is used on the payment dates is (here) the six-month LIBOR that prevailed six months earlier. The first payment date occurs six months after the inception of the swap, so the first payment is known at inception, the second payment is known six months after inception, and so on. For instance, suppose that the LIBOR is 11 percent six months prior to a payment date. From Figure 21.3, and assuming semiannual compounding for all interest rates, firm A would be required to pay the intermediary the following amount on the next payment date:

Swaps can be expressed as portfolios of forward contracts.

$$.50(.1105 - .0980)NP = .00625NP,$$

where NP is the notional principal of the swap. In turn, the intermediary would pay firm B the following amount:

$$.50(.1120 - .1005)NP = .00575NP.$$

Thus, the intermediary's profit is $.0005NP$ per six months, or 10 bps per year.

To generalize this process, denote L as the six-month LIBOR on any previous payment (or inception) date. Thus, the payoff to firm A on each payment date is

$$NP/2[0.098 - (L + 5bps)].$$

This expression is nothing more than a forward contract on six-month LIBOR that is settled up six months in arrears. For firm A, therefore, the swap can be represented by a portfolio of these forward contracts. If the swap (debt instrument) has a ten-year maturity, then there are twenty of these in-arrears forward contracts.

For firm B, the payoff on each payment date is given by the following in-arrears forward contracts:

$$NP/2[(L + 20\ bps) - .1005].$$

At the swap's inception, the *sum* of the values of these forward contracts should be zero. But *each* forward contract's value is not necessarily equal to zero, as is the case for a normal forward contract. For example, suppose that the term structure of interest rates is upward-sloping, which is common. As a consequence, for firm A the

---

[8]Using a similar analysis, it is possible to demonstrate that a currency swap may be represented by a portfolio of forward contracts.

forward rate of interest is likely to be less than 9.8 percent when the forward contract's maturity is short, and vice versa. The values of the shorter-maturity forward contracts are therefore likely to be negative, while the values of the longer-term forward contracts are likely to be positive. The opposite is true for firm B.

Cash-flow patterns such as these have implications for default risk when considering swap arrangements. For instance, firm B is more likely to default later in the swap period if, as above, the term structure is upward-sloping. The above analysis of swaps as a portfolio of forward contracts implicitly assumes that the swap arrangement is free of default risk, discussed below.

SWAPS AS A PORTFOLIO OF DEFAULT-FREE BONDS

Swaps can be expressed as portfolios of default-free bonds.

Swaps can also be expressed as a portfolio of default-free bonds, assuming no default risk exists. Consider the arrangement between firm A and the financial intermediary in Figure 21.3,[9] wherein firm A borrows the notional principal, NP, from the intermediary at a fixed rate of 9.8 percent. In turn, the swap intermediary borrows NP from firm A at LIBOR plus 5 bps. Define B_1 as the value of a fixed-rate, default-free bond that pays 9.8 percent. Define B_2 as the value of a default-free bond paying LIBOR plus 5 bps. The value of the interest rate swap to the intermediary is thus $B_1 - B_2$. In other words, the swap value can be expressed as a portfolio of the two default-free bonds. Should interest rates increase, the value of the swap to firm A increases. The value of the swap to firm B can be similarly decomposed into a portfolio of default-free bonds. By finding a swap counterparty, the intermediary eliminates its interest rate risk.

DEFAULT RISK AND REGULATION

Swaps are typically arranged by financial intermediaries that have entered into offsetting contracts with the two firms involved. These intermediaries are fully hedged if neither firm defaults. For instance, in the interest rate swap illustrated in Figure 23.1, the intermediary earns 10 bps annually if A and B do not default, regardless of how the six-month LIBOR varies over the swap period.

However, should one firm default, the intermediary is no longer fully hedged. The intermediary must honor the swap arrangement with the remaining firm and is therefore exposed to risk. For instance, if firm B

---

[9]Using a similar analysis, it is possible to demonstrate that a currency swap may be represented as a portfolio of default-free bonds.

defaults and interest rates rise, the intermediary loses monies. This is evident from the above discussion of interest rate swaps as portfolios of bond instruments.

Given the present competitive nature of the swap market, the smaller spreads being earned by intermediaries, the off-balance sheet nature of swap arrangements, and the fact that commercial banks are becoming bigger players in swap intermediation, regulators of these banks are becoming more and more concerned with default risk as it relates to swaps.[10] Although bank supervisory authorities such as the Federal Reserve are only just beginning to grapple with this issue, some regulatory recommendations are being given intense consideration. These include

- *Risk weighting.* In a risk-weighting scheme, now used widely in the United Kingdom, a bank's capital adequacy requirement is determined by assigning to each balance and off-balance sheet item, including swaps, a weight reflecting the item's riskiness. The major determinants of this weight for asset items are the credit risk of the other party and the asset's maturity.

- *Marking-to-the-market.* As shown above, swaps are akin to a *series* of forward contracts. From Part 2 of this book we know that a significant difference between forwards and futures is that the latter require daily resettlement. This daily marking-to-the-market procedure helps to reduce the riskiness of a futures position relative to that of a forward position. Now notice that a swap entails a series of resettlements that fall somewhere between a listed futures contract and a normal forward contract. For example, the interest rate swap above entailed resettlement every six months. By shortening the interval between payment dates, therefore, the swap becomes less risky to the intermediary. This is obvious when one thinks of a swap intermediary as a type of futures clearinghouse. Thus, shortening the resettlement window on swaps may help to reduce the intermediary's risk exposure.

- *Performancing bonding.* Margins in a futures or options market represent a type of performance bond. Similar performance bonding occurs in swaps markets, although it is not required by legislation. For example, a low-credit-rated firm may have to post collateral in the form of financial securities in order to engage in the swap arrangement. Also, performance bonding through insurance has been used. For instance, the World Bank has established an arrangement in which the default risk of a swap is assumed by a private insurer, Aetna Casualty and Surety Company.

---

[10]However, it should still be kept in mind that swap defaults have far lighter consequences to commercial bank intermediaries than do straight loan defaults. Recall that the principal on an interest rate swap is only notional.

OTHER TYPES OF SWAPS

The currency and interest rate swaps presented in this chapter may be called *straight* or *plain* swaps. We now briefly describe a number of more elaborate swap arrangements:

- *Amortized swaps.* The principal reduces over time much the same way a home mortgage is amortized.

- *Deferred swaps.* Interest payments do not begin until a more deferred future date.

- *Circus swaps.* These are combinations of currency and interest rate swaps. The parties exchange fixed-rate debt denominated in one currency for floating-rate debt denominated in another currency. The swap arrangement described earlier in connection with Exhibit 21.3 — in which a British firm swapped fixed-rate pound-denominated debt for floating-rate dollar-denominated debt — was an example of a circus swap.

- *Extendable swaps.* One of the parties has the option to extend the swap's life beyond the originally prescribed period.

- *Puttable swaps.* One party has the option to terminate the swap before its originally prescribed period.

FUTURE OUTLOOK FOR THE SWAPS MARKET

In 1982 the combined value of dollar currency and interest rate swaps outstanding was about $5 billion. In 1984 the combined value grew to over $45 billion, and at year-end 1987 it was over $703 billion. The swaps market has exhibited astonishingly rapid growth, attesting to its vital role in integrating international capital markets. Swaps have effectively created a single unified international capital market from what was earlier a set of segmented capital markets due to restrictions on capital flows.

At the current time, the development of the swaps market is akin to the early development of the futures and options markets. That is, swaps are initiated through an informal network of brokers and dealers, are tailored contracts, and exhibit little secondary market trading. Recently, however, there has been a concentrated effort to offer more standardized swap contracts — known as *master agreements* — in order to reduce the time and costs associated with swap contracting and to enhance the trading liquidity of swaps in secondary markets.

Master agreements reduce the costs associated with swap contracting.

Much of this effort has been initiated by the *International Swap Dealers Association* (ISDA), which is an organization of leading swap intermediaries originally founded in 1985. During this year, the ISDA published *The Code of Standard Wording, Assumptions, and Provisions for Swaps*, a document that has been revised and expanded annually since 1985. The purpose of the code was to establish master agreements from which every swap transaction could be created as a supplement. In other words, these master agreements provided a set of terms applicable to any swap transaction; the parties could then tailor the transaction by appending specific terms to the master agreement.

Today, two master agreements exist: the *Interest Rate Swap Agreement* and the *Interest Rate and Currency Exchange Agreement*. The former agreement relates to U.S. dollar–denominated interest rate swaps, and the second to currency and circus swap transactions. The actual swap contract that is negotiated between the parties typically represents some extension of these basic agreements. In this way, the costs of negotiation are limited to these extensions.

The swaps market will likely continue to expand. Swaps provide for interest rate and exchange rate risk reallocation, help to create synthetic instruments that serve to complete the market, and play a major role in the integration of the world's capital markets. As this market expands, swap transactions are becoming more and more standardized. It appears that the market is moving towards standardization, much the way markets for futures and options did earlier this century.

SUMMARY

Currency swaps enable multinational corporations to exchange currencies at periodic intervals and are typically used to complement debt issues in which payments are made in a foreign currency. The currency swap market is unorganized and growing, and its existence can be clearly linked to exchange-exposure management and to international market segmentation, including regulatory barriers to capital flows.

An interest rate swap generally occurs when two firms agree to trade interest payments on each other's outstanding debt. The debt issues are denominated in the same currency, and the trade typically involves both fixed-rate and floating-rate debt. This market is growing very rapidly. In the classical example of an interest rate swap, a credit-market comparative advantage gives rise to gains from trade. However, such gains should not persist because of arbitrage restrictions and may instead represent compensation for lost prepayment options. The existence and growth of this market likely result from the ability of interest rate swaps to facilitate interest rate risk reallocation and to create synthetic financial instruments.

Both currency and interest rate swaps can be expressed as a portfolio of forward contracts or default-free bonds in the absence of default risk. Financial intermediaries who facilitate swaps, as well as their supervisory authorities, are currently grappling with the issue of default risk.

The organization of the swaps market is becoming more structured as parties seek standardized swap arrangements in order to reduce the costs of transacting. To this extent, the International Swap Dealers Association is playing a major role in the development of consistent swap terms.

Selected References

Arak, M., A. Estrella, L. Goodman, and A. Silver. "Interest Rate Swaps: An Alternative Explanation." *Financial Management* 17 (Summer 1988):12–18.

Arnold, T. "How to Do Interest Rate Swaps." *Harvard Business Review* 62 (September–October 1984):96–101.

Beckstrom, R. "The Development of the Swap Market" in *Swap Finance*, vol. 1, ed. Boris Antl. London: Euromoney Publications, 1986.

Beidleman, C. *Financial Swaps*. Homewood, Ill.: Dow Jones–Irwin, 1985.

Bicksler, J., and A. Chen. "An Economic Analysis Of Interest Rate Swaps." *Journal Of Finance* (July 1986):645–655.

Felgran, S. "Interest Rate Swaps: Use, Risk, and Prices." *New England Economic Review.* Federal Reserve Bank of Boston, November 1987, 22–32.

Gary, R., W. Kruz, and C. Strupp. "Interest Rate Swaps" in *Swap Financing Techniques*, ed. B. Antl. London: Euromoney Publications, 1983, 11–15.

Kidwell, D., W. Marr, and R. Thompson. "Eurodollar Bonds: Alternative Financing For U.S. Companies." *Financial Management* 14 (Winter 1985). 18–27.

Lipsky, J., and S. Elhalaski. "Swap-Driven Primary Insurance in the International Bond Market." Salomon Brothers, Inc., January 1986.

Park, Y. "Currency Swaps as a Long-Term International Financing Technique." *Journal of International Business Studies* 15, no. 3 (Winter 1984):47–54.

Powers, J. "The Vortex of Finance." *Intermarket Magazine*, 3, no. 2 (February 1986):27–38.

Price, J., J. Keller, and M. Nelson. "The Delicate Art Of Swaps." *Euromoney* N/A (April 1983):118–125.

Shirreff, D. "The Fearsome Growth of Swaps." *Euromoney* (October 1985):247–261.

Smith, C., C. Smithson, and L. Wakeman. "The Evolving Market for Swaps." *Midland Corporate Finance Journal* 41 (Winter 1986):20–32.

Smith, C., C. Smithson, and L. Wakeman. "The Market for Interest Rate Swaps." *Financial Management* 17 (Winter 1988):34–44.

Turnball, S. "Swaps: A Zero Sum Game." *Financial Management* 16 (Spring 1987):15–22.

Wall, L. "Interest Rate Swaps in an Agency Theoretic Model with Uncertain Interest Rates." Working paper No. 86–6. Federal Reserve Bank of Atlanta, July 1986.

Wall, L., and J. Pringle. "Alternative Explanations of Interest Rate Swaps." Working paper No. 87–2. Federal Reserve Bank of Atlanta, April 1987.

Whittaker, J. "Interest Rate Swaps: Risk and Regulation." Federal Reserve Bank of Kansas City. *Economic Review* 72, no. 3 (March 1987):3–13.

Questions and Problems

1. Define a currency swap and an interest rate swap.
2. Define a back-to-back loan and a parallel loan.
3. Name two reasons for the existence of currency swaps.

4. Name two reasons for the existence of interest rate swaps.

5. Give two criticisms of the credit-market comparative-advantage argument for the existence of interest rate swaps.

6. Given the following parameters, what are the potential "gains from trade" from an interest rate swap? Devise a swap in which both firms and a swap intermediary gain.

	Firm A	Firm B
Fixed:	10.0%	10.75%
Floating:	LIBOR + 10 bps	LIBOR + 30 bps

7. Discuss how swaps can be expressed as a portfolio of forward contracts in the absence of default risk.

8. Suppose that a firm can borrow at a fixed rate of 11.25 percent, or at a floating rate of LIBOR plus 60 bps. On the other hand, the firm can enter into a fixed-for-floating interest rate swap in which the intermediary would pay LIBOR flat while the firm would pay 10.00 percent. Should the firm issue fixed-rate debt directly, or should it issue floating and swap to fixed? Why?

9. Consider the indication pricing schedule for interest rate swap transactions appearing in Exhibit 21.2. Suppose that a U.S. corporation issues $25 million of seven-year debt, at par, that is nonamortizing and exhibits a semiannual coupon payment of 9.30 percent. If the corporation engages in a swap in which the intermediary pays fixed and receives floating, then (a) what will be the floating rate cost to the corporation, (b) what rates will the intermediary receive and pay, and (c) if the corporation could issue floating-rate debt directly at LIBOR + 0.25%, should it engage in the fixed-to-floating interest rate swap?

10. In Question 9, how would the intermediary likely try to offset the swap? In other words, describe the ideal swap counterparty.

11. Consider the following indication pricing schedule for Swiss Franc/U.S. Dollar swaps:

Maturity (Years)	Midrate[a]
3	6.19%sa
4	6.35
5	6.49

[a]Deduct 5 bps if the intermediary is paying fixed, and add 5 bps if it is receiving fixed.

Suppose that a Swiss firm wants to convert SF1,000,000 four-year semiannual fixed-rate debt into floating-rate dollar-denominated debt: (a) What does the Swiss firm pay the intermediary, and what does the intermediary pay the firm? (b) Why might the firm seek to undertake this circus swap?

12. Describe the intermediary's ideal swap counterparty for the swap arrangement of Question 11.

Self-Test Problems

ST-1. Given the following parameters, what are the potential "gains from trade" from an interest rate swap? Devise a swap arrangement in which both firms and a swap intermediary gain.

	Firm A	Firm B
Fixed:	10.75%	11.70%
Floating:	LIBOR + 25 bps	LIBOR + 37-½ bps

ST-2. Consider the following indication pricing schedule for interest rate swaps:

	Fixed Rate		
Maturity (Years)	Intermediary Pays	Intermediary Receives	U.S. Treasury Note Rate
4	4 yr TN sa + 30 bps	4 yr TN sa + 45 bps	9.00%
5	5 yr TN sa + 35 bps	5 yr TN sa + 58 bps	9.08
6	6 yr TN sa + 40 bps	6 yr TN sa + 66 bps	9.12

Suppose that a firm can issue fixed-rate five-year debt directly with a semiannual coupon rate of 9.75 percent, or it can issue floating-rate five-year debt directly at six-month LIBOR + 0.50 percent. Should the firm issue floating-rate debt directly or issue fixed-rate debt and engage in a swap?

Solutions to Self-Test Problems

ST-1.

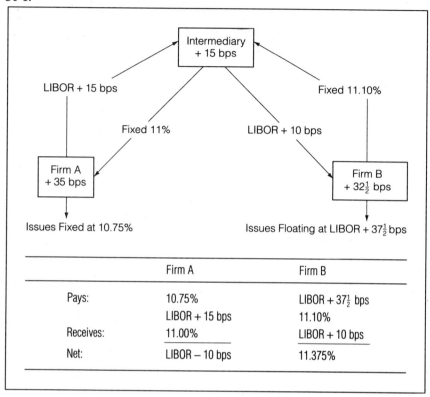

	Firm A	Firm B
Pays:	10.75%	LIBOR + $37\frac{1}{2}$ bps
	LIBOR + 15 bps	11.10%
Receives:	11.00%	LIBOR + 10 bps
Net:	LIBOR − 10 bps	11.375%

ST-2. The intermediary will pay 9.43 percent: five-year TN rate + 35 bps. For the firm, therefore, the resulting debt cost is LIBOR + 0.3156 percent: (9.75% + LIBOR − 9.43 percent) × (360/365). Since this cost is lower than that associated with issuing floating-rate debt directly (LIBOR + 0.50 percent), the firm should engage in the swap.

Appendix 1:

SIMPLE LINEAR REGRESSION

Suppose that we are interested in the relation between two variables, X and Y. Let X be our independent, or explanatory, variable, and Y be our dependent variable. To describe this relation statistically, we need a set of observations for each variable and a hypothesis concerning the mathematical form of the relation between X and Y. Assume that this form is linear. That is, the relation between X and Y is best described by a straight line. Given this assumption, we want to specify a criterion that generates the best straight line fitting X and Y.

The generally accepted criterion is the *least-squares criterion:* the line of best fit is that which minimizes the sum of the squared deviations of the sample points from the line. Mathematically, it can be stated as

$$\text{(A.1-1)} \qquad \text{Minimize} \sum_{i=1}^{N} (Y_i - \hat{Y}_i)^2,$$

where $\hat{Y}_i = a + bX_i$ represents the equation for a straight line with intercept a and slope b. Here Y_i is the sample value of Y for observation i. It corresponds to X_i, the sample value of X for observation i. N is the number of observations (sample size).

The problem is to simultaneously choose values for a and b such that Equation A.1-1 is minimized. Using elementary calculus or algebra, it is easy to show that the least-squares solutions for the slope and intercept are[1]

$$\text{(A.1-2)} \qquad b = \frac{N\Sigma X_i Y_i - \Sigma X_i RY_i}{N\Sigma X_i^2 - (\Sigma X_i)^2},$$

$$\text{(A.1-3)} \qquad a = \bar{Y} - b\bar{X},$$

where $\bar{Y}$ and $\bar{X}$ are the sample means of Y and X, respectively. Defining $x_i = X_i - X$ and $y_i = Y_i - Y$, we can rewrite Equation A.1-2 as follows:

$$\text{(A.1-4)} \qquad b = \Sigma x_i y_i / \Sigma x_i^2.$$

---

[1]All summation signs range over all observations 1, 2, . . ., N.

The *sample covariance* indicates whether X and Y are directly, inversely, or independently related. An unbiased estimate of the sample covariance, $COV(X,Y)$, is given by

(A.1–5)
$$COV(X,Y) = \Sigma(X_i - \bar{X})(Y_i - \bar{Y})/(N - 1).$$

The *sample correlation coefficient*, ρ_{XY}, provides one measure of the power of the association between X and Y. It ranges between -1 and $+1$, and its unbiased estimate is given by

(A.1–6)
$$\rho_{XY} = COV(X,Y)/\sqrt{VAR(X)VAR(Y)},$$

where $VAR(X)$ and $VAR(Y)$ are the sample estimates of the variances of X and Y, respectively. They are given by

(A.1–7)
$$VAR(X) = \Sigma(X_i - \bar{X})^2/(N - 1)$$

(A.1–8)
$$VAR(Y) = \Sigma(Y_i - \bar{Y})^2/(N - 1).$$

Next consider the expression obtained by dividing sample covariance by the sample variance of X. Specifically, by dividing Equation A.1-5 by Equation A.1-7, and recalling that $x_i = X_i - X$ and $Y_i = Y_i - Y$, we have

(A.1–9)
$$COV(X,Y)/VAR(X) = \Sigma x_i y_i/\Sigma x_i^2.$$

This ratio is identical to the estimate of the slope b obtained in Equation A.1-4. Thus, for any sample of data points, the least-squares slope estimator can be measured by the ratio of the sample covariance and the variance of the independent variable.

Our concern thus far in this appendix has focused on the algebra of parameter estimation rather than the statistics of model testing. We now turn to a discussion of the statistical testing of the least-squares regression model that contains one dependent and one independent variable. This model is often called the *simple linear regression*.

To understand the probabilistic nature of the regression model, we expand the analysis to allow for the fact that for a given observed value of X, we may observe many possible values of Y. More formally, we have

(A.1–10)
$$Y_i = a + bX_i + \epsilon_i,$$

where ϵ_i is a random error term. This error term may arise from a variety of sources, including omitted explanatory variables, errors in data measurement, and the like.

Under the simple linear regression model, the error term is assumed to exhibit the following properties: (1) it has zero expected value and constant variance; (2) it is normally distributed; and (3) errors corresponding to different observations have zero correlation. If these assumptions are accurate, then it can be verified that the intercept and slope parameters given by Equations A.1-2 and A.1-3 exhibit the following properties: (1) they are unbiased estimates; that is, their expected values equal the actual values of the parameters being estimated; (2) they are the most efficient estimates; that is, the variances of the estimates are smaller than the variances of any other unbiased estimators; and (3) they are normally distributed; specifically, it can be shown that

(A.1–11) $$b \sim N(b, \sigma_\epsilon^2 / \Sigma x_i^2)$$

(A.1–12) $$a \sim N(a, \sigma_\epsilon^2 \Sigma X_i^2 / N \Sigma x_i^2),$$

where σ_ϵ^2 is the variance of the error term. It is estimated by the following:

(A.1–13) $$\sigma_\epsilon^2 = \sigma_{\epsilon_i}^2 / (N - 2),$$

where $\epsilon_i = Y_i - \hat{Y}_i = (Y_i - \hat{a} - \hat{b}X_i)$. It is common to refer to ϵ_i as the *regression residual* and σ_ϵ^2 as the *sample residual variance*.

Given we know the distribution of the least-squares estimators a and b, it is now possible to discuss statistical testing of the linear model. The statistical test for rejecting the null hypothesis associated with a regression coefficient is usually based upon the t distribution. The t distribution is relevant because for statistical testing we need to utilize a sample estimate of the error variance rather than its true value.

To use the t distribution to construct confidence intervals for the estimated parameters, we first standardize the estimated regression parameter, a or b, by subtracting its hypothesized value, a_0 or b_0, and dividing by the estimate of its standard error:

(A.1–14a) $$t_{N-2} = \frac{b - b_0}{\sigma_\epsilon / \sqrt{\Sigma x_i^2}}$$

(A.1–14b) $$t_{N-2} = \frac{a - a_0}{\sigma_\epsilon \sqrt{\Sigma X_i^2} / \sqrt{N \Sigma x_i^2}}.$$

The standardized variable t_{N-2} will follow a t distribution with $N - 2$ degrees of freedom. Since this distribution is known, we can make statistical statements about the range of values likely to contain the true parameter. For instance, if $t_{N-2} > 1.96$, the 95 percent critical value for the normal distribution when sample size is large, then we conclude that the estimated value of the parameter differs from its hypothesized true value, and we can do so with a high degree of confidence (95 percent).

Besides testing the individual estimates a and b for statistical significance, it is useful to measure the overall goodness of fit of the estimated regression line. The residuals of a regression can help to provide a useful measure of the degree to which the estimated regression line fits the sample data points. Large (small) residuals generally imply poor (good) fit. Specifically, it is possible to show that

(A.1–15) $\Sigma(Y_i - \bar{Y})^2 \quad = \quad \Sigma(\hat{Y}_i - \bar{Y})^2 \quad + \quad \Sigma(Y_i - \hat{Y}_i)^2$

Total variation of Y (or total sum of squares)	Explained variation of Y (or regression sum of squares)	Residual variation of Y (or error sum of squares)
TSS =	RSS +	ESS.

Equation A.1-15 divides the total variation of Y into two distinct parts, the first accounted for by the regression equation (RSS) and the second associated with the unexplained portion (the error term) of the linear model (ESS). To normalize, we divide both sizes of Equation A.1-15 by the TSS to get

(A.1–16) $\qquad\qquad 1 = RSS/TSS + ESS/TSS.$

We define R squared (R^2), known as the *coefficient of determination* of the regression equation, as

(A.1–17) $\qquad\qquad R^2 = 1 - (ESS/TSS) = RSS/TSS.$

R^2 is the proportion of the total variation in Y explained by the regression of Y on X. R^2 ranges between 0 and 1. An R^2 of 0 occurs when the linear regression model does nothing to help explain the variation in Y; Y and X are independent, and the slope coefficient is zero. An R^2 of 1 can occur only in the case of a perfect fit when all sample points lie exactly on the estimated regression line. Thus, low (high) values of R^2 are associated with poor (good) fit. It can be shown that R^2 is equal to the square of the sample correlation coefficient, ρ_{XY}.

The procedure of dividing the total variation in Y into two components suggests a statistical test of the existence of a linear relation between Y and X. Specifically, we expect that a strong relation will result in a large ratio of explained to unexplained variance. Consider the following ratio:

(A.1–18) $\qquad F_{1,N-2} = \dfrac{explained\ variance}{unexplained\ variance} = \dfrac{RSS/1}{ESS/(N-2)}.$

$F_{1,N-2}$ follows the F distribution, a known distribution, with 1 (numerator) and $N - 2$ (denominator) degrees of freedom. The value of the F statistic will be zero only when the explained variance in the regression is zero ($R^2 = 0$). Thus, a low (high) value of the F statistic is associated with a weak (strong) linear association between Y and X. It is possible to make statistical statements about the strength of this association since, again, the F distribution is known.

The F and t distributions can be found in most statistics and econometrics textbooks. Indeed, it can be demonstrated that $F_{1,N-2} = t^2_{N-2}$.

Appendix 2

DIFFERENTIATION

The average rate of change for a linear function is constant and equal to the slope of the function. Contrastingly, the average rate of change for a curvilinear function varies with successive movements along the curve. Hence, the slope of a curvilinear function is nonconstant, varying at different points along the curve.

The slope of a curvilinear function at any given point is equal to the slope of a line drawn tangent to the curve at that point. In the figure below, three different tangents are drawn at points A, B, and C on the curve. The slopes of these tangents provide the slope of the function at the given points.

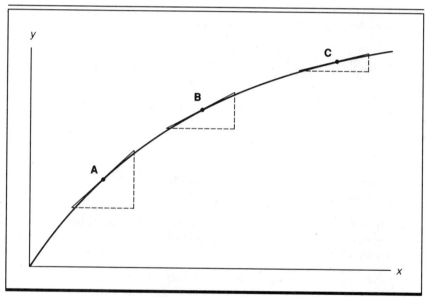

The *derivative* measures the instantaneous rate of change of a function; that is, how the dependent variable, y, changes in response to a very small unit change in the independent variable, x. The formal terminology for the derivative is

(A.2–1)
$$dy/dx = \lim_{\Delta x \to 0} \Delta y/\Delta x.$$

This expression states that the derivative of y with respect to x (dy/dx) equals the limit of the ratio $\Delta y/\Delta x$ as Δx (the change in x) approaches zero. The derivative measures the slope of a function and is therefore particularly helpful in measuring the slope of a curvilinear function.

Differentiation is the process of determining the derivative of a function; that is, determining the change in y in response to a change in x when Δx approaches zero. Below we provide some common rules of differentiation. Some of these rules employ auxiliary functions such as u and v, where u is an unspecified function of x, $u(x)$, and v is an unspecified function of x, $v(x)$.

- *Constant function rule.* The derivative of a constant function, $y = c$, where c is any constant, is zero.

  Given $y = c$, $dy/dx = 0$.
  Example: $y = 5$, $dy/dx = 0$.

- *Linear function rule.* The derivative of a linear function, $y = a + bx$, is equal to b, the coefficient of x, which is constant.

  Given $y = a + bx$, $dy/dx = b$.
  Example: $y = 8 + 3x$, $dy/dx = 3$.

- *Power function rule.* The derivative of a power function, $y = ax^p$, is equal to the exponent p times the coefficient a, multiplied by the variable x raised to the $(p - 1)$ power.

  Given $y = ax^p$, $dy/dx = pax^{p-1}$.
  Example: $y = 3x^3$, $dy/dx = (3)3x^{3-1} = 9x^2$.

- *Rule for sums and differences.* The derivative of a sum, $y = u(x) + v(x)$, is equal to the sum of the derivatives of the individual functions. The derivative of a difference, $y = u(x) - v(x)$, is equal to the difference of the derivatives of the individual functions.

  Given $y = u(x) \pm v(x)$, $dy/dx = du/dx \pm dv/dx$.
  Example: $y = 2x^2 - 3x$, $dy/dx = 4x - 3$.

- *Product rule.* The derivative of a product, $y = u(x) \cdot v(x)$, is equal to the first function multiplied by the derivative of the second plus the second function multiplied by the derivative of the first.

  Given $y = u(x) \cdot v(x)$, $dy/dx = u(dv/dx) + v(du/dx)$.
  Example: $y = 2x^4(x - 5)$, where $u = 2x^4$ and
  $y = (x - 5)$, $dy/dx = 2x^4(1) + (x - 5)8x^3 = 10x^4 - 40x^3$.

- *Quotient rule.* The derivative of a quotient, $y = u/v$, is equal to the denominator times the derivative of the numerator, minus the numerator times the derivative of the denominator, all divided by the denominator squared.

  Given $y = u(x)/v(x)$, $dy/dx = [v(du/dx) - u(dv/dx)]/v^2$.
  Example: $y = 3x^3/5x + 1$, where $u = 3x^3$ and $y = 5x - 1$,
  $dy/dx = [(5x - 1)(9x^2) - (3x^3)(5)]/(5x + 1)^2$.

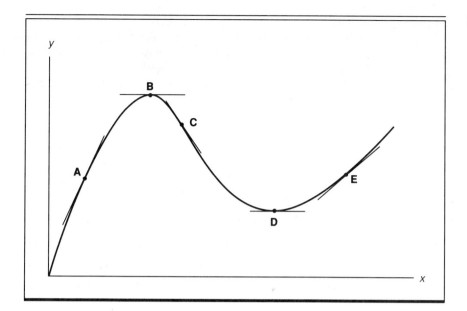

■ *Chain rule.* The derivative of a function of a function, $y = f(u)$, where $u = g(x)$, is equal to the derivative of the first function with respect to u times the derivative of the second function with respect to x.

Given $y = f(u)$ and $u = g(x)$, $dy/dx = (dy/du)(du/dx)$.
Example: $y = u^3$ and $u = x^2 - 8$, $dy/dx = 3u^2(2x)$.

Just as the first derivative (dy/dx) measures the rate of change of the original function, the second-order derivative, d^2y/dx^2, measures the rate of change of the first derivative (and so on). Higher-order derivatives are found simply by applying the rules of differentiation to the previous derivative. For instance, the second derivative of $y = 4x^5$ is $d^2y/dx^2 = 80x^3$.

Differentiation has many applications to most sciences. For our purposes, it is useful in determining a *relative maximum* or *minimum* of a function. To be at a relative maximum or minimum, a function must be at a plateau, implying that the first derivative is equal to zero. The second (and sufficient) condition is that the second derivative be negative for a relative maximum, and positive for a relative minimum. Thus, we have for a relative maximum:

$$dy/dx = 0 \text{ and } d^2y/dx^2 < 0,$$

and for a relative minimum:

$$dy/dx = 0 \text{ and } d^2y/dx^2 > 0.$$

From Figure A.1, points B and D indicate a relative maximum and minimum, respectively. At each of these points the slope of the tangent line is equal to zero; that is, $dy/dx = 0$. If the first derivative is zero and the second derivative is negative, it means that the function is moving down from the plateau and must have been at a relative maximum (B). If the first derivative is zero and the second is positive, then the function is moving upward from a plateau and must have been at a relative minimum (D).

GLOSSARY

All-or-none order A transaction order in which the broker must fill all of the order at a prescribed price.

American option An option contract that allows for premature exercise.

Anticipatory hedge A futures hedge in which a long futures position is undertaken in order to protect a spot transaction to occur at a future date.

Arbitrage A trading process designed to exploit violations of the Law of One Price.

Arbitrager A person who engages in arbitrage.

Ask price The price at which a market maker offers to sell a primary or derivative security.

At-the-money An option where the underlying asset price is equal to the option's exercise price.

Back-to-back loan A loan between two national firms, each making the other a loan in its respective currency.

Barone-Adesi and Whaley model A quadratic approximation to value American options written on continuous-leakage assets.

Basis The difference between the spot and futures prices.

Basis risk The risk associated with variation in the basis over time.

Bear money spread An option spread designed to profit from a forecast of declining prices.

Beta A measure of the responsiveness of a security's returns to returns of the market portfolio.

Bid-ask spread The difference between the bid and ask prices.

Bid price The price at which a market maker offers to buy a primary or derivative security.

Binomial option-pricing model (BOPM) A model for valuing options in which the underlying asset price can take on two possible values at the end of any one period of time.

Black's approximation An approximation for pricing American stock options.

Black's model A model for pricing European futures options.

Black-Scholes model A model for pricing European option contracts.

Boundary condition A condition limiting the value of an option contract due to arbitrage restrictions.

Bounded-payoff put A currency put option where the payoff is limited to less than the exercise price.

Brady Commission A commission appointed by President Reagan to study the causes of the October 1987 stock market crash.

Bucket trading An illegal futures trading scheme in which a broker and dual trader conspire to skim profits from public market orders.

Bull money spread An option spread designed to profit from a forecast of rising prices.

Butterfly spread An option combination designed to profit from a forecast of spot price stability.

Calendar spread An option combination consisting of the purchase of an option with a given expiration and the sale of an otherwise equivalent option having a different expiration date.

Call option An option giving the buyer the right to purchase the underlying asset at the prescribed exercise price.

Capital Asset Pricing Model (CAPM) An equilibrium model proporting a linear relation between the expected return of an asset and the return on the market portfolio.

Carrying-charge model A model used to determine futures or forward prices. It holds that such prices are given by the asset's spot price plus the costs of carrying the asset forward to delivery.

Carrying charges The total costs of carrying an asset forward in time, including storage, transportation, and financing costs.

Cash-and-carry arbitrage A theoretically riskless arbitrage trading strategy that underlies the carrying-charge model of futures prices.

Cash settlement A procedure applicable to certain futures and options contracts wherein a cash transfer is employed at contract settlement rather than the actual delivery of the asset in question.

Certainty equivalent The amount an individual would be willing to pay such that he is indifferent between the utility associated with a certain outcome and that associated with an uncertain outcome.

Characteristic line The linear regression relating a stock's return to the return on the market portfolio.

Cheapest to deliver That unique Treasury note or Treasury bond that the short trader will deliver against the Chicago Board of Trade's Treasury note or Treasury bond futures contract.

Circus swap A combination of a currency swap and an interest rate swap.

Clearing firm A firm that is a member of a futures or options clearinghouse.

Clearinghouse A firm that is associated with an options or futures exchange that guarantees contract performance and otherwise facilitates trading.

Coefficient of determination A measure of the strength of the linear association between two variables.

Commission broker A futures floor trader who executes public orders.

Commodity Futures Trading Commission (CFTC) A federal agency empowered to regulate futures trading.

Commodity pool *See* Futures fund.

Comparative statics A procedure for examining the effects of a marginal change in one particular variable while holding all other determinants constant.

Contango A condition in which the forward price is above the expected future spot price.

Convenience yield A premium embedded in the spot price of an asset that is in short supply.

Conversion An arbitrage trade consisting of a written call and the purchase of a synthetic call option.

Conversion factor Used by the Chicago Board of Trade to adjust the value of a deliverable Treasury note or Treasury bond.

Correlation A measure of the dependence of two variables that is bounded.

Cost of carry The cost of financing and storing an asset for a prescribed time period.

Covariance A measure of the dependence of two variables that is unbounded.

Covered call writing A strategy in which a call option is written on an underlying asset that is already held.

Covered interest arbitrage The currency market's version of the basic cash-and-carry arbitrage underlying the carrying-charge model of futures prices.

Critical asset price The price of the underlying asset that should trigger the premature exercise of an American option.

Cross hedge A futures hedge in which the asset underlying the futures contract differs from the asset being hedged.

Cross rate An exchange rate between two currencies that is implied from the exchange rates entailing a third currency.

Currency swap An arrangement in which two parties agree to exchange currencies at recurrent intervals, typically stemming from debt issues.

Daily price limits The maximum and minimum prices at which a futures contract may trade during a session.

Daily resettlement A futures market requirement that traders realize losses each trading day.

Day order An order to trade at a prescribed price that, if unfilled, is canceled at the end of the trading session.

Day trader A futures or options trader who closes all positions prior to the close of trading on any given day.

Delivery option The option that the short trader has to deliver the cheapest-to-deliver Treasury note or Treasury bond against the Chicago Board of Trade's Treasury note or Treasury bond futures contract.

Delta An elasticity measure of the sensitivity of an option's price to changes in the price of the underlying asset.

Designated Order Turnaround (DOT) A system at the New York Stock Exchange that expedites the trading of large amounts of stocks, such as amounts associated with program trading.

Diminishing marginal substitutability A condition applicable to risk-averse investors where more units of an alternative good are required to maintain a certain utility level when removing a good already held.

Diminishing marginal utility A condition applicable to risk-averse investors where the incremental utility derived from the consumption of an additional good will be progressively smaller.

Diversification A process of adding assets to a portfolio that reduce correlation in order to reduce risk.

Dividend-protected A feature of over-the-counter stock options where the exercise price is reduced by the dividend per share.

Dividend yield The ratio of the dividend per share to the share price.

Dual trading A futures trading practice in which a floor trader can trade both for his or her own account and for the public during the same trading session.

Duration A measure of the sensitivity of a bond's price to changes in market rates of interest.

Dynamic hedging A strategy in which an equity portfolio is insured through the continual trading of stock index futures contracts.

Dynamic-hedge ratio The ratio that determines the number of index futures contracts such that the equity portfolio is continually hedged.

Early-exercise premium The premium that an American option commands over an otherwise identical European option because of the ability of traders to exercise American options prior to their maturity.

Efficient market A market in which asset prices reflect the true intrinsic values of assets.

Efficient portfolio formation The process of obtaining portfolios from a given opportunity set that yield the highest expected returns for a given level of return variance.

Equity option An option written on a common stock.

Eurodollar A dollar-denominated deposit in an overseas bank.

European Currency Unit An index that measures the value of the dollar against a basket of currencies of the members of the European Community (EC).

European option An option that can be exercised only at expiration.

Ex-dividend date A date that, for all intents and purposes, denotes the investor who is entitled to a stock dividend.

Exercise limit The maximum number of options that a trader may exercise during a specified time period.

Exercise price The price at which an option owner may buy or sell the underlying asset if the option is exercised.

Expectations model An approach for determining futures prices that stresses the role of market expectations.

Expectations theory A theory of the term structure of interest rates in which forward rates of interest represent the market's unbiased expectation of future interest rates.

Fiduciary call writing A strategy in which call options are written in such a way as to make a spot asset position continually hedged against unanticipated spot price changes.

Financial engineering The process of designing new financial instruments, especially derivative securities.

Financial futures contract A futures contract written on a financial asset such as a bond, stock index, or unit of foreign exchange.

Financing cost A component of the cost of carry relating to the purchase of the underlying asset.

Foreign currency futures A futures contract written on a foreign currency that is useful for hedging against exchange rate risk.

Foreign currency option An option written on foreign exchange that is useful for immunizing against exchange rate risk when international trade agreements are contingent.

Forward contract An agreement between two parties to trade foreign currency at a future date and at a prescribed exchange rate which is determined today.

Frontrunning An illegal trading scheme in which brokers place orders in front of public market orders that are large enough to likely change prices.

Futures commission merchant A firm that executes futures trades for public clients.

Futures contract A contract between two parties to trade a specified asset in the future for a prescribed price determined at contract inception.

Futures fund A mutual fund that specializes in the trading of futures contracts.

Futures option An option that is written on a futures contract.

Futures-style options Currency options that entail margins and daily resettlement and are currently traded on the London International Financial Futures Exchange.

Geske-Johnson model An analytic approximation useful for pricing American put stock options.

Hedge A transaction in which a trader tries to protect a preexisting position in the spot asset market through the trading of derivative securities.

Hedged portfolio A combination of an asset and its derivative security such that the return is ensured to be risk-free.

Hedge ratio A ratio that determines the number of derivative securities to trade such that a hedged portfolio is attained.

Hedger An investor who executes a hedge transaction.

Hedging premium A premium observed in a futures or forward price due to the risk-averse nature of investors.

Historical volatility The variance of the returns of an asset that is derived from historical asset-price data over a recent time period.

IMM Index The method of quoting Treasury bill and Eurodollar futures prices at the International Monetary Market division of the Chicago Mercantile Exchange.

Implied repo rate The repo rate that effectively forces the carrying-charge model to perfectly fit the observed futures price.

Implied volatility The variance of the returns of an asset that is derived by equating an observed option price with a theoretical model price.

Index option An option written on an index of securities.

Indication pricing schedule A schedule used by swap intermediaries to quote swap prices.

Indifference curve A curve denoting the same utility derived from different combinations of assets.

Indifference map A set of indifference curves.

Initial margin The amount that must be posted in order to originally engage in a futures transaction.

Insatiability A quality exhibited by rational investors in which more of an asset is preferred to less.

Institutional investor A term describing an investor that is a firm rather than an individual person.

Interbank market An informal network of banks that execute transactions in currency, currency forwards, and currency options.

Intercommodity spread A futures combination entailing long and short positions in contracts written on two different assets but having the same delivery dates.

Interest rate futures Futures contracts written on fixed-income securities such as Treasury bills, notes, and bonds.

Interest rate parity The currency market's version of the carrying-charge model of futures prices.

Interest rate swaps An arrangement in which two parties agree to swap periodic interest payments on outstanding debt.

International Swap Dealers Association An informal association of large swap intermediaries that seeks to provide greater standardization of swap transactions.

In-the-money A call (put) option where the underlying asset price is greater (less) than the option's exercise price.

Intracommodity spread A futures combination entailing long and short positions in contracts written on the same asset but having different delivery dates.

Invoice price The amount the long party must pay the short party for delivering Treasury notes or Treasury bonds against the Chicago Board of Trade's Treasury note or Treasury bond futures contract.

Joint probability distribution Provides the probabilities of getting various pairs of returns on two securities at the same time.

Law of One Price An economic law stating that two identical assets cannot sell for different prices.

Limit down Occurs when the futures price moves down to its daily lower limit.

Limit up Occurs when the futures price moves up to its daily upper limit.

Liquidity preference theory A theory of the term structure that contends that longer-term interest rates exceed shorter-term rates due, in part, to a liquidity premium demanded by risk-averse investors for making longer-term loans.

Local A trader on the floor of a futures exchange who trades for his own account.

London Interbank Offer Rate The variable interest rate earned on Eurodollar deposits.

Long position Denotes the position of one who buys a primary or derivative security.

Long hedge *See* Anticipatory hedge.

Macro hedging A hedging strategy wherein a firm hedges the combined exposure of all assets and liabilities on its balance sheet.

Maintenance margin The margin that must be maintained after the initial day of trading in the futures contract; it is typically about 75 percent of the initial margin.

Margin Collateral that must be posted to transact in a futures or options contract in order to insure the clearinghouse against credit risk.

Margin call Indicates that a futures trader must post additional margin in order to continue trading in the contract.

Market completion A benefit offered by derivative-security trading in which an investor's opportunity set and utility are enhanced.

Market imperfections Taxes, transaction costs, imperfect security divisibility, restrictions on short selling, and any other such real-world frictions that frustrate arbitrage trading.

Marking-to-the-market *See* Daily resettlement.

Market maker A trader on an exchange who is charged with the duty of filling public market orders.

Market order An order to trade a security at the best currently available price.

Market portfolio A theoretical portfolio in which each risky asset in the economy is held in proportion to the total market value of all risky assets.

Market-segmentation theory A theory that proports that the shape of the term structure is dictated by the supply and demand conditions prevailing in the segmented maturity sectors of the debt market.

Markowitz model A formula for determining the variance of the returns of a portfolio of assets.

Master agreements Standardized forms that provide the basic makeup of currency and interest rate swap arrangements.

Micro hedging A common form of hedging in which a firm hedges specific transactions only.

Minimum-variance hedge ratio A hedge ratio commonly used in conjunction with stock index futures contracts that indicates the number of futures contracts to trade in order to immunize the portfolio against systematic market risk.

Money spread An option combination entailing a long position in one option and a short position in another option that differs only in exercise price.

Naive hedge ratio A simple hedge ratio in which one unit in the futures market is matched with each unit of spot asset held; it is commonly used in conjunction with currency futures hedging applications.

Naked call A risky position in which a call option is written on an asset that is not owned.

National Futures Association An organization of firms involved in futures trading that self-regulates the industry.

Normal backwardation A condition in which the forward price is below the expected future spot price.

Normal probability distribution Gives the probability that a normally distributed random variable will be less than or equal to some value.

Notional principal The principal underlying an interest rate swap; it is notional in the sense that it is never exchanged.

On the close order An order to execute a trade near the end of the trading session.

On the open order An order to execute a trade near the beginning of a trading session.

Open interest The number of futures or options contracts that have been initiated but not yet closed out or exercised.

Option A derivative security that gives the buyer the right to trade an underlying asset at a prescribed exercise price on or before a specified maturity date.

Option fund A mutual fund that specializes in writing covered calls.

Options Clearing Corporation The corporation that serves as the clearinghouse for all options traded on U.S. markets except futures options.

Order book official An employee of the Chicago Board Options Exchange who manages public limit orders.

Out-of-the-money A call (put) option where the underlying asset price is below (above) the option's exercise price.

Over-the-counter (OTC) market A less structured market where securities are traded that exhibit less standardized features.

Parallel loan Occurs when each of two multinationals makes a loan to the other's subsidiary; each loan is made in the multinational's respective currency, and each subsidiary is located in the other's country.

Pit An area on the trading floor of a futures or options exchange where contracts are traded.

Portfolio insurance A strategy using combinations of options, futures, and/or other securities designed to ensure a minimum future value of an equity portfolio.

Position limit The maximum allowable number of futures or options contracts that an investor may hold at any time.

Position trader A futures speculator who maintains a position for longer than one trading session.

Price discovery A function of the futures market wherein future price information can be gleaned from current futures prices.

Price-sensitivity hedge ratio A hedge ratio commonly used in applications entailing interest rate futures contracts; it determines the number of futures contracts to trade such that a fixed-income security is immunized from unanticipated changes in interest rates.

Prime A security created through the establishment of a trust that receives all dividend payments on a stock as well as any stock appreciation up to a termination value.

Program trading The use of computers to assimilate real-time data in order to detect arbitrage opportunities.

Protective put An investment strategy in which put options are purchased to provide a minimum future value for a spot asset held.

Put A derivative security giving the buyer the right to sell an underlying asset at a prescribed exercise price on or before a specified maturity date.

Puttable stock A stock that may be sold back to the issuing company for a specified price at a later date.

Put-call-futures parity A pricing relation between calls, puts, and futures that follows from arbitrage restrictions.

Put-call parity A pricing relation between puts and calls that follows from arbitrage restrictions.

Range forward A combination of a purchased currency put and a written currency call such that a zero price results at contract inception.

Registered option trader An options floor trader at the American Stock Exchange who trades for his or her own account.

Reinvestment-rate premium A premium contained in futures prices attributable to daily resettlement and nonconstant interest rates.

Repo rate The interest rate applicable to repurchase agreements.

Repurchase agreement A transaction in which an investor sells a security with the obligation to repurchase it at a specified later date, often the next day.

Residual variance A measure of the propensity of an asset to generate returns that deviate from its expected return.

Reversal An arbitrage strategy consisting of a written put and the purchase of a synthetic put.

Reversing trade A trade that unwinds an existing position; the vast majority of all futures positions are closed out via reversing trades.

Risk aversion A characteristic exhibited by rational investors in which disutility is associated with increasing outcome dispersion.

Risk neutrality A state in which investors are indifferent toward risk.

Risk premium The added return that risk-averse investors command for assuming risk.

Risk seeking A characteristic exhibited by irrational investors in which utility is enhanced as outcome dispersion is increased.

Roll-Geske-Whaley model An exact formula for pricing American call options written on dividend-paying common stocks.

Scalper A futures floor trader who trades for his or her own account and who maintains positions for very short periods of time.

Score An instrument created through the establishment of a trust that receives all stock appreciation beyond a termination value; it is akin to a long-term European option written on the stock.

Seat A membership of a securities exchange.

Securities and Exchange Commission (SEC) A federal agency charged with the regulation of all U.S. security and option markets.

Settlement committee A futures committee that establishes settlement prices for a contract each trading day.

Settlement price The futures price established at the end of each trading day upon which daily resettlement is based.

Short hedge A hedge transaction in which a short position in a futures contract is undertaken to protect a long position in the underlying asset.

Short position Denotes the position of one who sells a primary or derivative security.

Short sale A transaction in which a security is borrowed and sold, with the obligation to return the borrowed security at a later date.

Simple probability distribution Portrays the probabilities of obtaining various rates of return over some time period.

Single-index model A formula to approximate the return variance of a portfolio.

Specialist A floor trader charged with the duty of making a market in certain securities or options.

Speculation Investment strategies characterized by large risks that usually do not entail the trading of a spot asset.

Speculator One who engages in speculation.

Spot market The market for assets that entail immediate delivery.

Spot price The current price of an asset traded in the spot market.

Spread An options or futures combination entailing a long and short position in similar contracts.

Standard deviation A popular measure of the dispersion of an asset's returns about its expected return.

Stock index A weighted average of stock prices designed to proxy the entire stock market.

Stock index futures Futures contracts written on stock indices that are cash-settled.

Stock index option An option giving the owner the right to buy or sell an entire stock index at a prescribed exercise price.

Stock option *See* Equity option.

Stop order An order to trade securities when their prices reach a prescribed level; it is typically used to limit losses on extant positions.

Storage costs The costs of storing an asset for a given period.

Straddle An option combination entailing long positions in corresponding calls and puts.

Strap An option combination entailing long positions in two calls and one corresponding put.

Strike price *See* Exercise price.

Strip An option combination entailing a long position in two puts and a corresponding call.

Swaps A negotiated agreement between two parties to exchange cash flows at specified future dates according to a prescribed manner.

Synthetic call A securities combination that replicates the price action of a call option.

Synthetic futures A securities combination that replicates the price action of a futures contract; the combination typically entails call and put options.

Synthetic put A securities combination that replicates the price action of a put option.

Synthetic short call A securities combination that replicates the behavior of a written call position.

Systematic risk The risk of a security that is attributable to general market conditions.

Term premium A premium in a futures price that is associated with liquidity premia in the term structure.

Term structure of interest rates The relation between yields and maturities of bonds of a similar risk class.

Tick The smallest permissable price fluctuation of a security.

Time spread *See* calendar spread.

Time value The difference between an option's current price and its minimum possible value as given by arbitrage restrictions.

Transaction costs The costs of transacting in securities, including commissions.

Transaction exposure Represents the degree to which the value of future cash transactions can be affected by exchange rate fluctuations.

Transportation costs The costs involved in the actual delivery of an asset underlying a futures contract.

Uncovered call *See* Naked call.

Unsystematic risk The risk of a security that is not attributable to general market conditions.

Upside capture The percentage of the uninsured appreciation in an up market that is captured by the insured portfolio.

Uptick An increase in security price equal to one tick.

Utility A measure of the satisfaction derived from consumption or wealth.

Utility function Defines a relation between an individual's utility level and the amounts of goods and services consumed.

Utility theory The study and modeling of rational economic behavior.

Variance A measure of the dispersion of a security's return about its expected return; it is the square of standard deviation.

Variation margin The cash deposit required to satisfy a futures margin call.

Wash sale A stock sale and subsequent repurchase deemed to be executed to realize a tax loss only; tax law disallows the loss deduction.

Wild-card option An option enjoyed by the short trader of a Treasury note or Treasury bond futures contract on the Chicago Board of Trade; it arises because of the contract's unique delivery system, and presumably the value of this option confounds the futures price.

Writer The seller of an option contract.

Zero-beta asset An asset that exhibits no systematic risk; in equilibrium it should earn the riskless rate of interest.

Zero-sum game Refers to securities trading where the gains (losses) exhibited by long-position holders are equal to the losses (gains) exhibited by short-position holders.

INDEX